# BALKAN MILITARY HISTORY

MILITARY HISTORY BIBLIOGRAPHIES
(General Editors: Robin Higham
Jacob Kipp)
Vol. 8

GARLAND REFERENCE LIBRARY
OF SOCIAL SCIENCE
Vol. 234

# MILITARY HISTORY BIBLIOGRAPHIES

*Advisory Editors:*
Robin Higham
Jacob W. Kipp

1. *Israeli Military History: A Guide to the Sources*
   by Jehuda L. Wallach

2. *German Military Aviation: A Guide to the Literature*
   by Edward H. Homze

3. *German Military History: 1648–1982: A Critical Bibliography*
   by Dennis E. Showalter

4. *The Military in Imperial History: The French Connection*
   by Alf Andrew Heggoy and John M. Haar

5. *Japanese Military History: A Guide to the Literature*
   by Shinji Kondo

6. *French Military History, 1661–1799: A Guide to the Literature*
   by Steven T. Ross

7. *German Naval History: A Guide to the Literature*
   by Keith W. Bird

8. *Balkan Military History: A Bibliography*
   by John E. Jessup

9. *Napoleonic Military History: A Bibliography*
   edited by Donald D. Horward

# BALKAN MILITARY HISTORY
*A Bibliography*

John E. Jessup

GARLAND PUBLISHING, INC. • NEW YORK & LONDON
1986

**Library of Congress Cataloging-in-Publication Data**

Jessup, John E.
  Balkan military history.

  (Military history bibliographies ; vol. 8) (Garland
reference library of social science ; v. 234)
  Includes indexes.
  1. Balkan Peninsula—History, Military—Bibliography.
I. Title.  II. Series.  III. Series: Garland reference
library of social science ; v. 234.
Z2851.M5J47  1986  [DR37]  016.9496  83-49304
ISBN 0-8240-8963-4 (alk. paper)

Cover design by Renata Gomes

Printed on acid-free, 250-year-life paper
Manufactured in the United States of America

# CONTENTS

General Editors' Introduction vii

Preface ix

1. The Balkans in General 1

2. The Late 14th and the 15th Centuries 37

3. The 16th Century 63

4. The 17th Century 89

5. The 18th Century 121

6. 1800–1850 167

7. 1850–1899 211

8. 1900–1936 283

9. 1936–1984 349

Abbreviations 423

Index of Subjects 429

Index of Authors 449

# THE GENERAL EDITORS' INTRODUCTION

Military history is a vast international field touching upon all aspects of society, yet guides to the immense literature it contains, essential for anyone writing in the field, have largely been conspicuous by their absence. Over fifteen years ago an international start was made by Robin Higham with *Official Histories* (1970), which for the first time enabled even official historians to check what other offices had produced. That work established a pattern of historical essays, some by the original authors, followed by a checklist of the works published. While this was in process, *A Guide to the Sources of British Military History* (1971) was commenced along slightly different lines. In this each author was asked to provide a bibliographic essay over a segment of the military, naval or air history of one country, with a numbered alphabetical list by authors of those cited following. A further feature of each chapter was a short concluding section suggesting what research remained to be undertaken as well as what could profitably be reviewed. So successful was this volume, published simultaneously in the United States and in Britain, that not only did it become a standard library reference work, but also the editor was asked to undertake a similar compilation for U.S. military history. This latter guide was completed in 1975 on a more far-seeing scheme in which quinquennial supplements were planned to keep the work up to date (the first of these was issued in 1981). It was on the basis of these three successful volumes that the editors were approached by Garland in May 1978 to undertake the present series.

By that time both editors were involved in the United States and in the International Commissions for Military History, Dr. Higham being on the Editorial Advisory Board and Dr. Kipp on the Bibliographical Committee. They agreed with Garland that they would undertake to produce an international series of some thirty-odd volumes to provide scholars access to the vast collec-

*vii*

tions in all the countries of the world other than the United States and the United Kingdom. Those authors whose native language was not English should also produce a volume in their own tongue so that scholars of at least two major languages concerned with the military history of that country should benefit. No limits were set on length, though as with the two previous *Guides* it was not expected that these works would be either totally comprehensive or exhaustive, if for no other than the two very good reasons that in most cases there is a lot of repetitive material and that inevitably bibliographies are dated from the moment their sections are completed.

The very existence of the International Commission on Military History and the vigorous programs of the various national commissions that compose it confirm the vitality of the field of military history. Both editors believe that this bibliographic series can render a valuable service by facilitating the study of military history across national lines and in a comparative context. It is hoped that each volume will make explicit the general and particular historiographic approaches associated with an individual nation's military institutions. In such a manner researchers will be able to consult a single volume that will outline the historiographic developments for a particular nation's military experience or, in the case of major powers, of that of one of its principal armed services. Such a guide it is hoped will serve as a compass for further research, both enumerating what has been done and suggesting what still needs to be done.

Essentially the authors have been asked to provide readable essays that will guide the readers through the labyrinth of the most important sources as though walking through a library and archives, mentioning authors and titles, but leaving the details to be acquired by taking the works from the shelves, in this case the numbered lists at the back of each chapter. Both authors and Editors would be happy to have comments and suggestions from readers and users.

Robin Higham
Jacob Kipp
*Department of History*
*Kansas State University*
*Manhattan, KS 66506, USA*

The research and writing of a bibliography is considerably more complex than the efforts required to produce an acceptable monograph. I did not know this when I agreed to write this book. Bibliography preparation, I now suspect, is an art form unto itself and requires talents that are not a part of normal graduate preparation in history, nor easily learned. The problems associated with compiling a bibliography, when coupled with the intricacies of the Balkans, make the task overwhelming if not impossible. This is basically the case with this volume and will have to stand as my excuse for the inordinate delay in its completion and for its condition.

When I undertook this project, I did so without reservation and with the expectation that it would be, first of all, an education and, second, a challenge. It has been both of these things and more. The education came when I discovered how meager my knowledge was of where to find the sort of material I felt was needed for this work and, when I had gathered it, how to present it in the most usable fashion. The challenge came into clear focus when I viewed the thousands of entry forms, extracts, and other material that accumulated during the search phase of this project. The amount of research required convinced me that this was indeed a major and, possibly, a unique undertaking. There are, of course, a number of very fine bibliographic reference works that deal with various aspects of the subject of Balkan military history. For the most part, however, they do not convey the breadth of the subject and are usually either too explicit or too general in their coverage to be of real value to the military historian.

Not having a computer when I began the project, a mistake I later rectified, I felt I was condemned to do the job the old-fashioned way -- by hand. This was, of course, the way I was "brought up" in school as, although computers existed in those days, they were not usually found sitting in one's study with a half-eaten, multicolored fruit stenciled all over them. At the time I acquired the computer used to complete this work, I had already completed six chapters the old-fashioned way. I knew that I had enough left to do, however, to make it worthwhile investment and that it would be a most useful tool. For the record, this book was produced on an Apple //e computer using the Apple Writer // word processing program which was later replaced by a new program, Appleworks. The hardcopy printing was accomplished using a NEC 3530 letter-perfect printer, reinforced with a 64k Microbuffer. I really believe I could not have finished the job without these tools.

As my labors progressed I also discovered that, regardless of how meticulous I was in my research, and how broad I was in my coverage of sources, I had missed numerous important entries that absolutely had to be included. When one attempts to do a bibliography of this sort, something is bound to be left out or a national hero or scoundrel or important date or event is forgotten. Or, worst of all, some widely accepted scholar who has devoted his life to a particular facet of the study of the Balkans will be overlooked. It also became apparent, even as I worked, that whatever it was that I failed to do would undoubtedly cause consternation among scholars and apoplexy among patriots. For this I profusely apologize in advance to one and all knowing full well that, as Benjamin Disraeli pointed out, "Apologies only account for that which they cannot alter."

One question which the careful reader might justifiably ask is why studies that cover relatively broad periods of time are mentioned only in relation to specific events or much more restrictive timeframes? The most simple answer that I can give is that I used works in these instances that were familiar to me or that I had used in previous research. Another reason is that I could only access segments of the works in time to complete this project. In one or two instances, especially in the case of some very recent publications, I added them at the point where they became available knowing that the conscientious reader will be able to backtrack much more easily than I could in preparing this manuscript to find their uses in earlier periods. The most difficult part of this whole endeavor was coming to grips with the requirement to cut off any further acquisitions. This caused the greatest number of problems as each day's mail seemed to bring the announcement of some new work, or a reissued one, that was absolutely vital to the entire fabric of this work. It took a strong will not to succumb to the temptation to go back and reopen a chapter but it was absolutely essential that I did not do so, if I ever expected to finish the book and if I ever expected it to have any continuity.

The nature of this undertaking also required access to a very broad data base. Fortunately, living in the Greater Washington D.C. area gave me the use of the Library of Congress with all of its many finding aids and its even finer staff who offered invaluable assistance in locating otherwise obscure, and often misfiled, books that needed to be looked at before being added to the list. I also had good luck at the libraries in Arlington and Fairfax counties in Virginia and, as I acquired the habit of carrying data sheets with me, at a number of other libraries in the area as well. Most important of all, was the valuable assistance rendered by a group of my students at George Mason University who gave of their time to collect titles from which I could choose the best for inclusion in the book.

To find a means of controlling the data and as a means of keeping it in a usable form, I designed a quite simple reporting sheet upon which all of the pertinent bibliographic data was recorded. Thereafter, a synopsis was written, or extracts were made and attached to the sheet. This allowed for easy sorting and for moving the individual references between chapters. This was important as each chapter was designed to be "free-standing" and capable of separate review and updating as required. This accounts for many of the redundancies that are evident throughout the book.

I was also faced with the problem of transliteration and this created a number of serious complications. It was apparent at the outset that titles in a number of languages would have to be included if this effort was to have any encompassing value. To solve this problem, I used the form of transliteration found in the Library of Congress or in the Union Catalog, in that order. If the title was not to be found in either source, and a number did not appear, I used the most authoritative source available to check the spelling. There are some mistakes but every effort was made to avoid them.

It should be noted also that the use of the particular computer word-processing programs, and the publisher's requirement for submission of a camera-ready copy of this manuscript did not permit the addition of diacritical marks used in a number of the included languages. This is unfortunate and unavoidable but, as each citation contains the name of the author and the place and date of publication, it should not create an insurmountable obstacle to effective utilization.

Although the form and fundamental structure of the volume was prescribed in advance by the general editors and follows a plan accepted for all of the works in this series, each volume is necessarily somewhat different. In the case of this volume, I have incorporated a rather extensive glossary of abbreviations as a means of conserving space. Secondly, a perusal of the individual bibliographical listings in each chapter will note instances where entries have obviously been "Omitted." These omissions are the result of an inability to confirm one or more elements of a citation or because the title proved to be a poor choice because of some overriding flaw. The initial compilation of references included, in addition to titles gathered especially for this effort, bibliographical material from a number of past efforts of mine, from lists compiled by several researchers who assisted me, and from a number of "donations" from well wishers, critics, patriots, dilettantes, and others interested in the project. The entries were compiled into the basic, numbered bibliographical listings found with each chapter. These obviously had to be prepared before work could begin on the chapter itself. As the research continued, and references were more thoroughly checked, it became apparent that some did not, in fact, exist, and that others were in error as to scope, authorship or other basic value. In those cases, I chose to omit the entry. In other cases, the entry was omitted from one chapter and included, if appropriate, at a more useful point in the volume. It was inevitable that duplications, poor choices, and erroneous entries would crop up; they did, and where discovered they were removed.

This review process was not used to judge the contents of the works that were to be included, however, either from the scholarly or ideological standpoint. In only one or two instances were works consigned to oblivion because they were either so misleading or so ideologically perverse as to make them useless. This was especially the case when works that were purported to be histories turned out to be travel guides or, in one case, the writings of someone who had determined, without qualification, the Godliness of the Balkan people solely through his reading of the Bible. Considering that all men do or should possess this Godliness, I felt that his knowledge of the history of this troubled area was bereft of historical value in the context of this effort. His work was one of those consigned to oblivion.

Another area that should be mentioned is that of how selections were made in the first place. The answer is both very carefully and, at the same time, quite haphazardly. No one can claim expertise in all facets of the general history of the Balkans no less its military heritage. Similarly, there are a number of approaches that might have been taken to illuminate the military history of this intriguing corner of Europe. It was necessary, therefore, to establish a definition of military history that would be broad enough to include a number of studies that might not have fitted into a more tightly structured disciplinary framework. Thus, the reader will find works on society, economics, and politics, in addition to pure military historical works. If one considers that war is the outgrowth of other conditions then it becomes obvious that these other conditions must be understood to be able to contemplate man's most destructive occupation. If there is to be a hope for the eventual comprehension of the futility of war then it is imperative that the preconditions of war be understood in hopes that the consequences may be avoided. Hopefully, a careful analysis of the material contained in the books listed in this volume will aid in that understanding.

Lastly, as is the practice, I need to convey my thanks to those who have helped me in this effort. In particular, I need to thank, in addition to those fine people at the Library of Congress, Robin Higham and Jake Kipp for their excellent support and advice, Julie Johnson of Garland for her patience, Marguerite Wagner for her editing of the often incomprehensible writing that formed the drafts of this work, Dick Sharp, without whose help I would still be on Chapter One, Sue Nason, who helped get me started and kept me at it through the early days, Marcia Markie for the excellent index and the last-minute corrections, and the numerous helpers who did much of the initial collection of titles. I thank them collectively in fear of forgetting someone if I try to remember all their names. To all of this fine group goes most of the credit for success of this effort. I alone am responsible for its failures.

# CHAPTER ONE

## THE BALKANS IN GENERAL

### GENERAL BACKGROUND

The term "Balkan" is derived from the Turkish word for mountain and, according to the ENCYCLOPAEDIA BRITANNICA (3:5), is the name given to the "most easterly of the three southern prolongations of the European continent." In fact, the Balkans (or Balkan Peninsula) are named after the Balkan mountains that form a belt across Bulgaria and extend into Yugoslavia as far as Vrska Cuka in the province of Serbia. Geographically, the Balkan Peninsula implies the region of southeastern Europe bounded by the Black Sea, the Sea of Marmara, the Aegean Sea on the east, the Mediterranean on the south, and the Ionian and Adriatic Seas on the west. In the present-day political demarcation of states, the Balkans include Albania, Bulgaria, European Turkey, Greece, Hungary, Romania, and Yugoslavia.

Over the course of centuries, and because of the continuing strategic importance of the Balkan Peninsula, these political subdivisions have undergone numerous changes as the lands were crossed and recrossed by alien invaders who entered the region from all directions bent on plunder, subjugation or passage to even more distant lands. The Balkans, from the earliest times, sat at the crossroads between east and west and served as an axis of advance for numerous armies who either despoiled the lands as they passed through them or used the lands as the theater of war itself, with all the usual destruction. There are few areas on the earth's surface that have witnessed more of the entire spectrum of war than the Balkans.

Yet, with this realization comes the equally significant fact that not much is known in the West about the Balkan lands or people except for those few specialists who form a circle devoted to the study of the region. Thus, any bibliography of Balkan military history must begin on the premise that a foundation of more fundamental information, data of a more general nature, is necessary before delving into the specifics of the Balkans' history of conflict.

A second factor that cannot be overlooked in studying the Balkans is the number of languages that are spoken in the region. In either the general, or the more specialized military, historical study of the Balkans, the reader is faced by a polyglot of languages including Albanian, Bulgarian, Hungarian, Greek, Romanian, Serbo-Croatian, Russian, and Turkish, all of which are used by segments of the population, and are the principal tools for the writing of military history. In addition, numerous works appear in

1

languages from outside the region that include Polish and Czech, as well as the easily accessible French, German, Italian, Spanish, and English. The student of the Balkans must, therefore, familiarize himself with a cross-section of these Balkan tongues or be prepared to rely upon western sources. This problem goes without saying, of course, but it is an important one nonetheless as there are few parts of the world where so many people speak so many languages in such a relatively small area. And this is doubly true as the history of each country is intimately intertwined with that of its neighbors.

## GEOGRAPHICAL REFERENCES

There are a number of good geographies and atlases available to aid both the casual reader and the serious student in familiarizing themselves with the "lay of the land" in the Balkans. It is especially important to understand the makeup of the terrain in the region so as to appreciate the strategic and tactical value that has been placed upon it by past political and military leaders. The Danube valley was, for example, the primary axis of advance for the Ottoman invaders of the 17th century who were bent upon capturing the heartland of a disunited western Europe. Following the river's course would have carried the the Turks into the heart of Christendom which they had vowed to subjugate.

Francis W. Carter's AN HISTORICAL GEOGRAPHY OF THE BALKANS [39] is extremely useful for the purpose. Professor Carter has edited a series of addresses, essays, and lectures into a single work dealing specifically with the region. Similarly, the appendices to the Department of Army's Pamphlet 550-8 [216], that was published in 1971, contains one of the best collections of maps and other geographical data available. The volume's scope extends over all of Eastern Europe and contains data on other countries often associated with, but not technically part of, the Balkans. In this sense, this makes this compendium extremely valuable to the military historian.

Another useful tool is Colin McEvedy's THE PENGUIN ATLAS OF MEDIEVAL HISTORY [136] that covers the 4th through the 15th centuries in maps and narrative. This is an unpretentious work that has a number of advantages, not the least of which is that it has been published inexpensively as a paperback. There are 40 maps in the atlas, most of which contain information on the Balkans.

Among other atlases that may be of benefit are EASTERN EUROPE [13], edited by John Bartholomew, that covers central Europe, Italy, and the Balkans. The maps in this atlas are sometimes difficult to read. SOUTHERN EUROPE: A SYSTEMATIC GEOGRAPHICAL STUDY [15], by Monica and Robert Beckinsale, might also be referred to, but may be too complicated for the average reader.

Of special importance to the study of European military history is David Chandler's ATLAS OF MILITARY STRATEGY [43]. Without question, this is a most valuable addition to any library devoted to the study of the history of war, and it has direct application to the study of the subject as it pertains to the Balkans. Professor Chandler has added a significant amount of valuable commentary, including sections on techniques, military organization and weaponry that increase this volume's overall worth.

## GENERAL STUDIES ON THE BALKANS

There are a number of general histories available about the Balkans. One of the best of this group is Charles and Barbara Jelavich's THE BALKANS [104]. The authors are diplomatic historians who see the Balkans as the cockpit of international rivalry in Europe. Their work is one of the most thorough expositions of this complex region and, probably better than any other single work, elucidates the two principal threads of continuity that pervade the entire historical process. The Jelavichs saw these as a steadily rising national awareness on the part of the inhabitants of each area, that engendered conflict in and of itself, and the repeated interventions from the outside, especially by the Great Powers: England, France, Austria–Hungary, and Russia. In this last regard, the continous overlordship of the Ottoman Empire from the 15th through the 19th centuries must also be considered, even though it was not a European power in the conventional sense. The point is well made that these factors, more than any others, charted the region's historical course. The Jelavich book is limited only by the fact that its coverage ends with the Second World War.

Another fine work is the HISTORY OF THE BALKAN PENINSULA FROM THE EARLIEST TIMES TO THE PRESENT DAY [175]. Written by Ferdinand Schevill, it was first published in 1922, and was revised and reissued in 1933 with the assistance of Professor Wesley Marsh Gewehr. The fact that it has remained an important source of information and was still being reprinted as late as 1971 seems to justify its being called the best general history of the Balkans available in English. In the first edition, Professor Schevill manages to cover, in 558 pages, some 3,000 years of history in a scholarly, often brilliant, fashion. For the military historian, this book serves well as the basis for an understanding of those phases of Balkan history that preceded the Ottoman overlordship, namely, the Roman period of the 1st to the 11th centuries, and the Greco-Byzantine phase of the 11th through the 14th centuries, that directly or indirectly brought the Balkans within the scope of the Mediterranean world.

Schevill gives considerable attention to the study of the Byzantine period that traditionally ended when Ottoman Turks, led by Sultan Mohammed II (1444-1446, 1451-1481), succeeded in breaking through the outer defenses of the Empire and capturing Constantinople in May 1453. The work's treatment of the ensuing Ottoman period is equally excellent and serves as a good foundation for the more expository writings of others that follow.

One of the more readable works on the Balkans is Stojan Pribicevic's WORLD WITHOUT END; THE SAGA OF SOUTH-EASTERN EUROPE [155]. This fondly written book is also a pre-World War II production that was published as Hitler's armies were crushing Poland. It is an informal history, written by the son of a leader of the ANCIEN REGIME in Yugoslavia, that has, as its strongest point, a recitation of the social, political, and economic conditions found in each of the countries in southeastern Europe just before the beginning of the war. The book is also attractive because of its

3

extensive bibliography, but the casual reader will find very few titles in English.

Perhaps the best books available on the subject is THE BALKANS SINCE 1453 [194], by the Balkan scholar Professor Leften Stavrianos. Few, if any, of the works in English match the quality of presentation that is found in this book. It should be on the shelf of every serious student of Balkan history. Although it was published in 1958, its coverage outweighs its timeliness. Another excellent choice is SOUTHEASTERN EUROPE UNDER OTTOMAN RULE, 1354-1804 [198], by the noted Balkan historian, Professor Peter Sugar. This book was published as Volume 5 in the HISTORY OF EAST CENTRAL EUROPE [200] series that is being edited by Professors Sugar and Donald Treadgold.

Another equally readable, if somewhat less authoritative, book is Rene Ristelhueber's A HISTORY OF THE BALKAN PEOPLE [157], which is directed more toward the casual reader than the scholar. It is, in any case, unfortunately not documented and is therefore of less value to the serious student. Any value that may be found in the book is achieved in its chronological treatment of many of the later, major political and military events in the history of the Balkans. Ristelhueber's study ends with 1950 and was originally published in French. It was reissued in 1971 with a summary of the intervening two decades by Professor Sherman Spector.

There are a number of articles of importance to all phases of the study of Balkan military history in the CAMBRIDGE ANCIENT HISTORY [35], the CAMBRIDGE MEDIEVAL HISTORY [36], and THE NEW CAMBRIDGE MODERN HISTORY [46]. It goes without saying, that the scholarship in these series is of the very highest standards.

The studies by Robert Seton-Watson, THE RISE OF NATIONALITY IN THE BALKANS [179], THE DANUBE: THE DRAMATIC HISTORY OF THE GREAT RIVER AND THE PEOPLE TOUCHED BY ITS FLOW [125], by Erwin and Ann Lessner, Oskar Halecki's BORDERLANDS OF WESTERN CIVILIZATION: A HISTORY OF EAST CENTRAL EUROPE [84], and Traian Stoianovich's A STUDY OF BALKAN CIVILIZATION [196], are all worthwhile reading. It should be remembered that Seton-Watson was the voice of the pro-national forces in the framing of British policy on the Balkans during World War I. The Lessner book is exceptionally easy to read because of its style and attention to detail. Norman Pounds' EASTERN EUROPE [154] is a good socio-economic geography, while Matthew Spinka's A HISTORY OF CHRISTIANITY IN THE BALKANS: A STUDY OF THE SPREAD OF BYZANTINE CULTURE AMONG THE SLAVS [192] elucidates one of the single most important elements of Balkan life.

In a German-language work, MANNER AM BALKAN, VON ALEXANDER DEM GROSSE BIS JOSIP TITO [207], Franz Thierfelder has produced a series of bibliographical summaries of Balkan personalities from the Macedonian conqueror of the known world to the late war hero and leader of Yugoslavia. The list contains a fair cross section of Balkan personalities, but Thierfelder is quick to admit that no such list will satisfy everyone (and not without good reason as there are some obvious omissions). There are also a number of serious mistakes in the text that distract from the book's overall usefulness and that require the reader to accept the data presented with some caution.

4

Maximilian Braun's DIE SLAWEN AUF DEM BALKANS BIS ZUR BEFREIUNG VON DER TURKISCHEN HERRSCHAFT [24] is another study in German that covers the history of the Balkan Slavs up to the time of their independence from Turkish rule. Franz Babinger's AUFSATZE UND ABHANDLUNGEN ZUR GESCHICHTE SUDOSTEUROPAS UND DER LEVANTE [8] is an interesting collection of essays that contains excellent bibliographic footnotes. Babinger's work is in three volumes, the last of which was published in 1976.

Edgar Hosch's THE BALKANS: A SHORT HISTORY FROM GREEK TIMES TO THE PRESENT DAY [95] was originally published in German in 1968, and was then translated and published in English. It is only 164 pages, yet it presents a good summary of the history of the Balkans as well as rather detailed discussions on Albania, Bulgaria, and Yugoslavia. Hosch fails to mention the other Balkan nations, although Romania is named in passing. This helps point up the range of opinion on what constitutes that region of the world. This book is more suited to the casual reader than the serious student.

Konrad Bercovici's THE INCREDIBLE BALKANS [16] follows the Hosch pattern except that here, after a brief outline of Balkan history in general, the author turns to more specific resumes of all the principal states. George Stadtmuller's GESCHICHTE SUDOSTEUROPAS [193] is very detailed, but somewhat pretentious. George Mylonas' THE BALKAN STATES: AN INTRODUCTION TO THEIR HISTORY [143], while purporting to outline the history of the peninsula is, in fact, an undisguised justification for Greek claims in the Balkans after World War II. The book also contains numerous inaccuracies.

On the other hand, NEAR EAST AFFAIRS AND CONDITIONS [149], written by Stephen Panaretoff, and published in 1922, is a skillfully composed, 215 page study prepared from a series of seven lectures on Balkan history. Panaretoff makes the point that the Balkan Slavs laid themselves open to foreign intrigue and attack through their inability to unify against common enemies. In making this assumption, the author undoubtedly laid himself open to criticism by those who would quickly point out that others besides Slavs dwell in the Balkans and that they too must share in the burden of the collective incapacity to unite in the face of adversity. Cyril Black's "The Balkan Slavs in the Middle Ages" [18] is excellent.

THE BALKANS; A HISTORY OF BULGARIA, SERBIA, GREECE, ROUMANIA AND TURKEY [72], by Neville Forbes and others, was first published in 1915, but was reissued in 1970. It covers all of the Balkans, except Hungary. Another book of similar type is William Miller's THE BALKANS: ROUMANIA, BULGARIA, SERBIA AND MONTENEGRO [140]. This is yet another example of the various criteria used by scholars in determining the composition of the Balkans. George Mylonas' article, "An Introduction to the History of the Southern Balkan States" [142], is good, but once again shows too much of the author's personal feelings.

The Royal Institute of International Affairs, in collaboration with the London and Cambridge Economic Service, has recently reissued SOUTH-EASTERN EUROPE:A POLITICAL AND ECONOMIC SURVEY [170] that deals with the politico-economic makeup of the

5

region. This volume has an excellent bibliography.

Among the other general readings that should not be overlooked is Josef Dragan's WE, THE THRACIANS AND THEIR MULTIMILLENARY HISTORY [61] which is a two-volume account of history and ethnography. THE BALKAN REVOLUTIONARY TRADITION, [60] by Dimitrije Djordjevic and Stephen Fisher-Galati, is a book that does much to explain what is to follow. Walter Kolarz' MYTHS AND REALITIES IN EASTERN EUROPE [114] is interesting but not essential reading.

## GENERAL HISTORICAL WORKS OF EACH NATION

There are a number of useful general histories and other works on each of the Balkan states. Among these, the Department of Army series of AREA HANDBOOKS [217] include volumes on all of the Balkan countries. The volume on Romania, for example, was published in 1972 as a 319-page DA Pamphlet 550-160. It provides, as do all of the others, sections on the social, political, economic, and national security aspects of the nation, including a brief history of their armed forces.

### ALBANIA

Without question, Albania is one of the least known and least understood countries on earth. The Albanians came from basic Illyrian stock and were, by the 8th century AD, overrun by Slavs. For almost three centuries, Albania remained under West Bulgarian domination until the lands were conquered by Byzantium. By the 13th century, parts of Albania were occupied by the Serbs and all of the country was annexed by Stephen Dusan in the 14th century. This arrangement was shortlived, however, as Dusan's empire crumbled after his death in 1355. Soon after, the Ottoman Turks began their conquest of the Balkans.

In addition to the AREA HANDBOOK already mentioned, there are a number of general histories available. Otto R. Liess' ALBANIEN ZWISCHEN OST UND WEST [127], which was published in German in 1968, is best suited to the casual reader. Stavro Skendi's ALBANIA [189] is a better choice for the serious student. One of the more comprehensive investigations of Albania's past is Joseph Swire's ALBANIA, THE RISE OF A KINGDOM [201], while Stefanaq Pollo's HISTOIRE DE L'ALBANIE, DES ORIGINES A NOS JOURS [153] is among the best written. Other general histories include ALBANIA AND THE ALBANIANS [134], by Ramadan Marmullaku, ALBANIA, PAST AND PRESENT [44], by Constantin A. Chekrezi, and THE ALBANIANS [129] by Anton Logoreci. A rather thorough bibliography may be found in E.L.J. Legrand's BIBLIOGRAPHIE ALBANAISE [121].

### BULGARIA

Bulgarian kingdoms arose in the Balkans in the 10th and again in the 13th-14th centuries. After that time, Bulgaria remained under the hand of the Ottoman Empire until 1878. Among the better general histories of Bulgaria are V.N. Zlatarski's GESCHICHTE DER BULGAREN [234], which is in two volumes, Nicholai Todorov's BULGARIA, HISTORICAL AND GEOGRAPHICAL OUTLINE [208], and Stanley

Evan's A SHORT HISTORY OF BULGARIA [66]. Todorov has also condensed 1,300 years of history into 98 pages in A SHORT HISTORY OF BULGARIA [209]. Dimitrie Mishev's THE BULGARIANS IN THE PAST [141], first published in 1919, has an excellent bibliography. Another somewhat outdated, but still useful work is HISTOIRE DU PEUPLE BULGARE, DEPUIS LES ORIGINES JUSQU'A NOS JOURS [20], which was written by George Bousquit. Mercia Macdermott's A HISTORY OF BULGARIA, 1393-1885 [132] is written in topical fashion, is somewhat stuffy, but is still probably the best work in English. Christ Anastasoff's THE BULGARIANS: FROM THEIR ARRIVAL IN THE BALKANS TO MODERN TIMES [5] is also worthwhile reading.

### HUNGARY

The history of Hungary is somewhat better known in the West, perhaps because of the 1956 revolution that caught worldwide attention and interest. Hungarians trace their beginnings from the 9th century when the Magyar Arpad dynasty was founded. From that point Hungary remained a monarchy, except for a brief period between the world wars under the Horthy regency. During this millennium, Hungary was almost constantly beset by internal strife and external attack, first from the Turks who occupied the country for nearly 150 years and then from the Austrians who held it until 1918. Hungary subsequently fell under Nazi domination and then, after World War II became a Soviet satellite.

THE EVOLUTION OF HUNGARY AND ITS PLACE IN EUROPEAN HISTORY [204], by P. Teleki, is outdated but still one of the better sources of general information about the events leading to the making of the state, the rule of Stephen I, the Turkish invasion, the age of dualism, and the nationality question. As it was written in 1923, it has none of Hungary's more recent history. By comparison, the somewhat more recently published book by Domonic Kosary, A HISTORY OF HUNGARY [116], is suitable only for the casual reader. Emil Lengyel's 1000 YEARS OF HUNGARY [124], Denis Sinor's HISTORY OF HUNGARY [187], and C.A. Macartney's HUNGARY, A SHORT HISTORY [131] are all better and of more recent vintage.

### ROMANIA

Romanians trace their ancestry to the times of Burebista in the 1st century BC. Like the Hungarians, the Romanians are not of Slavic origin. Rather, they are an autochthonous people who managed to resist all incursions, maintaining discernible national traits in the process, even though they have been under foreign domination for most of their two thousand years of existence.

Romanian historians have, in recent years, produced a wealth of material that deals with all phases of their historical development and which serves as a very useful supplement to sources found in the West. These native histories vary in quality predicated upon the author's desire to stress the notion that Romania has always been united, even though unity was not formalized until the 19th century.

Of the better general histories, the most important are Stephen Fisher-Galati's ROMANIA [70], which he edited in 1957, and THE NEW ROMANIA [69], that he wrote in 1967. Another of this quality is Robert Seton-Watson's THE HISTORY OF THE ROUMANIANS: FROM ROMAN TIMES TO THE COMPLETION OF UNITY [178]. This is an excellent record of Romania from the time of Diocletian to 1878, when the unification of 1859 was forged into national independence. Ian Matley's RUMANIA: A PROFILE [135] is also valuable for its penetrating insights, even if there is little originality in the effort. Henry L. Robert's RUMANIA [158], and RUMANIEN [23] by E. von Braun are both interesting. Von Braun's work is in German and may be considered by some to be outdated.

Two good chronologies exist on the general course of Romanian history. The more valuable of the two is the CHRONOLOGICAL HISTORY OF ROMANIA [79]. This work was prepared under the direction of the late, noted scholar Constantin Giurescu and is in English. There are a number of rather glaring omissions that are probably due more to the ubiquitous governmental editor, than to the dedication of Doctor Giurescu and his colleagues who compiled this multidisciplined chronology. In places the book also suffers from poor translation into its English form. Yet, it is extremely useful and has an extensive bibliography and numerous summaries. The second chronology is CHRONIQUE DES EVENEMENTS POLITIQUES ET ECONOMIQUES DANS LE BASSIN DANUBIEN: ROUMANIE [50], that was published in Paris in 1938. Apparently this is a part of a series although the other volumes do not appear to exist.

Another major work by Constantin Giurescu is his monumental ISTORIA ROMANILOR [80], that was coauthored by his son, Dinu Giurescu, who, it may be hoped, will be able to complete the project. The first volume of what is to be an eight-volume set covers the period from paleolithic times to the 14th century. This new series will serve to complement the four-volume ISTORIA ROMANIEI [168] that was produced by the Romanian Academy in the early 1960s.

The well known Romanian intellectual Nicolae Balcescu wrote a book that was published in 1844, the English title of which is THE ARMED FORCES AND MILITARY ART OF THE ROMANIANS, FROM THE FOUNDING OF THE PRINCIPALITY OF WALLACHIA UNTIL NOW [10]. This work is found only in Romanian but contains a great deal of information on the development of the conditions that led to the 1848 revolt in Romania. Another, more contemporary work on this same subject is Constantin Cazanisteanu's "Evolution de la structure d'organisation de l'armee roumaine sous l'influence du development socio-politique et des realisations techniques et scientifiques" [40]. This article was published in 1980 in REVUE INTERNATIONALE D'HISTOIRE MILITAIRE, the journal of the Commission Internationale d'Histoire Militaire. A larger, more comprehensive exposition of the same subject may be found in Constantin Olteanu's CONTRIBUTII LA CERCETEREA CONCEPTULUI DE PUTERE ARMATA LA ROMANI [147]. The study presents an extensive exposition of development of the Romanian armed forces.

In 1919, the noted Romanian historian, Nicolae Iorga, wrote a short monograph titled HISTOIRE DES ROUMAINS DE LA PENINSULE DES BALCANS [103]. This little gem was published in French under the auspices of the Societe des Macedo-Roumains in Bucharest. It is only 64 pages in length, but is well worth the effort to find a copy.

Ladislav Makkai's L'HISTOIRE DE TRANSYLVANIE [133], which outlines the history of that Romanian province, is a useful work.

Although related by blood and by language, Transylvania's history followed a quite different course from that of its two sister provinces, Wallachia and Moldavia. Until the end of the First World War, Transylvania was a part of the Austro-Hungarian Empire and only at the end of the war was it united, some would say reunited, with the rest of Romania.

### YUGOSLAVIA

Yugoslavia occupies a unique position in the community of Balkan states. It is, in fact, not a single nation at all but, rather, a conglomerate of Serbian, Croatian, Macedonian, Montenegran, and other groups who initially had separate aspirations and cultural affinities. They were, for most of their histories, independent of each other. Yugoslavia did not come into being until 1 December 1918, when it emerged following the end of World War I and the dissolution of the Austro-Hungarian Empire.

There are a number of good histories of Yugoslavia that include information on most, if not all, of the various national groups. YUGOSLAVIA [88], by Muriel Heppell and Frank Singleton, for example, outlines the histories of the six individual kingdoms and principalities that were formed into the present state. This book is divided into two parts, the first dealing with the history before the First World War and the second, with modern Yugoslavia.

A SHORT HISTORY OF YUGOSLAVIA [49], which was edited by Stephen Clissold, is formed from pertinent sections of a handbook published by British Naval Intelligence during World War II. Handled as it is, on a region-by-region basis, the text may confound anyone looking for a general history of the whole country. It is an extremely accurate account, however, in which the astute may learn the differences among the regions. Another worthwhile general historical treatment is Robert Kerner's YUGOSLAVIA [111]. One book that should be used with caution is Z. Kostelski's THE YUGOSLAVS: THE HISTORY OF THE YUGOSLAVS AND THEIR STATES TO THE CREATION OF YUGOSLAVIA [118]. It lacks documentation and suffers from poor editing. An unusually good history is, on the other hand, DEJINY JUGOSLAVIE [232], that was produced in Prague in 1970, by Vaclav Zacek and a group of Czech specialists who trace the history of Yugoslavia in all its parts from the earliest settlements until the establishment of the communist government in 1946. It is found, unfortunately, only in the Czech language.

THE HISTORY OF SERBIA [205], by Sir Harold W. Temperley, traces that nation's development from the time of the arrival of the Slavs to the period just before the victorious Balkan Wars and the tragedy of Sarajevo. For this long period of history Temperley's work is by the far the best available in English and brings an added bonus of an excellent bibliography. Vojislav Petrovic's SERBIA: HER PEOPLE, HISTORY AND ASPIRATIONS [151], has a historical survey to 1914 and a second section that describes the national characteristics of the Serbian people. Another work of the same type is Chedomille Mijatovich's SERVIA AND THE SERVIANS [138].

Montenegro is another of the six constituent republics that form Yugoslavia. Before 1918 it was an independent state with a history dating from 1355 when the Serbian empire of Stephen Nemanja

(Dusan) collapsed and the district of Zeta broke away to become a haven for Serbian rebels, especially after the terrible defeat at the hands of the Turks at Kosovo in 1389. Curiously, the doughty Montenegrans never came under the Turkish thrall although, for a period of time, they were the vassals of Venice. Constant fighting and not infrequent raids into Turkish territory gave the Montenegrans an independence not shared by the remainder of the Balkans. They were able to maintain this freedom until the end of World War I when they were again absorbed into Serbia and, subsequently, into the new Yugoslavian state.

Several general histories exist on the Kingdom of Montenegro, one of the better being the Reverend William Denton's MONTENEGRO; ITS PEOPLE AND THEIR HISTORY [58]. This treatment ends with the period of the Russo-Turkish War of 1877-1878, however, as do almost all of the other, better works in English. Among these are THE LAND OF THE BLACK MOUNTAIN [229], by Reginald Wyon and Gerald Prance, that was published in 1903 and chronicles the travels of the two Englishmen through the countryside, and Francis Stevenson's A HISTORY OF MONTENEGRO [195] that was published in 1915. The best book for the flavor of the land in the 20th century is Milovan Djilas' LAND WITHOUT JUSTICE [59] that, in addition to being a patriot's call for freedom, also outlines the author's childhood before 1939. HISTOIRE DU MONTENEGRO ET DE LA BOSNIA [51], by P. Coquelle, covers Montenegran history from 900 AD to the late 19th century when it was published. This book also outlines the histories of Bosnia and Herzogovina after 955 AD.

Another of the Yugoslavian republics is Croatia which has existed since the 6th century AD, when the original stock first occupied the lands of Pannonia and Dalmatia. Although Pannonia was made a part of the Frankish empire in 812 and Dalmatia became a vassal of Byzantium, the Croatians continued to rule themselves and to develop a strong national consciousness. After 1102, Croatia was under Hungarian hegemony and, after 1527, had an Austrian king on the throne. When the Turks invaded the Balkans, Croatia became a major part of the Habsburg defensive line.

There are few good works in English on Croatia. Probably the most useful for the majority of readers is Antun Boniface's THE CROATIAN NATION IN ITS STRUGGLE FOR FREEDOM AND INDEPENDENCE [19]. This work suffers from the author's patriotic bias, but is still a good choice. Ferdnand Sisac's GESCHICHTE DER KROATEN [188] was published in German in 1917. The six-volume POVJEST HRVATA [113], by Vjekoslav Klaic, was published in Serbo-Croatian between 1899 and 1922 and is excellent. Two works that outline Croatia's long association with the Habsburgs are Robert Seton-Watson's THE SOUTHERN SLAVS AND THE HABSBURG MONARCHY [180], and an enlarged German version of the same book, DIE SUDSLAVISCHE FRAGE IM HABSBURGEREICH [181], that was published in 1913. Cherubin Segvic's DIE KROATEN UND IHRE MISSION WAHREND DREIZEHN JAHRHUNDERT DER GESCHICHTE [177] is also worth reading.

The last of the republics that needs to be discussed here is Macedonia. Macedonia's history can be traced to the early centuries of the first millenium before Christ when it created such leaders as Philip of Macedon and his son, Alexander the Great. Macedonia fell under Roman dominance in the 2nd century, AD and, after the 4th

10

century, came under Byzantine control. Before the end of the 14th century, however, most of Macedonia was in Turkish hands and remained there until peace settlement following the Russo-Turkish War of 1877-1878 gave it to Bulgaria. As a result of the Treaty of Bucharest (10 August 1913), following the end of the Second Balkan War in 1913, Macedonia was partitioned among Greece, Serbia, and Bulgaria. After several additional territorial modifications, as a result of World War I and the interwar period, Macedonia remained divided, and the outcome of World War II did nothing to correct the situation.

Numerous historical works are available on Macedonia. One of the best is Mihail Rostovzeff's GREECE [169] that deals succinctly, but well, with the early period. Nicholas Hammond's A HISTORY OF MACEDONIA [86] is also a history of the Classical period, but some obvious flaws will become apparent to the discerning reader who understands the Hellenist times. Henry Brailsford's MACEDONIA: ITS RACES AND ITS FUTURE [22], was written in 1906, but is still a useful reference. A more recently produced monograph is Elizabeth Barker's MACEDONIA: ITS PLACE IN BALKAN POWER POLITICS [12], that was prepared for the prestigious Royal Institute of Foreign Affairs in London.

As a last recommendation, the volume prepared by the National Historical Institute of Skoplje, ISTORIJA NA MAKEDONSKOIT NAROD [190], was prepared by a group of Yugoslav scholars and covers the period from ancient times to the end of the 18th century. Although the work is Marxian, a more serious problem exists in its stated proposition -- that the Macedonia nation is more Slavic than Greek -- without the benefit of convincing argument.

GREECE

Although the borders of Greece encompass an area well beyond the normally accepted boundaries of the Balkans, the region of central Greece, Macedonia, and Thrace are a part of the peninsula. Greek history, and prehistory, passes through a number of distinct phases extending back into the Bronze Age. By 400 AD, Greece was a part of the Byzantine Empire and, through a long period of tumultuous events, remained in this thrall even after the capture of Constantinople by Crusaders in 1204 split Greece between Latin and Byzantine interests. This situation continued until 1453 when Constantinople fell to the Ottoman Turks who had already occupied much of Greece's territory. Thereafter, Greece remained under Turkish overlordship until 1830 when the Greek state emerged from the fires of revolution. The nation did not achieve its modern borders, however, until 1923.

Historical literature on Greece is found in abundance. A HISTORY OF GREECE TO THE DEATH OF ALEXANDER THE GREAT [33], by J.B. Bury, and Rostovtzeff's already mentioned GREECE [169], are the best works on the Classical period. George Finlay's seven-volume HISTORY OF GREECE FROM ITS CONQUEST BY THE ROMANS TO THE PRESENT DAY, B.C. 164 TO A.D. 1864 [68] is very good as a general history that covers approximately 18 centuries of development.

The Byzantine period is available in two classics, George Ostrogorski's HISTORY OF THE BYZANTINE STATE [148], and a second

11

volume by the same title by A.A. Vasiliev [222]. Dimitri Obolensky's THE BYZANTINE COMMONWEALTH. EAST EUROPE, 500-1453 [146] is excellent, as is Joan Hussey's little gem THE BYZANTINE WORLD [101]. This 188-page book presents a clear, concise picture of the Eastern Empire and can stand by itself as a source of general background for the average reader. BYZANTIUM: AN INTRODUCTION TO EAST ROMAN CIVILIZATION [236], by Baines and Moss, is also very well done.

THE GREEK PHOENIX [21], by Joseph Braddock, is an excellent account of the revolutionary fervor in Greece that developed over a long period of time and manifested itself in sufficient strength only in the early 19th century to force the lifting of the Turkish yoke. Jack Lindsay's BYZANTIUM INTO EUROPE [128] relates directly to the Eastern Empire's hegemony in the Balkans. Two other excellent sources are, of course, the CAMBRIDGE ANCIENT HISTORY [35], and the CAMBRIDGE MEDIEVAL HISTORY [36]. The former is valuable for the Classical period, while the latter, specifically volumes 1, 2, and 4, contain information relevant to the Byzantine Age.

A SHORT HISTORY OF MODERN GREECE, 1821-1956 [73], by E.S. Forster, gives a good account of the period between Greece's two major revolutions of the modern age. This is one of the best studies of this crucial time in Greek history. Dionysios Zakythinos' THE MAKING OF MODERN GREECE: FROM BYZANTIUM TO INDEPENDENCE [233] is an excellent narration of the Turkish period.

IMPERIAL RUSSIA AND THE SOVIET UNION

Russia's earliest entrance into the Balkans is probably unrecorded, but it definitely preceded the Ottoman invasion by several centuries. The RUSSIAN PRIMARY CHRONICLE records that, in 968 AD, the Rus' Kievan prince Sviatoslav I (962-972) entered the region in response to a call for aid from the Byzantine emperor, Nicephorus II Phocas (963-969). This came about as a result of the Eastern Empire's inability to put down a Bulgar revolt and a 25-year-old mutual assistance treaty. Sviatoslav's Varangian force was able to quell the uprising and, in doing so, the Rus' leader became attracted to the lands around the Danube and decided to settle in the Dobrudja area.

Not without provocation, the new emperor, John I Tzimisces (969-976), was forced to dislodge the Rus' in 971. The treacherous Pecheneg ambush and massacre of Sviatoslav's band as it returned to Kiev is well recorded. What is not as well recorded is the possible long-term implications of that action. Surely, it would be difficult to trace a direct causal relationship between the incident in the 10th century and the events that transpired from the 15th into the 20th century. But there does appear in the Russian mentality a desire to possess the Balkans and succeeding chapters of the study will illustrate that point in detail, along with some other theories involved in the Russian preoccupation with the Balkans and the Ottoman Empire.

Russia's history, especially its military history, is dealt with elsewhere in this bibliographic series, but there are one or two works that are of general interest and are worth mentioning here, if only to maintain the continuity of presentation. Good accounts of particular periods may always be found in any of the

CAMBRIDGE series. Other general histories will be mentioned in the course of succeeding chapters. One exceptionally good study is "Russia and the Balkans" in RUSSIAN FOREIGN POLICY: ESSAYS IN HISTORICAL PROSPECTIVE [120], which was edited by Ivo Lederer and published in 1962.

A most useful tool is AN ATLAS OF RUSSIAN AND EAST EUROPEAN HISTORY [1] that authoritatively illustrates the region encompassing the Soviet Union as we see today, and the lands bounded by the Baltic Sea, the Elbe River, the Adriatic, and the Turkish Straits. Although the scope is greater than the Balkans alone, the atlas is well worth its modest cost. Another good one is Martin Gilbert's RUSSIAN HISTORY ATLAS [77]. This is a very detailed work that graphically displays Russia's expansion through the centuries. RUSSIA ASTRIDE THE BALKANS [17], by Robert Bishop and E.S. Crayfield, is also good reading.

THE HABSBURG EMPIRE

The great Habsburg (Hapsburg) Empire was another major, outside influence and threat to the Balkans. Beginning as early as the last quarter of the 13th century, the Habsburgs sat on the throne of the Holy Roman Empire, and they held on to that largely theoretical realm until Napoleon brought its demise in 1806. By 1700, however, the lands of the Habsburgs included several parts of the Balkans proper, plus larger segments of the lands along the Balkan frontiers. Chief among this latter group was the Austro-Hungarian Empire that, through the 16th-20th centuries, posed a major threat to the status quo of the region. In part, Austro-Hungarian policies toward the Balkans were a reaction to the activities of Imperial Russia, but aggrandizement for its own sake was never overlooked in Vienna.

A study of Austria-Hungary presents one of the most fertile fields of research. There is a great deal written in the form of general histories, in the form of more specialized histories regarding Austro-Hungarian policies toward the Balkans, and in the form of Austro-Hungarian military history. Many of these last two categories of works will be pointed out in later chapters, but a few general histories ought to be mentioned here.

THE HOLY ROMAN EMPIRE [87], by Friedrich Heer, is a useful source of information on the overall picture of the state that claimed, if not exercised dominion over, all the Christian princes of Europe. Heer's book is somewhat ponderous but is worth the effort. The classic presentation of this subject is James Bryce's THE HOLY ROMAN EMPIRE [27] that was written in 1906.

There are many excellent histories of the Habsburg Empire. Among this number are Robert Kann's A HISTORY OF THE HABSBURG EMPIRE, 1526-1918 [108]. Published in 1974, this book breaks with the traditional presentation of the Habsburg family as the central theme of the narrative and concentrates instead upon the numerous peoples who were subject to them. William Coxe's HISTORY OF THE HOUSE OF AUSTRIA [52], which was first published in 1847, and reissued in 1971, takes the more traditional approach in its coverage of the period 1218-1792. Adam Wandruszka's THE HOUSE OF HABSBURG: SIX HUNDRED YEARS OF A EUROPEAN DYNASTY [227] was originally published in German in 1956, and was later translated into English. The English edition is very difficult to read because of the inflexible style used in the translation process. This is extremely unfortunate as it is a good book. THE PEOPLES OF THE EASTERN HABSBURG LANDS, 1526-1918 [109], by Robert Kann and Zdanec David, was recently published as a part of the HISTORY OF EAST CENTRAL EUROPE [200] series and is very valuable as a tool for gaining an understanding of the relationships between Vienna and the subject provinces in the Balkan region.

Victor Tapie's THE RISE AND FALL OF THE HABSBURG MONARCHY [202], which was originally published in French and later translated into English, is a pleasure to read. THE HABSBURG EMPIRE, 1790-1918 [130], by C.A. Macartney, is an excellent account of the century-long struggle for power that took place between the conservative regime and the nationalistic forces that were developing within the borders of the empire's multinational holdings.

### TURKEY

Turkish movement to the west began in the 13th century when Mongol forces overcame Seljuk and Kipchak tribes and were, themselves, absorbed and brought under Turkish leadership. These Turco-Mongols began their expansion as a dynamic of the prospect of the rich plunder known to exist in the Christian empire to the West and as a consequence of the Mohammedan concept of GHAZA, in which conquest also brings the defeat of the infidel, all in the name of Allah. This type of war in the name of religion or obligation to faith (JIHAD), as well as the more pragmatic desire for booty, led to the Ottomans confronting Byzantium which defended its borders with force and determination. It should be noted that the term "Ottoman" has no ethnic or specific meaning but is, rather, a corruption of the Arabic "Othman" that was to become the Turkish "Osman" as a dynastic term referring to Prince Osman I (d.1326). Ottoman is, therefore, a word that means "Osmanli," or followers of Osman.

This early Ottoman period is discussed in detail by Muzaffer Erendil in "Emergence of the Ottoman State; An Outline of the Period Between 1299-1453" [64]. Highlighted in this excellent report are comments about the early military organization of the Turks and the reign of Sultan Murad I (1360-1389) that led to the conquest of the Balkans. There are very good accounts of the 1389 Battle of Kosovo, the siege of Constantinople by Sultan Bayasid I, the Battle of Nicopolis (Nigbolu), and the important Battle of Varna (10 November 1444), where the European defeat confirmed Ottoman hegemony in the Balkans.

There are numerous general histories available that outline Ottoman, and later Turkish, developments. Wayne Vucinich's THE OTTOMAN EMPIRE: ITS RECORD AND LEGACY [226] is very good, as is William Eton's A SURVEY OF THE TURKISH EMPIRE [65], and Arnold Toynbee's TURKEY [211]. Among the other important works are Sir Edward Creasy's HISTORY OF THE OTTOMAN TURKS [54], Lord Kinross' THE OTTOMAN CENTURIES [112], Lord Eversley's THE TURKISH EMPIRE FROM 1288 TO 1914 [67], and Albert Habib Hourani's THE OTTOMAN BACKGROUND OF THE MODERN MIDDLE EAST [96]. Prince Dimitri Cantemir's THE

HISTORY OF THE GROWTH AND DECAY OF THE OTTOMAN EMPIRE [38] was first published in English in 1733-1734. Cantemir, who ruled as prince of Moldavia in 1693, 1710-1711, was a humanist scholar but his work is purely polemical and should be used with caution.

No such warning need be issued for the superb history written by Halil Inalcik. His THE OTTOMAN EMPIRE: THE CLASSICAL AGE [102] is a near perfect example of the art of writing history and must not be overlooked. As much may be said for Stanford Shaw's two_volume HISTORY OF THE OTTOMAN EMPIRE AND MODERN TURKEY. Volume 1 is EMPIRE OF THE GAZIS: THE RISE AND DECLINE OF THE OTTOMAN EMPIRE, 1280-1808 [185], and volume 2, which he wrote with his wife, REFORM, REVOLUTION AND REPUBLIC: THE RISE OF MODERN TURKEY: 1808-1975 [186]. These works all complement each other and each has an excellent bibliography. Two histories in French are also worth noting: Joseph Hammer-Purgstall's HISTOIRE DE L'EMPIRE OTTOMAN [85] and Mehmet Fuat Koprulu's LES ORIGINES DE L'EMPIRE OTTOMAN [115].

Another good choice is George Arnakis's THE NEAR EAST IN MODERN TIMES: THE OTTOMAN EMPIRE AND THE BALKANS TO 1900 [6]. Published in 1969, this is the first book of a two-volume set. The second volume, by Arnakis with Wayne Vucinich, is THE NEAR EAST IN MODERN TIMES: FORTY CRUCIAL YEARS, 1900-1940 [7]. It was published in 1972. THE OTTOMAN IMPACT ON EUROPE [50], by Paul Coles, and W.E.D. Allen's THE TURKS IN EUROPE [3], both relate directly to the Balkans. The latter work is somewhat outdated, but is still one of the best accounts of the Ottoman hegemony.

THE EMERGENCE OF MODERN TURKEY [126], by Bernard Lewis, is also a good selection. Written by a leading western authority on Turkey, and published by the prestigious Royal Institute of International Affairs, this work is a useful source for background information on the Balkans. Sir Charles Eliot's TURKEY IN EUROPE [62], written between 1896 and 1900, is the account of a British civil servant who spent many years in Constantinople.

## BIBLIOGRAPHIC AND OTHER REFERENCE SOURCES ON THE BALKANS

In addition to those already mentioned, there are a number of bibliographic and other reference sources about the Balkans that deserve comment. Only a few of these deal with military history as a subject, but all of them will serve as starting point for the astute researcher.

A most helpful reference is SOUTHEASTERN EUROPE: A GUIDE TO BASIC PUBLICATIONS [93]. This work was edited by Paul Horecky and was published in 1973. It presents an overview of the sources of historical, geographical, and political information on the region that deal, not only with policy, but also with people. Reference works, monographs, journals, and occasional papers are listed, most of which are in Balkan languages. There are, however, sufficient listings in western languages and in Russian to make it generally useful. This is probably the most exhaustive resource work available and covers the publication period 1930-1960. To anyone seriously interested in the study of the Balkans, this is a must. A second compilation by Horecky, EAST CENTRAL EUROPE: A GUIDE TO BASIC PUBLICATIONS [92], has a section on Hungary that is not included in the first work.

Another, most worthwhile reference is A DOCUMENTARY HISTORY OF EASTERN EUROPE [11], by Alfred Bannon and Achilles Edelenyi. This book contains 88 source documents including treaties, chronicles, letters and accounts of travelers, each with an interpretive preamble by the authors. Although it covers all of Eastern Europe, most of the selections deal with material directly related to the Balkans, with only Albania being completely ignored. Some items of military interest are included such as the declaration of war that began the 1885 conflict between Serbia and Bulgaria.

For anyone with access to the Washington, DC, area, the Library of Congress offers almost unlimited material on the Balkans. Although it is now substantially outdated, Paul Horecky's 1964 article in SLAVIC REVIEW, "The Slavic and East European Resources and Facilities of the Library of Congress" [94], is a tool in itself as it makes the way so much easier. The same year the Horecky article was published, the Library of Congress put out THE USSR AND EASTERN EUROPE: PERIODICALS IN WESTERN LANGUAGES [219]. This work is also outdated, but it, and the Horecky article, is offered here as an illustration of the type of reference that is available.

Although not unique to the Library of Congress, nor to the study of the Balkans, the NATIONAL UNION CATALOG has some 14,000,000 pre-1952 imprints among which most of what has been written about military history in the Balkans is recorded. Supplements to the catalog have been produced in several series since the original was produced and keep the entire process updated.

In 1974, the American Association for the Advancement of Slavic Studies produced BALKANISTICA: OCCASIONAL PAPERS IN SOUTHEAST EUROPEAN STUDIES [144]. This work, edited by Kenneth E. Naylor and others, contains a series of essays such as one by Kemal Karpat in which he espouses the theory that nationalism arose in the Balkans as a result of significant social changes in the Ottoman Empire itself. Specialists in Romanian, Greek and Bulgarian studies then offer their critical comments. Stephan Horak's JUNIOR SLAVICA: A SELECTED ANNOTATED BIBLIOGRAPHY OF BOOKS IN ENGLISH ON RUSSIA AND EAST EUROPE [91] is also useful, as is the CHECKLIST OF PAPERBOUND BOOKS ON RUSSIA AND EAST EUROPE [191], by Spector and Legters, though published in 1966 and now somewhat dated.

The SLAVIC REVIEW, the journal of AAASS, has, since 1975, published an annual selection of references from the preceding year in its September issue. The editors admit to the highly selective nature of the list but, at the same time, point to its preparation by specialists. Each year, the SLAVIC REVIEW also publishes a listing of pertinent doctoral dissertations in its December issue. These included dissertations approved at American, Canadian, and British universities. The 1971-1972 list, for example, contained 258 titles that include, for example, Jack Tucker's "The Peasant Revolt of 1907: Three Regional Studies," that was presented to and accepted by the University of Chicago in 1972.

Another source of information on the Balkans is the four-volume INDEX TO BOOK REVIEWS IN HISTORICAL PERIODICALS [25] that covers works published in the 1972-1975 period. RUSSIAN AND EAST

EUROPEAN PUBLICATIONS IN THE LIBRARIES OF THE UNITED STATES [171], prepared by Melville Ruggles and Vaslac Mastecky, is useful, while the ACADEMIC WRITER'S GUIDE TO PERIODICALS II: EAST EUROPEAN AND SLAVIC STUDIES [235], compiled and edited by Lewis Tambs and Alexander Birkos, furnishes a listing of periodicals that carry articles on East Europe and, specifically, the Balkans. An excellent reference in French is ENCYCLOPEDIE BALKANIQUE PERMANENTE [172], than was begun in 1936 under the directorship of Leon Savadjian.

There are numerous collections and other reference sources on Greece and Byzantium. The best collection in the United States is located at Dumbarton Oaks in Washington, DC. The Byzantine Empire is the subject of several periodicals that are devoted to its study. BYZANTINISCHE ZEITSCRIFT has been published almost continuously since 1892, and publishes an annual bibliography. ECHOS D'ORIENT began in 1897 and was published continuously until 1939 when World War II intervened. It started up again in 1943 as ETUDES BYZANTINES and ran for three more years before expiring in 1946. Three years later, in 1949, a new publication was produced that has continued to the present as REVUE DES ETUDES BYZANTINES. Three other useful publications are BYZANTINOSLAVICA, BYZANTION, and VIZANTISKY VREMENNIK.

Sources of reference data on Modern Greece include GREECE: A SELECTED LIST OF REFERENCES [26], by A.D. Brown and H.D. Jones. The GREEK BIBLIOGRAPHY [78], published in three volumes in Greek, and compiled by D.S. Gines and B.G. Mexas, deals with the period 1800-1863. Another publication by the same title, GREEK BIBLIOGRAPHY [82], is published periodically by the Greek Ministry of Press and Information and is in French and English. The well-known Institute of Balkan Studies at Thessalonike produces VALKANIKE VIVLIOGRAPHIA [206], an annual bibliographic series, often with supplements, it began in 1975. Obviously, more than Balkan military history is included, but a great number of pertinent sources may be discovered by careful perusal. G.I. Phousaras' BIBLIOGRAPHY OF GREEK BIBLIOGRAPHIES, 1791-1947 [152] is also found only in Greek.

Another bibliography of Greek material covering the period up to 1790 was produced in 11 volumes in Paris between 1885 and 1928. It is BIBLIOGRAPHIE HELLENIQUE [122] by E. Legrand. Legrand also compiled BIBLIOGRAPHIE IONIENNE [123], that was published in two volumes in 1910. This reference covers the period 1494-1900. The Institute Francaise d'Athenes publishes a periodical, BULLETIN ANALYTIQUE DE BIBLIOGRAPHIE HELLENIQUE, in French, while the Royal Research Foundation in Athens has published, since 1950, a series of bibliographies that covers various periods in Greek history.

There are also a number of bibliographic articles on Greece that have been published in western journals in English. Among these are: AHR: W. Miller, XXXVII (January 1932), 272-279; XL (July 1935), 688-693. BYZANTINE-METABYZANTINE: P.W. Topping, I (1949), 113-127. CHJ: W. Miller, II (1928), 229-247; IV (1938), 115-120. JMH: W. Miller, II (December 1930), 612-628; IX (March 1937), 56-63; P.W. Topping, XXXIII (June 1961), 167-173; S.H. Weber, XXI (September 1950), 250-266.

THE AMERICAN BIBLIOGRAPHY OF SLAVIC AND EAST EUROPEAN STUDIES [4], published annually since 1956, is another tool for finding data on the Balkans. Up to 1972, this publication was a part of the RUSSIAN AND EAST EUROPEAN SERIES published at the University of Indiana. A new publication, expected to be published every two years, is the BULLETIN DE BIBLIOGRAPHIE [49]. This is the work of the Comite de Bibliographie of the Commission Internationale d'Histoire Militaire. Four issues have already been published. Books selected for inclusion in this publication are chosen by the member national commissions in the CIHM such as the United States Commission on Military History. Each entry lists the title and other bibliographic matter and has a short description of the work, usually presented in two languages. Numerous entries on the Balkans are to be found in these issues.

There are also a number of other foreign language references worthy of attention. There are three volumes in the SUDOSTEUROPA-BIBLIOGRAPHIE [197], the first of which was published in 1956 by the Sudost Institut in Munich. The third volume, put out in 1968, contains, for example, more than 8,000 titles of books, articles and dissertations, in many languages, that deal with subjects on Albania, Slovakia, Hungary, Romania, Bulgaria, Yugoslavia, and the Southeastern European area in general. One should also look at the BIBLIOGRAPHIE DER ARBEITEN ZUR OSTEUROPAISCHEN GESCHICHTE AUS DEN DEUTSCHSPRACHIGEN FACHZEITSCHRIFTEN 1858-1964 [137], and the BIBLIOGRAPHIE DER SLAVISTISCHEN ARBEITEN AUS DEN DEUTSCHSPRACHIGEN FACHZEITSCHRIFTEN 1876-1963 [176]. Both are part of the BIBLIOGRAPHISCHE MITTEILUNGEN DES OSTEUROPA-INSTITUTS AN DER FREIEN UNIVERSITAT BERLIN, and both are selective compilations of thousands of entries, although not exclusively on the Balkans. Other foreign language works include the BIBLIOGRAPHIE D'ETUDES BALKANIQUES [32] that was published as a result of the First International Congress of Balkan Studies in 1966.

Among the more specialized references that apply to the general subject area are Roger E. Kanet's SOVIET AND EAST EUROPEAN FOREIGN POLICY: A BIBLIOGRAPHY OF ENGLISH AND RUSSIAN LANGUAGE PUBLICATIONS, 1967-1971 [107]. This work contains 3,237 listings of books and articles arranged by topic and geographic areas. The SUBJECT CATALOG OF MICRO EDITIONS; RUSSIA, USSR, EASTERN EUROPE [212], which is published in Switzerland, contains over 7,000 titles from the Inter Documentation Company's Slavic Microfiche Collections. Published periodically, this work is usually complete to within 12 months of the present date.

There are two good bibliographies that deal with Albania. Emilio Legrand's BIBLIOGRAPHIE ALBANAISE [121], and the KATALOG DER BIBLIOTHEK DES ALBANIEN [2], published by the Albanian Institute in Munich. Both are rather small, but so are the available sources.

Bulgarian references include a series called LA SCIENCE HISTORIQUE BULGARE [29], which is a part of the ETUDES HISTORIQUES published by the Academy of Science in Sofia. Among these studies are several bibliographies such as the one covering works published 1965-1969. This work contains 3,560 entries in Bulgarian, Russian, and French, many of which are on military history. This document also lists the various research centers, archives, and museums in Bulgaria. There is also one bibliography of Bulgarian military history that was published in Sofia in 1972-1973 in French. HISTOIRE

MILITAIRE DE LA BULGARIE, 681-1945. BIBLIOGRAPHIE [90] contains 2,470 entries in this first of a reported two-volume edition.

As a part of this same general program, the Bulgarian Academy of Science also published L'HISTOIRE BULGARE DANS LES OUVRAGES DES SAVANTS EUROPEENS [28], in 1969. This is a collection of the writings of other European scholars who have been engaged in research on Bulgaria. It is quite good. Another Bulgarian Academy source is DOCUMENTS AND MATERIALS ON THE HISTORY OF THE BULGARIAN PEOPLE [31]. This book contains English translations of documents beginning with a 7th-century tract from Miracula Sancti Demetrii to a 1940 letter to the Prime Minister discussing the Macedonian situation. In all, some 347 documents are revealed, many of them of military importance. A careful examination of the selections raises a few questions about the motivations behind some of the choices and, except for three facsimiles, there is no way to check the accuracy of the translations. They are obviously well done, however, and these few criticisms aside, the work is excellent. Marin Pundeff's BULGARIA: A BIBLIOGRAPHIC GUIDE [156] is divided into two sections, one that discusses sources by category and a second that lists the same references alphabetically.

As a last reference on Bulgaria, mention should be made of IZVESTIA NA BULGARSKOTO ISTORICHESKO DRUZHESTVO [30], a series that began in 1905, and which has been published rather steadily until 1951, when the Bulgarian Historical Society, although Marxist, came under Stalin's suspicion and was abolished. With the revival of the group in 1964, the series was renewed. Each issue contains a number of articles on national and local history, and on Bulgarian historiography. Volume 25, published in 1967, contains an index of the preceding 24 volumes.

A number of Hungarian sources are also available, the best of which is MONUMENTA HUNGARIAE HISTORICA [99]. This may be supplemented with IRATOK A NEMZETISEGI KERDES TORTENETEHEZ MAGYARORSZAGON A DUALIZMUS KORABAN 1867-1918 [110], a six-volume series of document collections compiled and annotated by Gabor Kemeny. Volume 5 was published in 1971 and covers the period 1906-1913. In all, over 2,000 documents are displayed in the five volumes that deal with the pervading issue of dualism and that led to many of the situations that are part of Hungary's military history. Two other valuable Hungarian bibliographical references are the two-volume BIBLIOGRAFIAI TAJEKOZTATO [98], and the HUNGARIAN BIBLIOGRAPHIC SERIES [117], which is published annually by the Kossuth Foundation in New York. Lastly, a comprehensive, 8,800 entry, bibliography exists in A MAGYAR TORTENETTUDOMANY VALOGATOTT BIBLIOGRAFIJA, 1945-1968 [100], which was produced by the Hungarian Academy of Sciences.

Romanian reference sources are quite plentiful. Stephen Fisher-Galati's "Romania, a Bibliographic Guide" [71], published by the Library of Congress' Slavic and Central European Division in 1963, is only 75 pages, but is excellent. Another small, but useful reference is Kenneth Rock's LIST OF MATERIALS FOR THE STUDY OF THE HISTORY OF ROMANIA SHOWING HOLDINGS IN THE LIBRARIES OF STANFORD UNIVERSITY [159]. The already-mentioned Chronological History of Romania [79] is also a good reference source, but not without its flaws. ISTORIA ROMANIEI. GHID BIBLIOGRAFIC [37], that was compiled

19

by Sanda Candea, is also a useful reference.

DOCUMENTA ROMANIAE HISTORICA [165] is another Romanian source of some importance. This reference is organized in three series, each dealing with the document resources of one of the three principal provinces -- Wallachia, Moldavia, and Transylvania. When completed, each series is to include the pertinent documents up to 1700 for Wallachia and Moldavia, and up to 1541 for Transylvania, This collection is supplemented by DOCUMENTA PRIVIND ISTORIA ROMANIEI [164], and DOCUMENTA PRIVIND ISTORIA MILITARA A POPORULUI ROMAN [163], the former being the precursor to the BHR series, while the latter deals with military historical documentation. In APARAREA PATRIEI, A INDEPENDENTA SI SUVERANITATII NATIONAL [161], documents are collected that deal with the struggle for Romanian independence. A second collection, APARAREA NATIONALA A ROMANIEI SOCIALIST [162], holds a selection of documents on national defense thinking by the present government.

A unique volume that ought to be mentioned is PAGES FROM THE HISTORY OF THE ROMANIAN ARMY [173], which is a monograph collection of 19 articles by some of Romania's leading military historians and theorists. This volume is a part of the BHR [166] series. This work contains articles covering Romanian military history from the Geto-Dacian period to present-day defense theories. FILE DIN ISTORIA MILITARA A POPORULUI ROMAN [41] is another series that contains numerous articles on Romanian military history in the Romanian language, but with summaries prepared in Russian, English, French, or German. A special multilanguage edition of this publication called PAGES FROM THE MILITARY HISTORY OF THE ROMANIAN PEOPLE [42] was published in 1980 in commemoration of the XV International Congress of Historical Sciences held in Bucharest that year. Another excellent series is STUDII SI MATERIALE DE MUZEOGRAFIE SI ISTORIA MILITARA [167], which is the source of many fine articles dealing primarily with artifactual history.

There are equally fertile fields of bibliographic sources available on Yugoslavia. The KATALOG KNJIGA NA JEZICIMA JUGOSLAVENSKIH NARODA [230] is a listing of some 3,050 titles printed between 1519 and 1867 in one of the Yugoslav languages. There are numerous indices and an additional bibliography included. VODIC KROZ ARHIVSKE FONDOVE [231] describes, in five volumes, the archival holdings of five of the eight major repositories in Yugoslavia. Three more volumes are expected which will complete the series and will cover the period from 1225 to 1971. Another Yugoslav bibliography, published in cyrillic Serbo-Croatian, ENGLESKA BIBLIOGRAFIJA O ISTOCNOM PITANJU V EVROPI [106]. This is a compilation of English language publications on the Balkan peninsula and on the Eastern Question. It also contains a number of useful references and is well indexed.

Turkish reference books include TURKISH AND MONGOLIAN STUDIES [48], by Sir Gerard Clauson, and Franz Babinger's DIE GESCHICHTSSCHREIBER DER OSMANEN UND IHRE WERKE [9]. Excellent bibliographies may be found in the ENCYCLOPEDIA OF ISLAM [74/97], which is found in two editions. Military historical documentation may be found in HARP TARIHI BELGELERI DERGISI [213], that is published by the Turkish General Staff. TURK SILAHLI KUVVETLERI TARIHI [214] is a serial published by the Department of War History of the Turkish General Staff in Ankara. This series is the official historical record of the Turkish armed forces and is, for the most part, of exceptional quality. Each volume in the series, which has thus far been published only in Turkish, is individually authored. The best overall source is ISLAM ANSIKLOPEDISI [215], an encyclopedic series that is also printed in Turkish.

In 1960, Stanford Shaw published an article, "Archival Sources for Ottoman History: The Archives of Turkey" [184], in JAOS. This article is a gazetteer of the holdings of the several archival repositories in that country and, although it is nearly a quarter-century old, it is still useful. The Library of Congress publishes REPORTS ON CURRENT RESEARCH ON THE MIDDLE EAST [218]. Among the articles carried in this publication was R.H. Davison's "European Archives as a Source of Later Ottoman History" [56]. The Soviet Institute of Eastern Affairs published BIBLIOGRAFIYA TURTSII (1917-1958) [220] in 1959. It contains a listing of works on Turkey published in the USSR in the Russian language.

Another Soviet publication, MATERIALY PO ISTORII BALKANSKIKH SLAVIAN V OTDEL RUKOPISEI I REDKIKH KNIG GPB: KATALOG [221], was published in 1978, by the Leningrad Public Library's Department of Manuscripts and Rare Books. It is in effect, a catalogue of catalogues on books dealing with the Southern Slavs and with the Balkans.

There is also a reference called BIBLIOGRAPHIC GUIDE TO SOVIET AND EAST EUROPEAN STUDIES [145], which is published annually since 1978. The 1980 edition, for example, is in three volumes and contains 2,700 pages of listings of material published throughout the world on the USSR and Eastern Europe, including the Balkans, except Turkey and Greece, for that year. In addition, a new guide to Russian and Soviet resources called THE RUSSIAN EMPIRE AND THE SOVIET UNION: A GUIDE TO MANUSCRIPTS AND ARCHIVAL MATERIAL IN THE UNITED STATES [81] was published in 1981. It doubles the Russian material described in the NATIONAL UNION CATALOG OF MANUSCRIPTS. Patricia Grimsted's ARCHIVES AND MANUSCRIPT COLLECTIONS IN THE USSR [83] makes available lists of finding aids, including archival guides, manuscript catalogues, and other reference literature.

The Czechoslovakian Academy of Sciences published BIBLIOGRAFIE CESKOSLOVENSKE BALKANISTIKY [55] in 1966. This work contains a listing of studies on the Balkans prepared in that country between 1945-1965. The Bulgarian Academy of Sciences has also produced a bibliography under the direction of its Balkan Institute. This 217-page volume is called PETNADESET GODINI INSTITUT ZA BALKANISTIKA, 1964-1978: ISTORICHESKA SPRAVKA I BIBLIOGRAFIIA [183], and includes entries in Bulgarian and French. It has an excellent index.

Lastly, another most valuable source of reference data is Anton Scherer's SUDOSTEUROPA-DISSERTATIONEN, 1918-1960 [174]. This report contains a listing of all German, Austrian, and Swiss-German dissertations produced over the last four decades. It is extremely useful as a source of additional bibliographical material.

## MILITARY HISTORY IN GENERAL

While there is a great deal written about the Balkans in general and a fair amount of material on specific Balkan military events, trends, and institutions, there are very few works in any language that deal with the overall military history of the region. Most western military historians seem to have avoided the Balkans in their pursuits. There are a few good works that deal specifically with the Balkans, of course, and these will be mentioned where appropriate. On the whole, however, most of the work that has been accomplished is presented in a number of broadly outlined studies from which both the scholar and the casual reader must draw whatever conclusions are to be found about war and the military in that corner of Europe. One of the better general sources is A GUIDE TO THE STUDY AND USE OF MILITARY HISTORY [105] which was produced in the U.S. Army's Center of Military History under the general editorship of John E. Jessup and Robert W. Coakley. There are numerous and extensive bibliographies throughout this volume. In Chapter 6, for example, Jeffrey Clarke lists and discusses over 300 works dealing with "World Military History, 1786-1945" [47]. Other military historical material relating to the Balkans will be discussed in each chapter.

## BIBLIOGRAPHIC LISTING

1. Adams, A.E., et al. AN ATLAS OF RUSSIAN AND EAST EUROPEAN HISTORY. New York: 1967 [1966].

2. Albanian Institute. KATALOG DER BIBLIOTHEK DES ALBANIEN. Munich: 1977.

3. Allen, W.E.D. THE TURKS IN EUROPE. London: 1919.

4. THE AMERICAN BIBLIOGRAPHY OF SLAVIC AND EAST EUROPEAN STUDIES. REES. Published annually. 1956-.

5. Anastasoff, C. THE BULGARIANS: FROM THEIR ARRIVAL IN THE BALKANS TO MODERN TIMES, THIRTEEN CENTURIES OF HISTORY. Hicksville, NY: c.1977.

6. Arnakis, G.G. THE NEAR EAST IN MODERN TIMES. Vol. 1: THE OTTOMAN EMPIRE AND THE BALKANS TO 1900. New York & Austin: 1969.

7. Arnakis, G.G., & Vucinich, W.S. THE NEAR EAST IN MODERN TIMES. Vol. 2: FORTY CRUCIAL YEARS, 1900-1940. New York & Austin: 1972.

8. Babinger, F.C.H. AUFSATZE UND ABHANDLUNGEN ZUR GESCHICHTE SUDOSTEUROPAS UND DER LEVANTE. 3 vols. Munich: 1962-1976.

9. _____. DIE GESCHICHTSSCHREIBER DER OSMANEN UND IHRE WERKE. Leipzig: 1927.

10. Balcescu, N. THE ARMED FORCES AND THE MILITARY ART OF THE ROMANIANS, FROM THE FOUNDING OF THE PRINCIPALITY OF WALLACHIA UNTIL NOW. Jassy: 1844.

11. Bannan, A.J., & Edelenyi, A. A DOCUMENTARY HISTORY OF EASTERN EUROPE. NEW YORK: 1970.

12. Barker, E. MACEDONIA: ITS PLACE IN BALKAN POWER POLITICS. RIFA. London: 1950.

13. Bartholomew, J., ed. EASTERN EUROPE. BWS. Edinburgh: 1968.

14. Omitted

15. Beckinsale, M., & Beckinsale, R. SOUTHERN EUROPE: A SYSTEMATIC GEOGRAPHICAL SURVEY. New York: 1975.

16. Bercovici, K. THE INCREDIBLE BALKANS. New York: 1932.

17. Bishop, R., & Crayfield, E.S. RUSSIA ASTRIDE THE BALKANS. New York: 1948.

18. Black, C.E. "The Balkan Slavs in the Middle Ages," HANDBOOK OF SLAVIC STUDIES. Edited by L.I. Strakhovsky. Harvard: 1949.

19. Boniface, A. THE CROATIAN NATION IN ITS STRUGGLE FOR FREEDOM AND INDEPENDENCE. Chicago: 1955.

20. Bosquit, G. HISTOIRE DU PEUPLE BULGARE, DEPUIS LES ORIGINES JUSQU'A NOS JOURS. Paris: 1909.

21. Braddock, J. THE GREEK PHOENIX. New York: 1973 [1972].

22. Brailsford, H.N. MACEDONIA: ITS RACES AND ITS FUTURE. London: 1906.

23. Braun, E. von. RUMANIEN. Leipzig: 1877.

24. Braun, M. DIE SLAWEN AUF DEM BALKAN BIS ZUR BEFREIUNG VON DER TURKISCHEN HERRSCHAFT. Leipzig: 1941.

25. Brewster, J.W., & McLeod, J.A. INDEX TO BOOK REVIEWS IN HISTORICAL PERIODICALS, 1972-1976. 5 vols. Metuchen, NJ: 1975-1977.

26. Brown, A.D., & Jones, H.D. GREECE: A SELECTED LIST OF REFERENCES. Washington: 1943.

27. Bryce, J. THE HOLY ROMAN EMPIRE. London: 1906.

28. Bulgaria, Academy od Sciences, L'HISTOIRE BULGARE DANS LES OUVRAGES DES SAVANTS EUROPEENS. REHPB 1. Sofia: 1969.

29. _____. LA SCIENCE HISTORIQUE BULGARE, 1965-1969. Supp. V to Biblio. II, ETUDES HISTORIQUES. Sofia: 1970.

30. _____. IZVESTIA NA BULGARSKOTO ISTORICHESKO DRUZHESTVO. 25 vols. Sofia: 1905-1948, 1964-.

31. _____. DOCUMENTS AND MATERIALS ON THE HISTORY OF THE BULGARIAN PEOPLE. Edited by M. Voynov et al. Sofia: 1968.

32. _____. BIBLIOGRAPHIE D'ETUDES BALKANIQUES, 1966. Edited by N. Todorov et al. Sofia: 1968.

33. Bury, J.B. A HISTORY OF GREECE TO THE DEATH OF ALEXANDER THE GREAT. 3rd ed. Revised by R. Meiggs. London: 1951 [1900].

34. Byrnes, R.F., ed. YUGOSLAVIA. New York: 1957.

35. CAMBRIDGE ANCIENT HISTORY. 12 vols. Cambridge: 1923-1939.

36. CAMBRIDGE MEDIEVAL HISTORY. 8 vols. Cambridge: 1911-1936.

37. Candea, S. ISTORIA ROMANIEI. GHID BIBLIOGRAFIC. Bucharest: 1968.

38. Cantimir, D., Prince. THE HISTORY OF THE GROWTH AND DECAY OF
    THE OTTOMAN EMPIRE. Trans. by N. Tindal. London:
    1733-1734.

39. Carter, F., ed. AN HISTORICAL GEOGRAPHY OF THE BALKANS. London
    & New York: 1977.

40. Cazanisteanu, C. "Evolution de la structure d'organization de
    l'armee roumaine sous l'influence du developpment
    socio-politique et des realizations techniques et
    scientifiques," RIHM 48 (1980), 108-120.

41. Ceaucescu, I. ed. FILE DIN ISTORIA MILITARA A POPORULUI ROMAN.
    Bucharest: 1973-.

42. _____. PAGES FROM THE MILITARY HISTORY OF THE ROMANIAN
    PEOPLE. Bucharest: 1980.

43. Chandler, D.G. ATLAS OF MILITARY STRATEGY. New York: 1980.

44. Chekrezi, C.A. ALBANIA, PAST AND PRESENT. New York: 1971
    [c.1919].

45. CIHM. BULLETIN DE BIBLIOGRAPHIE. Berne: 1978-.

46. Clark, G.N., Sir., et al. Advisory Comm. THE NEW CAMBRIDGE
    MODERN HISTORY. 14 vols. Cambridge: 1957-1970.

47. Clarke, J.J. "World Military History, 1786-1945," GSUMH.
    Washington: 1979.

48. Clauson, G.L.M., Sir. TURKISH AND MONGOLIAN STUDIES. PRASGI
    Vol. 22. 1962.

49. Clissold, S., ed. A SHORT HISTORY OF YUGOSLAVIA. Cambridge:
    1966.

50. Coles, P. THE OTTOMAN IMPACT ON EUROPE. LECS. New York &
    London: 1968.

51. Coquelle, P. HISTOIRE DU MONTENEGRO ET DE LA BOSNIA. Paris:
    1895.

52. Coxe, W. HISTORY OF THE HOUSE OF AUSTRIA: FROM THE FOUNDATION
    OF THE MONARCHY BY RHODLOPH OF HAPSBURGH TO THE DEATH OF
    LEOPOLD THE SECOND, 1218 TO 1792. 3 vols. New York: 1971
    [1847].

53. CPHEI. CHRONIQUE DES EVENEMENTS POLITIQUES ET ECONOMIQUES DANS
    LE BASSIN DANUBIEN: ROUMANIE. ETUDES DANUBIENS I. Paris:
    1938.

54. Creasy, E.S., Sir. HISTORY OF THE OTTOMAN TURKS; FROM THE
    BEGINNING OF THEIR EMPIRE TO THE PRESENT TIME. Beirut:
    1961 [1878].

55. Czechoslovakia. Academie vedenie ustav dejin evropskych
    socialistickych zemi. BIBLIOGRAFIE CESKOSLOVENSKE
    BALKANISTIKY, 1945-1965. Edited by Klement Benda et al.
    Prague: 1966.

56. Davison, R.H. "European Archives as a Source of Later Ottoman
    History," REPORT ON CURRENT HISTORY ON THE MIDDLE EAST
    1958. Washington: 1958.

57. Dellin, L.A.D., ed. BULGARIA. New York: 1957.

58. Denton, W., Rev. MONTENEGRO: ITS PEOPLE AND THEIR HISTORY. New
    York: 1977 [1877].

59. Djilas, M. LAND WITHOUT JUSTICE. London: [1958].

60. Djordjevic, D., & Fisher-Galati, S. THE BALKAN REVOLUTIONARY
    TRADITION. New York: 1981.

61. Dragan, J.C. WE, THE THRACIANS, AND OUR MULTIMILLENARY HISTORY.
    [Milan]: 1976.

62. Eliot, C., Sir. TURKEY IN EUROPE. 2nd ed. new. London: 1965
    [1908].

63. Epstein, F.T., ed. THE AMERICAN BIBLIOGRAPHY OF RUSSIAN AND
    EAST EUROPEAN STUDIES. Bloomington & London: 1957-.

64. Erendil, M. "Emergence of the Ottoman Empire: An Outline of the
    Period 1299-1453," RIHM 46 (1980), 31-61.

65. Eton, W. A SURVEY OF THE TURKISH EMPIRE. New York: 1972.

66. Evans, S.G. A SHORT HISTORY OF BULGARIA. London: 1960.

67. Eversley, G.J. Shaw-Levre, Lord. THE TURKISH EMPIRE FROM
    1288-1914. New York: 1969.

68. Finlay, G. HISTORY OF GREECE, FROM ITS CONQUEST BY THE ROMANS
    TO THE PRESENT DAY, B.C. 164 TO A.D. 1864. 7 vols. New
    rev. ed. by H.F. Tozer. Oxford: 1877.

69. Fisher-Galati, S. THE NEW ROMANIA. Cambridge: 1967.

70. _____., ed. ROMANIA. New York: 1957.

71. _____. "Romania, a Bibliographical Guide," Washington:
    Library of Congress, Slavic and East European Division,
    1963.

72. Forbes, N., et al. THE BALKANS; A HISTORY OF BULGARIA, SERBIA,
    GREECE, ROMANIA, AND TURKEY. New York: [1970].

73. Forster, E.S. A SHORT HISTORY OF MODERN GREECE, 1815-1956. 3rd
    ed. rev. New York: 1958 [1957].

74. Gibb, H.A.R., Sir, et al. ENCYCLOPEDIA OF ISLAM. 2nd ed.
    Leiden: 1954-.

75. Gibb, H.A.R.,Sir, & Bowen H. ISLAMIC SOCIETY AND THE WEST. 2 vols. London: 1957 [1950].

76. Gibbon, E. THE DECLINE AND FALL OF THE ROMAN EMPIRE. 7 vols. London: 1909.

77. Gilbert, M. RUSSIAN HISTORY ATLAS. New York: 1972.

78. Gines, D.S., & Mexas, B.G. GREEK BIBLIOGRAPHY (1860-63). 3 vols. Athens: 1939-1957.

79. Giurescu, C., et al. CHRONOLOGICAL HISTORY OF ROMANIA. Bucharest: 1972.

80. Giurescu, C., & Giurescu, D. ISTORIA ROMANILOR. Vol. 1. Bucharest: 1974.

81. Grant, S.A., & Brown, J.H. THE RUSSIAN EMPIRE AND THE SOVIET UNION: A GUIDE TO MANUSCRIPTS AND ARCHIVAL MATERIAL IN THE UBITED STATES. Boston: 1981.

82. Greece. Ministry of Press and Information. GREEK BIBLIOGRAPHY. Athens: 1960-.

83. Grimsted, P.K., ed. ARCHIVES AND MANUSCRIPT COLLECTIONS IN THE USSR. Series 1: MOSCOW AND LENINGRAD. FINDING AIDS, SERIALS AND LARGE SETS, AND DIRECTORIES OF SOVIET LIBRARIES AND MUSEUMS. On microfiche. Zug: 1980.

84. Halecki, O. BORDERLANDS OF WESTERN CIVILIZATION: A HISTORY OF EAST CENTRAL EUROPE. New York: 1952.

85. Hammer-Purgstall, J. von. HISTOIRE DE L'EMPIRE OTTOMAN. 18 vols. Paris: 1835-1843.

86. Hammond, N.G.L. A HISTORY OF MACEDONIA. Vol. 1: HISTORICAL GEOGRAPHY AND PREHISTORY. Oxford: 1973.

87. Heer, F. THE HOLY ROMAN EMPIRE. New York & Washington: 1968 [1967].

88. Heppell, M., & Singleton, F.B. YUGOSLAVIA. New York: 1961.

89. Heurtley, W.A., et al. A SHORT HISTORY OF GREECE FROM EARLY TIMES TO 1964. New York: 1965.

90. HISTOIRE MILITAIRE DE LA BULGARIE, 681-1945. BIBLIOGRAPHIE. Sofia: 1972-1973.

91. Horak, S.M. JUNIOR SLAVICA: A SELECTED ANNOTATED BIBLIOGRAPHY OF BOOKS IN ENGLISH ON RUSSIA AND EAST EUROPE. Rochester: 1968.

92. Horecky, P.L., ed. EAST CENTRAL EUROPE: A GUIDE TO BASIC PUBLICATIONS. Chicago: 1969.

93. _____. SOUTHEASTERN EUROPE: A GUIDE TO BASIC PUBLICATIONS. Chicago: 1969.

94. _____. "The Slavic and East European Resources and Facilities of the Library of Congress," SR XXIII (June 1964), 309-327.

95. Hosch, E. THE BALKANS: A SHORT HISTORY FROM GREEK TIMES TO THE PRESENT DAY. New York: 1972 [1968].

96. Hourani, A.H. THE OTTOMAN BACKGROUND OF THE MODERN MIDDLE EAST. 3rd Carreras Arab Lectures of the University of Essex., November 27, 1969. Harlow: 1970.

97. Houtsma, T., ed. ENCYCLOPEDIA OF ISLAM. 1st ed. 4 vols. w/supplt. Leiden: 1913-1938.

98. Hungary. Academy of Sciences. BIBLIOGRAFIAI TAJEKOZTATO. Budapest: 1953.

99. _____. MONUMENTA HUNGARIAE HISTORICA. Budapest: 1868-1917.

100. _____. A MAGYAR TORTENETTUDOMANY VALOGATOTT BIBLIOGRAFIJA, 1945-1968. Budapest : 1971.

101. Hussey, J.M. THE BYZANTINE WORLD. New York: 1961.

102. Inalcik, H. THE OTTOMAN EMPIRE: THE CLASSICAL AGE. London: 1973.

103. Iorga, N. HISTOIRE DES ROUMAINES DE LA PENINSULE BALCANS. Bucharest: 1919.

104. Jelavich, C., & Jelavich, B. THE BALKANS. Englewood Cliffs: 1965.

105. Jessup, J.E., & Coakley, R.W., eds. A GUIDE TO THE STUDY AND USE OF MILITARY HISTORY. Washington: 1979.

106. Jovanovic, V.M. ENGLESKA BIBLIOGRAFIJA O ISTOCNOM PITANJU U EVROPI. Belgrad: 1978.

107. Kanet, R.E. SOVIET AND EAST EUROPEAN FOREIGN POLICY: A BIBLIOGRAPHY OF ENGLISH AND RUSSIAN LANGUAGE PUBLICATIONS, 1967-1971. Santa Barbara: 1974.

108. Kann, R.A. A HISTORY OF THE HABSBURG EMPIRE, 1526-1918. Berkeley: 1974.

109. Kann, R.A., & David, Z. THE PEOPLES OF THE EASTERN HABSBURG LANDS, 1526-1918. HECE VI. Seattle & London: 1983.

110. Kemeny, G.G. IRATOK A NEMZETISEGI KERDES TORTENETEHEZ MAGYARORSZAGON A DUALIZMUS KORABAN, 1867-1918. 5 vols. Budapest: 1952-1971.

111. Kerner, R.J. YUGOSLAVIA. UNS. Berkeley & Los Angelos: 1949.

112. Kinross, J.P.D. Balfour, Lord. THE OTTOMAN CENTURIES: THE RISE AND FALL OF THE TURKISH EMPIRE. London: 1977.

113. Klaic, V. POVJECT HRVATA. 6 vols. Zagreb: 1899-1919.

114. Kolarz, W. MYTHS AND REALITIES IN EASTERN EUROPE. Port Washington: 1971 [1946].

115. Koprulu, M.F. LES ORIGINES DE L'EMPIRE OTTOMAN. Philadelphia: 1978.

116. Kosary, D.G. A HISTORY OF HUNGARY. New York: 1941.

117. Kossuth Foundation. HUNGARIAN BIBLIOGRAPHIC SERIES. 3 series. New York: c.1960.

118. Kostelski, Z. THE YUGOSLAVS: THE HISTORY OF THE YUGOSLAVS AND THEIR STATES TO THE CREATION OF YUGOSLAVIA. New York: 1952.

119. Krallert-Sattler, G., ed. ALBANIEN, BULGARIEN, JUGOSLAWIEN, SUDOSTEUROPA UND GROSSERE TEILRAUME. SOB III:2 (1956-1960). Munich: 1968.

120. Lederer, I.J., ed. RUSSIA AND THE BALKANS IN RUSSIAN FOREIGN POLICY: ESSAYS IN HISTORICAL PERSPECTIVE. New Haven: 1962.

121. Legrand, E.L.J. BIBLIOGRAPHIE ALBANAISE. Leipzig: 1973.

122. _____. BIBLIOGRAPHIE HELLENIQUE (AU 1700). 11 vols. Paris: 1885-1928.

123. _____. BIBLIOGRAPHIE IONIENNE (1494-1900). 2 vols. Paris: 1910.

124. Lengyel, E. 1000 YEARS OF HUNGARY. New York: 1958.

125. Lessner, E.C., & Lessner, A.M.L. THE DANUBE: THE DRAMATIC HISTORY OF THE GREAT RIVER AND THE PEOPLE TOUCHED BY ITS FLOW. Garden City: 1961.

126. Lewis, B. THE EMERGENCE OF MODERN TURKEY. London: 1961.

127. Liess, O.R.I. ALBANIEN ZWISCHEN OST UND WEST. Hannover: 1968.

128. Lindsay, J. BYZANTIUM INTO EUROPE. London: 1952.

129. Logoreci, A. THE ALBANIANS. London: 1977.

130. Macartney, C.A. THE HABSBURG EMPIRE, 1790-1918. New York: 1969.

131. _____. HUNGARY, A SHORT HISTORY. Chicago: 1962.

132. Macdermott, M. A HISTORY OF BULGARIA, 1393-1885. London: 1962.

133. Makkai, L. L'HISTOIRE DE TRANSYLVANIE. Paris: 1946.

134. Marmullaku, R. ALBANIA AND THE ALBANIANS. Hamden, Conn.: 1975.

135. Matley, I. RUMANIA: A PROFILE. New York, Washington & London: 1970.

136. McEvedy, C. THE PENGUIN ATLAS OF MEDIEVAL HISTORY. Harmondsworth, Middlesex: 1961.

137. Meyer, K. BIBLIOGRAPHIE DER ARBEITEN ZUR OSTEUROPAISCHEN GESCHICHTE AUS DEN DEUTSCHSPRACHIGEN FACHZEITSCHRIFTEN, 1858-1964. VOL. IX: BIBLIOGRAPHISCHE MITTEILUNGEN DES OSTEUROPA-INSTITUTS AN DER FREIEN UNIVERSITAT BERLIN. Berlin: 1966.

138. Mijatovich, C. SERVIA AND THE SERVIANS. London & New York: 1915.

139. Miller, W. GREECE. London: 1928.

140. _____. THE BALKANS, ROUMANIA, BULGARIA, SERVIA, AND MONTENEGRO. Freeport: 1972.

141. Mishev, D. THE BULGARIANS IN THE PAST: PAGES FROM THE BULGARIAN CULTURAL HISTORY. New York: 1971 [1919].

142. Mylonas, G.E. "An Introduction to the History of the Southern Balkan States," ATHENE, VI (1945), 2:21-29, 4:25-31.

143. _____. THE BALKAN STATES: AN INTRODUCTION TO THEIR HISTORY. Washington: 1947.

144. Naylor, K.E., et al., eds. BALKANISTICA: OCCASIONAL PAPERS IN SOUTHEAST EUROPEAN STUDIES. AAASS. Ann Arbor: 1974.

145. New York Public Library Research Libraries. BIBLIOGRAPHIC GUIDE TO SOVIET AND EAST EUROPEAN STUDIES. 1978-3 vols., 1979-2 vols., 1980-3 vols. New York: 1979-1981.

146. Obolensky, D. THE BYZANTINE COMMONWEALTH. EASTERN EUROPE, 500-1453. New York: 1971.

147. Olteanu, C. CONTRIBUTII LA CERCETEREA CONCEPTULUI DE PUTERE ARMATA LA ROMANI. Bucharest: 1979.

148. Ostrogorski, G. HISTORY OF THE BYZANTINE STATE. Oxford: 1956.

149. Panaretoff, S. NEAR EAST AFFAIRS AND CONDITIONS. New York: 1922.

150. Papadopoullos, T.H. STUDIES AND DOCUMENTS RELATING TO THE HISTORY OF THE GREEK CHURCH AND PEOPLE UNDER TURKISH DOMINATION. Brussels: 1952.

151. Petrovic, V.M. SERBIA; HER PEOPLE, HISTORY, ASPIRATIONS. New York: 1915.

152. Phousarus, G.I. BIBLIOGRAPHY OF GREEK BIBLIOGRAPHIES, 1791-1947. Athens: 1961.

153. Pollo, S. HISTOIRE DE L'ALBANIE, DES ORIGINES A NOS JOURS. Rouanne: 1974.

154. Pounds, N.J.G. EASTERN EUROPE. Chicago: 1969

155. Pribicevic, S. WORLD WITHOUT END; THE SAGA OF SOUTH-EASTERN EUROPE. New York: 1939.

156. Pundeff, M.V. BULGARIA: A BIBLIOGRAPHICAL GUIDE. Washington: 1965.

157. Ristelhueber, R. A HISTORY OF THE BALKAN PEOPLE. Edited and trans. by Sherman D. Spector. New York: 1971 [1950].

158. Roberts, H.L. RUMANIA. New Haven: 1951.

159. Rock, K.W. LIST OF MATERIALS FOR THE STUDY OF THE HISTORY OF ROMANIA SHOWING THE HOLDINGS OF STANFORD UNIVERSITY. Stanford: 1962.

160. Ropp, T. "Military History to the End of the Eighteenth Century," GSUMH. Washington: 1979.

161. Romania. Center for Military History and Theory Studies and Research. APARAREA PATRIEI, A INDEPENDENTEI SI SUVERANITATII NATIONALE. 2nd ed. Bucharest: 1977.

162. _____. APARAREA NATIONALA A ROMANIEI SOCIALISTE. DOCUMENTE 1965-1977. Bucharest: 1978.

163. _____. DOCUMENTA PRIVIND ISTORIA MILITARA A POPORULUI ROMAN. Bucharest: 1974-.

164. _____. Institute of History of the Romanian Academy. DOCUMENTA PRIVIND ISTORIA ROMANIEI. 26 vols. Bucharest: 1951-1957.

165. _____. DOCUMENTA ROMANIAE HISTORICA. 3 series. Bucharest: 1965-.

166. _____. BIBLIOTHECA HISTORICA ROMANIEI. 2 series: Monographs - c.18, Studies - c.61. Each under separate title. Edited by Stefan Pascu & Stefan Stefanescu. Bucharest: 1967-.

167. _____. STUDII SI MATERIALE DE MUZEOGRAFIE SI ISTORIE MILITARA. Annual. Bucharest: 1968-.

168. _____. ISTORIA ROMANIEI. Bucharest: c.1960.

169. Rostovtzeff, M. GREECE. Trans. by J.D. Duff. New York: 1963.

170. Royal Institute of International Affairs. Information Department. SOUTH-EASTERN EUROPE; A POLITICAL AND ECONOMIC SURVEY. New York: 1972 [1939].

171. Ruggles, M.J., & Mastecky, V. RUSSIAN AND EAST EUROPEAN
     PUBLICATIONS IN THE LIBRARIES OF THE UNITED STATES. Vol.
     11: Columbia University Studies in Libraries. New York:
     1960.

172. Savadjian, L., ed. ENCYCLOPEDIE BALKANIQUE PERMANENTE. Paris:
     1936-.

173. Savu, A.G., ed. PAGES FROM THE HISTORY OF THE ROMANIAN ARMY.
     BHR Monograph 15. Bucharest: 1975.

174. Scherer, A. SUDOSTEUROPA-DISSERTATIONEN, 1918-1960. EINE
     BIBLIOGRAPHIE DEUTSCHER, OSTERREICHISCHER UND
     SCHWEIZERISCHER HOCHSCHULSCHRIFTEN. Graz, Vienna, Cologne
     & Bohlau: 1968.

175. Schevill, F. HISTORY OF THE BALKAN PENINSULA FROM THE EARLIEST
     TIMES TO THE PRESENT. New York: 1971 [c.1922].

176. Seemann, K.-D., & Siegmann, F. BIBLIOGRAPHIE DER SLAVISTISCHEN
     ARBEITEN AUS DEN DEUTSCHSPRACHIGEN FACHZEITSCHRIFTEN,
     1876-1963. Vol. 8: BIBLIOGRAPHISCHE MITTEILUNGEN DES
     OSTEUROPA INSTITUTS AN DER FREIEN UNIVERSITAT BERLIN.
     Berlin: 1965.

177. Segvic, C. DIE KROATEN UND IHRE MISSION WAHREND DREIZEHN
     JAHRHUNDERTE DER GESCHICHTE. Zagreb: 1941.

178. Seton-Watson, R.W. A HISTORY OF THE ROUMANIANS; FROM ROMAN
     TIMES TO THE COMPLETION OF UNITY. Cambridge: 1934.

179. _____. THE RISE OF NATIONALITIES IN THE BALKANS. London:
     1917.

180. _____. THE SOUTHERN SLAVS AND THE HABSBURG MONARCHY.
     LONDON: 1911.

181. _____. DIE SUDSLAVISCHE FRAGE IM HABSBURGERREICH. Berlin:
     1913.

182. _____. A HISTORY OF THE CZECHS AND SLOVAKS. London: 1943.

183. Shandanova, L. PETNADESET GODINI INSTITUT ZA BALKANISTIKA,
     1964-1978: ISTORICHESKA SPRAVKA I BIBLIOGRAFIIA. Sofia:
     1979.

184. Shaw, S.J. "Archival Sources for Ottoman History: The Archives
     of Turkey," JAOS 80 (1960), 1-12.

185. _____. HISTORY OF THE OTTOMAN EMPIRE AND MODERN TURKEY.
     Vol. 1: EMPIRE OF THE GAZIS: THE RISE AND DECLINE OF THE
     OTTOMAN EMPIRE, 1280-1808. Cambridge & New York: 1976.

186. Shaw, S.J., & Shaw, E.K. HISTORY OF THE OTTOMAN EMPIRE AND
     MODERN TURKEY. Vol. 2: REFORM, REVOLUTION AND REPUBLIC:
     THE RISE OF MODERN TURKEY: 1808-1975. Cambridge, London &
     New York: 1977.

187. Sinor, D. HISTORY OF HUNGARY. New York: 1961.

188. Sisac, F. "Geschichte der Kroaten," DIE WECHTIGSTEN QUELLEN UND
WERKE. [Zagreb], I (1917), 1-19.

189. Skendi, S. ALBANIA. London: 1957.

190. Skoplje. National Historical Institut of Skoplje. ISTORIJA NA
MAKEDONSKIOT NAROD. Vol. 1. Skoplje: 1969.

191. Spector, S.D., & Legters, L. CHECKLIST OF PAPERBACK BOOKS ON
RUSSIA AND EAST EUROPE. 2nd ed. rev. Albany: 1966.

192. Spinka, M. A HISTORY OF CHRISTIANITY IN THE BALKANS: A STUDY OF
THE SPREAD OF BYZANTINE CULTURE AMONG THE SLAVS. Chicago:
1933.

193. Stadtmuller, G. GESCHICHTE SUDOSTEUROPAS. Munich: 1950.

194. Stavrianos, L.S. THE BALKANS SINCE 1453. New York: 1958.

195. Stevenson, F.S. A HISTORY OF MONTENEGRO. London: 1912.

196. Stoianovich, T. A STUDY OF BALKAN CIVILIZATION. New York: 1967.

197. Sudost Institut. SUDOSTEUROPA-BIBLIOGRAPHIE. 3 vols. Munich:
1956-1968.

198. Sugar, P.F. SOUTHEASTERN EUROPE UNDER OTTOMAN RULE, 1354-1804.
HECE 5. Seattle & London: 1977.

199. Sugar, P.F., & Lederer, I.J., eds. NATIONALISM IN EASTERN
EUROPE. Seattle: 1969.

200. Sugar, P.F., & Treadgold, D.W., eds. HISTORY OF EAST CENTRAL
EUROPE. 11 vols. Seattle & London: 1975-.

201. Swire, J. ALBANIA, THE RISE OF A KINGDOM. New York: 1971.

202. Tapie, V.L. THE RISE AND FALL OF THE HABSBURG MONARCHY. Trans.
by Stephen Hardman. New York, Washington and London: 1971.

203. Taylor, A.J.P. THE HABSBURG EMPIRE. New York: 1949.

204. Teleki, P. THE EVOLUTION OF HUNGARY AND ITS PLACE IN EUROPEAN
HISTORY. New York: 1923.

205. Temperley, H.W.V., Sir. HISTORY OF SERBIA. New York: 1969
[c.1910].

206. Thessalonike. HMCH. VALKANIKE VIVLIOGRAPIA. Thessalonike:
1975-.

207. Thierfelder, F. MANNER AM BALKANS: VON ALEXANDER DEM GROSSE BIS
JOSIP TITO. Graz, Vienna & Cologne: 1961.

208. Todorov, N. BULGARIA; HISTORICAL AND GEOGRAPHICAL OUTLINE.
Sofia: 1968.

209. _____. A SHORT HISTORY OF BULGARIA. Trans. by L. Dimitrova. Sofia: 1975.

210. Omitted.

211. Toynbee, A. TURKEY. New York: 1927.

212. Trypucko, J. SUBJECT CATALOG OF MICRO EDITIONS: RUSSIA, USSR, EASTERN EUROPE. Zug: 1980.

213. Turkey. Turkish General Staff. HARP TARIHI BELGELERI DERGISI. Ankara: 1976.

214. _____. Department of War History. TURK SILAHLI KUVVETLERI TARIHI. 6 vols. Ankara: c.1977.

215. Turkiye Cumhuriyeti, Maarif Vekaleti. ISLAM ANSIKLOPEDISI. Istanbul & Ankara: 1940-.

216. United States. Department of Army. COMMUNIST EASTERN EUROPE: ANALYTIC SURVEY OF LITERATURE. DA Pamphlet 550-8. Washington: 1971.

217. _____. Foreign Area Studies, The American University. AREA HANDBOOKS: ALBANIA. DA Pamph. 550-98, 1971; BULGARIA. DA Pamph. 550-168, 1974; GREECE. DA Pamph. 550-87, 1977; HUNGARY. DA Pamph. 550-165, 1973; ROMANIA. DA Pamph. 550-160, 1972; TURKEY. DA Pamph. 550-80, 1970; YUGOSLAVIA. DA Pamph. 550-99, 1973.

218. _____. Library of Congress. REPORTS IN CURRENT RESEARCH ON THE MIDDLE EAST. Produced in cooperation with the Middle East Institute, Washington, DC., 1955-1957.

219. _____. THE USSR AND EASTERN EUROPE: PERIODICALS IN WESTERN LANGUAGES. Compiled by P.L. Horecky & R.G. Carlton. Washington: 1964.

220. USSR. Akademi nauk. BIBLIOGRAFIYA TURTSII (1917-1958). Moscow: 1959.

221. _____. Publichnaya biblioteka. MATERIALY PO ISTORII BALKANSKIKH SLAVIAN V OTDEL RUKOPISEI I REDKIKH KNIG. GPB: KATALOG. Compiled by L.I. Buchina. Leningrad: 1978.

222. Vasiliev, A.A. HISTORY OF THE BYZANTINE EMPIRE, 324-1453. 2nd English ed. rev. Madison: 1952.

223. _____. ORIGINS OF THE GREEK NATION: THE BYZANTINE PERIOD, 1204-1461. New Brunswick: 1970.

224. Vaughn, D.M. EUROPE AND THE TURK: A PATTERN OF ALLIANCES, 1350-1700. Liverpool: 1954.

225. Vryonis, S. BYZANTIUM AND EUROPE. New York: 1967.

226. Vucinich, W.S. THE OTTOMAN EMPIRE, ITS RECORD AND LEGACY. Huntington: 1979 [c.1965].

227. Wandruszka, A. THE HOUSE OF HABSBURG: SIX HUNDRED YEARS OF A EUROPEAN DYNASTY. Trans. by C. & H. Epstein. Garden City: 1964.

228. Wanklyn, H.G. CZECHOSLOVAKIA. New York: 1954.

229. Wyon, R., & Prance, G. THE LAND OF THE BLACK MOUNTAIN. London: 1905.

230. Yugoslavia. Narodna biblioteka SR Srbije. KATALOG KNJIGA NA JEZICIMA JUGOSLAVENSKIH NARODA, 1519-1867. Edit. by S. Duric. Belgrad: 1973.

231. _____. VODIC KROZ ARHIVSKE FONDOVE. 6 vols. Compiled by V. Djonlic. Belgrad: 1972-.

232. Zacek, V., et al. DEJINY JUGOSLAVIE. Prague: 1970.

233. Zakythinos, D. THE MAKING OF MODERN GREECE: FROM BYZANTIUM TO INDEPENDENCE. Totowa, NJ: 1976.

234. Zlatarski, V.N. GESCHICHTE DER BULGAREN. 2 vols. Sofia: 1917-1918.

ADDITIONS

235. Tambs, L.A., & Birkos, A.S. eds. ACADEMIC WRITER'S GUIDE TO PERIODICALS, II: EAST EUROPEAN AND SLAVIC STUDIES. Kent, Ohio: 1973. Also listed as Birkos & Tambs.

236. Baines, N.H., & Moss, H.St.L.B. BYZANTIUM: AN INTRODUCTION TO EAST ROMAN CIVILIZATION. Oxford: 1948.

# CHAPTER TWO

# THE LATE 14TH AND THE 15TH CENTURIES

## GENERAL DISCUSSION

The transition from medieval to modern times was marked by the demise of feudal overlordship and the rise of strong, centralized monarchical national realms. These early states, England, France, Spain, Portugal, and The Netherlands became the great empire builders in the West, and it was through their actions that the future course of western civilization was to grow and flourish.

The close of the Middle Ages was also a time of great intellectual and cultural growth that is best exemplified by the rise of a spirit of inquiry, criticism, and skepticism. The attending rapid expansion of commercialism in Europe led to an ever-increasing demand for foreign goods and this, in turn, led to greater exploration, especially after the Ottoman Turks cut the overland routes to Cathay. In this way, the New World was discovered as explorers sought the elusive Northwest Passage.

Another manifestation of those times was the withering away of the Byzantine Empire which lived out its last days squandering what little strength it still had in incessant civil war. Byzantium's final passing, especially the Turkish capture of the Seat of Constantine, set into motion forces that are still felt today and that have altered the course of events in the intervening centuries in ways neither clearly understood nor appreciated.

There are a number of good general histories of this period but none is better than William McNeill's THE RISE OF THE WEST [71]. This is a monumental study of man's history and its coverage of the "Era of Western Dominance, 1500 A.D. to the Present" is among the very best. Professor McNeill's A WORLD HISTORY [72] is, on the other hand, much easier reading and may be more suited to the casual reader.

Other good accounts of this last phase of the Middle Ages may be found in volumes VII [119] and VIII [95] of the CAMBRIDGE MEDIEVAL HISTORY. Volume VIII, for instance, has articles covering 15th—century Bohemia, Hungary, and the Holy Roman Empire. It also contains Sir Charles Oman's "The Art of War in the Fifteenth Century" [82], which is very good. In addition to Oman's article, Dupuy's introduction to Chapter XII in his ENCYCLOPEDIA OF MILITARY HISTORY [33], and Chapters V and VI in A SHORT HISTORY OF WARFARE [130], by David Zook and Robin Higham, are good military overviews of this period. In THE TOOLS OF WAR [78], James Newman traces the history of military arms from the earliest times, while ARMAMENT AND HISTORY [36], by the distinguished British historian J.F.C. Fuller, studies the influence of weaponry on history from the dawn of classical warfare to the Second World War. Dudley Pope's GUNS: FROM THE INVENTION OF GUNPOWDER TO THE 20TH CENTURY [93] is also useful. As a final suggestion, J.H. Parry's THE ESTABLISHMENT OF THE EUROPEAN HEGEMONY, 1415-1715: TRADE AND EXPLORATION IN THE AGE OF THE RENAISSANCE [87] will serve as an excellent foundation for this period.

Colin McEvedy's PENQUIN ATLAS OF MEDIEVAL HISTORY [70] and David Chandler's ATLAS OF MILITARY STRATEGY [20] will suffice as geographical references. Ferdinand Schevill's HISTORY OF THE BALKAN PENINSULA FROM THE EARLIEST TIMES TO THE PRESENT [103], Leften Stavrianos' THE BALKANS SINCE 1453 [109], and Trian Stoianovich's A STUDY OF BALKAN CIVILIZATION [113] are the best general histories available in English for this early time.

For the reader untrained in military arts and sciences, Henry Lee Scott's MILITARY DICTIONARY [106] is an indispensable tool that will aid in understanding the military techniques and terminology of this and succeeding periods to the mid-19th century. WAR AND ECONOMIC DEVELOPMENT [127], which was edited by J.M. Winter, is composed of six essays that consider the impact of war on the economic development of Europe from the 13th century. Of similar relevance is Richard Lewinsohn's THE PROFITS OF WAR THROUGH THE AGES [66]. Although it was published before World War II, it is still worth reading.


## THE SECOND HALF OF THE 14TH CENTURY

### THE OTTOMAN THREAT

During the last 50 years of the 14th century, the Ottoman Turks captured the important Byzantine fortress at Gallipoli (Galibolu) (1354) thereby establishing a lodgement on the European continent. By 1362, Turkish forces had seized Adrianople and, three years later, Sultan Murad I (1359?-1389) established his residence there. The Turks were raiding across the Danube into Wallachia by November-December 1369 and, on 26 September 1371, an Ottoman army defeated Lazar I's (1371-1389) Serbian army which had been reinforced by Wallachian contingents. The battle took place near Cirmen (Cernomen) on the Maritza River. Its outcome marked the decline of South Serbian power and turned Macedonia into an Ottoman vassal.

In 1376, the despot of Dobrudja, Dobrotich (c.1348-1386), with Venetian help and in consort with the Byzantine emperor, John V Paleologus, opened a long campaign to install his son-in-law (John V's son) on the throne in Constantinople. Three years later, in 1379, Dobrotich's fleet participated in the blockade of Constantinople in which he fought the Genoese. In the meantime, of course, the Ottomans, aware of the internicene fighting, were making steady progress into the Balkans pushing northward in Bulgaria and westward into Macedonia.

These events are all reported in a number of the general sources already discussed. Especially interesting in this regard are

38

Finlay's HISTORY OF GREECE [35], Erendil's article on early Ottoman development [34], and in Giurescu's CHRONOLOGICAL HISTORY OF ROMANIA [39]. Inalcik's "Ottoman Methods of Conquest" [50] is also important reading at this point. Nicolae Iorga presents a vivid description of the battles of this period in an article [55] published in 1900 in CONVORBIRI LITERATURE. Andrew Urbansky's BYZANTIUM AND THE DANUBE FRONTIER [124] should also be read. Additional information on Dobrotich may be found in DOBROGEA: ISTORIA ROMANILOR DINTRE DUNARE SI MARE [96], by Adrian Radulescu and Ion Bitoleanu, and in Stefanescu's "Comments Upon the Romanian Military History of the 3rd-14th Centuries" [112].

Dobrotich passed from the scene without notice and was replaced by his son, Ivanco, who managed to remain independent of outside influence by signing a treaty with the Turks in 1386, and with the Genoese the following year. In 1388, however, a large Turkish force, commanded by the Grand Vizier Ali Pasha, threatened Dobrudja and would have turned it into a pashalik had it not been for the timely intervention of the voivode of Wallachia, Mircea the Old (1386-1418).

## THE HUNGARIAN THREAT

At the same time the Danubian provinces faced a Turkish attack from the south, they also faced an equally dangerous adversary in the west and north. In 1368, for example, King Louis I the Great (of Anjou)(1342-1382), opened a Hungarian campaign against Wallachia in which he was supported by the Szekler voivode of Transylvania, Nicolae Lackfy (1367-1368). This was but a single round in what was to be a long-term struggle for control of Transylvania. Although the Wallachians were successful in driving off the Hungarians and their allies in 1368, the conflict continued; and, in 1373-1377, a new outbreak of fighting occurred. The CHRONOLOGICAL HISTORY OF ROMANIA [39] covers this period, and Nicholae Stoicescu's "The Greater Army of Wallachia and Moldavia (14th-16th Centuries)" [114] identifies the makeup and form of the Wallachian forces, including a description of 10,000 knights dressed "in armours bought in Venice."

The close of the 14th and beginning of the 15th centuries are very carefully reviewed in Peter Sugar's SOUTHEASTERN EUROPE UNDER OTTOMAN RULE, 1354-1804 [117], and by M. Dinic in "The Balkans: 1018-1499" [30], in volume 4 of the NEW CAMBRIDGE MODERN HISTORY. Another good study is Franz Babinger's BEITRAGE ZUR FRUHGESCHICHTE DER TURKENHERRSCHAFT IN RUMELIEN (14.-15. JAHRHUNDERT) [8], that also has an excellent bibliography. Not all of the conflicts were caused by outside influence, however, as there were numerous uprisings among the Romanian and Hungarian peasantry as well. There were peasant revolts against the nobility in Transylvania, for instance, in 1380 and again in 1382-1383.

## THE BATTLE OF KOSSOVO

The most important military event to occur in the Balkans during the last quarter of the 14th century was the Ottoman victory at the First Battle of Kossovo on 15 June 1389. When the allied army of Serbs, Bosnians, and Macedonians was defeated, the Ottoman Turks took control of the western and southwestern parts of Serbia and the fate of the Balkans was sealed. The best account of this battle is found in Maximilian Braun's KOSSOVO [17] which was published in 1937 in German.

## THE OTTOMAN BULGARIAN CAMPAIGN

Seven months after Kossovo, on 20 January 1390, the Romanians and Poles signed the Treaty of Lublin that pledged mutual assistance in case of an attack, principally from Hungary, against either country. At that same moment, the Turks opened a new campaign north of the Danube. Wallachian forces under the Mircea the Old and Bulgarian troops commanded by Tsar Ivan Srazhimir (1371-1396), of the Tsarate of Vidin, defeated the Turks and were able to recapture the strategically important terrain around Vidin itself. This campaign lasted until 1391. In the brief respite that followed, Mircea was able to reinforce the Danube river line, especially around Turnu (near present-day Turnu Magurele), where he built new fortifications upon the ruins of a fortress that had stood since Roman times. By mid-summer, 1393, however, the Turks had returned in force and had seized the remaining Romanian territories south of the Danube and had sacked the Bulgarian capital at Turnovo, most likely killing the Turnovo Tsar, Ivan Shishman (1371-1393) in the process. This fighting seesawed back and forth into 1394 when Sultan Bayazid I Iildirium (1389-1402) sent 40,000 Ottomans and 8,000 vassal troops, most of whom were Serbs, against the Wallachians.

The military activities of Mircea the Old are touched upon by Constantin Giurescu in "Premise istorice ale redobindirii independentei poporului Roman" [40] while Stoicescu's "Organizational Structure of the Armies in the Romanian Principalities in the 14th-18th Centuries" [115] suggests that as many as 50,000 troops were under arms on occasion and that, between 1394 and 1601, over 90 separate campaigns were fought.

Sultan Bayazid I led his Turkish forces into the first of these campaigns and, on 10 October 1394, was defeated by Mircea the Old at Rovine where the Wallachians were apparently outnumbered 4 to 1. The Turks prevailed, however, and in continued fighting eventually forced Mircea to flee to Transylvania, while a Turkish puppet (known as Vlad the Usurper, or Iron Vlad (1394-1397)) was put on the throne. Before the end of the year, Turkish raiding parties had entered Transylvania.

The situation in Transylvania is discussed by the noted Romanian scholar, Stefan Pascu, in his MAREA ADUNARE NATIONALA DE LA ALBA IULIA: INCUNUNAREA IDEII, A TENDITELOR SI A LUPTELOR DE UNITATE A POPORULUI ROMAN [90]. This is a comprehensive study that carries the reader through the historical process that culminated in the union of Transylvania with Romania following the end of the First World War. A second book by Professor Pascu is of similar importance. VOIEVODATUL TRANSYLVANIEI [91] traces the history of that region from the 9th through the 14th centuries and stresses the multi-ethnic origins of the populace, which included Romanians, Hungarians, Saxons, Szeklers, and Teutonic Knights, that frequently were the cause of both internal and external conflict. Stefan Stefanescu's "Romanian Countries' Military Effort in Their Fight for Independence During the Middle Ages" [111] presents an overview of the military situation in the other Danubian Principalities from about the 10th to the 17th centuries. A good work in German is DAS RUMANISCHE FURSTENTUM MOLDAU UND DIE OSTSLAVEN IM 15. BIS 17. JAHRHUNDERT [126]. This study was produced by the East European Institute in Munich and deals with the relationships between the Romanians in Moldavia and the Eastern Slavs across the Dneister.

SERBSKAIA GOSUDARSTVENNOST' V X-XIV VV. (KRITIKA TEORII "ZHUPNOI ORGANIZATSII") [41] is a good history of the medieval Serbs. Although this work, by the Soviet medieval scholar V.P. Grachev, stresses the controversial problem of the organization of specific Slavic groups, there is sufficient material on the general historical developments to make it worthwhile. The best coverage of this period is found in Konstantin Jirecik's GESCHICHTE DER SERBEN [58].

The Ottoman story of this crucial period is told in a number of sources. One of the best of these in English is Stanford Shaw's EMPIRE OF THE GAZIS: THE RISE AND DECLINE OF THE OTTOMAN EMPIRE [108], which is the first of a two-volume set. THE FOUNDATIONS OF THE OTTOMAN EMPIRE [38], by H.A. Gibbons, is old but excellent. These two, plus two in French both of which are titled HISTOIRE DE L'EMPIRE OTTOMAN, are more than sufficient for the most serious scholar. Of the French works, the one written by A. de Juchereau de Saint-Denys [60] was published in 1844, while A. de la Jonquiere [59] wrote his version just before the start of the First World War. Lastly, a chronology in Romanian, CRONICILI DINASTICI OTOMANI [1], by Ordaz Bin Adil, is a good source document, especially about the reign of the Bayazid reign (1389-1403).

## THE BATTLE OF NICOPOLIS

By the end of 1394, Ottoman forces had probably occupied most of Dobrudja, the region between the Black Sea and Danube. Stefanescu [112] states that "shortly before the Battle of Nicopolis, Dobrudja was subjected to the Turks, but was again conquered by Mircea the Old in 1404." Radelescu and Bitoleanu [96] mention this situation only in passing. Then, in 1395, the Hungarians opened a campaign against Moldavia but were defeated at Hindov, by Stefan I, Voivode of Moldavia (1394-1399), in a protracted battle that lasted from 2 to 14 February. This invasion began as a result of Hungarian reaction to Stefan's pledge of fealty to Poland's Queen Jadwiga (1384-1399). Sigismund of Luxembourg was King of Hungary (1387-1437) at this time but would later become King (1410-1433), and then Emperor (1433-1437), of the Holy Roman Empire. He also served as King of Bohemia (1420-1437).

The battle at Nicopolis came about as a result of one of the last attempts to revive what had been the crusading spirit in Europe in preceding centuries. After Pope Boniface IX (1389-1404) had preached a crusade against the Ottoman Turks because of their almost unchecked expansion in the Balkans, a Crusade army of about 130,000 men, led by Sigismund, and with a large contingent of European nobles including Jean Sans Peur, Duke of Burgundy, marched into the Danube valley. At Nicopolis (Nikopol, Bulgaria), this force, which included Burgundy's 10,000 Frenchmen, was met and decisively defeated by a Turkish army commanded by Sultan Bayazid I on 25 September 1396. Mircea the Old fought in this battle as Sigismund's ally having thrown over the Polish-Wallachian Alliance in favor of a pact with Hungary that was signed at Brasov on 7 March 1395. The Serbian ruler, Stefan Lazarevich (1389-1427), fought on the Turkish side and would do so again at the Battle of Angora (Ankara) in 1402.

Erendil [34] has a excellent account of this battle and the various alliances associated with it. The CHRONOLOGICAL HISTORY OF ROMANIA [39] covers Mircea's activities, while Beckman describes Sigismund's military campaigns against the Turks in his DER KAMPF KAISER SIGMUNDS GEGEN DIE WERDENDS WELTMACHT DER OSMANEN, 1392-1437 [11]. THE CRUSADE OF NICOPOLIS [7], by A. Atiya, is also an especially good study of the entire episode.

Reverberations of the defeat were widespread; and nowhere was the impact felt more keenly than at Vidin where, subsequent to the action at Nicopolis, the Turks assaulted and captured the citadel of Tsar Ivan Srazimir, who was taken prisoner. With the capture of the Tsarate of Vidin, the last physical vestige of Bulgarian independence disappeared. Mercia Macdermott's A HISTORY OF BULGARIA, 1393-1885 [69] gives an excellent account of those early times and is valuable for the later periods as well, covering the five centuries of Bulgarian subjugation in excellent detail. This may be supplemented by Sir Stephen Runciman's HISTORY OF THE FIRST BULGARIAN EMPIRE [100], that serves as an excellent background for the period between the 9th and 12th centuries, and "The 'Second Bulgarian Empire,' Its Origins and History" [129], by R.L. Wolff.

Following the defeat at Nicopolis, Mircea recrossed the Danube and, by December 1396, had positioned his forces to cut off the retreat of Vlad the Usurper who was fleeing a Transylvanian army. With his escape thwarted, Vlad took his troops into the Dimbovita fortress where he was besieged and finally captured. Mircea emerged from the incident as the sole ruler of Wallachia.

## THE OTTOMAN INVASION OF GREECE

During the next year, 1397, a Turkish invasion of Greece began which is discussed in Nicholas Hammond's MIGRATIONS AND INVASIONS IN GREECE AND ADJACENT AREAS [43] and in the introduction to THE GREEK NATION, 1453-1669 [125], by Apostollos Vacalopoulos. Paul Coles' THE OTTOMAN IMPACT ON EUROPE [23] is a particularly valuable reference as it describes not only the invasion of Europe in great detail, especially the Turk's unsuccessful campaign of September-October 1397, but also the structure of Turkish society and the Ottoman government.

Another work that does a good job of illuminating this period is BULGARO-RUMUNSKI VRUZKI I OTNOSHENIIA PREZ VEKOVETE: IZSLEDOVANIIA [4]. Among other things, it compares the development of Wallachia and Bulgaria during the 13th and 14th centuries. Constantin Olteanu's "On the Organization of the Army of the Romanian Countries" [81] outlines the need for the establishment of a military structure within the feudal state to defend against attacks from its immediate neighbors, especially Hungary and the Turks in Bulgaria. "The Strife Among the Paleologi and the Ottoman Turks, 1370-1402" [21], by P. Charnaris, is a most worthwhile discussion of the Turco-Byzantine confrontation that spanned this period.

The 15th century opened on a less than auspicious note in the Balkans, and during the first decade a number of militarily important events took place. In 1401, for instance, a Wallachian army defeated and drove off a Turkish force commanded by Evrenos-Bey that had penetrated into Wallachia and Transylvania causing much destruction as it went. At the same time, the Turks attacked into Moldavia in spite of the fact that the Ottoman Sultan found himself in conflict with the Mongol Timur (Tamerlane) over Turkish expansion in Asia Minor. Moldavian forces under Alexandru the Kind (1400-1432) repelled what was to be the first of many attacks by the Turks on his princedom. To accomplish this, however, the Moldavian prince was forced to acknowledge suzereignty to the King of Poland as a means of gaining the additional strength necessary to fight the growing Ottoman threat.

By 1404, Mircea had succeeded in recapturing the greater part of the eastern provinces (Dobrudja and Silistra), using the difficulties that had arisen within the Ottoman empire to his own advantage. Within two years, Mircea had established himself as the most powerful ruler on the Christian frontier and, in November-December 1406, met with Sigismund to plot a major campaign against the Turks.

A truism of history is that a relatively obscure event may produce results of major proportion. Such was the case in 1409 when Sigismund ennobled a minor Romanian knaz named Voicu, as a reward for his military service. Along with his brothers, Voicu was given leadership over the county of Hunedoara where, among other things, he raised a son, Iancu, who was to become one of the great Balkan military leaders of the century. These events are discussed in the CHRONOLOGICAL HISTORY OF ROMANIA [39] and by Mircea Musat in "Sur le pas de luttes du peuple roumain pour son unite et son independence" [77].

## THE OTTOMAN STRUGGLE IN THE EAST

The Turkish Asia Minor campaign was the result of a need for more Muslim support for further expansion into Christian Europe. Previous restraint in annexing the Turkish amirates was abandoned by Bayazid; and direct force was used to seize more territory and, in turn, more men for the army. This led to conflict, not only from the Muslims who lived in those lands, but also from his own Ghazi supporters. Much of Bayazid's Asian conquest was, therefore, the result of the use of Janissaries, or by Christian units such as the Serbian detachment led by Stefan Lazarevich, simply because Turkish-manned Ghazi units often failed to perform, or their employment was deemed politically inappropriate. The Janissaries were quite often slaves of non-Turkish, non-Muslim origin. Information on this subject may be found in J.A.B. Palmer's "The Origins of the Janissaries" [85].

Many of the Christian vassal troops still supported Bayazid, and fought with great courage, when large numbers of the Ghazi went over to Timur's Mongol army at the Battle of Angora on 28 July 1402. Bayazid lost the battle and was taken prisoner by Timur. LA CAMPAGNE DE TIMUR EN ANATOLIA, 1402 [2] by M. Alexandrescu-Dersca discusses this campaign. This action well outside the confines of the Balkans is mentioned here only because of the employment and importance of Balkan troops in the Ottoman army.

## CIVIL WAR IN THE WAKE OF BAYAZID'S DEATH

One year after the battle, Bayazid died in captivity. His death, along with the defeat and ouster of the Ottomans from Asia Minor, led to a partitioning of the empire among his sons. Almost immediately, the sons fell to fighting among themselves; and, from 1403 to 1413, a three-way civil war raged. One of the sons, Musa, was able to seize control of the Balkans (1409-1413) and established his capital at Adrianople with the assistance of Wallachian troops.

In anticipation of better treatment of his people and his lands by Musa (over that which had been received from Musa's brother, Suleiman) Mircea negotiated a treaty with the Turks that led to the employment of Wallachian troops in the capture of Adrianople that put Musa on the Rumelian throne. The reign turned out to be one based upon terror and was shortlived, however, as another brother, Mohammed -- or Mehmet, put an end to it at the Battle of Ciamurli, that was fought near Sofia on 5 July 1413. Musa was killed in the battle and Mohammed was able to consolidate the Ottoman Empire as a result.

Turkish historical development during those critical times is covered in LE MONDE OTTOMAN DES BALKANS, 1402-1566 [13], by Nicoara Beldiceanu, and in Halil Inalcik's THE OTTOMAN EMPIRE: THE CLASSICAL AGE, 1300-1600 [49]. Inalcik organizes his material into topical sections the most important of which, for purposes of this subject, is "The State." This work also includes an excellent bibliography and several useful maps and charts. Erendil's article [34] is also quite useful at this point.

A new Polish-Moldavian alliance was sealed at Roman on 25 May 1411. While this compact was satisfactory to the Moldavians, it was even more important to the Poles as it protected their flank from attack. Moldavian troops had taken part in the great Battle of Tannenberg the preceding year (15 July 1410) in which the Teutonic Knights had been defeated. This affair is mentioned in Giurescu [39].

The reign of Sultan Mohammed I the Restorer (1413-1421) was a period of recovery for the Ottoman Turks; and soon after he assumed the throne, the march against Christendom was renewed. In 1416, Mircea the Old refused to pay the tribute that had been imposed upon Wallachia and actively supported a pretender to the Ottoman throne, Mustafa, in his bid to take it by force. As a consequence of Mustafa's subsequent defeat by an Ottoman army, the hope for a new government faded and Wallachia was laid open to further depredation. Even so, Mircea again supported a new pretender in 1417 when Sheikh Bedr-ed-Din, a social and religious reformer, attempted to seize power. Mohammed's forces were successful, however, and Wallachia was subjected to severe reprisals. Turkish forces established themselves north of the Danube, and Dobrudja was annexed in the Sultan's name. Mircea was forced to yield and to agree to pay the tribute in return for a guarantee of peace. That same year, a series of disorders broke out in Transylvania that took more than two years to put down.

## THE TURKS FIGHT THE VENETIANS

While the Ottoman Empire endured the series of attempts upon the throne, it was still undertaking a number of foreign ventures. In 1416, for example, there was a naval war with Venice that ended in a Turkish disaster off Gallipoli. This was followed by a long struggle with the Venetians (1425-1430), in which the Turks, under the rule of Murad II (1421-1451), were more successful, capturing several important trading centers along the Albanian coast and the important port of Thessaloniki. Murad's reign is presented in great detail by Inalcik in his article, "Murad II" [48]. The naval engagements are mentioned in Saim Besbelli's "Ottoman Naval Superiority in the Mediterranean" [15].

## CONFLICT IN THE BALKANS

The Balkans were not spared during this period. In 1419, the Turks attacked Wallachia where they failed to reduce the powerful fortress at Severin and were subsequently defeated by Mircea's son and heir, Mihail I (1418-1420), with aid from Sigismund. The Hungarian ruler then annexed Severin and entrusted its defense to one of his lieutenants, Filippo de Scolari. Two years later, the Turks renewed their attack on Wallachia, defeating and killing Mihail and devastating the land. The Ottomans then turned on Moldavia, which had not suffered from the Turks up to this time. A Turkish fleet attempted the seizure of Cetatea-Alba (today Belgorod-Dnestrovski, USSR) but was defeated. The land campaign in Moldavia continued and, in September 1420, another Turkish force defeated the Transylvanian defenders at the "Iron Gates" on the Danube.

In 1425, however, the Turks were handed a setback when a Wallachian army, led by Prince Dan II (1421-1431 intermittently) and supported by de Scolari and by a Bulgarian contingent, retook Vidin. While the victory was important, a more interesting aspect of this campaign was Romanian use for the first time of mercenaries. Dan's army of Wallachians also participated in the Battle of Golbac (in Yugoslavia) on the side of Sigismund. This indecisive action was followed by the conclusion of a Turko-Hungarian armistice that also reinstated the Turkish guarantee of peace in Wallachia in return for the payment of tribute.

William Cooke's THE OTTOMAN EMPIRE AND ITS TRIBUTARY STATES [24] and George Arnakis' THE NEAR EAST IN MODERN TIMES: THE OTTOMAN EMPIRE AND THE BALKANS TO 1900 [5] are both good reading in this area. Ilie Ceaucescu's THE ENTIRE PEOPLE'S WAR FOR THE HOMELAND'S DEFENCE WITH THE ROMANIANS [18] might also be of use, but its coverage of this period is not very strong. ISTORIA TURCO-BIZANTINA (1341-1462) [32], by I. Ducas, is good supplemental reading. So are "Obzor srednevekovykh voennykh struktur v rumynskikh knyazhestvakh" [57], by Sergei Iosipescu and Viktor Eskenasi, and Gheorghe Romanescu's "Grosse mittelalteriche Schlachten des rumanischen Volkes fur die Verteidigung der Unabhangigkeit und des uralten Heimatsbodens" [98].

TROUBLE IN TRANSYLVANIA AND THE BATTLE OF BOBILNA

All of the troubles of the times in the Balkans did not come from outside forces. A number of internal disorders also broke out over these decades, some of them quite violent. Among those that took place in 1417 was one led by Kardas Janos and was aimed at the Saxon patricianship in southeastern Transylvania. This uprising took two years to quell and was only put down when Prince Nicolae Csaki (1415-1426) stepped in. The problem of Hungarian overlordship in Transylvania broke out again in 1435 when salt miners revolted against their royal overseers. Other troubles began in the following year when the form of the church's tithe was changed. Then, in either April or May 1437, a great uprising took place in the region of the Somes river because of church taxes and the general oppressiveness of the feudal system. When a delegation of peasants was murdered at the direction of the Transylvanian viovode, Ladislau Csaki (1426-1437), a general revolt began that led to the Battle of Bobilna (sometimes Bobolna) Mountain at the end of June. The rebel army was victorious, and an agreement was reached that was later repudiated by a coalition of Saxon and Szekler chieftains. A second battle was then fought, this time at Apatiu, that ended inconclusively. The rebels again took the field in November 1437 in what had, by then, assumed the appearance of a peasant war.

This uprising is admirably described in "The Peasant Revolt of Bobolna" [44], by Joseph Held. Additional information may be found in the CHRONOLOGICAL HISTORY OF ROMANIA [39]. There is also some evidence that a tenuous tie existed between these troubles and the Bohemian Hussite movement that fomented open warfare between 1419 and 1436. Some background material on the Hussite movement may be found in Howard Kaminsky's THE HISTORY OF THE HUSSITE REVOLUTION [61].

IANCU OF HUNEDOARA

The year 1437 also marked the beginning of the short and troubled reign over Hungary of Sigismund's son-in-law, Albert of Habsburg (1437-1439), and marked the emergence of Iancu of Hunedoara (variously Janos or John Hunyadi). Iancu's prestige rose to a point where he was revered as the defender of Hungary, hence the West, against the Turks. His life and exploits are described in Camil Muresan's IANCU DE HUNEDOARA [76], in Kosary [63], and in Lengyel [65]. Lengyel points out that the Turks considered Iancu a worthy foe, as did those among his countrymen who opposed him during the Hungarian Civil War of 1439-1440. This internal struggle was fought over the right to the throne after the death of Albert. Iancu's success in this endeavor was matched by his successes over the Turks during the long campaign that followed his appointment as the Transylvanian voivode (1441) and during his service as captain of the fortress at Belgrad.

His victories and defeats included Semendria (Smederevo, Yugoslavia) in which he defeated a Turkish army commanded by Ishak Bey in the autumn of 1441. The fortress at Semendria had been used until 1439 as the headquarters and capital of George Brankovic (1427-1456), the Despot of Bulgaria. The Battle of Sintimbru (near Alba Iulia, Romania), which was fought on 18 March 1442, was a loss for Iancu, but within a week (either 21 or 25 March) he defeated the

Turks under Mezit Beg of Vidin at Hermannstadt (Sibiu, Romania). This battle is described by Mihail Dan in UN STEGAR AL LUPTEI ANTIOTOMANE -- IANCU DE HUNEDOARA [28].

## THE CAMPAIGN AGAINST THE TURKS IN BULGARIA

The Long (or Bulgarian) Campaign was fought in the autumn of 1443-January 1444 when Iancu's army of some 35,000 troops, including a Wallachian detachment sent by Vlad Dracul (Dracula), Voivode of Wallachia (1436-1442, 1443-1447), and a Polish force, crossed into Bulgaria and won at least six victories over the Turks, including the capture of Sofia and of Nis. As a result, the Sultan, Murad II, was forced to agree to a ten-year truce. The truce lasted only until 20 September 1444, however, when what has been called the Last Crusade began; and an army led by Ladislas III (Poland, 1434-1444; Hungary, 1440-1444) crossed the Danube into Bulgaria. In response, Murad moved his main forces back into Europe from Asia by crossing the Bosphorus with the aid of the Genoese fleet. Venetian naval units, sent by Ladislas to prevent the crossing, failed in their mission. On 10 November 1444, the Crusader army, including the Wallachians and Transylvanians led by Vlad Dracul, was decisively defeated at Varna and Ladislas was killed. Hunedoara and Dracul were able to escape with the remnants of the army, but Turkish domination was reasserted in the Balkans.

Inalcik describes the processes that led to the Crusade in his "1444 Burham" [46], which is found only in Turkish. Franz Babinger approaches the same subject in his MEHMET THE CONQUEROR AND HIS TIMES [9] but uses only western European sources which leads to the consideration by some that it is less than objective. Nevertheless, it is worth reading and is found in the original German, as well as French and Italian, in addition to the more recent English version that was published in 1978. In may be well to read Inalcik's review "Mehmed the Conqueror and His Time" [47] in conjunction with Babinger. THE ENCYCLOPEDIA OF MILITARY HISTORY [33], by Trevor N. Dupuy, and his father, R. Ernest Dupuy, contains short descriptions of some of these actions, but the data is often too sketchy to be of any real use. If supplemented with Erendil [34], the CHRONOLOGICAL HISTORY OF ROMANIA [39], Shaw [108], Kosary [63], Babinger [8,9], and Lengyel [65], a complete picture of this crucial period in Balkan history may be seen and understood. Oskar Halecki's THE CRUSADE OF VARNA [42] should also be studied.

Mihail Dan's article, "The Multinational People's Army of Iancu of Hunedoara" [27], is interesting but places too much emphasis on the presently fashionable theme of the unitary nature of Romanian society. Dan attempts to make the point that it "was mainly a people's army" that fought and that, somehow, the feudal nobility had little or no part in the affair. Even so, Professor Dan's study does expose some interesting information, especially about the Crusader volunteers and the use of mercenaries. For a general review of the Crusade, Nicolae Iorga's NOTES ET EXTRAITS POUR SERVIR A L'HISTOIRE DES CROISADES AU XVe SIECLE [56] is worth reading.

After the Varna failure, Hunedoara and Vlad Dracul withdrew north of the Danube where they were joined by a Burgundian naval force reinforced with some ships from the Papal navy. This flotilla had been able to sail up the Danube and was in position to attack the Turkish-held forts along the course of the river. This action was only partially successful; however, and the whole affair was soon overtaken by a period of intense diplomatic activity aimed at establishing a new anti-Ottoman coalition. See Frederick Pall's "Interventia lui Iancu de Hunedoara in Tara Romaneasca si Moldava in anii 1447-1448" [84] for another aspect of Iancu's campaigning during this period.

## SKANDERBEG AND THE SIEGE OF ALBANIA

When the anticipated coalition failed to materialize, Iancu, who had been installed as Regent of Hungary (5 June 1446) on 28 September 1448, set out with his army down the Morava valley intent upon linking up with the Albanian forces of Skanderbeg (Gjergj Kastrioti) who were also in a struggle against the Turks for their independence. Hunedoara had about 90,000 Hungarian, German, Polish, Transylvanian, and Wallachian troops (some sources say there were only 20,000); and the time seemed auspicious for victory as the Sultan's army had its hands full with Skanderbeg.

In 1443, Skanderbeg, an experienced soldier with service in the Ottoman army, had rallied the Albanians to fight a holy war against the Turks. By 1448, he had managed to almost completely free Albania of Turkish influence and was, more than likely, confounded when Murad suddenly broke contact and appeared to withdraw. In fact, the Turks were moving toward the northeast to meet the Hungarians. Murad's forces arrived at Kossovo, by way of Sofia, and there, on 17-19 October 1448, the Turk's defeated Iancu in what has been termed the Second Battle of Kossovo. This success all but sealed the fate of the Balkans, and it would be centuries before the Ottomans could be dislodged from European territory.

As for Skanderbeg and the Albanians, the Turks made yearly attempts to retake the country and were, for the next quarter century, thwarted every time. In 1451, Skanderbeg was required to establish a military alliance with Naples that meant the stationing of a Neopolitan garrison at Kruje. Finally, however, in 1466, Sultan Mohammed II (1451-1481) threw 200,000 troops against Kruje which still managed to hold out until 1478, when the Turks finally captured the citadel, ten years after Skanderbeg's death from disease. Albania was then swallowed up and a deliberate program undertaken to destroy all symbols of the past, especially all Christian and Latin monuments. For the next 400 years, Albania literally ceased to exist as a socio-political entity in the western concept of that term. The second battle at Kossovo is described in Erendil [34] and in Dan [28]. Skanderbeg's story is told in Fan Noli's GEORGE CASTRIOTI SCANDERBEG [79] while the campaigns in Albania are outlined in Athanase Gegaj's L'ALBANIE ET L'INVASION TURQUE AU XV$^e$ SIECLE [37].

Before the Albanian drama could play itself out, however, other events were taking place that would have an even more profound effect upon the Balkans and the course of European history. The Ottoman successes at Varna and in the Second Battle of Kossovo led to a Turkish attempt to capture Morea (the Peloponnesus) in 1447, the onset of the already discussed Albanian campaign, and the fall of Constantinople. When Constantinople did fall to the Turks in 1453, it forever brought to an end the notion of Byzantium as the

Second Rome, and began, for those willing to believe, the myth of Moscow as the Third Rome. In the not too distant future, therefore, Imperial Russia began to play a role as the protector of the Christian Balkans, a role often considered by scholars to be a conscious desire to gather the inheritances Russia then felt it deserved as the seat of the true Orthodoxy. While it is not a military history, the reading of Cyril Toumanoff's "Moscow the Third Rome: Genesis and Significance of a Politico-Religious Idea" [121] will help explain much that is to follow.

## THE BATTLE OF VASLUI

Any detailed analysis of the military history of the Balkans brings out one important point -- there was always someone to fight, even if it meant fighting among themselves. A good example of this is seen in the feud that developed between Iancu of Hunedoara and George Brankovic, the Despot of Serbia, who was restored to his throne in 1443 through the military exploits of Iancu and Ladislas. In 1449, however, Iancu led a punitive expedition against the Serbian. Then, in another incident, in September 1450, a battle took place in the Crasna village woods near Vaslui when Polish feudal lords attempted to replace the Bogdan II (1449-1451) as Voivode of Moldavia with a previously ousted Polish favorite. Bogdan was subsequently killed by his successor, Petru Aron, who was, in turn, thrown out by the Poles one year later.

In a slightly different form, the events of the autumn of 1452 and the spring of 1453 also illustrate the growing complexity of the situation. Beginning in the fall, Iancu and the Byzantine emperor opened negotiations to establish a new anti-Ottoman coalition. The enterprise again failed, however, because of Byzantine intransigence in refusing to meet Iancu's demands. This turn of events led directly and inexorably to the fall of Constantinople. That same year also witnessed the waning of Iancu's power.

## THE END OF THE ROMAN EMPIRE IN THE EAST

On 6 April 1453, one of the century's great dramas began to unfold when Sultan Mohammed II laid siege to Constantinople. Mohammed's force consisted of perhaps 150,000 troops, four heavy cannon, and 14 batteries of light artillery. In addition, the Turks had about 150 ships of various types. The Byzantine garrison has been estimated to have been about 11,400 men, which was too few by all accounts to have adequately defended the city. Riza Bozkurt, in his "Sultan Mehmet II and the Conquest of Constantinople" [16], disputes this figure and gives a rather convincing argument as to why it had to be larger. Others, such as Dupuy [33], claim the number was even smaller, but present no convincing arguments to defend the assertion and a study of the length of the fortifications would tend to deny its validity.

Regardless of these points, the siege was laid and was not broken until 29 May 1453 when the city fell and was mercilessly put to the sword by the Turks. The last Byzantine Emperor, Constantine XI Paleologus, was killed in action preceding the capture. In addition, a large number of prisoners were taken. The Turks did not attempt to destroy the Christian religion and the many religious shrines, even though they visited other depredations upon the city. Eventually the Turks selected Constantinople as the seat of the Sublime Porte. Bozkurt [16] tells the story of the siege and the victory from the Turkish view and tells it in sufficient detail to make it extremely interesting reading. Unfortunately, however, he does not document his findings. TURK SILAHLI KUVVETLERI TARIHI [123] also portrays the Turkish side of these momentous events. Volume III of this official historical series, published in Ankara, outlines the period from 1451 to 1566 in a systematic manner and is replete with source references. The siege and capture of Constantinople is discussed in great detail. Robert Schwoebel's THE SHADOW OF THE CRESCENT: THE RENAISSANCE IMAGE OF THE TURK (1453-1517) [105] uses the downfall of Constantinople as the basis upon which he builds the Ottoman development over the following 60 years. While the book is useful, the unwary will fall victim to the numerous small errors it contains. Another work in Turkish on the conquest is ISTANBUL'UN FETHI [31], by Feridun Dirimtekin.

The fall of the Byzantine capital is also portrayed in Runciman [99], in Sir Edwin Pears' THE DESTRUCTION OF THE GREEK EMPIRE AND THE STORY OF THE CAPTURE OF CONSTANTINOPLE BY THE TURKS [92], in Schlumberger's LE SIEGE, LA PRISE ET LE SAC DE CONSTANTINOPLE PAR LES TURCS EN 1453 [104], in ISLAM, FROM THE PROPHET MOHAMMED TO THE CAPTURE OF CONSTANTINOPLE [67], edited by Sir Bernard Lewis and others, and in Mordtmann's BELAGERUNG UND EROBERUNG CONSTANTINOPELS DURCH DIE TURKEN IN JAHRE 1453 NACH ORIGINALQUELLEN BEARBEITET [75]. Two works on Byzantine history that discuss the fall are George Ostrogorski's HISTORY OF THE BYZANTINE STATE [83] and BYZANTIUM: GREATNESS AND DECLINE [29] by Charles Diehl. Another interesting study of the affair is Bistra Tsvetkova's LA BATAILLE MEMORABLE DES PEUPLES: LE SUD-EST EUROPEEN ET LA CONQUETE OTTOMANS [122] published in French in 1971.

THE FIRST ATTACK ON BELGRAD

Even though the downfall of the Byzantine state marked the end of an age (indeed, to some, it was the end of the world), mankind did somehow continue, and this was no more evident anywhere than in the Balkans where the struggle to overthrow the Turkish yoke was only really getting underway. At the same time, of course, the Turks were in full cry to complete the Jihad .

By June 1456, the Turks had placed Belgrad in danger as they moved farther up the Danube valley into Central Europe. Hunedoara gathered a force of about 25,000 men, mainly Germans, Poles, Czechs, Transylvanians, and Hungarians, and prepared to defend the city. In doing this, Iancu asked Vlad Tepes (Vlad the Impaler) (1448, 1456-1462, 1476) the former voivode of Wallachia, to undertake the defense of southern Transylvania in place of the Transylvanian troops under Iancu's command. On 4 July 1456, Mohammed II opened his attack and began the siege of the city that he considered to be an absolutely vital objective. On 14 July, in a naval engagement fought on the Danube near Slankamen, Iancu's forces defeated the Turks and were able to reinforce the city garrison.

The Turks began their general attack on 21 July and, although they gained some penetration of the defenses, were thrown back. The following day, Iancu carried out a brilliantly executed infantry and artillery counterattack that forced a general Turkish withdrawal back as far as Constantinople. Less than one month later, Iancu of Hunedoara died of the plague. The military aspects of this siege of Belgrad have not received adequate coverage. There are mentions of the event in Romanescu [98], in Dan [27], in Shaw [108], in Inalcik [47, 49], and in Ladislau Banyai's excellent article [10]. Banyai points out that among the reinforcements Iancu managed to get into the city were Wallachians, Czechs, Hungarians, and Poles.

## VLAD THE MERCILESS AND STEFAN THE GREAT

Within a month of the successful defense of Belgrad, Vlad Tepes had routed the usurper on the Wallachian throne and reassumed that duty. As his appelation implies, Vlad was a merciless ruler who broke anyone refusing to submit to him. He was, at the same time, a valiant military leader who, throughout his reign, fought outside interference in his domain. Stoicescu's VLAD TEPES, PRINCE OF WALLACHIA [116] contains a great amount of material on his military exploits, but it is published only in Romanian. Serban Papacostea's article, "Vlad l'Empaleur, precise de la Valachie (1456-1462)" [86], is a good synopsis of his rule and is in French. Most of the general histories of Romania, such as Roberts [97], and Seton-Watson [107], have good coverage and Giurescu's CHRONOLOGICAL HISTORY OF ROMANIA [39] has numerous entries about him. Vlad is also discussed in Nicoara Beldiceanu's "Sur la Valaques des Balkans slaves a l'epoque ottoman, 1450-1550" [14].

At about the same time Vlad Tepes ruled Wallachia, Moldavia was favored by the advent of the regal leadership of Stefan the Great (1457-1504), a gifted politician and military commander. It was not too long before these two Romanian leaders began to feel the weight of the Turkish advance, with Wallachia being the first to be attacked. In May 1458, a large Turkish force, commanded by the Grand Vizier, Mohammed Pasha, penetrated into Wallachia, plundering and taking slaves. It is quite possible that this campaign was diversionary and that the real Turkish objective was to end the tenuous existence of Serbia as a free state. A massive attack in that direction accomplished this goal in 1459.

For the next two years, Vlad was forced to defend his throne against another usurper put forward by the Transylvanian Saxons. At the same time, Stefan was engaged in a war with Poland over a similar attempt to take his throne from that quarter. This war ended when a treaty was agreed upon on 4 April 1459, but it did not really end the fighting or the Polish interference. As a result, Stefan attacked the Szekler region of Transylvania for its part in offering safehaven to the would-be usurper, Petru Aron. These accounts may be found in the CHRONOLOGICAL HISTORY OF ROMANIA [39].

Having secured his throne in Wallachia, Vlad Tepes opened a new campaign against the Turks in the winter of 1461. Vlad crossed the Danube and fought a number of engagements, the chief result of which was, as Vlad later confessed, the annihilation of some 25,000 Turkish subjects, most of whom were civilians. In retaliation, Mohammed II, now carrying the appelation, "the Conquerer," for his success at Constantinople, sent a very large force, often exaggerated as being in excess of 200,000 men, against Wallachia. By the end of June 1462, Vlad had this Ottoman force in flight. But, while Vlad was fighting the Turks, his brother, Radu the Handsome, with Turkish connivance, and the help of disgruntled Wallachian boyars, put himself on the throne. Vlad was forced to flee to Transylvania where he hoped to gain aid from Mathias Corvinus, Iancu's second son, who was then King of Hungary (1458-1490). Instead, Vlad was imprisoned by the Hungarians and remained in confinement for 12 years. Stoicescu [116] has a good account of these events, while Papacostea [86] ends his account with Vlad's capture and imprisonment.

## TURKISH EXPANSION CONTINUES

During this period, the Ottoman Empire had continued its advance into southeastern Europe and had invaded and conquered Bosnia (1463), the Herzogovina (1483), and Montenegro (1499). At the same time, the Turks had fought a major war with Venice (1463-1479), had attacked Italy (1480), had laid siege to, but failed to capture, Rhodes (1480-1481), had invaded Carniola and Styria (1492-1494), and had won a great naval victory over the Venetians at the First Battle of Lepanto (28 July 1499). These actions are outlined in Dupuy [33], and are discussed in detail in Shaw [108], Inalcik [49], and Kinross [62]. A generalized account of the situations in Bosnia and Montenegro can be found in Coquelle's HISTOIRE DU MONTENEGRO ET DE LA BOSNIA [25].

## THE BATTLE OF BAIA AND THE RISE OF STEFAN THE GREAT

This was also the time of Stefan's rise to prominence as a great military captain. In 1467, the nobility and some of the populace in Transylvania rose against the Hungarian king. Without the full support of the peasantry, however, the revolt was doomed, even though Stefan had furnished aid to the rebels from Moldavia, an act that did not go unnoticed by Mathias Corvinus. On 11 November 1467, with a Hungarian army of about 40,000 men, he invaded Moldavia. The invasion ended in a great battle fought at Baia where Stefan defeated the Hungarians with a force of about 8,000 men. This campaign, along with a discussion of Stefan's military programs in Moldavia, is presented in Ion Cuspa's article on "The Contribution of Stephen the Great to the Development of Romanian Military Art" [26]. The action at Baia constituted the last major attempt of the Hungarian crown to reestablish hegemony over Moldavia by force of arms. Both Cuspa [26], and Romanescu [98] discuss this battle.

Although there were some minor incidents in Moldavia over the next nine years, the situation remained relatively stable until another Turkish invasion began. The result of this attack was that Suleiman-Pasha, with an army of about 120,000 men, was defeated in the Vaslui marsh midpoint between Rahova and Lipovat on 10 January 1475, by Stefan the Great and an allied force of Szeklers, Hungarians, Poles, and Moldavians. Although the Battle of Vaslui is hardly mentioned in accounts of Turkish military operations of this period, the event was a stunning victory for the Romanian prince, and it led to a Hungarian alliance, and more fighting. Nicholae Iorga's ISTORIA ARMATEI ROMANESTI [52] and Romanescu [98] have good accounts of the battle.

On 13 May 1476, Sultan Mohammed II again set out from Adrianople with an army sometimes estimated at 150,000 troops, including a 10,000-12,000 man Wallachian detachment, to attack Moldavia. The Turks were to be supported by a Tatar attack from the east. By 10 June, the Ottoman force was advancing up the Siret valley when the Tatars crossed the Dniester. Stefan was able to force an almost immediate Tatar withdrawl and then went to meet the Turks at Valea-Alba (Razboieni). There, on 26 July 1476, the Ottomans were again defeated. Stefan was then able to withdraw to a series of fortresses where he held out until the approach of Mathias Corvinus, and the effects of starvation and disease, forced Mohammed to withdraw. With the Turks thus momentarily out of the way, Stefan, along with Stefan Batory I (1479-1493), the Transylvanian viovode, and Vlad Tepes moved to dispose of the pro-Ottoman regime in Wallachia. Bucharest was taken by the coalition in November 1476 and one year later a new ruler was put on the throne. The Wallachian issue was not settled, however, and intermittent fighting continued between Moldavia and Wallachia for the next five years.

This period is covered in some detail in Cuspa [26], and in Romanescu [98]. The best account of the various alignments involved in these affairs is in the CHRONOLOGICAL HISTORY OF ROMANIA [39], and the best overall study of Mohammed's military campaigns during this period is Salahaddin Tansel's OSMANLI KAYNAKLARINA GORE FATIH SULTAN MEHMED'IN SIYASI ASKERI FAALIYETI [120]. This work also details Mohammed's political activities, but it is, thus far, published only in Turkish. Vasile Parvan's RELATIILE LUI STEFAN CEL MARE CU UNGARIA [89] explains the rather complex cooperative arrangements that appeared from time to time between Stepfan and the Hungarian throne. Makkai [74] touches upon the life and times of Stefan Batory I, who was to be overshadowed by his more famous namesake in the 16th century.

THE RISE OF A NEW TURKISH SULTAN

The last two decades of the century witnessed a renewal of Turkish attacks in the Balkans. The new Turkish ruler, Bayazid II (1481-1512), ignoring the policy of caution that had prevailed for some time before, called upon his armies for more direct and comprehensive action. In 1482, an Ottoman force attacked the Banat, only to be beaten back. Then, in June 1484, a new campaign began in which Bayazid sent his troops into Moldavia. Soon, a joint Ottoman-Tatar-Wallachian army invested the great fortress at Chilia (7 July 1484), and one week later, it fell to the Turks. By 5 August, Turkish forces held Cetatea-Alba. These battles are discussed by Beldiceanu in his article, "Le conquete des cities marchandes de Kilia et de Cetatea-Alba" [12].

When the Turks learned that Stefan had journeyed to Poland (September 1485), they renewed their attacks, bent on enthroning a puppet before the prince could return. But Stefan's early arrival back in Moldavia derailed the plan and the Turks, along with their Wallachian allies, were forced to retire to Chilia. On 16 November 1485, a major battle was fought at Catlabuga in which Stefan's Moldavian army, reinforced with about 3,000 Polish cavalry, defeated a Turkish force commanded by Bali-Beg Malcoci Oglu, the Pasha of Silistra. Even though the victory was clear, Chilia and Cetatea-Alba remained in Ottoman hands, and a new campaign was mounted in 1486 that culminated in the Battle of Scheia (6 March 1486). These activities continued until 1489, when a treaty was concluded in which Stefan promised tribute in return for peace.

But the quiet was not to last for the Moldavians, and eight years after the treaty the Poles attacked into Moldavia intent upon bringing the province into the Polish hegemony. The Polish king, John Albert (1492-1501), at the head of an army of 100,000, crossed the Dniester on 9 August 1497, and, by 26 September, had laid siege to the fortress at Suceava. Stefan's army of about 40,000 Moldavians, plus a Turkish corps and one from Wallachia, withstood the attack for three weeks until a Transylvanian force sent by the King of Hungary, and commanded by the Viovode of Transylvania, arrived and lifted the investment. After some negotiation, the Poles withdrew only to again become engaged with Stefan's forces in the Cosmin Forest (Codrul Cosminului) (26 October). A pitched battle was fought that turned into a bloodbath. In a series of subsequent actions, the Polish army was badly mauled and forced to withdraw back across the Dniester. Then, in 1498, Stefan invaded Poland and after gathering much plunder withdrew back into Moldavia. He was then once again set upon by the Turks for failing to pay the tithe. Both Giurescu [39] and Cuspa [26] adequately cover these events.

As all of this was taking place, the stage was also being set for the opening of a new drama. In a campaign that lasted from 1463-1485, Bohenian and Hungarian forces had been attacking and plundering Austria to the northwest. By 1486, Mathias Corvinus had captured Vienna, and had annexed Austria, Stryia, and Carinthia in the Hungary empire. This action brought a reaction from the Germans and, in 1491, the Archduke Maximilian retook Vienna, forcing the Hungarians out of the country. The following year, Maximilian defeated a Turkish army that had invaded Austria and, in 1493, he took the German throne from his inept father. The Holy Roman Empire now directly confronted the forces of conflict in the Balkans.

"The Ottoman Empire (1491-1520)" [88], by V.J. Parry, deals with most aspects of this transitional period, while C.A. Macartney, in his "Eastern Europe" [68], discusses Hungary and deals with the Turkish advance into the Balkans. In the "Empire under Maximilian I" [64], R.G.D. Laffan describes the Turkish threat, the intervention into Hungary in 1506, and the Emperor's death. All of these articles are found in volume one of the NEW CAMBRIDGE MODERN HISTORY [94]. One additional work of some significance is DIE KAISERLICHEN KRIEGSVOLKER VON MAXIMILLIAN I. BIS PRINZ EUGEN, 1479-1718 [3], by the outstanding Austrian scholar J.C. Allmayer-Beck and E. Lessing. This work concerns itself with the Imperial army over a 250-year period, ending with the Treaty of Passarowitz. For the serious student who reads German there is nothing better and nothing that so adroitly combines straight military history with the socio-economic aspects of the times.

# BIBLIOGRAPHIC LISTING

1. Adil. O.B. CRONICILI DINASTICI OTOMANI. Vol. 1: CRONICI
   TURCESTI PRIVIND TARILE ROMANE. Bucharest: 1966.

2. Alexandrescu-Dersca(Bulgaru), M.M. LA CAMPAGNE DE TIMUR EN
   ANATOLIA, 1402. London: 1977 [1942].

3. Allmayer-Beck, J.C., & Lessing, E. DIE KAISERLICHEN
   KRIEGSVOLKER VON MAXIMILIAN I. BIS PRINZ EUGEN, 1497-1718.
   Munich: 1978.

4. Angelov, D.S., et al., eds. BULGARO-RUMUNSKI VRUZKI I
   OTNOSHENIIA PREZ VEKOVETE: IZSLEDOVANIIA. Vol. 1: XII-XIX
   centuries. Sofia: 1965.

5. Arnakis, G.G. THE NEAR EAST IN MODERN TIMES. Vol. 1: THE
   OTTOMAN EMPIRE AND THE BALKANS TO 1900. Austin & New York:
   1969.

6. Arnakis, G.G., & Vucinich, W.S. THE NEAR EAST IN MODERN TIMES.
   Vol. 2: FORTY CRUCIAL YEARS, 1900-1940. Austin & New York:
   1972.

7. Atiya, A.S. THE CRUSADE OF NICOPOLIS. London: 1938.

8. Babinger, F.C.H. BEITRAGE ZUR FRUHGESCHICHTE DER
   TURKENHERRSCHAFT IN RUMELIEN. Brunn: 1944.

9. _____. MEHMET THE CONQUEROR AND HIS TIMES. Trans. by Ralph
   Manheim. Princeton: 1978.

10. Banyai, L. "Formes de Collaboration de peuple Roumain avec les
    peuples voisons au moyen age dans la lutte pour la
    conservation de son entite d'etat, pour la defense de la
    liberte et de son independence." PMHRP. Bucharest: 1980.

11. Beckman, G. DER KAMPF KAISER SIGMUNDS GEGEN DIE WERDENDS
    WELTMACHT DER OSMANEN, 1392-1437. Gotha: 1902.

12. Beldiceanu, N. "La conquete des cites marchandes de Kilia et de
    Cetatea Alba par Bayezid II." SOF, XXIII (1964), 36-105.

13. _____. LE MONDE OTTOMAN DES BALKANS 1402-1566. London:
    1976.

14. _____. SUR LES VALAQUES DES BALKANS SLAVES A L'EPOQUE
    OTTOMANE 1450-1550. Paris: 1967.

15. Besbelli, S. "Ottoman Naval Superiority in the Mediterranean,
    Barbaros Hayreddin and the Prevesa Naval Victory." RIHM ,
    46 (1980), 93-107.

16. Bozkurt, R. "Sultan Mehmet II and the Conquest of Constantinople." RIHM, 46 (1980), 61-71.

17. Braun, M. KOSSOVO. Leipzig: 1937.

18. Ceaucescu, I. THE ENTIRE PEOPLE'S WAR FOR THE HOMELAND'S DEFENCE WITH THE ROMANIANS. Bucharest: 1980.

19. _____., ed. PAGES FROM THE MILITARY HISTORY OF THE ROMANIAN PEOPLE. Bucharest: 1980.

20. Chandler, D.G. ATLAS OF MILITARY STRATEGY. New York: 1980.

21. Charnaris, P. "The Strife Among the Paleologi and the Ottoman Turks, 1370-1402." BYZANTION, I:XVI (1942-43), 286-314, II:XVII (1944-45), 330-335 passim.

22. Clark, G.N., Sir., et al. Advisory Comm. THE NEW CAMBRIDGE MODERN HISTORY. 14 vols. Cambridge: 1957-1970.

23. Coles, P. THE OTTOMAN IMPACT ON EUROPE. LECS. London: 1968.

24. Cooke, W.S. THE OTTOMAN EMPIRE AND ITS TRIBUTARY STATES. Chicago & Amsterdam: 1968.

25. Coquelle, P. HISTOIRE DU MONTENEGRO ET DE LA BOSNIA. Paris: 1895.

26. Cuspa, I. "The Contribution of Stephen the Great to the Development of Romanian Military Art." PHRA, Monograph XV. BHR. Bucharest: 1975.

27. Dan, M. "The Multinational People's Army of Iancu of Hunedoara." PHRA, Monograph XV. BHR. Bucharest: 1975.

28. _____. UN STEGAR AL LUPTEI ANTIOTOMANE - IANCU DE HUNEDOARA. Bucharest: 1974.

29. Diehl, C. BYZANTIUM: GREATNESS AND DECLINE. New Brunswick: 1960.

30. Dinic, M. "The Balkans: 1018-1499." CaMH IV. Cambridge: 1966.

31. Dirimtekin, F. ISTANBUL'UN FETHI. Istanbul: 1949.

32. Ducas, I. ISTORIA TURCO-BIZANTINA (1341-1462). Bucharest: 1952.

33. Dupuy, R.E., & Dupuy, T.N. THE ENCYCLOPEDIA OF MILITARY HISTORY. Rev. ed. New York: 1977.

34. Erendil, M. "Emergence of the Ottoman State: An Outline of the Period Between 1299-1453." RIHM, 46 (1980), 31-61.

35. Finlay, G. HISTORY OF GREECE, FROM ITS CONQUEST BY THE ROMANS TO THE PRESENT TIME, B.C. 164 TO A.D. 1864. 7 vols. New rev. ed. by H.F. Tozer. Oxford: 1877.

36. Fuller, J.F.C. ARMAMENT AND HISTORY. New York: 1945.

37. Gegaj, A. L'ALBANIE ET L'INVASION TURQUE AU XV^e SIECLE.
    Paris: 1937.

38. Gibbons, H.A. THE FOUNDATIONS OF THE OTTOMAN EMPIRE. New York:
    1916.

39. Giurescu, C., et al., eds. CHRONOLOGICAL HISTORY OF ROMANIA.
    Bucharest: 1972.

40. _____. "Premise istorice ale redobindirii independentei
    poporului Roman." ROMANIA IN RAZBOIUL DE INDEPENDENTA.
    Coord. by Ion Coman. Bucharest: 1977.

41. Grachev, V.P. SERBKAIA GOSUDARSTVENNOST' V X-XIV VV. (KRITIKA
    TEORII "ZHUPNOI ORGANIZATSII"). Moscow: 1972.

42. Halecki, O. THE CRUSADE OF VARNA. New York: 1943.

43. Hammond, N.G.L. MIGRATIONS AND INVASIONS IN GREECE AND ADJACENT
    AREAS. Park Ridge, NJ: c.1976.

44. Held, J. "The Peasant Revolt of Bobolna." SR XXXVI No. 1
    (March, 1977), 25-38.

45. Heymann, F.G. JOHN ZIZKA AND THE HUSSITE REVOLUTION. Princeton:
    1955.

46. Inalcik, H. "1444 Burham." FATILI DEVRI UZERINDE TETKIKLER VE
    VESIKALAR, Vol. 1. Ankara: 1954.

47. _____. "Mehmet the Conqueror and His Time - A Review."
    SPECULUM, XXXV (1960), 408-427.

48. _____. "Murad II." IA VIII, 598-615.

49. _____. THE OTTOMAN EMPIRE: THE CLASSICAL AGE, 1300-1600.
    Trans. by Norman Itzkowitz & Colin Imber. New York &
    Washington: 1973.

50. _____. "Ottoman Methods of Conquest." SI, II (1954),
    103-129.

51. Iorga, N. GESCHICHTE DES OSMANISCHEN REICHES. 5 vols. Gotha:
    1908-1913.

52. _____. ISTORIA ARMATEI ROMANESTI. 2 vols. Bucharest:
    1929-1930 [1910].

53. _____. ISTORIA LUI MIHAI VITEAZUL. 2 vols. Bucharest: 1935.

54. _____. ISTORIA LUI STEFAN CEL MARE PENTRU POPORUL ROMAN.
    Bucharest: 1966.

55. _____. "Lupta pentru stapinirea Viidinului in 1365-1369 si
    politica lui Vladislav voda fata de unguri." CL, XXXIV
    (1900), 962-999.

56. _____. NOTES ET EXTRAITS POUR SERVIR A L'HISTOIRE DES CROISADES AU XVe SIECLE. 2 vols. Paris: 1899.

57. Iosipescu, S., & Eskenasi, V. "Obzor srednevekovykh voennykh struktur v rumynskikh knyazhestvakh." PMHRP. Bucharest: 1980.

58. Jirecik, K. GESCHICHTE DER SERBEN. 2 vols. Gotha: 1911-1918.

59. Jonquiere, A. de la. HISTOIRE DE L'EMPIRE OTTOMAN. 2 vols. 3rd ed. Paris: 1914.

60. Juchereau de Saint-Denys, A. de. HISTOIRE DE L'EMPIRE OTTOMAN. Paris: 1844.

61. Kaminsky, H. THE HISTORY OF THE HUSSITE REVOLUTION. Berkeley & Los Angelos: 1967.

62. Kinross, J.P.D. Balfour, Lord. THE OTTOMAN CENTURIES: THE RISE AND FALL OF THE TURKISH EMPIRE. London: 1977.

63. Kosary, D.G. A HISTORY OF HUNGARY. New York: 1941.

64. Laffan, R.G.D. "The Empire Under Maximilian I." NCMH, I. Cambridge: 1971.

65. Lengyel, E. 1000 YEARS OF HUNGARY. New York: 1958.

66. Lewinsohn, R. THE PROFITS OF WAR THROUGH THE AGES. London: 1936.

67. Lewis, B., et al., eds. ISLAM FROM THE PROPHET MUHAMMED TO THE CAPTURE OF CONSTANTINOPLE. Vol. I: POLITICS AND WAR. DHWC. New York: 1973.

68. Macartney, C.A. "Eastern Europe." NCMH, I. Cambridge: 1971.

69. Macdermott, M. A HISTORY OF BULGARIA, 1393-1885. London: 1962.

70. McEvedy, C. PENGUIN ATLAS OF MEDIEVAL HISTORY. Harmondsworth, Middlesex: 1961.

71. McNeill, W.H. THE RISE OF THE WEST. New York & Toronto: 1965.

72. _____. A WORLD HISTORY. New York, London & Toronto: 1967.

73. _____. EUROPE'S STEPPE FRONTIER, 1500-1800. Chicago: 1964.

74. Makkai, L. HISTOIRE DE TRANSYLVANIE. Paris: 1946.

75. Mordtmann, A. BELAGERUNG UND EROBERUNG CONSTANTINOPELS DURCH DIE TURKEN IN JAHRE 1453 NACH ORIGINALQUELLEN BEARBEITET. Stuttgart: 1858.

76. Muresan, C. IANCU DE HUNEDOARA. Bucharest: 1968.

77. Musat, M. "Sur le pas de luttes de peuple roumain pour son unite et son independance." RIHM, 26 (1977), 17-29.

78. Newman, J.R. THE TOOLS OF WAR. Garden City: 1943.

79. Noli, F.S. GEORGE CASTRIOTI SCANDERBEG, 1405-1468. New York: 1947.

80. Odlozilik, O. THE HUSSITE KING: BOHEMIA IN EUROPEAN AFFAIRS. 1440-1471. New Brunswick: 1965.

81. Olteanu, C. "On the Organization of the Army in the Romanian Countries." PHRA, Monograph XV. BHR. Bucharest: 1975.

82. Oman, C., Sir. "The Art of War in the Fifteenth Century." CaMH VIII. Cambridge:

83. Ostrogorski, G. HISTORY OF THE BYZANTINE STATE. Oxford: 1956.

84. Pall, F. "Interventia lui Iancu de Hunedoara in Tara Romaneasca si Moldava in anii 1447-1448." STUDII ACADEMIEI, V (1963), 1049-1072.

85. Palmer, J.A.B. "The Origins of the Janissaries." BULLETIN OF THE JOHN RYLANDS LIBRARY, XXV (1956), 433-443.

86. Papacostea, S. "Vlad l'Empaleur, prince de la Valachie (1456-1462)." RIHM, 36 (1977), 202-211.

87. Parry, J.H. THE ESTABLISHMENT OF THE EUROPEAN HEGEMONY, 1415-1715: TRADE AND EXPLORATION IN THE AGE OF THE RENAISSANCE. New York: 1961.

88. Parry, V.J. "The Ottoman Empire (1481-1520)." NCMH, I. Cambridge: 1971.

89. Parvan, V. "Relatiile lui Stefan cel Mare cu Ungaria." CL, XXXIV (1900), 92.

90. Pascu, S. MAREA ADUNARE NATIONALA DE LA ALBA IULIA: INCUNUNAREA IDEII, A TENDITELOR SI A LUPTELOR DE UNITATE A POPORULUI ROMAN. Cluj: 1968.

91. _____. VOIEVODATUL TRANSYLVANIEI. Vol. 1. 2nd ed. Cluz: 1972.

92. Pears, E., Sir. THE DESTRUCTION OF THE GREEK EMPIRE AND THE STORY OF THE CAPTURE OF CONSTANTINOPLE BY THE TURKS. London: 1903.

93. Pope, D. GUNS: FROM THE INVENTION OF GUNPOWDER TO THE 20TH CENTURY. New York: 1965.

94. Potter, G.R., ed. THE RENAISSANCE. Vol. 1 in NCMH. Cambridge: 1971.

95. Previte-Orton, C.W., & Brooke, Z.N. THE CLOSE OF THE MIDDLE AGES. Vol. 8 in CaMH. Cambridge: 1959.

96. Radulescu, A., & Bitoleanu, I. DOBROGEA: ISTORIA ROMANILOR DINTRE DUNARE SI MARE. Bucharest: 1979.

97. Roberts, H.L. RUMANIA. New Haven: 1951.

98. Romanescu, G. "Grosse mittelalterliche Schlachten des rumanischen Volkes fur die Verteidigung der Unabhangigkeit und des uralten Heimatsbodens." PMHRP. Bucharest: 1980.

99. Runciman, S., Sir. THE FALL OF CONSTANTINOPLE, 1453. Cambridge: 1965.

100. _____. A HISTORY OF THE FIRST BULGARIAN STATE. London: 1930.

101. Savu, A.G., ed. PAGES FROM THE HISTORY OF THE ROMANIAN ARMY. BHR, Monograph XV. Bucharest: 1975.

102. _____. THE ARMY AND ROMANIAN SOCIETY. Bucharest: 1980.

103. Schevill, F. HISTORY OF THE BALKAN PENINSULA FROM THE EARLIEST TIMES TO THE PRESENT. New York: 1971 [c.1922].

104. Schlumberger, G. LE SIEGE, LA PRISE ET LA SAC DE CONSTANTINOPLE PAR LES TURCS EN 1453. Paris: 1914.

105. Schwoebel, R. THE SHADOW OF THE CRESCENT: THE RENAISSANCE IMAGE OF THE TURK (1453-1517). New York: 1967.

106. Scott, H.L. MILITARY DICTIONARY. New York: 1861.

107. Seton-Watson, R.W. A HISTORY OF THE ROUMANIANS: FROM ROMAN TIMES TO THE COMPLETION OF UNITY. Cambridge: 1934.

108. Shaw, S.J. HISTORY OF THE OTTOMAN EMPIRE AND MODERN TURKEY. Vol. 1: EMPIRE OF THE GAZIS: THE RISE AND DECLINE OF THE OTTOMAN EMPIRE, 1280-1808. Cambridge & New York: 1976.

109. Stavrianos, L.S. THE BALKANS SINCE 1453. New York: 1958.

110. Stefanescu, S. "Participarea romanilor la lupta de la Grunewald." STUDII ACADEMIEI, I (1961), 5-22.

111. _____. "Romanian Countries' Military Effort in Their Fight for Independence During the Middle Ages." RIHM, 36 (1977), 30-44.

112. _____. "Comments upon the Romanian Military History of the 3rd-14th Centuries." PHRA, Monograph XV, BHR. Bucharest: 1975.

113. Stoianovich, T. A STUDY OF BALKAN CIVILIZATION. New York: 1967.

114. Stoicescu, N. "The Great Army of Walachia and Moldavia (14th-16th Centuries)." PHRA, Monograph XV, BHR. Bucharest: 1975.

115. _____. "Organizational Structure of the Armies in the Romanian Principalities in the 14th-18th Centuries." ARS. Bucharest: 1980.

116. _____. VLAD TEPES, PRINCE OF WALACHIA. BHR, Monograph XXI. Bucharest: 1978.

117. Sugar, P.F. SOUTHEASTERN EUROPE UNDER OTTOMAN RULE, 1354-1804. Vol.1 in HECE. Seattle: 1977.

118. Sugar, P.F., & Treadgold, D.W. HISTORY OF EAST CENTRAL EUROPE. 11 vols. Seattle & London: 1975-.

119. Tanner, J.R., et al., eds. DECLINE OF EMPIRE AND PAPACY. CaMH VII. Cambridge: 1958.

120. Tansel, S. OSMANLI KAYNAKLARINA GORE FATIH SULTAN MEHMED'IN SIYASE VE ASKERI FAALIYETI. Ankara: 1953.

121. Toumanoff, C.M. "Moscow the Third Rome: Genesis and Significance of a Politico-Religious Idea." CHR, XL No. 4 (January 1955), 411-447.

122. Tsvetkova, B. LA BATAILLE MEMORABLE DES PEUPLES: LE SUD-EST EUROPEEN ET LA CONQUETE OTTOMANS, FIN XIVe - PREMIERE MOITIE DU XVe SIECLES. Trans. by Jetcho Obbov. Sofia: 1971.

123. Turkey. Department of War History. TURK SILAHLI KUVVETLERI TARIHI. 6 vols. Ankara: c.1977.

124. Urbansky, A.B. BYZANTIUM AND THE DANUBE FRONTIER; A STUDY OF THE RELATIONS BETWEEN BYZANTIUM, HUNGARY, AND THE BALKANS DURING THE PERIOD OF THE COMNENI. New York: [c.1968].

125. Vacalopoulos, A. THE GREEK NATION, 1453-1669. THE CULTURAL AND ECONOMIC BACKGROUND OF MODERN GREEK SOCIETY. New Brunswick: 1976.

126. Volkl, E. DAS RUMANISCHE FURSTENTUM MOLDAU UND DIE OSTSLAVEN IM 15. BIS 17. JAHREHUNDERT. PEEI 42. Wiesbaden: 1975.

127. Winter, J.M. ed. WAR AND ECONOMIC DEVELOPMENT. Cambridge & New York: 1975.

128. Wittek, P. THE RISE OF THE OTTOMAN EMPIRE. London: 1938.

129. Wolff, R.L. "The 'Second Bulgarian Empire,' its Origins and History." SPECULUM, XXIV (1949), 167-206.

130. Zook, D.H., & Higham, R. A SHORT HISTORY OF WARFARE. New York: 1966.

CHAPTER THREE

THE 16TH CENTURY

GENERAL BACKGROUND

By the beginning of the 16th century, a number of powerful states had arisen in western Europe. The Holy Roman Empire had been in decline, however, as it lacked the cohesiveness and strength that had marked its course through the Middle Ages. The Empire's rebirth came about when Charles V (1519-1556) used its carcass to forge one of the greatest of empires ever controlled by a single ruler. In 1516, he took the Spanish territories of Ferdinand and, in 1519, the Austrian and Dutch lands of Maximilian. That same year he was crowned Holy Roman Emperor over French protestations. With his new title, Charles not only assumed great power but an equal number of great problems as well, not the least of which were those posed by the Balkans.

Austria's eastern neighbor, Hungary, was a nation at the crossroads. Controlled by a strong nobility and an embedded, self-serving feudal system on the inside and threatened by powerful assailants from without, there was little opportunity for any real concentration of power in a native monarchy. Austria, Poland and the Ottoman Empire all had designs on Hungary and all exerted their style of external pressure upon it.

Russia was still in its Muscovite period and the "Gathering of the Lands," that had begun in the old century, was still going on. With the death of Ivan III (1462-1505), his son, Vasili (1505-1533), continued the process of annexing additional territories to the west and southwest of Moscow. By the reigns of Ivan IV (1533-1584) and Feodar I (1584-1598), Moscovy had become Russia (Ivan IV had been crowned "Tsar of All the Russias" in 1547). Still, even all of this progress throughout the century left Russia a considerable distance from the Balkans, both in miles and in interest.

There are any number of good general historical reviews of the 16th century that should suffice for both the casual reader and the serious student. There are, for instance, three excellent articles in the first volume of the NEW CAMBRIDGE MODERN HISTORY [98], H.C. Darby's "The Face of Europe on the Eve of the Great Discoveries" [24], J.R. Hale's "International Relations in the West: Diplomacy and War" [48], and "Eastern Europe" [80], by C.A. Macartney. Darby's discussion includes sections on the Balkan peninsula, the mountains of central Europe, the Bohemian uplands, the Hungarian plain, and Transylvania. Macartney's article contains considerable information on the Balkans, while Hale's piece is replete with data on the art, style, and conditions of war. The second NCMH volume, THE REFORMATION, 1520-1559 [29], which was edited by G.R. Elton, and Richard Dunn's THE AGE OF RELIGIOUS WARS, 1559-1715 [26] are valuable in rounding out the general review of the century.

## MILITARY ARTS AND SCIENCES IN THE 16TH CENTURY

In addition to Hale's article [48], there are several good sources on the overall conduct of war in this century. Without question, one of the best treatises on the subject is Quincy Wright's A STUDY OF WAR [144] which is brilliantly written, well-documented, and thoroughly indexed. Of equal value is Sir Charles Oman's A HISTORY OF THE ART OF WAR IN THE SIXTEENTH CENTURY [91], as is the introduction to Chapter XIII in the Dupuys' ENCYCLOPEDIA OF MILITARY HISTORY [27], and Chapter V, "The Transition from Feudal to Modern Warfare," in a SHORT HISTORY OF WARFARE [145], by David Zook and Robin Higham. Professor Theodore Ropp's "Military History to the End of the Eighteenth Century" [106], found in A GUIDE TO THE STUDY AND USE OF MILITARY HISTORY [60], has an excellent bibliography in addition to much useful information on the period.

## THE BALKANS IN THE 16TH CENTURY

The Danubian Provinces in the Balkans were spending as much time fighting internal disorder and among themselves as they did in defending their frontiers against foreign encroachment. Bulgaria was in the Ottoman thrall and entering the second century of its dark era. Albania, too, was a Turkish captive, and many of its people were fleeing to Italy and to other Christian lands. As in Bulgaria, many of the Albanian landed gentry embraced Islam as a means of maintaining their position. Greece was also an occupied land, although pockets of independence still existed when the 16th century began. By the end of the century, however, only Crete and the Ionian isles would be free of Ottoman domination.

The Ottoman Empire itself was at the apex of its power and was still pressing forward up the Danube valley, its main axis of advance, into the heart of Christian Europe. By the beginning of the century, the paradoxical nature of Ottoman rule in the Balkans was beginning to be defined; and, although it was hard to rationalize, Christians had greater freedom in Islamic lands than Moslems had in the Christian World. At the same time, Ottoman justice was almost always swift and bloody, but no more so than that meted out by Christian kings and princes. Of all things, Ottoman rule was more capricious and erratic but, even so, for the Greeks for instance, it was less distasteful than the Venetian intolerance that they had also suffered.

## EARLY PROBLEMS IN THE BALKANS

Although the century began peacefully enough in the Balkans, there were problems that grew out of the need to select a successor for Stefan the Great, the Prince of Moldavia, who died on 2 July 1504. These problems spilled over into Wallachia as a consequence of Wallachian meddling. This issue was settled, however, in 1507, but the squabbling continued for another four years. STEFAN CEL MARE [132], by I. Ursu, and Manole Neagoe's STEFAN CEL MARE [89] are both excellent accounts of the life of the great Moldavian leader.

There were problems of a different sort in Hungary. Ladislas II of Bohemia (1471-1516) was also on the throne of Hungary as Ladislas VI (1490-1516). A weak ruler, he found himself torn between the desires of the feudal nobility and internal division caused by dynastic ties with the Habsburgs. Ladislas' daughter was married to the Archduke Ferdinand, brother of Emperor Charles V (1519-1556) of the Holy Roman Empire, and served as the empire's Austrian agent. The Hungarian nobility, in the process of developing a national consciousness, opposed both the crown and the influence of the Habsburgs. This nationalist movement was led by John Zapolya, the voivode of Transylvania (1510-1528), who would soon become a dominant figure in Balkan history.

In 1514, a vicious peasant revolt swept Transylvania that was not quelled until a severe toll was extracted from both sides. This revolt was led by a petty Szekler nobleman, Gheorghe Doja, who was a commander of the anti-Ottoman Crusader force being conscripted from among the peasantry. The excesses of the nobility toward the soldiery sparked the initial fighting, and soon portions of the Transylvanian and Hungarian populace joined in. It took over six months for John Zapolya to put down the revolt and only after a major battle was fought at Timisoara 15 July 1514. Although the rebellion continued sporadically for a period of time, the murder of Doja and other rebel leaders and the imposition of serfdom (1517) finally ended the struggle but not the unrest. One of the outcomes of this revolt was the abandonment of the plan for the crusade against the Ottoman Empire.

These events are outlined in the CHRONOLOGICAL HISTORY OF ROMANIA [36]. Lengyel [71] discusses the development of the Crusade and the underlying causes of the Hungarian revolt pointing out how the peasants sought the protection of the Cross from the bestial way they were treated by their masters. Lengyel also points out that neither side can be exonerated from charges of barbarism during the revolt.

## THE OTTOMAN EMPIRE AND THE WAR WITH VENICE

Turkey entered the century at war (1499-1503) with Venice. In this struggle, the First (1499) and Second (1500) Battles of Lepanto were fought in which the Turks defeated the Venetians. The 1500 action is briefly described in "The Battle of Lepanto and Its Place in Mediterranean History" [50] by A. Hess. This article deals primarily with the greater naval engagement fought at the same place in 1571. The 1500 battle is also discussed by H.A. von Burski in KEMAL RE'IS: EIN BEITRAGE ZUR GESCHICHTE DER TURKISCHEN FLOTTE [18]. How Turkish naval power developed and continued to constitute a significant threat to the empire's opponents is explained in Hess' "The Evolution of the Ottoman Seaborne Empire in the Age of Oceanic Discoveries" [51] and in THE HISTORY OF THE MARITIME WARS OF THE TURKS [64], by Hajji Khalifeh.

To appreciate properly the influences involved in the Sublime Porte's choice of the course of action taken at the time, Sidney Fisher's THE FOREIGN RELATIONS OF TURKEY, 1481-1512 [32] should be read. The life of the Ottoman Sultan of this period is covered in V.J. Parry's "Bayazid II" [94] and in Tansel's SULTAN II.

65

BAYAZID'IN SIYASI HAYATI [125].

## OTTOMAN PROBLEMS AT HOME

Another useful study by Sidney Fisher is "Civil Strife in the Ottoman Empire, 1481-1503" [31], in which the author points out that, while Bayazid II was restoring and adding to the empire abroad, he was also creating severe economic hardships at home. The economic conditions, coupled with the rivalries that abounded in the Turkish court (especially the ones between Bayazid and his brother, Cem Sultan) and between the aristocracy and the prestigious state service class (devsirme), eventually caused a revolt to erupt that turned into a civil war. For a different approach to this same general subject of balance between foreign and domestic policy, see W.E.D. Allen's THE PROBLEMS OF TURKISH POWER IN THE SIXTEENTH CENTURY [4].

The conscription of non-Moslem children for conversion to Islam and service to the Sultan either in administrative posts, or in the Kapikulu ("Slave to the Porte") military corps is detailed in "Devshirme" [83], by Victor Menage, and in OSMANLI DEVLETI TESKILATINDAN KAPULULU OCAKLARI [135], by Ismail Hakki Uzuncarsili. Two other works on this subject are Uzuncarsili's "Devshirme and Shari'a" [134] and Johannes Mordtmann's "Dewshirme" [85]. Schwoebel [110] has probably the best overall account of this period; while Shaw, in volume one of his two-volume HISTORY OF THE OTTOMAN EMPIRE AND MODERN TURKEY [112], discusses the dynamics of the development of the Ottoman military institution.

Internal disorder broke out again in the Ottoman Empire in 1509. This time it was between father and sons, when three of Bayazid's sons began squabbling over the right to the throne. This struggle soon turned into a major civil war. In 1513, one son, Selim, was victorious and forced his father to abdicate. Selim I ruled for seven years, from 1513 to 1520, spending most of his reign at war, especially with Persia and other countries in the Near East.

## THE REIGN OF SULEIMAN THE MAGNIFICENT

Immediately after Selim's death, however, his son, Suleiman I the Magnificent (1520-1566), embarked on a new course that was aimed at reducing dissidence and the unconquered pockets of resistance along the empire's European frontier. His first target was Hungary where he opened a major campaign in May 1521, with the capture of Belgrad as a prime objective.

## THE TURKISH CAMPAIGN AGAINST HUNGARY

Suleiman was encouraged in this decision by two factors: the knowledge that the Holy Roman Emperor, Charles V, was at war with France, and the fact that Louis (often Ludwig or Lajos) II (1516-1526) was as inept as his father had been before him at being King of Hungary. The Sultan chose that moment, therefore, to open a gateway to central Europe and what lay beyond. Only Belgrad stood in the way of accomplishing that first goal.

After an initial success at Shabotz (8 July 1521), the Turkish army proceeded to lay siege to the fortress at Belgrad and bombarded the town from heavy artillery emplacements on an island in the Danube. Forced to give up the town, the Hungarian defenders set fire to it before retiring to the fortress proper. After a gallant defense, however, the citadel fell to the Turks on 29 August.

Shaw [112] has a good account of this battle, as does Kinross [65], and Inalcik in his OTTOMAN EMPIRE: THE CLASICAL AGE [56]. Lessner [73] adds some interesting, but not necessarily vital, additional information. Another fine study of this particular campaign is found in HISTOIRE DE LA CAMPAGNE DE SULTAN SULEYMAN I$^{er}$ CONTRE BELGRADE EN 1521" [126], and there is an excellent account in Turkish in the official TURK SILAHLI KUVVETLERI TARIHI [131]. In his article, "The Ottoman Empire, 1520-1566" [95], V.J. Parry covers this period in great detail. Inalcik does the same in his "Ottoman Methods of Conquest" [57].

## THE SITUATION IN THE ROMANIAN PROVINCES

In addition to exposing Europe to Turkish assault, the capture of Belgrade threatened the precarious existence of Wallachia which lay just beyond the right flank of the Turkish axis of advance. From January through November 1522, the Wallachian voivode, Radu de la Afumati (1522-1529), beat off a series of Turkish attacks, often in consort with the Transylvanians under John Zapolya, who were also threatened by the Ottoman advance. Eventually, however, the Turks were able to defeat Afumati and the Wallachian leader was forced to flee to Transylvania. By October 1523, Afumati was able to return and oust the Turkish puppet, Vladislav III, from his throne. This was only a side-show for the Turks as it would appear their only interest in Wallachia was to secure their right flank preparatory to continuing the attack into the heart of Christendom.

But before Suleiman could continue his advance, his attention was diverted by internal problems in the eastern reaches of his empire and by his strategic decision to conquer the island of Rhodes. This did not really signal a respite for the Balkans. When disorders broke out in Moldavia in a dispute between the viovode, Stefanita (1517-1527), and the nobility and after the reimposed puppet, Vladislav, was again ousted by Afumati in Wallachia (this time for good), the Turks reacted but not with much enthusiasm. These relatively minor events are reported in sufficient detail in Giurescu [36].

## SULEIMAN'S SECOND CAMPAIGN INTO HUNGARY

By 1526, Suleiman was again ready to move on Hungary. With an army estimated to have been between 70,000 and 80,000 strong, he began his march out of Constantinople on 23 April 1526. Between May and July, clear signs were evident to the Hungarian crown that there was great danger; but the disruption caused by the 1514 revolt still gripped Hungary, and mobilization was hindered by the fact that the feudal lords were hesitant to entrust their armed forces to a single leader. John Zapolya found himself surrounded by an ever-increasing number of petty nobles who feared that fighting the Turks would play into the hands of the Catholic and Habsburg elements who vied with them over their nationalistic aims.

THE BATTLE OF MOHACS AND ITS AFTERMATH

After a series of delays caused by exceptionally foul weather, and by the stubborn defense of the 1,000-man garrison at Peterwardein (Petervarad) 15-27 July 1526, the Turkish army, under the command of the Grand Vizier Ibrahim, finally arrived with its 300 cannon in the vicinity of the village of Mohacs, on the southern edge of a large, swampy plain. The Hungarian army, under King Louis II, had left Buda (the ancient fortress and town on the right bank of the Danube across from the town of Pest) with an army of only 4,000 Hungarians, plus another 4,000 Bohemian and Moravian mercenaries sent by Pope Clement VII (1523-1534). At the last minute, another detachment of 5,000 men arrived led by Stefan Batory (later voivode of Transylvania, 1529-1533) and some additional Hungarian cavalry, Slavonians and Croatians. The Hungarians had decided that the Mohacs plain was the ideal place to meet the Turks. With both nearby rivers, the Danube and the Drava, swollen by heavy rains and the soggy fields, the Hungarians concluded the advantage would be with the defenders.

Unfortunately for the Hungarians, their estimates were wrong; and, in a climactic battle that lasted less than two hours on 29 August 1526, the Hungarian army was defeated -- destroyed, some say, on a day that the survivors claimed God had forsaken Hungary. The twenty-year old King Louis II was killed, as were hundreds of other nobles. Included in the losses was the Cardinal of Esztergom, who had largely financed the Hungarian venture. The defeat set into motion forces that could not be understood at the time but which changed the face of Europe.

This important battle is amply covered in the literature. Lessner [73] is exceptional in his vivid presentation. Dupuy [27] tells the story, but without detail. Lengyel [71] makes a number of solid points, not the least of which is his account of the traitorous absence of John Zapolya and his forces on that fateful Sunday. Shaw [112] hardly mentions the battle, while Lord Kinross tells the story with his customary eloquence. Inalcik, in his THE OTTOMAN EMPIRE: THE CLASSICAL AGE [56], reduces the battle to two or three lines of text.

The HISTOIRE DE LA CAMPAGNE DE MOHACZ PAR KEMAL PASHA [22], by Michel Pavet de Courteille, is probably the most thorough account. TURK SILAHLI KUVVETLERI TARIHI [131] presents the official Turkish report. An interesting vignette is provided by Paula Fichtner in "An Absence Explained: Archduke Ferdinand of Austria and the Battle of Mohacs" [30].

Another important study of the battle is found in MOHACS EMLEKEZETE. A MOHACSI CSATARA VONATKOZO LEGFONTOSABB MAGYAR, NYUGATI ES TOROK FORRASOK [53], that was published in 1979 by the Hungarian Academy of Sciences. This work contains all the significant data on the battle from the most influential sources and is rich in information gleaned from archeological investigations of the battlesite. A second work in Hungarian is A MOHACSI CSATA [123], by Ferenc Szakaly, that was published in 1977.

Warfare in general is the theme of Professor J.R. Hale's "Armies, Navies, and the Art of War" that may be found in volume II

[46], and volume III [47] of the NCMH. While the first of these two articles covers the specific period under discussion, the two together outline the subject over the entire century and discuss changes in armaments, the use of mercenaries and standing armies, prestige and glory as incentives in war, the treatment of prisoners and the care of the wounded, and discipline and morale in the Turkish army.

In the aftermath of the Mohacs battle, Suleiman occupied Buda (11 September) and then withdrew the bulk of his army to Constantinople (Istanbul) where he arrived on 13 November. The taking of Buda is the subject of ZUR KAPITULATION VON BUDA IN JAHRE 1526 [86], by Johannes Mordtmann. Lessner [73] tells the story in great detail, especially about the Turkish disaster on the bridge between Buda and Pest. Istvan Sugar's A BUDAI VAR ES OSTOMAI [120] is also worthwhile, but is found only in Hungarian.

## CIVIL WAR IN HUNGARY

Before departing Hungary, Suleiman accepted John Zapolya as his choice to rule the nation (September 1526), provided the necessary tribute was paid. Zapolya was, thereafter, duly elected king by his followers at Alba Regia (today Skekesfehervar, Hungary) on 10 November 1526 (reconfirmed on 16 September 1527). Thirty-seven days later, on 17 December 1526, another election was held at Pozsony, where the Austrians and Transylvanian Saxons put up their candidate, the Archduke Ferdinand of Habsburg, who was also duly elected king. As there was but one throne, a bitter civil war ensued that lasted 12 years. Lengyel [71] tells this story on the basis of "three Hungaries" –– the part in Austrian hands, the part in Hungarian hands, and the third part being Transylvania. Indeed, Transylvania figured prominently during those critical times. In 1527, an anti-feudal revolt erupted in that province that took nine months to put down and which, in turn, had weakened neighboring Moldavia's chances of defending itself against the Turks and Poles.

## SULEIMAN'S THIRD HUNGARIAN CAMPAIGN

Suleiman had kept a close eye on all of these developments; and, as soon he was able to suppress the Kalender revolt that raged in Anatolia, he once again mounted a campaign into Hungary to restore the order that he thought had prevailed before the Habsburgs had upset it. As a matter of fact, the Habsburgs had done little to influence the events, as Charles V was immersed in his second war with France (1527-1529), and the twenty-five-year old Ferdinand was trying to straighten out the problems he was having in Austria and Bohemia. Still, when Ferdinand met Zapolya at Tokay (Tokaj), on the Tisza river in northwest Hungary (26 September 1527), he was able to defeat him. Zapolya had requested aid from Poland, but it had failed to materialize.

## HABSBURG AUSTRIA MOVES INTO THE BALKANS

By December 1527, Ferdinand's forces had cleared most of Hungary and had retaken Buda. Only the Turkish garrisons in the south prevented him from liberating the entire country. It was at that point that Suleiman decided to move, especially after Zapolya had entreated him to do so (28 February 1528). During the year it took the Sultan to prepare, Zapolya was able to achieve a treaty with France against the Habsburgs and one with the Moldavians (1529), who were able to support him in the defeat of the Transylvanian Habsburg forces at Feldioara on 22 June 1529.

Already in May, Suleiman had begun moving his army of over 80,000 troops (some say as many as 270,000) into the Balkans enroute to Hungary. This occurred after Ferdinand had offered the Porte the dove of friendship and had been rebuffed. By 6 August, the Turks had been reinforced by 6,000 Magyar troops led by Zapolya; and, by 3 September, the Ottoman force was arrayed before Buda. After a short siege, the city capitulated (8 September); and, after gratuitously murdering most of the garrison, Suleiman began an advance on Vienna.

## THE OTTOMAN CAMPAIGN AGAINST AUSTRIA

Ferdinand had about 17,000 troops in the capital garrison. Awaiting the arrival of the Ottoman army, these troops were put to work strengthening the city's fortifications. Their labors were not wasted as the Turks could not substantially penetrate them once the battle began. From 27 September until 15 October 1529, the investment continued, but the early arrival of cold weather and other problems caused Suleiman to break off the siege at a critical moment when the decision could have gone either way. Leaving a strong force with Zapolya, the Turkish main army withdrew, pursued and harassed by the Austrians and Habsburg Hungarians. The battle was over, and a crucial shift in the balance of power in the Balkans was about to begin.

The First Siege of Vienna has excellent coverage. The best sources are J.H. Kramers' SULEIMAN, DER GESETZBERGERS TAGEBUCH AUF SEINEN FELDZUGE NACH WEIN [68] and THE SIEGES OF VIENNA BY THE TURKS, FROM THE GERMAN OF KARL AUGUST SCHIMMER AND OTHER SOURCES [28], which had been translated and edited by the Earl of Ellesmere. Lessner [73] has a good account of the siege, as does Dupuy [27], and Shaw [112]. Martin Luther's VOM KRIEGE WIDER DIE TURCKEN [78] is interesting, if only because of its authorship. BIBLIOGRAPHIE UND IKONOGRAPHIE DER TURKENBELAGERUNGEN WIENS, 1529 U. 1683 [119], by Walter Sturminger, serves as an excellent bibliographical source.

By the following year, 1530, Austro-Hungarian forces had advanced across Hungary capturing Gran and demonstrating in the vicinity of Buda. Fighting was widespread throughout the country, and in neighboring Wallachia, where warring factions, one of which supported Zapolya, fought each other. This squabbling meant the entire region was left open to foreign attack. By 1531, Buda was under Austrian siege; and Moldavia was under attack by the Poles, who sought to restore lands previously taken from them. Again, Suleiman seized upon the disorder as a sign that it was time to reassert his hegemony. On 25 June 1532, the Sultan led another large army through Belgrad into the heart of Hungary.

This time, however, Emperor Charles moved to ensure the security of Vienna and dispatched large numbers of imperial troops to Austria. Suleiman, not wishing a conclusive battle, sortied into southwestern Austria where he played havoc before withdrawing behind his own frontiers. An armistice followed that was accepted in part by the Turks because of increased problems in Persia, to which the

Sultan desired to give his full attention. In the agreement, Hungary is divided between Ferdinand and John Zapolya. The Holy Roman Emperor was not so easily gratified; however, and the war between the two empires continued.

Lessner [73] tells this story well, especially about the heroic defense of the small garrison at Guns (Koszeg), an insignificantly small Hungarian border village some 60 miles from Vienna. Shaw [112] adds very little information, while Kinross [65] describes the Turkish side in excellent detail. Inalcik [56] concentrates more on the Ottoman Empire's emergence as a world power as an outgrowth of its growing strength and position on the European continent. He does add the interesting assertion that Suleiman chose Guns carefully as the best locale for a main force battle against the Holy Roman forces.

## BARBAROSSA AND THE OTTOMAN NAVAL WAR AGAINST THE HOLY ROMAN EMPIRE

Inalcik also discusses the naval aspects of the continuing Ottoman struggle against Charles V. Suleiman was obliged to put all his naval forces under the command of his best admiral, Hayreddin Barbarossa, in order to meet the threat posed by the combined Holy Roman fleets. At this same juncture, France was attempting to conclude an alliance with the Sublime Porte that was finally initialled in 1536. With French insistence, Suleiman ordered Barbarossa to attack Italy as a means of gaining a successful conclusion to the war. Thus, in 1537, the Turks declared war on Venice and moved an army into Albania to attack and ravage the Venetian ports along its coast. Thereafter, the plan was to move on Corfu. The following year, the French made their peace with Charles abandoning the Turks in the process. Suleiman continued his campaign, however, capturing most of the Venetian holdings in the Aegean and carrying out raids as far as Crete. Peace was finally achieved in 1539.

Besbelli describes the naval actions of the Turks in his "Ottoman Naval Superiority in the Mediterranean" [16]. The Turkish naval commander is discussed in Enver Karal's "Barbaros Hayreddin Pasa" [63] and in Ali Riza Seyfi's BARBAROS HAYREDDIN [111]. DORIA ET BARBAROUSSE [39], by Jurien de la Graviere, compares Barbarossa against Admiral Andrea Doria, the Emperor's naval commander in the Mediterranean.

THE HOLY ROMAN EMPIRE [49], by Friedrich Heer, discusses the development of the empire, dwelling on the establishment of the Habsburg dynasty. Adam Wandruszka's THE HOUSE OF HABSBURG: SIX HUNDRED YEARS OF A EUROPEAN DYNASTY [141] is good but gives a rather one-sided account of the growth of the family that at one time or another ruled most of Europe. There is a rather poor bibliography included that is of value only to the most casual reader. Victor Mamatey's THE RISE OF THE HABSBURG EMPIRE, 1526-1815 [82] is good, but Kann's HISTORY OF THE HABSBURG EMPIRE, 1526-1918 [61] is even better. Kann concentrates on the histories of the various peoples that lived under Habsburg domination. THE PEOPLES OF THE EASTERN HABSBURG LANDS, 1526-1918 [62], by Kann and Zdanek David, is also most useful.

# THE STRUCTURE OF THE OTTOMAN STATE

There is a wealth of reference material covering the Ottoman side of this period. Halil Inalcik's "The Heyday and Decline of the Ottoman Empire" [54] is especially well written. Ismail Uzuncarsili's OSMANLI DEVLETI TESKILATINA MEDHAL [136] describes the administrative structure of the state and, more particularly, the military structure of the Turkish armed forces. In another study, OSMANLI IMPARATORLUGU TESKILATI, 1453-1575 SENESINE KADAR [137], Uzuncarsili discusses the organizational structure of the empire during this crucial period. In OSMANLI TARIHI [138], he outlines the historical development of the empire between 1299 and 1789. Albert Lybyer's classic THE GOVERNMENT OF THE OTTOMAN EMPIRE IN THE TIME OF SULEIMAN THE MAGNIFICENT [79] is an excellent source of information on the military institutions of the Turks. KUNH UL-AHBAR [1], by Ali Mustafa ben Ahmed, outlines the history of the Ottomans from the 13th century to 1597. Agah Sirri Levend's GAZAVATNAMELER VE MIHAILOGLU ALI BEY'IN GAZATVATNAMESI [74] discusses the types of forays and raids carried out by the Turks in the name of Islam and describes the system whereby the beys of the frontier regions had greater independence for military action than did the sanjaks who were under direct Ottoman control. The frontier regions were administered by beys (governors) from prominent families, such as the Mihal Ogullari clan, that Levend uses to describe in detail the operations of a raid into territory considered to be a part of the jihad . Another view of the same topic is found in F.A. Belin's DU REGIME DES FIEFS MILITAIRES DANS L'ISLAMISME ET PRINCIPALEMENT EN TURQUIE [15]. Leopold von Ranke compares the Spanish and Turkish situations in THE OTTOMAN AND SPANISH EMPIRES IN THE SIXTEENTH AND SEVENTEENTH CENTURIES [101]. The official Turkish historical interpretation of this period is found in TURK SILAHLI KUVVETLERI TARIHI [131].

The situation in the Romanian provinces is told in some detail in the CHRONOLOGICAL HISTORY OF ROMANIA [36], but the coverage of the overall events is somewhat spotty. Beldiceanu's SUR LES VALAQUES DES BALKANS SLAVES A L'EPOQUE OTTOMANE, 1450-1550 [14] is a better account of the period from the Romanian view. Bulgarian restiveness during this period is amply portrayed in Macdermott [81], but what is more interesting is his discussion of the levees of children (devsirme) that were imposed as taxes (ispendzh) , and how many of them found their way into the janissary corps. This is confirmed in C.L. Huart's "Janissaries" [52], in Weissmann's LES JANISSAIRES, ETUDE DE L'ORGANIZATION MILITAIRE DES OTTOMANS [142] and in Ahmed Djevad Bey's LE CORPS DE JANISSAIRES DEPUIS SA CREATION JUSQU'D SA SUPPRESSION [25].

## MORE TROUBLE IN THE ROMANIAN PROVINCES

Stoicescu [117] states that the decay of the "greater army" in the Romanian provinces in the mid-16th century came about because the concept was overtaken by technological advances and because of Ottoman domination, first in Wallachia by 1529 and in Moldavia after 1538. Indeed, Suleiman determined to punish Moldavia for having sided with the Habsburgs in past encounters and sent a large army into that country in August 1538. The Sultan felt secure in this action as the Peace of Oradea (24 February 1538), that had settled

72

the fighting between Ferdinand and Zapolya, had put the latter on the throne of Transylvania. Suleiman also knew that Moldavia was in revolt at the moment and could not, therefore, mount any real resistance. The campaign was short and bloody and, by the end of September 1538, Moldavia was in the Ottoman thrall.

The troubles in Moldavia were barely put to rest when another revolt broke out in Wallachia, this one between the voivode, Radu Paisie (1535-1545), and the great boyars. With Ottoman help, Radu was able to quell the uprising, but not before the Porte placed much more stringent restrictions upon both provinces.

## ANOTHER CIVIL WAR IN HUNGARY

The Romanian disturbances were insignificant in comparison to what occurred upon the death of King John I Zapolya of Hungary on 22 July 1540. Ignoring the secret treaty signed at Nagyvarad in 1538, that recognized Ferdinand as successor to the throne, Zapolya's followers elected John's son, John Sigismund, who was but a few months old at the time, to be the new king of Hungary. John II Sigismund (1540-1571) was also elected voivode of Transylvania (1540-1551, 1556-1571) in violation of the Oradea treaty, the provisions of which also put Ferdinand on that throne. The result was another civil war in Hungary that culminated in an Ottoman offensive in which Buda was once again taken by the Turks. In 1547, Suleiman granted Ferdinand a truce, giving him the northern and western regions of Hungary in return for tribute. Another provision of the truce established Transylvania as an independent Ottoman pashalik and made John II its prince. (During John's minority, his mother served as regent.)

## ACTION ALONG THE CHRISTIAN FRONTIER

From 1547 to 1568, clashes between the Turks and Habsburgs occurred intermittently. This frontier skirmishing flared into full-scale war when Ferdinand invaded Transylvania in 1551, forcing Isabella, the regent, to renounce her son's crown in favor of the Habsburgs. This struggle continued until 1556 when John was restored to power. Turkish troops employed in this war occupied the Romanian region known as the Banat (and part of Crisana, as well). These regions were converted into Turkish pashaliks in 1552 and remained as such until 1718.

## PEACE, RENEWED FIGHTING, AND THE DEATH OF SULEIMAN

In 1562, Ferdinand and Suleiman arranged a peace at Prague that momentarily put an end to the fighting in the Balkans in return for Ferdinand's agreement to continue paying tribute to the Porte. The war with the Holy Roman Empire continued, however, and flared into renewed fighting when the new emperor, Maximilian II (1564-1576), created a situation that allowed Suleiman to convince himself that he had been wronged. This was not too difficult as his recent misadventure on Malta, his agony from gout, and his advanced age (72) apparently led the Sultan to consider that he would die without achieving victory. It is probably for this latter reason, more than any other, that Suleiman set out, once again, in April 1566, with his army to invade Hungary.

About two weeks before Suleiman's arrival, Arslan Pasha of Buda opened the campaign (5 June 1566) with an attack on the Habsburg fortress at Varpolota (west of Stuhlweissburg). When this attack was repulsed, the Austrians failed to take the offensive thereby allowing Suleiman to bring the main body of his troops into the arena of conflict. The Sultan crossed the Danube at Belgrad on 20 June and moved on to Zemun. He then ordered the capture of the fortress at Gyula and a continuation of the attack at the fortress town of Szigeth (Szigetvar). The Turks moved slowly and did not invest the town until 5 August. In the final assault on the town (7-8 September) which was defended by about 2,000 Hungarians and a small, untrained militia, a powder magazine blew up disrupting the Turkish attack. The fort was taken, however, and its defenders put to the sword. Thereafter, the Turks immediately broke off operations, ostensibly upon the orders of Suleiman (but actually upon the orders of Ibraham, the Grand Vizier). Suleiman had died the day before the final assault, but his death had been kept secret from all. Thus, the Ottoman army returned to Constantinople not knowing it was without a sovereign leader.

There is a wealth of material on the life and times of Suleiman the Magnificent. Two of the better works are Franz Babinger's SULEJMAN [10], and Roger Merriman's SULEIMAN THE MAGNIFICENT [84]. The life of his Grand Vizier is recounted by H.D. Jenkins in his IBRAHAM PASHA: GRAND VIZIR OF SULEIMAN THE MAGNIFICENT [59]. The volume of TURK SILAHLI KUVVETLERI TARIHI [131] that covers the period 1451-1566 ends with a summation of Suleiman's last campaign. TEVARIH-I AL-I OSMAN [76], by Lufti Pasha, covers the Turkish history from the 13th century to 1553 and deals with all of Suleiman's Balkan campaigns, except the last one. The death of Suleiman marked the beginning of the decline of the Ottoman Empire.

One book that should not be overlooked when studying this period is Leften Stavrianos' THE BALKANS SINCE 1453 [115]. While the great strength of this work rests on its treatment of the 17th and 18th centuries, the coverage given the 16th century is in itself excellent. ISLAMIC SOCIETY AND THE WEST: A STUDY OF THE IMPACT OF WESTERN CIVILIZATION ON MOSLEM CULTURE [34], by Sir Harold Gibb and H. Bowen, should also be studied at this point with a view toward understanding the double-edged effect of the Turkish presence in the Balkans and how all of this played heavily upon later developments. Sidney M. Fisher's "Ottoman Feudalism and Its Influence Upon the Balkans" [33] is also worthwhile. Two other good references are Carl Gollner's TURCICA, DIE EUROPAISCHEN TURKENDRUCKE DES XVI JAHRHUNDERTS [38] and Kowalski's "Les Turcs balkaniques" [67].

One of the best accounts of the territorial changes that affected Transylvania as a result of the Habsburg-Ottoman conflicts, and because of internal disorders, is found in Imre Lukinich's ERDELY TERULETI VALTOZASAI A TOROK HODITAS KORABAN 1541-1711 [77]. Stanko Guldescu's THE CROATIAN-SLAVONIC KINGDOM [43] supplements his HISTORY OF MEDIEVAL CROATIA [44] and deals with the politico-military developments that led to a close alignment that would exist between that kingdom and Hungary by the 18th century. This work may be supplemented by Gunther Rothenberg's excellent study THE AUSTRIAN MILITARY BORDER IN CROATIA, 1522-1747 [108].

UPRISINGS, LARGE AND SMALL

The events reported thus far for this period encompass only
the major military actions that affected the Balkans in general.
There were, of course, numerous other, more localized, events of a
military nature that affected specific areas on the peninsula, not
the least of which were the Romanian Danubian Principalities. From
1558 to the end of the century, no less than a dozen major uprisings
took place within the three provinces. In most cases these were
purely internal affairs in which, for instance, the feudal boyars,
in an effort to retain their prerogatives, took up the sword against
their liege lords. Other rebellions centered upon the peasantry who
rose up against the grievous conditions in which they were forced to
live and against the burdensome taxes placed upon them by the often
extravagant nobility.

A last type of uprising often seen throughout this period
was that in which either the Porte, the Habsburgs, or the Poles,
wishing for more authority within a particular region, fostered
revolt so as to put their man on the throne. One such instance is
seen in the battles fought at Iezerul Cahului (today Kagul, USSR)
and Roscani (today Ryskany, USSR), on 10-11 June 1574, where the
Moldavian army was defeated by an Ottoman-Wallachian-Tatar force. In
retribution for the refusal to pay tribute, the Turks allowed the
Tatars to lay waste to the countryside while they installed a
puppet, Petru Schiopul (1574-1579, 1582-1591) on the Moldavian
throne.

THE RULE OF SELIM THE SOT

Indeed, the empire continued to exist for several centuries
more; but the passing of Suleiman opened the way for a procession of
sultans who were, at best, incapable of ruling. Suleiman's imperial
throne was taken by Selim II (1566-1574), who was known as "the Sot
(Sari)." In 1568, he authorized the Truce of Adrianople that
temporarily ended the warring with the Habsburgs that had gone on
for the past 21 years. Selim's reign was marked by considerable
activity that only peripherally involved the Balkans. A major war
broke out with the Venetians in 1570 that was followed in a year's
time by a conflict with the Russians over Astrakhan in which the
Turks were defeated.

In the war with Venice, the Turks laid siege to the town of
Farmagusta on the island of Cyprus. On hearing of this, Pope Pius V
(1566-1572) established the Holy League to conduct a crusade against
the Turks to relieve the city. In 1571, an Allied Christian fleet
was formed and set sail to find and defeat the Turks. This they
accomplished on 7 October 1571, at Lepanto in the Gulf of Corinth,
in a brilliant naval battle that signalled the end of galley warfare.
By 1573, the alliance was weakening, however; and more because of
that than any rejuvenation of Turkish strength, the Venetians made
peace. The treaty was not signed until after Selim's death in 1574.

SULTAN MURAD III AND THE RISE OF MICHAEL THE BRAVE

The Turkish throne was then taken by Murad III (1574-1593),
who regained some of the territory lost in the previous war. He also

fought another war against Persia that lasted almost 13 years (1577-1590). In 1590 when Emperor Rudolph refused to pay the annual tribute, Murad resumed the land war against the Habsburgs. This was an unspectacular affair that featured a considerable number of border clashes but no main force battles, until 1593.

By that year, Ottoman exploitation of its captive lands was at its highest point. Severe economic conditions and internal disorder were the chief causes of this situation, one result of which was the settlement of some Turks upon the lands of Wallachia and Moldavia. Turks had been settled much earlier south of the Danube but never before in the Principalities. The numbers were not large, but it did create an entirely new situation.

At that juncture, a new voivode of Wallachia was put on the throne, Michael the Brave (Mihai Viteazul) (1593-1601). Modern Romanian historians claim Michael "reunited" all of Romania in an anti-Ottoman coalition. Lessner [73], among others, points out that those who seek to prove the notion that there has always been a Romanian commonality find little more than one reference that "Michael the Brave freed and reunited all Romanian territory," and that he called himself "Prince of Hungro-Wallachia, Transylvania, and Moldavia." Shaw [112] mentions Micheal's role in aiding Seyr Bedreddin in his radical preachings in Rumelia against the Ottoman Empire.

## THE LONG WAR BETWEEN AUSTRIA AND THE TURKS

The year of Michael's ascendancy to the throne of Wallachia was also the beginning of what has been called the "Long War." On 20 June 1593, an Austrian army defeated the Turks in the Battle of Sissek in Bosnia. The weak Murad vacillated; but his Grand Vizier, Sinan Pasha, did not and led a large Ottoman army into Hungary and Austria. By October, the Turks had captured Vesprism (Beszprem), near Lake Balaton in west-central Hungary, and were on their way to Vienna. At that juncture, the Janissaries refused to continue the campaign because of the onset of cold weather.

The following February, Prince Sigismund Batory of Transylvania (1581-1601) concluded a treaty with the Habsburgs and joined a resusitated Holy League against the Turks. By summer both Michael of Wallachia and Aron the Tyrant (1592-1595), the prince of Moldavia, had also joined the anti-Ottoman coalition. In order to push back this gathering resistance, Sinan Pasha reopened his campaign early in 1594. But, before he could take the offensive against Vienna, a new crisis arose for the Turks in the Danubian Principalities.

In the fall of 1594 a general uprising took place in which the forces of each of the provinces took the field against the Turks. The revolt carried into 1595 where, in January, the Wallachians defeated a Tatar army that had entered its lands (Battle of Putineiu, 14 January 1595). In May, an agreement was reached between Sigismund and Michael (Treaty of Alba Iulia) in which the Wallachian leader acknowledged suzereignty to the Transylvanian prince.

THE BATTLE OF CALUGARENI

The Turks could not allow this coalition to continue and dispatched an army to punish the Wallachians. At that time, an Austrian army invaded Hungary rolling back the Ottoman frontier. The chief battle of this campaign was fought at Gran on 4 August 1595. Ten days later, at Calugareni, in Wallachia, Michael met and defeated Sinan Pasha (23 August 1595). Batory failed to reach the field in time, however, and Michael, victorious in the battle but too weak to consolidate his position, was forced to withdraw, leaving the Turks free to occupy and fortify a number of towns including Bucharest. In subsequent battles in October, however, Sinan Pasha was defeated at Bucharest, Tirgoviste, and Giurgiu. Following these successes, Michael repudiated the Alba Iulia agreement and began a series of independent, and generally successful, forays against the Turks, including one that threatened Sofia in 1596.

That same year, the Turks regained control of Hungary after a new sultan, Mehmet III (1595-1603), ordered his Grand Vizier, Ibraham, to mount another campaign. The initial successes of the Turks were challenged at Kerestes about 12 miles southwest of Erlau, Hungary by a force of about 40,000 Austrians under the Archduke Maximilian, with a large Transylvanian force under Sigismund Batory. The Turks, with about 80,000 men, were able to penetrate the Austrian rear with cavalry and routed the allies. About 50,000 soldiers on both sides lost their lives. In 1596, the Austrians renewed their invasion of Hungary and, after some initial successes, were again beaten back. In March 1599, Sigismund Batory was forced to abdicate his throne in Transylvania; and, by October, Michael had marched into Alba Iulia and had forced a Transylvanian acknowledgment of his hegemony.

These episodes are described in the CHRONOLOGICAL HISTORY OF ROMANIA [36], which has excellent detail at this point. It is also a fact, however, that it suffers from very poor translation into English. Stoicescu, in his "Organizational Structure of the Armies. . ." article [118], outlines the various Romanian military formations utilized during these times. Gheorge Romanescu, in his "Grosse Mittelalterliche Schlachten des rumanischen Volkes. . ." [104], discusses the entire century in relation to the military requirements each of the principalities had to meet. "The Battle of Calugareni (1595)" [88], by Manole Neagoe, deals with not only the battle itself but also the composition of the army of Michael the Brave and the general situation between the Habsburgs and the Turks that led to the Romanian decision to fight at that time and at that place. Another interesting study is presented by Eugen Stanescu in "Tarile Romane la sfersitul veacului al XVI-lea si prima lor unificare politica. Despre ecesitate si posibilitate in istorie" [114]. There are a number of good works on Michael the Brave. MIHAI VODA VITEAZUL [6], by D. Almas; MIHAI VITEAZUL [93], by P.P. Panitescu; and ISTORIA LUI MIHAI VITEAZUL [58], by Nicholae Iorga, are all good, but are all written in Romanian. Kinross [65] has numerous references to Michael in his narrative. Volume XI of the DOCUMENTA ROMANIAE HISTORICA [105] contains materials from Michael's reign that cover the period 1593-1600.

The reigns of the various Ottoman sultans are covered in "Selim II" [129], by Serafeddin Turan; "III Murad" [69], by Bekir

Kutukoglu; and "III Mehmet" [37], by M. Tayyip Gokbilgin. Turan also produced an article, "Sinan Pasha" [130], that is quite interesting. Some Ottoman internal problems are discussed in the "Celali Rebellions in the Ottoman Empire, 1596-1610" [35], by H.H. Girvidan, and in Mustafa Akdag's CELALI ISYANLARI, 1550-1603 [2]. These studies describe religious revolts in eastern Anatolia that created great problems for the Porte. R.C. Anderson's NAVAL WARS OF THE LEVANT, 1558-1853 [7], is exceptionally good in describing the Ottoman's other campaign against Europe. Of special note in this regard is Jurien de la Graviere's LA GUERRE DE CHYPRE ET LA BATAILLE DE LEPANTO [40], in which the Cyprus campaign and the great naval battle at Lepanto are exhaustively analyzed. A general discussion of the Turks, from the reign of Selim the Sot to the end of the century, may be found in V.J. Parry's "The Ottoman Empire, 1566-1617" [96]. In "Yeniciri Ocak Nizaminin Bozulmasi" [3], Mustafa Akdag describes the processes by which the Janissary Corps was brought under control and finally disbanded. Ahmed Refik's OCAK AGALARI [102] profiles some of the commanders of the corps.

Three works on Bulgaria are of some interest at this point. Alois Hajek's BULGARIEN UNTER DER TURKENHERRSCHAFT [45] is in German, while Michel Leo's LA BULGARIE ET SON PEUPLE SOUS LA DOMINATION OTTOMANE [72] is in French although it was produced in Bulgaria. This study deals with accounts of Western visitors from the 16th through the 19th centuries. The best of the three is Ahmed Refik's TURK IDARESINDE BULGARESTAN (973-1255) [103], which is in Turkish. Refik's work refers to the period 1565-1840 as reckoned by western calendars. Macdermott, in his HISTORY OF BULGARIA [81], clearly represents the fact that, regardless of the level of domination of the Turks, there were still those in Bulgaria who were prepared to fight for independence if the opportunity arose. This is demonstrated by Macdermott in his description of the great Turnovo uprising of 1598 that accompanied one of Micheal's raids below the Danube. DE L'EXPLOITATION FEODAL DANS LES TERRES DE POPULATION BULGARE SOUS LA DOMINATION TURQUE AU XVe ET XVIe SIECLES [87], by Vera Mutafeieva, should also be read as it helps understand the reasons for the revolts in Bulgaria during this and the preceding century. In a similar fashion, Gunther Rothenberg's study of other uprisings in the Turkish sphere in Europe, "Christian Insurrections in Turkish Dalmatia, 1580-96" [109], is interesting, not so much for its locale, as for its definitions of the causes.

Carl Kortepeter uses a number of good Turkish sources in his OTTOMAN IMPERIALISM DURING THE REFORMATION: EUROPE AND THE CAUCASUS [66] in his description of the Long War that ended the century. Dupuy [27] is sketchy, but good, in his description of military operations that occurred during the last quarter of the century in and around the Balkans. But to properly understand what transpired, Dupuy must be augmented with more detailed accounts of the period. Lessner [73], Kinross [65], Shaw [112], Stavrianos [115], and Inalcik [56] are all good for this purpose. Inalcik's book on the classical age in Ottoman history ends with the close of this century.

There is some good supplemental reading also to be found in Zook and Higham's A SHORT HISTORY OF WARFARE [145]. The principal value of this book at this point is its excellent synthesis of the military, especially the technological and tactical developments of the 16th century. It is even better on the 17th century. "Armies, Navies, and the Art of War" [46], by J.R. Hale, found in the second volume of the NEW CAMBRIDGE MODERN HISTORY [143], is a good general description of the military arts and sciences during the second half of the 16th century.

Among the numerous works on Austria and the Holy Roman Empire during this period, Heer [49] is good in his description of the Habsburg role in the unfolding drama of the Balkans. "The Austrian Habsburgs and the Empire" [100], by G.D. Ramsay, is also good. In the diary of Erich Lassota von Steblau, HABSBURGS AND ZAPOROZHIAN COSSACKS [116], the author, a Moldavian nobleman in the service of Rudolf II, tells of his recruiting Ukrainian Cossacks to serve in the Austro-Turkish War of 1593.

Two Romanian works that deal with military operations during this period are I. Pataki's "Ceva despre relatiile Tarii Romanesti cu Ungaria la sfirsitul veacului al XIV-lea" [97] and E. Stanescu's "Colaborarea militara dentre romani si cazaci in ultime sfert a veacului al XVI-lea" [113]. Another good work in Romanian is ISTORIA ARTEI MILITARA A ROMANILOR [107] that, among other things, describes the battle at Calugareni. Nicholae Stoicescu [117], in addition to discussing the decay of the greater army, also examines the development of the army in Transylvania. OCHERKI PO ISTORII MEZHDUNARODNYKH OTNOSHENII VOSTOCHNOI EVROPY XIV-XVI VV. [41], by I.B. Greckov, is a series of essays on the relations between the various states in eastern Europe during the 14th to the 16th centuries. This work may be supplemented by by MEZHDUNARODNYE OTNOSHENIIA V TSENTRAL'NOI I VOSTOCHNOI EVROPE I IKH ISTORIOGRAFIIA [133], which is a collection of essays on the international relations among the countries of eastern and southern Europe beginning with the end of the 15th century.

Gustav Bayerle's OTTOMAN DIPLOMACY IN HUNGARY: LETTERS FROM THE PASHAS OF BUDA, 1590-1593 [12] represents a collection of correspondence, 107 letters in all, written by the senior Ottoman civil and military administrators to their opposite numbers in Vienna, to the commanders of various Austrian fortresses along the frontier, and to the princes of Transylvania. A second volume of this type contains some 450 letters written between 1553 and 1589. These are published in A BUDAI BASAK MAGYAR NYELVU LEVELEZESE [124], which was edited by Sandor Takats and a group of associates. Bayerle has also produced another volume titled OTTOMAN TRIBUTES IN HUNGARY. ACCORDING TO THE 16TH CENTURY TAPU REGISTERS OF NOVIGRAD [13]. This work presents a clear picture of Hungary tributary financing from 1526 to the end of the century.

# BIBLIOGRAPHIC LISTING


1. Ahmed, A.M. KUNH UL-AHBAR. Istanbul: 1860.

2. Akdag, M. CELALI ISYANLARI, 1550-1603. Ankara: 1963.

3. _____. "Yeniciri Ocak Nizaminin Bozulmasi." DIL VE
   TARIH-COGRAFYA FAKULTESI, V (1947), 219-313.

4. Allen, W.E.D. THE PROBLEMS OF TURKISH POWER IN THE SIXTEENTH
   CENTURY. London: 1963.

5. Allmayer-Beck, J.C., & Lessing, E. DIE KAISERLICHEN
   KRIEGSVOLKER. VON MAXIMILIAN I. BIS PRINZ EUGEN,
   1497-1718. Munich: 1978.

6. Almas, D. MIHAI VODA VITEAZUL. Bucharest: 1966.

7. Anderson, R.C. NAVAL WARS OF THE LEVANT, 1558-1853. Princeton:
   1952.

8. Arnakis, G.G. THE NEAR EAST IN MODERN TIMES. Vol. 1: THE
   OTTOMAN EMPIRE AND THE BALKANS TO 1900. Austin & New York:
   1969.

9. Babinger, F.C.H. "Kaiser Maximiliens i. 'Geheime Prakteken' mit
   den Osmanen (1510/11)." SF XV (1956).

10. _____. SULEJMAN. Stuttgart: 1922.

11. Bastav, S. ORDO PORTAE. DISCRIPTION GRECQUE DE LA PORTE ET
    L'ARMEE DU SULTAN MEHMED II. Budapest: 1947.

12. Bayerle, G. OTTOMAN DIPLOMACY IN HUNGARY: LETTERS FROM THE
    PASHAS OF BUDA, 1590-1593. UAS 101. Bloomington: 1972.

13. _____. OTTOMAN TRIBUTES IN HUNGARY. ACCORDING TO THE 16TH
    CENTURY TAPU REGISTERS OF NOVIGRAD. The Hague: 1973.

14. Beldiceanu, N. SUR LES VALAQUES DES BALKANS SLAVES A L'EPOQUE
    OTTOMANE, 1450-1550. Paris: 1967.

15. Belin, F.A. DU REGIME DES FIEFS MILITAIRES DANS L'ISLAMISME ET
    PRINCIPALEMENT EN TURQUIE. Paris: 1870.

16. Besbelli, S. "Ottoman Naval Superiority in the Mediterranean:
    Barbaros Hayreddin and the Prevda Naval Victory." RIHM 46
    (1980), 93-107.

17. Bradford, E. THE SULTAN'S ADMIRAL. THE LIFE OF BARBAROSSA.
    London & New York: 1969 [1968].

18. Burski, H.A. von. KEMA RE'IS: EIN BEITRAGE ZUR GESCHICHTE DER TURKISCHEN FLOTTE. Bonn: 1928.

19. Cesar, J., ed. OSMANSKA MOC VE STREDNI A JIHOVYCHODNI EVROPE V 16.-17. STOLETI. ACTA of the 9th Joint Conference of the Czechoslovak-Yugoslav Historical Committee. Prague: 1978.

20. Coles, P. THE OTTOMAN IMPACT ON EUROPE. LECS. London: 1968.

21. Coquelle, P. HISTOIRE DU MONTENEGRO ET DE LA BOSNIA. Paris: 1895.

22. Courteille, M.L. Pavet de. HISTOIRE DE LA CAMPAGNE DE MOHACZ PAR KEMAL PASHA. Paris: 1859.

23. Cuspa, I. "The Contribution of Stephen the Great to the Development of Romanian Military Art." PHRA. BHR Monograph XV. Bucharest: 1975.

24. Darby, H.C, "The Face of Europe on the Eve of the Great Discoveries." NCMH I. Cambridge: 1971.

25. Djevad Bey. ETAT MILITAIRE DEPUIS LA FOUNDATION DE L'EMPIRE JUSQU'D NOS JOURS. Vol. 1: LE CORPS DE JANISAIRES DEPUIS SA CREATION JUSQU'D SA SUPPRESSION. Constantinople & Paris: 1882.

26. Dunn, R.S. THE AGE OF RELIGIOUS WARS, 1559-1715. 2d ed. NHME. New York: 1979 [1970].

27. Dupuy, R.E., & Dupuy, T.N. THE ENCYCLOPEDIA OF MILITARY HISTORY. Rev. ed. New York: 1977.

28. Ellesmere, Earl of., trans. & ed. THE SIEGES OF VIENNA BY THE TURKS, FROM THE GERMAN OF KARL AUGUST SCHIMMER AND OTHER SOURCES. London: 1847. Also listed under Karl August Schimmer.

29. Elton, G.R., ed. THE REFORMATION, 1520-1559. Vol. 2 in NCMH. Cambridge: 1958.

30. Fichtner, P.S. "An Absence Explained: Archduke Ferdinand of Austria and the Battle of Mohacs." AUSTRIAN HISTORY YEARBOOK II (1966), 11-16.

31. Fisher, S.N. "Civil Strife in the Ottoman Empire, 1481-1503." JMH XIII (1941), 448-466.

32. _____. THE FOREIGN RELATIONS OF TURKEY, 1481-1512. Urbana: 1948.

33. _____. "Ottoman Feudalism and Its Influence Upon the Balkans." HISTORY XV (1930), 3-22.

34. Gibb, H.A.R., Sir., & Bowen, H. ISLAMIC SOCIETY AND THE WEST: A STUDY OF THE IMPACT OF WESTERN CIVILIZATION ON MOSLEM CULTURE. Vol. 1. London& New York: 1950-1957.

35. Girvidan, H.H. "Celali Rebellions in the Ottoman Empire, 1596-1610." ACTA of the CIHM 1974. Sandhurst: 1975.

36. Giurescu, C.C., et al., eds. CHRONOLOGICAL HISTORY OF ROMANIA. Bucharest: 1972.

37. Gokbilgin, M.T. "III Mehmet." IA VIII, 537-547.

38. Gollner, C. TURCICA, DIE EUROPAISCHEN TURKENDRUCKE DES XVI JAHRHUNDERTS. Bucharest & Baden-Baden: 1968 [1961].

39. Graviere, J. de la. DORIA ET BARBAROUSSE. Paris: 1886.

40. _____. LA GUERRE DE CHYPRE ET LA BATAILLE DE LEPANTA. Paris: 1888.

41. Greckov, I.B. OCHERKI PO ISTORII MEZHDUNARODNYKH OTNOSHENII VOSTOCHNOI EVROPY XIV-XVI VV. Moscow: 1963.

42. Grenadier, R.L. "Zaporozhian Cossacks." Unpublished monograph, George Mason University. 1981

43. Guldescu, S. THE CROATIAN-SLAVONIC KINGDOM, 1526-1792. SEH 21. The Hague & Paris: 1970.

44. _____. HISTORY OF MEDIEVAL CROATIA. SEH 1. The Hague: 1964.

45. Hajek, A. BULGARIEN UNTER DER TURKENHERRSCHAFT. Stuttgart: 1925.

46. Hale, J.R. "Armies, Navies, and the Art of War." NCMH II. Cambridge: 1958.

47. _____. "Armies, Navies, and the Art of War." NCMH III. Cambridge: 1968.

48. _____. "International Relations in the West: Diplomacy and War." NCMH I. Cambridge: 1971.

49. Heer, F. THE HOLY ROMAN EMPIRE. Trans. by Janety Sondheimer. New York & Washington: 1968 [1867].

50. Hess, A. "The Battle of Lepanto and Its Place in Mediterranean History." PAST AND PRESENT LII (1972), 53-73.

51. _____. "The Evolution of the Ottoman Seaborne Empire in the Age of the Oceanic Discoveries." AHR LXXVV (1970), 1892-1919.

52. Huart, C. "Janissaries." EI 25 (1919), 572-574.

53. Hungary. MOHACS EMLEKEZETE. A MOHACSI CSATARA VONATKOZO LEGFONTOSABB MAGYAR, NYUGATI ES TOROK FORRASOK. Budapest: 1979.

54. Inalcik, H. "The Heyday and Decline of the Ottoman Empire." CHI I. Cambridge: 1970.

55. _____. "Osmanli-Rus rekabepinin mensei ve Don-Volga kanali tesebusu. BELLETIN XII (April 1948), 349-402.

56. _____. THE OTTOMAN EMPIRE: THE CLASSICAL AGE. Trans. by Norman Itzowitz & Colin Imber. London & New York: 1973.

57. _____. "Ottoman Methods of Conquest." SI II (1954), 103-129.

58. Iorga, N. ISTORIA LUI MIHAI VITEAZUL. Bucharest: 1970.

59. Jenkins, H.D. IBRAHAM PASHA: GRAND VIZIR OF SULEIMAN THE MAGNIFICENT. New York: 1911.

60. Jessup, J.E., & Coakley, R.W., eds. A GUIDE TO THE STUDY AND USE OF MILITARY HISTORY. Washington: 1979.

61. Kann, R.A. THE HISTORY OF THE HABSBURG EMPIRE, 1526-1918. Berkeley: 1974.

62. Kann, R.A., & David, Z. THE PEOPLES OF THE EASTERN HABSBURG LANDS, 1526-1918. HECE 6. Seattle & London: 1982.

63. Karal, E.Z. "Barbaros Hayreddin Pasa." IA II. Istanbul & Ankara: 1944.

64. Khalifeh, H. THE HISTORY OF THE MARITIME WARS OF THE TURKS. Trans. by James Mitchell. London: 1831.

65. Kinross, J.P.D. Balfour, Lord. THE OTTOMAN CENTURIES: THE RISE AND FALL OF THE TURKISH EMPIRE. London: 1977.

66. Kortepeter, C.M. OTTOMAN IMPERIALISM DURING THE REFORMATION: EUROPE AND THE CAUCASUS. New York: 1972.

67. Kowalski, T. "Les Turcs balkaniques." RIEB IV (1936), 420-430.

68. Kramers, J.H. SULEIMAN, DER GESETZBERGERS TAGEBUCH AUF SEINEN FELDZUGE NACH WIEN. Trans. by F.A. Behrnauer. Vienna: 1858. LC records indicate Kramers' (1891-1952) name appears on the book with the 1858 publication date. The book is in the Yale University collection.

69. Kutukoglu, B. "III Murad." IA VIII. Ankara & Istanbul: 1970.

70. Lamb, H. SULEIMAN THE MAGNIFICENT. New York: 1958.

71. Lengyel, E. 1000 YEARS OF HUNGARY. New York: 1958.

72. Leo, M. LA BULGARIE ET SON PEUPLE SOUS LA DOMINATION OTTOMANE. Sofia: 1949.

73. Lessner, E.C., & Lessner, A.M.L. THE DANUBE: THE DRAMATIC HISTORY OF THE GREAT RIVER AND THE PEOPLE TOUCHED BY ITS FLOW. Garden City: 1961.

74. Levend, A.S. GAZAVATNAMELER VE MIHAILOGLU ALI BEY'IN GAZATVATNAMESI. Ankara: 1956.

75. Lewis, B., ed. ISLAM FROM THE PROPHET MUHAMMED TO THE CAPTURE OF CONSTANTINOPLE. Vol. 1: POLITICS AND WAR. DCWC. New York: 1973.

76. Lufti Pasha. TEVARIH-I AL-I OSMAN. Istanbul: 1925.

77. Lukinich, I. ERDELY TERULETI VALTOZASAI A TOROK HODITAS KORABAN 1541-1711. Budapest: 1918.

78. Luther, M. VOM KRIEGE WIDER DIE TURKEN. Wittenberg: 1529.

79. Lybyer, A.H. THE GOVERNMENT OF THE OTTOMAN EMPIRE IN THE TIME OF SULEIMAN THE MAGNIFICENT. Cambridge: 1913.

80. Macartney, C.A. "Eastern Europe." NCMH I. Cambridge: 1971.

81. Macdermott, M. A HISTORY OF BULGARIA, 1393-1885. London: 1962.

82. Mamatey, V.S. RISE OF THE HABSBURG EMPIRE, 1526-1815. New York: 1971.

83. Menage, V.L. "Devshirme." EI(new) II (1965), 210-213.

84. Merriman, R.B. SULEIMAN THE MAGNIFICENT. Cambridge: 1944.

85. Mordtmann, J.H. "Dewshirme." EI 15 (1912), 952-953.

86. _____. ZUR KAPITULATION VON BUDA IN JAHRE 1526. Budapest & Constantinople: 1918.

87. Mutafeieva, V.P. DE L'EXPLOITATION FEODAL DANS LES TERRES DE POPULATION BULGARE SOUS LA DOMINATION TURQUE AU XV$^e$ ET XVI$^e$ SIECLES. Sofia: 1960.

88. Neagoe, M. "The Battle of Calugareni (1595)." PHRA BHR Monograph XV. Bucharest: 1975.

89. _____. STEFAN CEL MARE. Bucharest: 1970.

90. Olteanu, C. "On the Organization of the Army in the Romanian Countries." PHRA. BHR Monograph XV. Bucharest: 1975.

91. Oman., C., Sir. A HISTORY OF THE ART OF WAR IN THE SIXTEENTH CENTURY. New York: 1937.

92. Palmer, J.A.B. "The Origins of the Janissaries." BJRL XXV (1956), 433-443.

93. Panitescu, P.P. MIHAI VITEAZUL. Bucharest: 1936

94. Parry, V.J. "Bayazid II." EI(new) I (1960), 1119-1121.

95. _____. "The Ottoman Empire, 1520-1566." NCMH II. Cambridge: 1958

96. _____. "The Ottoman Empire, 1566-1617." NCMH III. Cambridge: 1968.

97. Pataki, I. "Ceva despre relatiile Tarii Romanesti cu Ungaria la sfirsitul veacului al XVI-lea." STUDII SI MATERIALE DE ISTORIA MEDIE, II (1957), 421-430.

98. Potter, G.R., ed. THE RENAISSANCE, 1493-1520. Vol. I in NCMH. Cambridge: 1957.

99. Prpic, G.J. CROATIA AND HUNGARY DURING THE TURKISH ERA. SHBS I. Cleveland: 1973.

100. Ramsay, G.D. "The Austrian Habsburgs and the Empire." NCMH III. Cambridge: 1968.

101. Ranke, L. von. THE OTTOMAN AND SPANISH EMPIRES IN THE SIXTEENTH AND SEVENTEENTH CENTURIES. London: 1843.

102. Refik, A. OCAK AGALARI. Istanbul: 1931.

103. _____. TURK IDARESINDE BULGARESTAN (973-1255). Istanbul: 1933.

104. Romanescu, G. "Grosse Mittelalterliche Schlachten des rumanischen Volkes fur die Verteidigung der Unabhangigkeit und des uralten Heimatsbodens." PMHRP. Bucharest: 1980.

105. Romania, Institute of History of the Romanian Academy. DOCUMENTA ROMANIAE HISTORICA. 3 series. Bucharest: 1977-.

106. Ropp, T. "Miltary History to the End of the Eighteenth Century." GSUMH. Washington: 1979.

107. Rossetti, R. ISTORIA ARTEI MILITARA A ROMANILOR. Bucharest: 1943.

108. Rothenberg, G.E. THE AUSTRIAN MILITARY BORDER IN CROATIA, 1522-1747. ISSS. Urbana: 1961.

109. _____. "Christian Insurrections in Turkish Dalmatia, 1580-96." SEER XL (December 1961), 136-147.

110. Schwoebel, R. THE SHADOW OF THE CRESCENT: THE RENAISSANCE IMAGE OF THE TURK (1453-1517). New York: 1967.

111. Seyfi, A.R. BARBAROS HAYREDDIN. Istanbul: 1910.

112. Shaw, S.J. HISTORY OF THE OTTOMAN EMPIRE AND MODERN TURKEY. Vol. 1: EMPIRE OF THE GAZIS: THE RISE AND DECLINE OF THE OTTOMAN EMPIRE, 1280-1808. Cambridge & New York: 1976.

113. Stanescu, E. "Colaborarea militara dentre romani si cazaci in ultime szert a veacului al XVI-lea." STUDII III (1954), 110-144; IV (1955), 187-213.

114. _____. "Tarile Romane la sfersital veacului al XVI-lea si prima lor unificare politica. Despre necesitate si posibilitate in istorie." FILE III. Bucharest: 1975.

115. Stavrianos, L.S. THE BALKANS SINCE 1453. New York: 1958.

116. Steblau, E.L. von. HABSBURGS AND ZAPOROZHIAN COSSACKS. Trans.
     by Orest Subtelny. New York: 1975.

117. Stoicescu, N. "The Greater Army of Walachia and Moldavia (14th
     - 16th Centuries)." PHRA. Bucharest: 1975.

118. _____. "Organizational Structure of the Armies in the
     Romanian Principalities in the 14th - 18th Centuries."
     ARS. Bucharest 1980.

119. Sturminger, W. BIBLIOGRAPHIE UND IKONOGRAPHIE DER
     TURKENBELAGERUNGEN WIENS, 1529 U. 1683. Graz & Cologne:
     1955.

120. Sugar, I. A BUDAI VAR ES OSTOMAI. Budapest: 1979.

121. Sugar, P.F. SOUTHEASTERN EUROPE UNDER OTTOMAN RULE, 1354-1804.
     HECE V. Seattle: 1977.

122. Sugar, P.F., & Treadgold, D.W., eds. HISTORY OF EAST CENTRAL
     EUROPE. 11 vols. Seattle & London: 1975-.

123. Szakaly, F. A MOHACSI CSATA. 2nd ed. Budapest: 1977.

124. Takats, S., et al., eds. A BUDAI BASAK MAGYAR NYELVU
     LEVELEZESE. Budapest: 1915.

125. Tansel, S. SULTAN II. BAYAZID'IN SIYASI HAYATI. Istanbul: 1966.

126. Tauer, F. HISTOIRE DE LA CAMPAGNE DE SULTAN SULEYMAN I$^{er}$
     CONTRE BELGRADE EN 1521. Prague: 1924.

127. _____. "Soliman's Wiener Feldzug." ARCHIV ORIENTALNI XXIV 4
     (1956), 507-563.

128. Turan, S. KANUNI'NIN OGLU SCHZADE BAYEZID. Ankara: 1961.

129. _____. "Selim II." IA X. Istanbul & Ankara: 1972.

130. _____. "Sinan Pasha." IA IX. Istanbul & Ankara: 1972.

131. Turkey. Department of War History. General Staff Headquarters.
     TURK SILAHLI KUVVETLERI TARIHI. Vol. III. Ankara: 1977.

132. Ursu, I STEFAN CEL MARE. Bucharest: 1925.

133. USSR. Institut slavianovedeniia. MEZHDUNARODNYE OTNOSHENIIA V
     TSENTRAL'NOI I VOSTOCHNOI EVROPE I IKH ISTORIOGRAFIIA.
     Moscow: 1966.

134. Uzuncarsili, I.H. "Devshirme and shari'a." BSOAS XVII (1955),
     271-278.

135. _____. OSMANLI DEVLETI TESKILATINDAN KAPULULU OCAKLARI. 2
     vols. Ankara: 1943-1944.

136. _____. OSMANLI DEVLETI TESKILATINA MEDHAL. Istanbul: 1941.

137. _____. OSMANLI IMPARATORLUGU TESKILATI, 1453-1575 SENESINE KADAR. Istanbul: 1936.

138. _____. OSMANLI TARIHI. 4 vols. Ankara: 1947-1960.

139. Vacalopoulos, A. THE GREEK NATION, 1453-1669. New Brunswick: 1976.

140. Volkl, E. DAS RUMANISCHEN FURSTENTURM MOLDAU UND DIE OSTSLAVEN IM 15. BIS 17. JAHREHUNDERT. PEEI 42. Wiesbaden: 1975.

141. Wandruszka, A. THE HOUSE OF HABSBURG: SIX HUNDRED YEARS OF A EUROPEAN DYNASTY. Trans. by Cathleen and Hans Epstein. Garden City: 1964.

142. Weissmann, N. LES JANISSAIRES, ETUDE DE L'ORGANIZATION MILITAIRE DES OTTOMANS. Paris: 1938.

143. Wernham, R.B., ed. COUNTER-REFORMATION AND PRICE REVOLUTION, 1559-1610. Vol. 3 in NCMH. Cambridge: 1968.

144. Wright, Q. THE STUDY OF WAR. London & Chicago: 1965 [1942].

145. Zook, D.H., & Higham, R. A SHORT HISTORY OF WARFARE. New York: 1966.

# CHAPTER FOUR

## THE 17TH CENTURY

### GENERAL BACKGROUND

The 17th century was marked by the rise of absolutism in France and by the dynastic rivalries that arose among the rulers of France and the Habsburgs. These rivalries helped foment many of the military conflicts that occurred during the century and that broke out at one time or another in every corner of the European continent. These wars, especially the Thirty Years' War, left Europe ravaged to an extent matched up to that time only by the destruction left in the wake of the Mongol invasions.

The period also witnessed the beginning of the dynamic reign of Peter I of Russia (1682-1725) that signalled his nation's emergence from centuries of isolation. His rule set into motion expansionist policies that would, in the future, place the Russian Bear at the Balkan's doorstep. His successors would develop policies that would be aimed directly at aggrandizement in southeastern Europe, and that would turn the Balkans into a theater of war in their attempts to carry them out.

The Ottoman Empire was engaged in almost constant warfare throughout the 17th century. Internal reforms came in quantities that were too little and too late. Yet, even though the empire showed clear evidence of deterioration, it was still a powerful adversary to its enemies and a pitiless master to its captives.

### GENERAL HISTORICAL COVERAGE

Several of the already mentioned general histories are especially good in their coverage of the 17th century. George Arnakis' THE OTTOMAN EMPIRE AND THE BALKANS TO 1900 [11], Paul Cole's THE OTTOMAN IMPACT ON EUROPE [39], and Sir Charles Eliot's TURKEY IN EUROPE [52] continue to detail the direct influence of the Turks on the Balkans and upon Europe in general. Stanford Shaw's THE EMPIRE OF THE GAZIS [132] is exceptional in its discussion of the reforms carried out within the structure of the Sublime Porte to meet the challenges that it had to address and that faced the nation both from within and from without.

The most thorough history of Turkey during this period is Ismail Hakki Uzuncarsili's OSMANLI TARIHI [159] that has only been published in Turkish up to this time. Lord Kinross, in THE OTTOMAN CENTURIES. . . [81], devotes a major part of his study to the description of the age of reform and does so with characteristic eloquence and skill. Leopold von Ranke's THE OTTOMAN AND SPANISH EMPIRES IN THE SIXTEENTH AND SEVENTEENTH CENTURIES [122] continues as an important means of comparing the eastern realm of the Turks with the Spanish world of the west that was also in decline. ISLAMIC SOCIETY AND THE WEST [61], by Sir Harold Gibb and H. Bowen, shows the impact of the numerous exposures to western culture and the effects these had upon the Turkish way of life. This work also discusses the attempts at westernization that were made by some of the Turkish rulers over the course of the century and the results of these efforts.

Leften Stavrianos' THE BALKANS SINCE 1453 [135] is still the single best source on the history of the Balkans. Peter Sugar's SOUTHEASTERN EUROPE UNDER OTTOMAN RULE, 1354-1804 [140] is also very good. Erwin and Ann Lessner's THE DANUBE. . . [93] is exceptionally well written and contains a wealth of detail, minutae, some would say, that adds flavor to the story. Lengyel's 1000 YEARS OF HUNGARY [91], Seton-Watson's A HISTORY OF THE ROUMANIANS [131], Mercia Macdermott's A HISTORY OF BULGARIA, 1393-1885 [97], Coquelle's HISTOIRE DU MONTENEGRO ET DE LA BOSNIA [43], YUGOSLAVIA [69], by Heppell and Singleton, and George Finlay's HISTORY OF GREECE [55] all have pertinent sections on this century.

The situation to the west especially as it may have affected the Balkans may be studied in THE HOLY ROMAN EMPIRE [68], by Frederich Heer; Robert Kann's A HISTORY OF THE HABSBURG EMPIRE [77], RISE OF THE HABSBURG EMPIRE [99], by Victor Mamatey; in Adam Wandruszka's THE HOUSE OF HABSBURGS [167], and in THE PEOPLES OF THE EASTERN HABSBURG LANDS [78], by Kann and Zdanec David. There are a number of worthwhile general studies on Russia during this period. Klyuchevsky [182] is the best. Jesse Clarkson's HISTORY OF RUSSIA [36], and another by the same title that was written by Nicholas Riasonovsky [125] are also both useful, and both have good bibliographies.

Historians have devoted considerable effort to studying the 17th century; and, consequently, there is a fairly broad selection of literature available that can be of use to a student of military history interested in those times. THE SEVENTEENTH CENTURY [35], by G.N. Clark; Basil Willey's THE SEVENTEENTH CENTURY BACKGROUND [172], HISTORY OF EUROPE, 1610-1715 [123], by W.F. Reddaway; David Ogg's EUROPE IN THE SEVENTEENTH CENTURY [105]; and A.J. Grant's A HISTORY OF EUROPE 1494-1610 [65] are all worth reading. Grant's work is mentioned here because it is useful in understanding the circumstances that culminated in the establishment of the Catholic League and that presaged war. CRISIS IN EUROPE, 1560-1660 [12], edited by Trevor Aston, does the same thing, and provides an analysis of the aftermath of the Peace of Westphalia (24 October 1648), which ended the Thirty Years' War. William Doyle's THE OLD EUROPEAN ORDER, 1660-1800 [48] is interesting at this point only because of its characterization of the people and the times in the last four decades of the century. THE ANCIEN REGIME IN EUROPE [173], by E.N. Williams, begins in 1648 with an excellent discussion of the governments and people of the various states in western Europe. A somewhat different approach to this period is taken in Carlo Cipolla's GUNS, SAILS AND EMPIRES: TECHNOLOGICAL INNOVATION AND THE EARLY PHASES OF EUROPEAN EXPANSION, 1400-1700 [190] and in G.V. Scammell's THE WORLD ENCOMPASSED: THE FIRST EUROPEAN MARITIME POWERS, C.800-1650 [186].

Using material from the Czech archives hitherto unavailable, J.V. Polisensky's DIE KRIEGE UND DIE GESELLSCHAFT IN EUROPA, 1618-1684 [116], is an excellent account of these crucial years. The volume is most illuminating in its discussion of the Thirty Years' War. There is an extensive listing of source documents included in this book that will make it a delight to the serious student. THE STRUGGLE FOR STABILITY IN EARLY MODERN EUROPE [118], by T.K. Rabb, and THE TRANSFORMATION OF EUROPE 1558-1648 [174], by C. Wilson, are also both worthwhile reading.

There is a French collection that should also be studied as it has a rich offering of documents on the military history of the 17th and 18th centuries. The 822-page volume, L'ANCIEN REGIME [57], was edited by Etienne Taillemite and is the work of Les Archives Nationales, Etat general des fonds. Series "K" is of special importance as it deals with military history in foreign lands. There is sufficient material that relates to events in the Balkans to make this a useful tool for the astute military historian.

The growing unrest in Greece is covered by Vacalopoulos in THE GREEK NATION, 1453-1669 [160]. The author outlines the cultural and economic developments in that region of the Balkans through most of the century. Ahmed Refik continues his study of Bulgaria in his TURK IDARESINDE BULGARESTAN (973-1255) [124]. Mustafa Akdag has written an excellent article called "Genel Cizgileriyle XVII yuzyil Turkiye Tarihi" [3] that condenses the general history of Ottoman Empire in the 17th century into just 46 pages. As is true about many of the better works about Ottoman history, this one is published only in Turkish. There are, however, in addition to those already mentioned, a number of works in English, or one of the other more easily acquired languages, that are useful at this point. There is, for example, a partial translation of the accounts of Mustafa Naima (1665-1716), the great Ottoman chronicler. His is the most important chronicle of his time, and significant portions were translated into English in the 19th century by Charles Fraser and published in London as the ANNALS OF THE TURKISH EMPIRE FROM 1591 TO 1659 [58]. Sir Paul Rycault's THE HISTORY OF THE TURKISH EMPIRE FROM THE YEAR 1623 TO THE YEAR 1677 [130] is well written and easily read, even though it was published in 1680. Rycault also produced a second volume some twenty years later that covers Turkish history from 1679 until 1699 [129]. Lastly, Michel Leo's LA BULGARIE ET SON PEUPLE SOUS LA DOMINATION OTTOMANE [92] is an interesting study that can be of benefit as background reading.

## THE MILITARY ARTS IN THE 17TH CENTURY

The 17th century was a time of change, especially in the style of warfare practiced almost without respite throughout the century. These changes were the result of technological advances that engendered revisions in doctrine, organization, and practice; and nowhere is this better illustrated than in the introduction of firearms into military formations.

Through the early decades of the century, the bow was replaced by the arquebus (also called variously the hagbut, hackbut, or harquebus). This was a portable firelock that, in its last stages of development, was called a matchlock. The forms of this weapon included a shoulder-fired model, which was usually equipped with a forked stick or pole to support the weight of the heavy barrel, and a pistol model, generally credited as being of English design. It should be remembered that firearms were known, and in military use, much before the 17th century. Cannon were reported to have been employed as early as Crecy (1346); and by the 15th century, the art of making firearms had reached a point where a few nations in Europe were seriously experimenting with individual weapons that might be issued to soldiers in lieu of a pike, spear, or bow. The French were among the first to see the military value of firearms, crude as they may have been by modern standards.

In addition to individual firearms, other forms of this weapon also gained acceptability during the 17th century. The cannon was already an acknowledged tool of war; and by century's end, men such as Gustavus Adolphus had made it not only better, but had also developed the doctrines and tactics for its proper employment to a point where artillery had become an arm of decision on the battlefield. Similar advances were made in siegecraft and in the design and employment of naval fighting craft. All of these advances required new methods of leadership, new doctrines, new tactics, and new military formations. The numerous conflicts of the 17th century speeded the processes of change and, indeed, made the changes necessary to survival.

These concepts were, of course, universal. They affected the Balkans as much as they did western Europe, although at a different pace and magnitude. There was little in the way of originality in arms or tactics developed in the Balkans, although the terrain and the situation did cause modifications to be made. The great battles of the 17th century that were fought in the Balkans came about primarily as a result of the meeting of two major, "outside" antagonists. Those battles incorporated many of the new technologies. The battle that involved local Balkan forces pitted against each other were of the more vintage variety.

To properly appreciate these few points, it would be useful for the reader to study the introduction to chapter 14 in Dupuy [50], and chapter 7 in Zook and Higham [179]. Quincy Wright discusses the developmental periods of civilization in THE STUDY OF WAR [176] and characterizes the 17th century as being equally divided between a period of religious wars (up to 1648), followed by a period of political absolutism that continued into the late 18th century. Professor Wright also presents some interesting charts that list the wars of the century and the countries involved. Most of the Balkan states are ignored in these lists probably because they were considered to be in the Turkish thrall, even though they fought their masters on numerous occasions.

WEAPONS OF WAR [37], by P.E. Cleator, and EUROPEAN WEAPONS AND WARFARE, 1618-1648 [165], by Major Eduard Wagner, are both good sources of data on arms and armaments of the period. The latter work dwells upon the time of the Thirty Years' War and is replete with facts about the developments of strategy and organization. "Military Forces and Warfare, 1610-1648" [171], by J.W. Wijn, presents the same data on the same period in capsule form. A MILITARY HISTORY OF THE WESTERN WORLD [59], by J.F.C. Fuller, is one of the best works on this period, especially the second volume. Another good choice is

Elbridge Colby's MASTERS OF MOBILE WARFARE [38], while J.P. Cooper's "Sea Power" [42] covers the trends in naval strategy and tactics as seen in the first half of the century, and relates details of the Turko-Venetian War.

Martin Van Creveld's SUPPLYING WAR: LOGISTICS FROM WALLENSTEIN TO PATTON [161] is of particular interest because of the changing nature of war during this period and the incurred increase in the problems of logistics. In his study, Van Creveld examines these problems in light of technological developments. A STUDY OF MILITARY METHODS. . . [134], by Oliver Spaulding and his colleagues, should be read for its fine insights into the larger issues involved in the evolution of war during this period.

There are several good histories and other accounts of the great captains of this period. Both Trevor Dupuy's MILITARY LIFE OF GUSTAVUS ADOLPHUS. . . [51] and GUSTAVUS ADOLPHUS, THE NORTHERN HURRICANE [100], by Sir George McMunn, are good. GUERRA E POLITICA NEGLI SCRITTORI ITALIANI [113], by Piero Pieri, is a comparative study of the military thought of a number of important military personalities, historians and authors — including Machiavelli, Montecuccoli, Palmieri, De Christoforus, Pisacane, and Marselli. Pieri concludes that if one studies the subject closely, especially the political and other related factors, it will be seen that the roots of war are found in the prevailing socio-economic strata as it exists.

David Chandler's ATLAS OF MILITARY STRATEGY [33] is excellent not only for its maps but also for its narrative. Another most useful tool is Andre Corvisier's ARMEES ET SOCIETES EN EUROPE DE 1494 A 1789 [44]. This work by an eminent French military historian and scholar is a must for any program of reading on the early centuries of the modern age. It has been translated into English. Hans Delbruck's GESCHICHTE DER KRIEGSKUNST IM RAHMEN DER POLITISCHEN GESCHICHTE [45] is also very valuable as it presents the German view on war as a function of politics. This work is also available in English. Hajji Khalifeh's THE HISTORY OF THE MARITIME WARS OF THE TURKS [79] and R.C. Anderson's NAVAL WARS OF THE LEVANT, 1558-1853 [8] both give thorough accounts of Ottoman naval campaigning during the century. Halil Inalcik's "Ottoman Methods of Conquest" [72] is also important, as is LES JANASSAIRES, ETUDE DE L'ORGANIZATION MILITAIRE DES OTTOMANS [169], by N. Weissmann. This last work discusses the Turkish military during the century. Another excellent study on the Janissaries is Ahmed Djevad Bey's ETAT MILITAIRE OTTOMAN [47].

Many of these works, as well as others, are discussed in Theodore Ropp's chapter on "Military History to the End of the Eighteenth Century" [126], in A GUIDE TO THE STUDY AND USE OF MILITARY HISTORY [76], by Jessup and Coakley. Other portions of the guide may also be of value at this point.

## THE BEGINNING OF THE CENTURY IN THE BALKANS

By 1600, Michael the Brave of Wallachia had brought both Transylvania and Moldavia under his control. This hegemony was not to last, however; and, by September 1600, the union of the principal Romanian provinces had already begun to crumble. In Transylvania, the Hungarian nobility rose against Michael and the Austrian garrison, under General George Basta, sided with the rebels. On 18 September 1600, Michael fought the Hungarians and Austrians at Miraslau and was beaten. He was then obliged to withdraw into Wallachia. Sigismund Batory was returned to the Transylvanian throne.

Michael's situation in Moldavia was much the same. In early September, a Polish army under John Zamoyski invaded Moldavia and reenthroned Ieremia Movila (1595-1600, 1600-1606). The Poles then invaded Wallachia and, on 20 October, defeated Michael at Bucov. Simion Movila (1600-1601, 1601-1602) was then placed on the Wallachian throne. A final battle was fought at Curtea de Arges where Michael was again defeated. Thereafter he traveled to Vienna where he sought the aid and protection of Emperor Rudolph (1576-1612).

Rudolph accepted Michael's pleas and reconciled the differences between the Wallachian and General Basta, hoping, as an outcome, to regain the influence that had been lost to Vienna when Batory regained his crown. Of the utmost importance was the fact that Batory had removed Transylvania from the anti-Ottoman coalition in May 1601. The reconciliation of Michael and Basta was aimed at ousting Batory and, more importantly, restoring the Transylvanian flank of the Austrian defensive alignment.

Word spread throughout the Romanian provinces that Michael was returning with an army, and a popular uprising (June-July 1601) ensued that saw the flight of Simeon Movila and the restoration of Michael's crown. This was followed by the defeat of Batory on 3 August at Goraslau. Michael's victory was shortlived, however, as Basta murdered him within the week at Cimpia Turzii. The general then carried out a reign of terror that was aimed primarily at Transylvanian Catholics. A resistance organization quickly sprang up under the leadership of Stefan Bocskai that sought to end the persecution. Possibly heeding the words of Dionysius of Halicarnassus that "Necessity is stronger than human nature," Bocskai sought and received an alliance with the Turks. Sigismund Batory was able to regain momentarily the throne but was forced to yield the crown to Rudolph in June 1602. In return Batory received several duchies and 50,000 florins. For the next year, Transylvania was ruled by a royal commission headed by George Basta.

The unrest caused by the death of Michael continued in Wallachia until July 1602, when Radu Serban (1602-1610) seized the throne. In the spring of 1603, Serban mounted a military campaign against the Turks in Dobrudja. Then, in the summer, the Wallachian prince aided Basta in putting down an uprising among the Hungarian nobility. Serban defeated the insurgent force led by Moise Secuiul in a battle fought in the mountainous terrain near Brasov. Serban then proceeded to take the rest of Transylvania, as Michael had done before him. All this changed again, however, when another Hungarian force chased both the Austrians and Serban out of the country and elected Stefan Bocskai (1605-1606) as the new prince. The Sublime Porte acknowledged Bocskai's crown before the end of the year.

## THE TREATY OF ZSITVATOROK

On 11 November 1606, the long war that had begun in 1593 between the Ottomans and the Austrians was concluded by the Treaty of Zsitvatorok (Zsitva-Torok). Little was changed by the treaty, however, except that both sides acknowledged the independence of Transylvania. Rudolph had, in fact, already done that on 23 June 1606 and had accepted Bocskai's rule. One month after the signing of the treaty, however, in December 1606, Bocskai was murdered and another mad scramble began for the throne.

All of this confusion in the Balkans must have seemed a respite to the Turks. From 1602, they had been involved in a major conflict with Persia and, from 1603, had to deal with a major revolt among Kurdish and Druse tribesmen. Also, in 1603, a fourteen-year-old was put on the Ottoman throne. Ahmed I (1603-1617) was to rule an empire that was showing all of the signs of decline. It was a rule marked by revolt and discord at home, and the Zsitvatorok treaty and the squabbling in the Balkans gained precious time for the Porte.

## THE PROTESTANT UPRISING IN BOHEMIA

This was also an interesting time in the Austrian realm. The efforts of the Jesuits had begun to pay off and Catholicism was having a resurgence, especially in Vienna. In 1608, the court returned to Vienna from Linz; and Matthias (1606-1612) (King of Austria, Bohemia, and Habsburg Hungary) already seemed destined to be emperor. Four years later, the hope became reality when the intolerant Matthias deposed his brother, Rudolph, for granting religious freedom to Bohemian Protestants. Thus, Matthias became emperor of the Holy Roman Empire (1612-1618). This led to trouble in Bohemia where, in 1617, the Catholics elected the Archduke Ferdinand of Stria (Matthias' cousin) as heir to the throne. The Protestants refused to accept this; and, after the defenestration incident at Prague (22 May 1618), a revolt began under the Protestant banner of Count Matthias of Thurn. Thurn's attack and capture of Krummau in July 1618, opened the first, or Bohemian phase, of the Thirty Years' War.

There is a wealth of information on the military history of these first two decades of the 17th century in the Balkans. The CHRONOLOGICAL HISTORY OF ROMANIA [62] has good detail on those incidents involving the Romanian principalities; but there are numerous transpositions of dates, apparently the result of faulty translation and technical editing. From this point forward, as the historical record becomes more complex, the reader who uses this otherwise excellent reference must do so with caution.

The three sources mentioned in the last chapter on the life of Michael the Brave, Iorga [74], Almas [6], and Panitescu [109] are all worthwhile reading on this last phase of his life. Imre Lukinich's ERDELY TERULETI VALTOZASAI A TOROK HODITAS KORABAN 1541-1711 [95] is a good source on the Transylvanian events, although it has been published, thus far, only in Hungarian. It does have an excellent set of maps and a very good cross-index of place names and subject matter.

DAS RUMANISCHE FURSTENTUM MOLDAU UND DIE OSTSLAVEN IM 15. BIS 17. JAHREHUNDERT [164], by Ekkehard Volkl, is an interesting account of Moldavia's affairs in relation to its Slavic neighbors in Southeastern Europe. OSMANSKA MOC VE STREDNI A JIHOVYCHODNI EVROPE V 16.-17. STOLETI [32], which was prepared from the papers presented at the Ninth Joint Conference of the Czechoslovak-Yugoslav Historical Committee, deals with the Ottoman rule in middle Europe during this century, especially the affairs in the Serbia-Croatia-Bosnia area.

Mercia Macdermott calls these early decades of the 17th century "The Dark Years" in A HISTORY OF BULGARIA [97] and explains this by graphic descriptions of Turkish depredations. Lessner [93], Kinross [81], Macartney, in his HUNGARY: A SHORT HISTORY [96], and Lengyel [91] all discuss this period. Lengyel's comments are especially good.

Evliya Celebi wrote an exhaustive account of 17th century travel through the Ottoman lands in SEYAHATNAME [30]. Part of the ten-volume account has been translated into German and, as it is an account of travel through Thrace, is of some interest as background reading. The translation of Celebi's work is found in Hans Kissling's BEITRAGE ZUR KENNTNIS THRAKIENS IM 17. JAHRHUNDERTS [82]. Volume four of the NEW CAMBRIDGE MODERN HISTORY [41] contains two excellent articles, one by V.J. Parry titled "The Ottoman Empire, 1617-48" [111], and one by V.J. Tapie "The Habsburg Lands, 1618-57" [145], that will serve as quick refreshers on the first half of the century.

The life of Ahmed I is sketched by Mohammed Cavid Baysun [16] in an article in ISLAM ANSIKLOPEDICI. The internal troubles of the Ottoman Empire are discussed in some detail in A. Tveritinova's VOSSTANIYE KARA YAZIDJI-DELI CHASANA VE TURTSII 1599-1603 [154] and in Mustafa Akdag's CELALI ISYANLARINDA BUYUK KACGUNLUK (1603-1606) [2]. The first work discusses the role of Kara-Yaziji and his brother, Deli Hassan (Hassan the Mad), in the early stages of the great Celali (Jelali) uprising that began in Anatolia among the members of the irregular provincial army. That force was made up primarily of Turkomens, Kurds, Sipahis, and Sekhans -- the last two being categories of Turks, rather than separate ethnic groups. Specifically because of the disruption caused by this revolt, the Persian Shah Abbas reopened the war against the Turks and was able to recapture much territory that had been previously lost. Both Shaw, in his HISTORY OF THE OTTOMAN EMPIRE [132], and Kinross [81] have adequate coverage of this situation. In his ZUR GESCHICHTE DES TURKEN KRIEGEN VON 1593-1606 [94], Alfred Loebl discusses the course of the Austro-Turkish conflict that ended in the Treaty of Zsitvatorok. Macartney [96] and Sugar [140] deal concisely with the aftermath of that treaty.

## CONTINUED DISORDER IN THE BALKANS

The peace treaty was of little consequence in the Balkans, especially in those regions that were not already incorporated into the Ottoman pashalik system. From 1607 until 1611, one struggle after another for the throne took place in Moldavia. These conflicts were often fostered and abetted by the Poles or Crimean Tatars, each of whom wanted hegemony over the province.

In Transylvania, Gabriel Bathory was elected prince (1608-1613), replacing Sigismund Rakoczi (1607-1608). Bathory's reign was poor, but he did manage to defeat Radu Serban and seize control of Wallachia. Bathory then established himself as ruler of Wallachia (January 1611) but was only able to hold on to it until March when the Turks imposed a more congenial puppet on the throne. In June 1611, Radu Serban defeated Bathory at Brasov, when the Transylvanian army broke and ran. Serban was not able to dislodge the Turks, however, and their puppet (Radu Mihnea (1611-1616)) was able to establish a government in which he surrounded himself with high ranking officials of Greek (Phanariot) extraction.

Although most historians rate this period as one featuring a nonaggressive Ottoman Empire, the Porte's resolve to maintain order on the frontier and to maintain its hegemony was amply demonstrated. In October 1613, for example, a Turkish army obliged the Diet of Cluj to elect Gabriel Bethlen (Bethlen Gabor)(1613-1629) as their prince. Then, in August 1616, another Turkish force put an end to the Polish protectorship in Moldavia by defeating a Moldo-Polish army at Dracsani. These incidents are amply reported in Giurescu [62], in Macartney [96], and in Macdermott [97], where a lengthy explanation of the role of the Phanariot Greeks in both Greek and Romanian history may be found.

## TURKEY AND POLAND AT WAR

Except as already noted, Turkish interests lay elsewhere during this period. Internal revolt flared in 1610 when the Drusian prince, Fakhir-ad-Din, with the connivance of a number of western powers including the Holy See, moved to recapture Syria. This revolt, from which the west hoped to regain the Holy Land, was not put down until 1613. The following year, the Turks went to war with Poland in a struggle that was provoked by Polish Cossack raids upon Turkish Black Sea towns and by the Porte's desire to rid Moldavia and Wallachia of Polish influence. This conflict lasted seven years, until 1621; but little was accomplished as the Cossack raiding continued. Turkey did manage to regain its hegemony in the Romanian provinces, albeit tenuously. In addition to the war with the Poles, the Turks were forced to fight the Persians once again in 1616. That struggle lasted two years and marked a further deterioration in Ottoman power and influence.

## THE RULES OF MUSTAFA I, OSMAN II & MURAD IV

In 1617, Ahmed I died and was succeeded by his imbecile brother Mustafa I (1617-1618, 1622-1623), who had languished in the Seraglio dungeons for 14 years. Deprived as he was of his senses, Mustafa was also deprived of his throne within a year. He was replaced by a nephew, Osman II (1618-1622), who was Ahmed's 14-year-old son. Osman's reign was marked by a very serious Janissary revolt that led eventually to his assassination in 1622 at the hands of henchmen of the Sultana Valide. Upon Osman's death, Mustafa returned to the throne for one more year. Mustafa's life is recorded by Munir Aktepe [4], while an account of Osman's life may be found in an article by Sinasi Altundag [7]. Kinross [81] gives a scholarly and interesting account of the various changes in Ottoman rule that occurred during this brief period, pointing out the almost absolute power the Janissaries had achieved in Constantinople.

The new sultan of the Ottoman Empire was Murad IV (1623-1640). His relatively long rule was punctuated by a renewal of the conflict with Persia (1623-1638) and by another uprising among the Druse, when Fakhir-ad-Din returned from Italy where he had sought refuge after the last abortive revolt. This time he managed to take Syria but was eventually defeated, captured, and beheaded by the Turks in 1633.

## THE THIRTY YEARS' WAR

While these incidents were taking place, other events were taking place in Europe that were to have a direct effect on the Balkans. They began in July 1618, when Count Matthias of Thurn captured Krummau. This marked the beginning of the hostilities that became known as the Thirty Years' War. Within four months, Pilsen was taken by Protestant forces (21 November 1618). Over the next several months, a series of minor engagements took place that did much damage to the countryside but did very little to settle the issue. Then, in March 1619, Emperor Matthias died, vacating not only the Holy Roman throne he had held since 1612 but also the thrones of Hungary (1608) and Bohemia (1611).

It was five months before Ferdinand II (1619-1637) was elected emperor. At the same time, however, the Bohemian Protestants, disregarding imperial threats, elected Frederick, the Elector of the Palatine, to be their king. This election was declared invalid by imperial decree on 30 April 1620. When the Bohemian Protestants rejected the invalidation, war was declared. Before the empire could move, however, Frederick invaded Austria with the help of a group of insurgent Austrian nobles. By the end of the year, Bavarian and Spanish troops had entered the campaign under the imperial banner.

At the same time, Thurn had opened a campaign of his own into Austria (May-June 1619) that was supported by a Transylvanian army led by Gabriel Bethlen. The Transylvanians laid siege to Vienna but were driven off. Bethlen was able to seize most of the Habsburg region of Hungary, however, and the fighting went on sporadically until 1626. The main issues of this campaign were settled by the Treaty of Miklov (Nicholsburg) on 6 January 1622. The Austrians acknowledged Bethlen as the prince of Transylvania and ceded him seven counties of Habsburg Hungary.

In Moldavia during this same period, the voivode, Gaspar Gratiani (1619-1620), rose up against the Porte with the aid of the Poles but was unsuccessful in the last battle at Tutora (September 1620). Gratiani was killed by his own boyars as a result. The Poles were then obliged to acknowledge Turkish hegemony over Moldavia (9 October 1621).

In the main war, the Bavarians took Austria by the beginning of August 1620 and then invaded Bohemia where they routed a large army under King Frederick in the battle at White Hill (Weisser Berg), near Prague. Frederick and the Bohemians fled, and imperial forces entered and sacked Prague. Although the war continued for another 28 years, the theater of active operations shifted away from the frontiers of the Balkans. This did not mean, however, that peace settled over the peninsula.

## TATARS ATTACK FROM THE EAST

In the fall of 1623, for example, an invasion by Bugeac Tatars caused great destruction in Wallachia. The Bugeacs were a part of the larger Crimean Tatar population that inhabited, along with the Christian Cossacks, the vast steppe wilderness that lay between Turkey, Russia, and Poland. After the 15th century, these Tatars were generally vassals of the Ottomans and often carried out raids at the Porte's bidding. It must also be remembered, however, that raids for plunder were a way of life on the steppe. After some initial successes, the Tatars were driven off by Moldavian reinforcements who were able to recapture most of the booty held by the Tatars.

## RAKOCZY AND ANOTHER WAR WITH THE HABSBURGS

With the Tatars driven back onto the steppe, a period of relative calm settled upon the Balkans that lasted until 1645. In that year, Prince George Rakoczy (1630-1648) of Transylvania began a new war against the Habsburgs -- this time as the protector of Protestant rights in Hungary. Rakoczy defeated the Habsburgs; and, by the Treaty of Linz (16 December 1645), forced the Austrian crown to grant religious freedom to the Protestants.

## TRANSYLVANIA'S WAR WITH POLAND

Upon his death, Rakoczy's son, George II (1645-1660), assumed the throne. Macartney [96] points out that Sweden's Charles X (1654-1660) seduced George into believing that the throne of Poland would be his, if he supported the Swede in his Polish schemes. The subsequent Transylvanian expedition into Poland in January 1657 was a disaster. Although George was able to occupy Warsaw for a short time, he was eventually defeated by a force of Crimean Tatars dispatched by the Ottoman Porte, who had no previous notification of his Transylvanian vassal's intentions. Rakoczy escaped with his neck, but with most of forces scattered or destroyed. When Rakoczy returned home, he was greeted with the news that the weak Sultan, Mehmet IV (1648-1687), had allowed his Grand Vizier, Mohammed Koprulu (d.1661), to send a force to punish the him. The Turks took five years to accomplish their mission. Rakoczy had some successes with his mixed Transylvanian-Wallachian-Moldavian army, such as at Lippa (May 1657), but he was finally defeated by a combined Turkish-Tatar force at Czerny Ostrov on 22 July 1657.

Thereafter, the Turks attempted to replace the viovodes in all three principalities. In Transylvania a series of puppets was put on the throne, even though Rakoczy was still actively campaigning, using his estates in Hungary as his base of operations. In 1659, for example, he ran Akos (Acatiu) Barcsai (1659-1660) off the throne for a time, but the Turks rescued him and drove Rakoczy out of the country. In the process, the Turks plundered the lands. In the meantime, Rakoczy had appealed for Habsburg assistance, offering in return the cession of several border provinces. The Habsburgs did not respond in time, however, as Rakoczy was again defeated by a new Turkish force commanded by Ahmed Sidi Pasha, that had come out of Ottoman Hungary. After a defeat at Fenes (Floresti) on 22 May 1659, Rakoczy was besieged at Nagyvarad where he died of wounds received in earlier fighting. After a four month siege, the citadel fell, although an Austrian force was at the scene but refused to fight. In the other Romanian provinces, similar campaigns were carried out by the Turks against stiff resistance. In the end, the Turks were successful and both Wallachia and Moldavia were sacked.

These events are discussed in Macartney [96], and in Sugar [140]. Kinross [81], and Shaw [132] have sound accounts of the Turkish Koprulu period, while Cavid Baysun deals with the lives of Murad IV [19], and Mehmet IV [18]. Some of the documents involved in the selection of Barcsai as prince in Transylvania are found in Ismail Uzuncarsili's "Barcsai Akos-un Erdel Kiralligini ait bazi orijinal vesikalar" [157]. There is, in addition, an excellent article titled "Ottoman Empire Under Mehmet IV" [87], by A.N. Kurat, in volume five of the NEW CAMBRIDGE MODERN HISTORY [28]. For a somewhat different view, Tadeusz Nowak's "Polish Warfare Techniques in the 17th Century" [103] outlines Polish artillery employment against the Turks in the 1621 war, especially in the defense of Chocim Castle on the Dniester river. This is an extremely well documented article.

Although the Thirty Years' War was a western European conflict, except for a brief period in the opening phases, its impact on the Balkans, both during the fighting and afterward, makes it proper to mention a few of the numerous studies available so that the reader may gain the proper perspective of the period. The THIRTY YEARS' WAR [168], by C.V. Wedgewood, is excellent for this purpose. THE THIRTY YEARS' WAR: PROBLEMS OF MOTIVE, EXTENT, AND EFFECT [119], a volume edited by Theodore Rabb, contains a number of interesting essays on all aspects of the war. Another fine study of the war is Samuel R. Gardiner's THE THIRTY YEARS' WAR, 1618-1648 [60]. J.V. Polisensky's THE THIRTY YEARS' WAR [115] focusses on the conditions in Moravia and Bohemia as a reflection of the larger struggle in western Europe. Belder's article [20] on the war in NCMH is more than sufficient for the casual reader.

Other interesting works that deal with the period include Bistra Tsvetkova's L'EVOLUTION DU REGIME FEODAL TURC DU LA FIN DU XVI$^e$ JUSQU'AU MILIEU DU XVIII$^e$ SIECLE [149] that was published as a part of the ETUDES HISTORIQUES series in Sofia. "Certains aspects de la conquete des peuples balkaniques par les Turcs" [9] is also interesting. Carsten's article in NCMH on "The Empire After the Thirty Years' War" [29] is a good primer for the conditions that faced the continent at the beginning of the second half of the century. Gerard Tingas wrote an excellent study of Turko-French relations during this period in his LES RELATIONS DE LA FRANCE AVEC L'EMPIRE OTTOMAN DURANT LA PREMIERE MOITIE DU XVII$^e$ SIECLE [147]. Josef Zacher's account of Laszlo Bercenyi's role in the Rakoczy struggles against the Austrians is told in his BERCSENYI LASZLO, A RAKOCZI-SZABADSAGHARC KAPITANYA. FRANCIAORSZAG MARSALLYA. VALOGATOTT FORRASOK [177].

The Cretan campaign is discussed in volume 3 of TURK SILAHLI KUVVETLERI TARIHI [153], the official history of the Turkish armed forces. This study points out that it took the Venetians 24 years to conquer the island. Two well-done studies on the Ottoman army during this time are Cenzig Orhonlu's OSMANLI IMPARATORLUGUNDA ASERETLERI ISKAN TESEBUSU, 1691-1698 [108] that deals with the organization of the small, outlying detachments that were scattered all over the empire, and Ismail Uzuncarsili's OSMANLI DEVLETININ MERKEZ VE BAHRIYE TESKILATI [158]. Uzuncarsili discusses the central structure of the army and the organization of the Turkish navy.

The events in the Romanian principalities are outlined in the CHRONOLOGICAL HISTORY OF ROMANIA [62] and in Stoicescu's "Organizational Structure of the Armies of the Romanian Principalities in the 14th-18th Centuries" [137]. Other works having a bearing on the military history of the Balkans during this period include Paul Cernovodeanu's SOCIETATA FEUDALA ROMANESCA VAZUTA DE CALATORI STRAINI (SECOLELE XV-XVIII) [31]. This work describes the society of the various Romanian principalities during the 15th through the 18th centuries as perceived by foreign travelers. One of the four sections of this book deals with the political, social and military organizations found in each province. Another most interesting article is "Spatharus Nicolae Milescu About Some Asian Realities of the Second Half of the 17th Century" [75]. Published in RIHM in 1977, it is primarily important because of its excellent bibliographic material in the form of footnotes that deal with Milescu's leadership of the Wallachian army in 1660. The article also points out the keen interest taken by Peter the Great of Russia in the Milescu odyssey into Asia.

Two works that deal with popular movements during this period are Bistra Tsvetkova's KHAIDUTSTVOTO V BULGARSKITE ZEMI PREZ 15/18 VEK [151], the first volume of which was published in Sofia in 1971, and SARUHAN'DA ESKIYALIK VE HALK HAREKETLERI: XVII. ASIRDA [155], by Mohammed Cagatay Ulucay. In the first of these volumes, Tsvetkova attempts to prove a social significance in the brigandage that was rampant in Bulgaria from the 15th to the 18th centuries. The work falls short of its goal, however, but is still an important source of data on a major concern of the Porte. A concern that developed at a time when the Turks could ill-afford the numbers of troops necessary to control all of the chief axes of commercial and military traffic through the realm, let alone patrol the entire countryside as well. Stavrianos [135] sums up the banditry question in the most succinct terms. Ulucay's work is, on the other hand, generally more straightforward in its discussion of banditry and popular movements through the 17th century, especially as they occurred in the Ottoman's European possessions where bandits gained some measure of credibility by sharing parts of the loot with the local populace.

Another dimension is added to the study of these times in Helmut Lahrkamp's KRIEGSABENTEUER DES RITTMEISTERS HIERONYMUS CHRISTIAN VON HOLSTEIN, 1655-1666 [90] that presents a clear picture of the battlefields of the 17th century from one who fought upon them. Especially significant to this effort is Holsten's reflections upon the atrocities committed by Wallachian troops and other barbarities he observed.

## MONTECUCCOLI IN THE BALKANS

As a part of the general campaign for reclamation of control in the Balkans, the Ottomans moved to again pacify Transylvania after the election of Ioan (Janos) Kemeny (1661-1662) as prince following Barcsai's departure. Kemeny's reign was short as he immediately took to the field against the Turks. Even with the aid of Austrian forces under the command of Raimondo Montecuccoli, Kemeny was defeated. In the final battle, fought at Seleusul Mare (now a part of Oradea), in Transylvania, on 22 January 1662, Kemeny was killed. The Turks then installed another puppet, Mihai Apafi (1662-1690), on the Transylvanian throne.

## A NEW TURKISH CAMPAIGN INTO AUSTRIA

These incidents in Romania acted almost as a respite between larger conflicts. In 1663, the Turks mounted another invasion of Austria. The new Grand Vizier, Fazil Ahmed Koprulu, was intent upon taking Vienna; but the momentum of the advance was slowed and finally stopped by the stubborn defense of the fortress of Nove Zamky (Neuhaus). The fortress did not surrender until September 1663, and the Turks thereupon postponed further operations until the following year. When the new attack began, it brought a reaction from the Holy Roman Empire; and, on 1 August 1664, about 25,000 allied troops (of a total force estimated to be about 65,000) led by Montecuccoli, met about 100,000 Turks at a ford over the Raab river, near St. Gotthard Abbey. The Turks were defeated; but when they withdrew, the allies failed to pursue, possibly because of the disparity in size between the winners and the losers. Negotiations were soon underway, and this latest in the series of conflicts between the Turks and the Austrians was settled by a treaty signed at Vasvar on 11 August 1664.

This conflict is covered by Thomas Barker in his DOUBLE EAGLE AND CRESCENT: VIENNA'S SECOND TURKISH SIEGE AND ITS HISTORICAL SETTING [14] and in John Stoye's THE SIEGE OF VIENNA [138]. Two Turkish accounts may be found in Ferik Ahmed Muhtar Pasa's SENGOTARDA OSMANLI ORDUSU [101] and in SENGOTAR SEFERI, 1662-1664 [120], by Raif and Ekren. Information may also be found in Rudolph Kindinger's "Die Schlacht bei St. Gotthard am 1. August 1664" [80]; in Georg Wagner's "Raimund Montecuccoli, die Schlacht an der Raab und der Friede von Eisenburg (Vasvar)" [166]; in "Der 1. August 1664 bei St. Gotthard" [70], by Walter Hummelberger; and in Kurt Peball's DIE SCHLACHT BEI ST. GOTTHARD-MOGENDORF, 1664 [112]. Peball's work has a good bibliography. The life of Raimondo Montecuccoli is outlined in Luciano Tomassino's RAIMONDO MONTECUCCOLI, CAPITANO E SCRITTORE [148]. Thomas Barker's THE MILITARY INTELLECTUAL AND BATTLE: RAIMONDO MONTECUCCOLI AND THE THIRTY YEARS' WAR [15] might also be looked at for insight.

Information on the Transylvanian prince, Mihai Apafi I, may be found in Ladislas Makkai's HISTOIRE DE TRANSYLVANIE [98]. Denis Sinor's HISTORY OF HUNGARY [133] is very good in its coverage of this period. Max Immich's GESCHICHTE DES EUROPAISCHEN STAATENSYSTEM [71] has good coverage of the military side of the history of this period. Though published in 1905, it is still excellent.

## DISCONTENT IN HUNGARY AND THE SIEGE OF VIENNA

Following the peace at Vasvar, a wave of unrest spread across Hungary in a reaction to the unfavorable settlement the treaty afforded. Many Magyar nobles, dissatisfied with the Habsburg rule, conspired to revolt; but the movement did not gain sufficient strength and was easily crushed by the Austrians. One interesting, first-hand account of these events was reported in Vienna in 1671 and was subsequently published in English in London in 1692. The work is called THE HUNGARIAN REBELLION: OR, AN HISTORICAL ACCOUNT OF THE LATE WICKED PRACTICES OF THE THREE COUNTS, NADASDI, SERINI AND FRANGEPANI [13]. The most notable of these three conspirators, all of whom were executed, was Count Ference Nadasdi (1625-1671) who called for the national uprising against the Emperor. The "Serini" mentioned in this English form of the original German title is Count Miklos Zrinyi who led guerrilla-style operations against the Turks in the latest war. Frangepani was Zrinyi's relative who had backed him in the plot with the Turks after the the Holy Roman Emperor, Leopold I (1658-1705), had refused to appoint him palatine. Lessner [93] has a good account of this incident.

The revolts in Habsburg Hungary continued until 1682 and spread through most of the northern and western provinces. By the beginning of 1680, the leader of the guerrilla forces was Count Imre Thokoly, who had help from the Poles, French, and Turks. Soon, however, French assistance dissipated as Louis XIV tired of the affair. For a short time, Thokoly ruled major portions of Hungary and Transylvania causing a much greater deflation of Austrian prestige than any real increase in that of the Turks who had backed him. These uprisings, and recent Ottoman good fortune, led to resumption of war between the two great empires and to the great siege of Vienna. All of these events are discussed in great detail in Barker [14], Lengyel [91], Sinor [133], William Munson's THE LAST CRUSADE [102], and in the opening pages of John Stoye's THE SIEGE OF VIENNA [138].

The Turkish successes in the decades of the 1660s and the 1670s included a number of military victories, not the least of which was their defeat of the French and Venetians at Candia on Crete. This battle is the topic of W. Bigg's DER KAMPF VON CANDIA IN DEN JAHREN 1667-1669 [23]. The Turks also had limited success in the long war with Poland (1671-1677) and had, for all intents and purposes, defeated Imperial Russia in the first of the many conflicts that would follow. With these successes, perceived or real, Mehmet IV ordered his Grand Vizier, Kara Mustafa (who had been restored to his post in 1678) to prepare for war against Austria and Poland. By May 1683 the Turkish army, with Mehmet in personal (if not actual) command, had passed through Belgrad and was close upon the Austrian border. The Turkish force included a Transylvanian army commanded by Mihai Apafi and a Hungarian force under Imre Thokoly. In all the Ottoman army numbered about 200,000 men.

Following the course of the Danube, Kara Mustafa left a strong garrison at the confluence of the Danube and the Raab, at Gyor, and proceeded to cross into Austrian territory. The Austrians were ill-prepared to meet this attack; and the forces south of the river, under the command of Duke Charles V of Lorraine, were eventually required to withdraw north of the Danube after several sharp engagements. This left the approaches to the city open to the unopposed advance of the Turks. The Emperor, and his court, had long since fled the city for the safety of Passau, leaving behind the populace and a garrison under the command of Count Rudiger von Starhemberg that stood at about 15,000, plus some city militia. By

14 July, the Turkish investment of the city had begun and was complete within three days. From then until 12 September, they laid siege to Vienna but were hampered by a lack of sufficient numbers of heavy artillery pieces and by the stubborn Austrian defense.

The Turks were also harried at every turn by other forces in the area. Lorraine maintained contact with the Turks and prevented them from advancing farther up the Danube valley. By 1 September, the attacking force was reduced by almost one-half and was short of all supplies, including ammunition. Even though they had penetrated the Austrian defenses in several places, their steadily weakening condition made it impossible for them to clearly break into the city. A week later, the Ottomans received a second shock.

Having been already confronted by an enemy more determined than had been expected, Kara Mustafa was then informed that a Polish army was closing on the battle area and posed a direct threat to the Turkish camp. Poland's king, John III Sobieski, had honored his alliance with the Austrians and had marched an army of about 15,000 men over 200 miles in 15 days to a point where he could link up with Lorraine's forces. After much bickering between the two over who had overall command and after the diplomatic intervention of the Papal representative, Sobieski was named supreme commander of a mixed force of Austrians, Poles, Bavarians, and Saxons. This force is variously reported as having been up to 70,000 in strength. Even so, the Turks were still numerically stronger even if not stronger in effectiveness.

On 12 September 1683, Sobieski correctly evaluated the enemy's situation; and, instead of stopping for the night preparatory to attacking the next morning (as was the usual practice), he ordered his army to attack from the march. Thus, at 5 P.M., the general attack began and was coordinated with a sortie by the city's doughty defenders. At about 6 P.M., when Sobieski saw no immediate decision in sight, he led his Polish cavalry in a charge into the heart of Kara Mustafa's camp. The Turks fled, leaving their wounded and much of their equipment behind. Ottoman losses were extremely high. The remainder of the Turkish army was able to break contact only because Sobieski refused to pursue in the darkness. When the allies did take up the pursuit, they were able to clear much of northern Hungary of Ottoman influence. The following year, in March, Pope Innocent XI preached another crusade against the Ottoman; and a new Holy League was formed around the original membership of the empire, Poland, and Venice. Imperial Russia joined two years later in 1686.

In September 1686, Charles of Lorraine took Buda, the seat of Ottoman administration in Hungary. Then, in 1687, a 60,000-man army, jointly commanded by Charles and the Elector of Bavaria, met and defeated the Turks near Harkany (Nagyharsany), near the location of the former Battle of Mohacs that was fought in 1526. By September 1688, Belgrade had been taken by the allies; and much of the Serbian countryside had been cleared of Turkish troops. Thereafter, the fighting shifted into Transylvania where it continued for some time.

Romania had been deeply involved in the fighting up to this point with troops from all of the principalities participating in the siege of Vienna as a part of the Turkish army. As a result of these and other factors there were a number of internal alliances concluded among the Romanians that would be used in later times as a part of the basis for unification. The CHRONOLOGICAL HISTORY OF ROMANIA [62] maintains that even though the Romanians fought on the Turkish side, they maintained secret communications with the Austrians during the siege. Even so, the Turkish withdrawal left the Romanian lands open to attack by the Austrians and their allies. In 1686, Polish troops had entered Moldavia but had been driven off by Tatar forces allied with the Porte. Also, in 1686 (1 June), Transylvania was formally "acknowledged" by the Emperor and garrisoned with Austrian troops. Fifteen months later, under the terms of the Treaty of Blaj (27 October 1687), large tracts of Transylvanian land were placed under direct Austrian control.

## SLANKAMEN AND THE TREATY OF KARLOWITZ

Trouble broke out again in Transylvania when Mihai Apafi died. The Diet, with Austrian backing, elected Apafi's son as the hereditary heir to the throne. The Turks, on the other hand, nominated Thokoly. Obviously, a battle ensued in which the combined forces of Thokoly, the Turks, and some Wallachians defeated the Austrians at Zarnesti, near Brasov, on 11 August 1690. Thokoly was then put on the Transylvanian throne.

During the late summer and fall of 1690, the new Turkish Grand Vizier, Mustafa Koprulu, under orders of the sultan, Suleiman II (1687-1691), moved again into Serbian territory recapturing a number of strategically important points, including Belgrad. The following year, in August, the tide of battle turned once again and an Imperial army under Louis of Baden decisively defeated a Turkish-Transylvanian force led by Thokoly and Mustafa Koprulu at Slankamen (19 August 1691), a short distance from Belgrad. Over 20,000 Turks were reported killed in the engagement, including the Grand Vizier. The survivors fled the field leaving the Ottoman camp intact, along with its artillery.

For the next five years, sporadic fighting took place along the frontier. The Turkish force that had invaded Transylvania was expelled. This loss, coupled with the deaths of Koprulu and Suleiman, who died soon after the campaign began and the de facto loss of Hungary, all but eliminated Turkish presence in the north Balkans. There had been some Ottoman successes in the Aegean; but there was little to console the Porte in the Balkans, except possibly their show of stamina. In 1696, with Mustafa II (1695-1703) on the throne, the Turks again marched into the Danube valley and, after a short campaign, went into winter quarters. In the spring of 1697, Mustafa again took to the field where he was met and defeated at Zenta on the Tisza river by Prince Eugene of Savoy and an allied army. In this battle the Turkish army was nearly annihilated, and with its destruction the last real threat to Hungary ended.

Peace was finally achieved at Karlowitz on 26 January 1699. By the terms of the treaty, Austria took possession of Hungary and most of Transylvania. The Venetians were given Morea and much of the Dalmatian coastal area. Poland had the Podolian region returned, but Turkey managed to keep Serbia, especially the key city of Belgrad. The map of the Balkans was changed considerable and Austria had become the dominant power in Balkan affairs.

This long period of fighting is amply covered in the general literature on the Balkans, in addition to a number of specialized studies. The lives of the three Sultans who reigned during those times are covered in three articles in ISLAM ANSIKLOPEDISI: "Suleyman II" [89], by Bekir Kutukoglu; "Ahmed II" [17], by Cavid Baysum; and "II Mustafa" [107], by Cenzig Orhonlu. One eyewitness account of some of the events that transpired may be found in Sir Paul Rycault's THE HISTORY OF THE TURKS BEGINNING WITH THE YEAR 1679 . . . UNTIL THE END OF THE YEAR 1698 AND 1699 [129] that was published in 1700 following Rycault's tour as a English diplomat in Istanbul.

One account that helps explain French military personnel with the Ottoman forces is V.L. Tapie's LES RELATIONS ENTRE LA FRANCE ET L'EUROPE CENTRALE DE 1661 A 1715 [146]. An article titled "Timar" [46], written by J. Deny, and published in the ENCYCLOPEDIA OF ISLAM, outlines Turkish organization in 1683. George Kunitz' DIARIUM, WELCHES DER AM TURKISCHEN HOFF UND HERNACH BEYM VIZIER IN DER WIENISCHEN BELAGERUNG GEWESTER KAYSERB [86] describes life in a Turkish military camp. This work was produced in 1684.

Without question the best single work on the military aspects of these events is Thomas Barker's DOUBLE EAGLE AND CRESCENT [14], which may be supplemented with Munson's THE LAST CRUSADE [102]. Munson stresses the diplomatic side of the affair. Lessner's THE DANUBE [93] is the easiest to read and is full of those small details that add color to the otherwise awful business of war. Lord Kinross' work [81] adds a touch of elegance to the wealth of data that is available about this remarkable struggle. Sobieski's role in these affairs is amply covered in Otto Forst de Battaglia's JAN SOBIESKI, KONIG VON POLEN [183] and in Marian Kukiel's ZARYS HISTORII WOJSBOWOSCI [184].

One of the most exhaustive analyses of the printed sources relating to the 1683 siege of Vienna is found in Max Vansca's "Quellen und Geschichtesschreibung" [162], that is found in the 1911 edition of GESCHICHTE DER STADT WIEN. Albert Camesina's WIENS BEDRANGNIS IM JAHRE 1683 [27] and Kurt Koehler's DIE ORIENTALISCHE POLITIK LUDWIGS XIV., IHR VERHALTNIS ZUM TURKENKRIEG VON 1683 [83] both add distinctive elements to the story. Another work that should not be overlooked is Gunther Rothenberg's THE AUSTRIAN MILITARY BORDER IN CROATIA, 1522-1747 [127]. Professor Rothenberg is one of the very few western scholars who has specialized in the military history of southeastern Europe. Because of this and his excellent writing style, his works are unique and extremely important to the proper study of this subject.

There are two good works on the Augsburg Alliance. The first, in German, is Hans von Zwiedinech-Sudenhorst's DIE AUGSBURGER ALLIANZ VON 1686 [181]. The second is "La Dislocation de la Ligue d'Augsbourg et l'acheminement vers la Paix de Ryswick" [40], by the late French soldier-scholar Colonel Aime Constantini, which was presented in his honor at the 1981 Colloquy on Military History held at Paul Valery University in Montpellier, France.

THE SIEGES OF VIENNA BY THE TURKS, FROM THE GERMAN OF KARL AUGUST SCHIMMER AND OTHER SOURCES [54], translated and edited by the

Earl of Ellesmere in 1847, presents a number of interesting, first-hand accounts of the second siege as witnessed or assessed from the Austrian side. The English version of this work is often credited to Schimmer although the original manuscript was prepared by him in German. Another first-hand account, this time from the Turkish view, is found in the translation of the diary of the Master of Ceremonies of the Sultan's court entitled "Vakayi-i-Bec." This work is found in German under the title KARA MUSTAFA VOR WIEN: DAS TURKISCHE TAGEBUCH DE BELAGERUNG WIENS VERF. VOM ZEREMONIENMEISTER DER HOHEN PFORTE [85]. IKINCI VIYANA SEFERI, 1683 [143], by Necati Salim Tacan, deals with the Turkish perception of the expedition to Vienna, as does Asir Arkayin's "The Second Siege of Vienna (1683) and its Consequences" [10], which was published in English in issue number 46 of the REVUE INTERNATIONALE D'HISTOIRE MILITAIRE, by the Turkish Military History Commission in 1980. One should also look at Walter Sturminger's BIBLIOGRAPHIE UND IKONOGRAPHIE DER TURKENBELAGERUNGEN WIENS, 1529 U. 1693 [139] and at Nowak [103], for his Polish account of artillery employment at Vienna.

Akdes Kurat follows up his excellent article on "The Ottoman Empire Under Mehmed IV" [87], that was published in volume V of the NEW CAMBRIDGE MODERN HISTORY, with an equally important contribution in volume VI titled "The Retreat of the Turks, 1683-1730" [88]. This latter article traces not as much the Ottoman military withdrawals from the field of battle as the political and diplomatic retreats of an empire pulling in its horns in the face of the growing strength of the more united states of Europe and in the face of the growing Russian threat from the north.

Necati Salim Tacan's NIS - BELGRAD - SALANKAMEN - PETRO - VARADIN - LUGO TIMISVAR KUSATMA VE MEYDAN MUHAREBELERI, 1690-1696 [144] discusses the numerous battles that took place in the aftermath of the great siege as the two sides maneuvered for the most advantageous positions. PRINZ EUGEN VON SAVOYEN, EINE BIOGRAPHIE [24], which was published in five volumes, covers the long and illustrious career of the outstanding Imperial commander. Thomas M. Barker's volume [14] has an extensive bibliography that contains references to other memoires of the allied commanders in this great struggle. Barker's work on Montecuccoli [15] is important to the understanding of his part in the conflict. J.B. Wolf's THE EMERGENCE OF THE GREAT POWERS, 1685-1717 [175] gives a clear interpretation of the interrelationship between the Habsburg-Turkish war and the feud that went on between the Habsburgs and the Valois. This work has an excellent bibliography and good footnoting. Cenzig Orhonlu's OSMANLI IMPARATORLUGUNDA ASIRETLERI ISKAN TESEBBUSU, 1691-1698 [108] deals with the period of the frontier fighting that fitted between the two periods of main force combat.

Refik Abou El-Haj's article in the JOURNAL OF THE AMERICAN ORIENTAL SOCIETY titled "Ottoman Diplomacy of Karlowitz" [1] and M.R. Popovic's DER FRIEDE VON CARLOWITZ [117], which was published in 1893, are both good sources of information on the negotiations and the treaty that ended the fighting. Both Barker [14] and Munson [102]] also give this subject good treatment. So does Stavrianos in his THE BALKANS SINCE 1453 [135], that also has an excellent bibliography. Another interesting study is Giovanni Benaglia's AUSFUHRLICHE REIS-BESCHREIBUNG: VON WIEN NACH CONSTANTINOPEL [21]. This travel report was written in 1687 and gives a very clear picture of the regions through which the writer was guided. It is rich in the kind of detail that makes it easier to understand the effects of war at that time and place.

Traian Stoianovich's article on the "Factors in the Decline of Ottoman Society in the Balkans" [136] traces the antecedents of the fall to the period under discussion. Robert Gragger's TURKISCHEUNGARISCHE KULTURBEZIEHUNGEN [64] outlines the cultural impact of Ottoman occupation upon the Hungarians. Three other works that deal with the impact of the Turkish hegemony are E. Pittara's "Les Peuples que des Turcs ont amenes les Balkans" [114], T. Kowalski's "Les Turcs balkaniques" [84], and Sidney Fisher's "Ottoman Feudalism and Its Influence upon the Balkans" [56].

Among other sources useful to an understanding of this period is Bistra Tsvetkova's "Recherches sur le systeme d'affermage (Ittizam) dans l'Empire Ottoman au cours du XVI$^e$-XVIII$^e$ siecles par rapport aux contrees Bulgares" [152], that discusses the means used by the Ottomans to strengthen their rule over their widespread possessions. Tsvetkova looks at this subject in a slightly different perspective in LES INSTITUTIONS OTTOMANES EN EUROPE [150], as does Braun in his article "Turkenherrschaft und Turkenkampf bei den Balkanslawen" [25]. The efforts to settle the numerous nomadic tribes in the Ottoman Empire is outlined in Cenzig Orhonlu's OSMANLI IMPARATORLUGUNDA ASIRETLERI ISKAN TESEBUSU, 1691-1698 [108]. Although these activities did not deal directly with the Balkans, the indirect effects were felt there because of the Turkish dissipation of strength used in the effort and the fact that the Porte did actually attempt to settle some tribes in Rumelia. Tayyip Gokbilgim discusses this in his book RUMELI'DE YUKUKLER, TARTARLAR VE EVLAD-I FATIHAN [63] that was published in 1957. Ahmed Refik's TURK IDARESINDE BULGARESTAN (973-1255) [124] describes Bulgaria under Turkish rule from 1565 until 1840. Vicko Zmajevic looks at the sources available on the history of Albania during the 17th and 18th centuries in his QUELLEN UND MATERIALIEN ZUR ALBANISCHEN GESCHICHTE IM 17. UND 18. JAHREHUNDERT [178].

Another, most interesting work is RELATIILE ISTORICE DINTRE POPOARELE U.R.S.S. SI ROMINIA IN VEACURILE XV-INCEPUTUL CELUI DE AL XVIII-LEA [156]. This work was edited and published by the Soviet Academy of Sciences as a joint Soviet-Romanian effort. Despite the ridiculous title that suggests the Soviet Union existed as long ago as the 15th century, this work, the third of a series of volumes, is worth the ideological assault on the intelligence. The volume is printed in Romanian and Russian and contains 115 documents from the period 1673-1711, that include a number of interesting pieces of data. Not the least of these are the secret requests of various Romanian princes for Russian intervention against the Turkish overlordship. Some will see this volume, and the included documentation, as nothing more than a Soviet attempt at justifying Russian, and later Soviet, expansionism into the Balkans. Be that as it may, and the arguments are not without merit, the volume of documents, especially with the helpful notations, is worthwhile.

This question of Russo-Romanian relations is only one aspect of the much larger question of increasing interest in the Balkans that developed in the late 17th century. Without doubt, Russia was aware of the Balkans from much earlier times, as in the case of the

Kievan Prince Svyatoslav. But only after the assumption of the Imperial Russian throne by Peter I (1682-1725), was there any systematic involvement in the affairs of southeastern Europe.

By the mid-17th century, the foreign policy of Russia was aimed at breaking out of the isolation that had surrounded the country for centuries. At first these attempts were directed against the Baltic, where Russia found itself confronted by Sweden, and against Poland-Lithuania. In 1648, an uprising began in the Ukraine that was led by a Cossack, Bogdan Khmelnitsky. For three years the rebels plundered the Ukraine taking a heavy toll in lives. In 1651, fresh Polish troops were sent to clear out the rebels, who took that opportunity to appeal to Moscow for help. A war followed that was not settled until 1667 when the Ukraine east of the Dnieper, along with other strategic points, was annexed by the Tsar. The Cossacks were unhappy with the settlement and, because of internal disagreement, split into two groups -- one that favored the Russian overlordship, while the other favored the Ottomans who also laid claim to much of the annexed territory. This whole episode led to military conflict between Russia and the Turks in 1672-1676 and again in 1677-1681, from which Russia profitted at Polish expense and, to an almost equal degree, at Ottoman expense as well.

On the death of Feodar III (1676-1682), Russia was in the hands of Sophia, who ruled as regent. The half-sister of the young Peter, Sophia chose Prince Basil Golitsen as her foreign minister. It was Golitsen who put Russia on a collision course with the Ottoman Empire. In doing so, the Balkans were marked as the arena for more and even bloodier wars.

There are a number of good general histories that deal with Russia's emergence from isolation and especially with its relationships with the Balkans. Of special note in this regard are George Vernadsky's "On Some Parallel Trends in Russian and Turkish History" [163] and "Russia and Turkey, 1677-1681: The Treaty of Bakhchisaray" [104], by C.B. O'Brien, that appeared in 1953. Benedict Sumner's PETER THE GREAT AND THE OTTOMAN EMPIRE [142] begins its account with the last years of the 17th century but concentrates more on the 18th century. OCHERKI IZ ISTORII MALORUSSII V XVII V. [53] was published in 1899 and deals with problems in the Ukraine in the 17th century that were directly to affect the Balkans. Another indication of rising Russian power and influence in the Balkans may be found in LE PEUPLE SERBE ET SON EGLISE SOUS LA DOMINATION TURQUE [66] that points out the Serbian requests to Peter the Great to lift the Turkish yoke. Finally, PETER THE GREAT [106], edited by L. Jay Oliva, contains an excellent, albeit short, section on Peter's early confrontation with the Turks presaging the new century that was about to dawn. An even better choice is in Reinhard Wittram's PETER I, CZAR UND KAISER: GESCHICHTE PETERS DEN GROSSEN [191].

# BIBLIOGRAPHIC LISTING

1. Abou El-Haj, R.A. "Ottoman Diplomacy at Karlowitz." JAOS, LXXXVII (1967), 498-512.

2. Akdag, M. CELALI ISYANLARINDA BUYUK KACGUNLUK (1603-1606). Istanbul: 1969.

3. _____. "Genel Cizgileriyle XVII yuzyil Turkiye Tarihi." TAD, IV (1966), 201-247.

4. Aktepe, M. "Mustafa I." IA, VIII, 692-695.

5. Allmayer-Beck, J.C., & Lessing, E. DIE KAISERLICHEN KRIEGSVOLKER. VON MAXIMILIAN I. BIS PRINZ EUGEN, 1479-1718. Munich: 1978.

6. Almas, D. MIHAI VODA VITEAZUL. Bucharest: 1966.

7. Altundag, S. "Osman II." IA, IX, 443-448.

8. Anderson, R.C. NAVAL WARS OF THE LEVANT, 1558-1853. Princeton: 1952.

9. Angelov, D.S. "Certains aspects de la conquete des peuples balkaniques par les Turcs." BYZANTINOSLAVICA, XVII (1956), 220-275.

10. Arkayin, A. "The Second Siege of Vienna (1683) and Its Consequences." RIHM, 46 (1980), 107-119.

11. Arnakis, G.G. THE NEAR EAST IN MODERN TIMES. Vol. 1: THE OTTOMAN EMPIRE AND THE BALKANS TO 1900. New York & Austin: 1969.

12. Aston, T.H., ed. CRISIS IN EUROPE, 1550-1660. New York: 1965.

13. Ayres, P., trans. THE HUNGARIAN REBELLION: OR, AN HISTORICAL ACCOUNT OF THE LATE WICKED PRACTICES OF THE THREE COUNTS, NADASDI, SERINI AND FRANGEPANI. London: 1692.

14. Barker, T.M. DOUBLE EAGLE AND CRESCENT: VIENNA'S SECOND TURKISH SIEGE AND ITS HISTORICAL SETTING. Albany: 1967.

15. _____. THE MILITARY INTELLECTUAL AND BATTLE: RAIMONDO MONTECUCCOLI AND THE THIRTY YEARS' WAR. Albany: 1975.

16. Baysum, C. "Ahmed I." IA, I, 161-164.

17. _____. "Ahmed II." IA, I, 164-165.

18. _____. "Mehmet IV." IA, VII, 547-557.

19. _____. "Murad IV." IA, VIII, 625-647.

20. Belder, E.A. "The Thirty Years' War." NCMH IV. Cambridge: 1970.

21. Benaglia, G. AUSFUHRLICHE REISEBESCHREIBUNG: VON WIEN NACH CONSTANTINOPEL. Frankfurt: 1687.

22. Betts, R.R. "The Habsburg Lands." NCMH V. Cambridge: 1961.

23. Bigg, W. DER KAMPF VON CANDIA IN DEN JAHREN 1667-1669. Berlin: 1889.

24. Braubach, M. PRINZ EUGEN VON SAVOYEN, EINE BIOGRAPHIE. 5 vols. Vienna: 1963-1965.

25. Braun, M. "Turkenherrschaft und Turkenkampf bei den Balkanslawen." WaG, VI (1940), 124-139.

26. Bromley, J.S., ed. THE RISE OF GREAT BRITAIN AND RUSSIA, 1688-1715/25. Vol. 6 in NCMH. Cambridge: 1970.

27. Camesina, A. WIENS BEDRANGNIS IM JAHRE 1683. Vienna: 1865.

28. Carsten, F.L., ed. THE ASCENDANCY OF FRANCE, 1648-88. Vol. 5 in NCMH. Cambridge: 1961.

29. _____. "The Empire after the Thirty Years' War." NCMH V. Cambridge: 1961.

30. Celebi, E. SEYAHATNAME. 10 vols. Istanbul: 1928-1938.

31. Cernovodeanu, P. SOCIETATA FEUDALA ROMANESCA VAZUTA DE CALATORI STRAINI (SECOLELE XV-XVIII). Bucharest: 1973.

32. Cesar, J., ed. OSMANSKA MOC VE STREDNI A JIHOVYCHODNI EVROPE V 16.-17. STOLETI. ACTA of the 9th Joint Conference of the Czechoslovak-Yugoslav Historical Committee. Prague: 1978.

33. Chandler, D.G. ATLAS OF MILITARY STRATEGY. New York: 1980.

34. Clark, G.N., Sir, et al, Advisory Comm. THE NEW CAMBRIDGE MODERN HISTORY. 14 vols. Cambridge: 1957-1970.

35. _____. THE SEVENTEENTH CENTURY. New York: 1960.

36. Clarkson, J.D. A HISTORY OF RUSSIA. 2nd ed. New York: 1969 [1961].

37. Cleator, P.E. WEAPONS OF WAR. New York: 1968.

38. Colby, E. MASTERS OF MOBILE WARFARE. Princeton: 1943.

39. Coles, P. THE OTTOMAN IMPACT ON EUROPE. LECS. London: 1968.

40. Constantini, A. "La Dislocation de la Ligue d'Augsbourg et l'acheminement vers la Paix de Ryswick." Paper presented (postumously) at Colloquy of CIHM. Montpellier: 1981.

41. Cooper, J.P., ed. THE DECLINE OF SPAIN AND THE THIRTY YEARS' WAR, 1609-48/59. Vol. 4 in NCMH. Cambridge: 1970.

42. _____. "Sea Power." NCMH IV. Cambridge: 1970.

43. Coquelle, P. HISTOIRE DU MONTENEGRO ET DE LA BOSNIA. Paris: 1895.

44. Corvisier, A. ARMEES ET SOCIETES EN EUROPE DE 1494 A 1789. Paris: 1976. Found in English with trans. by Abigail T Siddall. Bloomington: 1979.

45. Delbruck, H. GESCHICHTE DER KRIEGSKUNST IM RAHMEN DER POLITISCHEN GESCHICHTE. Berlin: 1920.

46. Deny, J. "Timar." EI, VI:2 Leyden: 1929.

47. Djevad Bey, A. ETAT MILITAIRE OTTOMAN DEPUIS LA FOUNDATION DE L'EMPIRE JUSQU'D NOS JOURS. Vol. 1: LE CORPS DE JANISSAIRES DEPUIS SA CREATION JUSQU'D SA SUPPRESSION. Constantinople & Paris: 1882.

48. Doyle, W. THE OLD EUROPEAN ORDER, 1660-1800. SOHMW. Oxford: 1978.

49. Dunn, R.S. THE AGE OF RELIGIOUS WARS. 2nd ed. NHME. New York: 1979 [1970].

50. Dupuy, R.E., & Dupuy, T.N. THE ENCYCLOPEDIA OF MILITARY HISTORY. Rev. ed. New York: 1977.

51. Dupuy, T.N. MILITARY LIFE OF GUSTAVUS ADOLPHUS: FATHER OF MODERN WAR. New York: 1970.

52. Eliot, C., Sir. TURKEY IN EUROPE. London: 1965 [1900].

53. Einhorn, V. OCHERKI IZ ISTORII MALORUSSII V XVII V. Moscow: 1899.

54. Ellesmere, Earl of., ed. & trans. THE SIEGES OF VIENNA BY THE TURKS, FROM THE GERMAN OF KARL AUGUST SCHIMMER AND OTHER SOURCES. London: 1847. Sometimes listed under the name of Karl August Schimmer.

55. Finlay, G. HISTORY OF GREECE, FROM ITS CONQUEST BY THE ROMANS TO THE PRESENT DAY, B.C. 164 TO A.D. 1864. 7 vols. New revised edition by H.F. Tozer. Oxford: 1877.

56. Fisher, S.N. "Ottoman Feudalism and Its Influence Upon the Balkans." HISTORIAN, XV (Autumn, 1952), 3-22.

57. France. Les Archives Nationales. Etat general des fonds. L'ANCIEN REGIME. T.I Paris, la Documentation Francaise. Series K. Paris: 1978.

58. Fraser, C., trans. ANNALS OF THE TURKISH EMPIRE FROM 1591-1659.
    2 vols. London: 1832-1836.

59. Fuller, J.F.C. A MILITARY HISTORY OF THE WESTERN WORLD. 3 vols.
    New York: 1954-1955.

60. Gardiner, S.R. THE THIRTY YEARS' WAR, 1618-1648. New York:
    1949.

61. Gibb, H.A.R., Sir, and Bowen, H. ISLAMIC SOCIETY AND THE WEST:
    A STUDY OF THE IMPACT OF WESTERN CIVILIZATION ON MOSLEM
    CULTURE. Vol. 1: PROVINCIAL AND MILITARY ORGANIZATION.
    London & New York: 1950.

62. Giurescu, C, et al., eds. CHRONOLOGICAL HISTORY OF ROMANIA.
    Bucharest: 1972.

63. Gokbilgim, T. RUMELI'DE YUKUKLER, TARTARLAR VE EVLAD-I FATIHAN.
    Istanbul: 1957.

64. Gragger, R. "Turkisch-ungarische Kulturbeziehungen."
    LITERATURDENKMALER AUS UNGARN TURKENZEIT. Berlin: 1927.

65. Grant, A.J. A HISTORY OF EUROPE, 1494-1610. New York: 1951.

66. Hadrovics, L. LE PEUPLE SERBE ET SON EGLISE SOUS LA DOMINATION
    TURQUE. Paris: 1947.

67. Hale, J.R. "Armies, Navies, and the Art of War." NCMH III.
    Cambridge: 1968.

68. Heer, F. THE HOLY ROMAN EMPIRE. Trans. by Janet Sondhiemer. New
    York & Washington: 1968 [1967].

69. Heppell, M., & Singleton, F.B. YUGOSLAVIA. New York: 1951.

70. Hummelberger, W. "Der 1. August 1664 bei St. Gotthard."
    TRUPPENDIENST, IV (1964), 309-312.

71. Immich, M. GESCHICHTE DES EUROPAISCHEN STAATENSYSTEM. Munich &
    Berlin: 1905.

72. Inalcik, H. "Ottoman Methods of Conquest." SI, II (1954),
    103-129.

73. _____. THE OTTOMAN EMPIRE: THE CLASSICAL AGE. Trans. by
    Norman Itzowitz & Colin Imber. London & New York: 1973.

74. Iorga, N. ISTORIA LUI MAHAI VITEAZUL. Bucharest: 1970.

75. Iosipescu, S. "Spatharus Nicholae Milescu About Some Asian
    Realities in the Second Half of the 17th Century." RIHM,
    36 (1977), 218-227.

76. Jessup, J.E., & Coakley, R.W. A GUIDE TO THE STUDY AND USE OF
    MILITARY HISTORY. Washington: 1979.

77. Kann, R.A. A HISTORY OF THE HABSBURG EMPIRE, 1526-1918.
Berkeley: 1974.

78. Kann, R.A., & David, Z. THE PEOPLES OF THE EASTERN HABSBURG
LANDS, 1526-1918. HECE 6. Seattle & London: 1982.

79. Khalifeh, H. THE HISTORY OF THE MARITIME WARS OF THE TURKS.
Trans. by James Mitchell. London: 1831.

80. Kindinger, R. "Die Schlacht bei St. Gotthard am 1. August 1664.
Ein Wurdigungsversuch der Feldherrnkunst Montecuccolis
unter neuen Gesichtpunkten." ZHVS (1957), 145-155.

81. Kinross, J.P.D. Balfour, Lord. THE OTTOMAN CENTURIES: THE RISE
AND FALL OF THE TURKISH EMPIRE. London: 1977.

82. Kissling, H.J., ed. BEITRAGE ZUR KENNTNIS THRAKIENS IM 17.
JAHRHUNDERT. Weisbaden: 1956.

83. Koehler, K. DIE ORIENTALISCHE POLITIK LUDWIGS XIV., IHR
VERHALTNIS ZUM TURKENKRIEG VON 1683. Leipzig: 1907.

84. Kowalski, T. "Les Turcs balkaniques." RIEB, IV (1936), 420-430.

85. Kreutel, R., trans. KARA MUSTAFA VOR WIEN: DAS TURKISCHE
TAGEBUCH DE BELAGERUNG WIENS VERF. VOM ZEREMONIENMEISTER
DER HOHEN PFORTE. In OSMANISCHE GESCHICHTESCHREIBER No. 1.
Graz, Vienna & Cologne: 1955.

86. Kunitz, G.C. DIARIUM, WELCHES DER AM TURKISCHEN HOFF UND
HERNACH BEYM VIZIER IN DER WIENISCHEN BELAGERUNG GEWESTER
KAYSERB. Vienna: 1684.

87. Kurat, A.N. "The Ottoman Empire Under Mehmed IV." NCMH, V.
Cambridge: 1961.

88. _____. "The Retreat of the Turks, 1683-1730." NCMH, VI.
Cambridge: 1970.

89. Kutukoglu, B. "Suleyman II." IA, XI, 155-170.

90. Lahrkamp, H., ed. KRIEGSABENTEUER DES RITTMEISTERS HIERONYMUS
CHRISTIAN VON HOLSTEIN, 1655-1666. Vol. 6 in QUELLEN UND
STUDIEN ZUR GESCHICHTE DES OSTLICHEN EUROPA. Wiesbaden:
1971.

91. Lengyel, E. 1000 YEARS OF HUNGARY. New York: 1958.

92. Leo, M. LA BULGARIE ET SON PEUPLE SOUS LA DOMINATION OTTOMANE.
Sofia: 1949.

93. Lessner, E.C., & Lessner, A.M.L. THE DANUBE: THE DRAMATIC
HISTORY OF THE GREAT RIVER AND THE PEOPLE TOUCHED BY ITS
FLOW. Garden City: 1961.

94. Loebl, A. ZUR GESCHICHTE DES TURKENKRIEGES VON 1593-1606. 2
vols. Prague: 1899-1904.

95. Lukinich, I. ERDELY TERULETI VALTOZASAI A TOROK HODITAS KORABAN 1541-1711. Budapest: 1918.

96. Macartney, C.A. HUNGARY, A SHORT HISTORY. Chicago: 1962.

97. Macdermott, M. A HISTORY OF BULGARIA, 1393-1885. London: 1962.

98. Makkai, L. HISTOIRE DE TRANSYLVANIE. Paris: 1946.

99. Mamatey, V.S. RISE OF THE HABSBURG EMPIRE, 1526-1815. New York: 1971.

100. McMunn, G.F., Sir. GUSTAVUS ADOLPHUS, THE NORTHERN HURRICANE. London: 1930.

101. Muhtar Pasha, F.A. SENGOTARDA OSMANLI ORDUSU. Istanbul: 1908.

102. Munson, W.B. THE LAST CRUSADE. Dubuque: 1969.

103. Nowak, T. "Polish Warfare Technique in the 17th Century." MILITARY TECHNIQUE POLICY AND STRATEGY. Edited by Witold Bieganski. Warsaw: 1976.

104. O'Brien, C.B. "Russia and Turkey, 1677-1681: The Treaty of Bakchisaray." RR, XI (1953), 259-268.

105. Ogg, D. EUROPE IN THE SEVENTEENTH CENTURY. 8th ed. New York: 1960.

106. Oliva, L.J., ed. PETER THE GREAT. In the GREAT LIVES OBSERVED series. Englewood Cliffs: 1970.

107. Orhonlu, C. "II Mustafa." IA, VIII, 695-700.

108. _____. OSMANLI IMPARATORLUGUNDA ASIRETLERI ISKAN TESEBUSU, 1691-1698. Istanbul: 1963.

109. Panitescu, P.P. MIHAI VITEAZUL. Bucharest: 1936.

110. Parry, V.J. "The Ottoman Empire, 1566-1617." NCMH III. Cambridge: 1968.

111. _____. "The Ottoman Empire, 1617-48." NCMH IV. Cambridge: 1970.

112. Peball, K. DIE SCHLACHT BEI ST. GOTTHARD-MOGENDORF, 1664. MS 1. Vienna: 1964.

113. Pieri, P. GUERRA E POLITICA NEGLI SCRITTORI ITALIANI. Milan: 1952.

114. Pittara, E. "Les peuples que des Turcs ont amenes dans les Balkans." RIEB, II, (1935), 195-200.

115. Polisensky, J.V. THE THIRTY YEARS' WAR. Trans. by Robert Evans. Berkeley: 1971.

116. _____. DER KRIEGE UND DIE GESELLSCHAFT IN EUROPA, 1618-1648. Vienna, Cologne, Bohlau & Graz: 1971.

117. Popovic, M.R. DER FRIEDE VON CARLOWITZ. Leipzig: 1893.

118. Rabb, T.K. THE STRUGGLE FOR STABILITY IN EARLY MODERN EUROPE. New York: 1975.

119. _____., ed. THE THIRTY YEARS' WAR: PROBLEMS OF MOTIVE, EXTENT, AND EFFECT. PEC. Boston: 1967.

120. Raif (fnu), & Ekrem (fnu). SENGOTAR SEFERI, 1662-1664. Istanbul: 1934.

121. Ramsay, G.D. "The Austrian Habsburgs and the Empire." NCMH III. Cambridge: 1968.

122. Ranke, L. von. THE OTTOMAN AND SPANISH EMPIRES IN THE SIXTEENTH AND SEVENTEENTH CENTURIES. London: 1843.

123. Reddaway, W.F. HISTORY OF EUROPE, 1610-1715. New York: 1948.

124. Refik, A. TURK IDARESINDE BULGARESTAN (973-1255). Istanbul: 1933.

125. Riasonovsky, N.V. A HISTORY OF RUSSIA. 2nd ed. New York: 1969.

126. Ropp, T. "Military History to the End of the Eighteenth Century." GSUMH. Washington: 1979.

127. Rothenberg, G.E. THE AUSTRIAN MILITARY BORDER IN CROATIA, 1522-1747. ISSS. Urbana: 1961.

128. Roy, I. "Les forces armees de l'Angleterre et les traites d'alliance - 1604-1649." Paper presented at Colloquy of CIHM. Montpellier: 1981.

129. Rycault, P., Sir. THE HISTORY OF THE TURKS BEGINNING WITH THE YEAR 1679 . . . UNTIL THE END OF THE YEAR 1698 AND 1699. 2 vols. London: 1700.

130. _____. THE HISTORY OF THE TURKISH EMPIRE FROM THE YEAR 1623 TO THE YEAR 1677. London: 1680.

131. Seton-Watson, R.W. A HISTORY OF THE ROUMANIANS; FROM ROMAN TIMES TO THE COMPLETION OF UNITY. Cambridge: 1934.

132. Shaw, S.J. HISTORY OF THE OTTOMAN EMPIRE AND MODERN TURKEY. Vol. 1: EMPIRE OF THE GAZIS: THE RISE AND DECLINE OF THE OTTOMAN EMPIRE, 1280-1808. CAMBRIDGE & NEW YORK: 1976.

133. Sinor, D. HISTORY OF HUNGARY. New York: 1961.

134. Spaulding, O.L., et al. A STUDY OF MILITARY METHODS FROM THE EARLIEST TIMES. New York: 1925.

135. Stavrianos, L.S. THE BALKANS SINCE 1453. New York: 1958.

136. Stoianovich, T. "Factors in the Decline of Ottoman Society in the Balkans." SR, XXI No. 4 (December 1962), 623-632.

137. Stoicescu, N. "Organizational Structure of the Armies in the Romanian Principalities in the 14th-18th Centuries." ARS. Bucharest: 1980.

138. Stoye, J. THE SIEGE OF VIENNA. London: 1964.

139. Sturminger, W. BIBLIOGRAPHIE UND IKONOGRAPHIE DER TURKEN BELAGERUNGEN WIENS 1529 U. 1693. Graz & Cologne: 1955.

140. Sugar, P.F. SOUTHEASTERN EUROPE UNDER OTTOMAN RULE, 1354-1804. HECE 5. Seattle: 1977.

141. Sugar, P.F., & Treadgold, D.W. HISTORY OF EAST CENTRAL EUROPE. 11 vols. Seattle & London: 1975-.

142. Sumner, B.H. PETER THE GREAT AND THE OTTOMAN EMPIRE. Hamden: 1965.

143. Tacan, N.S. IKINCI VIYANA SEFERI, 1693. Istanbul: 1945.

144. _____. NIS-BELGRAD-SALANKAMEN-PETRO-VARADIN-LUGO TIMISVAR KUSATMA VE MEYDAN MUHAREBELERI, 1690-1696. Istanbul: 1939.

145. Tapie, V.L. "The Habsburg Lands, 1618-57." NCMH IV. Cambridge: 1970.

146. _____. LES RELATIONS ENTRE LA FRANCE ET L'EUROPE CENTRALE DE 1661 A 1715. 2 vols. Paris: 1958.

147. Tingas, G. LES RELATIONS DE LA FRANCE AVEC L'EMPIRE OTTOMAN DURANT LA PREMIERE MOITIE DE XVII$^e$ SIECLE. Toulouse: 1942.

148. Tomassino, L. RAIMONDO MONTECUCCOLI, CAPITANO E SCRITTORE. Rome: 1978.

149. Tsvetkova, B.A. L'EVOLUTION DU REGIME FEODAL TURC DU LA FIN DU XVI$^e$ JUSQU'AU MILIEU DU XVIII$^e$ SIECLE. Sofia: 1960.

150. _____. LES INSTITUTIONS OTTOMANES EN EUROPE. Wiesbaden: 1978.

151. _____. KHAIDUTSTVOTO V BULGARSKITE ZEMI PREZ 15/18 VEK. Vol. 1. Sofia: 1971.

152. _____. "Recherches sur le systeme d'affermage (Ittizam) dans l'Empire Ottoman au cours XVI$^e$-XVIII$^e$ siecles par rapport aux contrees bulgares." RO, XXVII (1964), 111-132.

153. Turkey. Department of War History. TURK SILAHLI KUVVETLERI TARIHI. Vol. 3: GIRIT SEFERI (1645-1669). Edited by K. Yukep. Ankara: 1977.

154. Tveritinova, A. VOSSTANIYE KARA YAZIDJI-DELI CHASANA VE TURTSII 1599-1603. Moscow: 1964.

155. Ulucay, M.C. SARUHAN'DA ESKIYALIK VE HALK HAREKETLERI: XVII. ASIRDA. Istanbul: 1944.

156. USSR. RELATIILE ISTORICE DINTRE POPOARELE U.R.S.S. SI ROMINIA IN VEACURILE XV-INCEPUTUL CELUI DE AL XVIII-LEA. Vol. 3. Moscow: 1970.

157. Uzuncarsili, I.H. "Barcsay Akos-un Erdel Kiralligini ait bazi orijinal vesikalar." TD, V (1952), 51-68.

158. _____. OSMANLI DEVLETININ MERKEZ VE BAHRIYE TESKILATI. Ankara: 1948.

159. _____. OSMANLI TARIHI. 4 vols. Ankara: 1947-1960.

160. Vacalopoulis, A. THE GREEK NATION, 1453-1669. New Brunswick: 1976.

161. Van Creveld, M.L. SUPPLYING WAR: LOGISTICS FROM WALLENSTEIN TO PATTON. New York: 1977.

162. Vansca, M. "Quellen und Geschichtesschreibung." GSW, No. 1 (1911), 1-108.

163. Vernadsky, G. "On Some Parallel Trends in Russian and Turkish History." TCAAS, XXXVI (July 1945), 25-36.

164. Volkl, E. DAS RUMANISCHE FURSTENTUM MOLDAU UND DIE OSTSLAVEN IM 15. BIS 17. JAHRHUNDERT. PEEI 42. Wiesbaden: 1975.

165. Wagner, E. EUROPEAN WEAPONS AND WARFARE, 1618-1648. London: 1979.

166. Wagner, G. "Raimund Montecuccoli, die Schlacht an der Raab und der Friede von Eisenberg (Vasvar)." OGL, VIII No. 5 (May 1964), 201-221.

167. Wandruszka, A. THE HOUSE OF HABSBURG: SIX HUNDRED YEARS OF A EUROPEAN DYNASTY. Trans. by C. & H. Epstein. Garden City: 1964.

168. Wedgewood, C.V. THE THIRTY YEARS' WAR. New York: 1961.

169. Weissmann, N. LES JANASSAIRES, ETUDE DE L'ORGANIZATION MILITAIRE DES OTTOMANS. Paris: 1938.

170. Wernham, R.B., ed. COUNTER-REFORMATION AND PRICE REVOLUTION 1559-1610. NCMH. Cambridge: 1968.

171. Wijn, J.W. "Military Forces and Warfare, 1610-1648." NCMH IV. Cambridge: 1970.

172. Willey, B. THE SEVENTEENTH CENTURY BACKGROUND. New York: 1953.

173. Williams, E.N. THE ANCIEN REGIME IN EUROPE: GOVERNMENT AND SOCIETY IN THE MAJOR STATES, 1648-1789. New York: 1980.

174. Wilson, C. THE TRANSFORMATION OF EUROPE, 1558-1648. Berkeley: 1976.

175. Wolf, J.B. THE EMERGENCE OF THE GREAT POWERS, 1685-1715. New York: 1951.

176. Wright, Q. THE STUDY OF WAR. London & Chicago: 1965 [1945].

177. Zacher, J. BERCSENYI LASZLO, A RAKOCZI-SZABADSAGHARC KAPITANYA. FRANCIAORSZAG MARSALLYA. VALOGATOTT FORRASOK. Vaja: 1979.

178. Zmajevic, V. QUELLEN UND MATERIALIEN ZUR ALBANISCHEN GESCHICHTE IM 17. UND 18. JAHREHUNDERT. 2 vols. Wiesbaden: 1975-1979.

179. Zook, D.H., & Higham, R. A SHORT HISTORY OF WARFARE. New York: 1966.

180. Zwiedineck-Sudenhorst, H. von. DEUTSCHE GESCHICHTE IM ZEITRAUM DER GRUNDUNG DES PREUSSISCHEN KONIGTUMS. 2 vols. Stuttgart: 1890-1894.

181. _____. DIE AUGSBURGER ALLIANZ VON 1686. Vienna: 1890.


ADDITIONS


182. Klyuchevski, V. KURS RUSSKOI ISTORII. 5 vols. Moscow: 1937 [1921-1923].

183. Forst de Battaglia, O. JAN SOBIESKI, KONIG VON POLEN. Einseldeln: 1946.

184. Kukiel, M. ZARYS HISTORII WOJSKOWOSCI. 5th ed. London: 1949.

185. Anderson, R.C. "The First Russian Fleet, 1695-1711." JRUSI LXI:441 (February 1916), 41-46.

186. Scammell, G.V. THE WORLD ENCOMPASSED: THE FIRST EUROPEAN MARITIME EMPIRES, c, 800-1650. Berkeley: 1981.

187. Tushin, Y.P. RUSSKOE MOREPLAVANIE NA KASPIISKOM, AZOVSKOM I CHERNOM MORIAKH, (XVII VEK). Moscow: 1978.

188. Elagin, S.I. ISTORIA RUSSKOGO FLOTA: PERIOD AZOVSKII. St. Petersburg: 1864.

189. Viskovatov, A.V. KRATKII ISTORICHESKII OBZOR MORSKIKH PODKHODOV RUSSKIKH I MOREKHODSTVA DO ISKHODA XVII STOLETII. St. Petersburg: 1964.

190. Cipolla, C. GUNS, SAILS AND EMPIRE: TECHNOLOGICAL INNOVATION AND THE EARLY PHASES OF EUROPEAN EXPANSION, 1400-1700. New York: 1966 [c.1965].

191. Wittram, R. PETER I, CZAR UND KAISER: ZUR GESCHICHTE PETERS DEN GROSSEN. Gottingen: 1964.

CHAPTER FIVE

THE 18TH CENTURY

GENERAL BACKGROUND

The 18th century has been characterized as the time of
colonial rivalry between England and France for domination of the
New World and as the "Age of Enlightenment." It was also an age of
revolution; and, because of this, it was also a period of stagnation
in military technological development. Theodore Ropp, in his WAR IN
THE MODERN WORLD [221], explains this by pointing out that "monarchs
could not reorganize their potential resources without social
revolutions which would be more dangerous to themselves than their
enemies." Put in other terms, it was a period that called for
"status quo" in all things, especially among the European monarchs
who were more interested in retaining their crowns, and their heads,
than they were in promulgating reforms that would lift some of the
burden from the shoulders of their common subjects.

Of course, to say that these fears of social upheaval so
dominated the times that there were no modifications to military
doctrine and technology would be incorrect. Many significant changes
occurred throughout the century in both land and sea warfare that
affected the outcomes of the numerous conflicts that took place.
These changes may be best appreciated by reading chapter VIII in
Zook and Higham [318] and the introduction to chapters XV and XVI in
Dupuy [78].

The development of a professional army loyal to the king is
also a manifestation of the period from the mid-17th to almost the
end of the 18th centuries. Quincy Wright [312] discusses this point
briefly but succinctly. Spaulding, Nickerson, and Wright [250] note
that the chief developments in defense and in the construction of
fortifications during the 18th century were directly linked to the
establishment of the professional army. Other interesting works that
discuss these factors are John W. Wright's article in the AMERICAN
HISTORICAL REVIEW, "Sieges and Customs of War at the Opening of the
Eighteenth Century" [311]; David Chandler's "The Art of War on Land"
[53]; John Stoye's "Soldiers and Civilians" [257]; and "Armies and
Navies" [45], by Bromley and Ryan. All of these works are in volume
VI of the NEW CAMBRIDGE MODERN HISTORY [42] that was edited by J.S.
Bromley. Professor Chandler's article has a brief discussion of the
military situation in the Balkans, while Stoye's well-done article
does much to capture the feeling of the times. Bromley and Ryan
point out the rapid development of the Russian navy under Peter the
Great (1692-1725), a growth that eventually constituted a threat
against the Black Sea forces of the Ottoman Empire. Volume VII [162]
in the NCMH series is devoted to the period 1713-1763 and contains
"The Armed Forces and the Art of War" [219] by Professor Eric Robson
of the University of Manchester. This article is so well prepared

that it may serve as a general, short reference on the military history of that crucial 50-year period.

Volume VIII [98] of the NCMH deals primarily with the American and French Revolutions but does contain entries that deal with general military events in Europe. Volume IX [65] covers the period 1793-1830; but, as those last seven years of the 18th century are so important, the articles by N.H. Gibbs [93] and C.C. Lloyd [163] are of value. THE AGE OF RELIGIOUS WARS, 1550-1715 [77], by Richard Dunn, ends with the beginning decades of the century but is well worth reading for the insights into the future that it offers. Similarly, R.G. Albion's FORESTS AND SEA POWER [5] presents a chapter on the mid-century that is an interesting account of the factors that allowed for the development of naval power. Another excellent work on naval affairs during this period is Paul Kennedy's THE RISE AND FALL OF BRITISH NAVAL MASTERY [330].

THE HISTORY OF 18TH-CENTURY EUROPE

There are many good sources on the general history of Europe in this century. Isser Woloch's EIGHTEENTH CENTURY EUROPE: TRADITION AND PROGRESS [310] is a good place to start. EUROPE IN THE EIGHTEENTH CENTURY [307], by R.J. White, provides excellent analytic coverage. Another excellent source are the volumes in Harper and Row's fine series, THE RISE OF MODERN EUROPE [153] edited by Professor William L. Langer. Langer, a distinguished Coolidge professor of history at Harvard, served as the director of the Research and Analysis Branch of OSS in World War II before resuming his academic career. Five of the volumes in this series deserve individual mention: John B. Wolf's THE EMERGENCE OF THE GREAT POWERS, 1685-1715 [309]; Penfield Roberts' THE QUEST FOR SECURITY, 1715-1740 [218]; Walter Dorn's COMPETITION FOR EMPIRE, 1740-1763 [71]; Crane Brinton's A DECADE OF REVOLUTION, 1789-1799 [335]; and Geoffrey Bruun's EUROPE AND THE FRENCH IMPERIUM, 1799-1814 [46]. These books are all of equal quality and are valuable for background reading.

Another good choice is William Doyle's "The Old European Order, 1660-1800" [72]. A relatively new work by E.N. Williams is THE ANCIEN REGIME IN EUROPE: GOVERNMENT AND SOCIETY IN THE MAJOR STATES [308]. It is very worthwhile, as is T.K. Rabb's THE STRUGGLE FOR STABILITY IN EARLY MODERN EUROPE [210], and THE EUROPEAN NOBILITY OF THE EIGHTEENTH CENTURY [97], edited by A. Goodwin. EIGHTEENTH CENTURY EUROPE, 1713-1789 [12], by M.S. Anderson, and W.F. Reddaway's A HISTORY OF EUROPE FROM 1715 TO 1814 [215] are both useful for the periods they cover. Eugen Weber's EUROPE SINCE 1715 [305] is an excellent account of the last two and one-half centuries, but the most important part is the section that covers the revolutionary period of 1715-1848.

A fair account of the economic conditions in Europe may be found in Herbert Kellenbenz's THE RISE OF THE EUROPEAN ECONOMY [137]. A somewhat better selection is Alan Hodgart's THE ECONOMICS OF EUROPEAN IMPERIALISM [114]. An excellent political survey of Europe during the 18th century is presented in Preclin and Tapie's first of a two-volume set, CLIO: INTRODUCTION AUX ETUDES HISTORIQUES [207]. Leonard Krieger's KINGS AND PHILOSOPHERS [146] and Edward Gulick's EUROPE'S CLASSICAL BALANCE OF POWER [102] are also good for this purpose. David Ogg's EUROPE OF THE ANCIEN REGIME [194] is an especially lucid account of the period and goes into the major military activities in great detail.

There are a number of source references available that either relate specifically to the 18th century or at least touch upon it. One of these is A SELECTED LIST OF WORKS ON EUROPE AND EUROPE OVERSEAS [44], by J.S. Bromley and A. Goodwin. This is a readily usable compilation of sources on the period that is still of value even though it is somewhat outdated. A source of the military literature of the period is Max Jahn's GESCHICHTE DER KRIEGSWISSENSCHAFTEN [131]. BIBLIOGRAPHY, MACHINE READABLE CATALOGUING, AND THE ESTC [6] was done by R.C. Alston and M.J. Janetta and is half-titled as EIGHTEENTH CENTURY SHORT TITLE CATALOGUE. It has a summary of the period plus a listing of works published between 1711-1800. How valuable it can be depends upon what the reader is looking for. Anton Scherer's SUDOSTEUROPA-DISSERTATIONEN, 1918-1960. EINE BIBLIOGRAPHIE DEUTSCHER, OSTERREICHISCHER UND SCHWEIZERISCHER HOCHSCHULSCHRIFTEN [231] is a excellent source for dissertations which act as a guide to the Balkans done by graduate students and other research material dealing with the Balkans that was accomplished in Germany, Austria and Switzerland during the 42-year period indicated in the title. A BIBLIOGRAPHY OF BRITISH HISTORY: THE EIGHTEENTH CENTURY, 1714-1789 [199], by Stanley Pargellis contains a few references to the Balkans that might be of some use. Of more specific value are Liliana Shandanova's PETNADESET GODINI INSTITUT ZA BALKANISTIKA, 1964-1978: ISTORICHESKA SPRAVKA I BIBLIOGRAFIIA [238], published in Bulgarian, and VALKANIKE VIVLIOGRAPHIA [273] that began to appear periodically, beginning in 1975, in Thessaloniki, Greece.

## HISTORIES ON THE BALKANS IN THE 18TH CENTURY

There are a numerous historical works on the Balkans in the 18th century. Without question, the best coverages of this century are found in Leften Stavrianos' THE BALKANS SINCE 1453 [254]; in Peter Sugar's SOUTHEASTERN EUROPE UNDER OTTOMAN RULE, 1354-1804 [261], which is a part of the very fine HISTORY OF EAST CENTRAL EUROPE series [262], edited by Professors Sugar and Donald Treadgold; and in Erwin and Ann Lessner's THE DANUBE: THE DRAMATIC HISTORY OF THE GREAT RIVER AND THE PEOPLE TOUCHED BY ITS FLOW [160]. The Lessners' book is highly entertaining and very easy to read and follow. Edgar Hosch's THE BALKANS: A SHORT HISTORY [117] is also valuable but is not as strong on the later centuries as on the earlier times. Ferdinand Schevill's HISTORY OF THE BALKAN PENINSULA [232] is old but excellent in all regards. WAR AND SOCIETY IN EAST CENTRAL EUROPE [322] edited by Bela Kiraly and Gunther Rothenberg should not be overlooked. Professor Kiraly's EAST CENTRAL EUROPEAN SOCIETY AND WAR IN THE PREREVOLUTIONARY EIGHTEENTH CENTURY [326] is also excellent. BALKAN ECONOMIC HISTORY, 1550-1950: FROM IMPERIAL BORDERLANDS TO DEVELOPING NATIONS [321], by J.R. Lampe and M.R. Jackson, provides the needed coverage of the important economic factors involved in much of the 18th century's history in the Balkans.

The Ottoman Empire is discussed in a number of fine works, several of which are devoted to the eighteenth century. Two of these are STUDIES IN EIGHTEENTH CENTURY ISLAMIC HISTORY [192], prepared

under the editorship of Thomas Naff and Roger Owen, and ISLAMIC
SOCIETY IN THE EIGHTEENTH CENTURY [92], by Sir Harold Gibb and R.
Bowen. Naff and Owen is a 450-page compilation of papers presented
at a colloquy sponsored by the Near East History Group from Oxford
and the Middle East Study Group of the University of Pennsylvania.
The text is in English and French, and there is an extensive
bibliography.

Another interesting work on the Turks is Norman Itzkowitz'
"Eighteenth Century Ottoman Realities" [128] which is actually a
summary of the times of the Grand Vizier Mehmed Raghib Pasha
(1699-1763). Traian Stoianovich's "Factors in the Decline of Ottoman
Society in the Balkans" [255], Sidney N. Fisher's "Ottoman Feudalism
and Its Influence upon the Balkans" [87], and Maximilian Braun's
"Turkenherrschaft und Turkenkampf bei die Balkanslawen" [39] are all
worthwhile reading at this point. George Arnakis does an above
average job of detailing the importance of the Greek movement in the
18th century in his THE NEAR EAST IN MODERN TIMES: THE OTTOMAN
EMPIRE AND THE BALKANS TO 1900 [17]. Walter Wright's OTTOMAN
STATECRAFT [313] does much to explain the rather spectacular
recovery made by the Turks following Karlowitz. Similar praise
cannot be given to Lavender Cassels' THE STRUGGLE FOR THE OTTOMAN
EMPIRE, 1717-1740 [49] that fails to come to grips with the problem
because of an almost total lack of objectivity and a reliance on
something less than the best sources available.

For the best general histories on the Turks, one needs look
no further than Stanford Shaw's EMPIRE OF THE GAZIS: THE RISE AND
DECLINE OF THE OTTOMAN EMPIRE, 1280-1808 [241], which is the first
of two volumes titled HISTORY OF THE OTTOMAN EMPIRE AND MODERN
TURKEY. A better-written, and more carefully edited, alternative is
Lord Kinross' THE OTTOMAN CENTURIES: THE RISE AND FALL OF THE
TURKISH EMPIRE [140]. Josef von Hammer-Purgstall's monumental
18-volume HISTOIRE DE L'EMPIRE OTTOMAN [103] was published in the
middle of the last century but is still one of the most thorough
studies available. GESCHICHTE DES OSMANISCHEN REICHS IN EUROPA
[316], by J.W. Zinkeisen, was also published in the mid-19th
century, but must be considered among the better selections. There
are two works by Bistra Tsvetkova that are also useful to review at
this point: L'EVOLUTION DU REGIME FEODAL TURC DE LA FIN DU XVIᵉ
JUSQU'AU MILIEU DU XVIIIᵉ SIECLE [279], and LES INSTITUTIONS
OTTOMANES EN EUROPE [278]. A HISTORY OF THE OTTOMAN EMPIRE TO 1730
[61], edited by M.A. Cook, contains one chapter, "The Retreat of the
Turks, 1683-1730" [151], by A.N. Kurat and J.S. Bromley, that is
also found in the same form in volume VI [42] of the NCMH.

One of the more valuable documents available is I.M.
d'Ohsson's TABLEAU GENERALE DE L'EMPIRE OTHMAN [70] which was
published in seven volumes between 1788 and 1824. The author was a
Swede of Armenian birth who served as Sweden's minister in
Constantinople from 1796 to 1799. For many years this work was the
standard reference on the Ottoman Empire's structure and system of
operations. THE OTTOMAN BACKGROUND TO THE MODERN MIDDLE EAST [118],
by Albert Habib Hourani, has some material on this period; while
William Eton's 1799 report [83] on the government, provincial
organization, and causes of decline is an excellent firsthand
account of conditions in the Turkish empire. Paul Coles' THE OTTOMAN
IMPACT ON EUROPE [60], if used at all, should be used with caution.

Coles' obviously anti-Ottoman sentiments permeate his work. There are some perceptive insights into Turkish affairs in Europe that should not be overlooked, but the warning still stands. As a final work in English, the newest edition of the ENCYCLOPEDIA OF ISLAM [119] is always a most useful source of information. Nicolae Iorga's GESCHICHTE DES OSMANISCHEN REICHES [125], which was published in five volumes between 1908 and 1913, is one of the most thorough accounts of the Ottoman Empire even though it is outdated by modern interpretive standards.

The best general source in Turkish is the ISLAM ANSIKLOPEDISI [283], while Ismail Uzuncarsili's OSMANLI TARIHI [287] is the best all-around historical treatment in that language. One might also consider RASID TARIHI [214], which was prepared in five volumes in 1867, by Mehmet Rasid. BIBLIOGRAFIYA TURTSII (1917-1958) [285] was produced by the Soviet Academy of Sciences' Institute of Eastern Affairs. There are a number of entries on the 18th century.

Historical documentation on Albania is always difficult to find, and general coverage of the 18th century is no exception. QUELLEN UND MATERIALEN ZUR ALBANISCHEN GESCHICHTE IM 17. UND 18. JAHRHUNDERT [317], by Vicko Zmajecic, is a good compilation of sources, as is F.L.J. Legrand's BIBLIOGRAPHIE ALBANAISE [156]. Joseph Swire's ALBANIA, THE RISE OF A KINGDOM [265] has good coverage of the latter part of the 18th century.

George Finlay's HISTORY OF GREECE [85] is excellent. Another interesting work that relates to the entire period of the Ottoman's Balkan tenure is ESSAYS ON THE HISTORICAL GEOGRAPHY OF THE GREEK WORLD IN THE BALKANS DURING THE TURKOKRATIA [252] by Basile Spiridonakis that was published by the Institute of Balkan Studies at Thessaloniki. Elizabeth Barker's MACEDONIA: ITS PLACE IN BALKAN POWER POLITICS [20] is also valuable at this point.

Romania in the 18th century is highlighted in Robert Seton-Watson's A HISTORY OF THE ROUMANIANS; FROM ROMAN TIMES TO THE COMPLETION OF UNITY [236]. The CHRONOLOGICAL HISTORY OF ROMANIA [95], edited by Constantin Giurescu and a group of leading Romanian scholars, contains a rather complete listing of the events of the 18th century but suffers here, as it has before, from imperfect translation into English. Ladislas Makkai's HISTOIRE DE TRANSYLVANIE [176] is the best study of that province's unique historical development. HISTOIRE DES ROUMAINES DE LA PENINSULA DES BALCANS [126], by Nicolae Iorga, produced in French in 1919, deals with the spread of Romanians throughout the Balkans, especially into Macedonia where they played a large part in the overall development of the region. The last part of this monograph deals with the economic and cultural renovation of these folk in southern mountainous regions of the peninsula.

Mustafa Mehmet's CRONICI TURCESTI PRIVIND TARILE ROMANE (EXTRASE, SEC. XV - MIJLOCUL SEC. XVIII) [184] gives a chronological account of Ottoman events in Wallachia up to the mid-18th century. Paul Cernovodeanu's SOCIETATA FEUDALA ROMANEASCA VAZUTA DE CALATORI STRAINI (SECOLELE XV-XVIII) [52] deals with the same general period. RELATIILE ISTORICE DINTRE POPOARELE U.R.S.S. SI ROMANE IN VEACURILE XV-INCEPUTUL CELUI DE AL XVIII-LEA [284] is a joint Soviet-Romanian effort that has thus far produced three volumes, the last of which concentrates upon the events of 1683-1711. More than two-thirds of the documents cover the 1700-1711 period. The ridiculous title notwithstanding, this is a most useful document that contains, among other things, records of Russian pursuit of the Swedes into Moldavia after Poltava (1709). Many, although not all, of the documents were hitherto unpublished.

The general histories of Hungary that have been written by Sinor [246], Macartney [173], and Lengyel [157] are more than adequate as background reading. HUNGARY IN THE EIGHTEENTH CENTURY [178], by H. Marczali, is also worth reading because of its concentration on the period under discussion. BOHEMIA IN THE EIGHTEENTH CENTURY [138], by Robert Kerner, gives a thorough account of a country that was directly involved in a large part of Balkan history even through it is not technically considered a part of the region. Similarly, the article by Paul Ignotus, "Czechs, Magyars, Slovaks" [124], traces the antagonisms that developed among these three groups and the differences that existed in their societies.

The history of the states that today comprise Yugoslavia is found in YUGOSLAVIA [110], by Muriel Heppell and Frank Singleton. This work has some overall flaws but is adequate as background reading. The history of Serbia, one of Yugoslavia's integral parts, is covered in Vojislav M. Petrovic's SERBIA; HER PEOPLE, HISTORY, ASPIRATIONS [202]. HISTOIRE DU MONTENEGRO ET DE LA BOSNIA [62], by P. Coquelle, discusses the course of events in two of the other Yugoslav states. Mercia Macdermott's A HISTORY OF BULGARIA, 1393-1885 [174] has excellent coverage of the 18th century, as does Ahmed Refik's TURK IDARESINDE BULGARISTAN (973-1255) [216]. The dates in the title refer to the Moslem calendar for the approximate period 1565-1840. Michel Leo's LA BULGARIE ET SON PEUPLE SOUS LA DOMINATION OTTOMANE [159] is an interesting account told through the reports of visitors to Bulgaria at various times over a three-century period. Bistra Tsvetkova's "Recherches sur la system d'affermage (Ittizam) dan l'Empire Ottoman au cours XVIe-XVIIIe siecles par rapport aux contrees Bulgares" [281] discusses the measures taken to consolidate the Turkish hold on Bulgaria. Tsvetkova's KHAIDUTSVOTO V BULGARSKITE ZEMI PREZ 15/18 VEK [280] is a commentary on the banditry that was widespread throughout Bulgaria, Macedonia and Serbia during the Ottoman period. DOCUMENTS AND MATERIALS ON THE HISTORY OF THE BULGARIAN PEOPLE [47], compiled by the Bulgarian Academy of Sciences, is another handy tool but contains only five documents dealing with the 18th century.

Imperial Austrian history can be studied in a myriad of standard works. Two respectable sources on the 18th century are THE IMPERIAL CROWN: THE STORY OF THE RISE AND FALL OF THE HOLY ROMAN AND AUSTRIAN EMPIRES [89], by P. Frischauer, and Victor Mamatey's THE RISE OF THE HABSBURG EMPIRE, 1526-1815 [177]. Mamatey's book is the better of the two for the general reader, especially as it focuses on Austria, Bohemia, and Hungary, although not to the exclusion of the rest of the empire. THE PEOPLES OF THE EASTERN HABSBURG LANDS, 1526-1918 [134], by Robert Kann and Zdanek David, is another fine choice as it, too, centers on the areas of direct concern in southeastern Europe. Robert Kann's A HISTORY OF THE HABSBURG EMPIRE, 1526-1918 [133] is also a worthwhile choice, as is Adam Wandruszka's THE HOUSE OF HABSBURG: SIX HUNDRED YEARS OF A EUROPEAN DYNASTY [302]. DAS GESCHICHTE OSTERREICHS [106], by H. Hantsch, is a two-volume work that is extremely thorough in its coverage. John Stoye's "The Austrian Habsburgs" [258] in volume VI of the NCMH concentrates on the period 1688-1725. Volume VII has C.A. Macartney's "The Habsburg Dominions" [171] for the period from the end of the War of the Spanish Succession (1714) to the aftermath of the Treaty of Aix-la-Chapelle (1748). Wangerman's "The Habsburg Possessions and Germany" [303] is found in volume VIII but does not really fulfill the same role as the preceding articles. In volume IX, Macartney discusses "The Austrian Monarchy, 1792-1847" [170] emphasizing the Hungarian, Bohemian, and Slavic national issues.

The 18th century also marked the emergence of Imperial Russia's direct interest in the Balkans, and a number of sound histories exist that will suit the needs of any reader. A few of the better ones are Clarkson [56], Riasanovsky [217], and Florinsky [88]. Michael Florinsky's work is generally considered to be among the best available, and it has almost 30 pages of bibliography. Another of the very best histories of Russia is Vasili Klyuchevski's KURS RUSSKOI ISTORII [143] that has been translated into a number of languages with various degrees of success and completeness. RUSSLAND WEG NACH EUROPA [183], written by W. Mediger, is a German account of Russian expansion westward. RUSSIA IN THE EIGHTEENTH CENTURY [158], by A. Lentin, is of particular interest, as is Portal's L'OURAL AU XVIII$^e$ SIECLE [205]. Alfred Rambaud's THE EXPANSION OF RUSSIA [212] is particularly useful at this juncture and so is "Russia and the Balkans" in RUSSIAN FOREIGN POLICY: ESSAYS IN HISTORICAL PERSPECTIVE [154], edited by Ivo Lederer. George Vernadsky's article "On Some Parallel Trends in Russian and Turkish History" [298] points out the lack of an energetic policy on the part of the Turks to enforce uniformity over their various holdings in the Balkans and how this emboldened the Russians to seek greater influence there. S.L. Pestich's three-volume RUSSKAYA ISTORIOGRAFIYA XVIII VEKA [201] is a must for any serious student of this period.

Benedict Sumner's excellent little book, PETER THE GREAT AND THE OTTOMAN EMPIRE [264] presents important information on Russian relations with the Turks, Tatars, and the people of the Balkans, especially the Slavs who lived there. This book should be supplemented with Kontogiannes' study [145] that deals primarily with Russo-Greek relations during the reign of Catherine the Great (1762-1796) at the time of the Russo-Turkish War of 1768-1774. Of particular interest is the introductory section on Russo-Greek relations during the time of Peter I and afterward. RUSSIAN IMPERIALISM FROM IVAN THE TERRIBLE TO THE REVOLUTION [120], edited by Taras Hunczak, offers the reader a comprehensive assessment of the various imperialistic schemes put forward by the Tsars and Tsarinas of Russia from the end of the 16th to the beginning of the 20th centuries. The contributions of the various authors in this work are uniformly good with the exception of the article by Sarkisyanz that should be ignored as it serves no respectable purpose. Colonel Aleksandr Z. Myshlaevskii's PETR VELIKII. VOENNIE ZAKONII I INSTRUTSII [323] is also very interesting in its discussion of Russian military rules and regulations. Naval affairs are discussed in R.C. Anderson's "The First Russian Fleet, 1695-1711." [337].

A number of pertinent works exist on the Russian military in the 18th century that include Bruce Menning's "Military Institutions and the Steppe Frontier in Imperial Russia, 1700-1861" [185], and M. Lyons' THE RUSSIAN IMPERIAL ARMY [169]. Professor Menning's work was presented as a paper at the conference of the Commission Internationale d'Histoire Militaire held in Bucharest in 1980. Luibomir.G. Beskrovnyi's RUSSKAYA ARMIYA I FLOT V XVIII VEKE [327] studies the military affairs of Russia through this century.

## MILITARY HISTORY ON EIGHTEENTH-CENTURY EUROPE

The principal wars on the European continent during this century were: the Great Northern War (1700-1721), fought primarily between Russia and Sweden; The War of the Spanish Succession (1701-1714), a struggle over the Spanish Habsburg crown; the War of the Quadruple Alliance (1718-1720), another dynastic struggle, this time over the succession to the French throne; and the War of the Polish Succession (1733-1738), a conflict between France and Russia over influence in Poland that eventually involved much of Europe. This latter struggle was fought on the periphery of the Balkans, and many of the struggles that preceded and followed it saw the Balkans as the theater of war, or the axes along which contending armies passed. The Austro-Russo-Turkish War of 1736-1739, which grew out of the struggle in Poland, had much of its fighting take place in the Balkans and was typical of this phenomenon.

Another major European conflict, the War of Austrian Succession (1740-1748), began upon the death of Emperor Charles VI (1711-1740) when the formula provided in the Pragmatic Sanction (19 April 1713) placed Maria Theresa (1740-1780) upon the throne. This procedure was challenged by Charles Albert, the Elector of Bavaria, by Philip V of Spain, and by Augustus III of Saxony based upon mutually exclusive yet similar desires to see themselves on the Austrian throne. When Frederick II (the Great) (1740-1786) offered Maria Theresa aid against these claimants in return for Silesia, Maria refused thereby setting off a series of incidents that resulted in eight years of war.

The next major conflict began in 1756 with the start of the Seven Years' War. The war involved the military forces of most of the major powers in Europe and has been called in recent years "The Great War for Empire," especially by British historians who view it as an extension of the French and Indian War (1754-1763) fought between England and France for dominance in the New World and in India. The last great struggle in 18th century Europe was the Wars of the French Revolution (1792-1800) fought in attempt to restore the monarchy to France. Indeed, the French Revolution was the last in a series of European revolts against the established order that occurred throughout the course of the century. These rebellions rocked the continent and the world and signalled even more widespread disorder in the future. Not the least of the other 18th century revolts was the American Revolution (1775-1783), that fired the imaginations of succeeding generations of people all over the world who desired to be free. The American and French Revolutions have had lasting impacts upon the course of history that can never be accurately measured.

There are numerous accounts of both the socio-economic and the military historical events of the 18th century. The best place to start is the HISTORICAL ATLAS [245], by W.R. Shepherd. David

Chandler's ATLAS OF MILITARY STRATEGY [54] which has an extremely well written and illustrated section on this century. Of special interest is the chapter titled "Islam versus Christianity" that carries the reader through 1717 and the siege of Belgrad of that year. This atlas should be on the shelf of every serious military historian. AN ATLAS OF RUSSIAN AND EAST EUROPEAN HISTORY [2], by Adams, Matley and McCagg, is also useful although its coverage of this century is not extensive.

For a stimulating look at the military historical background to the 18th century, Geoffrey Blainey's THE CAUSES OF WAR [30] is an excellent choice. Professor Blainey begins his general survey of international wars in 1700 and has compiled a factual, albeit controversial, study of war that emphasizes the complexities that were developing in the art of armed conflict at that juncture in history. A STUDY OF MILITARY METHODS FROM THE EARLIEST TIMES [250], by Spaulding, Nickerson, and Wright, is the selection for those desiring a general discussion of the military art during the century; but Robert Quimby's THE BACKGROUND OF NAPOLEONIC WARFARE: THE THEORY OF MILITARY TACTICS IN THE EIGHTEENTH CENTURY [209] is even better for the purpose. Quimby points out that the differences between revolutionary and imperial warfare were not really so different after all.

An interesting study of 18th−century military social structures may be found in "Militarism in the Eighteenth Century" [251], by H. Speire. Another more general work on this theme is Alfred Vagts' A HISTORY OF MILITARISM [289] which is far superior to either KRIEG UND KRIEGFUHRUNG IM WANDEL DER WELTGESCHICHTE [234], by P. Schmitthenner, or GESCHICHTE DER KRIEGSKUNST IM RAHMEN DER POLITISCHEN GESCHICHTE [69], by Hans Delbruck. Quincy Wright's STUDY OF WAR [312] discusses the "Period of Absolutism (1648-1789)" in the context of its being the second part of the "Reign of War" expounded by Van Vollenhaven [293] in describing the period 1492-1780. Three other useful books are MEN IN ARMS [208], by Preston, Wise, and Werner; Cyril Falls' THE ART OF WAR [84]; and J.F.C. Fuller's A MILITARY HISTORY OF THE WESTERN WORLD [90]. Fuller's book is a major accomplishment in the field and is an exceptionally well written minor classic.

Probably the best discussion of the interaction between war, the military and 18th-century society is found in ARMEES ET SOCIETES EN EUROPE DE 1494 A 1789 [63], by the preeminent French military historian, Professor Andre Corvisier of the Sorbonne. This work has recently been translated into English. John Rose's THE INDECISIVENESS OF WAR AND OTHER ESSAYS [222] deals primarily with naval warfare, but there is also enough information of the land conflicts of the period to make it generally worthwhile reading. Other useful studies include WEAPONS OF WAR [57], by P.E. Cleator; Elbridge Colby's MASTERS OF MOBILE WARFARE [59]; and R.C. Anderson's NAVAL WAR OF THE LEVANT, 1559-1853 [13], which has a chapter devoted to this century. Martin Van Creveld's SUPPLYING WAR: LOGISTICS FROM WALLENSTEIN TO PATTON [290] has excellent coverage of the ever-increasing demands for provisions and transport for the military forces.

Among all things, great and small, that were produced during the 18th century, none would have a greater impact on future military history and upon the art of war than the great military thinkers and commentators who came forward during those years. The eminent American military historian, Professor Jay Luvaas, outlines the growth of the military intellectual class and discusses their writings in his "The Great Military Historians and Philosophers" [168]. The bibliography to this article, which is found in A GUIDE TO THE STUDY AND USE OF MILITARY HISTORY [132], provides a wealth of references to these writings. THE MAKERS OF MODERN STRATEGY: MILITARY THOUGHT FROM MACHIAVELLI TO HITLER [80], edited by E.M. Earle, is also worthwhile at this point. Chapter II of this book outlines the work of the Marquis Sabastien le Prestre de Vauban (1633-1707) who was a marshal of France and one of the greatest military engineers of his or any other age. Although he was of the 17th century, his various treatises gained currency after his death, and his ideas on fortifications were used throughout the 18th century. Earle's book also has an excellent bibliography. The two best general references are Zook and Higham [318] and Dupuy [78]. Together, these two works serve most of the requirements of the average reader.

## THE MILITARY HISTORY OF THE BALKANS IN THE 18TH CENTURY

Although the century opened with the Great Northern War raging in north central Europe, the lands south of the Carpathians were relatively calm. By 1703, however, two events occurred that did affect the Balkans, each in its own way. The first of these was the Janissary revolt that took place as a result of Sultan Mustafa II's (1695-1703) refusal to reside in Constantinople and his subsequent failure to pay the army. Thus, in what has been called the "Adrianople Affair," the army forced Mustafa to abdicate in favor of his brother, Ahmed III (1703-1730). Mustafa was then publicly and brutally tortured and executed.

The second event was the anti-Habsburg uprising of the Curutzi of Hungary and Transylvania that was led by Francis Rakoczi (elected prince in 1704-1711) and Nicholas Berczenyi, who was called the Hungarian Cromwell. The course of the Great Northern War made it possible for Rakoczi to occupy most of Hungary west of the Danube. In April 1707 Transylvania reaffirmed Rakoczi's leadership at Targul-Mures (Maros-Vasarkely). The following month the Magyars followed the Transylvanians by dethroning Joseph I as king of Hungary.

Internal problems and growing Austrian strength led to the eventual defeat of Rakoczi at Zsibo on 11 November 1705. Thereafter, Rakoczi's forces were defeated in one battle after another as the imperial strength under Prince Eugene continued to grow. After a decisive loss at Trentschin (Trencin) in August 1707, Rakoczi did manage to continue the struggle until 1711 but was finally forced to flee (February). The ensuing Peace of Szatmar (Satu Mare, 26 April 1711) did much to strengthen the power of the dual monarchy.

The Rakoczi saga is portrayed in Ladislas Freiherr Hengelmuller von Hengervar's FRANZ RAKOCZY UND SEIN KAMPF FUR UNGARN FRIEHEIT [108], published in 1913 in Stuttgart and Berlin. An almost exact English version was published in London that same year under the title HUNGARY'S FIGHT FOR NATIONAL EXISTENCE: OR, THE HISTORY OF THE GREAT UPRISING LED BY FRANCIS RAKOCZI II, 1703-1711 [109].

Imre Lukinich's ERDELEY TERULETI VALTOZASAI A TOROK HODITAS KORABAN 1541-1711 [166] deals with the territorial changes that occurred in the century and one-half that preceded the uprising. This is a most valuable work as it contains an excellent place name and subject index. Luckinich also wrote A SZATMARI BEKE TORTENETE ES OKIRATTARA [167] published in 1925. This is a history of the treaty plus a compilation of the archival sources from both Vienna and Budapest. A more recent account may be found in "AD PACEM UNIVERSALEM" - THE INTERNATIONAL ANTECEDENTS OF THE PEACE OF SZATMAR [294], by A.R. Varkonyi, published in 1980. There is also UNGARISCH-SERBISCHE VERSOHNUNGVERSUCHE WAHREND DES RAKOCZI-AUFSTANDES [27] by K. Benda. The biography, PRINZ EUGEN VON SAVOYEN [18], by A. von Arneth, describes the Rakoczi movement and gives portrayals of the leading characters. John Stoye's "The Austrian Habsburgs" [258] in volume VI [42] of the NCMH gives a fine outline of the rebellion but without any real detail. William Doyle, in his "The Old European Order, 1660-1800" [72], makes the point that Rakoczi was looked upon as the Messiah by many of the Hungarian peasants. The CHRONOLOGICAL HISTORY OF ROMANIA [95] mentions the Rakoczi affair but only to point out the participation of numbers of Romanians in support of his cause. One other work of some interest at this point is PRINZ EUGEN VON SAVOYEN, EINE BIOGRAPHIE [38] in five volumes by M. Braubach. Dupuy [78] mentions these incidents but without much substance.

In THE EMERGENCE OF THE EUROPEAN WORLD [31], the authors point out that Rakoczi was aided by France's Louis XIV (1643-1715) and that the Hungarian uprising "broke out during the War of the Spanish Succession." The implication presented here is that the Rakoczi incident was a part of a larger struggle. The article, "The War of the Spanish Succession in Europe" [296], by A.J. Veenendal, outlines the causes of that war and adds some credence to the notion that France instigated a diversion in the Balkans. A more detailed account of the war may be found in Arthur Parnell's THE WAR OF SUCCESSION IN SPAIN DURING THE REIGN OF QUEEN ANNE, 1702-1711 [200] which was produced in 1905.

## THE RUSSO-TURKISH WAR OF 1710-1711

Hungary and Transylvania were not alone in their troubles during the first decade of the new century. In 1703, for instance, the Sublime Porte ordered a drastic increase in the tributes expected from the Danubian provinces. Wallachia, for one, under the leadership of Constantin Brincoveanu (1688-1714), was forced to accept the new taxation but it also led to his making a secret agreement (1709) with Tsar Peter I to support the Russians in a planned campaign against the Turks. This was followed by the Russo-Moldavian alliance of Luck-Volhynia signed on 13 April 1711 that established the same understandings.

With the aid of the French and with money he received from the Zaporozhian Cossacks, Charles XII (1697-1718) of Sweden was able to convince Sultan Ahmed III to declare war on Russia (November 1710). Although Peter had, indeed, threatened war if the Porte refused to expel Charles from his safehaven in Constantinople, he was not in an immediate position to back up the threat with force of arms. Instead, he called for a Balkan uprising and made the already mentioned treaties with Wallachia and Moldavia. By July 1711 a Tsarist army was on the move south entering Moldavia in the first Russian intervention into the region since the Rurikide Grand Duke, Svyatoslav I (962-972), conquered the Bulgarians in support of the Byzantine Empire.

Now, in 1711, the Russian army took the circuitous route through the Polish Ukraine to avoid the perilous region between the Dnieper and Dniester rivers. Occupying Jassy, the Russians then moved south along the Pruth to the vicinity of Stanilesti-Falcui (Staneliste) (near Vaslui) where the combined Russo-Moldavian force of some 40,000 troops found themselves surrounded by an allied Turkish army estimated at 260,000 men, led by the Grand Vizier Baltaji Mehmed Pasha. With his back to the east bank of the Pruth and the combined Turkish-Tatar-Polish force on commanding terrain on all sides, Peter had little alternative but to surrender. On 21 July 1711, the white flag was raised just in time to prevent what would most likely have been a battle of annihilation. The ensuing Treaty of the Pruth gave back to the Ottomans much that they had lost earlier to the Russians, including the great fortress at Azov. The key element in the outcome of this shortlived campaign was probably Baltaji Pasha's lack of aggressiveness. It is also possible that his lack of enthusiasm in attacking and crushing the Russian Tsar changed the course of European history.

This battle and its consequences are covered in a number of sources. Chandler presents a vivid schematic array of the forces involved in his ATLAS OF MILITARY STRATEGY [54]. The best single account of the battle is found in Sumner's PETER THE GREAT AND THE OTTOMAN EMPIRE [264], although Sumner's style of writing is somewhat difficult to follow. The article by Kurat and Bromley, "The Retreat of the Turks, 1683-1730" [151], in both NCMH VI [42] and in Cook's A HISTORY OF THE OTTOMAN EMPIRE TO 1730 [61], has excellent detail. The CHRONOLOGICAL HISTORY OF ROMANIA [95] contributes a few details not readily available elsewhere, while the DESPATCHES OF SIR ROBERT SUTTON, AMBASSADOR TO CONSTANTINOPLE (1710-1714) [147], edited by the noted Turkish Professor Ardes N. Kurat, provide a firsthand account of the events by an obviously pro-Russian eyewitness. Riasanovsky [217] and Clarkson [56] also discuss the battle. Kurat's ISVEC KIRALI XII KARL' IN TURKIYEDE KALISI VE BU SIRALARDA OSMANLI IMPARATORLUGI [148] discusses Charles XII, his stay in Constantinople, and the state of the Ottoman Empire. An article by R.M. Hutton, "Charles XII in Turkey 'Narrative of the King of Sweden's Movements, 1709-1714'" [123], provides additional information on Charles' part in the ill-fated Russian campaign. In "XVIII Yuzyil Basi Avrupa Umumi Harbinde Turkiye Nin Tarafsizligi" [150], Professor Kurat maintains that the Pruth treaty was not at all in Turkey's favor and was a mistake. He goes on to estimate the advantages to Turkey if the Porte had sided with Sweden in its struggle with Imperial Russia. Kurat further states that Turkey's second mistake of the period was its maintenance of neutrality during the War of the Spanish Succession, when it had the opportunity to gain much from the French. The value of this article is not so much in its tendentious nature but in its insights into the inner workings of the Porte. Another work by Kurat on this subject is PRUT SEFERI VE BARISI 1123/1711 [149]. This two-volume work deals directly with the battle.

PETER THE GREAT [195], by L. Jay Oliva, quotes from Peter's
JOURNAL DE PIERRE LE GRAND DEPUIS L'ANNEE 1698 JUSQU'A LA CONCLUSION
DE LA PAIX DE NEUSTADT in discussing the campaign against the Turks.
Vasili Klyuchevsky's KURS RUSSKOI ISTORII [143] has been translated
into English, is probably the best account of the Tsar's life, and
has an exceptionally good discussion of the 1711 campaign. Benedict
Sumner has also produced PETER THE GREAT AND THE EMERGENCE OF RUSSIA
[263] that takes a much broader view of Imperial Russian development
than his previously mentioned PETER THE GREAT AND THE OTTOMAN EMPIRE
[264]. Another excellent account is Robert K. Massey's Pulitzer
Prize — winning PETER THE GREAT: HIS LIFE AND WORLD [181]. Reinhard
Wittram's Peter I, CZAR UND KAISER: ZUR GESCHICHTE PETERS DEN
GROSSEN [336] is one of the best. Two other works on Peter the Great
by Eugene Schuyler [235] and K. Waliszewski [301] are both of some
interest at this point. An article, "Iz russko-serbskikh otnoshenii
pri Petre Velikom" [33], by S. Bogaiavlenskii, contains information
about the attention that Peter gave to the Serbs during his reign.
Before 1711, the Russian Tsar sent agents into Serbia, Bulgaria,
Romania, and Montenegro seeking to arouse the populace to revolt in
advance of the arrival of the Russian army. The disaster at the
Pruth spelled the end of this plan and set for the Balkan people
another 65 years of degradation before they could hope for relief
from the Turkish yoke. Macdermott explains this situation quite well
in A HISTORY OF BULGARIA, 1393-1885 [174]. Finally, there is an
article on the Turkish Sultan, "Ahmed III" [136], by Enver Z. Karal,
in ISLAM ANSIKLOPEDISI [283]. There are also two excellent
biographies on the life of the great Austrian general, Prince Eugene
of Savoy. The best is the already mentioned, five-volume, PRINZ
EUGEN VON SAVOYEN, EINE BIOGRAPHIE [38], by M. Braubach. The other
work, also of good quality, is Nicholas Henderson's PRINCE EUGENE OF
SAVOY [107].

## THE TURKO-VENETIAN-AUSTRIAN WAR OF 1715-1718

With the end of the Russo-Turkish conflict, a new era in the
relations between the Porte and its subject Balkan states began. On
the one hand, the Turks were interested in regaining Morea which had
been lost at Karlowitz. This meant a new conflict with Venice that
required a concentration of effort. To accomplish this required a
decision, on the other hand, to reduce the level of dissension in
the Balkans so that the required resources could be mustered for the
campaign in Greece.

One of the first moves in this direction occurred in October
1711 with the nomination of Nicolae Mavrocordata, to be viovode of
Moldavia. Mavrocordata was a Phanaroit Greek, so-called because they
lived in the district near the Constantinople lighthouse. From this
point until 1821 Phanaroits ruled the Danubian principalities. This
period represents the height of Turkish exploitation and control in
the Balkans.

As a second move, Ahmed III allowed a war party led by his
son-in-law, Silahdar Ali Pasha, to seize the power that had been
held by Chorlulu Ali and Baltaji Mehmed. In April 1713 Silahdar
became Grand Vizier. The following year, in March 1714, Constantin
Brincoveanu (1688-1714), the Wallachian prince, was taken to
Constantinople where he and his sons were beheaded. He was replaced
on the Wallachian throne by Stepan Cantacuzino (1714-1715) who was,

in turn, also executed by the Turks. Nicolae Mavrocordat (1715-1716), a Phanaroit, was then installed on the throne. As a final step leading to war, the Turks worked assiduously to undermine the Venetian administration in Morea to the extent that when war did break out, there was little or no popular support for the Venetians.

The war began on two pretexts, Turkish claims that the Venetians were supplying arms to rebels in Montenegro; and, secondly, that the Venetians refused to turn over to the Turks the considerable wealth of the executed Constantin Brincoveanu held in the Bank of Venice. Although fighting broke out in 1714, war between Turkey and Venice was not formally declared until 11 January 1715. The Turks were initially successful and, by July 1715, had taken the fortress at Corinth after which one important Morean port after another fell. In July 1716, the Turks attacked Corfu where Marshal Johann Mathias von der Schulenberg, a friend of Prince Eugene, was in command. Not only Corfu, but the entire Dalmatian coast appeared in danger of falling into Turkish hands. It was this situation, plus the implicit strategic threat to Croatia and Styria, that led the Austrians to go to the aid of the Venetians on 13 April 1716. The ultimatum issued by the Austrian crown dismayed the Turks who were not overly enthused at the prospect of their campaign of restoration turning into a major war.

The first major action of the Turko-Austrian war was the battle fought at Peterwardein where a Turkish force of about 120,000-150,000 was defeated by Prince Eugene and an Austrian Imperial force of 60,000-70,000 men. After a pitched battle on 5 August 1716 with the Turks losing about double the 5,000 Austrian casualties, the Ottoman army was routed. Curiously, Eugene did not pursue but, rather, moved his forces through difficult terrain to lay siege to the very strong Turkish fortress at Timisoara (Temesvar) in the Banat region of Transylvania. When this fortress fell on 12 October, the Turks did not release the information for some time in Constantinople fearing a revolt. At the same time, the Sultan broke off the attack on Corfu and withdrew his army.

After the fall of the "Gazi" fort at Timisoara, Prince Eugene raided Bucharest with a small force and moved to lay siege to Belgrad, the Ottoman citadel in the Balkans. Throughout July and August 1717 the siege continued. Eugene had about 20,000 troops, while the bastion's defenders numbered about 30,000. In mid-August a relief column of about 200,000 Turks under the command of Khalil Pasha, the new Grand Vizier, arrived at Belgrad. Eugene, with typical boldness, turned his small army to meet this Turkish force and, on 16 August, in a fierce battle defeated the Turks. Austrian losses numbered about 2,000 while the Turkish casualties were over 20,000 killed and wounded. Four days later, Belgrad surrendered giving up over 150 cannon and 60 battle standards.

In the aftermath of this success, Prince Eugene turned his forces southward and occupied much of Serbia and western Wallachia. Bosnia was not overrun, however, because of the stubborn and gallant defenses of the fortresses at Zvornik, Bihach, and Novi. Remembering the situation after Karlowitz, the Serbs did not rise up against the Turks this time, nor did the Romanians; but this did not really affect the outcome. By that point the Turks had already decided they had had enough and were ready to discuss peace.

Although the Venetians were determined to continue the war, the other European powers, especially England and Holland, desired a a quick and peaceful solution. Even though Venice verged on complete victory, the Emperor decided upon peace, as much to pacify the English and the Dutch who wanted to reopen the Levant trade, as because of growing troubles elsewhere in the empire. Thus, the treaty of Passarowitz (Pozarevac) was initialed on 21 July 1718. Austria retained Timisoara, thereby completing the liberation of Hungary from Turkish rule. The Turks were allowed to keep Morea. It was a case of a return to the status quo ante bellum in which everyone profitted except the Venetians. Austria was now the dominant power in the Balkans.

Stavrianos' [254] account of this period is short but solid, while Kurat and Bromley's article [151] in the NCMH conveys a great deal of information in a very small space. Dupuy's reference [78] is short but complete, while Schevill [232] hardly mentions the affair and the CHRONOLOGICAL HISTORY OF ROMANIA [95] brings out a number of interesting sidebars to the main events of the war.

More precise information may be found in "He anakatalepsis tes Peloponnesou hypo ton Tourkon en etei 1715" [227], by M.B. Sakellariou,which deals with the conquest of Morea by the Turks in 1715. Leopold von Ranke also discusses these incidents in his ZUR VENETIANISCHEN GESCHICHTE [213] which was published in 1878. The war in general is the topic of two volumes in the 21-volume FELDZUG DES PRINZEN EUGEN VON SAVOYEN [182], which was prepared by L. Matuschka. THE HISTORY OF THE MARITIME WARS OF THE TURKS [139], that was written by Hajji Khalifeh and later translated by James Mitchell in 1831. Along with R.C. Anderson's NAVAL WARS OF THE LEVANT [13], these works give a complete account of the naval aspects of this period. LES RELATIONS ENTRE LA FRANCE ET L'EUROPE CENTRALE DE 1661-1715 [267], by V.L. Tapie, goes into the background of the struggle. Another view is presented in I. Jacobs' BEZIEHUNGEN ENGLANDS ZU RUSSLANDS UND DER TURKEI IN DEN JAHREN 1718-1724 [130] which offers a number of interesting sidebars to the main events of the war. Finally, William Miller's THE TURKISH RESTORATION IN GREECE, 1718-97 [188] discusses the reestablishment of Turkish rule in that country following this war.

## THE AFTERMATH OF PASSAROWITZ

The signing of the treaty signalled a relatively long period of peace, if not tranquility, for the Balkans. Turkey had concerns in the east and problems at home that diverted attention away from its errant subjects, at least for a while. In the eastern part of the Ottoman realm, the Turks, along with the Russians, attempted to partition Persia. The Persians were, however, involved in a revival of nationalism and proved this when their leader, Nadir Shah, handed the Turks a disastrous defeat at Hamadan. This led to an eventual Russo-Turkish withdrawal (1735) from the area; but, in the meantime, in September 1730, a major Janissary revolt broke out in Constantinople as a result of the Persian victory, which turned out to be one of the bloodiest in Turkish history.

Even though he attempted to placate the mob by having a number of his chief advisors executed, Ahmed III was forced to abdicate on 1 October 1730 and was replaced by his nephew, Mahmud I (1730-1754), who had been held in captivity since 1703. The revolt continued, however, and spread throughout the region with the rebels demanding both internal reforms and the destruction of the infidel Russians. As is so often the case, the rebel ardor began to flag, largely due to the excesses of their leader, Patrona Halil. Although the fighting continued for about two years, Patrona and his lieutenants lasted only until 25 November 1730 when they were murdered in the Sultan's presence. By 28 November some 7,000 more rebels had been summarily executed. By the end of the revolt, about 50,000 were reported to have been killed or banished from Constantinople alone.

There are two works in Turkish on this episode: PATRONA ISYANI (1730) [4], by M. Munir Aktepe; and Abdi's 1730 PATRONA IHTILALI HAKKINDA BIR ESER [1]. The first of these deals primarily with the social aspects of the revolt and provides little in the way of background. The latter work is a more rounded account but is found only in Turkish. Harold Bowen's "Ahmed III" [37] is useful at this point as it describes how the Sultan was more interested in raising tulips than he was in the affairs of state. Aktepe's "Mahmud I" [3] should not be overlooked. The same is true of J.W. Zinkeisen's GESCHICHTE DES OSMANISCHEN REICHS IN EUROPE [316] that appeared in the mid-19th century in seven volumes. Volume five has a solid section on the Turko-Persian War of Nadir Shah. Also known as Nadir Kuli Beg, he was regent to his son Shah Abbas III and was assassinated in 1747. He is a legend in Persian history.

This period is also covered in great detail in Mary Lucille Shay's THE OTTOMAN EMPIRE FROM 1720 TO 1734 AS REVEALED IN THE DESPATCHES OF THE VENETIAN BAILI [244]. This work is found as a 1978 reprint of a 1944 University of Illinois publication and deals with the reigns of Ahmed III and Mahmud I. Another history of this period is found in TARIH-I SUBHI, SAMI VE SAKIR [259] which was published in Turkish in 1793.

## THE WAR BETWEEN TURKEY, RUSSIA, AND AUSTRIA

The quiet in the Balkans was shattered by a large-scale uprising in the Danubian principalities and in Transylvania that was led by Pero Seghedinat. Beginning in 1735, the revolt soon spread into Hungary. There were some local successes; but, for the most part, the rebels were rather quickly suppressed and many were forced to flee south of the Danube to escape the Austrian authorities.

Another set of circumstances also caused trouble for the Balkans. The War of the Polish Succession, that began in 1733, came about as a result of a dispute over whether Russia and Austria, or France should have their candidate on the throne in Warsaw. Trouble for the Balkans grew out of this struggle when France induced the Porte to enter the war as its ally against the Turk's two traditional enemies.

For Russia's part, the time also appeared ripe for war against the Turks as the Tsarina Anna (1730-1740) had become convinced that an outlet onto the Black Sea was a prime strategic objective. War was declared when the Ottomans reacted, following a Russian attack on the Crimean Tatars. Russia then invoked the term of a secret 1726 alliance with Austria and, by 1737, the Empire was also in the struggle. This action sent Austrian troops into Bosnia, Wallachia, and Serbia where they were defeated by the Turks primarily because of a lack of coordination by the Austrians with the Russians.

Fighting broke out again in 1738 when the Turks crossed the Danube in the Banat region and moved toward Belgrad. Although there were no decisive battles, there were a large number of engagements in which the Austrian forces were commanded by Colonel Lothar J.G. Konigsegg-Rothenfels. Another Austrian force, under the command of Count Georg O. von Wallis, was defeated in 1739 by a numerically superior Turkish army and was driven back into Belgrad where the Turks laid siege to the city and its defenders. The principal battle in this campaign was fought at Kroszka, near the capital. Although there had been some intermittent discussions of peace during the course of the fighting up to this time, it was only after the disastrous turn of events near Belgrad that the Austrians were willing to undertake the humiliating agreement signed on 18 September 1739. As a result of this Treaty of Belgrad, almost all that Austria had won at Passarowitz was lost. Three weeks later, bereft of its ally, Russia sued for peace. The subsequent Treaty of Nissa, signed on 3 October 1739, stripped Russia of its hard-won territorial gains around Azov; and, although it remained somewhat closer to the Black Sea, in the final analysis, Russia was still deprived of the right to operate in those waters.

There is a great deal written about this important war. Stavrianos' account [254] is thorough but without any real detail. Dupuy [78] is good but as always lacks depth. The accounts of Macartney [173] and Schevill [232] are both useful. More detailed sources include Theodor Tupetz' "Der Turkenfeldzug von 1739 und der Friede von Belgrade" [282] published in 1878, and DER KRIEG MIT DER PFORTE, 1736 BIS 1739 [14], by Moritz von Angeli, published in 1880. This latter work also deals with the death of Prince Eugene in April 1736. Antonio Bezoin's "La guerra russo-turca del 1736-1739" [29] looks at the war through Venetian diplomatic material. Another solid work, this one in English, is THE RELUCTANT ALLY: AUSTRIA'S POLICY IN THE AUSTRO-TURKISH WAR OF 1736-1739 [220], which was Karl A. Roider's doctoral dissertation at Stanford in 1970 and was subsequently published in 1972. An excellent paper on the topic of this war, "L'Alliance Austro-Russe contre la Turquie 1736-1739" [193] was presented by Jean Nouzille at the 1981 colloquy of the CIHM held by the Center of Military History at Paul Valery University, Montpellier, France. Yet another interesting work in French that touches on this subject is Auguste Boppe's "La France et le militaire turc' au XVIII<sup>e</sup> siecle" [36].

## MARIE THERESA AND THE HABSBURG EMPIRE

On 29 October 1740, Charles VI, the Emperor, died and the 23-year-old Maria Theresa took the Habsburg throne. There was, of course, a dispute over this and the War of the Austrian Succession (1740-1748) ensued. This war affected Bohemia but did not spill over into the Balkans proper. In effect, the Balkans enjoyed three decades of peace marred only by the periodic uprisings of the peasantry seeking redress of their problems. Turkey, on the other hand, was not so fortunate and had to fight a four-year war with

Persia (1743-1747) that cost the Ottomans almost all of their territorial gains of the last 20 years in the Iranian region.

There are any number of good studies on the rule of Maria Theresa. Robert Pick's EMPRESS MARIA THERESA: THE EARLY YEARS [204] is excellent for the period it covers, as are Edward Crankshaw's MARIA THERESA [64], and Lady Constance Morris' MARIA THERESA, THE LAST CONSERVATIVE [190]. Of special importance is Christopher Duffy's THE ARMY OF MARIA THERESA. THE ARMED FORCES OF IMPERIAL AUSTRIA, 1740-1780 [76] published in 1975. Professor Duffy's study is a companion piece to THE ARMY OF FREDERICK THE GREAT [75]. These volumes are indispensable to the serious military historian who is interested in this period. They are both written in a historiographical style and are full of order of battle information that will be of great assistance to the reader.

In addition to the standard references on Turkish history that are mentioned elsewhere in this chapter, Suleyman Izzi's IZZI TARIHI [129] is important as it deals specifically with the period 1744-1747. This work was written by Suleyman Izzi and was published in 1782. It is rare and difficult to find but quite interesting.

BONNEVAL PASHA

It is worthwhile to note here the passing of Claude Alexandre Bonneval (1675-1747) who was known to the Turks as Bombardier Ahmed Pasha or Bonneval Pasha after his entrance into the Sultan's service in 1729. Bonneval did much to modernize the Turkish army. There are a number of interesting studies about this man that need to be referred to by the serious student. Count Bonneval's memoires were published in 1806 [35], while Albert Vandal's work, LE PACHA BONNEVAL [291], was published in 1885. BONNEVAL PACHA [99], by Septima Gorceix; DER PASCHA-GRAF ALEXANDER VON BONNEVAL, 1675-1747 [28], by Heinrich Benedict; and "Bonneval und Prinz Eugen" [34] are also quite valuable for understanding the role played by this man in the course of Ottoman history.

This period also marked the beginning of the rule of Frederick the Great (1740-1786), King of Prussia. Frederick's influence on the military events of future generations cannot be overlooked as they affected the Balkans as much as anywhere else. There are, of course, many fine works on Frederick; Thomas Barker's FREDERICK THE GREAT AND THE MAKING OF PRUSSIA [21] should not be overlooked. George Gooch's FREDERICK THE GREAT [96] and G.B. Volz's FRIEDRICH DER GROSSE IM SPIEGEL SEINER ZEIT [299] are both very good. Volz's work is in three volumes and is exhaustive in its coverage. An interesting article in Turkish is Salahuddin Tansel's "Buyuk Friedrich devrinde Osmanli Prusya munasebetleri hakkinda" [266] that deals with Turko-Prussian relations during Frederick's reign.

As a final recommendation, Gunther Rothenberg ends THE AUSTRIAN MILITARY BORDER IN CROATIA, 1522-1747 [223] with this period and starts his even better MILITARY BORDER IN CROATIA, 1740-1881: A STUDY OF AN IMPERIAL INSTITUTION [225] with it. Granting Croatia's distance from the Balkan heartland, so much of Professor Rothenberg's work is pertinent to the Balkans that it cannot be overlooked.

THE RUSSO-TURKISH WAR OF 1768-1774

The second half of the 18th century was a time when the earth shook. The great wars for empire that took place between England and France culminated in the American Revolution. It was a time of great change although few probably realized it as the events transpired. For Europe the period opened with the Seven Years' War (1756-1763) in which England relied upon Frederick to fight the land war on the continent while it conquered the New World. This massive struggle was followed by a civil war in Poland (1768-1774) that led to a Russian invasion and, eventually, the First Partition.

At the same time that the Confederation of Bar was leading the insurrection in Poland, events were developing to the south that were to lead Russia into another war with Turkey that would involve the Balkans. To some extent the struggle in Poland and the conflict in the Balkans were connected. As the French supported the Polish dissidents, so too did they goad the Turks into undertaking a war against Russia. Using the pretext of increased Russian activity in the Balkans as the cause for the most recent rash of uprisings, particularly in Montenegro and Wallachia (1764-1767), the Turks took on a hostile attitude toward Russia, even though caution would have shown that Russia was now a vastly superior military power to what it had been in the past. When Russian forces crossed into Turkish territory in pursuit of a group of Polish rebels, the Porte declared war (30 October 1768). Crimean Tatars immediately attacked into the Ukraine and the war was on.

This struggle began during the reign of Sultan Mustafa III (1757-1773) who has been judged to have been out of his mind when he opened hostilities against the Russians. Regardless of this fact, the war began in the Balkans after a delay of several months that allowed the Russians the opportunity to make ample preparations while, at the same time, the Turks did little to strengthen the forces and fortifications. One Russian army under the command of Prince Alexandre Golitsyn was directed to attack and capture the Turkish fortress at Khotin (today in the USSR near Kamenets Podolsk). A second army was to screen the Russian frontier between the Dnieper and the Sea of Azov to prevent further Tatar encroachments. Another army was to occupy Poland, while two others were to operate in the Caucasus. In addition, all available aid and comfort was to be afforded the Montenegrans.

After a dilatory start, the Turkish army under the Grand Vizier, Emin Mohammed (Mehmet Emin Pasha), the Sultan's son-in-law, moved from Constantinople toward the Danube. In the meantime, Golitsyn began his attack on Khotin, he failed, and immediately withdrew behind the Dniester. Meanwhile the Grand Vizier's army had moved slowly forward, making frequent stops while the inexperienced Emin held councils of war to determine what to do. Finally, it was decided to cross the Danube into the provinces and place the Turkish army between Gallitsin and the Moldavian capital of Jassy (Iasi).

By the second half of 1769, after Russia forced the Poles to declare war on the Porte, a second series of skirmishes took place around Khotin that seemed to prove Frederick's comment that it was a war "between the one-eyed and the blind." Finally, the Sultan ordered Emin's relief and execution (August 1769), and replaced him with the Ali Moldowandji (Ali the Moldavian), who had been the Sultan's gardener). After several offensives, Ali was unable to break the Russian lines around Khotin; and the fortress capitulated on 18 September 1769. Even though he had been ultimately successful, Golitsyn was relieved by the Empress Catherine II (1729-1796) and replaced by Count Petr Rumiantsev. The new Russian commander immediately struck into Moldavia capturing Jassy. Then on 2 February 1770, he entered Bucharest only to find the city in Romanian hands as a group of partisans had taken it in advance of the Russian columns. Additional battles were fought at Giurgiu and Comona Monastery in the succeeding months.

Thereafter the Turks massed for a large battle and were decisively defeated in the vicinity of Larga and Cahul (Kartal) by a Russian army reinforced with Romanian units. This battle took place on 1 August 1770 and claimed one-third of the Turkish force killed in action and another third drowned while trying to escape across the Danube. The Russians cleared the remainder of Turkish resistance from the principalities and then went into winter quarters where they prepared for an offensive into Bulgaria the following spring. On other fronts the Russians were equally successful, and the Ottoman Empire appeared to be helpless to stop them.

Although the war continued another four years, there were no more major battles fought in the Balkans. The Russians were able to stir rebellion in Greece, however, when an imperial naval squadron, commanded by Admiral Orlov, arrived in April 1770; but it was a small revolt with only one real success at Navarino. Albanian troops in the service of the Porte forced a Russian withdrawal and then ran amok killing the Greek population indiscriminately. It took the Turks nine years to restore order in the region.

Where Orlov's forces failed on land, they were highly successful at sea. On 6 July 1770 the Russian fleet, officered by a number of Englishmen in key positions, destroyed the Turkish fleet as it lay at anchor at Chesme near the island of Chios. Although senior English officers, led by Admiral Elphinstone, recommended the fleet move immediately on Constantinople, Orlov chose not to follow their advice. Debate continues to this day over his judgment, or lack of it, in this matter.

What happened during the remainder of the war might be of interest to the military historian but it had very little to do with the Balkans until the very last phases of the struggle. During that interim, the Romanians, in conferences held in both principalities between July 1772 and March 1773, voted to swear allegiance to Catherine and sent delegations to St. Petersburg for that purpose. By that juncture, however, the Pugachev revolt at home and pressure from Prussia and Austria was forcing Catherine into a position of having to seek a peace with the Porte.

To hasten this process, Rumiantsev crossed the Danube in 1773 near Shumla, Varna, and Silistria. The Turks were defeated at Kizluca (Korludzha) by another Russian force commanded by Alexandre Suvorov in June 1774 at the same moment that peace negotiators were already meeting. A peace accord was concluded at Kuchuk Kainardji

(Kucuk Kaynarca) on 16 July 1774. By its terms Russia withdrew from the principalities but reserved the right to intercede on the behalf of the Romanians should the need arise. The full scope of the treaty was extensive, and its implementation was to have far-reaching effects.

One of the best accounts of this war is found in Sir Edward Creasy's HISTORY OF THE OTTOMAN TURKS [66], that was reprinted in 1961. It is replete with otherwise unavailable detail. Shaw's account [241] summarizes the war, as does Stavrianos [254]. Schevill's work [232] is useless at this point for the serious military historian. Dupuy's ENCYCLOPEDIA OF MILITARY HISTORY [78] is accurate. The reign of Mustafa III is covered in "Bekir Sidki Baykal" [211], by Ragib Pasha, and in Baykal's "Mustafa III" [23]. The internal situation in the Ottoman Empire during this reign is described in "XVIII-inci yuzyilda cikarilan adalet-namelere gore Turkiye'nin ic durumu" [196], by Yucel Ozkaya. Uzuncarsili's "Cezayirli Gazi Hasan Pasa'ya dair" [286] emphasizes the naval reforms that followed the disaster at Chesme. Two other Turkish histories of some interest are MAHASIN AL-ASAR VE HAQAYIK AL-AHBAR [295], by Ahmed Vasif Efendi, that was published in part in 1830 and apparently never completed. The two volumes that were printed cover 1752-1774 and summarize HAKIM TARIHI (Hakim's History) for the period 1747-1766. There are at least five more manuscript volumes that are yet to be published. The second work of interest is CESMIZADE TARIHI [315], by Cesmi Zade Mustafa Resid Efendi, that covers the period 1766-1768.

The Russian side of the battle is found in a number of excellent works: Viktor F. Golovachev's CHESMA; EKSPEDITSIYA RUSSKOGO FLOTA V ARKHIPELAG I CHESMENSKOE SRAZHENIE [334] and F.S. Krinitsyn's CHESMANSKAYA POBEDA [324] follow the course of the battle. PODVIG LEITENANTA DMITRIYA SERGEIEVICH IL'INA I EGO LOVARISHCHEI [338] is the 20 page personal account of Lieutenant Il'in. V PAMYAT CHESMENSKOI POBEDY, 24-26 IUNIA 1770 GODA [339] is a collection of documents on the battle and on the expedition's operations around the island of Chios. There are two works by Evgenie Tarle that also should be read: CHESMENSKII BOI I PERVAYA RUSSKAYA EKSPEDITSIYA V ARKHIPELAG, 1769-1774 [332] and EKSPEDITSIYA RUSSKOGO FLOTA V ARKHIPELAG V 1769-1774 [333].

THE OTTOMAN EMPIRE AND ITS SUCCESSORS [187], by William Miller, covers from the last part of the 18th century up to World War II. FELDMARSHAL RUMIANTSEV V PERIOD RUSSKO-TURETSKOI VOINY 1768-1774 [142], by I.R. Klokman, was published in Moscow in 1951. The article, "Great Britain and the Russo-Turkish War of 1768-1774" [9], by M.S. Anderson, is a good account of English policy during the struggle. Allen Fisher's THE RUSSIAN ANNEXATION OF THE CRIMEA [86] deals only peripherally with the Balkans but is an interesting report of another phase of the conflict. Another interesting study is Douglas Dakin's THE UNIFICATION OF GREECE, 1770-1923 [68].

There are any number of works on Russia's Catherine the Great. Probably the best for its discussion of matters relevant to the Balkans is Gladys Scott Thomsom's CATHERINE THE GREAT AND THE EXPANSION OF RUSSIA [274]. Russia's constant struggle with the Ottoman Empire during Catherine's reign is extensively covered in this relatively small book. Andreas Bode's DIE FLOTTENPOLITIK

KATHERINAS II UND DIE KONFLIKTE MIT SCHWEDEN UND DER TURKEI (1768-1792) [328] is also important reading. Another excellent study is Isalda De Maderiaga's RUSSIA IN THE AGE OF CATHERINE THE GREAT. Two of the best works on Suvorov are also among the most difficult to find: HISTOIRE DES CAMPAGNES DU MARECHAL DE SUVOROV [112], which was published in Paris in 1802; and Johann F. Anthing's HISTORY OF THE CAMPAIGNS OF PRINCE ALEXANDER SUVOROV RYMNIKSKI [15]. The latter work was published in New York in 1800. The two works are quite similar. David Ransel's THE POLITICS OF CATHERINIAN RUSSIA: THE PANIN PARTY [320] is also well-worth reading.

The military reforms of Mustafa III are covered by Baron Francois de Tott (1730-1793) in his MEMOIRES SUR LES TURCS ET TARTARES [276]. This work describes de Tott's role in reforming the Turkish army. He also wrote MEMOIRES DU BARON DE TOTT SUR LES TURCS [275] which was published in 1795. De Tott is also discussed in Shaw [241] and in Creasy [66]. Finally, Geoffrey Blainey's THE CAUSES OF WAR [30] focuses on the struggle in the context of the "Vendetta of the Black Sea" and is essential reading for a full understanding of the events.

THE RULE OF ABDULHAMIT I

The treaty of 1774 dealt a serious blow to the Ottoman Empire even though the Turks lost little in the way of territory. Russia was back in Azov and now controlled the territory between the Dniester and the Bug; but it did have to evacuate the Danubian Principalities, the Caucasus, and the Aegean islands taken by Orlov. Still, for Turkey, the price was extremely high. A large indemnification was ordered, and the Porte was required to grant the Russians what amounted to authority to intercede on the behalf of orthodox Christians all over the Turkish empire.

The year of the treaty also witnessed the assumption of power of Abdulhamit I (Abdul Hamid) (1774-1789) following the death of his brother, Mustafa III, after a long illness. Abdulhamit was 50 years old and had lived most of his life in seclusion. He was, however, probably better prepared for his task than most of his predecessors. He personally directed a series of reforms designed to improve the conditions of not only his armed forces but his country as well. Creasy [66] deals with Abdulhamit's reign in great detail. The reign is also discussed by Cavid Baysun [24] in ISLAM ANSIKLOPEDISI. Bekir Kutukoglu discusses the reforms in a three-part article, "Murerrih Vasifin kaynaklarindan Hakim Tarihi" [152], published in TARIH DERGISI. This article discusses the reforms in light of the HISTORY OF HAKIM (HAKIM TARIHI), which is also one of the sources used by Vasif Efendi [295] in his history of this period which was published in Arabic in Cairo in 1930 in.

There were in addition to the Turkish reforms a number of other events that were of significance in the Balkans. On 7 May 1775, for instance, the Turks under pressure from the Austrians, who had assisted the Sultan by threatening the Russian right flank, ceded the Bukovina district of Moldavia to Vienna. As was the custom, neither the populace of the district nor Prince Grigore Ghica III (1774-1777) were consulted about the transfer. The Turks, in fact, had Ghica murdered in 1777 in retaliation for his protesting the cession and for his dealings with the Russians.

Bukovina remained under Austro-Hungarian control until 1918.

Trouble also began in Transylvania in 1779 when a delegation led by Vasili Ursu Nicola Horea travelled to Vienna to inform the imperial court of the corruption within the administration of the province. Little was accomplished by this or subsequent imperial visits (1783 & 1784) after the death of Maria Theresa, when Joseph II (1780-1790) sat on the throne. Then in May 1784, Vienna declared that henceforth the official language in Transylvania would be German. Two months after that in July 1784, the province was redivided so as to break up the centers of resistance to Austrian rule. Finally, at the end of October, the emperor decreed that Transylvanians could serve as border guards, apparently oblivious of the fact that a great revolt was in the offing.

The peasant uprising began on 2 November. Local forces were unable to check the revolt, and Joseph had to send imperial troops into the rebellious area. The revolt ended with the execution of Horea and a number of others; but its effect was felt in Vienna, and the emperor was forced to make a number of concessions including the lifting of the yoke of serfdom from the Transylvanians in 1785. This affair is discussed in "The Organization of the Peasant Army Led By Horea, Closca and Crisan (1784)" [81], by Nicolai Edriou. Even though the Transylvanians were still in the Austrian thrall they were at least emancipated.

## THE EASTERN QUESTION AND THE BALKANS

At this juncture the Balkans entered into a new episode of its history and became a key element in the most important issue of the age, the Eastern Question. This problem would remain alive in Europe, and especially in the southeastern part of the continent until the very eve of World War I. The scope and complexity of the issues involved go well beyond military history so it will have to suffice to state that the Balkans, along with the question of access to the Straits and the equally nettlesome problem of who was to control the Transcaucasian region between Russia and the Ottoman Empire, were the cause of almost all of the major conflicts that would involve central and southeastern Europe from the last decades of the 18th to the beginning of the 20th centuries. Certainly there were wars of independence fought during this period, but they were also a part of the Eastern Question; and, insofar as the Balkans were concerned, the outcomes of these struggles were tied directly to great power politics and not to the desires of the people to be free.

In 1780, after the death of Maria Theresa and the ascension of Joseph II to the Austrian throne, a reevaluation of French support was made in Vienna. Perceiving that France seemed more intent on its conflict with England than upon a continuation of diplomatic support of Austria, Joseph sought to renew the ties that had existed between his country and Imperial Russia. Russia viewed this as an opportunity to gain greater leverage in its almost constant warfare with the Turks even though Austria was its chief rival and primary opposition in the Balkans. Catherine used this moment to divest herself of the alliance with Prussia, that was about to expire anyway, to begin negotiations that culminated in an Austro-Russian defensive alliance (1781). Prussia, isolated, began to court England; and England, concerned with Russia's increasingly more powerful attacks upon the Turks, began seeking ways of bolstering the sagging Ottoman Empire thereby preventing Russia from reaching the eastern Mediterranean.

Since the signing of the Treaty of Kuchuk-Kainardji, Catherine and her advisors had been working on what became known as the "Greek Plan." This had several parts, one of which dealt with the ejection of Turkey from the European continent and the subsequent division of the liberated territory into three segments. The area under discussion was, of course, the Balkan peninsula. The western part was to go to Austria. Russia was to sponsor a buffer state to be called Dacia that was to be composed of Moldavia, Wallachia, and Bessarabia. The remaining third was to form the new Byzantine Empire with its capital at Constantinople and with Catherine's grandson, appropriately named Constantine, upon its throne. The other great powers were to all receive a small largesse as a palliative. Even though somewhat ill-at-ease over the plan, Joseph II agreed to its goals.

## THE RUSSO-TURKISH WAR OF 1787-1792

In 1783 Russia annexed the Khanate of the Crimea and a crisis arose in which the French and Prussians were able to dissuade the Turkish Sultan, Abdulhamit I, from immediately declaring war -- a war that almost certainly would have gone badly for the Ottomans. Also, a new Grand Vizier, Halil Hamid, had just been appointed and wished to use the time for a major overhaul of the armed forces. There were strong elements in the Turkish court that sought war, but eventually the Porte acknowledged the annexation in the Agreement of Aynali Kavak (9 January 1784).

Almost immediately the Russians began other activities designed to draw the Turks into open conflict. Russian interference in the Danubian Principalities was but a lesser part of these acts, but they played an important part in the ultimate Turkish decision once again to make war on Russia. The war came about because the Ulema, the chief council to the Sultan, became dominated by a war party led by Koca Yusuf Pasha, who had become Grand Vizier in 1786. At his insistence the Turks issued an ultimatum to the Russians demanding their immediate evacuation of the Crimea and the Caucasus. When this failed, the Porte declared war (14 August 1787). Russia responded some thirty days later (15 September) with its own declaration: Austria did not formally enter the conflict until 19 February 1788.

As neither side was prepared for war, the conflict was slow in starting. In 1788 a coordinated offensive began with widely separated attacks on the Turks. Suvorov had already been successful in beating off an Ottoman attack to reconquer the Crimea. Austria's armies, with Joseph II in personal command, suffered initial setbacks. Russian forces were more successful and moved into Moldavia, capturing the important cities of Chocim and Jassy.

At sea a Russian Black Sea flotilla under John Paul Jones inflicted serious losses on Turkish naval units in the two battles at Liman (17 & 27 June 1788), near the mouth of the Dnieper. To add to Turkish difficulties, a major uprising broke out that year that was led by Prince Peter of Montenegro. In 1789 new offensives began with Austro-Russian attacks unto Moldavian territory and Austrian attacks into Serbia. In the Moldavian campaign, Russian forces commanded by the Empress' lover, Potemkin, and Count Rumiantsev were unsuccessful against the Turks; but those led by Suvorov and Austrian forces under Prince Friedrich of Saxe-Coburg defeated the Turks at Focsani on 1 August, Rimnik on 22 September, and occupied Bucharest on 11 November. These defeats forced a Turkish withdrawal south of the Danube. In the Serbian campaign, the Austrian army commanded by General Gideon von Laudon -- Joseph had wisely decided not to campaign that year, was able to repulse a strong Turkish attack into Bosnia and was then able to lay siege to, and eventually capture, Belgrad (8 October).

## AUSTRIA MAKES PEACE

During the winter of 1789-1790, a general desire for peace pervaded in all the capitals of Europe. Russia needed to be free to respond to a Swedish assault into Finland. Austria was beset by revolts, notably in the Netherlands and in Hungary. But, most of all, the onset of revolution in France required the specific attention of the great powers who saw in it the seeds of their own destruction.

For Turkey, this was an opportunity, given the offers of support made by the great powers. The new Sultan, Selim III (1789-1807), was, however, in no particular hurry to concede anything as, having cast aside the impediments of reform, he saw the situation as favorable for a return of all Ottoman territory as a concession for peace, rather than the guarantees that had been promised by the great powers. Regardless of this Turkish intransigence, the Triple Alliance was able to hammer out a separate peace between the Porte and Austria (Treaty of Sistova - 4 August 1791). Neither side was very happy with the terms that had been forced upon them by the Prussians. Austria was required to relinquish its holds on Bosnia, Serbia, and the Principalities, while Selim had to guarantee the rights of Christians and to allow an Austrian overwatch of Christian affairs in the Balkans. Once again, Austria had abandoned Russia at a critical moment; and, once again, Russia faced the Turks alone.

Alone may not be the right word, however, as a major revolt in Greece seriously interfered with Turkish planning for a new campaign against the Russians. Fighting continued after the Austrians had entered into a truce (27 July 1790) and up to the time of the Sistova treaty. During that period Suvorov was able to take the powerful Turkish fort at Ismail on the Kilia river (the north branch of the Danube, at a point 40 miles inland from the Black Sea). In four days of plundering following the Russian entrance into the fortress city (22 December 1790), it has been estimated that 40,000 Turkish troops, along with uncounted thousands of civilians, perished by the sword. This was the last great battle of the war; and Russia, anxious for peace, opened negotiations that culminated in the Treaty of Jassy on 9 January 1792. Russia was required to surrender Moldavia and Bessarabia to the Turks but was able to retain the territories it had taken east of the Dniester.

There is some very good coverage of this period in English-language books. Creasy's [66] account of the war is complete but somewhat biased. Shaw [241] gives a concise review of the events from the Turkish viewpoint. Schevill's [232] rendition is also very good. Dupuy [78] gives the basic facts and little more. Stavrianos' [254] telling of the war is the best short account. THE EASTERN QUESTION, 1774-1923 [11], by Matthew Anderson, also has a solid history of the war along with excellent coverage of European diplomatic relations involving the Balkans. Anderson has also edited THE GREAT POWERS AND THE NEAR EAST, 1774-1923 [10] that reviews much of the earlier writings about the international relations involved in the Eastern Question. Together his two works encompass most of the information that the average student should need to know.

An earlier study by Albert Sorel, THE EASTERN QUESTION IN THE EIGHTEENTH CENTURY; THE PARTITION OF POLAND AND THE TREATY OF KAINARDJI [249], was published in French in 1889. It was subsequently published under the English version of the same title in 1969 [247]. The gist of Sorel's study concerns Austria's failure to exert sufficient influence in attempting to solve the problem. Sir John Marriott's history [179] is, at best, a sketchy second choice, as is the French work by Edouard Driault [73]. Even the omnipresent Karl Marx wrote on the subject [180]. As a final selection, and a solid one, Jacques Ancel's MANUEL HISTORIQUE DE LA QUESTION D'ORIENT: 1792-1923 [8] should not be overlooked.

There are a number of good works on Europe during this critical period. Leo Gershoy's FROM DESPOTISM TO REVOLUTION, 1763-1789 [100]; Norman Hampson's THE FIRST EUROPEAN REVOLUTION, 1776-1815 [104]; George Rude's REVOLUTIONARY EUROPE, 1783-1815 [226]; E.J. Hobsbawm's THE AGE OF REVOLUTION: EUROPE, 1789-1848 [113]; and Charles Breunig's THE AGE OF REVOLUTION AND REACTION, 1789-1850 [41] are all worth reading. Albert Sorel's monumental eight-volume L'EUROPE ET LA REVOLUTION FRANCAISE [248] is excellent, while Nicholae Iorga's LA REVOLUTION FRANCAISE ET LE SUD-EST EUROPE [127] is a superficial treatment of the impact of the events in France upon revolutionary spirits in eastern Europe.

CATHERINE THE GREAT AND THE EXPANSION OF EUROPE [274], by G.S. Thomson, is the best account of Imperial Russia in this period. RUSSIA AND EUROPE, 1789-1825 [164], by A. Lobanov-Rostovsky, is very interesting reading even if the reader may come away with questions still unanswered. Norman Saul's RUSSIA AND THE MEDITERRANEAN, 1797-1807 [228] deals with that phase of the Eastern Question that was seen in the emerging foreign policy of Imperial Russia. A useful article by J.C. Hurowitz appeared in 1962 in WORLD POLITICS, "Russia and the Straits: A Reevaluation of the Origins of the Problem" [122]. This is reinforced with Hurowitz' 1964 article in the Turkish BELLETIN titled "The Background of Russia's Claims to the Turkish Straits" [121]. Of particular interest is Demetreous Dvoichenko-Markov's "Russia and the First Accredited Diplomat in the Danubian Principalities, 1779-1808" [79]. De Maderiaga [325] and Rancel [320] should be studied along with Bode [328]. Tarle's ADMIRAL USHAKOV NA SREDIZEMNOM MORE, 1798-1800 GG. [331] is also very important at this point.

The Austrian side of this story is told in C.A. Macartney's THE HABSBURG EMPIRE, 1790-1918 [172] and in his article in NCMH, "The Austrian Monarchy, 1792-1847" [170]. Saul Padover concentrates on the reign of Joseph II in his THE REVOLUTIONARY EMPEROR, JOSEPH II OF AUSTRIA [197]. Sir Harold Temperley compares and differentiates between FREDERICK THE GREAT AND KAISER JOSEPH [271], while DIE ORIENTALISCHE POLITIK OSTERREICHS SEIT 1774 [25], by A. Beer, studies the Eastern Question from the Austrian viewpoint.

The reforms carried out in Turkey by Halil Hamid Pasha, who was Grand Vizier from 1782 until 1785, are discussed in "Sadrazam Halil Hamid Pasa" [288] for TURKIYAT MECMUASI by Ismail Uzuncarsili. This excellent article stresses the modernization program and other internal reforms carried out during the reign of Abdulhamit I. Another solid article on the reform movement during this general period is T. Naff's "Reform and the Conduct of Ottoman Diplomacy in the Reign of Selim III, 1789-1807" [191]. Stanford Shaw has contributed two articles on this period: "The Origins of Ottoman Military Reform: The Nizam-i Cedid Army of Sultan Selim III" [242]; and "The Established Ottoman Army Corps Under Selim III (1789-1807)" [240]. Shaw also wrote "Selim III and the Turkish Navy" [243] in 1969. An important study of the council structure in the Porte is found in Uriel Heyd's "The Ottoman 'Ulema and Westernization in the Time of Selim III and Mahmud II" [111]. One of the most useful works on the Ottoman Empire during this period is Shaw's BETWEEN OLD AND NEW: THE OTTOMAN EMPIRE UNDER SELIM III, 1789-1807 [239]. It has excellent coverage of the war and an exhaustive bibliography. A. Cevat Eren's "Selim III" [82] is excellent but it is in Turkish. So is Ahmed Asim's TARIH-I ASIM [19] published in 1866, which covers the period 1791-1808 in two volumes. Lastly, there is Bernard Lewis' "The Impact of the French Revolution on Turkey" [161] a prime example of this outstanding scholar's work.

THE SOUTHERN SLAV QUESTION AND THE HABSBURG MONARCHY [237], by Robert Seton-Watson, is very good, as is BALCANICA: A GUIDE TO THE POLISH ARCHIVES RELATIVE TO THE HISTORY OF THE BALKAN COUNTRIES [300]. This latter work is only 79 pages, but it contains numerous sources that are of great interest on this current period. Professor Bela Kiraly's HUNGARY IN THE LATE EIGHTEENTH CENTURY: THE DECLINE OF ENLIGHTENED DESPOTISM [141] is the best work available on Hungary for these times. There are a few obvious shortcomings in the volume, but these will only be noticeable to the dedicated scholar. For the ordinary reader and for the military historian, Kiraly's study is better than anything else presently available. Peter Sugar's article, "The Influence of the Enlightenment and the French Revolution in Eighteenth Century Hungary" [260] is also worthwhile. An interesting work on foreign trade in Austria-Hungary is DER AUSSENHANDEL DES KONIGREICHS UNGARN (1700-1848) [186], by G. Merei. Finally, there are two articles on the Jacobin Movement that are of some interest, "The Hungarian Jacobin Conspiracy of 1794-5" [32], by P. Body; and K. Benda's "Les Jacobins hongrois" [26]. These two pieces demonstrate the effect that the French Revolution and Jacobin ideas for revolution had upon the people of east-central Europe.

The British view of the Eastern Question is explained in Temperley's ENGLAND AND THE NEAR EAST [269]. This study focusses on the Crimea rather than on the Balkans but is still excellent reading. Stavrianos [254] has excellent coverage of the period and emphasizes the repercussions felt in the Balkans following Napoleon's invasion of Egypt and after Selim III joined forces with the French ruler.

Mercia Macdermott's A HISTORY OF BULGARIA, 1393-1885 [174] contains extensive coverage of the Kurdzhali movement that started in 1792 as an outgrowth of the brigandage discussed earlier. Another document on Bulgaria is NATSIONALNOOSVOBODITELNI DVIZHENIIA NA BALKANSKITE NARODI: VTORATA POLOVINA NA XVIII V.-1878 G. [48] a bibliography dealing with military armaments. Finally, there is THE MOVEMENT FOR GREEK INDEPENDENCE, 1779-1821 [58] that is a collection of documents edited by Richard Clogg. This is an excellent source of data.

The end of the 18th century witnessed a number of changes in the style and intensity of warfare. These changes only confirmed what many were already well aware of, that war was a serious business and it was being waged more and more by people willing to fight to be free.

# BIBLIOGRAPHICAL LISTING

1. Abdi, (fnu). 1730 PATRONA IHTILALI HAKKINDA BIR ESER. Ankara: 1943.

2. Adams, A., et al. AN ATLAS OF RUSSIAN AND EAST EUROPEAN HISTORY. New York: 1967 [1966].

3. Aktepe, M.M. "Mahmud I." IA VII, 154-165.

4. _____. PATRONA ISYANI (1730). Istanbul: 1958.

5. Albion, R.G. FORESTS AND SEA POWER. Cambridge: 1929.

6. Alston, R.C., & Janetta, M.J. BIBLIOGRAPHY, MACHINE READABLE CATALOGUING, AND THE ESTC. London: 1978.

7. Altindag, S. "Osman III." IA VII, 448-450.

8. Ancel, J. MANUEL HISTORIQUE DE LA QUESTION D'ORIENT: 1792-1923. Paris: 1923.

9. Anderson, M.S. "Great Britain and the Russo-Turkish War of 1768-1774." EHR 64 (1964), 39-38.

10. _____., ed. THE GREAT POWERS AND THE NEAR EAST (1774-1923). London: 1970.

11. _____. THE EASTERN QUESTION, 1774-1923. London & New York: 1966.

12. _____. EIGHTEENTH CENTURY EUROPE, 1713-1789. New York: 1966.

13. Anderson, R.C. NAVAL WARS OF THE LEVANT, 1559-1853. Princeton: 1952.

14. Angeli, M.E. von, DER KRIEG MIT DER PFORTE, 1736 BIS 1739. Vienna: 1880.

15. Anthing, J.F. HISTORY OF THE CAMPAIGNS OF PRINCE ALEXANDER SUVOROV RYMNIKSKI. New York: 1800.

16. Anthony, K. CATHERINE THE GREAT. New York: 1927 [1925].

17. Arnakis, G.G. THE NEAR EAST IN MODERN TIMES: THE OTTOMAN EMPIRE AND THE BALKANS TO 1900. Austin & New York: 1969.

18. Arneth, A. von. PRINZ EUGEN VON SAVOYEN. Vienna: 1864.

19. Asim, A. TARIH-I ASIM. 2 vols. Istanbul: 1866.

20. Barker, E. MACEDONIA: ITS PLACE IN BALKAN POWER POLITICS. RIIA. Westport: 1980 [1950].

21. Barker, T.M. FREDERICK THE GREAT AND THE MAKING OF PRUSSIA. New York: [1971, c. 1972].

22. _____. "Military Entrepreneurship and Absolutism: Habsburg Models." JES 4 (1974), 19-42.

23. Baykal, B.S. "Mustafa III." IA VII, 700-708.

24. Baysun, C. "Abdulhamid I." IA I, 73-76.

25. Beer, A. DIE ORIENTALISCHE POLITIK OSTERREICHS SEIT 1774. Prague: 1883.

26. Benda, K. "Les Jacobins hongrois." ANN. HIST. DE LA FRANC. (1959), 38-60.

27. _____. UNGARISCH-SERBISCHE VERSOHNUNGVERSUCHE WAHREND DES RAKOCZI-AUFSTANDES 1703-1711. EHH I. Budapest: 1980.

28. Benedict, H. DER PASCHA-GRAF ALEXANDER VON BONNEVAL, 1675-1747. Graz & Cologne: 1959.

29. Benzoin, A. "La guerra russo-turca del 1736-1739." ARCHIVIO VENETA V xiii (1933), 186-202.

30. Blainey, G. THE CAUSES OF WAR. New York: 1973.

31. Blum, J., et al. THE EMERGENCE OF THE EUROPEAN WORLD. Boston: 1966.

32. Body, P. "The Hungarian Jacobin Conspiracy of 1794-5." JCEA XXII (1962), 3-26.

33. Bogaiavlenskii, S. "Iz russko-serbskikh otnoshenii pri Petre Velikom." VI Nos. 8-9 ( 1946), 11-28.

34. "Bonneval und Prinz Eugen." MIOG 18 (1950), 470-502.

35. Bonneval, Comte de. MEMOIRES DU COMTE DE BONNEVAL, OFFICIER GENERAL, AU SERVICE DE LOUIS XIV ... Paris: 1806.

36. Boppe, A. "La France et le militaire turc' au XVIIIe siecle." FH VIII (1912), 386-402, 490-512.

37. Bowen, H. "Ahmed III." EI I, 286-271.

38. Braubach, M. PRINZ EUGEN VON SAVOYEN, EINE BIOGRAPHIE. 5 vols. Vienna: 1963-1965.

39. Braun, M. "Turkenherrschaft und Turkenkampf bei die Balkanslawen. WaG VI (1940), 124-139.

40. Omitted

41. Breunig, C. THE AGE OF REVOLUTION AND REACTION, 1789-1850. 2nd ed. NHME. New York: c.1977 [1970].

42. Bromley, J.S., ed. THE RISE OF GREAT BRITAIN AND RUSSIA, 1688-1715/25. Vol. 6 in NCMH. Cambridge: 1970.

43. Omitted.

44. Bromley, J.S., & Goodwin, A. A SELECTED LIST OF WORKS ON EUROPE AND EUROPE OVERSEAS, 1715-1815. Oxford: 1956.

45. Bromley, J.S., & Ryan, A.N. "Armies and Navies." NCMH 6. Cambridge: 1970.

46. Bruun, G. EUROPE AND THE FRENCH IMPERIUM, 1799-1814. New York & London: 1938.

47. Bulgaria. Academy of Sciences. DOCUMENTS AND MATERIALS ON THE HISTORY OF THE BULGARIAN PEOPLE. Compiled by M. Voynov, et al. Sofia: 1969.

48. _____. NATSIONALNOOSVOBODITELNI DVIZHENIIA NA BALKANSKITE NARODI: VTORATA POLOVINA NA XVIII V. -- 1878 G.: VUORUZHENA BORBA: BIBLIOGRAFIIA, 1966-1976. Compiled by Liudmila Genova. Sofia: 1978.

49. Cassels, L. THE STRUGGLE FOR THE OTTOMAN EMPIRE, 1717-1740. London: 1966.

50. Ceaucescu, I. THE ENTIRE PEOPLE'S WAR FOR THE HOMELAND'S DEFENCE WITH THE ROMANIANS. Bucharest: 1980. Also found in Romanian as RAZBOIUL INTREGULUI POPOR PENTRU APARAREA PATRIEI LA ROMANI. Bucharest: 1980.

51. _____., ed. PAGES FROM THE MILITARY HISTORY OF THE ROMANIAN PEOPLE. Bucharest: 1980.

52. Cernovodeanu, P. SOCIETATA FEUDALA ROMANEASCA VAZUTA DE CALATORI STRAINI (SECOLELE XV-XVIII). Bucharest: 1973.

53. Chandler, D.G. "Armies and Navies: 1. The Art of War on Land." NCMH VI. Cambridge: 1970.

54. _____. ATLAS OF MILITARY STRATEGY. New York: 1980.

55. Clark, G.N., Sir., et al. Advisory Comm. NEW CAMBRIDGE MODERN HISTORY. 14 vols. Cambridge: 1957-1970.

56. Clarkson, J.D. A HISTORY OF RUSSIA. New York: 1969 [1961].

57. Cleator, P.E. WEAPONS OF WAR. New York: 1968.

58. Clogg, R., ed. THE MOVEMENT FOR GREEK INDEPENDENCE, 1779-1821. LSSEES. London & Basingstoke: 1973 [1970].

59. Colby, E. MASTERS OF MOBILE WARFARE. Princeton: 1943.

60. Coles, P. THE OTTOMAN IMPACT ON EUROPE. LECS. London: 1968.

61. Cook, M.A., ed. A HISTORY OF THE OTTOMAN EMPIRE TO 1730. Berkeley: 1976

62. Coquelle, P. HISTOIRE DU MONTENEGRO ET DE LA BOSNIA. Paris: 1895.

63. Corvisier, A. ARMEES ET SOCIETES EN EUROPE DE 1494 A 1789. Paris: 1976. Also found in English.

64. Crankshaw, E. MARIA THERESA. New York: 1970.

65. Crawley, C.W., ed. WAR AND PEACE IN THE AGE OF UPHEAVAL. Vol. IX in NCMH. Cambridge: 1965.

66. Creasy, E.S., Sir. HISTORY OF THE OTTOMAN TURKS. Oriental Reprints No. 1. Beirut: 1961.

67. Crouzenac, S. de. (Saunier de Beaumont) HISTOIRE DE LA DERNIERE REVOLUTION ARRIVEE DANS L'EMPIRE OTTOMAN. Paris: 1970.

68. Dakin, D. THE UNIFICATION OF GREECE, 1770-1923. London: 1972.

69. Delbruck, H. GESCHICHTE DER KRIEGKUNST IM RAHMEN DER POLITISCHEN GESCHICHTE. 4 vols. Berlin: 1920.

70. d'Ohsson, I.M. TABLEAU GENERALE DE L'EMPIRE OTHMAN. 7 vols. Paris: 1788-1824.

71. Dorn, W. COMPETITION FOR EMPIRE, 1740-1763. RME 9. New York: 1940.

72. Doyle, W. "The Old European Order, 1660-1800". SOHMW. Oxford: 1978.

73. Driault, E. LA QUESTION D'ORIENT. Paris: 1912.

74. Duggan, S.P.H. THE EASTERN QUESTION. New York: 1970.

75. Duffy, C. THE ARMY OF FREDERICK THE GREAT. New York: 1974.

76. _____. THE ARMY OF MARIA THERESA. THE ARMED FORCES OF IMPERIAL AUSTRIA, 1740-1780. New York: 1977.

77. Dunn, R.S. THE AGE OF RELIGIOUS WARS, 1550-1715. 2nd ed. NHME. New York: 1979 [1970].

78. Dupuy, R.E., & Dupuy, T.N. THE ENCYCLOPEDIA OF MILITARY HISTORY. Rev. ed. New York: 1977.

79. Dvoichenko-Markov, D. "Russia and the First Accredited Diplomat in the Danubian Principalities, 1779-1808." SEES VIII, 3-4 (1963), 200-229.

80. Earle, E.M. THE MAKERS OF MODERN STRATEGY: MILITARY THOUGHT FROM MACHIAVELLI TO HITLER. Princeton: 1943.

81. Edroiu, N. "The Organization of the Peasant Army Led by Horea, Closca and Crisan (1784)." ARS. Bucharest: 1980.

82. Eren, A.C. "Selim III." IA X, 441-457.

83. Eton, W. A SURVEY OF THE TURKISH EMPIRE. 2nd. ed. London: 1972 [1799].

84. Falls, C.B. THE ART OF WAR. New York: 1961.

85. Finlay, G. HISTORY OF GREECE, FROM ITS CONQUEST BY THE ROMANS TO THE PRESENT TIME, B.C. 164 TO A.D. 1864. New rev. ed. by H.F. Tozer. Oxford: 1877.

86. Fisher, A. THE RUSSIAN ANNEXATION OF THE CRIMEA, 1772-1783. Cambridge: 1970.

87. Fisher, S. "Ottoman Feudalism and Its Influence Upon the Balkans." HISTORIAN, XV (Autumn 1952), 3-22.

88. Florinsky, M.T. RUSSIA: A HISTORY AND AN INTERPRETATION. 2 vols. New York: 1953.

89. Frischauer, P. THE IMPERIAL CROWN: THE STORY OF THE RISE AND FALL OF THE HOLY ROMAN AND AUSTRIAN EMPIRES. London: 1939.

90. Fuller, J.F.C. A MILITARY HISTORY OF THE WESTERN WORLD. 3 vols. New York: 1954-1955.

91. Gibb, H.A.R., Sir, et al. ENCYCLOPEDIA OF ISLAM. New ed. Leiden: 1913-1938.

92. Gibb, H.A.R., Sir, & Bowen, H. ISLAMIC SOCIETY AND THE WEST: ISLAMIC SOCIETY IN THE EIGHTEENTH CENTURY. London: 1950.

93. Gibbs, N.H. "Armed Forces and the Art of War: Armies." NCMH IX. Cambridge: 1965.

94. Gilbert, M. RUSSIAN HISTORY ATLAS. New York: 1972.

95. Giurescu, C.C., et al. CHRONOLOGICAL HISTORY OF ROMANIA. Bucharest: 1972.

96. Gooch, G. FREDERICK THE GREAT. London: 1947.

97. Goodwin, A. THE EUROPEAN NOBILITY OF THE EIGHTEENTH CENTURY. London: 1953.

98. _____. THE AMERICAN AND FRENCH REVOLUTIONS, 1763-93. Vol. VIII in NCMH. Cambridge: 1965.

99. Gorceix, S. BONNEVAL PACHA. Paris: 1953.

100. Omitted.

101. Gossip, R. TURKEY AND RUSSIA, THEIR RACES, HISTORY ANND WARS. Edinburgh: 1879.

102. Gulick, E.V. EUROPE'S CLASSICAL BALANCE OF POWER. Ithaca: [1955].

103. Hammer-Purgstall, J. von. HISTOIRE DE L'EMPIRE OTTOMAN. 18 vols. Paris: 1835-1843.

104. Hampson, N. THE FIRST EUROPEAN REVOLUTION, 1776-1815. LWC. New York & London: 1969.

105. _____. THE FRENCH REVOLUTION: A CONCISE HISTORY. London: 1975.

106. Hantsch, H. DAS GESCHICHTE OSTERREICHS. 2 vols. Vienna: 1950.

107. Henderson, N. PRINCE EUGENE OF SAVOY. London: 1964.

108. Hengelmuller von Hengervar, L. Freiherr. FRANZ RAKOCZY UND SEIN KAMPF FUR UNGARN FRIEHEIT. Stuttgart & Berlin: 1913.

109. _____. HUNGARY'S FIGHT FOR NATIONAL EXISTENCE; OR, THE HISTORY OF THE GREAT UPRISING LED BY FRANCIS RAKOCZY II, 1703-1711. London: 1913.

110. Heppell, M., & Singleton, F.B. YUGOSLAVIA. New York: 1961.

111. Heyd, U. "The Ottoman 'Ulema and Westernization in the Time of Selim III and Mahmud II." SIHC 9 (1961), 63-96.

112. HISTOIRE DES CAMPAGNES DU MARECHAL DE SUVOROV, PRINCE ITALIKSKI. 3 vols. Paris: 1802.

113. Hobsbawm, E.J. THE AGE OF REVOLUTION: EUROPE 1789-1848. New York: 1969 [1962].

114. Hodgart, A. THE ECONOMICS OF EUROPEAN IMPERIALISM. FMES. New York: 1978 [1977].

115. Hodgetts, E.A.B. THE LIFE OF CATHERINE THE GREAT. London: [1914].

116. Horecky, P.L., ed. EAST CENTRAL EUROPE: A GUIDE TO BASIC PUBLICATIONS. Chicago: 1969.

117. Hosch, E. THE BALKANS: A SHORT HISTORY. New York: 1972.

118. Hourani, A.H. THE OTTOMAN BACKGROUND OF THE MODERN MIDDLE EAST. Harlow: 1970.

119. Houtsma, T., ed. ENCYCLOPEDIA OF ISLAM. 2nd ed. 4 vols. w/supplt. Leiden: 1954-.

120. Hunczak, T., ed. RUSSIAN IMPERIALISM FROM IVAN THE TERRIBLE TO THE REVOLUTION. New Brunswick: 1974.

121. Hurowitz, J.C. "The Background of Russia's Claims to the Turkish Straits." BELLETIN XXVIII (1964), 459-503.

122. _____. "Russia and the Straits: A Reevaluation of the
     Origins of the Problem." WP XIV (1962), 606-632.

123. Hutton, R.M. "Charles XII in Turkey 'Narrative of the King of
     Sweden's Movements, 1709-1714.'" TAD I (1957), 83-143.

124. Ignotus, P. "Czechs, Magyars, Slovaks." TPQ (June 1969),
     187-204.

125. Iorga, N. GESCHICHTE DES OSMANISCHEN REICHES. 5 vols. Gotha:
     1908-1913.

126. _____. HISTOIRE DES ROUMAINS DE LA PENINSULE DES BALCANS.
     Bucharest: 1919.

127. _____. LA REVOLUTION FRANCAISE ET LE SUD-EST DE L'EUROPE.
     Bucharest: 1934.

128. Itzkowitz, N. "Eighteenth Century Ottoman Realities." SI 16
     (1969), 73-94.

129. Izzi, S. IZZI TARIHI. 2 vols. Istanbul: 1782.

130. Jacobs, I. BEZIEHUNGEN ENGLANDS ZU RUSSLAND UND ZUR TURKEI IN
     DEN JAHREN 1718-1724. Basel: 1945.

131. Jahn, M. GESCHICHTE DER KRIEGSWISSENSCHAFTEN. Berlin: 1891.

132. Jessup, J.E., & Coakley, R.W., eds. A GUIDE TO THE STUDY AND
     USE OF MILITARY HISTORY. Washington: 1979.

133. Kann, R.A. A HISTORY OF THE HABSBURG EMPIRE, 1526-1918.
     Berkeley: 19974.

134. Kann, R.A., & David, Z. THE PEOPLES OF THE EASTERN HABSBURG
     LANDS, 1526-1918. HECE 6. Seattle & London: 1982.

135. Kaplan, H.H. RUSSIA AND THE OUTBREAK OF THE SEVEN YEARS' WAR.
     Berkeley & Los Angelos: 1968.

136. Karal, E.Z. "Ahmed III." IA I, 165-168.

137. Kellenbenz, H. THE RISE OF THE EUROPEAN ECONOMY. Rev. & edited
     by Gerhard Benecke. New York: 1976.

138. Kerner, R.J. BOHEMIA IN THE EIGHTEENTH CENTURY. New York: 1932.

139. Khalifeh, H. THE HISTORY OF THE MARITIME WARS OF THE TURKS.
     Trans. by James Mitchell. London: 1831.

140. Kinross, J.P.H., Lord. THE OTTOMAN CENTURIES: THE RISE AND FALL
     OF THE TURKISH EMPIRE. London: 1977.

141. Kiraly, B. HUNGARY IN THE LATE EIGHTEENTH CENTURY: THE DECLINE
     OF ENLIGHTENED DESPOTISM. New York & London: 1969.

142. Klokman: I.R. FELDMARSHAL RUMIANTSEV V PERIOD RUSSKO-TURETSKOI VOINY, 1768-1774. Moscow: 1951.

143. Klyuchenski, V.O. KURS RUSSKOI ISTORII. 5 vols. Moscow: 1937 [1921-23].

144. _____. PETER THE GREAT. Trans. by Liliana Archibald. New York: 1958.

145. Kontogiannes, P.M. HOI HELLENES KATA TON PROTON EPI AIKATERINES II ROSSOTOURKIKOM POLEMON (1768-1774). Athens:1903.

146. Kreiger, L. KINGS AND PHILOSOPHERS, 1689-1789. NHME. New York: 1970.

147. Kurat, A.N., ed. DESPATCHES OF SIR ROBERT SUTTON, AMBASSADOR TO CONSTANTINOPLE (1710-1714). London: 1953.

148. _____. ISVEC KIRALI XII KARL' IN TURKIYEDE KALISI VE BU SIRALARDA OSMANLI IMPARATORLUGI. Istanbul: 1943.

149. _____. PRUT SEFERI VE BARISI 1123/1711. 2 vols. Ankara: 1951.

150. _____. "XVIII Yuzyil Basi Avrupa Umumi Harbinde Turkiye Nin Tarafsizligi." BELLETIN VII (April 1943), 245-272.

151. Kurat, A.N., & Bromley, J.S. "The Retreat of the Turks, 1683-1730." NCMH 6. Cambridge: 1970.

152. Kutukoglu, B. "Murerrih Vasifin kaynaklarindan Hakim Tarihi." TD V (1953), 69-76; VI (1954), 91-122; VII (1954), 79-192.

153. Langer, W.L., ed. THE RISE OF MODERN EUROPE. 20 vols. New York & London: 1936-.

154. Lederer, I.J., ed. "Russia and the Balkans." In RUSSIAN FOREIGN POLICY: ESSAYS IN HISTORICAL PERSPECTIVE. New Haven: 1962.

155. Lefebvre, G. THE FRENCH REVOLUTION. 2 vols. Trans. by E.M. Evanson. London & New York: 1962-1964.

156. Legrand, E.L.J. BIBLIOGRAPHIE ALBANAISE. Leipzig: 1973.

157. Lengyel, E. 1000 YEARS OF HUNGARY. New York: 1958.

158. Lentin, A. RUSSIA IN THE EIGHTEENTH CENTURY. London & New York: 1973.

159. Leo, M. LA BULGARIE ET SON PEUPLE SOUS LA DOMINATION OTTOMANE. Sofia: 1949.

160. Lessner, E.C., & Lessner, A.M.L. THE DANUBE: THE DRAMATIC HISTORY OF THE GREAT RIVER AND THE PEOPLE TOUCHED BY ITS FLOW. Garden City: 1961.

161. Lewis, B. "The Impact of the French Revolution on Turkey." JWH I (1953), 105-125.

162. Lindsay, J.O., ed. THE OLD REGIME, 1713-1763. Vol. VII in NCMH.
     Cambridge: 1957.

163. Lloyd, C. "Navies in the Armed Forces and the Art of War." NCMH
     IX. Cambridge: 1965.

164. Lobanov-Rostovsky, A. RUSSIA AND EUROPE, 1789-1825. Durham:
     1947.

165. Omitted.

166. Lukinich, I. ERDELY TERULETI VALTOZASAI A TOROK HODITAS
     KORABAN, 1541-1711. Budapest: 1918.

167. _____. A SZATMARI BEKE TORTENETE ES OKIRATTARA. Budapest:
     1925.

168. Luvaas, J. "The Great Military Historians and Philosophers."
     GSUMH. Washington: 1979.

169. Lyons, M., et al., eds. THE RUSSIAN IMPERIAL ARMY. Stanford:
     1968.

170. Macartney, C.A. "The Austrian Monarchy, 1792-1847." NCMH IX.
     Cambridge: 1965.

171. _____. "The Habsburg Dominions." NCMH VII. Cambridge: 1957.

172. _____. THE HABSBURG EMPIRE, 1790-1918. New York: 1969.

173. _____. HUNGARY, A SHORT HISTORY. Chicago: 1962.

174. Macdermott, M. A HISTORY OF BULGARIA, 1393-1885. London: 1962.

175. Omitted.

176. Makkai, L. HISTOIRE DE TRANSYLVANIE. Paris: 1946.

177. Mamatey, V.S. THE RISE OF THE HABSBURG EMPIRE, 1526-1815. New
     York: 1971.

178. Marczali, H. HUNGARY IN THE EIGHTEENTH CENTURY. Cambridge:
     1910.

179. Marriott, J.A.R., Sir. THE EASTERN QUESTION. Oxford: 1930.

180. Marx, K. THE EASTERN QUESTION. New York: 1969.

181. Massie, R.K. PETER THE GREAT: HIS LIFE AND WORLD. New York:
     1981.

182. Matuschka, L. DER TURKEN-KRIEGE, 1716-1718. Vols. VII & VIII in
     FELDZUG DES PRINZEN EUGEN VON SAVOYEN. 2nd ed. Vienna:
     1876-1892.

183. Mediger, W. RUSSLANDS WEG NACH EUROPA. Brunswick: 1952.

184. Mehmet, M.M. CRONICI TURCESTI PRIVIND TARILE ROMANE (EXTRASE, SEC. XV - MIJLOCUL SEC. XVIII). Bucharest: 1966.

185. Menning, B.W. "Military Institutions and the Steppe Frontier in Imperial Russia, 1700-1861." CIHM ACTA No. 5. Bucharest: 1980.

186. Merei, G. DER AUSSENHANDEL DES KONIGREICHS UNGARN (1700-1848). Edited by D. Nemes, et al. Budapest: 1980.

187. Miller, W. THE OTTOMAN EMPIRE AND ITS SUCCESSORS. 4th ed. Cambridge: 1936.

188. _____. THE TURKISH RESTORATION IN GREECE, 1718-97. London: 1921.

189. Montagu, M.W., Lady. LETTERS AND WORKS. 2 vols. New ed. London: 1887.

190. Morris, C., Lady. MARIA THERESA, THE LAST CONSERVATIVE. New York: 1937.

191. Naff, T. "Reform and the Conduct of Ottoman Diplomacy in the Reign of Selim III, 1789-1807." JAOS LXXXIII/3 (1963), 295-315.

192. Naff, T., & Owen, R., eds. STUDIES IN EIGHTEENTH CENTURY ISLAMIC HISTORY. Carbondale: c.1977.

193. Nouzille, J. "L'Alliance Austro-Russe contre la Turquie 1736-1739." Paper presented at CIHM Colloquy, Montpellier, September 1981.

194. Ogg, D. EUROPE OF THE ANCIEN REGIME, 1715-1783. HES. New York: 1965.

195. Oliva, L.J., ed. PETER THE GREAT. Englewood Cliffs: 1970.

196. Ozkaya, Y. "XVIII-inci yuzyilda cikarilan adalet-namelere gore Turkiye'nin ic durumu." BELLETIN 38 (1974), 445-491.

197. Padover, S.K. THE REVOLUTIONARY EMPEROR, JOSEPH II OF AUSTRIA. 2nd ed. rev. London: 1967.

198. Pajol, C.V.P. LES GUERRES SOUS LOUIS XV. 7 vols. Paris: 1881-1891.

199. Pargellis, S.M. BIBLIOGRAPHY OF BRITISH HISTORY: THE EIGHTEENTH CENTURY, 1714-1789. Oxford: 1951.

200. Parnell, A. THE WAR OF THE SUCCESSION IN SPAIN DURING THE REIGN OF QUEEN ANNE, 1702-1711. London: 1905.

201. Pestich, S.L. RUSSKAYA ISTORIOGRAFIYA XVIII VEKA. 3 vols. Leningrad: 1965-1971.

202. Petrovic, V.M. SERBIA; HER PEOPLE, HISTORY, ASPIRATIONS. New York: 1915.

203. Petrovich, M.B. A HISTORY OF MODERN SERBIA, 1804-1918. 2 vols.
New York & London: 1976.

204. Pick, R. EMPRESS MARIA THERESA: THE EARLY YEARS. New York:
1966.

205. Portal, R. L'OURAL AU XVIIIᵉ SIECLE. Paris: 1950.

206. Pounds, N.J.G. AN HISTORICAL GEOGRAPHY OF EUROPE, 1500-1840.
Cambridge: 1979.

207. Preclin, E., & Tapie, V.L. CLIO, INTRODUCTION AUX ETUDES
HISTORIQUES. Vol. I. Paris: 1952.

208. Preston, R.A., et al. MEN IN ARMS. New York: 1956.

209. Quimby, R.S. THE BACKGROUND OF NAPOLEONIC WARFARE: THE THEORY
OF MILITARY TACTICS IN THE EIGHTEENTH CENTURY. New York:
1968 [1957].

210. Rabb, T.K. THE STUGGLE FOR STABILITY IN EARLY MODERN EUROPE.
New York: 1975.

211. Ragib Pasa. "Bekir Sidki Baykal." IA VII, 594-596.

212. Rambaud, A.N. THE EXPANSION OF RUSSIA. Boston: 1978.

213. Ranke, L. von. ZUR VENETIANISCHEN GESCHICHTE. Leipzig: 1878.

214. Rasid, M. RASID TARIHI. 5 vols. Istanbul: 1867.

215. Reddaway, W.F. A HISTORY OF EUROPE FROM 1715 TO 1814. 4th ed.
London: 1951 [1936].

216. Refik, A. TURK IDARESINDE BULGARISTAN (973-1255). Istanbul:
1933.

217. Riasanovsky, N.V. A HISTORY OF RUSSIA. 2nd ed. New York: 1969.

218. Roberts, P. THE QUEST FOR SECURITY, 1715-1740. RME. New York:
1947.

219. Robson, E. "The Armed Forces and the Art of War." NCMH VII.
Cambridge: 1957.

220. Roider, K.A. THE RELUCTANT ALLY: AUSTRIA'S POLICY IN THE
AUSTRO-TURKISH WAR OF 1736-1739. Baton Rouge: 1972.

221. Ropp, T. WAR IN THE MODERN WORLD. Durham: 1959.

222. Rose, J.H. THE INDECISIVENESS OF MODERN WAR, AND OTHER ESSAYS.
Port Washington: [1968].

223. Rothenberg, G.E. THE AUSTRIAN MILITARY BORDER IN CROATIA,
1522-1747. Urbana: 1960.

224. _____. "The Croatian Military Border and the Rise of Yugoslav Nationalism." SEER XLII/100 (December 1965), 34-45.

225. _____. THE MILITARY BORDER IN CROATIA, 1740-1881: A STUDY OF AN IMPERIAL INSTITUTION. Chicago: 1966.

226. Rude, G.F. REVOLUTIONARY EUROPE, 1783-1815. London: 1967.

227. Sakellariou, M.B. "He anakatalepsis tes Peloponnesou hypo ton Tourkon en etei 1715." HELLENIKA IX (1936), 241-260.

228. Saul, N.E. RUSSIA AND THE MEDITERRANEAN, 1797-1807. Chicago: [1970].

229. Savu, Al. Gh., ed. PAGES FROM THE HISTORY OF THE ROMANIAN ARMY. BHR Monograph XV. Bucharest: 1975.

230. _____. THE ARMY AND THE ROMANIAN SOCIETY. Bucharest: 1982.

231. Scherer, A. SUDOSTEUROPA-DISSERTATIONEN, 1918-1960. EINE BIBLIOGRAPHIE DEUTSCHER, OSTERREICHISCHER UND SCHWEIZERISCHER HOCHSCHULSCHRIFTEN. Graz, Vienna, Koln, Bohlau: 1968.

232. Schevill, F. HISTORY OF THE BALKAN PENINSULA. New York: 1971 [c.1922].

233. Schmitt, B.E. ENGLAND AND GERMANY, 1740-1914. Princeton: 1916.

234. Schmitthenner, P. KRIEG UND KRIEGFUHRUNG IM WANDEL DER WELTGESCHICHTE. Potsdam: 1930.

235. Schuyler, E. PETER THE GREAT. New York: 1967 [1884].

236. Seton-Watson, R.W. A HISTORY OF THE ROUMANIANS; FROM ROMAN TIMES TO THE COMPLETION OF UNITY. Cambridge: 1934.

237. _____. THE SOUTHERN SLAV QUESTION AND THE HABSBURG MONARCHY. New York: 1969.

238. Shandanova, L. PETNADESET GODINI INSTITUT ZA BALKANISTIKA, 1964-1978: ISTORICHESKA SPRAVKA I BIBLIOGRAFIIA. Sofia: 1979.

239. Shaw, S.J. BETWEEN OLD AND NEW: THE OTTOMAN EMPIRE UNDER SELIM III, 1789-1807. Cambridge: 1971.

240. _____. "The Established Ottoman Army Corps Under Selim III (1789-1807)." DER ISLAM 40 (1965), 142-184.

241. _____. HISTORY OF THE OTTOMAN EMPIRE AND MODERN TURKEY. Vol. 1: EMPIRE OF THE GAZIS: THE RISE AND DECLINE OF THE OTTOMAN EMPIRE, 1280-1808. Cambridge: 1976.

242. _____. "The Origins of Ottoman Military Reform: The Nizam-i Cedid Army of Sultan Selim III." JMH XXXVII (1965), 291-306.

243. _____. "Selim III and the Turkish Navy." TRET I (1969), 212–241.

244. Shay, M.L. THE OTTOMAN EMPIRE FROM 1720 TO 1734 AS REVEALED IN THE DESPATCHES OF THE VENETIAN BAILI. ISSS. Westport: 1978.

245. Shepherd, W.R. HISTORICAL ATLAS. 8th ed. London: 1956.

246. Sinor, D. HISTORY OF HUNGARY. New York: 1961.

247. Sorel, A. THE EASTERN QUESTION IN THE EIGHTEENTH CENTURY; THE PARTITION OF POLAND AND THE TREATY OF KAINARDJI. New York: 1969.

248. _____. L'EUROPE ET LA REVOLUTION FRANCAISE. 8 vols. Paris: 1895–1904.

249. _____. LA QUESTION D'ORIENT AU XVIII$^e$ SIECLE. LE PARTAGE DE LA POLOGNE ET LA TRAITE DE KAINARDJI Paris: 1889.

250. Spaulding, O.L., et al. A STUDY OF MILITARY METHODS FROM THE EARLIEST TIMES. New York: 1925.

251. Speire, H. "Militarism in the Eighteenth Century." SoR III (1936), 304–336.

252. Spiridonakis, B.G. ESSAYS ON THE HISTORICAL GEOGRAPHY OF THE GREEK WORLD IN THE BALKANS DURING THE TURKOKRATIA. Thessaloniki: 1977.

253. Stan, A. RENASTEREA ARMATEI NATIONALE. Craiova: 1979.

254. Stavrianos, L.S. THE BALKANS SINCE 1453. New York: 1958.

255. Stoianovich, T. "Factors in the Decline of Ottoman Society in the Balkans." SR XXI/4 (December 1962), 623–632.

256. Stoicescu, N. "Organizational Structure of the Armies in the Romanian Principalities in the 14th-18th Centuries." ARS. Bucharest: 1980.

257. Stoye, J.W. "Armies and Navies: 2. Soldiers and Civilians." NCMH VI. Cambridge: 1970.

258. _____. "The Austrian Habsburgs." MCMH VI. Cambridge: 1970.

259. Subhi, M., et al. TARIH-I SUBHI, SAMI VE SAKIR. Istanbul: 1783.

260. Sugar, P.F. "The Influence of the Enlightenment and the French Revolution in Eighteenth Century Hungary." JCEA XVII (1958), 331–355.

261. _____. SOUTHEASTERN EUROPE UNDER OTTOMAN RULE, 1354–1804. HECE 5. Seattle: 1977.

262. Sugar, P.F., & Treadgold, D.W. HISTORY OF EAST CENTRAL EUROPE. 11 vols. Seattle & London: 1974-.

263. Sumner, B.H. PETER THE GREAT AND THE EMERGENCE OF RUSSIA. London: 1950.

264. _____. PETER THE GREAT AND THE OTTOMAN EMPIRE. Hamden: 1965.

265. Swire, J. ALBANIA, THE RISE OF A KINGDOM. London: 1929.

266. Tansel, S. "Buyuk Friedrich devrinde Osmanli Prusya munasebetleri hakkinda." BELLETIN X (1946), 133-165.

267. Tapie, V.L. LES RELATIONS ENTRE LA FRANCE ET L'EUROPE CENTRALE DE 1661-1715. 2 vols. Paris: 1958.

268. _____. THE RISE AND FALL OF THE HABSBURG MONARCHY. Trans. by Stephen Hardman. New York, Washington & London: 1971.

269. Temperley, H.W.V., Sir. ENGLAND AND THE NEAR EAST. London: 1936.

270. _____. FOUNDATIONS OF BRITISH FOREIGN POLICY FROM PITT TO SALISBURY. Cambridge: 1939.

271. _____. FREDERICK THE GREAT AND KAISER JOSEPH. 2nd ed. New York: 1968.

272. Thessaloniki. SYMPOSIUM SUR L'EPOQUE PHANAROITE. ACTA of 1970 Symposium. Thessaloniki: 1974

273. _____. VALKANIKE VIVLIOGRAPHIA. 1975-.

274. Thomson, G.S. CATHERINE THE GREAT AND THE EXPANSION OF RUSSIA. New York: 1962 [1947].

275. Tott, Baron de. MEMOIRES DU BARON DE TOTT SUR LES TURCS. 4 vols. Amsterdam: 1785.

276. _____. MEMOIRES SUR LES TURCS ET TARTARES. 3 vols. Amsterdam: 1794.

277. Trowbridge, W.R.H. A BEAU SABREUR: MAURICE DE SAXE, MARSHAL OF FRANCE. New York: 1910.

278. Tsvetkova, B.A. LES INSTITUTIONS OTTOMANES EN EUROPE. Wiesbaden: 1978.

279. _____. L'EVOLUTION DU REGIME FEODAL TURC DE LA FIN DU XVI$^e$ JUSQU'AU MILIEU DE XVIII$^e$ SIECLES. EH. Sofia: 1960.

280. _____. KHAIDUTSVOTO V BULGARSKITE ZEMI PREZ 15/18 VEK. Sofia: 1971.

281. _____. "Recherches sur la system d'affermage (Ittizam) dan l'Empire Ottoman au cours XVI<sup>e</sup>-XVIII<sup>e</sup> siecles par rapport aux contrees Bulgares." RO 27 (1964), 111-132.

282. Tupetz, T. "Der Turkenfeldzug von 1739 und der Friede von Belgrade." HZ 40 (1878).

283. Turkiye Cumhuriyeti, Maarif Vekaleti. ISLAM ANSIKLOPEDISI. Istanbul & Ankara: 1940-.

284. USSR. RELATIILE ISTORICE DINTRE POPOARELE U.R.S.S. SI ROMANE IN VEACURILE XV-INCEPUTUL CELUI DE AL XVIII-LEA. Vol. III. Edited by A.A. Novosel'sky & L.V. Cherepnin. Moscow: 1970.

285. _____. Academy of Sciences, Institut Vostokogovedeniya. BIBLIOGRAFIYA TURTSII (1917-1958). Moscow: 1959.

286. Uzuncarsili, I.H. "Cezayirli Gazi Hasan Pasa'ya dair." TM VII-VIII (1940-1942), 17-40.

287. _____. OSMANLI TARIHI. 4 vols. Ankara: 1947-1960.

288. _____. "Sadrazam Halil Hamid Pasa." TM V (1936), 213-267.

289. Vagts, A. A HISTORY OF MILITARISM. New ed. New York: 1957.

290. Van Creveld, M.L. SUPPLYING WAR: LOGISTICS FROM WALLENSTEIN TO PATTON. New York: 1977.

291. Vandal, A. LE PACHA BONNEVAL. Paris: 1885.

292. _____. UNE AMBASSADE FRANCAISE EN ORIENT SOUS LOUIS XV. LA MISSION DU MARQUIS DE VILLENEUVE, 1728-1741. Paris: 1887.

293. Van Vollenhaven, C. THE LAW OF PEACE. London: 1936.

294. Varkonyi, A.R. "AD PACEM UNIVERSALEM" - THE INTERNATIONAL ANTECEDENTS OF THE PEACE OF SZATMAR. EHH. Budapest: 1980.

295. Vasif, A, Efendi. MAHASIN AL-ASAR VE HAQAYIK AL-AHBAR. 2 vols. Cairo: 1930.

296. Veenendal, A.J. "The War of the Spanish Succession in Europe." NCMH 6. Cambridge: 1970.

297. Ventre-Nouvel, J. "L'Alliance Franco-Bavaroise-Prusso-Saxonne contre l'Autriche pendant la campagne de Boheme de 1742." Paper presented at CIHM Colloquy, Montpellier, 1981.

298. Vernadsky, G. "On Some Parallel Trends in Russian and Turkish History," TCAAS XXXVI (july 1945), 25-36.

299. Volz, G.B. FRIEDRICH DER GROSSE IM SPIEGLE SEINER ZEIT. Berlin: 1934.

300. Walichnowski, T. BALCANICA: A GUIDE TO THE POLISH ARCHIVES RELATIVE TO THE HISTORY OF THE BALKAN COUNTRIES. Warsaw: 1979.

301. Waliszewski, K. PETER THE GREAT. Trans by Lady Mary Ford. New York: 1897.

302. Wandruszka, A. THE HOUSE OF HABSBURGS: SIX HUNDRED YEARS OF A EUROPEAN DYNASTY. Trans. by Cathleen & Hans Epstein. Garden City: 1964.

303. Wangerman, E. "The Habsburg Possessions and Germany." NCMH 8. Cambridge: 1965.

304. _____. FROM JOSEPH II TO THE JACOBIN TRIALS. London: 1959.

305. Weber, E. EUROPE SINCE 1715: A MODERN HISTORY. New York: 1972.

306. Western, J.R. "Armies in Armed Forces and the Art of War." NCMH 8. Cambridge: 1965.

307. White, R.J. EUROPE IN THE EIGHTEENTH CENTURY. New York: 1965.

308. Williams, E.N. THE ANCIEN REGIME IN EUROPE: GOVERNMENT AND SOCIETY IN THE MAJOR STATES, 1648-1789. New York: 1980.

309. Wolf, J.B. THE EMERGENCE OF THE GREAT POWERS, 1685-1715. RME. New York: 1951.

310. Woloch, I. EIGHTEENTH CENTURY EUROPE: TRADITION AND PROGRESS. New York: 1982.

311. Wright, J.W. "Sieges and Customs of War at the Opening of the Eighteenth Century." AHR 39 (July 1934), 629-644.

312. Wright, Q. STUDY OF WAR. London & Chicago: 1965 [1942].

313. Wright, W.L. OTTOMAN STATECRAFT. Princeton: 1935.

314. Zachar, J. BERSENYI LASZLO, A RAKOSZI-SZABADSAGHARC KAPITAYA FRANCIAORSZAG MARSALLJA. Vaja: 1979.

315. Zade, C.M.R. Efendi. CESMIZADE TARIHI. Istanbul: 1959.

316. Zinkeisen, J.W. GESCHICHTE DES OSMANISCHEN REICHS IN EUROPA. 7 vols. Hamburg & Gotha: 1840-1863.

317. Zmajevic, V. QUELLEN UND MATERIALEN ZUR ALBANISCHEN GESCHICHTE IM 17. UND 18. JAHRHUNDERT. 2 vols. Wiesbaden: 1975-1979.

318. Zook, D.H., & Higham, R. A SHORT HISTORY OF WARFARE. New York: 1966.


ADDITIONS


319. Kukiel, M. CZARTORYSKI AND EUROPEAN UNITY, 1770-1861. Princeton: 1955.

320. Ransel, D.L. THE POLITICS OF CATHERINIAN RUSSIA: THE PANIN
PARTY. New Haven: 1975.

321. Lampe, J.R., & Jackson, M.R. BALKAN ECONOMIC HISTORY,
1550-1950. Bloomington: 1982.

322. Kiraly, B.K., & Rothenberg, G., eds. WAR AND SOCIETY IN EAST
CENTRAL EUROPE. New York: 1981.

323. Myshlaevskii, A.Z. PETR VELIKII. VOENNIE ZAKONII I INSTRUKTSII.
St. Petersburg: 1894.

324. Krinitsyn, F.S. CHESMENSKAYA POBEDA. Moscow: 1962 [1951].

325. De Maderiaga, I. RUSSIA IN THE AGE OF CATHERINE THE GREAT. New
Haven & London: c.1981.

326. Kiraly, B.K. EAST CENTRAL EUROPEAN SOCIETY AND WAR IN THE
PREREVOLUTIONARY EIGHTEENTH CENTURY. New York: 1982.

327. Beskrovnyi, L.G. RUSSKAYA ARMIYA I FLOT V XVIII VEKE; OCHERKI.
Moscow: 1958.

328. Bode, A. DAS FLOTTENPOLITIK KATHERINAS II UND DIE KONFLIKTE MIT
SCHWEDEN UND DIE TURKEI (1768-1792). Wiesbaden: 1979.

329. Omitted.

330. Kennedy, P. THE RISE AND DECLINE OF BRITISH NAVAL MASTERY. Rev.
ed. : 1983 [1976].

331. Tarle, E.V. ADMIRAL USHAKOV NA SREDIZEMNOM MORE, 1798-1800.
Moscow: 1948.

332. _____. CHESMENSKII BOI I PERVAYA RUSSKAYA EKSPEDITSIYA V
ARKHIPELAG, 1769-1774. Moscow: 1945.

333. _____. EKSPEDITSIYA KUSSKOGO FLOTA V ARKHIPELAG V
1769-1774. Moscow: 1945.

334. Golovachev, V.F. CHESMA; EKSPEDITSIYA RUSSKOGO FLOTA V
ARKHIPELAG I CHESMENSKOE SRAZENIE. Moscow: 1944.

335. Brinton, C.C. A DECADE OF REVOLUTION, 1789-1799. RME XI. London
& New York: 1934.

336. Wittram, R. PETER I, CZAR UND KAISER, ZUR GESCHICHTE PETERS DEN
GROSSEN. 2 vols. Gottingen: 1964.

337. Anderson, R.C. "The First Russian Fleet, 1695-1711." JRUSI
LXI:441 (February 1916), 41-46.

338. Il'in, D.S. PODVIG LEITENANTA DMITRIYA SERGEIEVICH IL'INA I EGO
LOVARISHCHEI. A.K. Kronstadt: 1885.

339. V PAMYAT CHESMENSKOI POBEDY, 24-26 IUNIA 1770 GODA. SBORNIK
DOKUMENTOV' O SRAZHENIYAKH V KHIOSKOM PROLIVA I
CHESMENSKOI BUKHTA. Odessa: 1886.

# CHAPTER SIX

## 1800–1850

### GENERAL BACKGROUND

The first half of the 19th century must be considered one of the momentous periods in modern history. In 1789 the French middle class began the process of sweeping away the Ancien Regime with all of its abuses and inequalities. In doing so, they also swept away the monarchy and set the French republic against most of the rest of Europe. The succession of events that followed made Napoleon Bonaparte the master of France and led to a period of revolution and war that lasted until 1815. When Napoleon was finally overthrown, the chief beneficiaries were Russia, Great Britain, and the United States: Russia, through its occupation of Finland and Poland; England, through its mastery of the seas; and America, through its acquisition of the Louisiana territories, even though it had failed to take Canada during the war of 1812.

Also of importance during this period was the beginning of the Industrial Revolution that changed the fundamental structure of life in the western world. Although the roots of this epoch are found in the activities of past centuries and the movement is still going forward at perhaps an even greater pace, the large scale and basic nature of the changes that took place upon the European continent after 1815 marked the times as the most significant in history. As a result of the Industrial Revolution dependent proletariats who were for the most part propertyless and illiterate were concentrated in the cities of Europe.

The rapid growth of the industrial cities, the lack of protection for the worker, and the greed of the capitalist and his agents created situations where men, women, and children worked long hours for low pay and lived in horrible squalor. As the labor pool grew at the same time that fewer and fewer workers were needed to tend the machines, mass unemployment resulted and social unrest grew.

The Industrial Revolution also had, as a far-reaching consequence, a direct effect upon war. The development of new weapons through the use of advanced technologies rendered war immensely more destructive and created a new balance of power as it became clear that military strength depended on the industrial strength of the nation. Thus, western European nations such as England, France, and Prussia became powerful and, consequently, dominant in the affairs of the continent, while Russia and the nations of eastern Europe lagged behind in industrialization and tended toward envy and self-delusion. This situation would continue until the beginning of the 20th century, and there is evidence that it continues to this day.

There is a wealth of good material that deals with the events of this period. William McNeill's A WORLD HISTORY [203] is the best overall history. McNeill stresses the interaction among the chief Old World civilizations and portrays the events of the time with typical erudition. Other histories of value that deal with the more generalized situations of the first half of the 19th century include: THE ECONOMICS OF EUROPEAN IMPERIALISM [125], by Alan Hodgart; THE EMERGENCE OF THE EUROPEAN WORLD [29], by Jerome Blum and others; and David Vital's THE SURVIVAL OF SMALL STATES: STUDIES IN SMALL POWER/GREAT POWER CONFLICT [339]. Much can be learned from these works that can serve as a foundation for the more specific information that follows.

Under this rubric it would also be wise to study Edward Gulick's EUROPE'S CLASSICAL BALANCE OF POWER: A CASE HISTORY OF THE THEORY AND PRACTICE OF ONE OF THE GREAT CONCEPTS OF EUROPEAN STATECRAFT [115]. This study examines, defines, and traces the history of the "balance of power" and its effect on history. Another good work that is of particular value at this point is William Woodruff's THE STRUGGLE FOR WORLD POWER, 1500-1980 [349]. This volume focusses on the changing nature of the factors involved in the makeup of the balance and emphasizes the role of superiority as opposed to cooperative effort.

Professor Clive Trebilcock's THE INDUSTRIALIZATION OF THE CONTINENTAL POWERS, 1780-1914 [327] presents a series of historical models structured around a comparative historical framework that allows the author a means of discussing several areas of direct interest. The case study on Austria-Hungary is especially relevant, while the treatments of Germany, Russia, and France make valuable contributions to the understanding of the outside influences that directly affected the course of events in the Balkans.

Another interesting work is Eugen Weber's EUROPE SINCE 1715: A MODERN HISTORY [343]. The first part of this book deals with the revolutionary period from 1715 to 1848. It is replete with passages from diaries, journals, and other firsthand accounts of the period. EUROPE: A BRIEF HISTORY [258], by George Rothrock and Tom Jones, is an excellent background for the events leading to Napoleon's final defeat and the ensuing Congress of Vienna with all that it portended for the future of Europe.

EARLY MODERN EUROPE, 1500-1815 [49] is also a good background source. This volume is a series of essays that explains in general terms the French Revolution and the Industrial revolution, among other things. These two parts alone make the book worthwhile. A DOCUMENTARY HISTORY OF MODERN EUROPE [19], by Thomas Barnes and Gerald Feldman, is in four volumes. The second and third of these contain extensive selections of documents dealing with the periods 1660-1815 and 1815-1914, respectively. They are an excellent supplement to the general outlines of history of this period.

Similarly, A SELECTED LIST OF WORKS ON EUROPE AND EUROPE OVERSEAS, 1715-1815 [40], that was edited by J.S. Bromley and A. Goodwin, while somewhat dated, is still a solid source of additional reading. Bromley and Goodwin are two of the prestigious group of scholars who participated in the preparation of the outstanding NEW

CAMBRIDGE MODERN HISTORY series [64]. Two volumes from this series, volume 9: WAR AND PEACE IN AN AGE OF UPHEAVAL 1793-1830 [77] and volume 10: THE ZENITH OF EUROPEAN POWER 1830-1870 [46], are particularly well suited to the casual reader who seeks a quick appraisal of these periods. They are among the most competent works available.

Some of the more specific surveys of this period include: A HISTORY OF EUROPE FROM 1715 TO 1814 [242], by W.F. Reddaway; THE FIRST EUROPEAN REVOLUTION, 1776-1815 [117], by Norman Hampson; and George Rude's REVOLUTIONARY EUROPE, 1783-1815 [259]. Other works dedicated to this period are E.J. Hobsbawn's THE AGE OF REVOLUTION: EUROPE, 1789-1848 [124], which is, although 20 years old, one of the more original and suggestive offerings of interest in this period. THE AGE OF REVOLUTION AND REACTION, 1789-1850 [38], by Charles Breunig, which is found in the Norton series, is one of the mainstays of this complex period.

Solid works on the post-Napoleonic period include THE SOVEREIGN REMEDY: EUROPE AFTER WATERLOO [344], by M. Weiner, that highlights the era of the Congresses by focussing on the personalities involved -- Alexander, Metternich, Castlereagh, and others. ROMANTICISM AND REVOLT, 1815-1850 [316], by J.L. Talmon, outlines the events leading to the 1848 revolt in sufficient detail for the most serious reader. DEBATE IN EUROPE, 1815-1850 [260], by G. Rude, is a history of the histories written by others and stresses the different themes and interpretations put forward in those works. Another series of interpretations can be found in THE MAKING OF THE MODERN WORLD, 1815-1914 [51], which is edited by Norman F. Cantor and Micheal Werthman. THE NINETEENTH CENTURY, 1815-1914 [231], edited by David Pinkney, has an excellent bibliographic essay; while THE MODERN ERA, 1815 TO THE PRESENT [50], edited by Cantor and Samuel Berner, deals with events up to the pre-World War II period in a series of nine essays that deal with, among other things, the 1848 revolt.

One of the best accounts of the relations among the nations of Europe is found in THE GREAT POWERS AND THE EUROPEAN STATES SYSTEM, 1815-1914 [45], by Roger Bullen and Roy Bridge. The authors point out the conservative nature of great power relations and the effects of domestic changes as underlying the diplomatic alignments of the period. Another good account is Gordon Craig's EUROPE SINCE 1815 [75] that stresses the interrelationships among the political, social, economic, and intellectual histories of the times.

A DOCUMENTARY HISTORY OF MODERN EUROPE [19], by Thomas Barnes and Gerald Feldman, was produced in four volumes; numbers 2 and 3 of which apply to the general period. Each volume includes extensive selections of pertinent documents of the respective periods being examined. Horecky's EAST CENTRAL EUROPE: A GUIDE TO BASIC PUBLICATIONS [129] is always a good place to start, even though it is now somewhat outdated.

Some of the series that are valuable include, in addition to those already discussed: THE NORTON HISTORY OF MODERN EUROPE [107], edited by Felix Gilbert; PROBLEMS IN CIVILIZATION [232], prepared under the general editorship of David Pinkney; THE WORLD OF EUROPE [250], edited by Karl Roider; and THE RISE OF MODERN EUROPE series

[163], edited by W.L. Langer.

There are a number of general cartographic works that are of benefit to the casual reader and the ardent scholar. AN ATLAS OF RUSSIAN AND EAST EUROPEAN HISTORY [1], by Adams, Matley, and McCagg, is very good. So is W.R. Shepherd's HISTORICAL ATLAS [289] which is in its 8th edition. For a view from the Russian perspective Martin Gilbert's RUSSIAN HISTORY ATLAS [108] is worthwhile. One of the best of the military historical atlases is David Chandler's ATLAS OF MILITARY STRATEGY [62], while N.J.G. Pounds' AN HISTORICAL GEOGRAPHY OF EUROPE, 1500-1840 [236] is especially good as it covers most of the period under discussion. ESSAYS ON THE HISTORICAL GEOGRAPHY OF THE GREEK WORLD IN THE BALKANS DURING THE TURKOKRATIA [299], by Basile Spiridonakis, is interesting as background to the Greek revolution that occurs during this time.

## THE GREAT POWERS

There is little argument that Napoleon affected all of the nations of Europe, including those in the Balkans. Literature on Napoleon abounds and covers all aspects of his life and times. NAPOLEON'S MARSHALS [89], by R.P. Dunn-Pattison; THE ANATOMY OF GLORY [161], by Henri Lachouque; and NAPOLEON: HISTORICAL ENIGMA [230], edited by David Pinkney, are all excellent works that will give sufficient background to the casual reader. Alistair Horne's NAPOLEON: MASTER OF EUROPE, 1805-1807 [130] rebuts some recent denigations of Bonaparte's role in shaping European history. EUROPE AND THE FRENCH IMPERIUM, 1779-1814 [41], by Geoffrey Bruun, is in the RISE OF EUROPE series and is very good. Alexander Niven's NAPOLEON AND ALEXANDER I: A STUDY OF FRANCO-RUSSIAN RELATIONS, 1807-1812 [220] is a brief yet thorough analysis of the interaction between two of the most powerful men in Europe after Tilsit up to the French invasion of Russia.

Ernst Birke's FRANKREICH UND OSTMITTELUROPA IM 19. JAHRHUNDERT; BEITRAGE ZUR POLITIK UND GESCHICHTE [26] is important as an intellectual history of French policy toward Poland, Bohemia, Hungary, and Romania from the French Revolution to the end of the 19th century. There is an extensive bibliography and helpful sections by scholars of the French Slavic school.

## THE EASTERN QUESTION

If Napoleon was the most influential individual of his time then certainly the Eastern Question was the most burning issue and nothing affected the course of Balkan history more directly than did the events that transpired as a result of the Great Powers acting in response to the stimuli induced by the Question. Literature abounds on the subject, and no single listing could account for it all. Sir John Marriott's THE EASTERN QUESTION [199] is at best sketchy but is sufficient to the needs of the casual reader. Another presentation of the facts may be found in in Matthew Anderson's THE GREAT POWERS AND THE NEAR EAST (1774-1923) [7] that deals more with the Turkish Empire than with the Balkans but is still extremely useful at this point. A much better source of information is his THE EASTERN QUESTION, 1774-1923 [6]. Other useful works include THE EUROPEAN POWERS AND THE NEAR EASTERN QUESTION, 1806-1807 [290], by Paul Shupp; Jacques Ancel's MANUEL HISTORIQUE DE LA QUESTION

D'ORIENT: 1792-1923 [5]; and Edouard Driault's LA QUESTION D'ORIENT [87].

Works dealing with specific nations or aspects of the Eastern Question include J.C. Hurowitz's "Russia and the Turkish Straits: A Revaluation of the Origins of the Problem" [135] and his somewhat similar "The Background of Russia's Claims to the Turkish Straits" [136]. Gerald Clayton's BRITAIN AND THE EASTERN QUESTION: MISSOLONGHI TO GALLIPOLI [67] does a good job of explaining the English role. THE EASTERN QUESTION [88], by Stephen Duggan, discusses the international aspects of the problem, while the ubiquitous Karl Marx, as might might have expected, also wrote about it in his THE EASTERN QUESTION [200], using 656 pages to do so. Marx's work was still in print as late as 1969.

Austria's role in the events dealing with the Eastern Question are admirably covered in a number of works that include: Victor Mamatey's THE RISE OF THE HABSBURG EMPIRE, 1526-1815 [187]; THE HABSBURG EMPIRE, 1804-1918 [156], by Hans Kohn; THE HABSBURG EMPIRE, 1790-1918 [183], by C.A. Macartney; Robert Kann's excellent A HISTORY OF THE HABSBURG EMPIRE, 1526-1918 [149]; THE HOUSE OF HABSBURG: SIX HUNDRED YEARS OF A EUROPEAN DYNASTY [342], by Adam Wandruszka; THE IMPERIAL CROWN: THE STORY OF THE RISE AND FALL OF THE HOLY ROMAN AND AUSTRIAN EMPIRES [100], by P. Frischauer; and THE HABSBURG MONARCHY [52], by F.L. Carsten and others. This last work is in two volumes, one of which deals with the eastern lands under Austrian dominion.

Robert Kann's THE HABSBURG EMPIRE: A STUDY IN INTEGRATION AND DISINTEGRATION [147] is not so much a history as it is an investigation into the dynamics of the empire. Alan Sked's THE SURVIVAL OF THE HABSBURG EMPIRE: RADETZKY, THE IMPERIAL ARMY AND CLASS WAR [293] contains much new information not previously considered by scholars. Of special interest is Sked's coverage of the events leading to the 1848 revolt and life in the Austrian army. Robert Seton-Watson's THE SOUTHERN SLAV QUESTION AND THE HABSBURG MONARCHY [284] deals with issues directly affecting the Balkans. Lastly, C.A. Macartney's "The Austrian Monarchy, 1792-1847" [182], found in Volume 9 of the NEW CAMBRIDGE MODERN HISTORY, summarizes this period in Austro-Hungarian history as well as anything that can be found in English.

Two good works in German are DAS GESCHICHTE OSTERREICHS [118], by H. Hantsch, and HANDBUCH DER GESCHICHTE OSTERREICHS UND SEINER NACHBARLANDER BOHMEN UND UNGARN [331], by Matilde and Karl Uhlirz. This latter work is important as it has, in its five volumes, a wealth of bibliographic material and excellent indices. Volume five is best left aside as it was written during the Nazi period (1944) and is unabashedly anti-semitic. There is supposedly a revision to these works but it has not been evident.

Of the pertinent English histories of this period, probably the most useful is Sir Harold Temperley's ENGLAND AND THE NEAR EAST [320]. In this work Temperley undertakes the task of explaining British policy from the end of the Napoleonic period through the 1878 Congress of Berlin. Volume one covers the period up to the Crimean War and is one of the best treatises available on the Eastern Question.

BRITISH POLICY AND THE TURKISH REFORM MOVEMENT; A STUDY OF ANGLO-TURKISH RELATIONS, 1826-1853 [15] is an important discussion of British influence in the Turkish reforms that preceded the Crimean War, while John Marlow outlines British and French policies in the Near East in his PERFIDIOUS ALBION: THE ORIGINS OF ANGLO-FRENCH RIVALRY IN THE LEVANT [189]. Bernodotte Schmitt's ENGLAND AND GERMANY, 1740-1914 [277] is a somewhat shallow and often biased account of England's dealings with Germany.

A much broader view of England's foreign policy is presented in FOUNDATIONS OF BRITISH FOREIGN POLICY FROM PITT TO SALISBURY [321]. This work, edited by Temperley and Lillian Penson, assembles the primary documents and speeches that presented the ideas and the forces that motivated the English opinion of the period. Equally important are the BRITISH DIPLOMATIC BLUEBOOKS RELATING TO THE RUSSIAN EMPIRE, 1801-1899 [39] that are assemblages of the dispatches of the Foreign and Colonial Offices that were published for the House of Commons as "Bluebooks" or Parlimentary Papers. The collection includes some 22,000 pages which have been indexed and microfiched. One of the six sections of this set deals with Turkish affairs. Lastly, Hugh Egerton's BRITISH FOREIGN POLICY IN EUROPE TO THE END OF THE 19TH CENTURY [92] is somewhat difficult to follow because of its style of presentation. It is, however, impartial and is very useful.

Vasili Klyuchevski's KURS RUSSKOI ISTORII [154] is still one of the best among the Russian histories. Micheal Florinsky's RUSSIA: A HISTORY AND AN INTERPRETATION [96], Nicholas Riasonovsky's A HISTORY OF RUSSIA [248], and Jesse Clarkson's A HISTORY OF RUSSIA [66] are all quite good. Alfred Rambaud's THE EXPANSION OF RUSSIA [239] goes more directly to Russia's propensity for aggrandizing its neighbors. Another approach to that subject is RUSSLANDS WEG NACH EUROPA [204] that was written by M. Mediger. RUSSIA AND THE BALKANS IN RUSSIAN FOREIGN POLICY: ESSAYS IN HISTORICAL PERSPECTIVE [166], that was edited by Ivo Lederer, and Robert Gossip's TURKEY AND RUSSIA, THEIR RACES, HISTORY AND WARS [112] are both good. The Russo-Turkish situation is also discussed by George Vernadsky in his "On Some Parallel Trends in Russian and Turkish History" [338].

Hugh Seton-Watson attempts to chronicle the reigns of the last five Tsars in his THE RUSSIAN EMPIRE: 1801-1917 [281]. It is not very good. Neither is Graham Stephenson's RUSSIA FROM 1812 TO 1945: A HISTORY [304] that suffers the same imprecision that plagues the Seton-Watson book. These two are not of much value.

Much better use can be made of Norman Saul's RUSSIA AND THE MEDITERRANEAN, 1798-1807 [269]. While it is primarily a naval history and covers only the first decade of the century, it is a detailed account of the unprecedented alliance between the Russian and Ottoman Empires that caused great consternation in the courts of western Europe. Another work covering this same general time period is RUSSIA AND EUROPE, 1789-1825 [177], by A. Lobanov-Rostovsky. This work deals primarily with Russia's participation in the coalitions against Napoleon and in the policies of Alexander I and his brother-successor, Nicholas I.

ENDURANCE AND ENDEAVOUR: RUSSIAN HISTORY, 1812-1880 [345], by J.N. Westwood, and RUSSIAN IMPERIALISM FROM IVAN THE TERRIBLE TO THE REVOLUTION [134], by T. Hunczak, are both interesting. The latter work was edited by Taras Hunczak and is generally of excellent quality, but not without some glaring faults such as Emanuel Sarkisyanz's poorly balanced equation of Russian imperialism to those varieties found elsewhere in the world. In general, however, the book is worthwhile.

Of particular importance to the serious student of Russian military history is Bruce Menning's paper on "Military Institutions and the Steppe Frontier in Imperial Russia, 1700-1861" [205], which was presented at the International Conference on Military History at Bucharest in 1980. The paper was subsequently published in the proceedings of that meeting. THE RUSSIAN IMPERIAL ARMY [180], which was edited and compiled by M. Lyons, is also valuable. A relatively new and important work in Russian is ISTORIA OTECHESTVENNOI VOENNO-ENTSIKLOPEDICHESKOI LITERATURII [13], by A.I. Babin, and others. This is an historical resume of the progress of military literature from the beginning of the 18th century and contains a wealth of material on relevant dictionaries and encyclopedias.

There are a number of good works about the Russian leadership, among which THE EMPEROR ALEXANDER I [4], by E.M. Almedingen, and TSAR ALEXANDER I: PATERNALISTIC REFORMER [202], by Allen Mcconnell, are readable. This latter work focuses upon many points of interest specific to the turn of events in Balkan history. NICHOLAS I, EMPEROR AND AUTOCRAT OF ALL THE RUSSIAS [175], which was written by W. Bruce Lincoln, gives the same type of coverage to the reign of the second ruler to sit upon the Russian throne in the first half of the 19th century.

Lastly, there is an extraordinary collection of titles of books and other works on Russia and Eastern Europe to be found on microfiche in the IDC's RUSSIA, U.S.S.R., EASTERN EUROPE: ALPHABETICAL CUMULATIVE CATALOGUE [261]. This compendium contains over 6,500 titles, many of which are germane to this period and subject.

## GENERAL HISTORIES OF THE BALKANS

There are a number of excellent works on the Balkan history of this period. One of the best is L.S. Stavrianos' THE BALKANS SINCE 1453 [301]. Another is Edgar Hosch's THE BALKANS: A SHORT HISTORY [131]. This latter book centers on Albania, Bulgaria, and Serbia and has excellent maps. Bernard Schevill's HISTORY OF THE BALKAN PENINSULA FROM THE EARLIEST TIMES TO THE PRESENT DAY [276] is also very good. Erwin and Ann Lessner's THE DANUBE: THE DRAMATIC HISTORY OF THE GREAT RIVER AND THE PEOPLE TOUCHED BY ITS FLOW [170] is extremely easy to read and is very informative. For those interested in understanding the problems of the Balkans, THE BALKANS IN TRANSITION [142], edited by Charles and Barbara Jelavich, presents a series of essays by some of the best scholars in Balkan studies. THE PEOPLES OF THE EASTERN HABSBURG LANDS, 1526-1918 [150], by Robert Kann and Zdanec David, is a concise account of those lands under Austro-Hungarian control. Peter Sugar's SOUTHEASTERN EUROPE UNDER OTTOMAN RULE, 1354-1804 [311] tells about the rest of the Balkans that were under Turkish domination; and, although it barely touches the 19th century, it establishes a firm background for the events that were to transpire during that time.

Franz Babinger's AUFSATZE UND ABHANDLUNGEN ZUR GESCHICHTE SUDOSTEUROPAS UND DER LEVANTE [14] is another series of essays, all of first quality. Another work in German is Egon Heymann's BALKAN: KRIEGE, BUNDNISSE, REVOLUTIONEN; 150 JAHRE POLITIK UND SCHICKSAL [121]. This 440-page study deals with the wars, alliances and revolutions that affected the Balkans during the 19th and early 20th centuries. It covers in detail the Eastern Question that dominated the region during that time.

There are two excellent works by Robert Seton-Watson: THE SOUTHERN SLAV QUESTION AND THE HABSBURG MONARCHY [284] and THE RISE OF NATIONALITY IN THE BALKANS [283]. This latter history, initially published during the First World War, is one of the most useful in the English language. A very good alternative is Wesley M. Gewehr's THE RISE OF NATIONALISM IN THE BALKANS, 1800-1930 [104]. Either of these works can be supplemented by Peter Sugar's ETHNIC DIVERSITY AND CONFLICT IN EASTERN EUROPE [312] that is a compendium of ten essays covering a number of topical areas. One of these deals with the influence of state policy upon ethnic persistence and the formation of nationalities. Lastly, a number of excellent references can be found in Anton Scherer's SUDOSTEUROPA-DISSERTATIONEN, 1918-1960 [275] that was published in 1968 and which covers Swiss, German, and Austrian theses on the subject.

Works on Balkan economics include: BALKAN ECONOMIC HISTORY, 1550-1950 [162], by John R. Lampe and Melvin Jackson; and ECONOMIC DEVELOPMENT IN EAST-CENTRAL EUROPE IN THE 19TH AND 20TH CENTURIES [22], by Ivan T. Berend and Gyorgy Ranki. The first of these is especially good in its coverage of the 19th century when independent states began to emerge. The latter work covers the Austro-Hungarian Empire and the Balkans, less Greece, and is extremely readable although definitely Marxist in its outlook.

Looking at Balkan history from a different perspective, Neville Forbes' THE BALKANS: A HISTORY OF BULGARIA, SERBIA, GREECE, RUMANIA, TURKEY [98] is excellent. Forbes and his coauthors compiled a history of the Balkans that is very useful even though it is by some standards outdated. It looks closely at the Eastern Question in the context of the several nations and dwells upon the 19th century as a centerpiece. There is a most useful bibliography in this book.

### HUNGARY

A number of excellent histories of Hungary exist that deal with the nation rather than its association with the empire. Among these histories, C.A. Macartney's HUNGARY, A SHORT HISTORY [181], Emil Lengyel's 1000 YEARS OF HUNGARY [168] and Denis Sinor's HISTORY OF HUNGARY292] are all very good to excellent choices.

BEVEZETES MAGYARORSZAG TORTENETENEK FORRASAIBA ES IRODALMABA [157], a series that began publication in 1970 under the auspices of Institute of History of the Hungarian Academy of Sciences, was written by Domokos Kosary. Volume 5 of this introduction to sources of Hungarian history contains the entries for the period 1790-1848. This series is a revision of an earlier work by Kosary and is primarily in Hungarian although quite a few entries deal with works in some of the more accessible languages.

The ETUDES HISTORIQUES HONGROISES, 1980 [218], published on the occasion of the XV International Congress of Historical Sciences in Bucharest, contains a number of reference of interest to this period. HUNGARY AND TRANSYLVANIA [225], by John Paget, published in London in 1850, is a contemporary view of those areas at that crucial time. Paul Ignotus' "Czech, Magyars, Slovaks" [137] details the fundamental differences between the Czechs and Hungarians, with their Transylvanian appanage, especially in the forms of the soldiery they delivered to the empire. CZECHO-SLOVAKIA: A SHORT HISTORY [35], by J.F.N. Bradley, deals with this important period succinctly and forms an excellent foundation for the future course of events in the second half of the 19th and in the 20th centuries.

### ROMANIA

Lucian Boia's RELATIONSHIPS BETWEEN ROMANIANS, CZECHS AND SLOVAKS [32] is another work that deals with the interrelationships among Balkan states and their neighbors. This study outlines the political relations among these groups during the struggle to assert national independence from the Austro-Hungarian Empire. The material is good but suffers from an overall lack of objectivity. Nicolae Iorga's HISTOIRE DES ROUMAINES DE LA PENINSULE DES BALCANS [139] is significantly better as a straight history of the times, even though it is only 64 pages. Robert Seton-Watson's A HISTORY OF THE ROUMANIANS; FROM ROMAN TIMES TO THE COMPLETION OF UNITY [282] is excellent as is Ladislas Makkai's HISTOIRE DE TRANSYLVANIE [185], that was published in 1946.

The CHONOLOGICAL HISTORY OF ROMANIA [109] has a considerable amount of information on the period and presents a few otherwise unknown facts that improve the view of the times. These are, of course, always favorable to the idea of Romanian unity. THE RUMANIAN NATIONAL MOVEMENT IN TRANSYLVANIA, 1780-1849 [122], by Keith Hitchins, traces the history of the national movement in the Romanian province whose course of development was markedly different from that of Wallachia or Moldavia. Transylvania, under Austro-Hungarian tutelage, learned different lessons that manifested national desires in slightly different ways from those witnessed in the Ottoman-held provinces.

Romanian scholars have written prolifically about this period. A good starting place for the serious student is the ENCICLOPEDIA ISTORIOGRAFIEI ROMANESTI [303], which was published in 1978. This reference work contains biographical notes and an excellent bibliography. THE ARMY AND THE ROMANIAN SOCIETY [273] was also published in Romanian as ARMATA SI SOCIETATEA ROMANEASCA. Edited by Alexandru Savu, this work is a collection of studies on the Romanian army. RAZBOIUL INTREGULUI POPOR PENTRU APARAREA PATRIEI LA ROMANI [56], by Ilie Ceaucescu, is a study of Romanian defense concepts. This work is also found in English [56]. General Ceaucescu has also edited a 510-page compilation of articles written by others called PAGES FROM THE MILITARY HISTORY OF THE ROMANIAN PEOPLE [57]. PAGES FROM THE HISTORY OF THE ROMANIAN ARMY [271] is a good source of military historical data on this period. This work was edited by

the ubiquitous Colonel Savu who has also edited another volume
titled STUDII DE ISTORIE SI TEORIE MILITARA. RETROSPECTIVE ISTORICE
ANALIZE CONTEMPORANE [272]. Lastly, Romanian naval affairs are
discussed in CONTRIBUTII LA ISTORIA MARINEI ROMANE. DIN CELE MAI
VECHI TIMPURI PINA IN 1918 [25]. A good work in French that is both
well written and contemporary is Elias Regnault's HISTOIRE POLITIQUE
ET SOCIALE DES PRINCIPANTS DANUBIENNES [246]. This study was
published in 1857.

## MONTENEGRO & SERBIA

There are a number of good works on Montenegro. Francis S.
Stevenson's A HISTORY OF MONTENEGRO [306] deals extensively with the
Eastern Question. HISTOIRE DES MONTENEGRO ET DE LA BOSNIA [73], by
P. Coquelle, is an excellent French history of the period in these
two provinces. This work was published in 1857 while LA SERBIE ET LA
MONTENEGRO [247], by Joseph Reinach, was published in 1876, just
before the great revolt that precipitated the Russo-Turkish War of
1877-1878. Lastly, MONTENEGRO [280], by B. Schwarz, is another
interesting 19th-century account of that province.

An encyclopedic work on Serbia is SERVIAN PEOPLE [165] by
the Prince Lazarovich-Hrebelianovich. This two-volume set is
excellent although outdated by some standards. Micheal Petrovich's A
HISTORY OF MODERN SERBIA [229] is also important, especially the
first volume which deals specifically with this period. YUGOSLAVIA
[120], by Muriel Heppell and Frank B. Singleton is a very good
outline history of the six nations that would be eventually united
into one state.

## BULGARIA

Bulgarian history is more than adequately described in
Mercia Macdermott's A HISTORY OF BULGARIA, 1393-1885 [184]; in
Micheal Leo's LA BULGARIE ET SON PEUPLE SOUS LA DOMINATION OTTOMANE
TELS QUE LES ONT VUS LES VOYAGEURS ANGLO-SAXONS (1586-1878) [169];
and in DOCUMENTS AND MATERIALS ON THE HISTORY OF THE BULGARIAN
PEOPLE [340]. A good bibliography can be found in
NATSIONALNOOSVOBODITELNI DVIZHENIIA NA BALKANSKITE NARODI: VTORATA
POLOVINA NA XVIII V. -- 1878 G. [43]. This work deals particularly
with the military aspects of the period and is a product of the
Bulgarian Academy of Sciences in 1978.

## ALBANIA

Joseph Swire gives a good account of Albania in ALBANIA, THE
RISE OF A KINGDOM [314] that deals specifically with this period.
Felice Cammarata's ALBANICA [47] is brief but useful as general
information, as is L'ALBANIE INDEPENDANTE ET L'EMPIRE KHALIFAL
OTTOMAN [20], by Basri Beg of Dukagjin. Lastly, the most valuable
source document is I.J. Legrand's BIBLIOGRAPHIE ALBANAISE [167].

## GREECE & MACEDONIA

MODERN GREECE, 1800-1931 [201], by J. Mavrocordato, deals
specifically with this period. George Finlay's HISTORY OF GREECE,
FROM ITS CONQUEST BY THE ROMANS TO THE PRESENT TIME, B.C. 164 TO
A.D. 1864 [94], and Richard Clogg's A SHORT HISTORY OF MODERN GREECE

[70] are both sufficient for general background reading. MACEDONIA: ITS PLACE IN BALKAN POWER POLITICS [18], by Elizabeth Barker, is excellent.

Another interesting document pertinent to this period is BRITISH DOCUMENTS ON THE HISTORY OF THE MACEDONIAN PEOPLE [234]. This book was published in 1968 in Yugoslavia. What is unique about it is the fact that the material is quite evenly handled and is a good source of data on the influence of the British in Greece, Turkey, Serbia, Bulgaria and Albania between 1797 and 1839. It even says a few words about Macedonia, but not in much detail; and there is no discussion at all about the Macedonian people. This is, of course, an indictment of the English officials who were stationed in the region during those critical years and whose dispatches were rather meticulously gathered in this collection. Still, there is a wealth of data and quite a great amount of it directly associated with military affairs. Lastly, Emile Kuepfer's LA MACEDOINE ET LES BULGARES [160] is interesting for this period in its opening sections that establish a good background for later events.

## THE OTTOMAN EMPIRE & TURKEY

The general history of Turkey through this period is covered in a number of excellent sources. Certainly, the ENCYCLOPEDIA OF ISLAM is good for the average reader in either its old [105] or new [133] editions. The best encyclopedia is ISLAM ANSIKLOPEDISI [330] which is found only in the Turkish language. Stanford Shaw's HISTORY OF THE OTTOMAN EMPIRE is in two volumes: Volume 1 is EMPIRE OF THE GAZIS: THE RISE AND DECLINE OF THE OTTOMAN EMPIRE, 1280-1808 [287], and Volume 2 is REFORM, REVOLUTION AND REPUBLIC: THE RISE OF MODERN TURKEY, 1808-1975 [288]. Both of these are excellent for this period. THE OTTOMAN CENTURIES: THE RISE AND FALL OF THE TURKISH EMPIRE [152], by Lord Kinross, is easily the most enjoyable to read. Sir Edward Creasy's HISTORY OF THE OTTOMAN TURKS [79] is quite good also, although the old-fashioned style of writing is occasionally disconcerting. Another good study is Albert Hourani's THE OTTOMAN BACKGROUND OF THE MODERN MIDDLE EAST [132]. OTTOMAN STATECRAFT [351], by W.L. Wright, and William Stillman's TURKISH RULE AND TURKISH WARFARE [308] give good accounts about the political and military policies of the Ottomans. THE OTTOMAN EMPIRE AND ITS SUCCESSORS, 1801-1927 [210] opens its account with the period under discussion, while George Arnakis' THE NEAR EAST IN MODERN TIMES: THE OTTOMAN EMPIRE AND THE BALKANS TO 1900 [11] concentrates on this period and upon the Balkans. It is especially good in its coverage of the Greek Question with emphasis on 1821. Two good articles that pertain to this period and subject are Trian Stoianovich's "Factors in the Decline of Ottoman Society in the Balkans" [309] and "Ottoman Feudalism and Its Influence Upon the Balkans" [95].

There are a number of foreign language works that also need to be considered. These include "Turkenherrschaft und Turkenkampf bei den Balkenslawen" [36], by M. Braun; Nicholae Iorga's GESCHICHTE DES OSMANISCHEN REICHES [138]; GESCHICHTE DES OSMANISCHEN REICHES IN EUROPA [355], in seven volumes by J.W. Zinkeisen; and Josef von Hammer-Purgstall's HISTOIRE DE L'EMPIRE OTTOMAN [116], which was published in 1835-1843 in 18 volumes and which closes with the beginning of this period. Bistra Tsvetkova's LES INSTITUTIONS OTTOMANES EN EUROPE [328]; GRANDEUR ET DECADENCE DE L'ASIA [114], by

Fernand Grinard; and CHARTE TURQUE EN ORGANIZATION RELIGIEUSE,
CIVILE ET MILITAIRE DE L'EMPIRE OTTOMAN [113], by M.A. Grassi, are
all good sources. TARIH-I ASIM [12], which covers the period
1791-1808, and TURK SILAHLI KUVVETLERI TARIHI (1793-1908) [329] are
both valuable sources in the Turkish language, as is Ahmed Refik's
TURK IDARESINDE BULGARISTAN (973-1255) [245], which covers the
period 1565-1840. Lastly, the Soviet Academy of Sciences has
published a useful reference called BIBLIOGRAFIYA TURTSII [333] that
can be of value. BALCANICA [341] is a guide to Polish sources on the
Balkans.

PERTINENT WORKS ON MILITARY HISTORY

A large number of studies on the various aspects of military
arts and sciences have application to this period. A MILITARY
HISTORY OF THE WESTERN WORLD [101], by J.F.C. Fuller; A STUDY OF
MILITARY METHODS FROM THE EARLIEST TIMES [296], by Spaulding,
Nickerson and Wright; Lynn Montross' WAR THROUGH THE AGES [212]; MEN
IN ARMS [237], by Preston, Wise, and Werner; Quincy Wright's THE
STUDY OF WAR [350]; and Theodore Ropp's WAR IN THE MODERN WORLD
[254] are all of excellent quality. Stanislav Andreski's MILITARY
ORGANIZATION AND SOCIETY [10] is also good reading as is Raymond
O'Connor's WAR, DIPLOMACY, AND HISTORY: PAPERS AND REVIEWS [221]. In
his work, Professor O'Connor discusses the use of foreign relations
and armed forces as instruments of national policy through an
assemblage of essays, commentaries, and reviews. Abbott Brayton and
Stephana Landwehr discuss the development of political-military
thought by surveying and comparing numerous soldiers, scholars and
statesmen in THE POLITICS OF WAR AND PEACE: A SURVEY OF THOUGHT
[37].

Among the best bibliographical sources are A GUIDE TO THE
STUDY AND USE OF MILITARY HISTORY [144], by John E. Jessup and
Robert W. Coakley, and Dale Floyd's excellent two-volume THE WORLD
BIBLIOGRAPY OF ARMED LAND CONFLICT [97]. Professor Ropp has numerous
valuable bibliographical footnotes in his WAR IN THE MODERN WORLD
[254].

Other works of direct interest include Ludwig Renn's
WARFARE: THE RELATION OF WAR AND SOCIETY [357] that was published
just before World War II; Edward Gulick's EUROPE'S CLASSICAL BALANCE
OF POWER: A CASE HISTORY OF THE THEORY AND PRACTICE OF ONE OF THE
GREAT CONCEPTS OF EUROPEAN STATECRAFT [115]; A HISTORY OF MILITARISM
[334], by A. Vagts; THE LAW OF PEACE [336], by C. Van Vollenhaven;
Cyril Falls' THE ART OF WAR [93]; and THE MAKERS OF MODERN STRATEGY:
MILITARY THOUGHT FROM MACHIAVELLI TO HITLER [91], that was edited by
E.M. Earle. William Balck's TACTICS [16] is quite good although it
centers on the end of the century rather than the beginning.
Clausewitz [240] and Jomini [145] need to be read now to understand
contemporary military thinking. Jomini's work is often considered
the greatest military textbook of the 19th century.

John Alger's THE QUEST FOR VICTORY: THE HISTORY OF THE
PRINCIPLES OF WAR [3] examines the ideas and the attitudes of
military writers, scholars, and leaders who have expounded on the
nature and factors involved in the art of war over the centuries.
Martin Van Creveld looks at the problems associated with the

logistics and transportation of armies during this period in his
SUPPLYING WAR: LOGISTICS FROM WALLENSTEIN TO PATTON [335]. Richard
Lewinsohn discusses THE PROFITS OF WAR THROUGH THE AGES [174], while
David Singer and Melvin Small have produced a statistical handbook
called THE WAGES OF WAR [291].

The two most important combat arms of the period are
discussed in Ian Hogg's A HISTORY OF ARTILLERY [126] and George
Denison's HISTORY OF CAVALRY [84]. Elbridge Colby expands upon this
theme in his MASTERS OF MOBILE WARFARE [72], as does P.E. Cleator in
his WEAPONS OF WAR [68]. Ian Hogg also examines the history of
defensive warfare in his FORTRESS: A HISTORY OF MILITARY DEFENSE
[127].

The best general chronology on war during this period is THE
ENCYCLOPEDIA OF MILITARY HISTORY [90], by Dupuy and Dupuy. Another
good one is A SHORT HISTORY OF WARFARE [356], by David Zook and
Robin Higham. WAR AND SOCIETY IN REVOLUTIONARY EUROPE, 1770-1870
[23], by Geoffrey Best, provides an in-depth analysis of the effects
of war in Europe during the years surrounding the Napoleonic period.
WAR AND PEACE IN AN AGE OF UPHEAVAL, 1793-1830 [77], edited by C.W.
Crawley, does much the same thing. Robert S. Quimby's THE BACKGROUND
OF NAPOLEONIC WARFARE [238] is written for the 18th century but lays
a good foundation for what was to transpire in the early decades of
the 19th.

There are three good works on naval warfare that are of use
at this point. TWENTY-FIVE CENTURIES OF SEA WARFARE [213], by
Jacques Mordal, and R.C. Anderson's NAVAL WARS OF THE LEVANT,
1559-1853 [8] are both good. THE INDECISIVENESS OF MODERN WAR AND
OTHER ESSAYS [255], by John H. Rose, was written in 1927 and
contains some naval material that is of peripheral value here.

Lastly, there are three additional works that deserve
mention here. These are David Chandler's excellent DICTIONARY OF THE
NAPOLEONIC WARS [61] that contains more than 1,200 entries relevant
to the period. KRIEG UND KRIEGFUHRUNG IM WANDEL DER WELTGESCHICHTE
[278], by P. Schmitthenner, which as the title implies deals with
the changes wrought by war upon man's history. And BIBLIOGRAFIA
MILITARA ROMANEASCA [253] which is now in a number of volumes that
cover Romanian military publications back to 1831.

## THE BALKANS IN THE FIRST HALF OF THE 19TH CENTURY

The beginning of the century witnessed the Russians, Turks,
and British allied against France. Russia was under the
schizophrenic rule of Paul I (1796-1801), while Selim III
(1789-1807) still sat on the throne in Constantinople. In France the
Consuls had proclaimed an end to the Revolution on 15 December 1799,
and the Third Estate seemed firmly in control. In 1800 Napoleon
raised a new army and, on 14 June, won a spectacular victory over
the Austrians at Marengo.

The War of the Second Coalition ended with the signing of
the Treaty of Amiens (27 March 1802), but not before the combined
naval forces of Russia and Turkey had cleared the French out of the
Ionian Islands. Stavrianos [301] points out that the loss of the
Ionians came about as a consequence of the French invasion of Egypt,

an action that led to a Turkish declaration of war and the subsequent Russo-Ottoman joint naval operations in the Aegean.

Although Russia had strengthened its strategic position in the Balkans, especially in the Danubian Principalities, during these early days, it was not until after the resumption of hostilities in 1803 and the ensuing formation of the Third Coalition (1805) that there was any real military activity in that region. This came about with the uprising of the Belgrad pashalik in Serbia which was led by George Petrovic who assumed the name Karageorge (Black George). The revolt actually began in 1804 as a result of the tyrannical conduct of the Janissaries. This tale is told admirably well in Creasy [79], whose footnotes are especially valuable as sources for further reading.

By December 1806 the Turks had been driven out, and Serbian independence was declared. This came about because the Janissaries in the Belgrad garrison would not answer to the Pasha and were ordered to withdraw by the Sublime Porte, but only after the Sultan had seen to the assassination of the Janissaries' Aga. The Serbian state lasted until 1812, when Russia made peace with the Turks thereby freeing the Porte to send an army to crush the rebels. Karageorge was forced to flee.

There are a number of works on this period, one of the most interesting of which is THE MEMOIRES OF PROTA MATIJA NENODOVIC [219], that was edited by Lovett Edwards. During this First Serbia Revolt, as the events following 1804 have been called, Father Nenodovic was a Serbian field commander of considerable skill and importance. Another excellent work is Dimitrije Djordjevic's REVOLUTIONS NATIONALES DES PEUPLES BALCANIQUES, 1804-1914 [85]. A good subsidiary work is Paul Shupp's EUROPEAN POWERS AND THE EASTERN QUESTION, 1806-1807 [290]. Karl Gladt does a most effective job of detailing the course of the Serbian struggle through this and subsequent revolts in his KAISERTRAUM UND KONIGSKRONE. AUFSTIEG UND UNTERGANG EINER SERBISCHEN DYNASTIE [110]. This work was produced in 1972 and is extremely valuable. Lastly, Herve Fuyet's HISTOIRE DES RELATIONS ENTRE LA SERBIE ET LA FRANCE PENDANT LA PERIODE D'INSURRECTION SERBE (1802-1813) [102] looks at some of the attempts made by the Serbs to gain recognition and the activities of France, which was more interested in its personal designs on the region than in the freedom of the Serbs.

THE RUSSO-TURKISH WAR OF 1806-1812

The war that broke out between Russia and the Ottoman Empire in 1806 was, in no small measure, the result of French meddling in the Balkans. The actual flare-up that triggered the war was the product of a long-standing dispute over the Principalities that was exacerbated by the arrival of General Sebastiani, Napoleon's minister to the Sublime Porte. His mission, thus the French design, was to create a situation in which Russian attention and, consequently, the Tsar's armies, were diverted from the struggle being waged in Prussian Poland, where Alexander I of Russia (1801-1825) was attempting to aid the Prussians against Napoleon's legions. Russia was already at war with Persia (1804-1813) over St. Petersburg's annexation of Georgia when Turkey declared its own war against the Tsar on 6 November 1806.

The Turkish declaration was followed, paradoxically, by a Russian one on 22 November that cited the Porte's banishment of Constantin Ypsilanti, the Prince of Wallachia (1802-1806), and the Turkish infringement upon the 1802 hettisherif as the causes for war. One month later, on 25 December 1806, Russian troops occupied Bucharest after a minimum of resistance. Ypsilanti was restored to his throne and immediately took advantage of the situation by establishing an independent state that included Wallachia, Moldavia, and Serbia. By that time over 35,000 Russian troops were in the Principalities, and a crossing of the Danube to attack the Turks in Bulgaria was expected at any moment.

While these events were transpiring in the field, the English minister in Constantinople was threatening the Porte with military intervention if the French minister, Sebastiani, was not forthwith dismissed and if the Ottomans did not renew their alliance with the Coalition. Selim III was unimpressed by the British threat, however, and refused to comply. Very soon thereafter, a British naval squadron forced a passage of the Dardenelles and narrowly missed capturing Constantinople (19 February 1807). Thereafter, on 30 June , the Turkish fleet was sunk at Lemnos, near Mount Athos, by a Russian naval squadron under the command of Admiral Senyavin. Eight days later, at Tilsit, Alexander of Russia and Napoleon reached an accommodation that was, of course, unacceptable to the British; and Senyavin and his fleet found themselves blockaded in the Aegean by Duckworth's English flotilla. Tilsit also witnessed Napoleon act the role of mediator and arrange an armistice between the Russians and Turks (Slobozia, 24 August 1807).

The struggle in the Balkans during this time included the previously discussed Belgrad uprising. Karageorge, the Serbian leader, sided with the Russians against the Turks and formally requested aid from the Tsar as protection from the French and Turkish forces in Bosnia. In June a number of the Balkan pashas, not necessarily out of loyalty to the Sultan, attacked the Russians. The Tsar's forces were thrown back in most areas although they fought successfully at Obilesti on 14 June 1807. Before the end of that month, the Russians were under siege in and around Bucharest. This situation changed rapidly, however, when the Janissaries in Constantinople mutinied and Selim II was overthrown. The August armistice followed, as much a result of the mutiny as it was a product of the Franco-Russian accord at Tilsit that left the Porte bereft of great power support.

Regardless of these events, the war started again in 1809, after it became obvious to the Porte that the Russians had no intention of withdrawing from the Principalities as prescribed in the Slobozia armistice. Thereafter, sporadic fighting continued until 1812 when British mediation led to the Treaty of Bucharest (28 May). Russia gained Romanian Bessarabia between the Pruth and Dniester rivers from this treaty without, of course, the consent of the Romanians.

This period is rather well reported in Stavrianos [301], and in Shaw [287-8]. The Turkish side is told in Creasy [79], while the second chapter of Karl Gladt's KAISERTRAUM UND KONIGSKRONE [110] discusses the Serbian role. Another important, if not totally impartial, work that deals with this area is Dimitrije Djordjevic's REVOLUTIONS NATIONALES DES PEUPLES BALCANIQUES, 1804-1914 [85].

Selim III's reign is exhaustively detailed in A. Cevad Eren's article [59] by that name in Islam Ansiklopedisi [330], while Ahmed Asim Efendi's history [12] covers the period just as well. Both of these works are in Turkish as is Ahmed Vasif Efendi's MAHASIN AL-ASAR VE HAQAYIK AL-AHBAR [337] which is extremely valuable, but still in manuscript form. Mehmed Ataullah Sani-zade's SANI-ZADE TARIHI [267] begins its coverage in 1808 and goes through 1821. Suleymen Sudi's DEFTER-I MUQTESID [310] describes the Ottoman administration of the period.

In NCMH's Volume 9, N.H. Gibbs [106] describes the armies of the period, while C.C. Lloyd [176] tells about the navies. These two accounts are centered upon the major powers in Europe but are still valuable. Dupuy and Dupuy [90] also outline the events of the era and have a good account of the style of warfare. C.W. Crawley's article on "The Near East and the Ottoman Empire" [76], which is also found in NCMH 9, is extremely valuable. So is Macdermott's A HISTORY OF BULGARIA [184] in which he discusses the Kurdzhali banditry that plagued the country from 1792 until 1815 and which contains a short but interesting account that helps in understanding Bulgaria's role in the war and in the Serbian uprising. Further references on this subject may be found in HISTOIRE MILITAIRE DE LA BULGARIE, 681-1945. BIBLIOGRAPHIE [44]. Gunther Rothenberg's THE MILITARY BORDER IN CROATIA, 1740-1881: A STUDY OF AN IMPERIAL INSTITUTION [256] is also valuable.

## THE GREEK REVOLUTION OF 1821 AND ITS CONSEQUENCES

Selim's reforms ended with his removal and the subsequent elevation of Mustafa IV (1807-1808) to the Turkish throne. Mustafa was the son of the late Abdul Hamid (1773-1789). In August 1807, once the peace of Slobozia allowed it, an army of some 40,000 Bosnian and Albanian supporters of Selim, led by Mustafa Bairactar Pasha, marched on Constantinople. After much fighting they arrived at the royal palace; but before they could force their way in, Selim, who had been under house arrest since his deposition, was killed by palace enuchs (28 July 1808). Mustafa IV was ousted, many Janissaries executed, and Mahmoud II (1808-1839) installed as Sultan. Mustafa Bairacter Pasha was named Grand Vizier and, as his first act, he set about breaking up the Janissary Corps and establishing of a new armed force, called Seymens, that was to be trained and outfitted in the European style. Bairacter's plan did not succeed, however, as a new Janissary revolt began that did not end until 17 March 1809 when Bairacter was killed. Mahmoud II was allowed to live and continue his reign as the last of the House of Othman. The Ottoman decline had now taken on a more precipitous angle, and throughout the empire the signs of decay emboldened those who sought freedom from the Turkish yoke to commit even more desperate acts of rebellion.

In one sense, the Greek revolt has its origins in Serbia where the murder of Karageorge by a rival clan leader, Milos Obrenovich, reopened fighting that had more of the color of a blood feud than that of an uprising against the Porte. Regardless, to put down the trouble, the newly installed pasha in Belgrade carried out a reign of terror that had far-reaching consequences. In 1817 Obrenovich was proclaimed hereditary prince of Serbia after he swore his allegiance to the Sultan. This was accomplished after the Serbian had deftly placed the entire blame for all of the troubles on the pasha.

Obrenovich's success in this matter was also the result of the Porte's knowledge that Russia, as well as the other great powers, was watching these events very closely. In Constantinople the conviction was strongly held that the armies, which had only recently defeated Napoleon, had to be carefully reckoned with so as to insure they did not march against the Sultan. In the meantime, the blood feud continued and did not abate until the end of World War II.

These events did not go unnoticed in the other Balkan principalities; and from this beginning secret organizations sprung up, such as the one in Odessa that formed in 1814 and called itself Heretiai (Philiki Etaireia, or Philhellene). This group had less than unanimity of purpose even though its avowed goal was the removal of the Ottoman Yoke. Because of this many saw the Heretiai as simply another form of Greek interference.

Among this latter group was Tudor Vladimescu and his followers who had long agitated for independence in their native Wallachia. In January 1821, after the death of Prince Alexandru Sutu, Vladimerescu seized the opportunity and issued the Proclamation of Pades (23 January 1821) that began the Romanian revolt. By 21 March, Vladimerescu had entered Bucharest. Fifteen days earlier, on 6 March, Alexandros Ypsilanti had, with Russia's blessing, crossed the Pruth into Moldavia and carried out a bloody campaign in which a number of Turkish civilians in Jassy and Galati were murdered. Ypsilanti and Vladimirescu met after that, but nothing was accomplished. Thereafter, Vladimirescu proclaimed himself Prince of Wallachia.

The Wallachian's success was short lived, however, as an Ottoman army crossed the Danube into the Principalities after Russia disavowed its previously promised support. Vladimirescu moved to engage the Turks but was instead betrayed and handed over to Ypsilanti who had in the meantime proclaimed himself Prince of Moldavia. Ypsilanti ordered that Vladimirescu be executed and attempted to rally the Pandour army to his banner. Although some did swear their allegiance, most broke away either going home or moving off to fight the Turks on their own.

Those who joined with Ypsilanti suffered their defeat at Dragasani on 7 June 1821, while those who chose to fight under native Wallachian leadership held out until 17 July, when they were defeated at Slobozia. The Turks then carried out an extremely cruel repression throughout the provinces until Great Power pressure caused the Ottomans to withdraw (2 March 1822).

The actual uprising in Greece began as a result of Albania's Ali Pasha, the "Old Lion of Janina's," successful defense of his territory against a large Turkish force sent to punish him for numerous real and imagined crimes and misdemeanors. These events ended at approximately the same time that Ypsilantis was entering Romania (March 1821). This fact, and the absence of Turkish troops sent to Albania, heartened the Greeks to rise up against their Turkish masters. Sporadic revolts began in Peloponnese and elsewhere that soon took on the proportions of a full-scale rebellion. On 5 October 1821, for instance, the 10,000-man Turkish garrison at Tripolitsa was massacred. This led to severe reprisals against Greeks everywhere in the empire, including the hanging of the Greek Orthodox Patriarch in Constantinople. Thereafter, the struggle continued until 1825 with the scales of success or failure constantly shifting.

Before the end of 1825, numerous foreign volunteers had joined the Greek ranks; and, at one point, both the Greek army and navy were commanded by Englishmen. At mid-point in that year, however, the siege of the Acropolis ended in a Turkish victory (5 June 1825) that was brought about in part by the arrival of Egyptian reinforcements sent by the Sultan's vassal, Mehmet Ali, the Bey of Egypt. On 6 July 1827, the Great Powers demanded an immediate withdrawal of the Egyptians and a Turkish promise of an armistice. When these demands were refused, the Allies sent large naval contingents into the eastern Mediterranean where, on 20 October, they cornered the combined Turkish-Egyptian fleets riding at anchor in Navarino Bay. Although some say it was actually an artillery duel, and not a true naval battle, the Allies scored a stunning victory.

Then, on 26 April 1828, Russia declared war on Turkey in support of the Greeks. Russia viewed this juncture as an ideal time to secure the greatest advantage it could. Russian forces entered the Danubian Principalities, and in less than one month helped gain complete control to the extent of establishing a Russian civil administration under Count Pahlen. This occupation lasted until April 1834.

Russia's war with Turkey ended after a series of successful engagements that included Kulevcha (11 June 1829), Silistra (30 June), and Adrianople (20 August). The Turks then sued for peace, and the Treaty of Adrianople was initialed on 16 September. Russia gained the mouth of the Danube and the eastern coast of the Black Sea. In the meantime, the Egyptians had withdrawn from Greece (August 1828) under French supervision. Following much negotiation that was swayed largely by public sentiment in the west, the Treaty of London was signed on 7 May 1832. By its terms an independent Kingdom of Greece was created. One of the upshots of this was the fact that John Capodistrias (Ioannins Kapodistrias), one of the real leaders of the Greek independence movement, was murdered amid the confusion of finding a ruler for the new kingdom. Finally, Otho of Bavaria was selected and Greece became a protectorate under the Bavarian crown. These moves were acknowledged by Turkey in the Treaty of Constantinople signed in July 1832.

This period is extremely well reported in a number of good and varied works. The background to the struggle is covered in Mavrocordato [201] and in Finlay [94]. Dakin uses the first four chapters of THE UNIFICATION OF GREECE, 1770-1923 [82] describing the events surrounding the rebellion. THE GREEK PHOENIX [34], by Joseph Braddock, is readable but not very informative. A better selection is Charles Crawley's THE QUESTION OF GREEK INDEPENDENCE, 1821-1831 [78].

Other good works include THE MAKING OF MODERN GREECE [353], by D.A. Zakythinos, which has an extensive bibliography, THE STRUGGLE FOR GREEK INDEPENDENCE [69], which was edited by Richard Clogg, and which contains ten excellent articles on all phases of the times; THE LAST PHASE OF THE WAR OF INDEPENDENCE IN WESTERN GREECE [86], by D. Dontas; A SHORT HISTORY OF MODERN GREECE, 1821-1956 [99], by E. Forster; A HISTORY OF THE GREEK PEOPLE, 1821-31 [209]; and GREECE IN THE NINETEENTH CENTURY [268], by L. Sargent. Also to be considered are "The Greek Revolution in the Ottoman Empire (1821-1829)" [352], by R. Yurtseven; C.M. Woodhouse's THE GREEK WAR OF INDEPENDENCE [346]; HISTORY OF THE GREEK REVOLUTION [111], by Thomas Gordon; and Douglas Dakin's THE GREEK STRUGGLE FOR INDEPENDENCE, 1821-1833 [83].

A CONTEMPORARY HISTORY OF THE GREEKS AND OF THE OTHER PEOPLES OF THE EAST FROM 1821 TO 1921 [151] is Volume 7 in a large history written by Professor P. Karolides. This work is of extreme value as it deals with the Serbs, Romanians and Bulgarians, as well as the Greeks. Djordjevic [85] is also useful here, as in Todorov's BALGARI UCHASTNICI V BORBITE ZA OSVOBOZDENIETO NA GARCIJA, 1821-1828 [325]. This last work is a compendium that includes a brief, concise history of the struggle along with documents and lists of participants. The book is in Bulgarian, but many records are in Greek and Russian. Part of the history is translated into French.

There are at least two good works on the revolt in Constantinople that led to the overthrow of Mustafa IV: Ottokar von Schechta-Wesseherd's DIE REVOLUTIONEN IN CONSTANTINOPLE IN DEN JAHREN 1807 UND 1808 [274] and Juchereau de St. Denys' LES REVOLUTIONS DE CONSTANTINOPLE EN 1807 ET 1808 [264]. The former was published in 1882, while the quite similar latter work was published in 1819. The life of Mustafa Bairactar Pasha, who led the revolt, is covered in A.F. Miller's MUSTAFA PASHA BAYRAKDAR [208] which was published in Moscow in 1947.

Three works deal with the situation in Albania: A. Boppe's L'ALBANIE ET NAPOLEON [33], Dennis N. Skiotes' "The Lion and the Phoenix: Ali Pasha and the Greek Revolution, 1819-1822" [295], and ALI THE LION [233], by W. Plomer. The war report of von Moltke is found in English in THE RUSSIANS IN BULGARIA AND RUMELIA IN 1828 AND 1829 [211], which was published in London in 1854. Another interesting work in English is Colonel F.R. Chesney's THE RUSSO-TURKISH CAMPAIGN OF 1828 AND 1829 [63]. An excellent account in Turkish is Ahmed Muktar Pasha's 1244 TURKIYE RUSYA SEFERI VE EDIRNE MUAHEDESI [215] which is in two volumes.

The Serbian role is amply covered in Danica Milic's TRGOVINA SRBIJE, 1815-1839 [207], in Gladt's work [110], and in the first volume of Micheal Petrovich's A HISTORY OF MODERN SERBIA, 1804-1918 [229]. The index to this last work mentioned is found in the second volume as is a short, but good, bibliography and numerous charts and tables. This publishing feature makes the finding of both volumes a necessity.

Most of the works discussed above mention the Philhellenes. There are several additional works that ought to be considered when dealing with this group. These include St. Clair's THAT GREECE MIGHT STILL BE FREE: THE PHILHELLENES IN THE WAR OF INDEPENDENCE [263], Dakin's BRITISH AND AMERICAN PHILHELLENES DURING THE WAR OF GREEK INDEPENDENCE, 1821-1833 [80], and Stephen Larrabee's HELLAS OBSERVED - THE AMERICAN EXPERIENCE OF GREECE, 1775-1865 [164]. Also of interest is Dakin's BRITISH INTELLIGENCE OF EVENTS IN GREECE, 1824-1827 [81].

The best overall history of the period is probably Stavrianos [301], which deals with events in the Balkans and how these events impact upon the rest of Europe. Another excellent choice is Arnold Toynbee's THE WESTERN QUESTION IN GREECE AND TURKEY [326]. Two works that deal with the Great Powers during those important times are THE GREAT POWERS AND THE EUROPEAN STATES SYSTEMS, 1815-1914 [45], by Roger Bullen and Roy Bridge, and EUROPE'S BALANCE OF POWER, 1815-1848 [294]. Eberhard Schultz's DIE EUROPAISCHE ALLIANZPOLITIK ALEXANDER I, UND DER GRIECHISCHE UNABHANGIGKEITSKAMPF, 1820-1830 [279], and "Napoleon et la liberation de la Grece" [270], by J. Savant, look at the roles assumed by two of the leaders of the European world, while RUSSIA AND EUROPE [177], by Lobanov-Rostovsky, presents a different view of Russia's role in these events.

The story of Tudor Vladimirescu is told in Doctor Dorina Rusu's article "The Army of the First Revolution in the Modern Epoch of Romania" [262]. S.I. Samoilov deals with the national uprising in Wallachia in 1821 in his "Narodno-osvoboditelnoe vosstanii 1821 g. v Valakhii" [266]. C.M. Woodhouse outlines the part played by Count John Capodistrias in the Greek liberation in CAPODISTRIA, THE FOUNDER OF GREEK INDEPENDENCE [348], while William Kaldis does much the same thing in his JOHN CAPODISTRIAS AND THE MODERN GREEK STATE [146]. THE MEMOIRES OF GENERAL MAKRIYANNIS, 1797-1864 [186], which were translated in 1966, are a first-class historical account of a number of important military actions involved in the revolution. THE MEMOIRS OF PROTA MATIJA NENADOVIC [219] tells of the priest's role as a gunrunner and a diplomat.

REFLECTARI ISTORICO-LITERARE ALE REZIZTENTEI ROMANESTI [300], by Nicholae Stan, deals with the general characteristics of revolution and resistance in the Romanian experience. Constantin Olteanu's "On the Organization of the Army in the Romanian Counties" [224], and his "Genese et developpement de l'armee permanente chez les Roumaines" [223] also deal with certain aspects of the Romanian part in this struggle. Dominic Kosary's MAGYAR TORTENETI BIBLIOGRAFIA, 1825-1867 [158] covers Hungarian publications of this period. Macdermott deals with the Bulgarian part in the Russo-Turkish war and in the revolt.

Three works on the Austro-Hungarian Empire during those times are A.J.P. Taylor's THE HABSBURG MONARCHY, 1809-1918 [317], which is interesting, if not overly reliable, and Hans Kohn's THE HABSBURG EMPIRE, 1804-1918 [156], which is somewhat better. Dupuy [90] gives a fair account of the chronology of the period. The CHRONOLOGICAL HISTORY OF ROMANIA [109] does not cover the period satisfactorily at all. C.M. Woodhouse's THE BATTLE OF NAVARINO [347] is a good account of that naval engagement.

## THE JANISSARY REVOLT AND THEIR MASSACRE

The obstinate disloyalty of the Janissaries finally forced the Sultan to act in 1826, at the height of the Greek Revolution. This came about when Mahmoud II ordered the Janissaries to practice regular military drills as a means of instilling the discipline they lacked. On 15 June 1826, the Janissaries of the capital garrison revolted. When they marched on the palace they were destroyed by the Sultan's artillery, with many more being put to death throughout the realm as a means of ending the Corps. With their destruction a new, modern army was begun that was built upon the European system. These events are covered in detail in Creasy [79] and in Stavrianos [301].

Three more works on the subject are "The Destruction of the Janissaries by Mahmud II in June 1826" [244], PRECIS HISTORIQUE DE LA DESTRUCTION DU CORPS DES JANISSAIRES PAR LE SULTAN MAHMOUD II EN 1826 [227], by Caussin de Perceval, and Ahmed Cevat Pasha Efendi's TARIH-I ASKERI-I OSMANLI I YENICERILER [60]. This last work was published in Istanbul in 1880 and is the first volume of a larger history of the empire. This volume deals with the history of the Janissary Corps from its inception to its demise.

## MEHMET ALI AND HIS REVOLT AGAINST CONSTANTINOPLE

On 4 July 1830, the French seized Algiers with the explicit intent of delivering the city from the Ottoman Yoke. More than anything else this act proved how weak the Turks were as a result of the recent war and the revolt at home. The Porte could neither fight nor even bargain with the French; and it was little wonder, therefore, when one of the Sultan's pashas, Mehmet Ali, the Bey of Egypt, rose against him. Aided and encouraged by the French, Mehmet Ali invaded Syria in 1832 and then turned upon Anatolia where, at Konya(Koniah), the Turkish army was defeated on 21 December. Fearing more successes, the Porte openly accepted the offers of assistance proffered by their erstwhile, and recurrent, enemy Imperial Russia. Soon afterward a Russian naval force appeared in the Bosphorus and one of the Tsar's divisions was put ashore near Constantinople (20 February 1833).

Alarmed by those events, the French attempted to persuade the Egyptian field commander, who was also Mehmet Ali's son, Ibrahim Pasha, to turn away from his drive on Constantinople. This attempt failed, but when Ibrahim determined that a second Russian force had landed at Scutari, the Egyptian advance was stopped. To put an end to the affair, the Sultan issued a firman that gave Mehmet Ali much of the land he had already taken. In turn the Russians demanded and received a defensive alliance with the Turks and a closure of the Straits to foreign men-of-war. These terms were codified in the Treaty of Unkiar-Skelessi on 8 July 1833.

The Turko-Egyptian peace lasted until 1839 when the Turks moved to take back Syria. A large Turkish army commanded by Hafiz Pasha, with Captain Helmuth von Moltke along as an advisor, moved from Bir on the Euphrates into Syrian Territory. On 25 June 1839, the Ottomans met Ibrahim's army near Nezib. Before the battle even began large numbers of the Sultan's army deserted, and the Turks were decisively defeated. One week later, the Turkish fleet surrendered at Alexandria (1 July). That same day, Mahmoud II died apparently not knowing of either disaster.

The courts of Europe looked somberly on what was transpiring and chose to once again shore up the sagging Ottoman Empire. British and Austrian forces moved to isolate Ibrahim's army in Syria; Beirut was occupied on 10 October 1840 and Acre on 3 November. The British then forced the Egyptians to withdraw from Syria (Convention of Alexandria, 27 November 1840) and to return the Turkish fleet. The evacuation was completed in February 1841 and was followed by the Straits Convention of 13 July 1841, in which the Great Powers forced the closure of the Straits and the Dardenelles to all warships in peacetime. Abdul Medjid (1839-1861) became Sultan of the Ottoman Empire.

The reign of Mahmoud II is reported in Creasy [79] and in Shaw [288]. There are also a number of other works dealing with Mahmoud's life. These include DIE MILITARISCHEN REFORMEN UNTER MAHMUD II [21], by J. Bastelberger; Avigdor Levy's " The Military Policy of Sultan Mahmud II, 1808-1839" [172]; and his "The Officer Corps in Sultan Mahmud II's New Ottoman Army, 1826-1839" [173]. Ahmed Cevad Eren's MAHMUD II ZAMININDE BOSNA-HERSEK [58] deals specifically with the Sultan's relations with Bosnia-Herzogovina, while Juchereau de St. Denys covers a broader view of the period in his HISTOIRE DE L'EMPIRE OTTOMAN DEPUIS 1792 JUSQU'EN 1844 [265].

Creasy [79] and Shaw [288] discuss the events surrounding Mehmet Ali, as do Charles and Barbara Jelavich in THE ESTABLISHMENT OF THE BALKAN NATIONAL STATES, 1804-1920 [143]. Additional coverage may be found in Stavrianos [301]. A chronology of the First and Second Turko-Egyptian War can be found in Dupuy [90].

Dakin [83] deals at length with the internal problems that occurred following the Greek independence and the arrival of King Otho in 1833 (d.1867). The Treaty of Unkiar-Skellesi is covered in Stavrianos [301], Jelavich [143], and almost any decent Russian history book.

THE REIGN OF ABDUL MEDJID

The new Sultan maintained the policies of his father, Mahmoud II, and, as his father had done, surrounded himself whenever possible with good advisors. One of these was Omar Pasha, one of his generals with a solid reputation for putting down insurrections in Albania, Bosnia, and elsewhere that started because of some of the Sultan's reforms and because of general dissatisfaction with Turkish overlordship. Most of these facts can be found in Creasy [79] who stresses the point that the treaty with Russia and a rather benign rule allowed the Ottoman Empire enough time to resusitate itself and, therefore, to survive a little while longer.

THE GREEK REVOLUTION OF 1843

It has already been noted that Greece suffered most of the usual problems associated with freedom when it finally won its independence. A number of outbreaks of lawlessness took place, for example, that generally followed factional lines and clearly illustrated the tenuous grip the interim central government had on the countryside. These events are well documented in Dakin [82]. Finally, in 1832, the Greeks settled upon Otho, son of Ludwig of Bavaria, to be their king. In addition to delivering the 17-year-old to the Greeks, Ludwig also offered a 3,500-man contingent of Bavarian troops; but before they could be sent, Greek constitutionalists attempted to seize the government. This move was foiled, however, by the intervention of French troops who still remained in Greece as a part of the Powers' guarantee. Otho's arrival early in 1833 aboard a British warship was hailed by the Greek people who apparently did not see in all of the symbolism the fact that they were still very much under foreign domination.

Otho's internal rule is well reported in Dakin [82] and elsewhere. What is more important here is the signing of the Straits Convention in 1841 that once again divided England and France over the Eastern Question. In this affair, Greece found itself firmly caught in the middle and bereft of outside support. Otho then found himself faced with growing discontent at home that finally brought about a bloodless revolt (14 September 1843) that was led by several senior military officers. Before dawn the next morning, the king, deserted by his army, including his personal bodyguard, was forced to accept the concept of constitutional government in Greece. Once again, the signs of what was happening were apparent, but few chose to recognize them.

THE REVOLUTION OF 1848

This great revolution that shook Europe from France to the Balkans did not have a common origin but, rather, spread as a fire igniting whatever tinder lay in its path. Both liberal and nationalistic causes can be discovered that were exacerbated by a poor harvest, a worsening commercial outlook, and a growing awareness by urban workers and artisans of their political power.

In Romania, for example, the revolutionary spirit was an outgrowth of an upsurge in centuries-old nationalistic fervor directly related to an almost universal desire to be free of foreign domination. The new awareness can be traced in part to the work of a number of liberal societies that had sprung up in the provinces. One of these, FRATIA (Fraternity), was founded in Wallachia in late 1843 and became associated with the publication of magazines that helped develop the national awareness that was to be crucial in 1848.

The first outbreak began in France in February 1848 when Louis Philip was forced to abdicate (25 February) and a republic was proclaimed. On 3 March, another revolt broke out in Pest that began the 1848-1849 Hungarian Revolt. Then, on 13 March, a popular uprising broke out in Vienna, and before the end of the month another one flared up in Moldavia. By June 1848, all of Romania was aflame with rebellion. In Transylvania, a near civil war situation surfaced as factions squabbled over whether to join the Principalities or to enter into a free association with Hungary. There was some fighting but mostly rhetoric; and, for a while, it appeared the Romanian revolt would be successful. The apparent victory was short-lived, however; as, on 19 July 1848, Ottoman troops crossed the Danube into Wallachia from Ruschuk and began a campaign to restore Turkish order. By 13 September, Turkish troops were in Bucharest despite stiff local resistance. Two days later, on 15 September, the Turks were reinforced by a Russian army commanded by General A.N. Luders. Even so, the Romanians continued to fight with the Transylvanian struggle continuing into 1849.

The great revolt that broke out in Hungary was led by Louis Kossuth (1802-1894) whose call for independence from the Austrian crown triggered the uprising in Vienna and probably helped in forcing Metternich to resign and flee. As a part of the overall plan for Hungarian autonomy (under the Habsburg crown), Kossuth attempted to annex Transylvania and Croatia and intended to do the same thing to the Serbs at a later time. These plans failed, however, even though Hungarian troops had occupied large sections of Transylvania by the end of 1848.

For the first six months of 1849, a Transylvanian peasant force led by Avram Iancu (1824-1872) held the Hungarians at bay in the Apuseni Mountains inflicting a number of telling defeats such as at Marisel (19 January), Rosia (6 May), and in the Apusenis on 3 June. On 6 June, the Austrian Emperor asked for and received Russian military aid and a large Russian force entered Transylvania almost immediately. Before their presence could be felt, however, the Hungarians suffered a stunning defeat at Fintinele on 24 June. Subsequently, the Kossuth forces were compelled to capitulate upon the arrival of the Russians (1 August); and, on 22 September, the Hungarian garrison at the stronghold of Komarno surrendered effectively ending the Kossuth uprising and returning Transylvania to provincial status in the Austrian realm. Both the Hungarians and the Transylvanians suffered as a result.

Bulgaria missed the main fury of the 1848 revolt but this is not to imply that there was no trouble in that country. Indeed, the first uprising of this period had its origins in 1841 in Braila that had to be put down by the Moldavian troops of Prince Sturdza, who used force to prevent a large group of rebels from crossing the river into Bulgaria. After a short battle, the Bulgarian leaders were tricked into surrendering, and the group was transported to Romanian salt mines. A second uprising took place in 1842 and was followed by a third in 1843. Many were killed in these incidents and many others sent into exile. In 1850 a very serious revolt began that encompassed most of the northwestern part of Bulgaria. This uprising ended in disaster as the Turks carried out a bloody repression once the ill-organized and equipped peasant army had been defeated near Belogradchik.

The Ottoman role in these affairs was really one of great restraint. Fearing Russian intervention should it overreact to the uprisings in its territories, the Porte used the time to continue its rebuilding program, knowing full well that a Russian army of almost 50,000 troops was just north of the Danube and could strike into Bulgaria at any time. The Turks did offer sanctuary to a number of the Hungarian leaders; and, although their return was demanded, the Sultan firmly refused. Russia went so far as to threaten war, but the first half of the 19th century ended without another conflict.

This very important period is covered extensively in any number of histories of Europe. It was, after all, a momentous time the reverberations from which would continue into the 20th century. Among the more generalized works devoted to this period, two good ones are Peter N. Stearn's 1848: THE REVOLUTIONARY TIDE IN EUROPE [303] and Lewis B. Namier's 1848: THE REVOLUTION OF THE INTELLECTUALS [217]. Both of these works devote considerable coverage to the Balkans. Jean L.E. Bujac's PRECIS DE QUELQUES CAMPAGNES CONTEMPORAIRES [42] covers Balkan history during this period, but a somewhat better job is done in Charles and Barbara Jelavich's THE BALKANS IN TRANSITION [142] which is a series of excellent essays. Stavrianos [301] is still among the best, while Dupuy [90] gives only sketchy coverage.

Robert Kann's THE MULTINATIONAL EMPIRE: NATIONALISM AND NATIONAL REFORM IN THE HABSBURG MONARCHY, 1848-1918 [148] is very comprehensive, while Rueben John Rath's THE VIENNESE REVOLUTION OF 1848 [241]; Rudolph Kissling's DIE REVOLUTION IM KAISERTUM OSTERREICH, 1848-1849 [153]; and William Stiles' AUSTRIA IN 1848-49 [307] are all very good. Stiles' work is contemporary and was published in 1852. THE HABSBURG MONARCHY; TOWARD A MULTINATIONAL EMPIRE OR NATIONAL STATES? [141], edited by Charles Jelavich, is a short work that brings together a few of the more important sources on the subject. The rule of Franz Joseph, who was Emperor of Austria for 68 years, having taken the crown in December 1848, is reported in Anatol Murad's FRANZ JOSEPH I OF AUSTRIA AND HIS EMPIRE [216]; Albert Margutti's EMPEROR FRANCIS JOSEPH AND HIS TIMES [188]; and in Gunther Rothenberg's excellent THE ARMY OF FRANCIS JOSEPH [257].

Russia's impact on the period may be gauged in Hans Kohn's PAN-SLAVISM; ITS HISTORY AND IDEOLOGY [155], in Philip Mosely's RUSSIAN DIPLOMACY AND THE OPENING OF THE EASTERN QUESTION IN 1838-1839 [214]; LA RUSSIE SUR LE DANUBE [171], by Armand Levy; Barbara Jelavich's RUSSIA AND THE GREEK REVOLUTION OF 1843 [140]; and Virginia Cowles' THE RUSSIAN DAGGER: COLD WAR IN THE DAYS OF THE CZARS [74]. Kohn's book is a good exposition of the causes of Russian involvement in the Balkans at that time. Levy's book uses this period as background but is still good reading. Djordjevic [85], Karolides [151], and Todorov [325] are of use in understanding the Austro-Russian arrangements that led to the intervention.

Three other works on the Russian intervention into Hungary are Ladislas Teleki's DE L'INTERVENTION RUSSE EN HONGROIE [319], that was published in 1849; Kenneth Rock's "Reaction Triumphant: The Diplomacy of Felix Schwarzenberg and Nicholas I in Mastering the Hungarian Insurrection, 1848-1850" [249]; and DIE UNGARISCHE KONSERVATIVEN HELFER DER OSTERREICHISCHEN UND DER ZARISTISCHEN ARMEE IM JAHRE 1848 [9], which was written by Mrs. E. Andics.

The life of Louis Kossuth, Hungary's great hero, is reported in numerous excellent works. One of some interest is THE LIFE OF LOUIS KOSSUTH [119], by Phineas Headley. This work was published in 1852. Lengyel [168], Macartney [181], and Sinor [292] all give good accounts. A very pro-Hungarian work is "Kossuth and Posterity" [298], by Gyorgy Spira, which was printed in 1980 in ETUDES HISTORIQUES HONGROISES. Also of interest is HUNGARY AND KOSSUTH: OR, AN AMERICAN EXPOSITION OF THE LATE HUNGARIAN REVOLUTION [318], by Benjamin Tefft, and "America and the Hungarian Revolution of 1848-1849" [315], by S. Szilassy. Spira also tells the story of A HUNGARIAN COUNT IN THE REVOLUTION OF 1848 [297] in which he recounts the public affairs of Count Stephen Szechenyi. DAS UNGARISCHE REGIERUNGSYSTEM VOR DEM VERFALL DER OSTERREICHISCH-UNGARISCHEN MANARCHIE [235], by F. Poloskei, touches on the Hungarian governmental system of those times.

John Campbell's "Eighteen Forty-eight in the Rumanian Principalities" [48] is a good introduction to the Romanian part of the uprising. An article written in 1869, "Hungary and Roumania" [28], by K. Blind, is an interesting view of the two nations as seen after 1848. "The Army and the 1848 Revolution" [103], by Maria Georgescu, is found in Savu's THE ARMY AND THE ROMANIAN SOCIETY [273]. REVOLUTIA DE LA 1848 IN TARILE ROMANE: CULEGERE DE STUDII [2], edited by Nichita Adaniloaie and Dan Berindei, is composite of 12 articles, seven of which deal specifically with the revolution, four speak of the revolt's effects on later Romanian development, and one discusses the historiography of the period. Cornelia Bodea's THE ROMANIAN STRUGGLE FOR UNIFICATION [31], which was translated into English in 1970, is an impressive account of the period, even if it is somewhat flawed by uneven outside editing.

ORTHODOXY AND NATIONALITY: ANDREIU SAGUNA AND THE RUMANIANS OF TRANSYLVANIA [123], by Keith Hitchins, is the story of the Bishop of the Orthodox Church in Transylvania who became the recognized leader of the Romanians in that Austro-Hungarian province during the revolt. Hitchins' history of THE NATIONAL MOVEMENT IN TRANSYLVANIA, 1780-1849 [122] is also extremely valuable. There are three articles by Constantin Cazanisteanu: "Tradition and Innovation in the Organization of the Modern Romanian Army" [53]; "People's War in Romanian Thought of the Mid-19th Century" [54]; and "On the Development of the Modern Romanian Army from the Revolution of Tudor Vladimirescu in 1821 to the 1859 Union" [55]. These three pieces are of varying quality.

Serbia's role is amply covered in Petrovich [229]. Another interesting source is Josef Thim's GESCHICHTE DES SERBISCHEN AUFSTANDER 1848-1849 [324]. Mercia Macdermott [184] covers the Bulgarian story. Turkey's role in the affair is covered in Creasy [79] and in Shaw [288]. Aladar Urban deals with the creation of the national guard and the Honved Army in A NEZMETORSEG ES HONVEDSEG SZERVEZESE 1848 NYARAN [332] which was published in Budapest in 1973. Lastly, Noel Barber's THE SULTANS [17] is useful.

## BIBLIOGRAPHIC LISTING

1. Adams, A.E., et al. AN ATLAS OF RUSSIAN AND EAST EUROPEAN HISTORY. New York: 1967 [1966].

2. Adaniloaie, N., & Berindei, D., eds. REVOLUTIA DE LA 1848 IN TARILE ROMANE: CULEGERE DE STUDII. Bucharest: 1974.

3. Alger, J. I. THE QUEST FOR VICTORY: THE HISTORY OF THE PRINCIPLES OF WAR. CMH 30. Westport: 1981.

4. Almedingen, E.M. THE EMPEROR ALEXANDER I. New York: 1964.

5. Ancel, J. MANUEL HISTORIQUE DE LA QUESTION D'ORIENT: 1792-1923. Paris: 1923.

6. Anderson, M.S. THE EASTERN QUESTION, 1774-1923. London & New York: 1966.

7. _____. THE GREAT POWERS AND THE NEAR EAST (1774-1923). London: 1970.

8. Anderson, R.C. NAVAL WARS OF THE LEVANT, 1559-1853. Princeton: 1952.

9. Andics, E. DIE UNGARISCHE KONSERVATIVEN HELFER DER OSTERREICHISCHEN UND DER ZARISTICHEN ARMEE IM JAHRE 1848. Vol. 1. Budapest: 1980.

10. Andreski, S. MILITARY ORGANIZATION AND SOCIETY. 2nd ed. Berkeley: 1968.

11. Arnakis, G.G. THE NEAR EAST IN MODERN TIMES. Vol. 1: THE OTTOMAN EMPIRE AND THE BALKANS TO 1900. Austin & New York: 1960.

12. Asim Efendi, A. TARIH-I ASIM. 2 vols. Istanbul: 1866.

13. Babin, A.I., et al. ISTORIA OTECHESTVENNOI VOENNO-ENTSIKLOPEDICHESKOI LITERATURII. Moscow: 1980.

14. Babinger, F.C.H. AUFSATZE UNF ABHANDLUNGEN ZUR GESCHICHTE SUDOSTEUROPAS UND DER LEVANTE. 3 vols. Munich: 1962-1976.

15. Bailey, F.E. BRITISH POLICY AND THE TURKISH REFORM MOVEMENT; A STUDY OF ANGLO-TURKISH RELATIONS, 1826-1853. New York: c.1982.

16. Balck, W. TACTICS. 2 vols. Trans. by Walter Krueger. Fort Leavenworth: 1911-1914.

17. Barber, N. THE SULTANS. New York: 1973.

18. Barker, E. MACEDONIA: ITS PLACE IN BALKAN POWER POLITICS. RIIA. Westport: 1980 [1950].

19. Barnes, T.G., & Feldman, G.D. NATIONALISM, INDUSTRIALIZATION, AND DEMOCRACY, 1815-1914. Vol. 3 in A DOCUMENTARY HISTORY OF MODERN EUROPE. Washington: 1980.

20. Basri Beg. L'ALBANIE INDEPENDANTE ET L'EMPIRE KHALIFAL OTTOMAN. Paris:      1920 [c.1919]

21. Bastelberger, J. DIE MILITARISCHEN REFORMEN UNTER MAHMUD II. Gotha: 1874.

22. Berend, I.T., & Ranki, G. ECONOMIC DEVELOPMENT IN EAST-CENTRAL EUROPE IN THE 19TH AND 20TH CENTURIES. New York: 1974.

23. Best, G. WAR AND SOCIETY IN REVOLUTIONARY EUROPE, 1770-1870. New York: 1982.

24. BIBLIOGRAPHIC GUIDE TO SOVIET AND EAST EUROPEAN STUDIES. New ed. Boston: 1982.

25. Birdeanu, N., & Nicholescu, D. CONTRIBUTII LA ISTORIA MARINEI ROMANE. DIN CELE MAI VECHI TIMPURI PINA IN 1918. Bucharest: 1979.

26. Birke, E. FRANKREICH UND OSTMITTELEUROPA IM 19. JAHREHUNDERT; BEITRAGE ZUR POLITIK UND GESCHICHTE. Koln & Bohlau: 1960.

27. Blainey, G. THE CAUSES OF WAR. New York: 1973.

28. Blind, K. "Hungary and Roumania." NAR CXI (1869), 176-196.

29. Blum, J., et al. THE EMERGENCE OF THE EUROPEAN WORLD. Boston: 1966.

30. Bodea, C. LUPTA ROMANILOR PENTRU UNITATEA NATIONALE, 1834-1849. Bucharest: 1967.

31. _____. THE ROMANIANS' STRUGGLE FOR UNIFICATION. BHR 25. Trans. by Liliana Teodoreanu. Bucharest: 1970.

32. Boia, L. RELATIONSHIPS BETWEEN ROMANIANS, CZECHS AND SLOVAKS. BHR Studies 54. Bucharest: 1977.

33. Boppe, A. L'ALBANIE ET NAPOLEON. Paris: 1914.

34. Braddock, J. THE GREEK PHOENIX. New York: 1973.

35. Bradley, J.F.N. CZECHO-SLOVAKIA: A SHORT HISTORY. Edinburgh: 1971.

36. Braun, M."Turkenherrschaft und Turkenkampf bei den Balkenslawen." WaG VI (1940), 124-139.

37. Brayton, A.A., & Landwehr, S.J. THE POLITICS OF WAR AND PEACE: A SURVEY OF THOUGHT. Washington: [1981].

38. Breunig, C. THE AGE OF REVOLUTION AND REACTION: 1789-1850. 2nd ed. NHME New York: 1977.

39. BRITISH DIPLOMATIC BLUE BOOKS RELATING TO THE RUSSIAN EMPIRE 1801-99. New York & Ontario: nd.

40. Bromley, J.S., & Goodwin, A., eds. A SELECTED LIST OF WORKS ON EUROPE AND EUROPE OVERSEAS, 1715-1815. Oxford: 1956.

41. Bruun, G. EUROPE AND THE FRENCH IMPERIUM, 1799-1814. RME. Edited BY W.L. Langer. New York & London: 1938.

42. Bujac, J.L.E. PRECIS DE QUELQUES CAMPAGNES CONTEMPORAIRES. Vol. 6. Paris: 1908 [1893].

43. Bulgaria. NATSIONALNOOSVOBODITELNI DVIZHENIIA NA BALKANSKITE NARODI: VTORATA POLOVINA NA XVIII V. -- 1878 G.: VUORUZHENA BORBA: BIBLIOGRAFIIA, 1966-1976. Edited by Liudmila Genova. Sofia: 1978.

44. _____. HISTOIRE MILITAIRE DE LA BULGARIE, 681-1945. BIBLIOGRAPHIE. Sofia: 1972.

45. Bullen, R., & Bridge, R. THE GREAT POWERS AND THE EUROPEAN STATES SYSTEM, 1815-1914. New York & London: 1980.

46. Bury, J.P.T., ed. THE ZENITH OF EUROPEAN POWER, 1830-1870. Vol. 10 in NCMH. Cambridge: 1960.

47. Cammarata, F. ALBANICA. Palermo: 1968.

48. Campbell, J.. "Eighteen Forty-eight in the Romanian Principalities." JCEA VIII/2 (July 1942), 181-190.

49. Cantor, N.F., & Berner, S., eds. EARLY MODERN EUROPE, 1500-1815. Vol. 2 in PEH. Arlington Heights: 1970.

50. _____. THE MODERN ERA, 1815 TO THE PRESENT. Vol. 3 in PEH. Arlington Heights: 1970.

51. Cantor, N.F., & Werthman, M.S., eds. THE MAKING OF THE MODERN WORLD, 1815-1914. SEH. Arlington Heights, IL: 1967.

52. Carsten, F.L., et al., eds. THE HABSBURG MONARCHY. Vol 1: AUSTRIA AND         BOHEMIA, 1835-1918. Vol 2: HUNGARY, 1835-1918. New York: 1979.

53. Cazanisteanu, C. "Tradition and Innovation in the Organization of the Modern Romanian Army." ARS. Bucharest: 1980.

54. _____. "People's War in the Romanian Thought of the Mid-19th Century." PHRA. BHR Monograph XV. Bucharest: 1975.

55. _____. "On the Development of the Modern Romanian Army from the Revolution of Tudor Vladimirescu in 1821 to the 1859 Union." PMHRP. Bucharest: 1980.

56. Ceaucescu, I. THE ENTIRE PEOPLE'S WAR FOR THE HOMELAND'S
    DEFENCE WITH THE ROMANIANS. Bucharest: 1980. Also found in
    Romanian as RAZBOIUL INTREGULUI POPOR PENTRU APARAREA
    PATRIEI LA ROMANI. Bucharest: 1980.

57. _____., ed. PAGES FROM THE MILITARY HISTORY OF THE ROMANIAN
    PEOPLE. Bucharest: 1980.

58. Cevad Eren, A. MAHMUD II ZAMININDE BOSNA-HERSEK. Istanbul:
    1965.

59. _____. "Selim III." IA X, pp.441-457.

60. Cevat Efendi, A. TARIH-I ASKERI-I OSMANLI I YENICERILER. Vol.
    1. Trans. by Fr. G. Mairides (French). Istanbul: 1880.

61. Chandler, D.G. DICTIONARY OF THE NAPOLEONIC WARS. London: 1979.

62. _____. ATLAS OF MILITARY STRATEGY. New York: 1980.

63. Chesney, F.R. THE RUSSO-TURKISH CAMPAIGN OF 1828 AND 1829. New
    York: 1854.

64. Clark, G.N., Sir. NEW CAMBRIDGE MODERN HISTORY. 14 vols.
    Cambridge: 1957-1970.

65. Clarke, J.J. "World Military History, 1786-1945." GSUMH.
    Washington: 1979.

66. Clarkson, J.D. A HISTORY OF RUSSIA. 2d ed. New York: 1969.

67. Clayton, G.D. BRITAIN AND THE EASTERN QUESTION: MISSOLONGHI TO
    GALLIPOLI. London and New York: 1974.

68. Cleator, P.E. WEAPONS OF WAR. New York: 1968.

69. Clogg, R., ed. THE STRUGGLE FOR GREEK INDEPENDENCE. LSSEES.
    London and Basingstoke: 1973 [1970].

70. _____. A SHORT HISTORY OF MODERN GREECE. Berkeley: 1979.

71. Codben, R. RUSSIA, TURKEY, AND ENGLAND. London: 1876.

72. Colby, E. MASTERS OF MOBILE WARFARE. Princeton: 1943.

73. Coquelle, P. HISTOIRE DES MONTENEGRO ET DE LA BOSNIA. Paris:
    1895.

74. Cowles, V. THE RUSSIAN DAGGER: COLD WAR IN THE DAYS OF THE
    CZARS. New York & Evanston: 1969.

75. Craig, G.A. EUROPE SINCE 1815. 3rd ed. New York: 1972 [c.1961].

76. Crawley, C.W. "The Near East and the Ottoman Empire." NCMH 9.
    Cambridge: 1965.

77. _____. WAR AND PEACE IN AN AGE OF UPHEAVAL, 1793-1830. Vol.
    9 in NCMH. Cambridge: 1965.

78. _____. THE QUESTION OF GREEK INDEPENDENCE, 1821-1831. New York: 1973.

79. Creasy, E., Sir. HISTORY OF THE OTTOMAN TURKS. Oriental Reprints No. 1. Beirut: 1961 [1878].

80. Dakin, D. BRITISH AND AMERICAN PHILHELLENES DURING THE WAR OF GREEK INDEPENDENCE, 1821-1833. Salonika: 1955.

81. _____. BRITISH INTELLIGENCE OF EVENTS IN GREECE, 1824-1827. Athens: 1959.

82. _____. THE UNIFICATION OF GREECE, 1770-1923. London: 1972.

83. _____. THE GREEK STRUGGLE FOR INDEPENDENCE, 1821-1833. London: 1973.

84. Denison, G.T. HISTORY OF CAVALRY. London: 1913.

85. Djordjevic, D. REVOLUTIONS NATIONALE DES PEUPLES BALCANIQUES, 1804-1914. Edited by Jorjo Tadic. Trans. by Margita Ristic. Belgrad: 1965.

86. Dontas, D. THE LAST PHASE OF THE WAR OF INDEPENDENCE IN WESTERN GREECE. Thessaloniki: 1966.

87. Driault, E. LA QUESTION D'ORIENT. 5th ed. Paris: 1912.

88. Duggan, S.P.H. THE EASTERN QUESTION: A STUDY IN DIPLOMACY. New York: 1970.

89. Dunn-Pattison, R.P. NAPOLEON'S MARSHALS. Totowa, NJ:

90. Dupuy, R.E., & Dupuy, T.N. THE ENCYCLOPEDIA OF MILITARY HISTORY. Rev. ed. New York: 1977 [1970].

91. Earle, E.M., ed. THE MAKERS OF MODERN STRATEGY: MILITARY THOUGHT FROM MACHIAVELLI TO HITLER. Princeton: 1943.

92. Egerton, H.E. BRITISH FOREIGN POLICY IN EUROPE TO THE END OF THE 19TH CENTURY. New York: 1917.

93. Falls, C.B. THE ART OF WAR. New York: 1961.

94. Finlay, G. HISTORY OF GREECE, FROM ITS CONQUEST BY THE ROMANS TO THE PRESENT TIME, B.C. 164 TO A.D. 1864. 7 vols. New rev. ed. by Rev. H.F. Tozer. Oxford: 1877.

95. Fisher, S.N. "Ottoman Feudalism and Its Influence Upon the Balkans." HISTORIAN XV (Autumn 1952), 3-22.

96. Florinsky, M.T. RUSSIA: A HISTORY AND AN INTERPRETATION. 2 vols. New York: 1953.

97. Floyd, D.E. THE WORLD BIBLIOGRAPHY OF ARMED LAND CONFLICT. Wilmington: 1979.

98. Forbes, N. THE BALKANS; A HISTORY OF BULGARIA, SERBIA, GREECE, RUMANIA, TURKEY. New York: [1970].

99. Forster, E.S.. A SHORT HISTORY OF MODERN GREECE, 1821-1956. 3rd ed. Edited by Douglas Dakin. London: 1958.

100. Frischauer, P. THE IMPERIAL CROWN: THE STORY OF THE RISE AND FALL OF THE HOLY ROMAN AND AUSTRIAN EMPIRES. London: 1939.

101. Fuller, J.F.C. A MILITARY HISTORY OF THE WESTERN WORLD. 3 vols. New York: 1954-1955.

102. Fuyet, H. HISTOIRE DES RELATIONS ENTRE LA SERBIE ET LA FRANCE PENDANT LA PERIODE D'INSURRECTION SERBE (1802-1813). Montreal, Unpublished dissertation, 1966.

103. Georgescu, M. "The Army and the 1848 Revolution." ARS. Bucharest: 1980.

104. Gewehr, W.M. THE RISE OF NATIONALISM IN THE BALKANS, 1800-1930. Hamden: 1967 [c.1931].

105. Gibb, H.A.R., Sir., et al. ENCYCLOPEDIA OF ISLAM. Leiden: 1913-1938.

106. Gibbs, N.H. "Armies." NCMH 9. Cambridge:1965.

107. Gilbert, F., ed. THE NORTON HISTORY OF MODERN EUROPE. 6 vols. New York:      1970-.

108. Gilbert, M. RUSSIAN HISTORY ATLAS. New York: 1972.

109. Giurescu, C.C., et al., eds. CHRONOLOGICAL HISTORY OF ROMANIA. Bucharest: 1972.

110. Gladt, K. KAISERTRAUM UND KONIGSKRONE. AUFSTIEG UND UNTERGANG EINER SERBISCHEN DYNASTIE. Graz, Vienna & Koln: 1972.

111. Gordon, T. HISTORY OF THE GREEK REVOLUTION. Edinburgh: 1832.

112. Gossip, R. TURKEY AND RUSSIA, THEIR RACES, HISTORY AND WARS. Edinburgh: 1879.

113. Grassi, M.A. CHARTE TURQUE ON ORGANIZATION RELIGIEUSE, CIVILE ET MILITAIRE DE L'EMPIRE OTTOMAN. Paris: 1925.

114. Grinard, F. GRANDEUR ET DECADENCE DE L'ASIA. Paris: 1947.

115. Gulick, E.V. EUROPE'S CLASSICAL BALANCE OF POWER: A CASE STUDY OF THE THEORY AND PRACTICE OF ONE OF THE GREAT CONCEPTS OF EUROPEAN STATECRAFT. Ithaca: 1955.

116. Hammer-Purgstall, J. von. HISTOIRE DE L'EMPIRE OTTOMAN. 18 vols. Paris: 1835-1843.

117. Hampson, N. THE FIRST EUROPEAN REVOLUTION, 1776-1815. New York: 1973.

118. Hantsch, H. DAS GESCHICHTE OSTERREICHS. 2 vols. Vienna: 1950.

119. Headley, P.C. THE LIFE OF LOUIS KOSSUTH. Auburn: 1852.

120. Heppell, M., & Singleton, F.B. YUGOSLAVIA. New York: 1961.

121. Heymann, E. BALKAN: KRIEGE, BUNDNISSE, REVOLUTIONEN; 150 JAHRE POLITIK UND SCHICKSAL. Berlin: 1938.

122. Hitchins, K. T. THE RUMANIAN NATIONAL MOVEMENT IN TRANSYLVANIA, 1780-1849. HHM 61. Cambridge: 1969.

123. _____. ORTHODOXY AND NATIONALITY: ANDREIU SAGUNA AND THE RUMANIANS OF TRANSYLVANIA. Cambridge: 1977.

124. Hobsbawn, E.J. THE AGE OF REVOLUTION: EUROPE, 1789-1848. New York: 1969 [1962].

125. Hodgart, A. THE ECONOMICS OF EUROPEAN IMPERIALISM. New York: 1978.

126. Hogg, I. A HISTORY OF ARTILLERY. London: 1974.

127. _____. FORTRESS: A HISTORY OF MILITARY DEFENSE. New York: 1977.

128. Holt, P.M., et al. "The Central Islamic Lands of the Ottoman Empire." CHI 1. Cambridge: 1977.

129. Horecky, P.L., ed. EAST CENTRAL EUROPE: A GUIDE TO BASIC PUBLICATIONS. Chicago: 1969.

130. Horne, A. NAPOLEON: MASTER OF EUROPE, 1805-1807. London: 1979.

131. Hosch, E. THE BALKANS: A SHORT HISTORY. New York: 1972.

132. Hourani, A.H. THE OTTOMAN BACKGROUND OF THE MODERN MIDDLE EAST. Harlow: 1970.

133. Houtsma, T., ed. ENCYCLOPEDIA OF ISLAM. 2nd ed. 4 vols. w/suppl. Leiden: 1954-.

134. Hunczak, T., ed. RUSSIAN IMPERIALISM FROM IVAN THE TERRIBLE TO THE REVOLUTION. New Brunswick, NJ: 1974.

135. Hurowitz, J.C. "Russia and the Turkish Straits: A revaluation of the Origins of the Problem." WP 14 (1962), 606-632.

136. _____. "The Background of Russia's Claims to the Turkish Straits." BELLETIN 28 (1964), 459-503.

137. Ignotus, P. "Czechs, Magyars, Slovaks." TPQ 40 (June 1969), 187-204.

138. Iorga, N. GESCHICHTE DES OSMANISCHEN REICHES. 5 vols. Gotha: 1908-1913.

139. _____. HISTOIRE DES ROUMAINES DE LA PENINSULE DES BALKANS. Bucharest: 1919.

140. Jelavich, B. RUSSIA AND THE GREEK REVOLUTION OF 1843. SA 65. Munich: 1966.

141. Jelavich, C., ed. THE HABSBURG MONARCHY; TOWARD A MULTINATIONAL EMPIRE OR NATIONAL STATES? New York: 1959.

142. Jelavich, C., & Jelavich, B., eds. THE BALKANS IN TRANSITION: ESSAYS ON THE DEVELOPMENT OF BALKAN LIFE AND POLITICS SINCE THE EIGHTEENTH CENTURY. REES. Berkeley: 1974 [c.1963].

143. _____. THE ESTABLISHMENT OF THE BALKAN NATIONAL STATES, 1804-1920. HECE 8. Seattle, Washington and London: 1977.

144. Jessup, J.E., & Coakley, eds. R.W. A GUIDE TO THE STUDY AND USE OF MILITARY HISTORY. Washington: 1979.

145. Jomini, H., Baron. THE ART OF WAR. Philadelphia: 1862.

146. Kaldis, W.P. JOHN CAPODISTRIAS AND THE MODERN GREEK STATE. Madison, Wisc.: 1963.

147. Kann, R.A. THE HABSBURG EMPIRE: A STUDY IN INTEGRATION AND DISINTEGRATION. New York: 1979.

148. _____. THE MULTINATIONAL EMPIRE: NATIONALISM AND NATIONAL REFORM IN THE HABSBURG MONARCHY, 1848-1918. 2 vols. New York: 1964.

149. _____. A HISTORY OF THE HABSBURG EMPIRE, 1526-1918. Berkeley: 1974.

150. Kann, R.A., & David, Z. THE PEOPLES OF THE EASTERN HABSBURG LANDS, 1526-1918. HECE 6. Seattle & London: 1982.

151. Karolides, P. CONTEMPORARY HISTORY OF THE GREEKS AND OF THE OTHER PEOPLES OF THE EAST FROM 1821 TO 1921. Athens: 1929.

152. Kinross, J.P.D., Lord. THE OTTOMAN CENTURIES: THE RISE AND FALL OF THE TURKISH EMPIRE. London: 1977.

153. Kissling, R. DIE REVOLUTION IM KAISERTUM OSTERREICH, 1848-1849. Vienna: [c.1948].

154. Klyuchevski, V.O. KURS RUSSKOI ISTORII. 5 vols. Moscow: 1937 [1921-23].

155. Kohn, H. PAN-SLAVISM; ITS HISTORY AND IDEOLOGY. Notre Dame: 1953.

156. _____. THE HABSBURG EMPIRE, 1804-1918. Princeton: 1961.

157. Kosary, D. BEVEZETES MAGYARORSZAG TORTENETENEK FORRASAIBA ES IRODALMABA. Vol. 1. Budapest: 1970.

158. _____. MAGYAR TORTENETI BIBLIOGRAFIA, 1825-1867. 4 vols. Budapest: 1950-59.

159. Koumoulides, J.T.A. ed. HELLENIC PERSPECTIVES: ESSAYS IN THE HISTORY OF GREECE. Washington: 1980.

160. Kuepfer, E. LA MACEDOINE ET LES BULGARES. Lausanne, 1918.

161. Lachouque, H. THE ANATOMY OF GLORY. London: 1982 [1961].

162. Lampe, J.R., & Jackson, M.R. BALKAN ECONOMIC HISTORY, 1550-1950. FROM IMPERIAL BORDERLANDS TO DEVELOPING NATIONS. Bloomington: 1982.

163. Langer, W.L., ed. THE RISE OF MODERN EUROPE. 20 vols. New York & London: 1936-.

164. Larrabee, S.A. HELLAS OBSERVED -- THE AMERICAN EXPERIENCE OF GREECE, 1775-1865. New York: 1957.

165. Lazarovich-Hrebelianovich, Prince. SERVIAN PEOPLE; THEIR PAST GLORY AND THEIR DESTINY. 2 vols. New York: 1910.

166. Lederer, I., ed. RUSSIA AND THE BALKANS IN RUSSIAN FOREIGN POLICY: ESSAYS IN HISTORICAL PERSPECTIVE. New Haven: 1962.

167. Legrand, E.L.J. BIBLIOGRAPHIE ALBANAISE. Leipzig: 1973.

168. Lengyel, E. 1000 YEARS OF HUNGARY. New York: 1958.

169. Leo, M. LA BULGARIE ET SON PEUPLE SOUS LA DOMINATION OTTOMANE, TELS QUE LES ONT VUS LES VOYAGEURS ANGLO-SAXONS (1586-1878). SOFIA: 1949.

170. Lessner, E.C. & A.M.L. THE DANUBE: THE DRAMATIC HISTORY OF THE GREAT RIVER AND THE PEOPLE TOUCHED BY ITS FLOW. Garden City: 1961.

171. Levy, A. LA RUSSIE SUR LE DANUBE, AVEC LA PROTESTATION DES ROUMAINS CONTRE L'INVASION DE LEUR PATRIE. Paris: 1853.

172. Levy, A. "The Military Policy of Sultan Mahmud II", 1808-1839. Harvard, Unpublished dissertation, 1968.

173. _____. "The Officer Corps in Sultan Mahmud II's New Ottoman Army, 1826-1839." IJMES 2 (1971), 21-39.

174. Lewinsohn, R. THE PROFITS OF WAR THROUGH THE AGES. New York: 1979.

175. Lincoln, W.B. NICHOLAS I: EMPEROR AND AUTOCRAT OF ALL THE RUSSIAS. Bloomington, Ind.: 1978.

176. Lloyd, C.C. "Navies." NCMH 9. Cambridge: 1965.

177. Lobanov-Rostovsky, A. RUSSIA AND EUROPE. Ann Arbor: 1954 [1949].

178. Omitted.

179. Luvaas, J. "The Great Military Historians and Philosophers." GSUMH. Washington: 1979.

180. Lyons, M., ed. THE RUSSIAN IMPERIAL ARMY. Stanford: 1968.

181. Macartney, C.A. HUNGARY, A SHORT HISTORY. Chicago: 1962.

182. _____. " The Austrian Monarchy, 1792-1847." NCMH 9. Cambridge: 1965.

183. _____. THE HABSBURG EMPIRE, 1790-1918. New York: 1969.

184. Macdermott, M. A HISTORY OF BULGARIA, 1393-1885. London: 1962.

185. Makkai, L. HISTOIRE DE TRANSYLVANIE. Paris: 1946.

186. Makriyannis. THE MEMOIRS OF GENERAL MAKRIYANNIS, 1797-1864. Edited and trans. by H.A. Lidderdale. London: 1966.

187. Mamatey, V.S. THE RISE OF THE HABSBURG EMPIRE, 1526-1815. New York: 1971.

188. Margutti, A.A.V., Freiherr von. EMPEROR FRANCIS JOSEPH AND HIS TIMES. London: 1921.

189. Marlow, J. PERFIDIOUS ALBION: THE ORIGINS OF ANGLO-FRENCH RIVALRY IN THE LEVANT. London: 1971.

190-198. Omitted.

199. Marriott, J.A.R., Sir. THE EASTERN QUESTION. Oxford: 1930.

200. Marx, K. THE EASTERN QUESTION. New York: 1969.

201. Mavrocordato, J. MODERN GREECE, 1800-1931. London: 1931.

202. McConnell, A. TSAR ALEXANDER I: PATERNALISTIC REFORMER. Arlington Heights: 1970.

203. McNeill, W.H. A WORLD HISTORY. 3rd ed. Oxford: 1979.

204. Mediger, W. RUSSLANDS WEG NACH EUROPA. Brunswick: 1952.

205. Menning, B.W. "Military Institutions and the Steppe Frontier in Imperial Russia, 1700-1861." CIHM ACTA No. 5. Bucharest: 1980.

206. Mickiewicz, A. LES SLAVES. HISTOIRE ET LITTERATURE DES NATIONS POLONAISE, BOHEME, SERBE ET RUSSE. Paris: 1849.

207. Milic, D. TRGOVINA SRBIJE, 1815-1839. Belgrad: 1959.

208. Miller, A.F. MUSTAFA PASHA BAYRAKDAR. Moscow: 1947.

209. Miller, W. A HISTORY OF THE GREEK PEOPLE, 1821-31. London: 1922.

210. _____. THE OTTOMAN EMPIRE AND ITS SUCCESSORS, 1801-1927.
     W/appendix for 1927-1936. Cambridge: 1936.

211. Moltke, H. von. THE RUSSIANS IN BULGARIA AND RUMELIA IN 1828
     AND 1829.    London: 1854.

212. Montross, L. WAR THROUGH THE AGES. New York: 1944.

213. Mordal, J. TWENTY-FIVE CENTURIES OF SEA WARFARE. New York:
     1965.

214. Mosely, P.E. RUSSIAN DIPLOMACY AND THE OPENING OF THE EASTERN
     QUESTION IN 1838-39. New York: 1969 [c.1934].

215. Muhtar Pasha, A. 1244 TURKIYE RUSYA SEFERI VE EDIRNE MUAHEDESI.
     2 vols. Ankara: 1928.

216. Murad, A. FRANZ JOSEPH I OF AUSTRIA AND HIS EMPIRE. New York:
     1968.

217. Namier, L.B. 1848: THE REVOLUTION OF THE INTELLECTUALS. London:
     1944.

218. Nemes, D., et al., eds. ETUDES HISTORIQUES HONGROISES, 1980. 2
     vols. Budapest: 1980:

219. Nenadovic, M. THE MEMOIRS OF PROTA MATIJA NENADOVIC. Edited and
     trans. by Lovett F. Edwards. Oxford: 1969.

220. Niven, A. NAPOLEON AND ALEXANDER I: A STUDY OF FRANCO-RUSSIAN
     RELATIONS, 1807-1812. Washington: 1978.

221. O'Connor, R.G. WAR, DIPLOMACY, AND HISTORY: PAPERS AND REVIEWS.
     Washington: 1979.

222. Olivier, L.P.F., ed. LA BOSNIA ET L'HERZEGOVINE. Paris:
     [1900?].

223. Olteanu, C. "Genese et developpement de l'armee permanente chez
     les Roumaines." RIHM 48 (1980), 75-83.

224. _____. "On the Organization of the Army in the Romanian
     Countries." PHRA BHR Monograph XV. Bucharest: 1975.

225. Paget, J. HUNGARY AND TRANSYLVANIA. 2 vols. London: 1850.

226. PENGUIN HISTORICAL ATLASES. NEW YORK: 1982.

227. Perceval, C. de. PRECIS HISTORIQUE DE LA DESTRUCTION DU CORPS
     DES JANISSAIRES PAR LE SULTAN MAHMOUD II EN 1826. Paris:
     1833.

228. Petrovic, V.M. SERBIA; HER PEOPLE, HISTORY ASPIRATIONS. New
     York: 1915.

229. Petrovich, M.B. A HISTORY OF MODERN SERBIA, 1804-1918. 2 vols.
     New York & London: 1976.

230. Pinkney, D.H., ed. NAPOLEON: HISTORICAL ENIGMA. Arlinton Heights: 1978.

231. _____. THE NINETEENTH CENTURY, 1815-1914. WE. St. Louis: c.1979.

232. _____., ed. PROBLEMS IN CIVILIZATION. 10+ vols. Lexington: 1977-.

233. Plomer, W. ALI THE LION. London: 1936.

234. Polianski, H.A. ed. BRITISH DOCUMENTS ON THE HISTORY OF THE MACEDONIAN PEOPLE. Vol. 1. Skopje: 1968.

235. Poloskei, F. DAS UNGARISCHE REGIERUNGSYSTEM VOR DEM VERFALL DER OSTERREICHISCH-UNGARISCHEN MANARCHIE. Edited by D. Nemes. EHH. 1980.

236. Pounds, N.J.G. AN HISTORICAL GEOGRAPHY OF EUROPE, 1500-1840. 2 vols. Cambridge: 1980.

237. Preston, R.A., et al. MEN IN ARMS: A HISTORY OF WARFARE. New York: 1956.

238. Quimby, R.S. THE BACKGOUND OF NAPOLEONIC WARFARE: THE THEORY OF MILITARY TACTICS IN THE EIGHTEENTH CENTURY. New York: 1968 [1957].

239. Rambaud, A.N. THE EXPANSION OF RUSSIA. Boston: 1978.

240. Rapoport, A., ed., CARL VON CLAUSEWITZ' ON WAR. New York: 1968.

241. Rath, R.J. THE VIENNESE REVOLUTION OF 1848. AUSTIN: 1957.

242. Reddaway, W.F. A HISTORY OF EUROPE FROM 1715 TO 1814. 4th ed. London: 1951 [1936].

243. Omitted

244. Reed, H.A. "The Destruction of the Janissaries by Mahmud II in June 1826." Princeton, Unpublished dissertation, 1951.

245. Refik, A. TURK IDARESINDE BULGARISTAN (973-1255), Istanbul: 1933.

246. Regnault, E. HISTOIRE POLITIQUE ET SOCIALE DES PRINCIPANTS DANUBIENNES. Paris: 1857.

247. Reinach, J. LA SERBIE ET LE MONTENEGRO. Paris: 1876.

248. Riasonovsky, N.V. A HISTORY OF RUSSIA. 2d ed. New York: 1969.

249. Rock: K.W. "Reaction Triumphant: The Diplomacy of Felix Schwarzenberg and Nicholas I in Mastering the Hungarian Insurrection, 1848-1850: A Study in Dynastic Power, Principles, and Politics in Revolutionary Times," Stanford, Unpublished dissertation, 1969.

250. Roider, K.A.,Jr., & Youngs, F.A., eds. THE WORLD OF EUROPE. 2 vols. St. Louis: c.1979.

251. Romanescu, Gh. "The Formation of the National Army and Its Development Down to the War of Independence." PHRA. BHR Monograph XV. Bucharest: 1975.

252. Romania. AUARUL INSTITUTULUI DE ISTORIE DIN CLUJ. 3+ Vols. Cluj: 1958-.

253. _____. BIBLIOGRAFIA MILITARA ROMANEASCA. Vols. 1-3. Edited by M. Andone. Bucharest: 1975-77.

254. Ropp, T. WAR IN THE MODERN WORLD. Durham: 1959.

255. Rose, J.H. THE INDECISIVENESS OF MODERN WARFARE, AND OTHER ESSAYS. New York: 1968 [1927].

256. Rothenberg, G. E. THE MILITARY BORDER IN CROATIA, 1740-1881: A STUDY OF AN IMPERIAL INSTITUTION. Chicago: 1966.

257. _____. THE ARMY OF FRANCIS JOSEPH. West Lafayette: 1976.

258. Rothrock, G.A., & Jones, T.B. EUROPE: A BRIEF HISTORY. Vol. 1: RENAISSANCE TO THE PRESENT. 2nd ed. rev. Washington: [1971].

259. Rude, G. REVOLUTIONARY EUROPE, 1783-1815. New York:

260. _____. DEBATE IN EUROPE, 1815-1850. New York: 1972.

261. RUSSIA, U.S.S.R., EASTERN EUROPE: ALPHABETICAL CUMULATIVE CATALOGUE. Cumulative IDC catalogue. Zug: nd.

262. Rusu, D.N. "The Army of the First Revolution in the Modern Epoch of Romania." ARS. Bucharest: 1980.

263. St. Clair, W. THAT GREECE MIGHT STILL BE FREE: THE PHILHELLENES IN THE WAR OF INDEPENDENCE. London, New York & Toronto: 1972.

264. St. Denys, A. de J. de. LES REVOLUTIONS DE CONSTANTINOPLE EN 1807 ET 1808. 2 vols. Paris: 1819.

265. _____. HISTOIRE DE L'EMPIRE OTTOMAN DEPUIS 1792 JUSQU'EN 1844. 4 vols. Paris: 1844.

266. Samoilov, S.I. "Narodno-osvoboditelnoe vostanie 1821 g. v Valakhii." VI (October 1955), 95-105.

267. Sani-zade, M.A. SANI ZADE TARIHI. 4 vols. Istanbul: 1875-76.

268. Sargent, L. GREECE IN THE NINETEENTH CENTURY. London: 1897.

269. Saul, N.E. RUSSIA AND THE MEDITERRANEAN, 1798-1807. Chicago & London:      1970.

270. Savant, J. "Napoleon et la liberation de la Grece," L'HELLENISME CONTEMPORAIN (July-October 1950), 320-341.

271. Savu, Al. Gh., ed. PAGES FROM THE HISTORY OF THE ROMANIAN ARMY. BHR Monograph XV. Bucharest: 1975.

272. _____. STUDII DE ISTORIE SI TEORIE MILITARA. RETROSPECTIVE ISTORICE ANALIZE CONTEMPORANE. Bucharest: 1980.

273. _____. THE ARMY AND THE ROMANIAN SOCIETY. Bucharest: 1980.

274. Schechta-Wesseherd, O. von. DIE REVOLUTIONEN IN CONSTANTINOPEL IN DEN JAHREN 1807 UND 1808. Vienna: 1882.

275. Scherer, A. SUDOSTEUROPA-DISSERTATIONEN, 1918-1960. Graz, Vienna, Koln & Bohlau: 1968.

276. Schevill, F. HISTORY OF THE BALKAN PENINSULA. Freeport, NY.: 1971 [1922].

277. Schmitt, B.E. ENGLAND AND GERMANY, 1740-1914. Princeton: 1916.

278. Schmitthenner, P. KRIEG UND KRIEGFUHRUNG IM WANDEL DER WELTGESCHICHTE. Potsdam: 1930.

279. Schutz, E. DIE EUROPAISCHE ALLIANZPOLITIK ALEXANDER I, UND DER GRIECHISCHE UNABHANGIGKEITSKAMPF, 1820-1830. Wiesbaden: 1975.

280. Schwarz, B. MONTENEGRO. Leipzig: 1883.

281. Seton-Watson, H. THE RUSSIAN EMPIRE: 1801-1917. Oxford: 1967.

282. Seton-Watson, R.W. A HISTORY OF THE ROUMANIANS; FROM ROMAN TIMES TO THE COMPLETION OF UNITY. Cambridge: 1934.

283. _____. THE RISE OF NATIONALITY IN THE BALKANS. New York: 1966.

284. _____. THE SOUTHERN SLAV QUESTION AND THE HABSBURG MONARCHY. New York: 1969.

285. Shandanova, L., ed. PETNADESET GODINI INSTITUT ZA BALKANISTIKA, 1964-1978: ISTORICHESKA SPRAVKA I BIBLIOGRAFIIA. Sofia: 1979.

286. Shaw, S.J. "The Ottoman View of the Balkans." THE BALKANS IN TRANSITION. Edited by Charles & Barbara Jelavich. Berkeley: 1963.

287. _____. HISTORY OF THE OTTOMAN EMPIRE AND MODERN TURKEY. Vol. 1: EMPIRE OF THE GAZIS: THE RISE AND DECLINE OF THE OTTOMAN EMPIRE, 1280-1808. Cambridge & New York: 1976.

288. Shaw, S.J., & Shaw, E.K., HISTORY OF THE OTTOMAN EMPIRE AND MODERN TURKEY. Vol. 2: REFORM, REVOLUTION AND REPUBLIC: THE RISE OF MODERN TURKEY, 1808-1975. Cambridge, London & New York: 1977.

289. Shepherd, W.R. HISTORICAL ATLAS. 8th ed. London: 1956.

290. Shupp, P.E. THE EUROPEAN POWERS AND THE NEAR EASTERN QUESTION, 1806-1807. New York: 1966.

291. Singer, J.D., & Small, M. THE WAGES OF WAR: A STATISTICAL HANDBOOK. New York: 1972.

292. Sinor, D. HISTORY OF HUNGARY. New York: 1961.

293. Sked, A. THE SURVIVAL OF THE HABSBURG EMPIRE: RADETZKY, THE IMPERIAL ARMY AND CLASS WAR. New York & London: 1979.

294. _____., ed. EUROPE'S BALANCE OF POWER, 1815-1848. Totowa: 1979.

295. Skiotes, D.N. "The Lion and the Phoenix: Ali Pasha and the Greek Revolution, 1819-1822". Harvard, Unpublished dissertation, 1974.

296. Spaulding, O.L., et al. A STUDY OF MILITARY METHODS FROM THE EARLIEST TIMES. New York: 1925.

297. Spira, G. A HUNGARIAN COUNT IN THE REVOLUTION OF 1848. Trans. and rev. by Richard E. Allen. Budapest: 1974.

298. _____. " Kossuth and Posterity," EHH, 1980.

299. Spiridonakis, B.G. ESSAYS ON HISTORICAL GEOGRAPHY OF THE GREEK WORLD IN THE BALKANS DURING THE TURKOKRATIA. Thessaloniki: 1977.

300. Stan, N. REFLECTARI ISTORICO-LITERARE ALE REZISTENTEI ROMANESTI. Bucharest: 1979.

301. Stavrianos, L.S. THE BALKAN SINCE 1453. New York: 1958.

302. _____. THE BALKANS, 1815-1914. Huntington, NY.: 1974 [1963].

303. Stefanescu, S., ed. ENCICLOPEDIA ISTORIOGRAFIEI ROMANESTI. Bucharest: 1978.

304. Stephenson, G. RUSSIA FROM 1812 TO 1945: A HISTORY. New York & Washington: 1970.

305. Sterns, P.N. 1848: THE REVOLUTIONARY TIDE IN EUROPE. New York:

306. Stevenson, F.S. A HISTORY OF MONTENEGRO. New York: 1971 [1912].

307. Stiles, W.H. AUSTRIA IN 1848-49. 2 vols. New York: 1852.

308. Stillman, W. TURKISH RULE AND TURKISH WARFARE. New York: 1877.

309. Stoianovich, T. "Factors in the Decline of Ottoman Society in the Balkans." SR XXI, 4 (December 1962), 623-632.

310. Sudi, S. DEFTER-I MUQTESID. 3 vols. Istanbul: 1891.

311. Sugar, P.F. SOUTHEASTERN EUROPE UNDER OTTOMAN RULE, 1354-1804. HECE 5, Seattle: 1977.

312. _____., ed. ETHNIC DIVERSITY AND CONFLICT IN EASTERN EUROPE. Santa Barbara: 1980.

313. Sugar, P.F., & Treadgold, D.W. HISTORY OF EAST CENTRAL EUROPE. 11 vols. Seattle & London: 1974-.

314. Swire, J. ALBANIA, THE RISE OF A KINGDOM. London: 1929.

315. Szilassy, S. "America and the Hungarian Revolution of 1848-1849." SEER XLIV, 102 (January 1966), 180-196.

316. Talmon, J.L. ROMANTICISM AND REVOLT; Europe, 1815-1848. LWC. New York:

317. Taylor, A.J.P. THE HABSBURG MONARCHY, 1809-1918. 2nd ed. London: 1948.

318. Tefft, B.F. HUNGARY AND KOSSUTH: OR, AN AMERICAN EXPOSITION OF THE LATE HUNGARIAN REVOLUTION. 3rd ed. Philadelphia: 1852.

319. Teleki, L. DE L'INTERVENTION RUSSE EN HONGROIE. Paris: 1849.

320. Temperley, H.W.V., Sir. ENGLAND AND THE NEAR EAST. 2 vols. London: 1936.

321. Temperley, H.W.V., Sir & Penson, L., eds. FOUNDATIONS OF BRITISH FOREIGN POLICY FROM PITT TO SALISBURY.London: 1939.

322. Thessaloniki, Institute of Balkan Studies. SYMPOSIUM L'EPOQUE PHANARIOTE, 1970. Thessaloniki: 1974.

323. _____. VALKANIKE VIVLIOGRAPHIE, 1975-.

324. Thim, J. GESCHICHTE DES SERBISCHEN AUFSTANDER, 1848-1849. 3 vols. Budapest: 1930.

325. Todorov, N. BALGARI UCHASTNICI V BORBITE ZA OSVOBOZDENIETO NA GARCIJA, 1821-1828. Sofia: 1971.

326. Toynbee, A.J. THE WESTERN QUESTION IN GREECE AND TURKEY. New York: 1970.

327. Trebilcock, C. THE INDUSTRIALIZATION OF THE CONTINENTAL POWERS. New York: 1981.

328. Tsvetkova, B.A. LES INSTITUTIONS OTTOMANES EN EUROPE. Wiesbaden: 1978.

329. Turkey. TURK SILAHLI KUVVETLERI TARIHI (1793-1908). Vol. 3. Ankara: 1978.

330. Turkiye Cumhuriyeti, Maarif Vekaleti. ISLAM ANSIKLOPEDISI.
     Istanbul & Ankara: 1940-.

331. Uhlirz, M, & Uhlirz, K. HANDBUCH DER GESCHICHTE OSTERREICHS UND
     SEINER NACHBARLANDER BOHMEN UND UNGARN. 4 VOLS. IN 5.
     GRAZ: 1927-1944.

332. Urban, A. A NEZMETORSEG ES HONVEDSEG SZERVEZESE 1848 NYARAN.
     Budapest: 1973.

333. USSR, Academy of Sciences, Institut Vostokovovedeniya.
     BIBLIOGRAFIYA TURTSII (1917-1958). Moscow: 1959.

334. Vagts, A. A HISTORY OF MILITARISM. New ed. New York: 1959.

335. Van Creveld, M.L. SUPPLYING WAR: LOGISTICS FROM WALLENSTEIN TO
     PATTON. New York: 1977.

336. Van Vollenhaven, C. THE LAW OF PEACE. London: 1936.

337. Vasif Efendi, A. MAHASIN AL-ASAR VE HAQAYIK AL-AHBAR. 2 vols in
     7. Cairo: 1930.

338. Vernadsky, G. "On Some Parallel Trends in Russian and Turkish
     History." TRANSACTIONS OF THE CONNECTICUT ACADEMY OF ARTS
     AND SCIENCES. XXXVI (July 1945), 25-36.

339. Vital, D. THE SURVIVAL OF SMALL STATES: STUDIES IN SMALL
     POWER/GREAT POWER CONFLICT. Toronto: 1971.

340. Voynov, M., et al. DOCUMENTS AND MATERIALS ON THE HISTORY OF
     THE BULGARIAN PEOPLE. Sofia: 1969.

341. Walichnowski, T., ed. BALCANICA: GUIDE TO THE POLISH ARCHIVES
     RELATIVE TO THE HISTORY OF THE BALKAN COUNTRIES. Warsaw:
     1979.

342. Wandruszka, A. THE HOUSE OF HABSBURG: SIX HUNDRED YEARS OF A
     EUROPEAN DYNASTY. Garden City, NY.: 1964.

343. Weber, E. EUROPE SINCE 1715: A MODERN HISTORY. New York: 1972.

344. Weiner, M. THE SOVEREIGN REMEDY: EUROPE AFTER WATERLOO. New
     York: 1971.

345. Westwood, J.N. ENDURANCE AND ENDEAVOUR: RUSSIAN HISTORY,
     1812-1880. New York: 1982.

346. Woodhouse, C.M. THE GREEK WAR OF INDEPENDENCE. London: 1952.

347. _____. THE BATTLE OF NAVARINO. Chester Springs: 1967
     [1965].

348. _____. CAPODISTRIA, THE FOUNDER OF GREEK INDEPENDENCE.
     London: 1973.

349. Woodruff, W. THE STRUGGLE FOR WORLD POWER, 1500-1980. New York: 1981.

350. Wright, Q. THE STUDY OF WAR. London & Chicago: 1965 [1942].

351. Wright, W.L. OTTOMAN STATECRAFT. Princeton: 1935.

352. Yurtseven, R. "The Greek Revolution in the Ottoman Empire (1821-1829)." CIHM ACTA Britannique. 1974.

353. Zakythinos, D.A. THE MAKING OF MODERN GREECE. Trans. by K.R. Johnstone. Totowa: 1976.

354. Zhilin, P.A. MIKHAIL ILLARIONOVICH KUTUZOV, ZHIZN' I POLKOVODCHESKAYA DEYATEL'NOST'. MOSCOW: 1978.

355. Zinkeisen J.W. GESCHICHTE DES OSMANISCHEN REICHES IN EUROPA. 7 vols. Hamburg & Gotha: 1840-1863.

356. Zook, D.H., & Higham, R. A SHORT HISTORY OF WARFARE. New York: 1966.

ADDITIONS

357. Renn, L. WARFARE: THE RELATION OF WAR TO SOCIETY. New York: 1939.

# CHAPTER SEVEN

GENERAL BACKGROUND

The second half of the 19th century may best be
characterized as the time of continued change. This period witnessed
an acceleration of the social, scientific, and technological
revolutions that had started earlier and which, as the second half
of the century began, showed no indication of having come close to
the full expression of the potentials each had for the future of
Europe. The acceleration that was manifested may be judged by the
fact that, during this 50-year period, the socio-economic structure
of Europe was more dramatically and rapidly changed than in the
whole of the preceding history of the continent.

The times were marked by a number of national revolutions
that struck in Ireland, Italy, and Germany, as well as in Poland and
in the Balkans. These upheavals were a continuation of the great
social revolution that had begun in 1848. The right formula for
social freedom and economic independence had not yet been found and
the only alternative to a return to the old ways was a continuation
of the struggle. The Second French Republic that had arisen from the
ashes of 1848 had been overpowered by Napoleon III who restored the
monarchy. The Frankfurt Assembly that had assembled to forge a
unification of the German states proved to be so ineffective that it
dissolved within its first year of existence. Italy's revolution
ended in anarchy. In Austria, where the revolt had been widespread
and extremely violent and specifically affected the Balkans, there
was little to show for the struggle except a belated abolition of
serfdom. Russia survived the events of 1848 shaken but fundamentally
untouched. The Ottoman Empire continued on its declining spiral, but
was still apparently too powerful for Imperial Russia to overwhelm,
even if it was still coveted.

Still there were important signs to be read in the outcome.
Socialism failed, but nationalism survived and grew. The apparition
of socialism and communism had badly frightened the monied classes
and the nobility but not enough to right all of the wrongs. Some
social progress was made, however, and what there was acted as both
a temporary salve and a taste of better things. New statesmen,
rulers, and military leaders also arose in this transitional period.
Napoleon III was to become one of the most significant and, at the
same time, one of the most paradoxical of them; but he was not the
only one of importance. Victor Emmanuel II and Garibaldi of Italy,
Germany's Otto von Bismarck and the brilliant Helmuth C.B. Moltke,
and Russia's Alexander II all shared in this distinction.

The aftermath of the 1848 revolt also allowed enough time
for Europe to continue its perennial enchantment with the

211

Apocalyptian horsemen. War during the second half of the 19th century once again crept into every corner of the continent beginning with the coup d'etat in France in 1851 and ending in some of the preparatory steps that were to lead to the Great War of 1914-1918. Most of these conflicts affected the Balkans and, indeed, this part of the continent rapidly earned its name as the "Cockpit of Europe."

## GENERAL HISTORIES

There is an abundance of good general histories of Europe that cover this period and that reflect on affairs in the Balkans. More and more, however, the astute reader will note the increased complexity of the situations that face the Balkans and should understand how the affairs of those peoples living in a backwater of the main course of European history were swept up in the mainstream of change that was rushing over the face of the continent. As before, the best general historiographical essay is Professor William McNeill's A WORLD HISTORY [349]. This is the best single-volume overview of the historical process available today.

Probably the second most valuable source of background information of the period of the second half of the 19th century is the two volumes of the NEW CAMBRIDGE MODERN HISTORY [115] that deal with various aspects and specific decades of the 1850-1898 period. Volume 10, THE ZENITH OF EUROPEAN POWER, 1830-1870 [89], which was edited by J.P.T. Bury; and volume 11, MATERIAL PROGRESS AND WORLD-WIDE PROBLEMS, 1870-1898 [231], which was edited by F.H. Hinsley, cover a wide range of subjects that relate directly to the course of historical development in the Balkans while, at the same time, being concise and skillfully written.

Still another valuable series is THE RISE OF MODERN EUROPE [300] that contains over 20 volumes that were prepared under the general editorship of William L. Langer. The six-volume series THE NORTON HISTORY OF MODERN EUROPE [193], prepared under the general editorship of Felix Gilbert, is also well prepared and contains a number of cogent studies. THE WORLD OF EUROPE [436] series, assembled under the editorship of Karl A. Roider, Jr. and Frederic A. Youngs, Jr. of Louisiana State University, contains THE NINETEENTH CENTURY, 1815-1914 [415] by David H. Pinkney. This volume deals with the problems caused by the Industrial Revolution and the social changes that were a part of it. It may serve as an excellent primer for the events that were to transpire before the end of the 19th century and lead the world into the great conflagration of 1914-1918. Pinkney also edited the PROBLEMS OF EUROPE [416] series, each volume of which contains a bibliographical essay of some value and other supplemental material such as glossaries and chronologies that will be of benefit to the reader. A similar effort is found in THE MODERN ERA, 1815 TO THE PRESENT [94], edited by Norman F. Cantor and Samuel Berner. This volume contains material on the rise of Napoleon III (Louis Napoleon Bonaparte) (1852-1870), the Second Empire that momentarily returned monarchical France to the "status quo," and the wave of new imperialism that dominated the late 19th century. Norman Cantor also edited, along with Micheal S. Werthman, THE MAKING OF THE MODERN WORLD, 1815-1914 [93] which is a collection of studies and interpretations. A better choice for a work of this type may be

Professor Gordon Craig's EUROPE SINCE 1815 [130] which is very thorough and extremely well written.

Yet another good choice of this genre is Eugen Weber's EUROPE SINCE 1715: A MODERN HISTORY [585] which is divided into two parts, the second of which deals with period after 1848. This book contains a wealth of firsthand information in the form of extracts of diaries, journals, and other records. EUROPEAN EMPIRE BUILDING: NINETEENTH CENTURY IMPERIALISM [122], edited by William B. Cohen, deals with the question of European expansion into Africa and Asia. These expansionistic tendencies on the part of the great powers helped foster the situation that led to World War I. WAR AND SOCIETY IN REVOLUTIONARY EUROPE, 1770-1870 [55], by Geoffrey Best, analyzes the effects of war on European society. This is a good book, written without scholarly pretensions but in a most scholarly manner. THE EMERGENCE OF THE EUROPEAN WORLD [64] by Blum, Cameron, and Burnes, and William Woodruff's THE STRUGGLE FOR WORLD POWER, 1500-1980 [594] are both good.

THE STRUGGLE FOR MASTERY IN EUROPE, 1848-1914 [538], written by A.J.P. Taylor, focusses more closely on the period under discussion. It is erratic in spots but is full of insight and has an excellent bibliography. Norman Rich's THE AGE OF NATIONALISM AND REFORM, 1850-1890 [433] is in its second edition and is greatly improved. The new version has a good bibliographical essay and is well illustrated. Another interesting selection is THE SOVEREIGN REMEDY: EUROPE AFTER WATERLOO [587], by M. Weiner, that assays many of the personalities that arose in the post-Napoleonic era.This book can assist in laying the groundwork for a detailed study of the second half of the century. The third volume of A DOCUMENTARY HISTORY OF MODERN EUROPE is NATIONALISM, INDUSTRIALIZATION, AND DEMOCRACY, 1815-1914 [42], by Thomas Barnes and Gerald Feldman.It is excellent in its use of archival material in explaining the phenomena associated with the rise of nationalism. The same topic is discussed in "Nationalities and Nationalism" [90] by J.P.T. Bury in an excellent article in NCMH.

Another good article in that same volume is Gordon Craig's "The System of Alliances and the Balance of Power" [131]. Professor Craig looks at a number of issues important to the Balkans in this incisive study of the pervasive desire among the great powers to maintain the status quo. Edward Gulick addresses this same problem in EUROPE'S CLASSICAL BALANCE OF POWER: A CASE STUDY OF THE THEORY AND PRACTICE OF ONE OF THE GREAT CONCEPTS OF EUROPEAN STATECRAFT [214]. THE GREAT POWERS AND THE EUROPEAN STATES SYSTEM, 1815-1914 [87] is an interpretive study of the development of this concept after the Congress of Vienna. The book has a good chronology that traces the events that earmark this progress. Matthew Anderson's THE GREAT POWERS AND THE NEAR EAST (1774-1923) [22] brings clarity to the struggle for balance as it affected the Balkans. Anderson has edited a number of excellent accounts of various themes that impact upon the problem into a single volume that is very much worth reading. A somewhat different approach to this same issue is taken in A.P. Thornton's "Rivalries in the Mediterranean, the Middle East and Egypt" [547]. Professor Thornton looks particularly at the extension of European great power interests into the realm of the Ottoman Empire in the last three decades of the 19th century and the changing roles assumed by the various players. A complementary piece in the same volume of NCMH is A.J.P. Taylor's "International Relations" [539] that deals more specifically with the Eastern Question in the context of the balance of power. Lastly, an excellent work that deals with the economic problems of this period is THE INDUSTRIALIZATION OF THE CONTINENTAL POWERS, 1780-1914 [551], by Clive Trebilcock.

## THE EASTERN QUESTION

The extent of the literature on the Eastern Question was illustrated in the preceding chapter. As this was a burning international issue that affected every corner of Europe, almost any competent history of the times will have some amount of detail on the subject. There are, however, several volumes that can be mentioned. THE EASTERN QUESTION [341] by Sir John Marriott is somewhat sketchy. Matthew Anderson's THE EASTERN QUESTION, 1774-1923 [21] expands on Marriott's efforts. Among other things, this highly authoritative volume on European diplomatic history contains ten very useful maps and a good bibliography. Although he centers his 19th century coverage on the Crimean War, his overall view of the entire period is excellent. Another possible choice is Stephen Duggan's THE EASTERN QUESTION; A STUDY IN DIPLOMACY [156]. Three works in French that are worth mentioning are Edouard Driault's LA QUESTION D'ORIENT [154] and Jacques Ancel's MANUEL HISTORIQUE DE LA QUESTION D'ORIENT: 1792-1923 [17]. Of these two the latter is better. The third work is Fernand Grinard's GRANDEUR ET DECADENCE DE L'ASIE [213]. This volume looks at the problem from a somewhat different perspective. Lastly, David Vital's THE SURVIVAL OF SMALL STATES: STUDIES IN SMALL POWER/GREAT POWER CONFLICT [575] is worth reading at this point.

## GENERAL HISTORIES ON THE BALKANS

Of the general surveys of Balkan history the best is still Leften Stavrianos' THE BALKANS SINCE 1453 [520]. Another, later work of his is THE BALKANS, 1815-1914 [521] that deals more directly with this period and illustrates the relationship between events in the Balkans and the remainder of Europe. Ferdinand Schevill's HISTORY OF THE BALKAN PENINSULA [476] is found in numerous editions and printings that have been published since 1922 and it is very good. Although Edgar Hosch's work is titled THE BALKANS: A SHORT HISTORY [238], it centers on Albania, Bulgaria, and Yugoslavia. This means that the crucial events in Greece and Romania are treated only superficially. THE PEOPLES OF THE EASTERN HABSBURG LANDS, 1526-1918 [273], by Robert Kann and Zdanek David, partially makes up for this in its coverage of the territory under Austro-Hungarian control. Erwin and Ann Lessner's THE DANUBE: THE DRAMATIC HISTORY OF THE GREAT RIVER AND THE PEOPLE TOUCHED BY ITS FLOW [315] is excellent in its story—telling. The British Foreign Office's THE BALKAN STATES [202] was published in two volumes in 1973. This work deals with the entire Balkan region and was originally printed in 1920 in the HISTORICAL SECTION HANDBOOK series. Another good selection is THE BALKANS; A HISTORY OF BULGARIA, SERBIA, GREECE, RUMANIA, TURKEY [179], written by Neville Forbes and others. This work was originally published in 1915 and was republished in 1970. It has a good bibliography.

THE BALKANS IN TRANSITION [263] which was edited by Charles and Barbara Jelavich for the RUSSIAN AND EAST EUROPEAN STUDIES series of the University of California is a collection of some 75 papers presented at a 1960 conference on the Balkans. Of special interest is one section by George Soulis that summarizes the best in bibliographical references on the Balkans. The Jelavichs also produced THE ESTABLISHMENT OF THE BALKAN NATIONAL STATES, 1804-1920 [264] which is found in the HISTORY OF EAST CENTRAL EUROPE series [532]. Peter Sugar, who along with Donald Treadgold has edited the HECE series, also edited ETHNIC DIVERSITY AND CONFLICT IN EASTERN EUROPE [531], a compilation of essays by leading scholars in the field. THE RISE OF NATIONALITY IN THE BALKANS [493] by Robert Seton-Watson is especially well suited as a detailed account of the second half of the 19th century and as an introduction into the momentous events in the Balkans in the early 20th century that altered the course of history. This work may be supplemented but not replaced by Seton-Watson's THE EMANCIPATION OF SOUTH-EASTERN EUROPE [491], which is a 38-page pamphlet. Wesley M. Gewehr's THE RISE OF NATIONALISM IN THE BALKANS, 1800-1930 [190] may be used instead of Seton-Watson although a better course is to read both for a full understanding of this important phenomenon. A CENTURY OF BALKAN TURMOIL [16] by Christ Anastasoff is also interesting as is William Murray's THE MAKING OF THE BALKAN STATES [370]. Murray's work was first produced in 1910 and was reprinted in 1967.

Two other works that should be taken together are Arnold Toynbee's THE WESTERN QUESTION IN GREECE AND TURKEY [550] and John Sanness' EUROPE AND THE BALKANS. PAST TERRITORIAL DISPUTES AND SOCIOPOLITICAL VARIETY [468]. Two good studies on Balkan economics are Ivan Berend and Gyorgy Ranki's ECONOMIC DEVELOPMENT IN EAST CENTRAL EUROPE IN THE 19TH AND 20TH CENTURIES [48] and BALKAN ECONOMIC HISTORY, 1550-1950 [299], by John Lampe and Marvin Jackson. There are three works in German that merit attention: Franz Babinger's AUFSATZE UND ABHANDLUNGEN ZUR GESCHICHTE SUDOSTEUROPAS UND DER LEVANTE [33]; Egon Heymann's BALKAN: KRIEGE, BUNDNISSE, REVOLUTIONEN; 150 JAHRE POLITIK UND SCHICKSAL [228]; and BALKAN AUS ESTER HAND. GESCHICHTE U. GEGENWART IN BERICHTEN VOM AUGENZEUGEN U. ZEITGENOSSEN [480], by George Schreiber. HISTOIRE POLITIQUE ET SOCIALE DES PRINCIPANTS DANUBIENNES [427], by Elias Regnault, was written in 1857 and sets the stage for this period. Dimitrije Djordjevic's REVOLUTIONS NATIONALES DES PEUPLES BALKANIQUES, 1804-1914 [151] looks at the problems of the Balkans in a different way. Professor Djordjevic contends that Balkan history emanates from within and is not necessarily a by-product of European history. PETNADESET GODINI INSTITUT ZA BALKANISTIKA, 1964-1978: ISTORICHESKA SPRAVKA I BIBLIOGRAFIIA [496], edited by Liliana Shandanova, is a product of the Bulgarian Academy of Science's Institute of Balkan Affairs. It is an excellent reference with entries in both Bulgarian and French.

The BIBLIOGRAPHIC GUIDE TO SOVIET AND EAST EUROPEAN STUDIES [58], published in Boston, contains a yearly cataloging of works that were themselves published in eastern Europe and the USSR, works published in a language of that area of the world, or works published in the west that deal with that region. There are about 40,000 entries listed each year. This may be supplemented by Horecky's two guides, one dealing with East Central Europe [235] and

215

one dealing with Southeastern Europe [236]. Anton Scherer's SUDOSTEUROPA-DISSERTATIONEN, 1918-1960. . . [475] is also a most useful reference. VALKANIKE VIVLIOGRAPHIA [545] is another useful bibliographical tool. Tadeus Walichnowski's BALCANICA: A GUIDE TO THE POLISH ARCHIVES RELATIVE TO THE HISTORY OF THE BALKAN COUNTRIES [582] adds yet another dimension to the reference sources available. The BIBLIOGRAPHICAL GUIDE TO MAPS AND ATLASES [57] is another yearly compilation that includes journal articles and other data on maps from nonmap sources, in addition to the obvious listings of maps and charts. THE PENGUIN HISTORICAL ATLASES [348] that were compiled by Colin McEvedy contain a volume on Europe since 1815. W.R. Shepherd's HISTORICAL ATLAS [500], which was in its eighth edition in 1956, is very good.

## MILITARY HISTORICAL WORKS

A number of the military works mentioned earlier in this guide are applicable to this period. MEN IN ARMS [421] by Richard A. Preston, Sidney Wise and Herman Werner is excellent reading even if only as background reading on the underlying factors of war. James T. Lowe's GEOPOLITICS AND WAR: MACKINDER'S PHILOSOPHY OF POWER [323] deals with the problem of war as a function of Mackinder's concept of the Heartland. This book gives one view of war in modern times that should not be overlooked. Lynn Montross' WAR THROUGH THE AGES [361] contains some of the best battle history that has been written. A MILITARY HISTORY OF THE WESTERN WORLD [185], by the noted military historian J.F.C. Fuller, is a must for any serious student. Another must is R. Ernest and Trevor N. Dupuy's THE ENCYCLOPEDIA OF MILITARY HISTORY [157]. This massive reference has some serious omissions and some errors but there is no better place to start when looking for data on a particular event. A SHORT HISTORY OF WARFARE [604], prepared by David Zook and Robin Higham, is also a good place to start.

Stanislav Andreski's MILITARY ORGANIZATION AND SOCIETY [24] is a minor military classic. Geoffrey Blainey's THE CAUSES OF WAR [62] deals at length with the Eastern Question. THE ART OF WAR [168] was written by Cyril Falls and must be read, as should Quincy Wright's THE STUDY OF WAR [597]. THE LAW OF PEACE [571] by C. Van Vollenhaven and Ludwig Renn's WARFARE: THE RELATION OF WAR TO SOCIETY [429] are both worthwhile reading. MILITARISM: THE HISTORY OF AN INTERNATIONAL DEBATE, 1860-1979 [49] was written by V.R. Berghahn and deals with the period from 1860 to the late 1970s. A HISTORY OF MILITARISM [569] by Alfred Vagts is also very good. KRIEG UND KRIEGFUHRUNG IM WANDEL DER WELTGESCHICHTE [479] is not as good as Vagts'. THE POLITICS OF WAR AND PEACE: A SURVEY OF THOUGHT [75] by Abbott Brayton and Stephana Landwehr looks at war in the framework of the ruler's and the citizen's responsibilities to the collective society. THE MAKERS OF MODERN STRATEGY: MILITARY THOUGHT FROM MACHIAVELLI TO HITLER [160] was edited by E.M. Earle and is excellent. This work may be complemented by "The Great Military Historians and Philosophers" [325] written by Jay Luvaas. Theodore Ropp's WAR IN THE MODERN WORLD [445] can serve the casual reader and the scholar with equal benefit. Major General Emory Upton's THE ARMIES OF ASIA AND EUROPE [564] is a very valuable tool in understanding the ways in which the American Civil War affected foreign military organization and preparations for conflict. Both Russia and Austria are discussed in detail. Also of interest is A

STUDY OF MILITARY METHODS FROM THE EARLIEST TIMES [515] by Spaulding, Nickerson, and Wright.

Details about the military between 1830 and 1870 may be found in Basil Liddell-Hart's "Armed Forces and the Art of War: Armies" [320] and Micheal Lewis' "Armed Forces and the Art of War: Navies" [319] that are companion articles in Volume 10 of the NCMH. Volume 11 contains Michael Howard's "The Armed Forces" [241] that contains information of the 1870-1898 period. Helmuth von Moltke's STRATEGY: ITS THEORY AND APPLICATION: THE WAR OF GERMAN UNIFICATION, 1866-1871 [358] is essential reading for an understanding of German military thinking up to World War I. William Balck's encyclopedic TACTICS [36] is also extremely valuable and is periodically revised. THE QUEST FOR VICTORY: THE HISTORY OF THE PRINCIPLES OF WAR [13], by J.I. Alger, is another important volume for the serious student of military history.

Jacques Mordal's TWENTY-FIVE CENTURIES OF SEA WARFARE [363] deals with all aspects of naval warfare in survey form. NAVAL WARS OF THE LEVANT, 1559-1853 [23], by R.C. Anderson, ends its coverage with the beginning of the Crimean War period but is still good background reading. George Denison deals with the use of horses in his HISTORY OF CAVALRY [149]. Elbridge Colby's MASTERS OF MOBILE WARFARE [123] is also important reading. Ian Hogg's A HISTORY OF ARTILLERY [232] deals with the development of that important combat arm through this period. WEAPONS OF WAR [119] deals with the development of military weaponry in more general terms. Jean Bujac's PRECES DE QUELQUES CAMPAGNES CONTEMPORAIRES [82] is a multi-volume collection of battle histories, many of which deal with the Balkans. Richard Lewinsohn's THE PROFITS OF WAR THROUGH THE AGES [316]; David Singer and Melvin Small's THE WAGES OF WAR: A STATISTICAL HANDBOOK [503]; and Martin Van Creveld's SUPPLYING WAR: LOGISTICS FROM WALLENSTEIN TO PATTON [570] all cover different aspects of the question of financing war and the inherent logistics involved. Jeffrey Clarke's "World Military History" [116] is an excellent bibliographic guide to this period. This article is found in A GUIDE TO THE STUDY AND USE OF MILITARY HISTORY [268], prepared under the general editorship of John E. Jessup and Robert W. Coakley. There are numerous other reference articles in this work that will be of value to the student and to the scholar. Dale Floyd's A BIBLIOGRAPHY OF NINETEENTH CENTURY ARMED LAND CONFLICT [175] is also extremely valuable. Lastly, Professor David Chandler's ATLAS OF MILITARY STRATEGY [110] is an essential part of any decent collection of works on military history

## THE NATIONS OF THE BALKANS

### YUGOSLAVIA

Although Yugoslavia did not exist as a nation between 1850-1899, the several states that would eventually form that nation did exist and were quite often heard from as they sought to find their independence. YUGOSLAVIA [225] is a good general history. Written by Muriel Heppell and Frank B. Singleton, this work outlines the history of the six states that would eventually be forcibly linked together. LA FORMATION DE LA YOUGOSLAVIE, XVe-XXe SIECLES [187] by E. Gaumant centers upon the Serbian rise to independence. The article, "Yugoslavia and Romania" [405] by K.S.

Pavlowitch deals with the relations between those two nations.

HISTOIRE DU MONTENEGRO ET DE LA BOSNIE [126] was written in 1895 by P. Coquelle. It deals with the period under discussion in both states. Francis Stevenson's A HISTORY OF MONTENEGRO [524] was published in 1912 but is still good. MONTENEGRO [483] by Bernhard Schwarz was first published in 1888 and is in German. Jaroslav Sidak has produced POVIJEST HRVATSKOG NARODA G. 1860-1914 [502] that relates the history of Croatia during the fifty years before the beginning of World War I. It is excellent. THE MILITARY BORDER OF CROATIA, 1740-1881: A STUDY OF AN IMPERIAL INSTITUTION [451], by Gunther Rothenberg, is supported by his "The Struggle Over the Dissolution of the Croatian Military Border, 1850-1871" [448].

Serbia's history is best covered in the two-volume A HISTORY OF MODERN SERBIA [413] by Micheal Petrovich. SERBIA; HER PEOPLE, HISTORY, ASPIRATIONS [412] was written by Vojislav Petrovic and is much less objective in its coverage. Sir Harold Temperley's HISTORY OF SERBIA [543] is very good. SERVIAN PEOPLE [305] was published in 1910 in two volumes. Written by Prince Lazarovich-Hrebelianovich, it is aimed at being an encyclopedic history of the Serbian people. Although obviously biased, both volumes, especially the second one, are very good. Count Carlo Sforza, who was the Italian envoy to the Serbian government when the country fell to the Central Powers in 1915, has written FIFTY YEARS OF WAR AND DIPLOMACY IN THE BALKANS: PASHICH AND THE UNION OF THE YUGOSLAVS [495]. This modest, often distorted work surveys Serbian history from 1848-1900 before dealing with the events in the public life of Nicola Pashich through a series of miniature studies of events and people associated with the times although not always associated with Serbia. DAS SERBISCHE BLAUBUCH, DAS RUSSISCHE ORANGEBUCH [488] was published in German in 1915 by the Serbian Foreign Office. Ivo Senkowitsch wrote DIE KULTURBEDEUTUNG SERBIENS [487] deals with the significance the Serbians place upon themselves as a people separate from all others.

Elizabeth Barker's MACEDONIA: ITS PLACE IN BALKAN POWER POLITICS [41] was originally published in 1950 by the Royal Institute of International Affairs and was reprinted in 1980. Another older work is Emile Kuepfer's LA MACEDOINE ET LES BULGARES [297] which was published in 1918. Lewis P.F. Olivier has edited LA BOSNIE ET L'HERZEGOVINE [382]. This may be supplemented by Vasa Pelagic's BORBA ZA OSVOBODJENJE: ISTORIJA BOSANSKO-HERCEGOVACHE BUNE I SOEZI SRPSKO-VLACHO-BUKGARSKO I RUSKO-TURKSIM RATOM [408] that deals with the 1875-1878 period in particular but has good background information. Two works that deal with peripheral areas are Paul Ignotus' "Czechs, Magyars, Slovaks" [248], that deals with the hostilities that existed among these groups, and J.F.N. Bradley's CZECHO-SLOVAKIA: A SHORT HISTORY [72], that covers the period under discussion in sufficient detail for the purpose of understanding its role in Balkan affairs.

## BULGARIA

The most valuable history in English on Bulgaria is Mercia Macdermott's A HISTORY OF BULGARIA, 1393-1885 [330] with the annexation of the province of Eastern Rumelia that led to the Serbo-Bulgarian War of 1885-1886. A good supplement to Macdermott is

G.P. Genoff's BULGARIJA I EVROPA [188] that appeared in 1940. An excellent bibliography on military history was published by the Bulgarians in 1973: HISTOIRE MILITAIRE DE LA BULGARIE, 681-1945. BIBLIOGRAPHIE [86] is in French and has about 2470 entries published to the end of 1972. Another Bulgarian government publication is DOCUMENTS AND MATERIALS ON THE HISTORY OF THE BULGARIAN PEOPLE [85]. This work was compiled by a team led by M. Voynov. This well-executed reference contains more than 125 English translations of documents dealing with this period. Michel Leo's LA BULGARIE ET SON PEUPLE SOUS LA DOMINATION OTTOMANE TELS QUE LES OUT VUS LES VOYAGEURS ANGLO-SAXONS (1586-1878) [314] is also quite interesting. Lastly, Liudmila Genova's bibliography [189] should be referred to as it is full of helpful source information.

## ROMANIA

There are a large number of histories about Romania in the second half of the 19th century. The best in English is Robert Seton-Watson's A HISTORY OF THE ROUMANIANS; FROM ROMAN TIMES TO THE COMPLETION OF UNITY [494]. This study ends in 1859 with the unification of Wallachia and Moldavia. Ladislas Makkai relates the events in the other principality in his HISTOIRE DE TRANSYLVANIE [336]. The NORTH AMERICAN REVIEW published a short article called "Romania Since 1848" [444] in 1869 while COLBURNS published "Roumania in 1866" [452] in 1866. A third article called "Romania" [443] was published in 1886 in THE NATION. Iorga's HISTOIRE DES ROUMAINES DE LA PENINSULE DES BALKANS [252] was published in 1919. ROMANIA IN SUD-ESTUL EUROPEI (1848-1886) [112], by Nicholae Ciachir, covers most of this period and includes a number of bibliographic references. The principal thrust of the book is Romania's foreign relations. A new book published in the United States is WAR, REVOLUTION, AND SOCIETY IN ROMANIA: THE ROAD TO INDEPENDENCE [107]. This book is a compilation of essays assembled under the direction of Ilie Ceaucescu and contains a number of articles on this period. Cornelia Bodea's THE ROMANIANS' STRUGGLE FOR UNIFICATION [65] is painstakingly prepared and cannot be overlooked. Originally published in Romanian in 1967 as a part of the BHR series, it was translated into English in 1970. Professor Lucian Boia's RELATIONSHIPS BETWEEN ROMANIANS, CZECHS AND SLOVAKS (1848-1914) [68] is a history of the political relations that were carried on among Romania and the other two states during the era. It is good but reflects too much of the present-day unitary policy of the Romanians. There is no bibliography, but the work contains numerous citations that will be of help to the diligent student. The CHRONOLOGICAL HISTORY OF ROMANIA [195] was compiled by Constantine Giurescu and others. Published in 1972 this reference is an excellent source of dates and pertinent information. It must be used with caution, however, as it has a number of errors and is often poorly translated.

With the passing of the centennial of Romanian independence in 1977 and the nation's subsequent hosting of the quinquennial International Congress of Historical Sciences in Bucharest in 1980, there has been a veritable avalanche of publications on military history produced not only in Romanian but in numerous other languages as well. In 1975 a BHR monograph entitled PAGES FROM THE HISTORY OF THE ROMANIAN ARMY [472] was published. This compilation was prepared under the direction of Alexandre Savu and contains 19 articles, two of which reference this period. Then, in 1978, Professor Stefan Stefanescu coordinated the preparation of an ENCICLOPEDIA ISTORIOGRAFIEI ROMANESTI [522] that contains biographical notes and bibliographical notations. In the following year REFLECTARI ISTORICO-LITERARE ALE REZISTENTEI ROMANESTI [518] was published. Authored by Nicolae Stan, this 231-page work analyzes the revolutionary and resistance characteristics of the Romanian people. It is polemical and contains numerous allusions to historic unity among the various principalities in what is today Romania. Much of the book is devoted to the 20th century period of Romania's interlude in the Nazi camp. Nicolae Birdeanu and D. Nicholescu's CONTRIBUTII LA ISTORIA MARINEI ROMANE. DIN CELE MAI VECHI TIMPURI PINA IN 1918 [60] was published in 1979 and deals with the development of the Romanian navy. PAGES FROM THE MILITARY HISTORY OF THE ROMANIAN PEOPLE [104] was published in 1980. This work is in the FILE DIN ISTORIA MILITARA A POPORULUI ROMAN series that is compiled under the direction of General Ceaucescu. This issue is a multi-language collection of 39 essays, five of which refer to this period. That same year THE ARMY AND ROMANIAN SOCIETY [473] was published which is a collection of 26 articles of which many refer to this period. This work was produced simultaneously in a number of languages including English. Another contribution of 1980 was THE ENTIRE PEOPLE'S WAR FOR THE HOMELAND'S DEFENCE WITH THE ROMANIANS [103]. Despite the awkward title, this collection, prepared under the direction of Ilie Ceaucescu, is a rather thorough exposition of Romanian defense concepts as they are perceived to have developed over the past centuries. This study was complemented by the concurrent publication of STUDII DE ISTORIE SI TEORIE MILITARA. RETROSPECTIVE ISTORICE ANALIZE CONTEMPORANE [471] that was coordinated by Doctor Savu. This work is a collection of studies on Romanian military thought and national defense policy.

Within these collective works are a number of articles that should be mentioned because of their general application. They are "On the Development of the Modern Romanian Army from the Revolution of Tudor Vladimirescu in 1821 to the 1859 Union" [97], "People's War in the Romanian Thought of the Mid-19th Century" [99], and "Tradition and Innovation in the Organization of the Modern Romanian Army" [98], all of which were written by Colonel Constantin Cazanisteanu. Nicholae Ciachir wrote "Military Cooperation Between Romanians and the Peoples of the South of the Danube During the Ottoman Period" [113] for TRTI. Christian Vladescu's UNIFORMELE ARMATEI ROMANE DE LA INCEPUTUL SECOLULUI AL XIX-LEA PINA LA VICTORIA DIN MAI 1945 [576] is a synthesis of the evolution of Romanian military uniforms from 1830.

## ALBANIA

There is an absence of literature on Albania. Several works do exist, however, such as John Swire's ALBANIA, THE RISE OF A KINGDOM [534]; L'ALBANIE INDEPENDANTE ET L'EMPIRE KHALIFAL OTTOMAN [45] by Basri Beg; Felice Cammarata's ALBANICA [91]; and E.L.J. Legrand's BIBLIOGRAPHIE ALBANAISE [311], and may be referred to for information on this country. Of this group, Swire's work is the best.

GREECE

A number of good studies exist that will be of assistance in understanding the Greek role in the military history of the Balkans during this period. A SHORT HISTORY OF MODERN GREECE, 1821-1952 [181], by E.S. Forster; George Finlay's HISTORY OF GREECE, FROM ITS CONQUEST BY THE ROMANS TO THE PRESENT TIME, B.C. 164 TO A.D. 1864 [171]; and Richard Clogg's A SHORT HISTORY OF MODERN GREECE [120] are good. THE MAKING OF MODERN GREECE [601], by D.A. Zakythinos; J. Mavrocordato's MODERN GREECE, 1800-1931 [344]; THE UNIFICATION OF GREECE, 1770-1923 [140]; GREECE IN THE NINETEENTH CENTURY [469], by Lyman T. Sargent; and Professor P. Karolides' CONTEMPORARY HISTORY OF THE GREEKS AND OTHER PEOPLES OF THE EAST FROM 1821 TO 1921 [277] are all significant, although Karolides' book is in Greek.

John T. Koumoulides has produced HELLENIC PERSPECTIVES: ESSAYS IN THE HISTORY OF GREECE [296] that contains information of interest in this period. ESSAYS ON THE HISTORICAL GEOGRAPHY OF THE GREEK WORLD IN THE BALKANS DURING THE TURKOKRATIA [516] deals with the demographics and historical geography of modern Greece. Stephen A. Larrabee presents a compilation of first hand reports on Greek life in his HELLAS OBSERVED - THE AMERICAN EXPERIENCE OF GREECE, 1775-1865 [304].

AUSTRIA-HUNGARY

The Austro-Hungarian Empire is reported abundantly in a number of good historical works. Hans Kohn's THE HABSBURG EMPIRE, 1804-1918 [292] and Robert A. Kann's A HISTORY OF THE HABSBURG EMPIRE, 1526-1918 [271] are both good places to start. Kann also wrote THE MULTINATIONAL EMPIRE: NATIONALISM AND NATIONAL REFORM IN THE HABSBURG EMPIRE, 1848-1918 [272] and THE HABSBURG EMPIRE: A STUDY IN INTEGRATION AND DISINTEGRATION [270]. Other good works are THE HABSBURG MONARCHY; TOWARD A MULTINATIONAL EMPIRE OR NATIONAL STATES? [259], edited by Charles Jelavich; THE HAPSBURG MONARCHY [95], a two-volume work with one volume covering Austria and Bohemia and the other about Hungary, edited by F.L. Carsten and others; THE IMPERIAL CROWN: THE STORY OF THE RISE AND FALL OF THE HOLY ROMAN AND AUSTRIAN EMPIRES [184], by P. Frischauer; A.J.P. Taylor's THE HABSBURG MONARCHY, 1809-1918 [537]; and Adam Wandruszka's THE HOUSE OF HABSBURG: SIX HUNDRED YEARS OF A EUROPEAN DYNASTY [583].

Macartney's THE HABSBURG EMPIRE, 1790-1918 [327] is also very good as is his "The Austrian Empire and Its Problems, 1848-67" [329] that appears in NCMH 10. This latter article may be supplemented by W.N. Medlicott's "Austria-Hungary, Turkey and the Balkans" [352] that is in NCMH 11 and deals with the 1870-1898 period. In HAPSBURG LEGACY 1867-1939 [403] the author, B. Pauley, takes a different approach by stating that the full impact of the Austro-Hungarian rule cannot be appreciated until the inter-world war period is studied. Alan Sked's THE SURVIVAL OF THE HABSBURG EMPIRE [507] ends with the beginning of this period, but his discussion of the roles of Marshal Josef Radetzky and the Imperial Army in the 1848 revolt give excellent insight into what happens in the latter half of the century. Stephan Fisher-Galati's "The Habsburg Monarchy and the Balkan Revolution" [173] is also useful at this point. Two works in German that are worthwhile are DAS

GESCHICHTE OSTERREICHS [220], by H. Hantsch, and HABSBURGERMONARCHIE 1848-1918: DIE WIRTSCHAFTLICHE ENTWICKLUNG [81], edited by Alois Brusatti. Brusatti's work contains a number of essays on the various economic progress made in each of the empire's states. Another work in German is DIE PROTOKOLLE DES OSTERREICHISCHEN MINISTERRATES, 1848-1867 [455]. Compiled by Helmut Rumpler, this is a collection of protocols submitted to the emperor during those years. Robert Seton-Watson's THE SOUTHERN SLAV QUESTION AND THE HABSBURG MONARCHY [492] deals with the national feeling among the Serbians and Croatians and how this grew into a movement that began to have an impact on Empire affairs near the turn of the century. This same theme is approached in Fran Zwitter's LES PROBLEMES NATIONAUX DANS LA MONARCHIE DES HABSBOURG [606] that was published in Belgrad in 1960. This work is a Marxist survey of the principal issues that faced Vienna as seen from a Yugoslav point of view.

Emil Lengyel's 1000 YEARS OF HUNGARY [313], Denis Sinor's HISTORY OF HUNGARY [506], and C.A. Macartney's HUNGARY, A SHORT HISTORY [328] are among the best historical treatments of Hungary available in English. DAS UNGARISCHE REGIERUNGSYSTEM VOR DEM VERFALL DER OSTERREICHISCH-UNGARISCHEN MONARCHIE, by F. Poloskei [418], deals with the governmental system as it existed in Hungary up to the time of the collapse of the empire. Domonic Kosary has produced a number of useful finding aids on Hungarian history. One of these is BEVEZETES MAGYARORSZAG TORTENETENEK FORRASAIBA ES IRODALMABA [293] an introduction to the sources. The other is MAGYAR TORTENETI BIBLIOGRAFIA, 1825-1867 [294]. This latter work contains over 72,000 entries in four volumes and is somewhat outdated. Sandor Petho's VILAGOSTOL TRIANONIG; A MAI MAGYARORSZAG KIALAKULASANAK TORTENETE [410] is an account of Hungarian events from 1848 to the collapse of Austria-Hungary in 1918. This work was produced in 1926.

THE OTTOMAN EMPIRE

A number of good histories exist that deal with the general course of Turkish history through this period. Lord Kinross' THE OTTOMAN CENTURIES: THE RISE AND FALL OF THE TURKISH EMPIRE [285] is always a good choice as are George Arnakis' THE NEAR EAST IN MODERN TIMES: THE OTTOMAN EMPIRE AND THE BALKANS TO 1900 [29]; Stanford Shaw's HISTORY OF THE OTTOMAN EMPIRE AND MODERN TURKEY: REFORM, REVOLUTION AND REPUBLIC: THE RISE OF MODERN TURKEY, 1808-1975 [499]; and William Miller's THE OTTOMAN EMPIRE AND ITS SUCCESSORS, 1801-1927 [354]. Miller's book has a supplement that covers 1927-1936. Other good works in English include Albert Hourani's THE OTTOMAN BACKGROUND OF THE MODERN MIDDLE EAST [239], THE EMERGENCE OF MODERN TURKEY [318], by Bernard Lewis, and Sir Edward Creasy's HISTORY OF THE OTTOMAN TURKS [136]. Robert Gossip's TURKEY AND RUSSIA, THEIR RACES, HISTORY AND WARS [199] is especially useful at this point. Barbara Jelavich's THE OTTOMAN EMPIRE, THE GREAT POWERS, AND THE STRAITS QUESTION, 1870-1887 [256] deals with the Bosphorus issue that directly affected the peace and security of the Balkans.

Bernard Lewis' "The Ottoman Empire in the Mid-Nineteenth Century: A Review" [317] is an excellent overview of the middle years of the century. OTTOMAN STATECRAFT [598], by W.L. Wright, is also important reading as is Stanford Shaw's "The Ottoman View of the Balkans" [499] and Sidney Fisher's "Ottoman Feudalism and Its Influence Upon the Balkans" [172]. Another interesting article is

Traian Stoianovic's "Factors in the Decline of Ottoman Society in the Balkans" [527]. Noel Barber's THE SULTANS [39] emphasizes the role of the ruler in Turkish affairs. William Stillman's TURKISH RULE AND TURKISH WARFARE [526] was published in 1877. Maximilian Braun's "Turkenherrschaft und Turkenkampf bei den Balkenslawen" [74], printed in DIE WELT ALS GESCHICHTE in 1940, is a good complementary piece. Nicolae Iorga's five-volume GESCHICHTE DES OSMANISCHEN REICHES [251] and Bistra Tsvetkova's LES INSTITUTIONS OTTOMANES EN EUROPE [555] are both interesting as is Fernand Grinard's GRANDEUR ET DECADENCE DE L'ASIE [213].

Histories in Turkish include TARIH-I LUFTI [324] that is a multi-volume, official chronicle found only in manuscript form. Volumes IX-XIII deal with the period 1846-1876 when this history stops. Ayvedis' TURK TARINDE OSMANLI ASRLAR [31] covers the period 1288-1918. OSMANLI TARIHI: NIZAM-I CEDIT VE TANZIMAT DEVIRLERI 1789-1856 [274], by E.K. Karal, deals with the Tanzimat epoch while Suleyman Sudi's DEFTER-I MUQTESID [530] covers the 19th century. TURK SILAHLI KUVVETLERI TARIHI [560] is the official military history of Turkey. Volume 3 covers 1793-1908. ISLAM ANSIKLOPEDISI [561] is the best encyclopedic source available.

The CAMBRIDGE HISTORY OF ISLAM [234] is a two-volume set that conforms to the normal high standards one has come to expect from this prestigious institution's historical series. Volume 1 is especially useful at this point. The ENCYCLOPEDIA OF ISLAM [240] is also an excellent reference. A Russian bibliography of 40 years of material on Turkey is BIBLIOGRAFIYA TURTSII (1917-1958) [567]. M.A. Grassi's CHARTE TURQUE EN ORGANIZATION RELIGIEUSE, CIVILE ET MILITAIRE DE L'EMPIRE OTTOMAN [200] is an important reference on the structure of the government of the military. Another good source on Turkish military organization is L. Lamouche's L'ORGANIZATION MILITAIRE DE L'EMPIRE OTTOMAN [298].

## IMPERIAL RUSSIA

Riasonovsky [432] and Clarkson [117] meet the requirements for general historical coverage of this period. Klyuchevski [286, 287] is still a classic as is Florinsky's RUSSIA: A HISTORY AND AN INTERPRETATION [174]. Graham Stephenson's RUSSIA FROM 1812 to 1945: A HISTORY [523] is at best a spotty product of haphazard scholarship and even more haphazard editing. A much more satisfactory choice is J.N. Westwood's ENDURANCE AND ENDEAVOUR: RUSSIAN HISTORY, 1812-1980 [591] which has a good bibliography. Alfred Rambaud's THE EXPANSION OF RUSSIA [424] is also very useful as is Barbara Jelavich's A CENTURY OF RUSSIAN FOREIGN POLICY, 1814-1914 [257]. RUSSIA, TURKEY, AND ENGLAND [121], by Richard Cobden, was published in 1876 as a reprint. Its period of coverage is limited; but, as a contemporary account, it is good background reading. Taras Hunczak edited RUSSIAN IMPERIALISM FROM IVAN THE TERRIBLE TO THE REVOLUTION [245] which was published in 1974. This is a collection of essays -- some good, some bad. Virginia Cowles' THE RUSSIAN DAGGER: COLD WAR IN THE DAYS OF THE CZARS [128] deals with the intrigues of Russia in the Balkans from 1840 to 1914. There are some distortions, but it is otherwise quite useful. Two articles in NCMH volumes 10 and 11, J.M.K. Vyvyan's "Russia in Europe and Asia" [580] and "Russia" [280], by J.L.H. Keep are excellent for the reader who wants a quick refresher on the course of Russian history in this period. George Vernadsky's

"On Some Parallel Trends in Russian and Turkish History" [574] is also interesting reading. RUSSIA AND THE BALKANS IN RUSSIAN FOREIGN POLICY: ESSAYS IN HISTORICAL PERSPECTIVE [309] was edited by Ivo Lederer and is very good. AN ATLAS OF RUSSIAN AND EAST EUROPEAN HISTORY [3] and RUSSIAN HISTORY ATLAS [194] are both useful references.

OCHERKI PO ISTORII YUZHNYKH SLAVIAN I RUSSKO-BALKANSKIKH SVYAZEI V 50-70-E GODY XIX V. [376] was written by S.A. Nikitin and published in Moscow in 1970. This is an interesting work dealing with Bulgaria that is quite apart from the normal and expected Marxist-Leninist dogma that appears in most present-day publications emanating out of the USSR. There is some, of course, but it is not enough to detract from the book's value. ISTORIA OTECHESTVENNOI VOENNO-ENTSIKLOPEDICHESKOI LITERATURII [32] is a 1980 publication that outlines the progress of Russian military literature throughout this period. Lastly, Ina Khitrova's CHERNOGORIYA V NATSIONALNO-OSVOBODITELNOM DVIZHENII NA BALKANAKH I RUSSO-CHERNOGORSKIE OTNOSHENIIA V 50-70-KH GODAKH XIX VEKA [281] is also a fairly recent publication (1979) and is fairly interesting but suffers from the heavy hand of the ideological editor.

## ENGLAND AND FRANCE

Although a majority of the literature covered in the section on the Great Powers deals with the policies and actions of England and France in the Balkans, there are a few works that deal specifically with one or the other of these two countries. ENGLAND IN THE NEAR EAST [541], for example, was written by Sir Harold Temperley and was published in 1936. Temperley also edited FOUNDATIONS OF BRITISH FOREIGN POLICY FROM PITT TO SALISBURY [542] that covers the period 1792 to 1902. Frank Bailey's BRITISH POLICY AND THE TURKISH REFORM MOVEMENT; A STUDY OF ANGLO-TURKISH RELATIONS, 1826-1853 [34] ends with the opening salvoes of the Crimean War. BRITISH FOREIGN POLICY IN EUROPE TO THE END OF THE 19th CENTURY [161], by H.E. Egerton, is a chronological index to the best sources of information on this important facet of England's role in the affairs of Europe. The book is for the Anglophile and there are some errors but it is still very good. The BRITISH DIPLOMATIC BLUEBOOKS: RUSSIA [203], and V.J. Puryear's ENGLAND, RUSSIA AND THE STRAITS QUESTION, 1844-1856 [423] deal with British relations with Imperial Russia. Bernadotte Schmitt's ENGLAND AND GERMANY, 1740-1914 [478] covers the Near East issues as well as the more central areas of contention between the two powers that led to the Great War. Gerald Clayton's BRITAIN AND THE EASTERN QUESTION: MISSOLONGHI TO GALLIPOLI [118] is also useful at this point. John Marlow's PERFIDIOUS ALBION: THE ORIGINS OF THE ANGLO-FRENCH RIVALRY IN THE LEVANT [340] outlines the ambivalence that existed between those two powers. Alyce Mange's THE NEAR EAST POLICY OF THE EMPEROR NAPOLEON III [337] is extremely useful because of the important role the French monarch played in Balkan affairs. FRANKREICH UND OSTMITTELEUROPA IM 19. JAHRHUNDERT; BEITRAGE ZUR POLITIK UND GESCHICHTE [61] covers French policy toward Romania, Hungary, Bohemia, and Poland to the end of the century.

## THE OPENING OF THE SECOND HALF OF THE 19TH CENTURY

There was little or no respite for the Balkans when the second half of the century began. Early in 1850, for instance,

British naval units blockaded Greek ports in an attempt to force payment of loans and claims. Although the matter was settled by compromise rather than bloodshed, this incident signalled the general tone that the next fifty years were to take. The primary cause of the problems in the Balkans came from the unresolved Eastern Question and its consequences, and the first attempt at its rectification took the form of the Crimean War. This war marked the ninth struggle between Imperial Russia and the Ottoman Turks and has been aptly called the dumbest war in history.

First of all, the war was not caused directly by a petty squabble concerning the protection of the Holy Places nor, as some claim, because Napoleon III instigated it nor because it was fulminated by Palmeston and Stratford. Rather it was the result of the smoldering discontent felt in Russia over the provisions of the Treaty of London (1840) and the Straits Convention of 1841 that effectively blocked the use of the Dardenelles to Russian warships. This discontent was pressed further when Nicholas I (1825-1855) deluded himself into believing that he had English support if he were to hasten the long-awaited demise of the Ottoman Empire. It is, of course, a fact that at that very moment, England was working to restore the health of "the Sick Man of Europe" so as to block further Russian aggrandizements in that region. This situation lasted from 1844 until 1852 when, in deference to French threats, the Sultan Abdul Medjid I (1839-1861) gave Louis Napoleon the keys to the Church of the Nativity. Russia took this as a direct affront and immediately demanded that the Porte acknowledge Russian rights to protect the Orthodox in Ottoman territory and recognition of Orthodox rights in the Holy Places. These demands were made in the full belief of English and Austrian support. After the British minister in Constantinople stiffened the Sultan's back, the Porte rejected the Russian ultimatum.

In July 1853 a Russian army commanded by General Field Marshal Prince Ivan Paskevich crossed the Pruth and began occupying the Danubian Principalities without a formal declaration of war. When Russia refused to answer the Porte's ultimatum (27 September) to withdraw these forces, a Turkish declaration of war followed. In the meantime, a Turkish army commanded by a Croatian named Michael Lattas (Omar Pasha) crossed the Danube and inflicted a defeat on the Russians near Oltenitza in Wallachia on 4 November 1853. Before the end of the month, however, Russia destroyed the Turkish fleet at Sinope (30 November). Within five weeks British and French squadrons were in the Black Sea in support of the Turks, although neither country immediately declared war. The declarations did not come until 28 March 1854, eight days after Russian forces crossed the Danube into Bulgarian territory. By 10 April an allied expeditionary force was ashore at Varna to block further Russian penetration into Bulgaria. Ten days later the Austrian government threatened Russia with war if it did not withdraw from the Principalities and entered into a defensive alliance with Prussia. An imperial army of about 50,000, that was massed in Transylvania and Galicia, moved into Wallachia and Moldavia (after 2 June and the signing of the Treaty of Boiacikoy). The Russian forces were obliged to withdraw and were out of the Balkans by mid-August. The Black Sea coastal ports in the Balkans were thereafter used as allied shipping bases.

Russia also refused an allied peace offer (often called the Vienna Four Points), and the war continued until after the death of Nicholas I in 1855 and the assumption of the Russian throne by Alexander II (1855-1881). After some hesitation, the fall of Sevastopol, and the threat of Austrian invasion, Alexander accepted terms on 17 January 1856. The Treaty of Paris was initialed on 30 March; and Russia stood the loser. A subsequent agreement that was signed on 15 April 1856 guaranteed English, French, and Austrian declarations of war in support of the Ottoman Empire if Russia violated the terms of the Paris treaty. To many the terms of the treaty marked the end of the conservative, monarchical association that had become the bastion against social change, and it brought an end to the Concert of Europe that had been the chief diplomatic instrument of stability on the continent since 1815.

There is a relatively massive amount of historical material available on this period. THE ORIGINS OF THE CRIMEAN WAR [198], by Brison Gooch, is a collection of interpretations about the genesis of the conflict. The Shaw's [498] do a very good job of explaining the Turkish side, as does Creasy [136]. Bekir Sidki Baykal discusses the problems of the Holy Places vis a vis the Porte in his "Makamat-i Mubareke Meselesi ve Babiali" [47]. Giurescu's CHRONOLOGICAL HISTORY OF ROMANIA [195] offers very little about the war, while G.H. Bolsover's "Nicholas I and the Partition of Turkey" [69] describes the Russian position that led it into the war.

A good general survey of the war is in Agatha Ramm's "The Crimean War" [425]. This article is in NCMH 10 and contains enough information to satisfy the average reader. A more thorough account may be found in Sir Edward Hamley's THE WAR IN THE CRIMEA [218] that has been reprinted from the original text which was first published in 1891. This is an excellent historical study by a well-known British military theorist of the last century. Colonel A.J. Barker's THE WAR AGAINST RUSSIA, 1854-1856 [40] must be used with some caution, on the other hand, as it is replete with a number of glaring errors that make it difficult to adhere to his other, seemingly accurate descriptions of the events upon the battlefield. Colonel Kadri Alasya's "The Turco-Russian War and the Crimean Expedition (1853-1856)" [9] deals at length with Russian operations in Wallachia and Moldavia. Wilhelm Treue's DER KRIMKRIEG UND SEINE BEDEUTUNG FUR DIE ENTSTEHUNG DER MODERNEN FLOTTEN [552] was written from research into records that were destroyed in World War II and may contain unique information. It is also important as it appraises the results of the war on western world military doctrinal development. Philip Warner attempts to reevaluate the war in THE CRIMEAN WAR: A REAPPRAISAL [584]. Once again, the details of battle appear accurate, but the author fails to understand the complex diplomatic situation that caused the war.

Sir Edward Hamley also wrote THE STORY OF THE CAMPAIGN OF SEBASTOPOL [217] which was first published in 1855. John Shelton Curtiss described the Russian forces in his "The Army of Nicholas I: Its Role and Character" [138], while Richard Delafield composed his REPORT ON THE ART OF WAR IN EUROPE IN 1854, 1855 & 1856 [146] in 1861. In Virginia Cowles' THE RUSSIAN DAGGER: COLD WAR IN THE DAYS OF THE CZARS [128], the author discusses subversion in the Balkans in the context of Russia's internal problems and external relations.

This is a good book for the general reader but not for the scholar. OCHERKI PO ISTORII YUZHNYKH SLAVIAN I RUSSKO-BALKANSKIKH SVYAZEI V 50-70-E GODY XIX V [376], by S.A. Nikitin, deals in part with the Balkan economic and political situation between 1853 and 1876. Paul Schroeder's AUSTRIA, GREAT BRITAIN, AND THE CRIMEAN WAR: THE DESTRUCTION OF THE EUROPEAN CONCERT [482] deals primarily with Austrian policy during the war, especially as it interacted with British foreign policy. This masterful work is an excellent source of information of the Eastern Question during the war years. Professor Schroeder's main point is that it was England that destroyed the Concert by preventing any meaningful negotiations that would have brought an earlier peace and a concommitant reduction in bloodshed. Ram Lakhan Shukla's BRITAIN, INDIA AND THE TURKISH EMPIRE, 1853-1882 [501] deals with another aspect of British relations with the Sublime Porte that was not directed toward the Balkans but impacted upon it nonetheless. FLORENCE NIGHTINGALE: REPUTATION AND POWER [513], by F.B. Smith, adds an interesting sidebar to the story of the war in its discussion of sanitary conditions in the field in those days.

## THE AFTERMATH OF THE CRIMEAN WAR

Kurt Rheindorf's DIE SCHWARZE-MEER-(PONTUS-) FRAGE VOM PARISER FRIEDEN VON 1856 BIS ZUM ABSCHLUSS DER LONDONER KONFERENZ VON 1871 [431] discusses the period from the Treaty of Paris, that ended the Crimean War, to the London Conference of 1871 in the context of the Black Sea as a part of the Eastern Question. THE RISE AND FALL OF THE CRIMEAN SYSTEM, 1855-71: THE STORY OF THE PEACE SETTLEMENT [366] is a collection of articles on the Eastern Question. This is a very good book. Another work of the same type is the EASTERN QUESTION FROM THE TREATY OF PARIS 1856 TO THE TREATY OF BERLIN 1878, AND TO THE SECOND AFGHAN WAR [92]. This book was written by George Douglas Campbell, the Eigth Duke of Argyll, and is more favorably disposed toward the British than either Mosse or Rheindorf appear to be. George Iseminger's doctoral dissertation "Britain's Eastern Policy and the Ottoman Christians, 1856-1877" [253] is also worth reading.

RUSSIA AND THE ROUMANIAN NATIONAL CAUSE, 1856-1859 [255], by Barbara Jelavich, deals with Russian diplomatic maneuvering in the period immediately following the war. Other aspects of the post-war period are discussed by M. Pinson in his "Ottoman Colinization of the Circassians in Rumeli After the Crimean War" [417], in R.H. Davison's REFORM IN THE OTTOMAN EMPIRE, 1856-1876 [142], and in Abdulhak Adnan's OSMANLI TURKLERINDE ILIM [7]. This last work deals with military reforms. Another interesting work is Monika Ritter's FRANKREICHS GRIECHENLAND-POLITIK WAHREND DES KRIMKRIEGES; IM SPIEGEL DER FRANZOSISCHEN UND DER BAYERISCHEN GESANDTSCHAFTSBERICHTE 1853-1857 [434]. The reign of Nicholas I is discussed in W. Bruce Lincoln's NICHOLAS I: EMPEROR AND AUTOCRAT OF ALL THE RUSSIAS [321].

## EVENTS IN THE BALKANS

A perusal of the foregoing works will clearly show that the post-war period was a time of intense activity in the Balkans. It should be remembered for instance that Russian troops withdrew across the Pruth between April and September 1854 following an Austrian ultimatum. Thereafter, Ottoman and Austrian troops occupied portions of the Principalities following a Turkish-Austrian Convention. By September the two princes who had fled to Vienna upon the arrival of the Russians were back on their thrones. In December, England, France, and Austria signed a treaty of alliance against Russia that, among other things, stipulated Austria's obligation to defend the Principalities and provided for the establishment of an allied commission to oversee the resolution of problems in that region. These terms were generally carried forward as a part of the Treaty of Paris that formally ended the war in March 1856. While those proceedings were underway, the Romanians were working to gain a union of the two Principalities and, at the same time, were protesting the continued allied insistence that the two were an integral part of the Ottoman Empire. In July 1857 the Turks rigged an election that put antiunionists in control of each of the provinces. These elections were immediately challenged by France, Russia, Prussia, and Sardinia; but not until after Napoleon III met with Queen Victoria in August 1857 were the Turks forced to void the elections. New elections were held almost immediately that cleared the way for the eventual unification of the Romanian provinces. At a subsequent Conference of the Seven Powers held in Paris in May 1858, further, if unwitting, steps were taken toward that end. The culmination of the movement came when both provinces elected the same prince, Colonel Alexandru Ioan Cuza (1859-1866), in January 1859 and the election was approved by the Seven Powers (September 1859). During that same year, Austria became involved in the Austro-French-Piemontese War that lasted about three months and was culminated in the Treaty of Zurich (10 November 1859). In 1860 Austria's emperor, Franz Joseph I, promulgated an edict called "The October Diploma" that declared Transylvania an autonomous state with the Austrian Empire.

In Bulgaria the struggle for independence from the Turks entered a new phase with the settlement of about 100,000 Tatars and Cicassians upon the lands and with the promulgation of a largely unenforced law granting equal rights to all subjects of the Sultan. The first result of these actions was the brutalization of the native population by the immigrants who used the Bulgarians to vent their anger and hatred for the Russians. The second result was a total breakdown of the economic system, such as it was, in Bulgaria that left the country destitute by 1875 and its people ready for revolt.

The attempted settlement of Turkish nationals affected not only the Bulgarians but the Serbians as well. Turkish garrisons in Serbia were surrounded by a proportionately large Moslem civilian population that rankled the natives. The situation was especially bad in Belgrad where trouble broke out in June 1862 after the garrison commander, Asir Pasha, threatened war if the Serbs attempted to prosecute Moslems in their courts. An incident at a water well led to the Turkish fortress opening fire on the city. A Serbian army converged on the city, but action by the Great Powers averted further bloodshed. What did come out of the incident was the clear fact that Turkish artillery was no good since the damage they had inflicted upon the city was almost negligible. Thereafter, the Turks set about upgrading their cannons. Of more particular importance was the Great Power alignment in the affair. England and Austria sided with the Turks while Russia and France stood in behalf of the Serbs. This was to be particularly important in the future.

This affair and the subsequent Kanlice Conference is discussed in great detail in Petrovich [413]. This book also discusses the series of alliances that developed among the Balkan states between 1860 and 1868 that were to be of extreme importance during the next few decades. Two works in Turkish that discuss some of these events are Bilal Siniser's RUMEL'I DEN TURK GOCLERI [505] and C. Orhonlu's "Balkan Turklerinin durumu" [392]. Siniser's work deals with Turk immigration in the Balkans while Orhunlu talks about the treatment of Turks in that region. Macdermott's A HISTORY OF BULGARIA, 1393-1885 [330] should not be overlooked.

THE SEVEN WEEKS' WAR

By June 1866 Europe again faced war this time over Bismarck's secret alliance with France that was roundly disapproved of by the members of the German Confederation. Austria suddenly found itself attacked by Prussian and Italian forces in what has been called the Austro-Prussian or Seven Weeks War of 1866. Although the war centered upon western Austria and Bavaria it had a direct impact upon the future of the Balkans. After the great battle at Koniggratz (Sadowa) on 3 July 1866, in which over 70,000 were lost or taken prisoner on both sides, Napoleon offered mediation. On 3 August 1866, the Treaty of Prague ended the conflict but not the animosity that existed between Berlin and Vienna. Thereafter, Bismarck rallied the new North German Confederation into an anti-French coalition that set the stage for the Franco-Prussian War.

When Bismarck viewed the success of Koniggratz he rightly reasoned that Napoleon would view the affair as a defeat for France. Bismarck set about, therefore, to incite a general enmity against the French and prepared for what appeared to be an inevitable conflict. In doing so, he left Austria to Russia's vengeful scrutiny. Still furious about Austria's treatment during the Crimean War, the Tsar took the occasion to seek once again to move on the Black Sea, an action that had been specifically prohibited by the Paris accords.

These events are reported in Colonel H.M. Hozier's THE SEVEN WEEKS' WAR: ITS ANTECEDENTS AND ITS INCIDENTS [244] and in Arthur Wagner's THE CAMPAIGN OF KONIGGRATZ: A STUDY OF THE AUSTRO-PRUSSIAN CONFLICT IN THE LIGHT OF THE AMERICAN CIVIL WAR [581]. Colonel Wagner was an American officer who was quite instrumental in the establishment of the U.S. Army's cavalry and infantry schools. Probably the best of all the accounts is Professor Gordon Craig's THE BATTLE OF KONIGGRATZ: PRUSSIA'S VICTORY OVER AUSTRIA, 1866 [129]. In this work Craig discusses the tactical considerations that affected the outcome of the battle pointing out that it was the brilliance of Moltke in ordering up Crown Prince Friedrich Wilhelm's Second Army at the crucial moment, rather than the assortment of new weapons the Prussians possessed, that won the field. Lastly, F.R. Bridge's FROM SADOWA TO SARAJEVO; THE FOREIGN POLICY OF AUSTRIA-HUNGARY, 1866-1914 [76] is not for the casual reader as the author often presumes knowledge without explanation.

Other works of interest on this period are Arthur May's THE HABSBURG MONARCHY, 1867-1914 [345] and Klaus Meyer's BIBLIOGRAPHIE

DER ARBEITEN ZUR OSTEUROPAISCHEN GESCHICHTE AUS DEN DEUTSCHSPRACHIGEN FACHZEITSCHRIFTEN 1858-1964 [353]. Gunther Rothenberg discusses the situation in Croatia in "The Struggle Over the Dissolution of the Croatian Military Border: 1850-1871 [448]. Another most useful source is HISTOIRE MILITAIRE DE LA BULGARIE, 681-1945. BIBLIOGRAPHIE [86] that was published in two volumes in 1973. Erich Eyck's BISMARCK AND THE GERMAN EMPIRE [167] and MOLTKE; A BIOGRAPHICAL AND CRITICAL STUDY [364], by William Morris, are both good sources on the Prussian leadership of this period. Gordon Craig's "The System of Alliances and the Balance of Power" [131]; J.M.K. Vyvyan's "Russia in Europe and Asia" [580]; and C.A. Macartney's "The Austrian Empire and Its Problems, 1848-67" [329] are all useful and are all found in NCMH 10. Two other worthwhile articles in that same publication are Micheal Lewis's "Armed Forces and the Art of War: Navies" [319] and B.H. Liddell-Hart's companion piece on "Armies" [320]. Gunther Rothenberg's THE ARMY OF FRANCIS JOSEPH [451] is very worthwhile at this point as is Albert Freiherr von Margutti's EMPEROR FRANCIS JOSEPH I AND HIS TIMES [338]. Anatol Murad's FRANZ JOSEPH I OF AUSTRIA AND HIS EMPIRE [369] is not worth the effort to read. Arthur Banks' A WORLD ATLAS OF MILITARY HISTORY, 1860-1945 [38] is also of some value. Some other works that discuss this period are Petrovich [413]; Dupuy [157]; Stavrianos [520, 521]; and Lessner [315]. Creasy's fine HISTORY OF THE OTTOMAN TURKS [136] deals with some of these issues in its last pages.

## THE SECOND GREEK WAR OF INDEPENDENCE

Also of importance were the events that transpired during this period in Greece. Parts of independent Greece had been occupied by British and French forces in 1854 after Greek forces had occupied Thessaly and Epirus. The allied intervention was carried out to prevent Greece from joining Russia in the Crimean War, but that affair ended well enough for the Greeks. In 1862, however, King Otho was deposed in a revolution that lasted from February to October and replaced by a Danish prince, George I, although there had been bitter debate over his choice or that of Leopold of Saxe-Coburg. Among George's first moves was the acquisition of the Ionian Islands. This was followed in early 1866 with the start of the so-called Second Greek War of Independence that began with the Cretan Revolution. Both Russia and Greece actively supported the rebels on the island. Turco-Egyptian forces numbered over 45,000 and eventually suppressed the uprising but not before suffering more than 20,000 killed and wounded. This activity is covered in great detail in Douglas Dakin's THE UNIFICATION OF GREECE, 1770-1923 [140] and is mentioned in Dupuy [157]. It is also discussed in GREECE AND THE GREAT POWERS, 1863-1875 [153], by Doman Dontas, and in Munir Aktepe's MEHMED SALAHI: GIRID MESLESI, 1866-1889 [8].

## ROMANIA FINDS A NEW PRINCE

Prince Cuza's reign over the unified Principalities ended in 1866 when he lost the coalition support that had made his reform program possible. His ouster was brought about by a palace coup involving a number of units in the capital garrison. Cuza was replaced by a triumvirate that ruled until the parliament was able to settle upon Carol of Hohenzollern-Sigmaringen (1866-1914) as the new prince (after 1888 as king). Other names had been proposed before his, but his election and subsequent acceptance would prove fortuitous. Romania's predicament during those days stemmed from the fact that the unification approved at Paris was conditional upon Cuza's remaining on the throne. Much of the activity concerned in Carol's assumption of office transpired at the same time that Austria was at war with Prussia and Italy. Carol was related to the king of Prussia and had to travel incognito across Austro-Hungarian territory to assume his throne. Austria's preoccupations elsewhere may have enabled all of this to transpire without a more vigorous response from Vienna. A Prussian on the Romanian throne was not something that lent itself to further Austrian aggrandizement in the region.

Carol's rule before and after 1877-1878 is covered in a number of sources. Giurescu's CHRONOLOGICAL HISTORY OF ROMANIA [195] has some data. Jessup's article entitled "Romanian Society and the Independence War of 1877-78" [267] describes Carol's role in the development of a fighting spirit in the army. Stavrianos [520] describes how Carol had to find Romania in an atlas when informed of his election to its throne. THE ESTABLISHMENT OF THE BALKAN STATES, 1804-1920 [263], by Charles and Barbara Jelavich, describes Carol's rule in some detail. Prince Cuza's influence upon the military is discussed in "The Military Reforms of Alexandru Ion Cuza and the Modernization of the Romanian Army" [53], by Dan Berindei. An article in Colburns' Magazine published in 1866 gives a contemporary view of "Roumania in 1866" [452]. A similar article, published in 1869, describes "Romania Since 1848" [444]. A third article, published in 1881, is entitled "Romania in 1866" [514]. Dumitru Preda's "The Status of Officers and Non-Commissioned Officers in the Romanian Army Over 1859-1877" [420] is also useful reading at this point.

## THE ESTABLISHMENT OF THE DUAL MONARCHY

Austria had been feeling the growing opposition of many of its subject states but none quite so strongly as that raised in Hungary. The Hungarians argued that they had the right to live under their own laws, even if under the protection of the Austrian crown. The crown felt, on the other hand, that Hungary was indivisibly a part of the kingdom and was answerable to the throne in all ways. By 1864 these arguments had become urgent as Vienna needed to know who could be counted upon in view of the threats it faced from France, Sardinia, and Prussia. Franz Joseph wanted the Hungarian crown firmly on his head but soon found it impossible without concessions that took some time to accomplish. Finally, on 8 June 1867 Franz Joseph was crowned king of Hungary, but Hungary was declared a constitutional monarchy, governed by its own laws and free of Austrian interference in its internal affairs. Defense and foreign policy were, however, concluded to be matters of common concern among all of the possessions. This meant, of course, that those actions would be dictated by Vienna. This affair is covered in detail by Macartney in his three works [327-329]. Another aspect of the activities involved in these events may be found in Gunther Rothenberg's "Toward a National Hungarian Army: The Military Compromise of 1868 and Its Consequences" [449]. Louis Eisenmann's LE COMPROMIS AUSTRO-HONGROIS DE 1867 - ETUDE SUR LE DUALISME [162] is exceptionally well written and has an excellent bibliography.

## THE DILESSI AFFAIR

More problems arose for Greece when brigandage along the Turkish border reached new heights. The Greek government had rejected plans to organize border forces to deal with the problem, and it might have continued unnoticed for years had it not been for an incident at Dilessi (near Marathon) on 11 April 1870 when a group of English and Italian diplomats was murdered by bandits who had taken them for ransom. Although there was much rhetoric, little was done. When the 1871 Conference on the Black Sea opened in London, the question was raised in terms dealing with a rectification of the Greco-Turkish border, but this move was rejected by the powers. This situation continued as a part of Greece's internal turmoil until the beginning of the 1876 crisis. Dakin [140] and Dontas [153] deal with this subject, but the best account is in Romilly Jenkins' THE DILESSI MURDERS, 1870 [266].

## THE FRANCO-PRUSSIAN WAR, 1870-1871

The basic cause of the Franco-Prussian War, like the Austro-Prussian War, was political power. France was attempting to regain lost power and prestige; Prussia sought to capitalize on its success against Austria and gain the unification of Germany. Some see an aura of inevitability in the actions of both nations between 1866 and 1870. Relations between France and Prussia, that had been deteriorating for the better part of a decade, now simply fell apart. The rapid advances in Prussian military power seriously concerned Napoleon III, and France became determined not to allow a shift in the European balance of power in Berlin's favor. Moltke assured Bismarck the Prussian army was ready, and clever diplomatic moves forced France to declare war on 19 July 1870.

There was little direct effect from the war on the Balkans. A number of Balkan officers, especially Romanians, are known to have fought in the war, apparently on both sides. The Romanian populace was favorable to the French, but the Hohenzollern on the throne in Bucharest probably helped sway some to the Prussian cause. Regardless, valuable combat experience accrued that would be of great importance in the near future.

As to the war itself, the Prussian victory changed the balance of the political and military power structures for all time in Europe. France was humiliated and was replaced as the dominant continental power; and the General Staff concept espoused by the Germans was emulated, with a few exceptions, around the world. Of equal importance was the fact that the change in Germany's status led to the alienation of England, Russia, and Italy and their eventual alignment against Germany in the Great War.

For the needs of the student in Balkan military history, Micheal Howard's THE FRANCO-PRUSSIAN WAR: THE GERMAN INVASION OF FRANCE [242] should suffice. Some additional works of interest include John Abbott's PRUSSIA AND THE FRANCO-PRUSSIAN WAR [1] which is a contemporary account, and Egmont Fehleisen's DER DEUTSCH FRANZOSISCHE KRIEG 1870-71, IN WORT UND BILD [169] that contains a number of large plates giving details of the war. The situation in France is discussed in THE FRENCH REVOLUTION OF 1870-1871 [592] by

Roger L. Williams while Richard Millman's BRITISH FOREIGN POLICY AND THE COMING OF THE FRANCO-PRUSSIAN WAR [355] describes the English position from Koniggratz to the French declaration of war on 15 July 1870. Lastly, William Langer's EUROPEAN ALLIANCES AND ALIGNMENTS, 1871-1890 [301] deals with the post-war balance of power structure that led directly into World War I.

## THE RUSSO-TURKISH WAR OF 1877-1878

The 1870s was truly one of the most exciting decades in Balkan history. Although Austria had maintained neutrality in the Franco-Prussian War, much to the dislike of France, it found itself in serious disarray when the bottom fell out of the stock market in 1873. This was due, in part, to the Austrian's propensity for issuing bogus stock, especially in the period immediately after the disastrous Austro-Prussian War of 1866. Therefore, when serious trouble broke out in the Balkans in 1875, the Viennese were licking their collective financial wounds.

Turkey had avoided involvement in the Franco-Prussian dispute but this is not to say that it was not affected by its outcome. Bismarck, in an attempt to keep France immobilized, sought Russia's support by denouncing the terms of the Paris Accords of 1856 that prevented Russia from building a Black Sea navy. In addition, events that transpired after 1869 threatened the Tanzimat reforms and led to the ouster of Abdulaziz (1861-1876) and his replacement with Abdulhamit II (1876-1909) after the very brief reign of Murad V (1876).

In Russia it was the time of Michael Bakunin and Peter Lavrov and the tendency toward radicalism and the Narodniki. Militarily, Russia had put down the Second Polish Revolution (1863-1864) and had conquered large sections of Central Asia, mainly as a result of the reforms instituted following the Crimean War. In 1874, for example, Russia instituted universal military service that required all male youths, irrespective of class, to be liable for six years of military service on their twentieth birthdays.

The problems that led to the outbreak of war in the Balkans are extremely complex and are beyond the scope of this brief discussion. It will have to suffice to point out that, in the military sense, the troubles began at the beginning of the decade when Napoleon III attempted to make territorial gains in the Balkans through an anti-Prussian alliance with Austria. Secret meetings involving the Archduke Albrecht took place in Paris but were overshadowed by the demise of Maximilian in Mexico. In addition to Franz Josef's distrust of Napoleon, his prime minister, Count Julius Andrassy, and his foreign minister, Count Friedrich von Beust, counseled caution lest the delicate balance of the Compromise of 1867 be upset. This culminated in the announcement of Austrian neutrality that helped trigger the Franco-Prussian War. One result of this was Napoleon's informing Romania that there would be no further financial support forthcoming.

With attention thus drawn elsewhere, discontent in many areas in the Balkans flared into open violence. During the Franco-Prussian War, for instance, Romanian mobs, unchecked by the police, attacked the Prussian quarter where the inhabitants were celebrating Prussian victories. Even in view of the end of the French largesse, sympathies still remained with France. The real trouble began when a Russian-inspired uprising broke out in Herzogovina in 1874. Turkish troops were employed to quell the disturbances in which many Christians were allegedly killed by the Muslim soldiers. The rebels, supplied with arms from Montenegro, then turned their wrath on the Muslims, killing many innocent civilians.

The revolt soon spread to Bosnia and was soon joined in September 1875 by an uprising in Bulgaria (called the Stara Zagora Uprising) that failed because of lack of coordination and communications. In April 1876, however, another revolt began in Bulgaria which was savagely suppressed by Midhat Pasha. The sensationalism attending the press reports of the brutality of the Ottoman response helped seal the region to the fatal prospect of another war. Before the major struggle began, however, Serbia and Montenegro had entered the fight against the Turks (July 1876) because of the wanton massacring of Christians in Bosnia and Herzogovina. The Serbian army, liberally salted with Russian "volunteers," was defeated at Alexinatz (1 September 1876) and at Djunas (29 October 1876). Although the fighting died down, the die was cast; Russia began mobilizing its armies north of the Pruth. These events could not be concealed from the Turkish population; and as early as May 1876, anti-government riots broke out that culminated in the deposition of Abdulaziz.

Despite eleventh-hour appeals from the powers, including the convening of the Constantinople Conference in December 1876, in hopes of averting war, little was accomplished and those demands that were placed before the Sublime Porte were rejected (18 January 1877). The one positive action taken, the granting of a constitution by the Porte, brought a vehement reaction from the Balkan nations and only further exacerbated the already dangerous situation. On 4 April 1877, a secret convention was signed between Romania and Russia granting the Russians permission to cross Romanian territory with its armies. In return Russia promised to preserve and defend Romanian rights and territories, a promise they forgot immediately after peace was restored. Two days later the Romanian army was ordered mobilized. On 24 April Russia declared war on the Turks. Expecting a quick and easy victory, the Russians moved through Romania and, in June, crossed the Danube into Bulgaria. The Russians opened a second front in Transcaucasia in July.

The Russian army in the Balkans was commanded by the Grand Duke Nicholas and was eventually visited by the Tsar. Good progress was made, especially by Gourko's cavalry (18-19 July at Shipka Pass), until the Russians came upon a series of very strong redoubts near the Bulgarian town of Plevna (Pleven). After a series of unsuccessful attempts, the Russians sensed their weakening position and took the unprecedented step of asking the untested Romanians to reinforce them with their four divisions. Carol used the occasion to test his new position -- Romania had declared its independence from the Ottoman Empire on 9 May 1877 and demanded a separate command rather than having his troops used as replacements for the Russian units. Nicholas finally accepted those terms, and the Romanians crossed into Bulgaria on 19 July. By 10 August Romanian units were in the fight at Plevna, and after several assaults succeeded in breaching the Ottoman defenses. After a pitched battle that lasted through the night, the Romanians, reinforced by Russian units, took the redoubt. The Ottoman commander, Osman Pasha, surrendered to the Romanians (28 November). Following the surrender at Plevna, Serbia again declared war on Turkey.

The war continued with several major battles being fought at Rahova (Orekhovo), Opanez, Sofia, Senova, and Smirdan. Thereupon, advance elements of the Russian army entered the outskirts of Constantinople (30 January 1878). The following day the Turks sued for peace, and the Treaty of San Stefano was signed on 3 March 1878. Turkey was forced to cede a number of strategically important towns in the Caucasus to Russia. Russia was also given the province of Dobrudja (present day Romanian district east of the Danube) which they forced Romania to accept in return for southern Bessarabia. Romania, Serbia, and Montenegro were recognized as independent as were Russian plans for a large Bulgarian territory that extended to the Aegean. Bosnia and Herzogovina were declared semi-autonomous states.

These terms brought what should have been expected in the way of reaction from the powers. During June and July of 1878 a conference was held in Berlin that wiped out most of Russia's gains. Bulgaria was denied access to the Aegean and was divided into two territories. Serbian, Montenegran, and Romanian independence was confirmed. Serbia accepted Austrian support, while the northern Bulgarian territory, called Bulgaria, was occupied by Russian troops and advisors. Bosnia and Herzegovina were made administrative dependents of Austria-Hungary.

All of this was a great blow to Russia who saw its plans for easy access to the Mediterranean dashed in Berlin. Twice in a generation, Russia had been forced to bend to the will of the other powers, and Russia's hatred for England and distrust of Austria grew apace. Russian gloom was further deepened when Austria concluded a military alliance with Germany in 1879. This treaty formed the basis for the onset of the First World War.

The Russo-Turkish War of 1877-1878 was indeed an important event, but a study of the available literature overwhelms the senses with its depth and variety. No war up to that time, with the possible exception of the American Civil War, had so much contemporary material formulated about it. As one English officer said, upon his request for orders to travel to the scene of war, "it is the only war we have. . ." Following that view, officers from almost every continental power and from the United States, observed and, on several occasions, actively participated in the conflict. Even more significant were the large number of press correspondents who viewed the war from different aspects from both sides of the lines. Lastly, because of its obvious importance scholars of the period, and ever since, have studied the war in infinite detail, especially as its results led inexorably to the tragedy of 1914-1918.

GENERAL ACCOUNTS OF THE WAR PERIOD

All competent histories that deal with these times and places discuss this war. Unfortunately, they all do not do it very well. Many, for instance, ignore the Romanian contribution at Plevna, while others gloss over or fail to mention the roles played by the Bulgarians or Serbians in bringing the war to a successful conclusion. Clearly, Russia would have won the war without Romanian help, although there appears to have been some doubt about that at the time, especially in the minds of the Russian staff. A delay until spring 1878 would have allowed for the arrival of fresh troops from Russia, but such a delay might not have been politically possible for the Russians in view of rising concern among the powers that an all-out assault might have carried the Russians into Constantinople with all that portended. The fact is, however, that accuracy and good scholarship demand a full disclosure of data. Probably the simplest method of understanding the overall situation at that point in time is to read Francis H. Hinsley's MATERIAL PROGRESS AND WORLD-WIDE PROBLEMS, 1870-1898 [231], which is volume 11 in the NCMH series. Also of value in this regard is Leften Stavrianos' "Antecedents to the Balkan Revolutions of the Nineteenth Century" [519], that was published in JMH in 1957.

Dupuy [157] pays only passing notice of the Romanian participation, while Zook and Higham [604] devote one paragraph to the entire war. There is a short account of the war in "Rivalries in the Mediterranean, the Middle East and Egypt" [547], by Professor A.P. Thornton, and in J.L.H. Keep's "Russia" [279], both of which are in NCMH 11. In that same volume, Professor W.N. Medlicott discusses a number of important points such as conditions in the Balkans and the Ottoman Empire in the 1870s in his "Austria-Hungary, Turkey and the Balkans" [352]. Uta Bindreiter's DIE DIPLOMATISCHEN UND WIRTSCHAFTLICHEN BEZIEHUNGEN ZWISCHEN OSTERREICH-UNGARN UND RUMANIEN 1875-1878 [59] and BIBLIOGRAPHIE DER SLAVISTISCHEN ARBEITEN AUS DEN DEUTSCHSPRACHIGEN FACHZEITSCHRIFTEN, 1878-1963 [484], by Klaus-Dieter Seemann and Frank Siegmann, are both useful as sources of German-language material. The HANDBOOK FOR THE DIPLOMATIC HISTORY OF EUROPE, ASIA, AND AFRICA, 1870-1914 [19], by Frank Meloy Anderson and Amos Hershey, is also useful.

Robert Seton-Watson's THE RISE OF NATIONALITY IN THE BALKANS [493] and his THE EMANCIPATION OF SOUTH-EASTERN EUROPE [491] are valuable at this point, as is THE BALKANS IN TRANSITION [263], by Charles and Barbara Jelavich. Also of use is A.P. Thornton's "Rivalries in the Mediterranean, the Middle East and Egypt" [547]. Other works of varying value include David Mackenzie's THE SERBS AND RUSSIAN PANSLAVISM, 1875-1878 [332]; F.J. Dwyer's "R.A. Cross and the Eastern Question of 1875-1878" [159]; and Antonello Biaggi's NOTE RELAZIONI DI VIAGGIO NEI BALCANI [56]. This last work is taken from the official records of reports of Italian officers who were in the Balkans from 1876 to 1900 and who reported on politico-military situations, customs, dress, and social conditions in the regions of their various assignments. George H. Rupp's A WAVERING FRIENDSHIP: RUSSIA AND AUSTRIA, 1876-1878 [458] is also good reading.

The war is discussed in varying degrees of detail in Jelavich [263], Stavrianos [520], and in Norman Rich's THE AGE OF NATIONALISM AND REFORM, 1850-1890 [433]. The affair is barely mentioned in Clarkson [117], and Riasonovsky [432] devotes no more than a paragraph to it. Lessner's [315] account is short but good. Shaw's [499] version of the events is very pro-Turkish. Creasy tells the story as a footnote at the very end of his narrative. Macdermott has an excellent account in his A HISTORY OF BULGARIA, 1393-1885 [330].

Probably the most thorough coverage of the war is found in Colonel Sir Henry M. Hozier's five-volume THE RUSSO-TURKISH WAR: INCLUDING AN ACCOUNT OF THE RISE AND DECLINE OF THE OTTOMAN POWER, AND THE HISTORY OF THE EASTERN QUESTION [243]. It is written as contemporary history and therefore lacks an appreciation of the events that can only be achieved after a passage of time. Nevertheless, it is still one of the best. Other works of value include Benedict H. Sumner's RUSSIA AND THE BALKANS, 1870-1880 [533], which is probably the most complete scrutinization of the readily available information; Mihailo D. Stojanovic's THE GREAT POWERS AND THE BALKANS, 1875-1878 [529]; and Barbara B. Jelavich's THE OTTOMAN EMPIRE, THE GREAT POWERS, AND THE STRAITS QUESTION, 1870-1887 [256] in which the author traces the evolution of English and Russian domination of Turkish affairs up to the Balkan crisis of 1887. David Harris' A DIPLOMATIC HISTORY OF THE BALKAN CRISIS OF 1875-1878 [222] is especially useful at this point as is Professor William Langer's EUROPEAN ALLIANCES AND ALIGNMENTS, 1871-1890 [301].

The "Aspects de la crise d'Orient, 1875-1878: Etudes" [10], by L. Aleksic-Pejkovic and others, has a good bibliography. Stuart F. Weld's THE EASTERN QUESTION AND A SUPPRESSED CHAPTER OF HISTORY; NAPOLEON III AND THE KINGDOM OF ROUMANIA [588] discusses France's role in the crisis, while Noel L. Leathers does the same in his 1963 University of Oklahoma dissertation entitled "France and the Balkans, 1871-1879" [307]. Two interesting firsthand accounts of French relations with the Porte are found in MEMOIRES SUR L'AMBASSADE DE FRANCE IN TURQUIE ET SUR LE COMMERCE LES FRANCAISE DAN LE LEVANT [463], by Saints-Priest, and MEMOIRES HISTORIQUE SUR L'AMBASSADE DE FRANCE A CONSTANTINOPLE [145], by the Marquis de Bonnac.

The English position is studied in Richard Millman's BRITAIN AND THE EASTERN QUESTION, 1875-1878 [356] and in BRITAIN AND THE BALKAN CRISIS, 1875-1878 [593], by Walter Wirthwein. David Harris discusses the Bulgarian massacres in his BRITAIN AND THE BULGARIAN HORRORS OF 1876 [223], while R.T. Shannon looks at the internal British political situation in his GLADSTONE AND THE BULGARIAN AGITATION, 1876 [497]. A more encompassing view of the Balkan crisis that is based upon secret correspondence between St. Petersburg and the Russian embassy in London and other sources is found in Robert Seton-Watson's DISRAELI, GLADSTONE AND THE EASTERN QUESTION [490]. Lastly, ANDRASSY UND DISRAELI IM SOMMER DES JAHRES 1877 [150] is a Hungarian view of the relations between these two great leaders.

The purely military histories of the war include Major General Sir Frederich B. Maurice's THE RUSSO-TURKISH WAR 1877; A STRATEGICAL SKETCH [343]; Lieutenant Colonel Howard M.E. Brunker's STORY OF THE RUSSO-TURKISH WAR, 1877-78 (IN EUROPE) [80], J.D. O'Connor's excessively overtitled HISTORY OF TURKEY . . . AND THE CAUSES OF THE WAR OF 1877 [379]; "The Turco-Russian War (1877-1878)" [381], by N. Okse, which presents a Turkish view of the war; R.A. Hammond's A HISTORY OF THE EMPIRE AND THE PEOPLE OF TURKEY AND THE WAR IN THE EAST [219]; and Alexander J Schem's THE WAR IN THE EAST [474]. Grant R. Barnwell's THE RUSSO-TURKISH WAR [43] was published in Philadelphia in 1877 under that title and it was published that same year in New York under a title that began the same but carried on for more than 50 words. Linus P Brockett and Porter C. Bliss' THE CONQUEST OF TURKEY; OR, THE DECLINE AND FALL OF THE OTTOMAN EMPIRE, 1877-78 [79] was also published in Philadelphia in 1878. Byron Andrews' THE EASTERN CONFLICT; A BRIEF HISTORY OF THE RUSSO-TURKISH WAR [25] was published in Chicago in 1877. This gives rise to the question of whether or not these are good histories or merely journalistic concoctions thrown together in a rush to print. They are indeed both in most cases simply because they present the prevailing attitudes and biases as they were perceived at the time of the war.

There are three good works in French which have quite similar titles: Ferdinand Lecomte's two-volume GUERRE D'ORIENT EN 1876-1877 [308]; Amedee J. Le Faure's HISTOIRE DE LA GUERRE D'ORIENT (1877-78) [310]; and Mouzaffer-Talaat Pasha Bey's GUERRE D'ORIENT [368]. RUSSKO-TURETSKAYA VOINA 1877-1878 [565] was published in Moscow in 1977 at the time of the one-hundredth anniversary of the war and presents the Soviet view that the only purpose of the war was freeing the Balkans from the Ottoman Yoke as "brothers in arms." Two Bulgarian works are also quite interesting: RUSKO-TURSKATA OSVOBODITELNA VOINA, 1877-1878: BIBLIOGRAFSKI UKAZATEL NA LITERATURA NA BULGARSKI EZIK ZA PERIODA 1879-1976, which contains 3,800 Bulgarian language titles, many of which are annotated, in two volumes; and LA GUERRE DE LIBERATION RUSSO-TURQUE, 1877-1878. RECUEIL D'ARTICLES SUR LES PROBLEMES DE LA GUERRE [84].

OTHER WORKS ON THE PERIOD

In addition to the already mentioned works there are a number of other documents that deserve mention for the various ways in which they approach the subjects of the Eastern Question, the Balkans, and the Russo-Turkish War fought during this period. Two of these studies are Virginia Cowles' THE RUSSIAN DAGGER: COLD WAR IN THE DAYS OF THE CZARS [128] and Edmund Ollier's CASSEL'S ILLUSTRATED HISTORY OF THE RUSSO-TURKISH WAR [383]. The latter work is full of maps and illustrations and is in two volumes.

There are three studies dealing with the war in Bosnia-Herzogovina: William Stillman's HERZOGOVINA AND THE LATE UPRISING; THE CAUSE OF THE LATTER AND THE REMEDIES [525]; Arthur Evan's eyewitness account in THROUGH BOSNIA AND THE HERZOGOVINA ON FOOT DURING THE INSURRECTION, AUGUST AND SEPTEMBER 1875 [166]; and Charles Yriarte's BOSNIA ET HERZOGOVINE: SOUVENIRS DE VOYAGE PENDANT L'INSURRECTION [600]. All of these are interesting.

A larger body of literature exists that deals with the Bulgarian participation in the war. Konstantin Kosev deals with THE UPRISING OF APRIL 1876 IN BULGARIA [295] that was published in 1976 in Romania. A contemporary account of these events may be found in Wentworth Huyshe's THE LIBERATION OF BULGARIA; WAR NOTES IN 1877 [246]. Dojno Dojnov has produced L'INSURRECTION DE 1878-1879 [152] which contains resumes of the text in a number of languages including English. Stojan Penkov authored LES BULGARES ET LA GUERRE DE LIBERATION, 1877-1878 [409] that deals with Bulgarian volunteers in the Russian army and other forms of participation by Bulgarians during the Russian campaign. Another document dealing with that subject is LA LANDWEHR BULGARE, 1877-1878. EFFECTIFS [454], by Rumen

Rumenin. The Soviet version of the events up to the declared war on Turkey by Russia is covered in OSVODOZHENIE BOLGARII OT TURETSKOGO IGA, volume one of which is called OSVOBODITELNAYA BORBA YUZHNYKH SLAVIAN I ROSSIYA [377] that was edited by S.A. Nikitin and others. DIE SEELE DES BULGARENTUMS [603], by Gorjanin Zmei, was published in Sofia in 1941. Zvetana Pavlovska's PROBLEMES DE L'ARMEMENT DES FORCES REBELLES DU MOUVEMENT NATIONAL-REVOLUTIONNAIRE BULGARE, 1868-1876. MONOGRAPHIE [404] compares Turkish and Bulgarian arms during that crucial period. Sir Harold Temperley's THE BULGARIAN AND OTHER ATROCITIES [540], which was published in 1931, exposed much of Lord Derby's manipulation of data that occurred in the 1870's to present the Turks in a more favorable light. Temperley also dispels some of the more sensational reports of atrocities as fabrications.

Also of some importance are Bistra Tsvetkova's LA BATAILLE MEMORABLE DES PEUPLES [554] and Khristo Khristov's OSVOBOZHDENIETO NA BULGARIIA I POLITIKATA NA ZAPADNITE DURZHAVI, 1876-1878 [282]. Khristov's thesis, as well as Tsvetkova's, appears to have been formulated in Party headquarters rather than through a thorough investigation of the information. The basic idea set forth here is that only Russia stood against the Turks and that fact, coupled with the popular "liberation" movement in Bulgaria, freed the country from the Ottoman yoke. Another work in the same genre is the English-language BULGARIA 1878-1978, 100 YEARS SINCE ITS LIBERATION FROM OTTOMAN DOMINATION [528]. DER KRIEG 1877-78 UND DEI BEFREIUNG BULGARIENS [182], by P. Fortunatow, was published in Berlin in 1953. An earlier study of this subject is Alois Hajek's BULGARIENS BEFREIUNG [215]. Hajek's work centers on the country's development under Prince Alexander I (of Battenberg) (1879-1893). Much of this same information can be found in Macdermott [330], but his coverage ends in 1885. Arnold Haskell's HEROES AND ROSES: A VIEW OF BULGARIA [224] might be looked at here but it is not a scholarly work. Of much greater interest is Bilal Siniser's CONTRIBUTION A L'HISTOIRE DES POPULATION TURQUES EN BULGARIE, 1876-1880 [504] which was published in Turkey in 1966. Professor Constantin Velicki's paper presented on the occasion of the centennial of Romanian Independence deals with "The Support Granted by the Romanian People to the Liberation Fight of the Bulgarian People" [572] and is quite good. OCHERKI PO ISTORII YUZHNYKH SLAVIAN I RUSSKO-BALKANSKIKH SVYAZEI V 50-70-E GODY XIX V. [376] deals with the period between the Crimean War and the 1875-1878 struggle. It has many useful references.

The course of history in Serbia during this period may best be understood by studying Petrovich [413] and by reading David Mackenzie's THE SERBS AND RUSSIAN PAN-SLAVISM, 1875-1878 [332]. These works may be supplemented by VOJVODA STEPA STEPANOVIC U RATOVIMA SRBIJE 1876-1918 [510] which was written by Savo Skoko and Petar Opacic. This work deals with Serbia's wars and the part played by one of its participants to whom the authors ascribe heroic proportions. Another interesting work is Joseph Reinach's LA SERBIE ET LE MONTENEGRO [428] which was publish just at the beginning of the period in 1876. There are five works that deal with the personal experiences of westerners in the Serbian conflict: SERVICE IN SERVIA UNDER THE RED CROSS [407], by Emma M. Pearson and Louisa McLaughlin; REPORT OF THE OPERATIONS OF THE BRITISH NATIONAL SOCIETY FOR AID TO THE SICK AND WOUNDED IN WAR DURING THE SERVIAN WAR AGAINST TURKEY, 1876 [77]; AMELIA PEABODY TILESTON AND HER CANTEENS FOR THE SERBS [548], which was edited by her daughter, Mary Wilder (Foote)

Tileston; Alfred Wright's ADVENTURES IN SERVIA; OR, THE EXPERIENCES OF A MEDICAL FREELANCER AMONG THE BASHI-BAZOUKS [596], that was edited by Alfred Farquhar-Bernard and deals with experiences in the medical service of the Turks in that war; and Philip H.B. Salusbury's TWO MONTHS WITH TCHERNAIEFF IN SERVIA [465]. Salusbury was a British army infantry officer (1st Royal Cheshire Light Infantry) who was posted to the war zone and who observed and participated in the war through 1878. His accounts are among the very best available. In this account he relates the tale of his visit to the headquarters of General Mikhail G. Cherniaev who was a retired Russian officer of some distinction who arrived in Serbia in 1876 as an emissary of the Pan-Slavic Committee in St. Petersburg who stayed to become commander of the Serbian eastern army and helped bring about the defeat of Serbia. Another look at this same information is provided in "Panslavism in Practice: Cherniaev in Serbia (1876) [333]. Another account of medical practices in the war will be found in LETTERS RELATING TO THE OPERATIONS OF THE SOCIETY IN THE RUSSO-TURKISH WAR [78], by the British National Society for Aid to the Sick and Wounded in War, and its REPORT OF THE OPERATIONS OF THE SOCIETY DURING THE SERVIAN WAR AGAINST TURKEY, 1876 [77].

Imperial Russia's part in the war may be studied in Lydia Narochnitskaya's ROSSIYA I NATSIONALNO-OSVOBODITELNOE DVIZHENIE NA BALKANAKH, 1875-1878 GG.: K STOLETIYU RUS.-TUR. VOINY 1877-1878 GG. [372] that was published in Moscow in 1979. In 1878 the EDINBURGH REVIEW published a long article entitled "Russia and Roumania" [459] which is an excellent recounting of the events leading to the war. Pavel Ignat'ev's RUSSIAN INTRIGUES: SECRET DESPATCHES OF GENERAL IGNATIEFF AND CONSULAR AGENTS OF THE GREAT PANSLAVIC SOCIETIES [247] discusses the record of the Imperial Russian representative in Constantinople, Count Nicholas Ignatiev, who was a leading proponent of the Pan-Slavist movement started by Nicholas Danilevsky. Ignatiev's exaggerated reports from his post in the seat of the Turkish government convinced St. Petersburg of the overall Ottoman weakness and led to the decision to begin the war. THE RUSSIAN IMPERIAL ARMY [326], that was edited and compiled by M. Lyons, is a collection of unit records that will help in any detailed analysis of the Russian forces involved in the war.

Edward King's "With the Russians in Bulgaria" [284] is a frequent eyewitness reporter's view of the conduct of the Imperial Russian army after it crossed the Danube in 1877. Archibald Forbes' CZAR AND SULTAN; THE ADVENTURES OF A BRITISH LAD IN THE RUSSO-TURKISH WAR OF 1877-78 [178] is excellent. Forbes was a correspondent for the London Daily News, and his reporting is very well written. Of equal interest is the often rancorous report of Frederich Boyle, another British correspondent who was unceremoniously expelled not only from the war zone but also from Romania by the Russian High Command because of fears he was a Turkish spy. His THE NARRATIVE OF AN EXPELLED CORRESPONDENT [71] is full of insights into the Russian and the Romanian character. Another very good report is found in Captain Hime's "The Russo-Turkish Campaign of 1877-78: From a German, an English, and an American Point of View [229] that is printed in three issues of the UNITED SERVICES MAGAZINE. A firsthand Russian account found in English is Colonel Nicholai Epanchin's OPERATIONS OF GENERAL GOURKO'S ADVANCE GUARD IN 1877 [163].

Some exceptionally interesting insights may be gained from the works of F.V. Greene who was an American army officer assigned to St. Petersburg as military attache. He accompanied the Tsar's army into combat and prepared some of the most meticulous reports available on the war. SKETCHES OF ARMY LIFE IN RUSSIA [208] was published in 1880 after his return to the United States. Many of his papers are in the collection at the United States Army Military History Institute at Carlisle Barracks, Pennsylvania, or in the National Archives. Among his numerous documents are facsimiles of his official reports [209, 210] both from Constantinople and from the field. "War Between Russia and Turkey: Official Despatches and Reports" [207] is actually two scrapbooks of clippings and other notes that were taken from French language newspapers in St. Petersburg. They contain a wealth of information. His REPORT ON THE RUSSIAN ARMY AND ITS CAMPAIGNS IN TURKEY IN 1877-1878 [206] is also in two volumes and was first published in 1879. Greene's THE CAMPAIGN IN BULGARIA, 1877-1878 [211] was published in London in 1903.

Other works on the Russian army during this campaign include Adolf von Horetsky's AN EPITOME OF THE RUSSO-TURKISH WAR, 1877/78 [237]; Major John H.V. Crowe's work of the same title [137]; Major General Sir Thomas Fraser's "Some Notes on Military Engineering Incidents in the War of 1877-78" [183]; Lieutenant Colonel John C. Fife-Cookson's WITH THE ARMIES IN THE BALKANS AND AT GALLIPOLI IN 1877-1878 [170]; "Russian Mines on the Danube" [73]; DIE RUSSISCHEN KAVALLERIE-DIVISIONEN UND DIE ARMEE-OPERATIONEN IM BALKAN FELDZUG, 1877-78 [586], by Cardinal von Weddern, who had served as a Captain and teaching professor at the military academy at Metz. His work was published in 1878 in Berlin. Major General J.C. Dalton wrote "The Russian Field Artillery in the War of 1877-78" [141] which was published in the U.S. Army's Ordnance Notes in 1883. In an earlier edition of the Ordnance Notes John L. Needham produced "Lessons from the Late War" [373]. Colonel M.T. Sale reported on THE CONSTRUCTION OF MILITARY RAILWAYS BY THE RUSSIANS DURING THE WAR OF 1877 AND 1878 [464]. Colonel, the Honorable Frederich A. Wellesley, who was British military Attache in Russia, and who often physically took part in fighting leading Russian troops, wrote WITH THE RUSSIANS IN PEACE AND WAR; RECOLLECTIONS OF A MILITARY ATTACHE [589]. It is simply excellent. Irving Montagu describes his view of the war in WANDERINGS OF A WAR ARTIST [359] and in his CAMP AND STUDIO [360]. Alexander Jomini's RUSSIA IN THE EAST, 1876-1880. . .LETTERS OF A.G. JOMINI TO N.K. GIERS [269] is quite interesting as is General Hippolyte Langlois' LESSONS FROM TWO RECENT WARS (THE RUSSO-TURKISH and SOUTH AFRICAN WAR) [302]. Olga Novikova wrote SKOBELEFF AND THE SLAVONIC CAUSE [378] that was published in London in 1883. The London Daily News produced THE WAR CORRESPONDENCE OF THE "DAILY NEWS," 1877 WITH A CONNECTING NARRATIVE FORMING A CONTINUOUS HISTORY OF THE WAR BETWEEN RUSSIA AND TURKEY TO THE FALL OF KARS [139] in 1878. George B. McClellan, of American Civil War fame, wrote "The War in the East" [346] that was published in the NORTH AMERICAN REVIEW in 1877. RUSSIAN ATROCITIES IN ASIA AND EUROPE DURING THE MONTHS OF JUNE, JULY, AND AUGUST 1877 [460] is an unsigned collection of official and private telegrams that was appropriately published in Constantinople in 1877 apparently as a means of softening the criticism leveled at the Turks. The question of Turkish atrocities is discussed by the noted English journalist Januarius Mac Gahan in THE TURKISH ATROCITIES IN BULGARIA. LETTERS

OF THE SPECIAL CORRESPONDENT OF THE "DAILY NEWS" [331] which was published in London in 1876.

The Turkish side of the story is presented in "Tanzimat" [607], by A. Cevad Eren, and in Halil Inalcik's TANZIMAT VE BULGAR MESELEI [250] that deals with the Bulgarian rebellion of 1876. "NOVYE OSMANI" I BORBA ZA KONSTITUTSIYU 1876 G. V TURTSII [411] is the Soviet version of the struggle over the Turkish constitution. The various reigns during the period are covered in SULTAN AZIZ, HAYATI, HAL'I OLUMU [485], by Haluk Y. Sehsuvaroglu; in I.H. Uzuncarsili's "Murad V" [568]; by Sir Bernard Pears in the LIFE OF ABDUL HAMID [406]; by F. McCullagh in THE FALL OF ABD-UL-HAMID [347]; in "Abdulhamit devrinde donanma" [391] by O. Ondes; and in the REFORM IN THE OTTOMAN EMPIRE, 1856-1876 [142], by R.H. Davison. Probably one of the most important documents is Lieutenant General Valentine Baker-Pasha's WAR IN BULGARIA: A NARRATIVE OF PERSONAL EXPERIENCE [35]. Baker-Pasha was a British army colonel who left Her Majesty's Service under a very dark Victorian cloud. Baker-Pasha served in the Ottoman army and was eventually put in command of the defenses around Constantinople. His service was exemplary, but he resigned in disgust over the Turkish failures. Whatever his crime in England possibly connected with the Crimean fiasco, he was held in high esteem by his fellow officers who, as late -- or as early , as 1888 were commenting openly about his poor treatment by the British crown.

RESIMLERLE 93 HARLI. 1877-78 TURK-RUS SAVASI [393], by T.Y. Oztuna, is an illustrated history of the war. Henry Dwight wrote about TURKISH LIFE IN WAR TIME [158] in 1881. DAS TURKISCHE HEER [477], by L. von Schlozer, discusses the Ottoman army. Army operations are described in "Turkish Tactics in the War of 1877" [562]. William Achtermeier tells an interesting part of the story in "The Turkish Connection: The Saga of the Peabody-Martini Rifle" [2]. Two lengthy works on medical support are REPORT AND OPERATIONS OF THE STAFFORD HOUSE COMMITTEE FOR THE RELIEF OF SICK AND WOUNDED TURKISH SOLDIERS, RUSSO-TURKISH WAR, 1877-78 [517], and UNDER THE RED CRESCENT; ADVENTURES OF AN ENGLISH SURGEON WITH THE TURKISH ARMY AT PLEVNA AND ERZEROUM, 1877-1878 [461], by Sir Charles Ryan with John Sandes. Major W.G. Knox's Aldershot lecture presented on 4 October 1888 relates his PERSONAL REMINISCENCES OF THE TURCO-RUSSIAN WAR [289]. Knox was later knighted and rose to the rank of general in the British army.

The activity at Plevna is covered in Rupert Furneaux's THE SIEGE OF PLEVNA [186], "The Siege of Plevna" [63], that was produced in 1881 by the then Lieutenant Tasker H. Bliss; PLEVNA AND THE DEFENSE THERE MADE BY THE TURKS AGAINST THE RUSSIANS IN THE WAR OF 1877-78 [535], by First Baron Colonel G.S. Sydenham; and Lieutenant Colonel Thilo von Trotha's TACTICAL STUDIES ON THE BATTLES AROUND PLEVNA [553] which was translated from the German version at Fort Leavenworth in 1896. John Formby wrote on THE FIRST TWO BATTLES OF PLEVNA [180], while THIRD BATTLE OF PLEVNA, AUGUST 26-31 O.S. (SEPT. 7-12) 1877 [546] is reported on in the Occasional Papers of the Royal Engineer Institute. General Count F.E. Todleben, in another REIOP, has written about THE INVESTMENT OF THE FORTIFIED POSITION OF PLEVNA AND THE SURRENDER OF THE TURKISH ARMY, NOVEMBER 28, 1877 [549]. Major General G. von Schroeder produced DAS VERSCHANZE LAGER VON PLEVNA UND DIE RUSSISCH-RUMANISCHE ANGRIFF DESSELBEN VON 19 JUNI

BIS 10 DEZEMBER 1877 [481] in 1878. In 1889, Mouzaffer-Talaat Pasha Bey wrote a two-volume DEFENSE DE PLEVNA D'APRES LES DOCUMENTS OFFICIELS ET PRIVE [367], while a similar work was published in Paris entitled LE BLOCUS DE PLEVNA D'APRES LES ACHIVES HISTORIQUES [342]. THE DEFENCE OF PLEVNA, 1877. WRITTEN BY ONE WHO TOOK PART IN IT [226], by Frederich W. von Herbert tells a part of the Turkish side of the siege. Colonel Vasile Aleksandrescu tells of the important battle at Vidin in an RIHM article entitled "Boi rumunskoi armii v raione Vidina" [12], while THE BATTLE OF LOVCHA, 22 AUGUST O.S. (3 Sept. 1877) may be found in the REIOP of 1879. Lastly, Major General Constantin Olteanu presented "The Romanian Army in the Fights at Pleven" [385] at the centennial of Romanian independence in 1977. This paper was subsequently published in RIHM 36 that same year.

## MATERIAL ON ROMANIA IN ITS WAR FOR INDEPENDENCE

There has been a veritable deluge of books, articles, and other forms of documentation on Romania's part in the war. Although a number of studies were produced over the years, the torrent began in the late 1970s in conjunction with the celebration of the centennial anniversary of that war and the subsequent affirmation of the the independence that had been achieved. Among the western works that deal with the Russo-Turkish War, there is very little said about the Romanians and their contribution. Thus, it is likely that the Romanians felt obligated for that and for other reasons to flood the market with new, often repetitive, material. Much that is written is quite good, but it requires the cautious reader to separate what is good from what is published as ideological justification. This is, of course, true of all literature; and it is probable that the very volume of Romanian-produced material presents a more predictable basis for spotting the heavy-handed political editor.

There are also a number of western works and works published by Romanians in the west that ought to be mentioned: Edward King's "In Roumanian Land" [283] was published in two parts in LIPPENCOTT'S MONTHLY in 1878. It is exceptionally good reading and is replete with excellent engravings. Richard Burks' THE DIPLOMACY OF THE ROMANIAN WAR OF INDEPENDENCE [88] was first published in 1937 and has a good bibliography. Frederick Kellogg's "The Historiography of Romanian Independence" [280] is very useful and is an excellent bibliographic source. Professor Kellogg is one of the leading western authorities on Romania. "Romanian Society and the Independence War of 1877-78" [267], by John Jessup, looks at the Romanian struggle for recognition and independence through the eyes of contemporary western observers, primarily military men and newspaper correspondents. Lastly, in this group is the extensive coverage given to Philip H.B. Salusbury's "With the Roumanians in the '77 Campaign" [466]. This is the most detailed account of the Romanian military presence in the war by a foreign observer. Salusbury's work is published in a number of parts in the British UNITED SERVICES MAGAZINE. There are also two articles published in western journals by the Cornelia Bodea. These are "The New York Times About the Struggle for Independence" [66], and "Contemporary American Recordings of Romania: Unity and Independence" [67].

243

The Romanian works include Nichita Adaniloaie "1877 - A Decisive Moment in Modern Romanian History" [5]; his "Unele probleme privind razboiul de independenta, 1877-1878" [6]; Colonel Constantin Nicholae's "Echos de la guerre d'independence de la Roumanie dans les Etats non-engages dans le conflict" [375]; and Mircea Muscat's "Sur le passe de luttes du peuple roumain pour son unite et son independence" [371]. Alexandre Rubin wrote LA PROCLAMATION DE L'INDEPENDENCE DE LA ROUMANIE [453] in 1903. Dan Berindei's EPOCA UNIRII [50] relates the unification of the Principalities to the eventual independence of the country. Berindei also produced INDEPENDENT ROMANIA, 1877 [51] that was published in English in 1976 and "The Romanian War of Independence (1877-1878) [52]. Along with others he wrote RAZBOIUL PENTRU INDEPENDENTA NATIONALA, 1877-1878 [54]. This work was published in 1971. Major Generals Constantin Antip and Eugen Bantea delivered a paper entitled "The Significance of Winning National Independence in the 1877-1878 War for the Development of Romania's Armed Power" [28] at the 1977 PCRI. Stefan Pascu wrote on "The Romanian Army and Society, 1878-1920" [400]. Nicholae Corivan's LUPTA DIPLOMATICA PENTRU CUCERIREA INDEPENDENTEI ROMANIEI [127] discusses the struggle in the context of the Eastern Question and the attitudes of the western powers toward Romania's unilateral declaration of independence. Another view of this aspect of the war is found in RAZBOIUL PENTRU INDEPENDENTA ROMANIEI IN CONTEXTUL EUROPEAN (1875-1878) [111] by N. Ciachir. DRUM DE GLORII [109] is the short title of a work by Lieutenant General Ilie Ceaucescu and others that deals with a representation of the most significant moments of the war. MASELE POPULARE IN RAZBOIUL PENTRU CUCERIREA INDEPENDENTEI ABSOLUTE A ROMANIEI, 1877-1878 [419] was edited by Ion Popescu-Puturi. MASELE POPULARE SI RAZBOIUL DE INDEPENDENTA [386] was written by Constantin Olteanu. These last two works present the case for the masses and their involvement in the war. Probably the best prepared of all the more recent works is ROMANIA IN RAZBOIUL DE INDEPENDENTA: 1877-1878 [124] that was prepared under the direction of the former Minister of Defense, General Ion Coman. While this work is excellent it is flawed in places with political rhetoric unbefitting the book's importance as a historical record. Professor Stefan Pascu has written "La Contribution economique du peuple roumain a la Guerre d'Independence" [398]. Florian Tuca wrote "Romanian Society During the War of Independence" [556]. Colonel Tuca, along with Cornel Skafesh, also wrote "Istoricheskie zhurnalii ruminskikh chastei i coedinenii, uchastvovavshikh v kampanii 1877-1878 godov." [557] which is in Russian. A chronology of the events of the war is presented in CRONICA PARTICIPARII ARMATIEI ROMANE LA RAZBOIUL PENTRU INDEPENDENTA, 1877-1878 [442]. ISTORICI ROMANI SI STRINI DESPRE RAZBOIUL DE INDEPENDENTA AL ROMANIEI (1877-1878) [26], that was edited by General Antip, is a summary of Romanian, Turkish and other foreign studies dealing with the diplomatic and military preliminaries to the war and to the army's participation in the campaign south of the Danube. "Romania's Share in the War of 1877" [447] was the work of R. Rosetti and was published in 1930. Liviu Maior's TRANSILVANIA SI RAZBOIUL PENTRU INDEPENDENTA (1877-1878) [335] discusses the part played by Romanians living in Transylvania, which was under Austro-Hungarian control during the war.

Works of a purely military nature include Major General Constantin Olteanu's "Genese et developpment de l'armee permanente chez les Roumains" [389]. He also wrote "On the Organization of the Army in the Romanian Countries" [388] and "The Strategy and Tactics of the Romanian Army During the Independence War" [387]. Olteanu collaborated with General Ilie Ceaucescu in writing THE ROMANIAN ARMY IN THE WAR FOR ROMANIA'S STATE INDEPENDENCE OF 1877-1878 [390]. General Ceaucescu also wrote "Rahova's Carrying by the Romanian Army in November 1877" [106] and "Romania's Military Effort in the War of Independence" [105]. Nichita Adaniloaie wrote "La participation de l'armee roumaine a la guerre russo-turque de 1877-1878" [4] while Colonel Vasile Alexandrescu discussed the broader aspects of the army's role in building the nation in "The Romanian Army's Adherence to the Ideal of Making the Unitary Romanian National State" [11]. "The Armament and War Material from the Equipment of the Romanian Troops over 1877-1878" [100] was written by Constantin Cazanisteanu. Colonel Cazanisteanu and Captain Micheal Ionescu wrote RAZBOIUL NEATIRNARII ROMANIEI 1877-1877 [102] which deals with the military operations of the Romanian army during the war and a number of other relevant topics. "The Formation of the National Army and Its Development Down to the War of Independence" [437] was prepared by Colonel Romanescu who also wrote "Permanent and Temporary Military Structures During the 1877-1878 War" [439]. Colonel Savu presented a paper entitled "Romanian Military Art During the War" [470] that was read at the PCRI. "Romanian-Russian Military Cooperation During the Independence War" [563] was presented at that same conference by General of Army Ion Tutoveanu. A chronology of the war is presented in INTINERARE EROICE 1877-1878. JURNALE DE OPERATII ALE UNOR UNITATI RAZBOIUL INDEPENDENTA [441]. This work presents the order of battle of the Romanian forces in the war and a large amount of other useful data and statistics. Colonel Gheorghe Sanda wrote "Pages of the History of Romanian Military Medicine (up to the War of 1877-1878) [467].

Among the bibliographic and other reference sources, THE INDEPENDENCE OF ROMANIA, SELECTED BIBLIOGRAPHY [402], by Professor Pascu and Jean Livescu, is the best. It contains over 2,600 entries of works published between 1856 and 1977 that deal with the events leading to the proclamation of independence. This work is also published in Romanian [401]. A collection of selected works of historical and documentary value is ROMANIA IN RAZBOIUL PENTRU INDEPENDENTA (1877-1878). CONTRIBUTII BIBLIOGRAFICE [440]. A very similarly titled work, ROMANIA IN RAZBOIUL PENTRU INDEPENDENTA NATIONALA 1877-1878: CONTRIBUTII BIBLIOGRAFICE [108] was compiled by General Ceaucescu and V. Mocanu. Colonel Gheorghe Romanescu wrote "Documents concernant la guerre de 1877-1878" [438] that is published in RIHM 36. Lastly, Elena Palanceanu and a group of specialists prepared 1877-1878. MARTURII MUZEISTICE PRIVIND RAZBOIUL PENTRU CUCERIREA INDEPENDENTEI DE STAT A ROMANIEI [395]. This work is a summary of the artifactual evidence of the war preserved in the several excellent military museums in Romania.

TURKEY'S WAR WITH GREECE, 1878

After the success against the Turks at Plevna, the Serbians once again entered the war and the Cretans again rose up. There had been hesitation when the Russian assaults foundered but, with the victory at the Grivitsa Redoubt and the continuation of the Russian offensive, the opportunities for throwing off the hated Ottoman yoke never appeared better. After some posturing on the part of the Greek king, the Kanaris government resigned leaving Greece without effective leadership. Mobs roamed the streets of Athens until Alexandros Koumoundouros formed a new government and immediately moved to occupy Thessaly. That same day, 31 January 1878, the San Stefano treaty was signed. The Greek force consisted of about 25,000 troops including 10,000 second-line reservists. After a successful occupation the Greeks were forced to withdraw because of pressure from the powers.

Many of the Greek troops refused to give up the fight, however, and deserted to form guerrilla bands whose guerrilla activities were coordinated out of Athens. After successes in Thessaly, Macedonia, and Pieria, Turkish forces under Asaf Pasha reacted with severe repressive measures. Nonetheless, the revolt grew and spread. When the terms of San Stefano became known and Russian treachery made obvious, Greece had been ignored and was in effect reduced in size by the Russian-promoted Great Bulgaria. At Berlin all Greek claims were brushed aside as English diplomacy refused any support for their cause. By August 1878 the rebellion, especially in Greek Macedonia, was in full fury. At that juncture, The Porte ordered 15 battalions of Asiatic troops into the fight. Winter reduced the fighting but not the repression of the countryside; the campaign died out when the Greek government withdrew support to the rebels for diplomatic reasons. These events are mentioned in Dupuy [157] and are described in some detail in Dakin [140]. Doman Dontas' GREECE AND THE GREAT POWERS, 1863-1875 [153] is good as background reading. Other interesting studies include "King George I and the Expansion of Greece, 1875-1881" [339], by G. Markopoulos; Evangelos Kofos' GREECE AND THE EASTERN CRISIS, 1875-1878 [290]; and his THE MACEDONIAN REVOLUTION OF 1878 [291]. This last work by Professor Kofos is a compilation of archival resources that is a most valuable source of the little known rebellion of the Greeks in Ottoman-held Macedonia. Lastly, the volume 3 of Professor P. Karolides CONTEMPORARY HISTORY OF THE GREEKS AND THE OTHER PEOPLES OF THE EAST FROM 1821 TO 1921 [277] covers the period from the end of 1864 to 1900 and deals with many of the events discussed in this section.

## THE CONTINUING TROUBLES IN THE BALKANS

The victory over the Turks rang hollow after the Congress of Berlin. The Great Powers may have come away satisfied, but the satisfaction did not extend to Russia whose relations with the other dominant European states still centered upon the Eastern Question. Russia was confirmed in its hatred of England and suspicious of Austria-Hungary. As for Germany, to whom Russia had looked for support, little remained except bitterness. Bismarck would have liked to renew Germany's friendship with St. Petersburg but felt compelled to first establish a rapprochement with Vienna. This was effected by the Austro-German Treaty of 1879. As the main thrust of this agreement focussed on mutual support in case of a Russian attack, and as this treaty remained the pivot of European diplomacy until 1918, Russia only felt that much more isolated and lonely. One bright note for Russia was the reinstitution of the Three Emperors League in 1881. Although this treaty did not offset the 1879 Austro-German Alliance, it did give Russia the benefit of the knowledge that the other two signators would remain neutral should another war with Turkey erupt.

In general, the Balkans were not much better off. Bulgaria was divided, Romania smarted from Russia's duplicity in taking Bessarabia, and Serbia was compelled to accept Austro-Hungarian tutelage. For Romania, the acceptance by the world's powers of its independent status prompted the Parliament (14 March 1881) to proclaim the country a kingdom and to crown Carol as its first king (10 May). In Transylvania, however, unrest was still apparent among the Romanian population which sought the Principality's autonomy and the right to use the Romanian language. Then, in March 1883, the London Conference produced a document dealing with the regulation of the Danube. The Kingdom of Romania was not included and was forced to declare the treaty illegal. In October of that year, Romania entered into a secret defensive alliance with Austria-Hungary. Germany soon joined in this treaty that stayed in force until 1913.

The Three Emperors League received its first test in 1885 when it attempted to settle the irreconcilable: Austria and Russia's desires in the Balkans. Upon the death of the Russian Tsar Alexander II in 1881, the rule passed to Alexander III (1881-1894). The new Tsar Emperor looked upon Bulgaria as a vassal and expected that its ruler, Alexander of Battenberg, would respect Russian counsel in all affairs. This was not the case, however, and in 1885, without consulting with St. Petersburg, Bulgaria carried out a coup d'etat in September by which the reunification of the province of Rumelia was effected. Turkey immediately began massing troops along its border and the Russian Tsar refused any assistance as long as Battenberg remained on the throne in Sofia. Alexander III emphasized his point by withdrawing all Russian officers from the Bulgarian army.

All of this greatly upset the Serbian government which had its own ideas about territorial divisions in the region; and, on 14 November 1885, after being refused compensation, King Milan Obrenovic declared war on Bulgaria. The Serbian army was generally considered superior to the Bulgarian army, especially since the latter had lost its Russian officers, and a quick Serbian victory was expected. The Bulgarian army was also deployed along the Turkish frontier and was in no position to defend the western borders. The Serbian soldiery were told they were on their way to fight the Turks when they invaded Bulgaria. They soon found, however, that their opponent was a Bulgarian population determined not to lose what they only so recently gained. Before the end of November, the Bulgarians had been decisively defeated in battles at Slivnitsa, Pirot, and Belogradchik. On 3 March 1886, The Treaty of Bucharest was signed that ended the war and returned the Balkans to a period of relative calm. Battenberg was forced out in Bulgaria after the Russian Tsar engineered a palace coup in Sofia; but the Bulgarians, still not of a mind to bend to the Russian will, chose as their new ruler, Ferdinand of Saxe-Coburg, who was pro-Austrian and pro-German. The upshot of all this was that when the Three Emperors League came up for renewal in 1887, it was allowed to die. Russia was once again without German friends, and many of the more influential Russians thought it time to foster better relations with France. In 1889 Milan of Serbia was forced to abdicate in favor of his 13-year-old son.

These events are reported in Dupuy [157], Petrovich [413],

247

Jelavich [263], Stavrianos [520, 521], Seton-Watson [493], Biaggi [56], and Macdermott [330]. Macdermott has many of his dates wrong. A detailed source list may be found in HISTOIRE MILITAIRE DE LA BULGARIE, 681-1945. BIBLIOGRAPHIE [86]. Professor J.L.H. Keep discusses the beginning of the Russian courtship of France in his "Russia" [280], while Virginia Cowles presents a view of the Russian character in THE RUSSIAN DAGGER: COLD WAR IN THE DAYS OF THE CZARS [128]. 100-LETIE OSVOBOZHDENIYA BOLGARII OT OSMANSKOGO IGA 1878-1978 [566] stresses the role of the Imperial Russian army in freeing the Bulgarians. It was published in Moscow in 1978. Charles Jelavich takes a more impartial look at this situation in his TSARIST RUSSIA AND BALKAN NATIONALISM: RUSSIAN INFLUENCE IN THE INTERNAL AFFAIRS OF BULGARIA AND SERBIA, 1879-1886 [262]. The role of Constantin Pobedonostsev, Alexander III's Overprocurator of the Holy Synod, is discussed in Melvin Wren's "Pobedonostsev and Russian Influence in the Balkans, 1881-1888" [595]. Turkey's eclipse of power is dealt with in Barbara Jelavich's THE OTTOMAN EMPIRE, THE GREAT POWERS, AND THE STRAITS QUESTION, 1870-1887 [256]. Arnakis' THE NEAR EAST IN MODERN TIMES: THE OTTOMAN EMPIRE AND THE BALKANS TO 1900 [29] should also be studied. Mladen Zujovic's LE POUVOIR CONSTITUANT DANS LES CONSTITUTIONS SERBES [605] is also interesting reading at this point. Charles Jelavich reports on "The Revolt in Bosnia-Hercegovina, 1881-1882" [261] which is not mentioned in any of the other standard sources.

Included in works of a more general nature are Sir Robert Graves' STORM CENTRES OF THE NEAR EAST: PERSONAL MEMORIES, 1879-1929 [201], Mieczysaw Tanty's KONFLIKTY BALKANSKIE W LATACH 1878-1918 [536], John Morris' EUROPE, 1880-1945 [435], Heinz Gollwitzer's EUROPE AND THE AGE OF IMPERIALISM, 1880-1914 [196], and William Langer's EUROPEAN ALLIANCES AND ALIGNMENTS, 1871-1890 [301]. Another good study is Christ Anastasoff's THE TRAGIC PENINSULA: A HISTORY OF THE MACEDONIAN MOVEMENT FOR INDEPENDENCE SINCE 1878 [15]. Anastasoff also wrote A CENTURY OF BALKAN TURMOIL [16] which was published in 1941. THE CONGRESS OF BERLIN AND AFTER [351], by W.N. Medlicott, lays out much of the groundwork for what transpired after 1878. Lucian Boia's RELATIONSHIP'S BETWEEN ROMANIANS, CZECHS AND SLOVAKS (1848-1914) [68] must be used with caution as it represents a latter-day ideological notion of an amicability among these peoples that did not really exist. There are some good features in the book, however, even if it does not have a bibliography. Both Henry Lazelle [306] and F.V. Greene [204] discuss military improvements during this period in a complementary article published in 1882 in JMSI.

Stavro Skendi wrote ALBANIAN POLITICAL THOUGHT AND REVOLUTIONARY ACTIVITY, 1881-1912 [508] in 1954. This short piece was followed by THE ALBANIA NATIONAL AWAKENING, 1878-1912 [509] that was published at Princeton in 1967. Another work on Albania is William Ash's PICKAXE AND RIFLE [30]. FROM SADOWA TO SARAJEVO; THE FOREIGN POLICY OF AUSTRIA-HUNGARY [76] is also important at this point. This book was written by F.R. Bridge and discussed the course of events from Koniggratz to Sarajevo and the beginning of the First World War. Arthur May's THE HABSBURG MONARCHY, 1867-1914 [345] is also useful, as is BISMARCKS PRESSPOLITIK IN DER BULGARISCHEN KRISE UND DER ZUSAMMENBRUCH SEINER REGIERUNGSPRESSE (1885-1890) [230], by Helma Hink. Gheorghe Cazan and Serban Radelescu-Zoner studied Romanian participation in the alliances of the period in their ROMANIA SI TRIPLA ALIANTI, 1878-1914 [96]. Constantin Cazanisteanu and others edited DOCUMENTE PRIVIND ISTORIA MILITARA A POPORULUI ROMAN , MAI 1888-JULIE 1891 [101] in 1975. Frederick Moore's THE BALKAN TRAIL [362] might be reviewed here to better understand the events that are about to unfold.

THE EMBASSY OF SIR WILLIAM WHITE AT CONSTANTINOPLE, 1886-1891 [512], by Colin Smith, reflects British policy toward Turkey. Germany's increased interest in Ottoman affairs is studied in Hajo Holborn's DEUTSCHLAND UND DIE TURKIE, 1878-1890 [233], while Pertev Demirhan wrote a biography of General Kolmar Baron von der Goltz who, as a major (later colonel), took over the German military mission in 1883 and who remained in Turkey for 33 years influencing every facet of the Ottoman military structure. Demirhan's work is in Turkish and is called GOLTZ PASANIN HATIRASI VE HAL TERCUMESI [148]. Von Scholzer's DAS TURKISCH HEER [477] is also of value at this point. Ibnulemin Mahmud Kemal Inal discusses the last Grand Viziers in the Ottoman Empire in his OSMANLI DEVRINDE SON SADRAZAMLAR [249]. Mehmed Ziki Pakalm does the same thing in his SON SADRAZAMLAR VE BASVEKILLER [394].

## ANOTHER OUTBREAK ON CRETE

Another uprising that had been brewing for some time broke out on Crete. In May 1896 Cretan rebels surrounded the Turkish garrison at Vamos. In reprisal the Turks began indiscriminately massacring civilians. Greece did nothing initially but did begin sending volunteers and arms to the rebels after the Turks strengthened their forces on the island. At this point (July), the powers stepped in and demanded a cessation of the flow of arms. The Greeks refused and war began on 17 April 1897. The struggle was marked by extraordinary ineptness on both sides and was short lived. An armistice was effected on 19 May and a formal treaty signed at Constantinople on 4 December. This war is amply covered in Dakin [140], Dupuy [157], and Karolides [277]. More detailed information can be found in "Osmanli Imparatorlugunda Girit isyanlari" [558], by C. Tukin; in DEVLET'I ALIYI'I OSMANIYI-YUNAN MUHAREBESI [544], by Suleyman Tevik and A. Zuhdi; and in A. Turat's L'INSURRECTION CRETOISE ET LA GUERRE GRECO-TURQUE [559]. A few other works of some importance include Carol's REMINISCENCES OF THE KING OF ROMANIA [276]; Thomas Duffy's RUSSIA'S BALKAN POLICY, 1894-1905 [155]; Frederic Morton's A NERVOUS SPLENDOR: VIENNA 1888/1889 [365]; ENGLAND AND THE NEAR EAST, 1896-1898 [396], by G.S. Papadopoulos; and R.N. Rundle's INTERNATIONAL AFFAIRS, 1890-1939 [456].

The chronological end of the century is an unsatisfactory separation in the flow of the events that were transpiring during those turbulent years. The outcome of the Franco-Prussian War opened an era that would not end until 1945 and may still be progressing today. Even so, the century ended and probably the only way to mark its passing is to quote Shakespeare: "What's past is prologue."

## BIBLIOGRAPHIC LISTING

1. Abbott, J.S.C. PRUSSIA AND THE FRANCO-PRUSSIAN WAR. Boston:
   1871.

2. Achtermeier, W.O. "The Turkish Connection: The Saga of the
   Peabody-Martini Rifle." MEN AT ARMS. (March/April 1979),
   12-21, 55-59.

3. Adams, A.E., et al. AN ATLAS OF RUSSIAN AND EAST EUROPEAN
   HISTORY. New York: 1967 [1967].

4. Adaniloaie, N. "La participation de l'armee roumaine a la
   guerre russo-turque de 1877-1878." RRH I No. 1 (1962).

5. _____."1877 - A Decisive Moment in Modern Romanian
   History." RRH II No.1 (1977), 64-105.

6. _____. "Unele probleme privind razboiul de independenta,
   1877-1878." STUDII X No. 6 (1957).

7. Adnan, A. OSMANLI TURKLERINDE ILIM. Istanbul: 1943.

8. Aktepe, M. MEHMED SALAHI: GIRID MESLESI, 1866-1889. Istanbul:
   1967.

9. Alasya, K. "The Turco-Russian War and the Crimean Expedition."
   RIHM 46 (1980), 119-136.

10. Aleksic-Pejkovic, L., et al. "Aspects de la crise d'Orient,
    1875-1878." RHMC 27. Paris: 1980.

11. Alexandrescu, V. "The Romanian Army's Adherence to the Ideal of
    Making the Unitary Romanian National State." ARS.
    Bucharest: 1980.

12. _____. "Boi rumunskoi armii v raione Vidina." RIHM 36
    (1977), 114-129.

13. Alger, J.I. THE QUEST FOR VICTORY: THE HISTORY OF THE
    PRINCIPLES OF WAR. CMH 30. Westport: 1981.

14. Allmayer-Beck, J.C., & Lessing, E. DIE KAISERLICHEN UND DIE
    KRIEGSVOLKER ARMEE, 1814-1914. Munich, Gutersloh, &
    Vienna: 1974.

15. Anastasoff, C. THE TRAGIC PENINSULA: A HISTORY OF THE
    MACEDONIAN MOVEMENT FOR INDEPENDENCE SINCE 1878. St.
    Louis: [c.1938].

16. _____. A CENTURY OF BALKAN TURMOIL. Indianapolis: 1941.

17. Ancel, J. MANUEL HISTORIQUE DE LA QUESTION D'ORIENT: 1792-1923. Paris: 1923.

18. Anderson, D.P. THE BALKAN VOLUNTEERS. London: 1968.

19. Anderson, F.M., & Hershey, A.S. HANDBOOK FOR THE DIPLOMATIC HISTORY OF EUROPE, ASIA, AND AFRICA, 1870-1914. New York: 1969 [1918].

20. Anderson, J.H. RUSSO-TURKISH WAR, 1877-8 IN EUROPE. London: 1910.

21. Anderson, M.S. THE EASTERN QUESTION, 1774-1923. London & New York: 1966.

22. _____. THE GREAT POWERS AND THE NEAR EAST (1774-1923). London: 1970

23. Anderson, R.C. NAVAL WARS OF THE LEVANT, 1559-1853. Princeton: 1952.

24. Andreski, S. MILITARY ORGANIZATION AND SOCIETY. 2nd ed. Berkeley: 1968.

25. Andrews, B. THE EASTERN CONFLICT; A BRIEF HISTORY OF THE RUSSO-TURKISH WAR. Chicago: 1877.

26. Antip, C., ed. ISTORICI ROMANI SI STRINI DESPRE RAZBOIUL DE INDEPENDENTA AL ROMANIEI (1877-1878). Bucharest: 1978.

27. _____. "The Idea of Partisan Warfare in a Romanian Work from the Mid-19th Century." PHRA. Bucharest: 1975.

28. Antip, C., & Bantea, E. "The Significance of Winning National Independence in the 1877-1878 War for the Development of Romania's Armed Power." PCRI. Bucharest: 1977.

29. Arnakis, G.G. THE NEAR EAST IN MODERN TIMES. Vol. 1: THE OTTOMAN EMPIRE AND THE BALKANS TO 1900. Austin & New York: 1969.

30. Ash, W. PICKAXE AND RIFLE. London: 1974.

31. Ayverdis, A. TURK TARINDE OSMANLI ASRLAR. Casalosu-Istanbul: 197?

32. Babin, A.I., et al. ISTORIA OTECHESTVENNOI VOENNO-ENTSIKLOPEDICHESKOI LITERATURII. Moscow: 1980.

33. Babinger, F.C.H. AUFSATZE UND ABHANDLUNGEN ZUR GESCHICHTE SUDOSTEUROPAS UND DER LEVANTE. 3 vols. Munich: 1962-1976.

34. Bailey, F.E. BRITISH POLICY AND THE TURKISH REFORM MOVEMENT; A STUDY OF ANGLO-TURKISH RELATIONS, 1826-1853. New York: 1982.

35. Baker-Pasha, V., Lt.Gen. WAR IN BULGARIA: A NARRATIVE OF PERSONAL EXPERIENCE. London: 1879.

36. Balck, W. TACTICS. 2 vols. Trans. by William Krueger. Fort Leavenworth: 1911-1914.

37. Balfour, M. THE KAISER AND HIS TIMES. New York: 1972.

38. Banks, A. A WORLD ATLAS OF MILITARY HISTORY, 1860-1945. New York: 1978.

39. Barber, N. THE SULTANS. New York: 1973.

40. Barker, A.J. THE WAR AGAINST RUSSIA, 1854-1856. New York: 1971.

41. Barker, E. MACEDONIA: ITS PLACE IN BALKAN POWER POLITICS. RIIA. Westport: 1980 [1950].

42. Barnes, T.G., & Feldman, G.D. NATIONALISM, INDUSTRIALIZATION, AND DEMOCRACY, 1815-1914. Vol. 3 in A DOCUMENTARY HISTORY OF MODERN EUROPE. Washington: 1980.

43. Barnwell, G.R. THE RUSSO-TURKISH WAR. New York & Philadelphia: 1877.

44. Basila, I. BIBLIOGRAFIA RAZBOIULI PENTRU INDEPENDENTA, 1877-1878. Bucharest: 1927.

45. Basri Beg. L'ALBANIE INDEPENDANTE ET L'EMPIRE KHALIFAL OTTOMAN. Paris: 1920 [c.1919].

46. "The Battle of Lovcha, 22 Aug. OS. (3 Sept. 1877)." REVUE MILITAIRE DE L'ETRANGER, REIOP (1879).

47. Baykal, B.S. "Makamat-i Mubareke Meselesi ve Babiali." BELLETIN 23 (1959), 241-266.

48. Berend, I.T., & Ranki, G. ECONOMIC DEVELOPMENT IN EAST CENTRAL EUROPE IN THE 19TH AND 20TH CENTURIES. New York: 1974.

49. Berghahn, V.R. MILITARISM: THE HISTORY OF AN INTERNATIONAL DEBATE, 1860-1979. New York: 1982.

50. Berindei, D. EPOCA UNIRII. Bucharest: 1979.

51. _____. INDEPENDENT ROMANIA, 1877. Ed. by R. Zaharia. Trans. by Dr. Leon Levitchi. Bucharest: 1976.

52. _____. "The Romanian War of Independence (1877-1878)." PHRA. BHR Monograph XV. Bucharest: 1975.

53. _____. "The Military Reforms of Alexandru Ion Cuza and the Modernization of the Romanian Army." TRTI. New York: 1983.

54. Berindei, D., et al. RAZBOIUL PENTRU INDEPENDENTA NATIONALA, 1877-1878. Bucharest : 1971.

55. Best, G. WAR AND SOCIETY IN REVOLUTIONARY EUROPE, 1770-1870.
New York: 1982.

56. Biaggi, A. NOTE E RELAZIONI DI VIAGGIO NEI BALCANI. Rome: 1979.

57. BIBLIOGRAPHIC GUIDE TO MAPS AND ATLASES: 1981. Boston: 1982.

58. BIBLIOGRAPHIC GUIDE TO SOVIET AND EAST EUROPEAN STUDIES: 1981.
Boston: 1982.

59. Bindreiter, U. DIE DIPLOMATISCHEN UND WIRTSCHAFTLICHEN
BEZIEHUNGEN ZWISCHEN OSTERREICH-UNGARN UND RUMANIEN
1875-1878. Vienna, Graz, Cologne: 1976.

60. Birdeanu, N., & Nicholescu, D. CONTRIBUTII LA ISTORIA MARINEI
ROMANE. DIN CELE MAI VECHI TIMPURI PINA IN 1918.
Bucharest: 1979.

61. Birke, E. FRANKREICH UND OSTMITTELEUROPA IM 19. JAHRHUNDERT;
BEITRAGE ZUR POLITIK UND GESCHICHTE. Koln & Bohlau: 1960.

62. Blainey, G. THE CAUSES OF WAR. New York: 1973.

63. Bliss, T. "The Siege of Plevna." JMSI 5 (1881),11-59.

64. Blum, J., et al. THE EMERGENCE OF THE EUROPEAN WORLD. Boston:
1966.

65. Bodea, C. THE ROMANIANS' STRUGGLE FOR UNIFICATION. BHR Studies
25. Bucharest: 1970.

66. _____. "The New York Times About the Struggle for
Independence." RESEE 3 (1977).

67. _____. "Contemporary American Reading of Romania: Unity and
Independence." EEQ XII No. 3 (1977), 359-367.

68. Boia, L. RELATIONSHIPS BETWEEN ROMANIANS, CZECHS AND SLOVAKS
(1848-1914). BHR Studies 54. Bucharest: 1977.

69. Bolsover, G.H. "Nicholas I and the Partition of Turkey." SEER
27 (1948), 115-145.

70. Borsody, S. "Modern Hungarian Historiography." JMH XXIV (),
398-405.

71. Boyle, F. THE NARRATIVE OF AN EXPELLED CORRESPONDENT. London:
1877.

72. Bradley, J.F.N. CZECHO-SLOVAKIA: A SHORT HISTORY. Edinburgh:
1971.

73. Brainard. A.P. "Russian Mines on the Danube." USNIP XCI,7 (July
1965), 51-66.

74. Braun, M. "Turkenherrschaft und Turkenkampf bei den
Balkenslawen." WaG VI (1940), 124-139.

75. Brayton, A.A., & Landwehr, S.J. THE POLITICS OF WAR AND PEACE: A SURVEY OF THOUGHT. Washington: [1981].

76. Bridge, F.R. FROM SADOWA TO SARAJEVO; THE FOREIGN POLICY OF AUSTRIA-HUNGARY, 1866-1914. Edited by C.J. Lowe. London & Boston: 1972.

77. British National Society for Aid to the Sick and Wounded in War. REPORT OF THE OPERATIONS OF THE . . . DURING THE SERVIAN WAR AGAINST TURKEY, 1876. London: 1877.

78. _____. LETTERS RELATING TO THE OPERATIONS OF THE SOCIETY IN THE RUSSO-TURKISH WAR. In two parts. 2nd ed. London: 1877-1878.

79. Brockett, L.P., & Bliss, P.C. THE CONQUEST OF TURKEY: OR, THE DECLINE AND FALL OF THE OTTOMAN EMPIRE, 1877-78. PHILADELPHIA: 1878.

80. Brunker, H.M.E. STORY OF THE RUSSO-TURKISH WAR, 1877-78 (IN EUROPE). London: 1911.

81. Brusatti, A., ed. DIE WIRTSCHAFTLICHE ENTWICKLUNG. Vol. 1 in HABSBURGERMONARCHIE, 1848-1918. Vienna: 1973.

82. Bujac, J.L.E. PRECIS DE QUELQUES CAMPAGNES CONTEMPORAINES. Vol. 6. Paris: 1908 [1893].

83. Bulgaria. Naroda Biblioteka "Kiril i Metodii." RUSKO-TURSKATA OSVOBODITELNA VOINA, 1877-1878: BIBLIOGRAFSKI UKAZATEL NA LITERATURA NA BULGARSKI EZIK ZA PERIODA 1879-1976. Edited by Aneliia Vulcheva. Sofia: 1978.

84. _____. Institute of Military History. LA GUERRE DE LIBERATION RUSSO-TURQUE, 1877-1878. RECUEIL D'ARTICLES SUR LES PROBLEMES DE LA GUERRE. Sofia: 1977.

85. _____. Academy of Sciences. DOCUMENTS AND MATERIALS ON THE HISTORY OF THE BULGARIAN PEOPLE. Sofia: 1969.

86. _____. HISTOIRE MILITAIRE DE LA BULGARIE, 681-1945. BIBLIOGRAPHIE. 2 vols. Sofia: 1973.

87. Bullen, R., & Bridge, R. THE GREAT POWERS AND THE EUROPEAN STATES SYSTEM, 1815-1914. New York: 1980.

88. Burks, R.V. THE DIPLOMACY OF THE ROMANIAN WAR FOR INDEPENDENCE. Chicago: 1939 [1937].

89. Bury, J.P.T., ed. THE ZENITH OF EUROPEAN POWER, 1830-1870. Vol. 10 in NCMH. Cambridge: 1960.

90. _____. "Nationalities and Nationalism." NCMH 10. Cambridge: 1960.

91. Cammarata, F. ALBANICA. Palermo: 1968.

92. Campbell, G.D. (8th Duke of Argyll). EASTERN QUESTION FROM THE
    TREATY OF PARIS 1856 TO THE TREATY OF BERLIN 1878, AND TO
    THE SECOND AFGHAN WAR. London: 1879.

93. Cantor, N.F., & Werthman, M.S., eds. THE MAKING OF THE MODERN
    WORLD, 1815-1914. Arlington Heights: 1967.

94. Cantor, N.F., & Berner, S., eds. THE MODERN ERA, 1815 TO THE
    PRESENT. PEH 3. Arlington Heights: 1970.

95. Carsten, F.L., et al., eds. THE HAPSBURG MONARCHY. 2 vols.
    SREEH. New York: 1979.

96. Cazan, G.N., & Radelescu-Zoner, S. ROMANIA SI TRIPLA ALIANTA,
    1878-1914. Bucharest: 1979.

97. Cazanisteanu, C. "On the Development of the Modern Romanian
    Army from the Revolution of Tudor Vladimirescu in 1821 to
    the 1859 Union." PMHRP. Bucharest: 1980.

98. _____. "Tradition and Innovation in the Modern Romanian
    Army." ARS. Bucharest: 1980.

99. _____. "People's War in the Romanian Thought of the
    Mid-19th Century." PHRA. BHR Monograph XV. Bucharest:
    1975.

100. _____. "The Armament and War Material from the Equipment of
     the Romanian Troops over 1877-1878." PCRI. Bucharest:
     1977.

101. _____., et al., eds. DOCUMENTE PRIVIND ISTORIA MILITARA A
     POPORULUI ROMAN, MAI 1888-JULIE 1891. Bucharest: 1975.

102. Cazanisteanu, C., & Ionescu, M. RAZBOIUL NEATIRNARII ROMANIEI
     1877-1878. Bucharest: 1977.

103. Ceaucescu, I. THE ENTIRE PEOPLE'S WAR FOR THE HOMELAND'S
     DEFENCE WITH THE ROMANIANS. Bucharest: 1980. Also found in
     Romanian as RAZBOIUL INTREGULUI POPOR APARAREA PATRIEI LA
     ROMANI. Bucharest: 1980.

104. _____., ed. PAGES FROM THE MILITARY HISTORY OF THE ROMANIAN
     PEOPLE. Bucharest: 1980.

105. _____. "Romania's Military Effort in the War of
     Independence." PCRI. Bucharest: 1977.

106. _____. "Rahova's Carrying by the Romanian Army in November
     1877." RIHM 36 (1977), 97-113.

107. _____., ed. WAR, REVOLUTION, AND SOCIETY IN ROMANIA: THE
     ROAD TO INDEPENDENCE. EEM CXXXV. New York: 1983.

108. Ceaucescu, I., & Mocanu, V. ROMANIA IN RAZBOIUL PENTRU
     INDEPENDENTA NATIONALA 1877-1878: CONTRIBUTII
     BIBLIOGRAFICE. Bucharest: 1972.

109. Ceaucescu, I., et al. DRUM DE GLORII. PAGINI DIN EROISMUL
     ARMATEI ROMANE IN RAZBOIUL NOSTRU PENTRU INDEPENDEN.
     Craiova: 1977.

110. Chandler, D.G. ATLAS OF MILITARY STRATEGY. New York: 1980.

111. Ciachir, N. RAZBOIUL PENTRU INDEPENDENTA ROMANIEI IN CONTEXTUL
     EUROPEAN (1875-1878). Bucharest: 1977.

112. _____. ROMANIA IN SUD-ESTUL EUROPEI: (1848-1886).
     Bucharest: 1968.

113. _____. "Military Cooperation Between Romanians and the
     Peoples of the South of the Danube During the Ottoman
     Period." TRTI. New York: 1983.

114. Cirilli, G. JOURNAL DU SIEGE D'ADRIANOPLE (IMPRESSIONS D'UN
     ASSIEGE). Paris: 1913.

115. Clark, G., Sir., et al. THE NEW CAMBRIDGE MODERN HISTORY. 14
     vols. Cambridge: 1957-1970.

116. Clarke, J.J. "World Military History." GSUMH. Washington: 1979.

117. Clarkson, J.D. A HISTORY OF RUSSIA. New York: 1961.

118. Clayton, G.D. BRITAIN AND THE EASTERN QUESTION: MISSOLONGHI TO
     GALLIPOLI. New York: 1974.

119. Cleator, P.E. WEAPONS OF WAR. New York: 1968.

120. Clogg, R. A SHORT HISTORY OF MODERN GREECE. Berkeley: 1979.

121. Cobden, R. RUSSIA, TURKEY, AND ENGLAND. London: 1876.

122. Cohen, W.B. EUROPEAN EMPIRE BUILDING: NINETEENTH CENTURY
     IMPERIALISM. St. Louis: c.1980.

123. Colby, E. MASTERS OF MOBILE WARFARE. Princeton: 1943.

124. Coman, I., coord. ROMANIA IN RAZBOIUL DE INDEPENDENTA:
     1877-1878. Bucharest: 1977.

125. "Conditions and Political Relations in Romania, 1857."
     WESTMINISTER REVIEW 67 (1856-1857), 486ff.

126. Coquelle, P. HISTOIRE DU MONTENEGRO ET DE LA BOSNIE. Paris:
     1895.

127. Corivan, N. LUPTA DIPLOMATICA PENTRU CUCERIREA INDEPENDENTEI
     ROMANIEI. Bucharest: 1977.

128. Cowles, V. THE RUSSIAN DAGGER: COLD WAR IN THE DAYS OF THE
     CZARS. New York & Evanston: 1969.

129. Craig, G.A. THE BATTLE OF KONIGGRATZ: PRUSSIA'S VICTORY OVER
     AUSTRIA, 1866. Philadelphia: 1964.

130. _____. EUROPE SINCE 1815. New York: 1972 [c.1961].

131. _____. "The System of Alliances and the Balance of Power."
     NCMH 10. Cambridge: 1960.

132. Crainiceanu, G., Gen. DESPRE ISTORIA ARMATEI. Bucharest: 1912.

133. Crankshaw, E. BISMARCK. New York: 1983.

134. _____. THE FALL OF THE HOUSE OF HABSBURG. New York: 1983.

135. Crawley, C.W. "The Mediterranean." NCMH 10. Cambridge: 1960.

136. Creasy, E., Sir. HISTORY OF THE OTTOMAN TURKS. Beirut: 1961.

137. Crowe, J.H.V. An Epitome of the Russo-Turkish War, 1877-78.
     Woolwich: 1904.

138. Curtiss, J.S. "The Army of Nicholas I: Its Role and Character."
     AHR LXIII, 4 (July 1958), 880-889.

139. Daily News, London. THE WAR CORRESPONDENT OF THE "DAILY NEWS,"
     1877, WITH A CONNECTING NARRATIVE FORMING A CONTINUOUS
     HISTORY OF THE WAR BETWEEN RUSSIA AND TURKEY TO THE FALLS
     OF KARS. London: 1878.

140. Dakin, D. THE UNIFICATION OF GREECE, 1770-1923. London: 1972.

141. Dalton, J.C. "The Russian Field Artillery in the War of
     1877-78." Ordnance Note No. 262. ORDNANCE NOTES, U.S. ARMY
     ORDNANCE DEPARTMENT, 1873-1884. 12 vols. Washington:
     1873-1884.

142. Davison, R.H. REFORM IN THE OTTOMAN EMPIRE, 1856-1876.
     Princeton: 1963.

143. Dawn, C.E. FROM OTTOMANSHIP TO ARABISM. Urbana: 1973

144. De Bazancourt, L. EXPEDITION DE CRIMEE: CHRONIQUES DE LA GUERRE
     D'ORIENT. Paris: 1856.

145. de Bonnac, Marquis. MEMOIRE HISTORIQUE SUR L'AMBASSADE DE
     FRANCE A CONSTANTINOPLE. Paris: 1884.

146. Delafield, R. REPORT ON THE ART OF WAR IN EUROPE IN 1854, 1855,
     & 1856. Washington: 1861.

147. del Vayo, J.A. "Balkan Triangle." NATION CLXXV No. 12
     (September 20, 1952), 224.

148. Demihan, P. GOLTZ PASANIN HATIRASI VE HAL TERCUMESI. Istanbul:
     1949.

149. Denison, G.T. HISTORY OF CAVALRY. 2nd ed. London: 1913.

150. Dioszegi, I. ANDRASSY UND DISRAELI IM SOMMER DES JAHRES 1877.
     EHH. Budapest: 1980.

151. Djordjevic, D. REVOLUTIONS NATIONALES DES PEUPLES BALKANIQUES, 1804-1914. Edited by Jorjo Tadic. Trans. by Margita Ristic. Belgrad: 1965.

152. Dojnov, D. L'INSURRECTION DE 1878-1879. Sofia: 1979.

153. Dontas, D. GREECE AND THE GREAT POWERS, 1863-1875. Thessaloniki: 1966.

154. Driault, E. LA QUESTION D'ORIENT. 5th ed. Paris: 1912.

155. Duffy, T.G. RUSSIA'S BALKAN POLICY, 1894-1905. New York: c.1975.

156. Duggan, S.P.H. THE EASTERN QUESTION; A STUDY IN DIPLOMACY. New York: 1970.

157. Dupuy, R.E., & Dupuy, T.N. THE ENCYCLOPEDIA OF MILITARY HISTORY. rev. ed. New York: 1977 [1970].

158. Dwight, H.O. TURKISH LIFE IN WAR TIME. New York: 1881.

159. Dwyer, F.J. "R.A. Cross and the Eastern Question of 1875-1878." SEER XXXIX,93 (June 1961), 440-458.

160. Earle, E.M., ed. THE MAKERS OF MODERN STRATEGY: MILITARY THOUGHT FROM MACHIAVELLI TO HITLER. Princeton: 1943.

161. Egerton, H.E. BRITISH FOREIGN POLICY IN EUROPE TO THE END OF THE 19TH CENTURY. London: 1917.

162. Eisenmann, L. LE COMPROMIS AUSTRO-HONGROIS DE 1867 - ETUDE SUR LE DUALISME Paris: 1904.

163. Epanchin, N.A. OPERATIONS OF GENERAL GOURKO'S ADVANCE GUARD IN 1877. Trans. by Henry Havelock. London: 1900.

164. Omitted

165. Eton, W. A SURVEY OF THE TURKISH EMPIRE. New York: 1972.

166. Evans, A.J. THROUGH BOSNIA AND THE HERZOGOVINA ON FOOT DURING THE INSURRECTION, AUGUST AND SEPTEMBER 1875. London: 1875.

167. Eyck, E. BISMARCK AND THE GERMAN EMPIRE. London: 1968.

168. Falls, C. THE ART OF WAR. New York: 1961.

169. Fehleisen, E. DER DEUTSCH FRANZOSISCHE KRIEG 1870-71, IN WORT UND BILD. Reutlingen: 1904.

170. Fife-Cookson, J.C. WITH THE ARMIES IN THE BALKANS AND AT GALLIPOLI IN 1877-1878. London & New York: 1880.

171. Finlay, G. HISTORY OF GREECE, FROM ITS CONQUEST BY THE ROMANS TO THE PRESENT TIME, B.C. 164 TO A.D. 1864. New rev. ed. Edited by the Rev. H.F. Tozer. Oxford: 1877 [1851].

172. Fisher, S.N. "Ottoman Feudalism and Its Influence Upon the
     Balkans." HISTORIAN XV (Autumn 1952), 3-22.

173. Fisher-Galati, S. "The Hapsburg Monarchy and the Balkan
     Revolution." AHY II (1966), 1-10.

174. Florinsky, M.T. RUSSIA: A HISTORY AND AN INTERPRETATION. 2
     vols. New York: 1953.

175. Floyd, D., ed. A BIBLIOGRAPHY OF NINETEENTH CENTURY ARMED LAND
     CONFLICT. Wilmington: 1979.

176. Foot, M. "The Origins of the Franco-Prussian War and the
     Remaking of German." NCMH 10. Cambridge: 1960.

177. Omitted.

178. Forbes, A. CZAR AND SULTAN; THE ADVENTURES OF A BRITISH LAD IN
     THE RUSSO-TURKISH WAR OF 1877-78. New York: 1894.

179. Forbes, N., et al. THE BALKANS; A HISTORY OF BULGARIA, SERBIA,
     GREECE, RUMANIA, TURKEY. New York: [1970].

180. Formby, J. THE FIRST TWO BATTLES OF PLEVNA. London: 1910.

181. Forster, E.S. A SHORT HISTORY OF MODERN GREECE, 1821-1952. 3rd
     ed. rev. Edited by Douglas Dakin. London: 1958.

182. Fortunatow, P. DER KRIEG 1877-78 UND DIE BEFREIUNG BULGARIENS.
     Berlin: 1953.

183. Fraser, T. Maj. Gen. Sir. "Some Notes on Military Engineering
     Incidents in the War of 1877-78." REIOP. 1881.

184. Frischauer, R. THE IMPERIAL CROWN: THE STORY OF THE RISE AND
     FALL OF THE HOLY ROMAN AND AUSTRIAN EMPIRES. London: 1939.

185. Fuller, J.F.C. A MILITARY HISTORY OF THE WESTERN WORLD. 3 vols.
     New York: 1954-1955.

186. Furneaux, R. THE SIEGE OF PLEVNA. London: 1958.

187. Gaumant, E. LA FORMATION DE LA YOUGOSLAVIE, XVe-XXe
     SIECLES. Paris: 1931.

188. Genoff, G.P. BULGARIJA I EVROPA. SOFIA: 1940.

189. Genova, L. NATSIONALNOOSVOBODITELNI DVIZHENIIA NA BALKANSKITE
     NARODI: VTORATA POLOVINA NA XVIII V.--1878 G.: VUORUZHENA
     BORBA: BIBLIOGRAFIIA, 1966-1976. Sofia: 1978.

190. Gewehr, W. M. THE RISE OF NATIONALISM IN THE BALKANS,
     1800-1930. Hamden: 1967 [c.1931].

191. Gibb, H.A.R., Sir., & Bowen, H. ISLAMIC SOCIETY AND THE WEST. 2
     vols. London: 1950, 1957.

192. Gilbert, F. THE END OF THE EUROPEAN ERA, 1890 TO THE PRESENT.
     New York: 1970.

193. _____., gen. ed. THE NORTON HISTORY OF MODERN EUROPE. 6 vols. New York: 1970-.

194. Gilbert, M. RUSSIAN HISTORY ATLAS. New York: 1972.

195. Giurescu, C., et al., eds. CHRONOLOGICAL HISTORY OF ROMANIA. Bucharest: 1972.

196. Gollwitzer, H. EUROPE AND THE AGE OF IMPERIALISM, 1880-1914. LWC. New York & London: 1969.

197. Gomoiu, G. "The People's National Character of the Independence War." PCRI. Bucharest: 1977.

198. Gooch, B.D. THE ORIGINS OF THE CRIMEAN WAR. Lexington: 1969.

199. Gossip, R. TURKEY AND RUSSIA, THEIR RACES, HISTORY AND WARS. Edinburgh: 1879.

200. Grassi, M.A. CHARTE TURQUE EN ORGANIZATION RELIGIEUSE, CIVILE ET MILITAIRE DE L'EMPIRE OTTOMAN. 2 vols. Paris: 1925.

201. Graves, R.W., Sir. STORM CENTRES OF THE NEAR EAST: PERSONAL MEMOIRES, 1879-1929. New York: 1975 [1933].

202. Great Britain. Foreign Office Historical Section. THE BALKAN STATES. 2 vols. Wilmington: 1973 [1920].

203. _____. BRITISH DIPLOMATIC PARLIMENTARY PAPERS: RUSSIA. Irish University Press Area Studies Series. Microfiche. Shannon: c.1971.

204. Greene, F.V. "The Important Improvements in the Art of War During the Past Twenty Years and their Probable Effect on Future Military Operations." JMSI 4/13 (1883), 1-54.

205. _____. "Recent Changes in the Art of War." PNYSHA. No. 15 (1916), 156-175.

206. _____. REPORT ON THE RUSSIAN ARMY AND ITS CAMPAIGNS IN TURKEY IN 1877-1878. 2 vols. New York: 1879.

207. _____. "War Between Russia and Turkey: Official Despatches and Reports." Unpublished note and scrapbooks. 2 vols. Presently in USMHI, Carlisle Barracks, PA.

208. _____. SKETCHES OF ARMY LIFE IN RUSSIA. New York: 1881.

209. _____. FACSIMILE OF OFFICIAL REPORT - CONSTANTINOPLE, July 1, 1878. Presently in USMHI, Carlisle Barracks, PA.

210. _____. FACSIMILE OF OFFICIAL REPORT - HQ. ARMY OF THE DANUBE, August 31, 1877. Presently in USMHI, Carlisle Barracks, PA.

211. _____. THE CAMPAIGN IN BULGARIA, 1877-1878. London: 1903.

212. Grey of Fallodon, Viscount. TWENTY-FIVE YEARS -- 1892-1916. 2 vols. London: 1925-1926.

213. Grinard, F. GRANDEUR ET DECADENCE DE L'ASIE. Paris: 1947.

214. Gulick, E.V. EUROPE'S CLASSICAL BALANCE OF POWER: A CASE STUDY OF THE THEORY AND PRACTICE OF ONE OF THE GREAT CONCEPTS OF EUROPEAN STATECRAFT. Ithaca: 1955.

215. Hajek, A. BULGARIENS BEFREIUNG. Munich & Berlin: 1939.

216. Halecki, O. BORDERLANDS OF WESTERN CIVILIZATION: A HISTORY OF EAST CENTRAL EUROPE. New York: 1952.

217. Hamley, E.B., Sir. THE STORY OF THE CAMPAIGN OF SEVASTOPOL. WRITTEN IN THE CAMP. London: 1855.

218. _____. THE WAR IN THE CRIMEA. 3rd ed. New York: 1891.

219. Hammond, R.A. A HISTORY OF THE EMPIRE AND PEOPLE OF TURKEY AND THE WAR IN THE EAST. Rockland, Mass.: 1878.

220. Hantsch, H. DAS GESCHICHTE OSTERREICHS. 2 vols. Vienna: 1950.

221. Hardoin, N. (Dick le Lonlay, pseud.) EN BULGARIE 1877-1878: PLOIESTI-MATCHINE-SISTOVA-TIRNOVA-KEGANLYK-SOUVENIRS DE GUERRE ET LE VOYAGE. Paris: 1883.

222. Harris, D. A DIPLOMATIC HISTORY OF THE BALKAN CRISIS OF 1875-1878. Hamden: 1969 [c.1936].

223. _____. BRITAIN AND THE BULGARIAN HORRORS. Chicago: 1939.

224. Haskell, A.L. HEROES AND ROSES: A VIEW OF BULGARIA. London: c.1966.

225. Heppell, M., & Singleton, F.B. YUGOSLAVIA. New York: 1961.

226. Herbert, F.W. von. THE DEFENCE OF PLEVNA, 1877. WRITTEN BY ONE WHO TOOK PART IN IT. London: 1895.

227. Heyd, U. "The Ottoman 'Ulema and Westernization in the Time of Selim III and Mahmud II." STUDIES IN ISLAMIC HISTORY AND CIVILIZATION. SCRIPTA HIEROSOLYMITANA 9 (1961), 60-96.

228. Heymann, E. BALKAN: KRIEGE, BUNDNISSE, REVOLUTIONEN; 150 JAHRE POLITIK UND SCHICKSAL. Berlin: 1938.

229. Hime, (fnu), Capt. R.A., F.S.S. "The Russo-Turkish Campaign of 1877-78: From a German, an English, and an American Point of View." USM DCXIII (December 1879), 423-434; DCXIV (January 1880), 20-32; DCXVI (March 1880), 330-340.

230. Hink, H. BISMARCKS PRESSPOLITIK IN DER BULGARISCHEN KRISE UND DER ZUSAMMERBRUCH SEINER REGIERUNGSPRESSE (1885-1890). Frankfurt a.M., Berne, Las Vegas: 1977.

231. Hinsley, F.H., ed. MATERIAL PROGRESS AND WORLD-WIDE PROBLEMS 1870-1898. Vol. 11 in NCMH. Cambridge: 1962.

232. Hogg, I. A HISTORY OF ARTILLERY. London: 1974.

233. Holborn, H. DEUTSCHLAND UND DIE TURKIE, 1878-1890. Berlin: 1926.

234. Holt, P.M., et al., eds. CAMBRIDGE HISTORY OF ISLAM. 2 vols. Cambridge: 1977-1978.

235. Horecky, P.L., ed. EAST CENTRAL EUROPE: A GUIDE TO BASIC PUBLICATIONS. Chicago: 1969.

236. _____. SOUTHEASTERN EUROPE: A GUIDE TO BASIC PUBLICATIONS. Chicago: 1969.

237. Horetsky, A. von. AN EPITOME OF THE RUSSO-TURKISH WAR, 1877/78. Trans. by Harry Bell. Vienna. 1915.

238. Hosch, E. THE BALKANS: A SHORT HISTORY. Trans. by Tania Alexander. New York: 1972.

239. Hourani, A.H. THE OTTOMAN BACKGROUND OF THE MODERN MIDDLE EAST. Harlow: 1970.

240. Houtsma, T., ed. ENCYCLOPEDIA OF ISLAM. 2d ed. Leiden: 1954-.

241. Howard, M.E. "The Armed Forces." NCMH 11. Cambridge: 1962.

242. _____. THE FRANCO-PRUSSIAN WAR: THE GERMAN INVASION OF FRANCE. New York: 1961.

243. Hozier, H. M., Col. Sir. THE RUSSO-TURKISH WAR: INCLUDING AN ACCOUNT OF THE RISE AND DECLINE OF THE OTTOMAN POWER, AND THE HISTORY OF THE EASTERN QUESTION. 5 vols. London: 1878.

244. _____. THE SEVEN WEEKS WAR: ITS ANTECEDENTS AND ITS INCIDENTS. Philadelphia: 1867.

245. Hunczak, T., ed. RUSSIAN IMPERIALISM FROM IVAN THE TERRIBLE TO THE REVOLUTION. New Brunswick: 1974.

246. Huyshe, W. THE LIBERATION OF BULGARIA; WAR NOTES IN 1877. London: 1894.

247. Ignat'ev, P.N. RUSSIAN INTRIGUES: SECRET DESPATCHES OF GENERAL IGNATIEFF AND CONSULAR AGENTS OF THE GREAT PANSLAVIC SOCIETIES. London: 1877.

248. Ignotus, P. "Czechs, Magyars, Slovaks." THE POLITICAL QUARTERLY 40 (June 1969), 187-204.

249. Inal, I.M.K. OSMANLI DEVRINDE SON SADRIAZAMLAR. 6 vols. Istanbul: 1940-1953.

250. Inalcik, H. TANZIMAT VE BULGAR MESELEI. Ankara: 1943.

251. Iorga, N. GESCHICHTE DES OSMANISCHEN REICHES. 5 vols. Gotha: 1908-1913.

252. _____. HISTOIRE DES ROUMAINES DE LA PENINSULE DES BALKANS. Bucharest: 1919.

253. Iseminger, G.L. "Britain's Eastern Policy and the Ottoman Christians, 1856-1877." DA XXVI No. 2 (August 1965), 1005.

254. Jaszi, O. THE DISSOLUTION OF THE HABSBURG MONARCHY. Chicago: 1929.

255. Jelavich, B. RUSSIA AND THE ROMANIAN NATIONAL CAUSE, 1856-1859. Bloomington: 1957.

256. _____. THE OTTOMAN EMPIRE, THE GREAT POWERS, AND THE STRAITS QUESTION, 1870-1887. Bloomington: 1973.

257. _____. A CENTURY OF RUSSIAN FOREIGN POLICY, 1814-1914. New York: 1964.

258. _____. "The Bulgarian Crisis of 1885-1887 in British Foreign Policy." In BULGARIA PAST AND PRESENT. Proceedings of the 1st International Conference on Bulgarian Studies. AAASS. Columbus: 1976.

259. Jelavich, C., ed. THE HABSBURG MONARCHY; TOWARD A MULTINATIONAL EMPIRE OR NATIONAL STATES? New York: 1959.

260. _____. "The Revolt in Bosnia-Herzogovina, 1881-1882." SEER XXXI (June 1953), 420-436.

261. _____. TSARIST RUSSIA AND BALKAN NATIONALISM: RUSSIAN INFLUENCE IN THE INTERNAL AFFAIRS OF BULGARIA AND SERBIS, 1879-1886. Westport: 1978.

262. Omitted

263. Jelavich, C., & Jelavich, B. THE BALKANS IN TRANSITION. REES. Berkeley: 1963.

264. _____. THE ESTABLISHMENT OF THE BALKAN NATIONAL STATES, 1804-1920. HECE 8. Seattle & London: 1977.

265. _____. THE BALKANS. Englewood Cliffs: 1965.

266. Jenkins, R. THE DILESSI MURDERS, 1870. London: 1961.

267. Jessup, J.E. "Romanian Society and the Independence War of 1877-78." TRTI. New York: 1983.

268. Jessup, J.E., & Coakley, R.W., eds. A GUIDE TO THE STUDY AND USE OF MILITARY HISTORY. Washington: 1979.

269. Jomini, A.G. RUSSIA IN THE EAST, 1876-1880...LETTERS OF A.G. JOMINI TO N.K. GIERS. Edit. by Charles & Barbara Jelavich. Leiden: 1959.

270. Kann. R.A. THE HABSBURG EMPIRE: A STUDY IN INTEGRATION AND DISINTEGRATION. New York: 1979 [c.1953].

271. _____. A HISTORY OF THE HABSBURG EMPIRE, 1526-1918. Berkeley: 1974.

272. _____. THE MULTINATIONAL EMPIRE: NATIONALISM AND NATIONAL REFORM IN THE HABSBURG MONARCHY, 1848-1918. 2 vols. New York: 1964 [1950].

273. Kann, R.A., & David, Z. THE PEOPLES OF THE EASTERN HABSBURG LANDS, 1526-1918. HECE 6. Seattle & London: 1983.

274. Karal, E.K. OSMANLI TARIHI. Vol. 5: NIZAM-I CEDIT VE TANZIMAT DEVIRLERI, 1789-1856. Ankara: 1956.

275. Karasz, A. HUNGARY IN THE DANUBIAN BASIN. Washington: 1953.

276. Karol of Romania. REMINISCENCES OF THE KING OF ROMANIA. Ed. by Sidney Whitman. New York: 1899.

277. Karolides, P. CONTEMPORARY HISTORY OF THE GREEKS AND OF THE OTHER PEOPLES OF THE EAST FROM 1821-1921. Vol. 3 (1864-1900). Athens: 1929.

278. Kaynar, R. MUSTAFA RESID PASA VE TANZIMAT. Ankara: 1954.

279. Keep, J.L.H., "Russia." NCMH 11. Cambridge, 1962.

280. Kellogg, F. "The Historiography of Romanian Independence. EEQ XII/3 (1977), 369-377.

281. Khitrova, I.I. CHERNOGORIYA V NATSIONALNO-OSVOBODITELNOM DVIZHENII NA BALKANAKH I RUSSO-CHERNOGORSKIE OTNOSHENIIA V 50-70-KH GODAKH XIX VEKA. Moscow: 1979.

282. Khristov, K. OSVOBODINIETO NA BULGARIIA I POLITIKATA NA ZAPADNITE DURZHAVI, 1876-1878. Sofia: 1968.

283. King, E. "In Roumanian Land." LMM XXI (May 1878), 536-555; (June 1878), 712-726.

284. _____. "With the Russians in Bulgaria." LMM XXI (February 1878), 177-191; XXII (March 1879), 265-289.

285. Kinross, J.P.D., Lord. THE OTTOMAN CENTURIES: THE RISE AND FALL OF THE TURKISH EMPIRE. London: 1977.

286. Klyuchevski, V.O. KURS RUSSKOI ISTORII. 5 vols. Moscow: 1937 [1921-1923].

287. _____. A HISTORY OF RUSSIA. 2 vols. Trans. by C.J. Hogarth. New York: 1911-1912.

288. Knapp, V.J. AUSTRIAN SOCIAL DEMOCRACY, 1889-1914. Washington: c.1980.

289. Knox, W.G., Gen. Sir. PERSONAL REMINISCENCES OF THE
     TURCO-RUSSIAN WAR. AMSL. Aldershot: 1888.

290. Kofos, E. GREECE AND THE EASTERN CRISIS, 1875-1878.
     Thessaloniki: 1975.

291. _____. THE MACEDONIAN REVOLUTION OF 1878. Thessaloniki:
     1969.

292. Kohn, H. THE HABSBURG EMPIRE, 1804-1918. Princeton: 1961.

293. Kosary, D. BEVEZETES A MAGYARORSZAG TORTENETENEK FORRASAIBA ES
     IRODALMABA. Vol. 1. Budapest: 1970.

294. _____. MAGYAR TORTENETI BIBLIOGRAFIA, 1825-1867. 4 vols.
     Budapest: 1950-1959.

295. Kosev, K. THE UPRISING OF APRIL 1876 IN BULGARIA. BHR 1 (1976),
     24-26.

296. Koumoulides, J.T.A., ed. HELLENIC PERSPECTIVES: ESSAYS IN THE
     HISTORY OF GREECE. Washington: 1980.

297. Kuepfer, E. LA MACEDONIE ET LES BULGARES. Lausanne: 1918.

298. Lamouche, L. L'ORGANISATION MILITAIRE DE L'EMPIRE OTTOMAN.
     Paris: 1895.

299. Lampe, J.R., & Jackson, M.R. BALKAN ECONOMIC HISTORY,
     1550-1950. Bloomington: 1982.

300. Langer, W.L., gen. ed. THE RISE OF EUROPE. 20+ vols. New York:
     1936-.

301. _____. EUROPEAN ALLIANCES AND ALIGNMENTS, 1871-1890. New
     York: 1950.

302. Langlois, H. LESSONS FROM TWO RECENT WARS (THE RUSSO-TURKISH
     AND THE SOUTH AFRICAN WAR). London: 1909.

303. _____. EUROPEAN ALLIANCES AND ALIGNMENTS, 1871-1890. New
     York: 1950.

304. Larrabee, S.A. HELLAS OBSERVED - THE AMERICAN EXPERIENCE OF
     GREECE, 1775-1865. New York: 1957.

305. Lazarovich-Hrebelianovich, Prince. SERVIAN PEOPLE. 2 vols. New
     York: 1910.

306. Lazelle, H. "Important Improvements in the Art of War During
     the Past Twenty Years and Their Probable Effects on Future
     Military Operations." JMSI 3/11 (1882), 307-373.

307. Leathers, N. "France and the Balkans, 1871-1879." University of
     Oklahoma DA XXIV (October 1963), p. 1594.

308. Lecomte, F. GUERRE D'ORIENT EN 1876-1877. 2 vols. Paris:
     1877-79.

309. Lederer, I.J., ed. RUSSIAN AND THE BALKANS IN RUSSIAN FOREIGN POLICY: ESSAYS IN HISTORICAL PERSPECTIVE. New Haven: 1962.

310. Le Faure, A.J. HISTOIRE DE LA GUERRE D'ORIENT (1877-78). Paris: 1878.

311. Legrand, E.L.J. BIBLIOGRAPHIE ALBANAISE. Leipzig: 1973.

312. _____. BIBLIOGRAPHIE IONIENNE (1494-1900). 2 vols. Paris: 1910.

313. Lengyel, E. 1000 YEARS OF HUNGARY. New York: 1958.

314. Leo, M. LA BULGARIE ET SON PEUPLE SOUS LA DOMINATION OTTOMANE TELS QUE LES ONT VUS LES VOYAGEURS ANGLO-SAXONS (1586-1878). Sofia: 1949.

315. Lessner, E.C., & Lessner, A.M.L. THE DANUBE: THE DRAMATIC HISTORY OF THE GREAT RIVER AND THE PEOPLE TOUCHED BY ITS FLOW. Garden City: 1961.

316. Lewinsohn, R. THE PROFITS OF WAR THROUGH THE AGES. New York: 1979.

317. Lewis, B. "The Ottoman Empire in the Mid-Nineteenth Century: A Review." MES. I/3 (April 1965), 283-295.

318. _____. THE EMERGENCE OF MODERN TURKEY. London: 1961.

319. Lewis, M. "Armed Forces and the Art of War: Navies." NCMH 10. Cambridge: 1960.

320. Liddell-Hart, B.H. "Armed Forces and the Art of War: Armies." NCMH 10. Cambridge: 1960.

321. Lincoln, W.B. NICHOLAS I: EMPEROR AND AUTOCRAT OF ALL THE RUSSIAS. Bloomington: 1978.

322. Omitted.

323. Lowe, J.T. GEOPOLITICS AND WAR: MACKINDER'S PHILOSOPHY OF POWER. Washington: c.1981.

324. Lufti, A. TARIH-I LUFTI. Vols. 9-13. THSA Ms 531/1-7, 5032-4, 4812. IAM Ms 1340-5, 1349.

325. Luvaas, J. "The Great Military Historians and Philosophers." GSUMH. Washington: 1979.

326. Lyons, M., ed. THE RUSSIAN IMPERIAL ARMY. Stanford: 1968.

327. Macartney, C.A. THE HABSBURG EMPIRE, 1790-1918. New York: 1969.

328. _____. HUNGARY, A SHORT HISTORY. Chicago: 1962.

329. _____. " The Austrian Empire and Its Problems, 1848-67." NCMH 10. Cambridge: 1960.

330. Macdermott, M. A HISTORY OF BULGARIA, 1393-1885. London: 1962.

331. Mac Gahan, J. THE TURKISH ATROCITIES IN BULGARIA. LETTERS OF THE SPECIAL CORRESPONDENT OF THE "DAILY NEWS." London: 1876.

332. Mackenzie, D. THE SERBS AND RUSSIAN PAN-SLAVISM, 1875-1878. Ithaca: [1967].

333. _____. "Panslavism in Practice: Cherniaev in Serbia (1876)." JMH 34 (September 1964), 279-297.

334. Madden, H.M. "The Diary of John Paget." SEER Yearbook Vol. 6, 1941.

335. Maior, L. TRANSILVANIA SI RAZBOIUL PENTRU INDEPENDENTA (1877-1878). Cluj-Napoca: 1977.

336. Makkai, L. HISTOIRE DE TRANSYLVANIE. Paris: 1946.

337. Mange, A.E. THE NEAR EAST POLICY OF EMPEROR MAXIMILIAN III. Westport: 1975.

338. Margutti, A.A.V., Freiherr von. THE EMPEROR FRANCIS JOSEPH I AND HIS TIMES. London: [1921].

339. Markopoulos, G. "King George I and the Expansion of Greece, 1875-1881." BS 9 (1968), 21-40.

340. Marlow, J. PERFIDIOUS ALBION: THE ORIGINS OF ANGLO-FRENCH RIVALRY IN THE LEVANT. London: 1971.

341. Marriott, J.A.R., Sir. THE EASTERN QUESTION. 3rd ed. Oxford: 1930.

342. Martinov, fnu. LE BLOCUS DE PLEVNA D'APRES LES ARCHIVES HISTORIQUES. Paris: 1904.

343. Maurice, F.B., Maj. Gen. Sir. THE RUSSO-TURKISH WAR 1877; A STRATEGICAL SKETCH. London: 1905.

344. Mavrocordato, J. MODERN GREECE, 1800-1931. London: 1931.

345. May, A.J. THE HABSBURG MONARCHY, 1867-1914. Cambridge: 1951.

346. McClellan, G.B. "The War in the East." NAR 125 (November 1877), 439-461.

347. McCullagh, F. THE FALL OF ABD-UL-HAMID. London: 1910.

348. McEvedy, C. THE PENQUIN ATLAS OF RECENT HISTORY. Hamondsworth: 1982.

349. McNeill, W.H. A WORLD HISTORY. 3rd ed. Oxford: 1979.

350. Mediger, W. RUSSLAND WEG NACH EUROPA. Brunswick: 1952.

351. Medlicott, W.N. THE CONGRESS OF BERLIN AND AFTER. London: 1938.

352. _____. "Austria-Hungary, Turkey and the Balkans." NCMH 11. Cambridge: 1962.

353. Meyer, K. BIBLIOGRAPHIE DER ARBEITEN ZUR OSTEUROPAISCHEN GESCHICHTE AUS DEN DEUTSCHSPRACHIGEN FACHZEITSCRIFTEN, 1858-1964. Berlin: 1966.

354. Miller, W. THE OTTOMAN EMPIRE AND ITS SUCCESSORS, 1801-1927. 4th ed. With appendix for 1927-1936. Cambridge: 1936.

355. Millman, R. BRITISH FOREIGN POLICY AND THE COMING OF THE FRANCO-PRUSSIAN WAR. Oxford: 1966.

356. _____. BRITAIN AND THE EASTERN QUESTION, 1875-1878. Oxford: 1979.

357. Milutinovic, K.N. STROSMAJER I JUGOSLOVENSKO PITANJE. Novi Sad: 1976.

358. Moltke, H.K.B., Graf von. STRATEGY: ITS THEORY AND APPLICATION: THE WAR OF GERMAN UNIFICATION, 1866-1871. Fort Leavenworth: 1907-1915.

359. Montagu, I. WANDERINGS OF A WAR ARTIST. London: 1889.

360. _____. CAMP AND STUDIO. London: 1890.

361. Montross, L. WAR THROUGH THE AGES. New York: 1944.

362. Moore, F. THE BALKAN TRAIL. New York: 1971 [1906].

363. Mordal, J. TWENTY-FIVE CENTURIES OF SEA WARFARE. New York: 1965.

364. Morris, W. O'C. MOLTKE; A BIOGRAPHICAL AND CRITICAL STUDY. New York: 1971.

365. Morton, F. A NERVOUS SPLENDOR: VIENNA, 1888/1889. Boston: c.1979 [c.1971].

366. Mosse, W.E. THE RISE AND FALL OF THE CRIMEAN SYSTEM, 1855-71: THE STORY OF THE PEACE SETTLEMENT. London: 1963.

367. Mouzaffer-Talaat Pasha Bey. DEFENSE DE PLEVNA D'APRES LES DOCUMENTS OFFICIELS ET PRIVE. London: 1889.

368. _____. GUERRE D'ORIENT, 1877-1878. Paris: 1889.

369. Murad, A. FRANZ JOSEPH I OF AUSTRIA AND HIS EMPIRE. New York: 1968.

370. Murray, W.S. THE MAKING OF THE BALKAN STATES. New York: 1967 [1910].

371. Muscat, M. "Sur le passe de luttes du peuple roumain pour son unite et son independance." RIHM 36 (1977), 17-29.

372. Narochniskaya, L.I. ROSSIYA I NATSIONALNO-OSVOBODITELNOE
DVIZHENIE NA BALKANAKH, 1875-1878 GG.: K STOLETIYU
RUS.-TUR. VOINY 1877-1878 GG. Moscow: 1979.

373. Needham, J.L. "Lessons from the Late War." Ordnance Notes No.
112. U.S. Army Ordnance Department Notes. 12 vols.
Washington: 1878-1884.

374. Nemes, D., et al., eds. ETUDES HISTORIQUES HONGROISES 1980. 2
vols. Budapest: 1980.

375. Nicholae, C. "Echos de la guerre d'independence de la Roumanie
dans les etats non-engages dans le conflict." RIHM 36
(1977), 144-162.

376. Nikitin, S.A. OCHERKI PO ISTORII YUZHNYKH SLAVIAN I
RUSSKO-BALKANSKIKH SVYAZEI V 50-70-E GODY XIX V. Moscow:
1970.

377. _____., et al. OSVOBOZHDENIE BOLGARII OT TURETSKOGO IGA.
Vol. 1. in OSVOBODITELNAYA BORBA YUZHNYKH SLAVIAN I
ROSSIYA. 3 vols. Moscow: 1961.

378. Novikova (Kireef), O.A. SKOBELEFF AND THE SLAVONIC CAUSE.
London: 1883.

379. O'Connor, J.D. HISTORY OF TURKEY, . . . AND THE CAUSES OF THE
WAR OF 1877. Chicago: 1877.

380. O'Connor, R.G. WAR, DIPLOMACY, AND HISTORY: PAPERS AND REVIEWS.
Washington: 1979.

381. Okse, N. "The Turco-Russian War (1877-1878)." RIHM 46 (1980),
137-163.

382. Olivier, L.P.F., ed. LA BOSNIE ET L'HERZOGOVINE. Paris:
[1900?].

383. Ollier, E. CASSEL'S ILLUSTRATED HISTORY OF THE RUSSO-TURKISH
WAR. 2 vols. London & New York: 1877-1878.

384. Olteanu, C. THE ROMANIAN ARMED POWER CONCEPT: A HISTORICAL
APPROACH. BUCHAREST: 1982.

385. _____. "The Romanian Army in the Fights at Pleven." PCRI.
Bucharest: 1977.

386. _____. MASELE POPULARE SI RAZBOIUL DE INDEPENDENTA.
Bucharest: 1977.

387. _____. "The Strategy and Tactics of the Romanian Army
During the Independence War." ARS. Bucharest: 1980.

388. _____. "On the Organization of the Army in the Romanian
Countries." PHRA. BHR Monograph XV. Bucharest: 1975.

389. _____. "Genese et developpment de l'armee permanente chez
les Roumains." RIHM 48 (1980), 75-83.

390. Olteanu, C., & Ceaucescu, I. THE ROMANIAN ARMY IN THE WAR FOR
     ROMANIA'S STATE INDEPENDENCE OF 1877-1878. New Dehli:
     1977.

391. Ondes, O. "Abdulhamid devrinde donanma." BTTD 19 (1969), 68-78;
     20 (1969), 71-75; 21 (1969), 70-73; 22 (1969), 78-80; 24
     (1969), 64-88.

392. Orhunlu, C. "Balkan Turklerinin durumu." TK II/12 (1964),
     49-60.

393. Oztuna, T.Y. RESIMLERLE 93 HARLI. 1877-78 TURK-RUS SAVASI
     Istanbul: 1969.

394. Pakalm, M.Z. SON SADRAZAMLAR VE BASVEKILLER. 5 vols. Istanbul:
     1940-1948.

395. Palanceanu, E., et al. 1877-1878. MARTURII MUZEISTICE PRIVIND
     RAZBOIUL PENTRU CICERIREA INDEPENDENTEI DE STAT A
     ROMANIEI. Bucharest: 1978.

396. Papadopoulos, G.S. ENGLAND AND THE NEAR EAST, 1896-1898.
     Thessaloniki: 1969.

397. Papavici, A. UN TEMOIGNAGE SERBE SUR LES ROUMAIN DE SERBIE.
     Paris: 1919.

398. Pascu, S. "La Contribution economique du peuple roumaine a la
     guerre d'independence." RIHM 36 (1977), 114-130.

399. _____., ed. THE INDEPENDENCE OF ROMANIA. BHR Monograph 18.
     Bucharest: 1977.

400. _____. "The Romanian Army and Society, 1878-1920." TRTI.
     New York: 1983.

401. Pascu, S., & Livescu, J., eds. INDEPENDENTA ROMANIEI,
     BIBLIOGRAFIE. Bucharest: 1979.

402. _____., eds. THE INDEPENDENCE OF ROMANIA, SELECTED
     BIBLIOGRAPHY. BHR Monograph 22. Bucharest: 1980.

403. Pauley, B. HAPSBURG LEGACY 1867-1939. New York: 1972.

404. Pavlovska, Z. PROBLEMES DE L'ARMEMENT DES FORCES REBELLES DU
     MOUVEMENT NATIONAL-REVOLUTIONNAIRE BULGAR, 1869-1876.
     MONGRAPHIE. Sofia: 1978.

405. Pavlowitch, K.S. "Yugoslavia and Romania." JCEA XXIII No. 4
     (January 1964), 451-485.

406. Pears, B., Sir. LIFE OF ABDUL HAMID. London: 1917.

407. Pearson, E.M., & McLaughlin, L.A. SERVICE IN SERVIA UNDER THE
     RED CROSS. London: 1877.

408. Pelagic, V. BORBA ZA OSVOBODJENJE: ISTORIJA BOSANSKO-
     HERZOGOVACHE BUNE U SOEZI SRPSKO-VLACHO-BULGARSKO I
     RUSKO-TURKSIM RATOM. 3rd ed. Belgrad: 1882.

409. Penkov, S. LES BULGARES ET LA GUERRE DE LIBERATION, 1877-1878.
     Sofia: 1979.

410. Petho, S. VILAGOSTOL TRIANONIG; A MAI MAGYARORSZAG
     KIALAKULASANAK TORTENETE. 5th ed. Budapest, 1926.

411. Petrosian, Y.A. "NOVYE OSMANI" I BORBA ZA KONSTITUTSIYU 1876 G.
     V TURTSII. Moscow: 1958.

412. Petrovic, V.M. SERBIA, HER PEOPLE, HISTORY, ASPIRATIONS. New
     York: 1915.

413. Petrovich, M.B. A HISTORY OF MODERN SERBIA, 1804-1918. 2 vols.
     New York & London: 1976.

414. Pheil-Burghaus, R.F.A., Graf von. EXPERIENCES OF A PRUSSIAN
     OFFICER IN THE RUSSIAN SERVICE DURING THE TURKISH WAR,
     1877-78. Trans. By Col. Cyril W. Bowdler. London: 1893.

415. Pinkney, D.H. THE NINETEENTH CENTURY, 1815-1914. WE Edited by
     Neil J Hackett. St. Louis: c.1979.

416. _____., ed. PROBLEMS OF CIVILIZATION. 10+ vols. Lexington:
     1977-.

417. Pinson, M. "Ottoman Colonization of the Circassians in Rumeli
     After the Crimean War." EB 3 (1975), 71-85.

418. Poloskei, F. DAS UNGARISCHE REGIERUNGSYSTEM VOR DEM VERFALL DER
     OSTERREICHISCH-UNGARISCHEN MANARCHIE. EHH. Budapest: 1980.

419. Popescu-Puturi, I. MASELE POPULARE IN RAZBOIUL PENTRU CUCERIREA
     INDEPENDENTEI ABSOLUTE A ROMANIEI, 1877-1878. Bucharest:
     1979.

420. Preda, D. "The Status of Officers and Non-Commissioned Officers
     in the Romanian Army Over 1859-1877." ARS. Bucharest:
     1980.

421. Preston, R.A., et al. MEN IN ARMS. New York: 1956.

422. Psomiades, H.J. THE EASTERN QUEST: THE LAST PHASE. A STUDY OF
     GREEK-TURKISH DIPLOMACY. Thessaloniki: 1968.

423. Puryear, V.J. ENGLAND, RUSSIA AND THE STRAITS QUESTION,
     1844-1856. Berkeley: 1931.

424. Rambaud, A.N. THE EXPANSION OF RUSSIA. Boston: 1978.

425. Ramm, A. "The Crimean War." NCMH 10. Cambridge: 1960.

426. Ranke, L. von. A HISTORY OF THE SERBIAN REVOLUTION. Trans A.
     Kerr. New York: 1973.

427. Regnault, E. HISTOIRE POLITIQUE ET SOCIALE DES PRINCIPANTS DANUBIENNES. Paris: 1857.

428. Reinach, J. LA SERBIE ET LE MONTENEGRO. Paris: 1876.

429. Renn, L. WARFARE: THE RELATION OF WAR TO SOCIETY. New York: 1939.

430. REVELATIONS FROM THE SEAT OF WAR: RUSSIANS, TURKS, BULGARIANS AND MR. GLADSTONE. London: 1877.

431. Rheindorf, K. DIE SCHWARZE-MEER-(PONTUS-) FRAGE VOM PARISER FRIEDEN VON 1856 BIS ZUM ABSCHLUSS DER LONDENER KONFERENZ VON 1871. Berlin: 1925.

432. Riasonovsky, N.V. A HISTORY OF RUSSIA. 2nd ed. New York: 1969.

433. Rich, N. THE AGE OF NATIONALISM AND REFORM, 1850-1890. 2nd ed. NHME. New York: 1976 [1970].

434. Ritter, M. FRANKREICHS GRIECHENLAND-POLITIK WAHREND DES KRIMKRIEGES; IM SPIEGEL DER FRANZOSISCHEN UND DER BAYERISCHEN GESANDTSCHAFTSBERICHTE 1853-1857. Munich: 1966.

435. Roberts, J.M. EUROPE, 1880-1945. New York: 1967.

436. Roider, K.A., & Youngs, F.A., eds. THE WORLD OF EUROPE. 9 vols. St. Louis: c.1979-.

437. Romanescu, G. "The Formation of the National Army and Its Development Down to the War of Independence." PHRA Monograph 15. BHR. Bucharest: 1975.

438. _____. "Documents concernant la guerre de 1877-1878." RIHM 36 (1977), 237-255.

439. _____. "Permanent and Temporary Military Structures During the 1877-1878 War. ARS. Bucharest: 1980.

440. Romania. Biblioteca centrala a Ministeralui Apararii Nationale. ROMANIA IN RAZBOIUL PENTRU INDEPENDENTA (1877-1878). CONTRIBUTII BIBLIOGRAFICE. Bucharest: 1979.

441. _____. Editura Militara. ITINERARE EROICE 1877-1878. JURNALE DE OPERATII ALE UNOR UNITATI RAZBOIUL INDEPENDENTA. Bucharest: 1977.

442. _____. Academy of Social and Political Science. STUDII SI MATERIALE DE ISTORIE MODERNA. Vol. 6. Edited by N. Adaniloaie & Dan Berindei. Bucharest: 1979.

443. "Romania." THE NATION. XLIII (11 November 1886), 387-388.

444. "Romania Since 1848." NAR 109 (1869), 176.

445. Ropp, T. WAR IN THE MODERN WORLD. Durham: 1959.

446. Rose, J.H. THE INDECISIVENESS OF WAR AND OTHER ESSAYS. Port
Washington: [1968].

447. Rosetti, R. "Roumania's Share in the War of 1877." SEER 8
(March 1930), 546-577.

448. Rothenberg, G.E. "The Struggle over the Dissolution of the
Croatian Military Border: 1850-1871." SR I (March 1964),
63-78.

449. _____. "Toward a National Hungarian Army: The Military
Compromise of 1868 and Its Consequences." SR XXXI No. 4
(December 1972), 805-816.

450. _____. THE MILITARY BORDER IN CROATIA, 1740-1881: A STUDY
OF AN IMPERIAL INSTITUTION. Chicago: 1966.

451. _____. THE ARMY OF FRANCIS JOSEPH. West Lafayette: 1976.

452. "Roumania in 1866." COLBURNS CXXXVIII (1866), 127.

453. Rubin, A. LA PROCLAMATION DE L'INDEPENDENCE DE LA ROUMANIE.
Bucharest: 1903.

454. Rumenin, Rumen. LA LANDWEHR BULGARE, 1877-1878. Sofia: 1978.

455. Rumpler, H. DIE PROTOKOLLE DES OSTERREICHISCHEN MINISTERRATES,
1848-1867. EINLEITUNGSBAND: MINISTERRAT UND
MINISTERRATS-PROTOKOLLE, 1848-1867. Vienna: 1970.

456. Rundle, R.N. INTERNATIONAL AFFAIRS, 1890-1939. New York: 1979.

457. _____. INTERNATIONAL AFFAIRS, 1939-1979. New York: 1981.

458. Rupp, G.H. A WAVERING FRIENDSHIP: RUSSIA AND AUSTRIA,
1876-1878. Philadelphia: 1976 [c.1941].

459. "Russia and Roumania." EDINBURGH REVIEW CCIII (July 1878),
100-113.

460. RUSSIAN ATROCITIES IN ASIA AND EUROPE DURING THE MONTHS OF
JUNE, JULY, AND AUGUST 1877. Constantinople: 1877.

461. Ryan, C.S., Sir., & Sandes, J. UNDER THE RED CRESCENT;
ADVENTURES OF AN ENGLISH SURGEON WITH THE TURKISH ARMY AT
PLEVNA AND ERZEROUM, 1877-1878. London: 1897.

463. Saints-Priest, M. le Comte. MEMOIRES SUR L'AMBASSADE DE FRANCE
IN TURQUIE ET SUR LE COMMERCE LES FRANCAISE DAN LE LEVANT.
Paris: 1977.

464. Sale, M.T. THE CONSTRUCTION OF MILITARY RAILROADS BY THE
RUSSIANS DURING THE WAR OF 1877 AND 1878. REIOP. 1881.

465. Salusbury, P.H.B. TWO MONTHS WITH TCHERNAIEFF IN SERVIA.
London: 1877.

466. _____. "With the Roumanians in the '77 Campaign." CUSM
    (March 1879), 348-357; (May 1879), 80-87; (August 1879),
    487-?; (September 1879) 71(?)-76(?), 206-209; (October
    1879), (October 1979), 202(?)-209(?); (November 1879),
    326-333; (December 1879), 482-488; (January 1880),
    56(?)-64(?); (February 1880), 219-228; (April 1880),
    431-439; (May 1880), 91-94; (June 1880), 167-175; (July
    1880), 330-335; (August 1880), 439-449; (October 1880),
    189-196; (November 1880), 329-338.

467. Sanda, G. "Pages of the History of the Roumanian Military
    Medicine (up to the War of 1877-1878). ARS. Bucharest:
    1980.

468. Sanness, J. EUROPE AND THE BALKANS. PAST TERRITORIAL DISPUTES
    AND SOCIOPOLITICAL VARIETY. Oslo: 1972.

469. Sargent, L. GREECE IN THE NINETEENTH CENTURY. London: 1897.

470. Savu, A.G. "Romanian Military Art During the War." PCRI.
    Bucharest: 1977.

471. _____., ed. STUDII DE ISTORIE SI TEORIE MILITARA.
    RETROSPECTIVE ISTORICE ANALIZE CONTEMPORANE. Bucharest:
    1980.

472. _____., ed. PAGES FROM THE HISTORY OF THE ROMANIAN ARMY.
    BHR XV. Bucharest: 1975.

473. _____., ed. THE ARMY AND ROMANIAN SOCIETY. Bucharest: 1980.
    Also in Romanian as ARMATA SI SOCIETATEA ROMANEASCA.
    Bucharest: 1980.

474. Schem, A.J. THE WAR IN THE EAST. New York & Cincinnati: 1878.

475. Scherer, A. SUDOSTEUROPA-DISSERTATIONEN, 1918-1960. EINE
    BIBLIOGRAPHIE DEUTSCHER, OSTERREICHISCHER UND
    SCHWEIZERIISCHER HOCHSCHULSCHRIFTEN. Graz, Vienna, Koln &
    Bohlau: 1968.

476. Schevill, F. HISTORY OF THE BALKAN PENINSULA. New York: 1971
    [c.1922].

477. Schlozer, L. von. DAS TURKISCHE HEER. Leipzig: 1901.

478. Schmitt, B.E. ENGLAND AND GERMANY, 1740-1914. Princeton: 1916.

479. Schmitthenner, P. KRIEG UND KRIEGFUHRUNG IM WANDEL DER
    WELTGESCHICHTE. Potsdam: 1933.

480. Schreiber, G. BALKAN AUS ESTER HAND. GESCHICHTE U. GEGENWART IN
    BERICHTEN VOM AUGENZEUGEN U. ZEITGENOSSEN. Wurzburg: 1971.

481. Schroder, G. von. DAS VERSCHANZTE LAGER VON PLEVNA UND DIE
    RUSSISCH-RUMANISCHE ANGRIFF DESSELBEN VON 19 JUNI BIS 10
    DEZEMBER 1877. London: 1878.

482. Schroeder, P.W. AUSTRIA, GREAT BRITAIN, AND THE CRIMEAN WAR: THE DESTRUCTION OF THE EUROPEAN CONCERT. Ithaca & London: 1972.

483. Schwarz, B. MONTENEGRO. Leipzig: 1888.

484. Seemann, K.-D., & Siegmann, F. BIBLIOGRAPHIE DER SLAVISTISCHEN ARBEITEN AÛS DEN DEUTSCHSPRACHIGEN FACHZEITSCHRIFTEN, 1878-1963. Vol. 8 of BIBLIOGRAPHISCHE MITTEILUNGEN DES OSTEUROPA-INSTITUTS AN DER FREIEN UNIVERSITAT BERLIN. Wurzburg: 1965.

485. Sehsuvaroglu, H.Y. SULTAN AZIZ, HAYATI, HAL'I, OLUMU. Istanbul: n.d.

486. Senior, N.W. A JOURNAL KEPT IN TURKEY AND GREECE IN THE AUTUMN OF 1857 AND THE BEGINNING OF 1858. New York: 1977.

487. Senkowitsch, I. DIE KULTURBEDEUTUNG SERBIENS. Zurich: 1917.

488. Serbia. Ministarstvo inostranih dela. DAS SERBISCHE BLAUBUCH, DAS RUSSISCHE ORANGEBUCH. Vienna: 1915.

489. Seton-Watson, H. THE DECLINE OF IMPERIAL RUSSIA, 1855-1914. New York: 1964.

490. Seton-Watson, R.W. DISRAELI, GLADSTONE AND THE EASTERN QUESTION. New York: 1972.

491. _____. THE EMANCIPATION OF SOUTH-EASTERN EUROPE. London: 1923.

492. _____. THE SOUTHERN SLAV QUESTION AND THE HABSBURG MONARCHY. New York: 1969.

493. _____. THE RISE OF NATIONALITY IN THE BALKANS. New York: 1966.

494. _____. A HISTORY OF THE ROUMANIANS; FROM ROMAN TIMES TO THE COMPLETION OF UNITY. Cambridge: 1934.

495. Sforza, C., Count. FIFTY YEARS OF WAR AND DIPLOMACY IN THE BALKANS: PASHISH AND THE UNION OF THE YUGOSLAVS. Trans. by J.G. Clemenceau LeClercq. New York: 1940.

496. Shandanova, L., ed. PETNADESET GODINI INSTITUT ZA BALKANISTIKA, 1964-1978: ISTORICHESKA SPRAVKA I BIBLIOGRAFIIA. Sofia: 1979.

497. Shannon, R.T. GLADSTONE AND THE BULGARIAN AGITATION, 1876. London & Paris: 1963.

498. Shaw, S.J. "The Ottoman View of the Balkans." In THE BALKANS IN TRANSITION. Edited by Charles and Barbara Jelavich. Berkeley: 1963.

499. Shaw, S.J., & Shaw, E.K. HISTORY OF THE OTTOMAN EMPIRE AND
     MODERN TURKEY. Vol. 2: REFORM, REVOLUTION AND REPUBLIC:
     THE RISE OF MODERN TURKEY, 1808-1975. Cambridge, London &
     New York: 1977.

500. Shepherd, W.R. HISTORICAL ATLAS. 8th ed. London: 1956.

501. Shukla, R.L. BRITAIN, INDIA AND THE TURKISH EMPIRE, 1853-1882.
     New Delhi: 1973.

502. Sidak, J., et al. POVIJEST HRVATSKOG NARODA G. 1860-1914.
     Zagreb: 1968.

503. Singer, J.D., & Small, M. THE WAGES OF WAR: A STATISTICAL
     HANDBOOK. New York: 1972.

504. Siniser, B. CONTRIBUTION A L'HISTOIRE DES POPULATION TURQUES EN
     BULGARIE, 1876-1880. Ankara: 1966.

505. _____. RUMELI' DEN TURK GOCLERI. 2 vols. Ankara: 1968-1970.

506. Sinor, D. HISTORY OF HUNGARY. New York: 1961.

507. Sked, A. THE SURVIVAL OF THE HABSBURG EMPIRE: RADETZKY, THE
     IMPERIAL ARMY AND CLASS WAR, 1848. New York & London:
     1979.

508. Skendi, S. ALBANIAN POLITICAL THOUGHT AND REVOLUTIONARY
     ACTIVITY, 1881-1912. Munich: 1954.

509. _____. THE ALBANIA NATIONAL AWAKENING, 1878-1912.
     Princeton: 1967.

510. Skoko, S., & Opacic, P. VOJVODA STEPA STEPANOVIC U RATOVIMA
     SRBIJE 1876-1918. 2nd ed. Belgrad: 1975.

511. Slijepcevic, D. THE MACEDONIAN QUESTION; THE STRUGGLE FOR
     SOUTHERN SERBIA. Chicago: 1958.

512. Smith, C.L. THE EMBASSY OF SIR WILLIAM WHITE AT CONSTANTINOPLE,
     1886-1891. Westport: 1979 [c.1957].

513. Smith, F.B. FLORENCE NIGHTINGALE: REPUTATION AND POWER. New
     York: 1982.

514. Soures, G.M. "Romania in 1866." TINSLEY'S MAGAZINE 29 (1881),
     169.

515. Spaulding, O.L., et al. A STUDY OF MILITARY METHODS FROM THE
     EARLIEST TIMES. New York: 1925.

516. Spiridonakis, B.G. ESSAYS ON THE HISTORICAL GEOGRAPHY OF THE
     GREEK WORLD IN THE BALKANS DURING THE TURKOKRATIA.
     Thessaloniki: 1977.

517. Stafford House Committee. REPORT AND OPERATIONS OF THE STAFFORD
     HOUSE COMMITTEE FOR THE RELIEF OF SICK AND WOUNDED TURKISH
     SOLDIERS, RUSSO-TURKISH WAR, 1877-78. LONDON: 1879.

518. Stan, N. REFLECTARI ISTORICO-LITERARE ALE REZISTENTEI
     ROMANESTI. Bucharest: 1979.

519. Stavrianos, L.S. "Antecedents to the Balkan Revolutions of the
     Nineteenth Century." JMH XXIX No. 4 (December 1957),
     335-348.

520. _____. THE BALKANS SINCE 1453. New York: 1958.

521. _____. THE BALKANS, 1815-1914. Huntington: 1974 [c.1963].

522. Stefanescu, S. ENCICLOPEDIA ISTORIOGRAFIEI ROMANESTI.
     Bucharest: 1978.

523. Stephenson, G. RUSSIA FROM 1812 TO 1945: A HISTORY. New York &
     Washington: 1970.

524. Stevenson, F.S. A HISTORY OF MONTENEGRO. New York: 1971.

525. Stillman, W. HERZOGOVINA AND THE LATE UPRISING; THE CAUSE OF
     THE LATTER AND THE REMEDIES. London: 1877.

526. _____. TURKISH RULE AND TURKISH WARFARE. New York: 1877.

527. Stoianovich, T. "Factors in the Decline pf Ottoman Society in
     the Balkans." SR XXI No. 4 (December 1962), 623-632.

528. Stoikov, A., et al. BULGARIA 1878-1978, 100 YEARS SINCE ITS
     LIBERATION FROM OTTOMAN DOMINATION. Edited by Boris
     Chalpanov. Trans. by Bovkitsa Grinberg. Sofia: 1978.

529. Stojanovic, M.D. THE GREAT POWERS AND THE BALKANS, 1875-1878.
     Cambridge: 1939.

530. Sudi, S. DEFTER-I MUQTESID. Istanbul: 1891.

531. Sugar, P.F. ETHNIC DIVERSITY AND CONFLICT IN EASTERN EUROPE.
     Santa Barbara: 1980.

532. Sugar, P.F. & Treadgold, D.W. HISTORY OF EAST CENTRAL EUROPE.
     11 vols. Seattle & London: 1974-.

533. Sumner, B.H. RUSSIA AND THE BALKANS, 1870-1880. Oxford: 1937.

534. Swire, J. ALBANIA, THE RISE OF A KINGDOM. London: 1929.

535. Sydenham, G.S., Col. First Baron. PLEVNA AND THE DEFENSE THERE
     MADE BY THE TURKS AGAINST THE RUSSIANS IN THE WAR OF
     1877-78. REIOP. 1880.

536. Tanty, M. KONFLIKTY BALKANSKIE W LATACH 1878-1918. Warsaw:
     1968.

537. Taylor, A.J.P. THE HABSBURG MONARCHY, 1809-1918. 2nd ed. London: 1964 [1948].

538. _____. THE STRUGGLE FOR MASTERY IN EUROPE, 1848-1918. Berkeley: 1931.

539. _____. "International Relations." NCMH 11. Cambridge: 1962.

540. Temperley, H.W., Sir. THE BULGARIAN AND OTHER ATROCITIES. PBA XVII (1931).

541. _____. ENGLAND AND THE NEAR EAST. 2 vols. London: 1936.

542. _____., ed. FOUNDATIONS OF BRITISH FOREIGN POLICY FROM PITT TO SALISBURY. London: 1939.

543. _____. HISTORY OF SERBIA. London: 1917.

544. Tevik, S., & Zuhdi, A. DEVLET'I ALIYI'I OSMANIYE-YUNAN MUHAREBESI. Istanbul: 1915.

545. Thessaloniki. Hidryma Meleton Chersonesou Tou Haimou. VALKANIKE VIVLIOGRAPHIA. Thessaloniki: 1975-.

546. THE THIRD BATTLE OF PLEVNA, AUGUST 26-31 O.S. (SEPT. 7-12), 1877. REIOP. 1878.

547. Thornton, A.P. "Rivalries in the Mediterranean, the Middle East and Egypt." NCMH 11. Cambridge: 1962.

548. Tileston, M.W. (Foote)., ed. AMELIA PEABODY TILESTON AND HER CANTEENS FOR THE SERBS. Boston: c.1920.

549. Todleben, F.E., Gen. Count. THE INVESTMENT OF THE FORTIFIED POSITION OF PLEVNA AND THE SURRENDER OF THE TURKISH ARMY, NOVEMBER 28, 1877. REIOP. London: 1878.

550. Toynbee, A.J. THE WESTERN QUESTION IN GREECE AND TURKEY. New York: 1970.

551. Trebilcock, C. THE INDUSTRIALIZATION OF THE CONTINENTAL POWERS, 1780-1914. New York & London: 1981.

552. Treue, W. DER KRIMKRIEGE UND SEINE BEDEUTUNG FUR DIE ENTSTEHUNG DER MORERNEN FLOTTEN. Herford: 1980.

553. Trotha, T. von. TACTICAL STUDIES ON THE BATTLE AROUND PLEVNA. Trans. by Lt. Carl Reichmann. Kansas City: 1896.

554. Tsvetkova, B.A. LA BATAILLE MEMORABLE DES PEUPLES. Sofia: 1971.

555. _____. LES INSTITUTIONS OTTOMANES EN EUROPE. Wiesbaden: 1978.

556. Tuca, F. "Romanian Society During the War for Independence." TRTI. New York: 1983.

557. Tuca, F., & Skafesh, C. ISTORICHESKIE ZHURNALII RUMINSKIKH CHASTEI I COEDINENII, UCHASTVOVAVSHIKH V KAMPANII 1877-1878 GODOV. RIHM 36 (1977), 265-269.

558. Tukin, C. "Osmanli Imparatorlugunda Girit isyanlari." BELLETEN 9 (1945), 163-206.

559. Turat, A. L'INSURRECTION CRETOISE ET LA GUERRE GRECO-TURQUE. Paris: 1898.

560. Turkey. Genelkurmay Harp Tarihi Baskanligi. TURK SILAHLI KUVVETLERI TARIHI. Vol. III. Ankara: 1978.

561. _____. Turkiye Cumhuriyeti, Maarif Vekaleti. ISLAM ANSIKLOPEDISI. Istanbul & Ankara: 1940-.

562. "Turkish Tactics in the War of 1877." USM (1877), 13.

563. Tutoveanu, I. "Romanian-Russian Military Cooperation During the Independence War." PCRI. Bucharest: 1977.

564. Upton, E. THE ARMIES OF ASIA AND EUROPE. New York: 1878.

565. USSR. RUSSKO-TURETSKAYA VOINA 1877-1878. Moscow: 1977.

566. _____. 100-LETIE OSVOBOZHDENIYA BOLGARII OT OSMANSKOGO IGA 1878-1978. SBORNIK STATEI. Moscow: 1978.

567. _____. Institut Vostokogovedeniya. BIBLIOGRAFIYA TURTSII (1917-1958). Moscow: 1959.

568. Uzuncarsili, I.H. "Murad V." IA VIII, 647-651.

569. Vagts, A. A HISTORY OF MILITARISM. New ed. New York: 1959.

570. Van Creveld, M.L. SUPPLYING WAR: LOGISTICS FROM WALLENSTEIN TO PATTON. New York: 1977.

571. Van Vollenhaven, C. THE LAW OF PEACE. London: 1936.

572. Velicki, C.N. "The Support Granted by the Romanian People to the Liberation Fight of the Bulgarian People." PCRI. Bucharest: 1977.

573. Veristchagin, A.V. AT HOME AND IN WAR 1853-1881: REMINISCENCES AND ANECDOTES. Trans. by I. Hapgood. New York: c.1888.

574. Vernadsky, G. "On Some Parallel Trends in Russian and Turkish History." TRANSACTIONS OF THE CONNECTICUT ACADEMY OF ARTS AND SCIENCES XXXVI (July 1945), 25-36.

575. Vital, D. THE SURVIVAL OF SMALL STATES: STUDIES IN SMALL POWER/GREAT POWER CONFLICT. Toronto: 1971.

576. Vladescu, C. M. UNIFORMELE ARMATEI ROMANE DE LA INCEPUTUL SECOLULUI AL XIX-LEA PINA LA VICTORIA DIN MAI 1945. Bucharest: 1977.

577. Vukcevic, R. TURIZAM U PRIVREDNOM RAZVOJU CRNE GORE. Kotor: 1977.

578. _____. RAZVOI PRIVREDE CRNE GORE. Titograd: 1974.

579. Vukmanovic-Tempo, S. REVOLUCIJA KOJA TECE: MEMOARI. Belgrade: 1971.

580. Vyvyan, J.M.K. "Russia in Europe and Asia." NCMH 10. Cambridge: 1960.

581. Wagner, A.L. THE CAMPAIGN OF KONIGGRATZ: A STUDY OF THE AUSTRO-PRUSSIAN CONFLICT IN LIGHT OF THE AMERICAN CIVIL WAR. Fort Leavenworth: 1889.

582. Walichnowski, T. BALCANICA: A GUIDE TO THE POLISH ARCHIVES RELATIVE TO THE HISTORY OF THE BALKAN COUNTRIES. Warsaw: 1979.

583. Wandruszka, A. THE HOUSE OF HABSBURG: SIX HUNDRED YEARS OF A EUROPEAN DYNASTY. Trans. by Cathleen and Hans Epstein. Garden City: 1964.

584. Warner, P. THE CRIMEAN WAR: A REAPPRAISAL. London: 1972.

585. Weber, E. EUROPE SINCE 1715: A MODERN HISTORY. NHME. New York: 1972.

586. Weddern, Cardinal von. DIE RUSSISCHEN KAVALLERIE-DIVISIONEN UND DIE ARMEE - OPERATIONEN IM BALKAN FELDZUG 1877-78. Berlin: 1878.

587. Weiner, M. THE SOVEREIGN REMEDY: EUROPE AFTER WATERLOO. New York: 1971.

588. Weld, S.F. THE EASTERN QUESTION AND A SUPPRESSED CHAPTER OF HISTORY; NAPOLEON III AND THE KINGDOM OF ROUMANIA. Boston: 1897.

589. Wellesley, F.A., Col. Hon. WITH THE RUSSIANS IN PEACE AND WAR; RECOLLECTIONS OF A MILITARY ATTACHE. London: 1905.

590. West, R. (pseud.) BLACK LAMB AND GREY FALCON. London & Melbourne: 1967

591. Westwood, J.N. ENDURANCE AND ENDEAVOUR: RUSSIAN HISTORY 1812-1980. 2nd ed.New York: 1982.

592. Williams, R.L. THE FRENCH REVOLUTION OF 1870-1871. RMW.

593. Wirthwein, W.G. BRITAIN AND THE BALKAN CRISIS, 1875-1878. New York: 1966.

594. Woodruff, W. THE STRUGGLE FOR WORLD POWER, 1500-1980. New York: 1981.

595. Wren, M.C. "Pobedonostsev and Russian Influence in the Balkans, 1881-1888." JMH. XIX (June 1947), 130-141.

596. Wright, A. ADVENTURES IN SERVIA; OR, THE EXPERIENCES OF A MEDICAL FREELANCER AMONG THE BASHI-BAZOUKS. Edited by Alfred G. Farquhar-Bernard. London: 1884.

597. Wright, Q. THE STUDY OF WAR. London & Chicago: 1965 [1942].

598. Wright, W.L. OTTOMAN STATECRAFT. Princeton: 1935.

599. Xanalatos, D. "The Greeks and the Turks on the Eve of the Balkan Wars." BS 3 (1973), 277-296.

600. Yriarte, C. BOSNIA ET HERZOGOVINE: SOUVENIRS DE VOYAGE PENDANT L'INSURRECTION. Paris: 1876.

601. Zakythinos, D.A. THE MAKING OF MODERN GREECE. Trans. by K.R. Johnstone. Totowa: 1976.

602. Zhilin, P.A. "Some Problems of Counteroffensive in Wars of the 19th-20yj Centuries." CIHM. Sandhurst: 1974.

603. Zmei, G. DIE SEELE DES BULGARENTUMS. Sofia: 1941.

604. Zook, D.H., & Higham, R. A SHORT HISTORY OF WARFARE. New York: 1966.

605. Zujovic, M.J. LE POUVOIR CONSTITUTANT DANS LES CONSTITIONS SERBES. Paris: 1928.

606. Zwitter, F. LES PROBLEMES NATIONAUX DANS LA MONARCHIE DES HABSBOURG. Belgrad: 1960.


ADDITIONS


607. Eren, A.C. "Tanzimat." IA XI, 709-765.

# CHAPTER EIGHT

## 1900-1936

## GENERAL BACKGROUND

There are those among the world's leading scholars and historians who place the 19th century's bounds as being the period from the Vienna Congress of 1815, that sought to restore pre-Napoleonic Europe, to 1914, when mankind once again set about to destroy itself. World War I is thus considered to be the point of departure into the contemporary world. There is little question that this formula may be applied to political and social developments and, as one uses war as an extension of political means, and social development is molded by it, it stands to reason that this definition might be applied to military history as well. For the purposes of this bibliography, however, it appears more proper to follow the chronological demarcation of the turn of the century to open the chapter. By a similar logic, 1936 was selected for the chapter's close. The reasoning here was that, in 1936, the efforts of von Ribbentrop bore fruit and the German-Italian Axis was formed. That same year saw Hitler launch his four-year rearmament plan that presaged the Second World War.

The opening of the 20th century witnessed an enormous shift in the balance of world power, as the United States found itself willingly or unwillingly thrust into the role of a major international force to be reckoned with and with new-found overseas interests to foster and protect. These times also saw Russia humiliated by the Japanese at Port Arthur and in the Tsushima Strait. It was a time when Great Power rivalries caused an arms race the only outcome of which could be war. The Great Powers exhibited this same rivalry over their interests in the Balkans, interests not altogether altruistic and based primarily upon the same features of the Eastern Question that had been so remarkable in their consistency during the preceding two centuries. This was, lastly, a time of unparalleled technological advances, advances which heralded great progress in communications, manned flight and ground transportation, all of which were to have a profound effect upon the future, not the least part of which was a heightened ability to make war.

## GENERAL HISTORIES OF THE PERIOD

Twentieth—century Europe is the topic of numerous works, any of which will be helpful as a means of refreshing the memory on the events that shaped the course of history. The period 1900-1936 is exceptionally well covered in many of these. Heinz Gollwitzer's EUROPE AND THE AGE OF IMPERIALISM, 1880-1914 [208] is a good place to start as is John Morris and J.M. Robert's EUROPE, 1880-1945 [367]. THE MODERN ERA, 1815 TO THE PRESENT [85], that was edited by

Norman Cantor and Samuel Berner, and Eugen Weber's EUROPE SINCE 1715: A MODERN HISTORY [557] are both good general accounts. Cantor, along with Michael Werthman, also edited THE MAKING OF THE MODERN WORLD, 1815-1914 [86]. Another worthwhile choice is Felix Gilbert's THE END OF THE EUROPEAN ERA, 1890 TO THE PRESENT [203] that was published in 1970. William Woodruff's THE STRUGGLE FOR WORLD POWER, 1500-1980 [568] is a more generalized version of the same theme. Alan Taylor's THE STRUGGLE FOR MASTERY IN EUROPE, 1848-1914 [505] focuses more specifically on the period under discussion and the important events that preceded it. While this book is full of insight it is, at the same time, contradictory and somewhat erratic. A somewhat more stable account may be found in THE GREAT POWERS AND THE EUROPEAN STATES SYSTEM, 1815-1914 [69]. The last two chapters of this book cover the period admirably. Sir Ernest Llewellyn Woodward's PRELUDE TO MODERN EUROPE, 1815-1914 [569], which was published in 1972, and David Pinkney's THE NINETEENTH CENTURY, 1815-1914 [391] give excellent appraisals of the period leading up to the Great War. INTERNATIONAL AFFAIRS, 1890-1939 [425], by R.N. Rundle, is an excellent review of the momentous events that marked the times up to the outbreak of World War II.

Clive Trebilcock's THE INDUSTRIALIZATION OF THE CONTINENTAL POWERS, 1780-1914 [523] presents historical models used in an economics framework for a different look at the Great Powers. The third volume of A DOCUMENTARY HISTORY OF MODERN EUROPE is called NATIONALISM, INDUSTRIALIZATION, AND DEMOCRACY, 1815-1914 [37] and contains essays and copies of the most important documents of the period. This volume and volume 4 of the series, BREAKDOWN AND REBIRTH, 1914 TO THE PRESENT [38] are the work of Thomas Barnes and Gerald Feldman. Frank Anderson and Amos Hershey prepared the HANDBOOK FOR THE DIPLOMATIC HISTORY OF EUROPE, ASIA AND AFRICA, 1870-1914 [16] for the National Board for Historical Science in 1918. It was reprinted in 1969 and again in 1974. Edward Gulick's EUROPE'S CLASSICAL BALANCE OF POWER: A CASE HISTORY OF THE THEORY AND PRACTICE OF ONE OF THE GREAT CONCEPTS OF EUROPEAN STATECRAFT [218] is extremely important at this point for a clear understanding of the dynamics that maintained the alignments of nations at the end of the 19th century and that led directly to the alliances of World War I. In this regard, THE SURVIVAL OF SMALL STATES: STUDIES IN SMALL POWER/GREAT POWER CONFLICT [545], by Daniel Vital, is also useful here. THE PENGUIN DICTIONARY OF TWENTIETH CENTURY HISTORY, 1900-1978 [382], which was compiled by A.W. Palmer, is also valuable for the reader who would like a handy, quick reference for data. The PENGUIN ATLAS OF RECENT HISTORY [353], by Colin McEvedy is also of great value as it deals with the changing face of Europe since 1815. The HISTORICAL ATLAS [467], by W.R. Shepherd, is an even better choice.

## GENERAL MILITARY WRITINGS OF IMPORTANCE

The best general works are Lynn Montross' WAR THROUGH THE AGES [362], J.F.C. Fuller's A MILITARY HISTORY OF THE WESTERN WORLD [188], Cyril Falls' THE ART OF WAR [166], Quincy Wright's THE STUDY OF WAR [570], and Spaulding, Nickerson and Wright's A STUDY OF MILITARY METHODS FROM THE EARLIEST TIMES [484]. THE ENCYCLOPEDIA OF MILITARY HISTORY [150], by R. Ernest and Trevor N. Dupuy, is still the best quick reference for information. A SHORT HISTORY OF WARFARE [583], by David Zook and Robin Higham, does the same thing but in a more narrative style. There is not a great deal of information on this particular period, so its chief value is in its overall approach to subject of warfare. Alfred Vagt's A HISTORY OF MILITARISM [538] and P. Schmitthenner's KRIEG UND KRIEGFUHRUNG IM WANDEL DER WELTGESCHICHTE [445] may be supplemented with THE HISTORY OF AN INTERNATIONAL DEBATE, 1860-1979 [47], that was published in 1982. Professor V.R. Berghahn, the work's author, has synthesized a number of widely diverging positions on the development of militarism into a readable treatise on the subject. Of special interest to this period is his treatment of the rise of militarism in Germany and Russia. Joel David Singer and a group of his associates have put together another interesting study entitled EXPLAINING WAR: SELECTED PAPERS FROM THE CORRELATES OF WAR PROJECT [473]. This book can be of great assistance in understanding the increasingly complex problems of international confrontations that faced Europe as it entered the 20th century. Ludwig Renn's WARFARE: THE RELATIONS OF WAR TO SOCIETY [410], Theodore Ropp's WAR IN THE MODERN WORLD [419], and the classic MEN IN ARMS [397], by R.A. Preston, Samuel Wise and H.O. Werner, are all useful in their several approaches to the study of warfare. Arthur Banks' A WORLD ATLAS OF MILITARY HISTORY, 1860-1945 [34] is an especially helpful tool at this point. THE LAW OF PEACE [542], by C. Van Vollenhaven, should also be referred to as it sets a tone definitely related to the period under discussion and helps to set the stage for the future.

Stanislav Andreski's MILITARY ORGANIZATION AND SOCIETY [19], THE MAKERS OF MODERN STRATEGY: MILITARY THOUGHT FROM MACHIAVELLI TO HITLER [155], that was edited by E.M. Earle, and Elbridge Colby's MASTERS OF MOBILE WARFARE [110] all have something to add to understanding the events that transpired in the Balkans. William Balck's TACTICS [29] is excellent in setting the parameters of the battlefield while Jean Bujac's PRECIS DE QUELQUES CAMPAGNES CONTEMPORAINES [61] describes the style of warfare at the beginning of the century. This work is in six volumes one of which is devoted to the Balkans. TWENTY-FIVE CENTURIES OF SEA WARFARE [365] is sufficiently detailed to provide whatever is necessary regarding the general activities at sea during this period. James Lowe's GEOPOLITICS AND WAR: MACKINDER'S PHILOSOPHY OF POWER [332] describes the views of the theoreticians who led Europe into the Great War. John Alger's THE QUEST FOR VICTORY: THE HISTORY OF THE PRINCIPLES OF WAR [11] is always interesting reading. UNIFORMEN EUROPAISCHER ARMEEN [181] by Gerhard Forster, Peter Hoch and Reinhard Muller, and UNIFORMS OF THE WORLD [304] describe the military dress of the various countries involved in the Balkans. The Forster book puts forth the novel idea that uniforms played an important role in shaping the socio-economic development of the nation. WEAPONS OF WAR [108], by P.E. Cleator, can be helpful in understanding some of the more important innovations in weaponry such as the machine gun, airplane, and the tank. THE WAGES OF WAR: A STATISTICAL HANDBOOK [474], by Singer and Small, and Martin Van Creveld's SUPPLYING WAR: LOGISTICS FROM WALLENSTEIN TO PATTON [541] are both very useful. Another good selection in that vernacular is Richard Lewinsohn's THE PROFITS OF WAR THROUGH THE AGES [328]. Finally, A GUIDE TO THE STUDY AND USE OF MILITARY HISTORY [278], which was edited by John E. Jessup and Robert W. Coakley, has numerous sections of interest, especially the articles by Jay Luvaas [335] and Jeffery Clarke [106].

WORKS ON THE GENERAL HISTORY OF THE BALKANS

Among the general histories of the Balkans, Leften Stavrianos' THE BALKANS SINCE 1453 [486] and his THE BALKANS, 1815-1914 [487] are both excellent. Ferdinand Schevill's critically acclaimed HISTORY OF THE BALKAN PENINSULA [440] ends with the World War I period but is extremely valuable for the period it does cover. THE BALKANS: A SHORT HISTORY [243], by Edgar Hosch, devotes only about 60 pages to this period but this may suffice for the casual reader who needs a little background information. THE BALKANS; A HISTORY OF BULGARIA, SERBIA, GREECE, RUMANIA, TURKEY [178], by Neville Forbes, Arnold Toynbee, David Mitrany, and D.G. Hodgarth traces the history of the Balkans up to 1915. It is excellent for this period. THE BALKAN STATES [214] is a two-volume study turned out by the British Foreign Office that was originally published in 1920 as a part of its Peace Handbooks series. William S. Murray's THE MAKING OF THE BALKAN STATES [368] was originally published in 1910 and reprinted in 1967. THE DANUBE: THE DRAMATIC HISTORY OF THE GREAT RIVER AND THE PEOPLE TOUCHED BY ITS FLOW [327], by Erwin and Ann Lessner, ends its coverage with the First World War.

THE RISE OF NATIONALITY IN THE BALKANS [462], by Robert Seton-Watson, has excellent coverage of the period after the Berlin settlement of 1878, while THE RISE OF NATIONALISM IN THE BALKANS, 1800-1930 [197], by Wesley M. Gewehr, covers the period implied in its title. THE BALKAN FEDERATION; A HISTORY OF THE MOVEMENT TOWARD BALKAN UNITY IN MODERN TIMES [485] is another excellent study by Leften Stavrianos. It is a history of the unity movements since the end of the 18th century. Charles and Barbara Jelavich have produced THE ESTABLISHMENT OF THE BALKAN NATIONAL STATES, 1804-1920 [276] as a part of the HISTORY OF EAST CENTRAL EUROPE [498] series prepared under the direction of Professors Peter Sugar and Donald Treadgold. John Sanness' EUROPE AND THE BALKANS. PAST TERRITORIAL DISPUTES AND SOCIOPOLITICAL VARIETY [428] looks at another aspect of the same problem. A CENTURY OF BALKAN TURMOIL [12] is a two-volume study by the prolific Yugoslav historian, Christ Anastasoff. Egon Heymann's BALKAN: KRIEGE, BUNDNISSE, REVOLUTIONEN; 150 JAHRE POLITIK UND SCHICKSAL [232] and Mieczysaw Tanty's KONFLIKTY BALKANSKIE W LATACH, 1878-1918 [504] both deal with the various issues involved in conflict in the Balkans. Tanty's work is in Polish. Arnold Toynbee's THE WESTERN QUESTION IN GREECE AND TURKEY [521] looks at this problem from yet another point of view. Robert Seton-Watson's THE EMANCIPATION OF SOUTH-EASTERN EUROPE [460] is also quite useful in understanding the conflicts that besieged the Balkans. George Schreiber's BALKAN AUS ESTER HAND. GESCHICHTE UND GEGENWART IN BERICHTEN VON AUSGENZUEGEN UND ZEITGENOSSEN [447] deals with eyewitness views of the events as they transpired.

Paul Horecky's SOUTHEASTERN EUROPE; A GUIDE TO BASIC PUBLICATIONS [240] is somewhat outdated but is still a good place to start in a search for material on this period. Another good reference source is that produced by the Zug-based I.D.C. called RUSSIA, U.S.S.R., EASTERN EUROPE: ALPHABETICAL CUMULATIVE CATALOGUE [426]. This is a listing of over 60,000 volumes on the subject that are found in microfiche editions. THE BALKANS IN TRANSITION [277], that was edited by Charles and Barbara Jelavich, contains a number of significant essays such as George Soulis' "Historical Studies in the Balkans in Modern Times." A listing of Polish documents on the

Balkans is found in BALCANICA: GUIDE TO THE POLISH ARCHIVES RELATIVE TO THE HISTORY OF THE BALKAN COUNTRIES [554]. Anton Scherer's SUDOSTEUROPA-DISSERTATIONEN, 1918-1960. EINE BIBLIOGRAPHIE DEUTSCHER, OSTERREICHISCHER UND SCHWEIZERISCHER HOCHSCHULSCHRIFTEN [439] and BIBLIOGRAPHIE DER SLAVISTISCHEN ARBEITEN AUS DEN DEUTSCHSPRACHIGEN FACHSEITSCHRIFT, 1876-1963 are also useful as sources. Lastly, BALKAN ECONOMIC HISTORY, 1550-1950 [317], by John Lampe and Marvin Jackson, is another excellent choice for examining the history of the Balkans from a different perspective.

## WORKS ON THE BALKAN NATIONS AND ON THE GREAT POWERS

Among the more general works on Austria-Hungary that have good coverage of the the empire's last days are Robert Kann's A HISTORY OF THE HABSBURG EMPIRE, 1526-1918 [286]; Adam Wandruszka's THE HOUSE OF HABSBURG: SIX HUNDRED YEARS OF A EUROPEAN DYNASTY [555]; Hans Kohn's THE HABSBURG EMPIRE, 1804-1918 [305]; THE HABSBURG EMPIRE, 1790-1918 [337], by C.A. Macartney; THE IMPERIAL CROWN: THE STORY OF THE RISE AND FALL OF THE HOLY ROMAN AND AUSTRIAN EMPIRES [184], by P. Frischauer; and DAS GESCHICHTE OSTERREICH [224], by H. Hantsch. THE HABSBURG MONARCHY, 1809-1918 [506], which somehow reached a second edition, was written by A.J.P. Taylor and is not reliable. THE HABSBURG EMPIRE: A STUDY IN INTREGRATION AND DISINTEGRATION [285], by Robert Kann, is not really a history but is, rather, a sociological analysis of the causes of its existence and demise. Kann's THE MULTINATIONAL EMPIRE; NATIONALISM AND NATIONAL REFORM IN THE HABSBURG MONARCHY, 1848-1918 [284] is, on the other hand, a two-volume encyclopedic work of great value. Another study of similar nature is THE HABSBURG MONARCHY; TOWARD A MULTINATIONAL EMPIRE OR NATIONAL STATES? [274], which was edited by Charles Jelavich. Fran Zwitter's LES PROBLEMES NATIONAUX DANS LA MONARCHIE DES HABSBOURG [584] is a different approach to the nationalities issue written by a Yugoslavian Marxist.

A number of other works have been written that deal with the fall of the empire. One of the best is Edward Crankshaw's THE FALL OF THE HOUSE OF HABSBURG [117] in which he studies the intrigues, strategies and personalities that helped destroy the empire. Professor Leo Valiani's THE END OF AUSTRIA-HUNGARY [539] concentrates on the Italian issues but also addresses the closely connected South Slav problems. This exceptional work was first published in Italian in 1966 and then in English in 1973. There is an excellent bibliography and extensive use of hitherto unpublished sources. Another good study of this same phenomenon is Oscar Jaszi's THE DISSOLUTION OF THE HABSBURG MONARCHY [272]. The HABSBURG LEGACY, 1867-1939 [384], by B. Pauley, proposes that the Austro-Hungarian empire cannot be properly assessed without a careful comparison of pre-World War I and interwar events.

THE PEOPLES OF THE EASTERN HAPSBURG LANDS, 1526-1918 [288], by Kann and David, deals primarily with the Hungarians, Croatians, and other ethnic groups living in or bordering on the Balkans. THE SOUTHERN SLAV QUESTION AND THE HABSBURG MONARCHY [463], by Robert Seton-Watson, deals with the rise of nationalism among the Croatians and Serbs in the Dual Monarchy, with Austrian politics, and with the Eastern Question. FROM SADOWA TO SARAJEVO. THE FOREIGN POLICY OF AUSTRIA-HUNGARY, 1866-1914 [56], by F.R. Bridge, is worthwhile but requires an extensive foreknowledge of events to understand.

AUSTRIA-HUNGARY AND GREAT BRITAIN, 1908-1914 [399] is less difficult to follow. A HABSBURG BIRDODALOM ES AZ OSTRAK-MAGYAR MONARCHIA TERKEPEINEK KATALOGUSA 1700-1919 [120] is a catalog of maps dealing with the empire between the given years. Gunther Rothenberg's THE ARMY OF FRANCIS JOSEPH [420] is probably the best study available on the multi-ethnic army of the empire. A broader view of the Emperor may be found in Albert Margutti's THE EMPEROR FRANCIS JOSEPH AND HIS TIMES [347].

Hungary's history is adequately covered in Sinor [475], Lengyel [325], or Macartney [338]. Sandor Petho's VILAGOSTOL TRIANONIG; A MAI MAGYARORSZAG KIALAKULASANAK TORTENETE [390] deals with the collapse of the Austro-Hungarian Empire in 1918 and its aftermath from the Hungarian perspective. The Trianon in the title refers to the treaty signed at that location in 1920 which confirmed Hungary's adherence to the Versailles-St. Germaine agreements. ETUDES HISTORIQUES HONGROIS [249] contains a number of articles that deal with this period, especially J. Galantai's "Austria-Hungary and the War - The October 1913 Crisis, Prelude to July 1914." Also of some importance at this point is Oscar Jaszi's REVOLUTION AND COUNTER-REVOLUTION IN HUNGARY [271] that looks at the empire's collapse, the October 1918 revolution, the character of Count Micheal Karolyi, the Hungarian Soviet Republic of 1919, and the "White Terror." This work was originally published in 1924 and is interesting even though it is without documentation.

There is relatively good coverage of the general historical development of Bulgaria in Stavrianos [486] and in THE ESTABLISHMENT OF THE BALKAN NATIONAL STATES, 1804-1920 [276], by Barbara and Charles Jelavich, and in Robert Seton-Watson's THE RISE OF NATIONALITY IN THE BALKANS [462]. Christ Anastasoff's THE BULGARIANS: FROM THEIR ARRIVAL IN THE BALKANS TO MODERN TIMES [14] is also worthwhile. A total of 128 documents dealing with this period are translated into English and reproduced in DOCUMENTS AND MATERIALS ON THE HISTORY OF THE BULGARIAN PEOPLE [65]. Among this number are many that are of direct military significance.

Greece's history through these times in discussed in a number of works. Douglas Dakin's THE UNIFICATION OF GREECE, 1770-1923 [126]; MODERN GREECE, 1800-1931 [350], by J. Mavrocordato; Richard Clogg's A SHORT HISTORY OF GREECE [109]; E.S. Forster's A SHORT HISTORY OF MODERN GREECE, 1821-1956 [180]; and D.A. Zakythinos' THE MAKING OF MODERN GREECE [578] are all good.

The history of Albania is adequately described in John Swire's ALBANIA, THE RISE OF A KINGDOM [500] which covers the period up to 1912. Stavro Skendi ends his account at the same point in his THE ALBANIAN NATIONAL AWAKENING, 1878-1912 [477]. This covers the period from the Congress of Berlin to the beginning of the Balkan Wars and has an extensive bibliography. Skendi's ALBANIAN POLITICAL THOUGHT AND REVOLUTIONARY ACTIVITY, 1881-1912 [476] is also valuable. Other useful works include Anton Logoreci's THE ALBANIANS [330], Felice Cammarata's ALBANICA [81], and E.L.J. Legrand's BIBLIOGRAPHIE ALBANAISE [324]. Logoreci's work deals with future events but is good reading here.

There are numerous works on Romanian history during the first four decades of the 20th century. Stephen Fisher-Galati's

TWENTIETH CENTURY RUMANIA [175] is useful and devotes the better part of three chapters to the pre-World War II period. Nicolae Iorga's HISTOIRE DES ROUMAINES DE LA PENINSULE DES BALKANS [258] is written in the more classical style but, as it was published in 1919, lacks the study of the interwar years. The CHRONOLOGICAL HISTORY OF ROMANIA [207] devotes about 80 pages to the period, but there is a positive lack of continuity to the entries. More space is devoted to the premiere of the first movie filmed in Romania in 1913 than is given to the discussion of Romania's role in the Second Balkan War. Coverage of the World War I period is generally very good.

STUDII DE ISTORIE SI TEORIE MILITARA. RETROSPECTIVE ISTORICE ANALIZE CONTEMPORANE [415] is a collection of studies dealing with Romanian military thought and art. Mihai Cucu's FACTORUL GEOGRAFIC IN ACTINUNILE MILITARE. SECVENTE DIN ISTORIA MILITARA ROMANEASCA [121] is an analysis of Romanian victories based upon the knowledge and use of terrain. Stefan Pascu's "The Romanian Army and Society, 1878-1920," that appears in Ilie Ceaucescu's THE ROAD TO INDEPENDENCE [99], is a short account of the Romanian role during the First World War. There is only a mention of the great peasant uprising of 1907, and of the Balkan Wars. PAGES FROM THE HISTORY OF THE ROMANIAN ARMY [436] contains two articles on the period, while PAGES FROM THE MILITARY HISTORY OF THE ROMANIAN PEOPLE [97] contains nine. THE ENTIRE PEOPLE'S WAR FOR THE HOMELAND'S DEFENCE WITH THE ROMANIANS [98] deals primarily with the role of the socialism and Communist Party and its ideology throughout this period. There are, however, some very interesting facts brought to light such as the military training given to children and data on compulsory military training before World War I. THE ARMY AND ROMANIAN SOCIETY [437] has at least six articles that are useful in the period. CONTRIBUTII LA ISTORIA MARINEI ROMANE. DIN CELE MAI VECHE TIMPURI PINA IN 1918 [51] deals with the development of Romanian naval forces to 1918 and was written by Nicolae Birdeanu and Dan Nicholescu. ENCICLOPEDIA ISTORIOGRAFIEI ROMANESTI [416] was published in 1978 and is a reference work containing biographical notes and extensive bibliographical references. Vasile Vesa discusses Franco-Romanian diplomatic relations from 1900-1916 in his ROMANIA SI FRANTA LA INCEPUTUL SECOLULUI AL XX-LEA [543]. Ladislas Makkai's HISTOIRE DE TRANSYLVANIE [344] and D. Draghicescu's LA TRANSYLVANIE [142] should suffice for general coverage of the Romanian province that remained under the Dual Monarchy until the close of the First World War.

Serbia's turbulent history during this period is portrayed in a number of good general studies. Sir Harold Temperley's HISTORY OF SERBIA [510], which was produced in 1917, is probably the most scholarly, while Professor Micheal Boro Petrovich's two-volume A HISTORY OF MODERN SERBIA, 1804-1918 [389] is both scholarly and readable. SERBIA; HER PEOPLE, HISTORY, ASPIRATIONS [388], by Vojislav Petrovic, is also good but its coverage ends in 1914. Prince Lazarovich-Hrebeliano's SERVIAN PEOPLE [320] is also interesting but may be too encyclopedic for some and too overly romantic for others. Of somewhat equally dubious quality is Count Carlo Sforza's FIFTY YEARS OF WAR AND DIPLOMACY IN THE BALKANS [464] which devotes about 70 of its 195 pages to the 1900-1914 period. Sforza's account deals heavily with the story of Nikola Pashich, the Serbian statesman. The book is uneven and quite often in error. SERBIA, NIKOLA PASIC, AND YUGOSLAVIA [143], by Alex N. Dragnic, has produced a very good biography of Pashich. Bernadotte Schmitt's SERBIA, YUGOSLAVIA, AND THE HABSBURG EMPIRE [443] which was published in the United Nations Series is also useful. Another good book that deals with Serbia's rise to independence and the events of the first decades of the 20th century is LA FORMATION DE LA YOUGOSLAVIE, XV$^e$-XX$^e$ [192] by E. Gaumant, published in 1931.

Macedonia's equally turbulent history is recounted in Elizabeth Barker's MACEDONIA: ITS PLACE IN BALKAN POWER POLITICS [36]; in Djoko Slijepcevic's THE MACEDONIAN QUESTION; THE STRUGGLE FOR SOUTHERN SERBIA [480]; and in MAZEDONIEN IN DER BULGARISCHEN GESCHICHTE [149], by Iwan Dujcev. Lastly, Alexandros Zannas' THE MACEDONIAN STRUGGLE, RECOLLECTIONS [579] is the personal account of a participant in the fight in Thessalonike after 1902. It is full of good data but, although it is reported as being in English, the only available forms seems to be in Greek. Christ Anastasoff's THE TRAGIC PENINSULA: A HISTORY OF THE MACEDONIAN MOVEMENT FOR INDEPENDENCE SINCE 1878 [13] is excellent, if somewhat outdated. Emile Kuepfer deals with the always volatile issue of cross-boundary relations in his LA MACEDOINE ET LES BULGARES [312].

Francis Stevenson's A HISTORY OF MONTENEGRO [490] is good for the general history of another of the fiercely independent provinces that would soon be forced into the Yugoslav union. Stevenson's book was originally published in 1912 so its value ends quite early in the new period. Jaroslav Sidak's PROIJEST HRVATSKOG NARODA G. 1860-1914 [469] gives approximately the same coverage to the development of Croatia. A glimpse of life in Bosnia is presented in Vladimir Dedijer's outstanding THE BELOVED LAND [128]. BLACK LAMB AND GREY FALCON [560] is a classic by Dame Rebecca West. While it tells of her journey through Yugoslavia in 1937, it should be read now as a primer on the nature of the country. Ruth Trouton's PEASANT RESISTANCE IN YUGOSLAVIA, 1900-1950 [524] tends to overplay Tito's role in later developments but is quite good during these early decades. Muriel Heppell and Frank B. Singleton's YUGOSLAVIA [229] is a good overall history while "Yugoslavia and Romania" [386] by K. St. Pavlowitch is interesting background reading at this point.

The works that are available about the Ottoman Empire include Lord Kinross' THE OTTOMAN CENTURIES: THE RISE AND FALL OF THE TURKISH EMPIRE [298], Stanford and E.K. Shaw's REFORM, REVOLUTION AND REPUBLIC: THE RISE OF MODERN TURKEY, 1808-1975 [466], Sir Bernard Lewis' THE EMERGENCE OF MODERN TURKEY [329], William Miller's THE OTTOMAN EMPIRE AND ITS SUCCESSORS, 1801-1927 [357], Nicholae Iorga's GESCHICHTE DES OSMANISCHEN REICHES [259], and Albert Hourani's THE OTTOMAN BACKGROUND OF THE MODERN MIDDLE EAST [244]. Stanford Shaw's "The Ottoman View of the Balkans" [465] and Traian Stoianovich's "Factors in the Decline of Ottoman Society in the Balkans" [492] are both useful for background reading. Wilbur White's THE PROCESS OF CHANGE IN THE OTTOMAN EMPIRE [562] is an account of the dissolution of an empire that spanned three continents at its zenith of power. Maximilian Braun's "Turkenherrschaft und Turkenkampf bei den Balkenslawen" [585] is of value as is Sidney Fisher's "Ottoman Feudalism and Its Influence Upon the Balkans" [174], Bistra Tsvetkova's LES INSTITUTIONS OTTOMANES EN EUROPE [526] and W.L. Wright's OTTOMAN STATECRAFT.

Some useful military organizational data may be found in M.A. Grassi's CHARTE TURQUE ON ORGANIZATION RELIGIEUSE, CIVILE ET MILITAIRE DE L'EMPIRE OTTOMAN [211]. DAS TURKISCHE HEER [441], by L. von Schlozer, is also quite useful. THE RISE OF TURKISH NATIONALISM, 1876-1908 [314] is only 138 pages, but it is a very valuable analysis of the closing decades of the Ottoman Empire. The last grand viziers and prime ministers of the empire are discussed in detail in Mehmed Zeki Pakalm's five-volume SON SADRAZAMLAR VE BASVEKILLER [380]. Noel Barber's THE SULTANS [586] covers the reigns of the last Sultans in sufficient detail for background reading. The best reference works are the two editions of the ENCYCLOPEDIA OF ISLAM [198, 245] and the CAMBRIDGE HISTORY OF ISLAM [238]. The Turkish-language ISLAM ANSIKLOPEDISI [531] is also very useful for anyone who can use it.

The history of Imperial Russia during this period may be found in Klyuchevski [301, 302], Riasonovsky [413], and Clarkson [107]. Micheal Florinsky's RUSSIA: A HISTORY AND AN INTERPRETATION [177] is also quite useful. Of more direct value are Hugh Seton-Watson's THE DECLINE AND FALL OF IMPERIAL RUSSIA, 1855-1914 [587] and J.N. Westwood's ENDURANCE AND ENDEAVOUR: RUSSIAN HISTORY, 1812-1980 [561]. Graham Stephenson's RUSSIA FROM 1812 TO 1945: A HISTORY [489] should not be trusted as it shamelessly misrepresents the history of these early 20th century decades. Of considerably better quality is Lionel Kochan and Richard Abraham's THE MAKING OF MODERN RUSSIA [589]. Barbara Jelavich's A CENTURY OF RUSSIAN FOREIGN POLICY, 1814-1914 [273] and RUSSIA AND THE BALKANS IN RUSSIAN FOREIGN POLICY: ESSAYS IN HISTORICAL PERSPECTIVE [321], that was edited by Ivo Lederer, are both worthwhile reading at this point. RUSSIAN REALITIES AND PROBLEMS [146], edited by James Duff, has an article by Paul N. Milyoukov entitled "The War and Balkan Politics." Virginia Cowles' THE RUSSIAN DAGGER: COLD WAR IN THE DAYS OF THE CZARS [115] relates the Russian intrigues in Bulgaria and Serbia and the role played by Nicholas II at the beginning of World War I. RUSSIAN IMPERIALISM FROM IVAN THE TERRIBLE TO THE REVOLUTION [249], edited by Taras Hunczak, barely touches on this last period of imperial rule. A resume of military literature on the period may be found in ISTORIYA OTECHESTVENNOI VOENNO-ENTSIKLOPEDICHESKOI LITERATURI [588] which was edited by a team of Soviet scholars and published in 1980. Patricia Grimsted's ARCHIVES AND MANUSCRIPT COLLECTION IN THE USSR [215] may be of some value as it contains finding aids for most major collections. Martin Gilbert's RUSSIAN HISTORY ATLAS [205] and AN ATLAS OF RUSSIAN AND EAST EUROPEAN HISTORY [3], by Adams, Matley and McCagg, are both of great benefit at this time.

Gerald Clayton's BRITAIN AND THE EASTERN QUESTION: MISSOLONGHI TO GALLIPOLI [590] deals with the period from the Greek War of Independence (1821-1832) to the disastrous campaign of 1915 that may have changed the course of history. J.F.N. Bradley's CZECHO-SLOVAKIA: A SHORT HISTORY [591] is valuable as it sheds a different light on Habsburg history during this period. Paul Ignotus's "Czechs, Magyars, Slovaks" [254] is also helpful reading.

THE BALKANS IN THE PRE-WORLD WAR I PERIOD

With the opening of the 20th century, the peace that
Bismarck had maintained in Europe began to change following his
dismissal by Wilhelm II in 1890. The Triple Alliance (1882) had
grown out of the 1879 Dual Alliance that had linked Germany and
Austria-Hungary together in a common cause against any third party
attack. When Italy, highly desirous of increasing its prestige and
irritated over the French annexation of Tunisia, sought an alliance
with Germany, the Kaiser's price was Italian military support if he
was attacked by France. In return, both Germany and Austria-Hungary
were to support Italy if it were attacked by France. Serbia had
entered into a Bismarck-instigated alliance with Austria-Hungary in
1881. Romania fell in with the Triple Alliance in 1883. When
Bismarck left office in 1890, he did so knowing that Germany's
position was secure. He may also have known that Austrian desires in
the Balkans were almost sure to bring a Russian reaction. Bismarck
also remarked that the Italians could not be trusted, and that they
too had designs on the Balkans that would eventually run counter to
Vienna's goals. When the Reinsurance Treaty between Germany and
Russia was not renewed in 1890, the Tsar was all but driven into the
arms of France.

Standing in opposition to the Triple Alliance was France
and, between 1891 and 1894, it was able to secure its first ally
since the disgrace of the Franco-Prussian War. Russia, always in
need of capital, was swayed by the blandishments of French bankers
and joined in a secret compact (1894) with France. Then, in 1898,
the new French foreign minister, Theophile Delcasse, began a
campaign that ended in the signing of an entente with Great Britain.
This was not totally unacceptable to the British as, by the turn of
the century, it had become clear they could no longer survive in
"splendid isolation." England's unpreparedness in the Boer War
(1899-1902) showed how much strong friends were needed. And the
results of the Russo-Japanese War (1904-1905) proved beyond question
to England and France that their respective alliances with Japan and
Russia could easily lead them into war on opposite sides thereby
clearing the way for German expansion at the expense of both. Thus,
the Anglo-French alliance of 1904 was followed by the Anglo-Russian
treaty of 1907 and the Triple Entente was born. Europe was now
divided into two armed camps.

As these events transpired, the Balkans were already feeling
increased Germanic pressure. Bismarck's successors seized upon the
possibility of exploiting the Ottoman Empire and in 1902 acquired
the rights to construct the Baghdad Railway between Constantinople
and the capitol of present-day Iraq. It was their hope that this new
line would link with the German and Austrian rail systems in the
west to create an overland route to the Indian ocean that would be
shorter and cheaper than the maritime routes maintained by England
and France. As a part of the arrangements, German officers began
training the Turkish army.

THE MACEDONIAN UPRISING OF 1903

There is a wealth of literature on this crucial period in
Balkan history. FROM SADOWA TO SARAJEVO. THE FOREIGN POLICY OF
AUSTRIA-HUNGARY, 1866-1914 [56], by F.R. Bridge, is appropriate

reading for this part of the period. Mary Edith Durham's TWENTY YEARS OF BALKAN TANGLE [152] deals with the first two decades of the century. Reginald Wyon's THE BALKANS FROM WITHIN [572] should also be studied. RUSSIA'S BALKAN POLICY, 1894-1905 [147] is interesting reading at this point. Sloane [481] builds an excellent picture of the conditions that existed on the eve of the Balkan Wars. Wayne Vucinich presents the background of the political factions at work in Serbia between 1905-1908 in his SERBIA BETWEEN EAST AND WEST [549]. Professor Vucinich also deals with the increasing rivalry that was growing between Russia and Austria over influence in Belgrad. These issues, of course, led directly to the start of the First World War. In addition, he discusses the conflict between Serbia's King Alexander and his father, the ex-king Milan that led to the Macedonia uprisings. Alexander was assassinated on 11 June 1903 by a band led by Dragutin Dimitrijevic, an officer under Russian influence. The aging Peter Kagageorgevic was proclaimed the new ruler and Austria-Hungary, disgusted with Alexander's earlier conduct, immediately recognized the new regime. Soon all of Europe followed, except England. Dimitrijevic was embraced by the new king, promoted to colonel and officially thanked by the Serbian parliament. There followed soon after an uprising in Macedonia in which Greek, Serbian, and Bulgarian insurgents took on the Turkish gendarmerie. Finally, in the fall of 1903, an international force was sent in to defuse the situation. Lessner [327] recounts this tale with his expected color and with more than a little imagination. Manol Pandevski tells the story from the modern Yugoslavian perspective in his ILINDENSKOTO VOSTANIE VO MAKEDONIJA 1903 [383]. THE ILINDEN-PREOBRAZHENIE UPRISING OF 1903 [248], by Hristov, Kossev, and Panayotov, highlights the continuity of events in Macedonia and in the area around Adrianople. Macedonia was disputed ground between Serbia and Bulgaria. This little book has some fascinating photographs from the times and has some very important information that needs to be separated from the rhetoric. Douglas Dakin discusses these events in his THE UNIFICATION OF GREECE, 1770-1923 [126] and in his THE GREEK STRUGGLE IN MACEDONIA, 1897-1913 [125]. ION DRAGHOUMIS AND THE MACEDONIAN STRUGGLE [164], by Dimitrios Evrygenis, tells of one of the Greek leaders of the period, but the work is in the Greek language. Another good work in Greek is OUR BALKAN NEIGHBORS [315], by Alexis Kyrou, that deals primarily with Bulgarian attempts to annex Macedonia following its annexation of Eastern Rumelia in 1885. Jacob Ruchti discusses the Russian and Austrian influences in the events in his DIE REFORMAKTION OSTRREICH-UNGARNS UND RUSSLANDS IN MAZEDONIEN 1903-1908 [424]. SARAEVSKOE UBIISTVO: ISSLEDOVANIE PO ISTORII A AVSTRO-CERSKIKH OTNOSHENII I BALKAMSKOE POLITIKI POSSII V PERIOD 1903-1914 [393], by N.P. Poletica, was published in Leningrad in 1930 and deals with Serbo-Austrian relations of the period.The so-called "Pig War" or Customs War that went on between Austria-Hungary and Serbia is discussed in Dimitrije Djordjevic's CARINSKI RAT AUSTRO-UGARSKE I SRBIJE, 1906-1911 [138]. Another aspect of these events may be found in Allen Upward's THE EAST END OF EUROPE: THE REPORT OF AN UNOFFICIAL MISSION TO THE EUROPAN PROVINCES OF TURKEY ON THE EVE OF REVOLUTION [535]. Croatian history during this period is discussed in Vladko Macek's THE STRUGGLE FOR FREEDOM [340]. Another similar work is Milan Zivanovic's DUBROVNIK U BORBA ZA UJEDINJENJEI 1908-1918 [582] that looks at the struggle of one Serbo-Croatian region during the time indicated.

# THE ROMANIAN UPRISING OF 1907

Romania's history during this period was relatively quiet. The treaty with Austria-Hungary was renewed in 1902 that kept Romania in the Triple Alliance. In 1904, following a strike by Transylvanian railway workers, an uprising began that was shortlived but which caused a number of casualties. Then, in July 1905, Romania became indirectly associated with the Russian Revolution when the mutinous crew of the Imperial Russian cruiser "Potemkin" brought their prize into Constanta harbor on Romania's Black Sea coast. In February 1907, an uprising began when peasants in the Botosani region demanded land. The trouble quickly spread throughout the country. Clashes between the rebels and the army soon became common with thousands being killed or arrested by the authorities before the revolt subsided. Gheorghe Cazan and Serban Radelescu's ROMANIA SI TRIPLA ALIANTA, 1878-1914 [95] is a compilation of two monographs that deal with Romania's adherence to the Triple Alliance in the face of its increasing conflict with Austria-Hungary over Transylvania. Giurescu [207] has a sketchy account of the events of 1907. A better assessment may be found in Philip Eidelberg's THE GREAT RUMANIAN PEASANT REVOLT OF 1907: ORIGINS OF A MODERN JACQUERIE [157]. Jack Tucker's dissertation, "The Rumanian Peasant Revolt of 1907: Three Regional Studies" [528], was accepted by the University of Chicago in 1972. Stefan Pascu speaks of "The Romanian Army and Society, 1878-1920" in TRTI that was edited by Ilie Ceaucescu. Vasile Vesa looks at Franco-Romanian relations in ROMANIA SI FRANTA LA INCEPUTUL SECOLULUI AL XX-LEA [543] which covers the period 1900 to 1916.

## THE BOSNIAN CRISIS AND THE YOUNG TURKS

When the Young Turk Association organized a revolutionary movement in 1908 and compelled Sultan Abdulhamit II (1876-1909) to restore the 1876 constitution, the Austrian government seized upon the opportunity to annex Bosnia-Herzogovina. This action displeased the Turks, but it infuriated the Serbs. Russia, still reeling from the disaster of the Russo-Japanese War could not help and England and France would not. Germany stood behind Austria and the crisis passed but was not forgotten.

THE AWAKENING OF TURKEY: A HISTORY OF THE TURKISH REVOLUTION [303], by E.F. Knight, Clair Price's THE REBIRTH OF TURKEY [400], E.E. Ramsaur's THE YOUNG TURKS; PRELUDE TO THE REVOLUTION OF 1908 [404], Charles Buxton's TURKEY IN REVOLUTION [75] and LA REVOLUTION TURQUE [46] are all useful in understanding the events that transpired in Turkey. THE BALKAN TRIAL [363], by Frederick Moore, describes the Balkan peninsula during this period and discusses Turkish politics and government. The Ottoman revolution is also discussed by Youssouf Fehmi in LA REVOLUTION OTTOMANE (1908-1910) [171]. Another interesting aspect of the revolt is found in the article by G. Jaschke entitled "Der Freiheitskampf des turkischen Volkes" [265]. BRITISH POLICY TOWARDS THE OTTOMAN EMPIRE 1908-1914 [226], by Joseph Heller, and "British Policy in the Balkans, 1908-1909" [112], by M.B. Cooper, are both important at this point. "Great Britain's Relations with the Young Turks, 1908-1914" [5], by F. Ahmad, is also useful as is AUSTRIA-HUNGARY AND GREAT BRITAIN, 1908-1914 [399], by A.F. Pribram. Zivanovic [582] deals with the Bosnia-Herzogovinian annexation, but a much more thorough account is found in Bernadotte Schmitt's THE ANNEXATION OF BOSNIA, 1908-1909. Paul Halpern deals with THE MEDITERRANEAN NAVAL SITUATION, 1908-1914 [222], while John Wesley Hoffman writes on the THE AUSTRO-RUSSIAN RIVALRY IN THE BALKANS, 1909-1912 [236].

## THE ITALO-TURKISH WAR, 1911-1912

On 29 September 1911, Italy declared war on Turkey following a 24-hour ultimatum it had issued the Porte over the alleged mistreatment of Italians in Tripoli on the North African coast. This ploy was the result of an Alliance attempt to counter French occupation of Tunisia. Although the Turks attempted conciliation the Tripoli War began and dragged on for a year, during which time the Italians sent naval forces into the Dardanelles (April 1912) and seized the Dodecanese islands (May 1912). Events in the Balkans contrived to force Italy to end its campaign. The ensuing treaty (Ouchy, 15 October 1912) ceded Libya, Rhodes, and the Dodecanese to Italy. This war on the periphery of the Balkans is covered in sufficient detail in Dupuy [150] and in Professor Kedourie's fine article [292] in NCMH 12.

## THE BALKAN WARS

### THE FIRST BALKAN WAR

Although the war between two Alliance partners, Italy and Turkey, provided secret satisfaction for the members of the Entente, the real test was to follow. The repercussions of the war in which the Ottoman Empire had once again proven how feeble it was were soon felt in the second Balkan crisis of the decade. In this case, the primary factors included Russian involvement in the treaty of alliance signed between Serbia and Bulgaria on 13 March 1912. The reasons for this alliance are manifold but center on fear of further Austro-Hungarian aggrandizement as much as any other reason. It was a fact, however, that a secret proviso called for the partition of Macedonia. Greece became a member of the new Balkan League by a separate treaty (29 May), to which Montenegro gave verbal adherence. With the Italo-Turkish War under way, insurrections broke out in Albania and Macedonia. Russia suddenly found itself without French support when Raymond Poincare, France's president and prime minister, discovered the secret Serbo-Bulgarian accords on Macedonia. At the same time, Austria-Hungary attempted diplomacy to settle the rising Balkan protests over alleged Turkish mistreatment of the Macedonians. Both Russia and Austria-Hungary warned the Balkan states that the powers would not recognize any dismemberment of the Ottoman Empire but the die was already cast. On 8 October 1912, Montenegro declared war on Turkey. Ten days later, Greek, Serbian and Bulgarian armies opened almost simultaneous offensives against the Turkish European provinces. About 310,000 troops, including more than 25,000 Montenegran irregulars were involved in campaigns directed against Adrianople in the east, Macedonia and Thrace.

In the Macedonian campaign, a Greek army under the Crown Prince Constantine defeated the Turks at Elasson (23 October). When the Turks withdrew toward Monastir (Bitola) (today just north of Yugoslavia's border with Greece), the Greeks failed to pursue moving instead toward Thessalonike (Salonika) in hopes of preventing a

Bulgarian takeover there. On 24 October, Serbian forces led by the Minister of War, General Radomir Putnik, defeated a second Turkish force at Kumanovo in the mountains east of Skoplje. The Turks were eventually forced to evacuate Skoplje and they too withdrew to Monastir. In the meantime, a Turkish holding action had blocked Constantine's Greeks at Venije Vardar. In two actions at Kastoria and Banitsa in northern Macedonia, the Greeks were defeated (2-3 November), but finally overcame the resistance at Venije Vardar (5 November) and pushed on to Thessalonike where they laid siege until 8 November when the 20,000 man Turkish garrison surrendered. The Bulgarians arrived too late on the following day.

At Monastir, the Ottoman garrison was reinforced by 40,000 additional troops. In a seesaw battle, that was joined on 5 November, but did not climax until 14-19 November, the Serbian First Army decisively defeated the Turks killing or capturing nearly 20,000 of them in the process. Fleeing the field, the Turks moved to Yannina (Ioannina) where the Greeks laid siege hoping to gain Epirus as a prize.

While this campaign progressed, a Bulgarian force of three armies under the command of General Radko Dimitriev had pushed toward Constantinople. After sharp actions at Kirk Kilissa and Seliolu (22-25 October), the Bulgarian Second Army with some Serbian reinforcements laid siege to Adrianople (Edirne) while two other Bulgarian armies maneuvered to face the main Turkish force under Abdalla Pasha in the vicinity of Lule' Burgas (Luleburgaz) that lies between Adrianople and Constantinople. As the battle grew in intensity between 28-30 October, the Turks were forced to withdraw behind permanent fortifications at Catalca about 20 miles from the Ottoman capital where poorly planned attacks by the Bulgarians caused very heavy casualties and little success. On 3 December, an armistice was concluded that was followed by the London Peace Conference that opened on 16 December. The Greeks and Montenegrans ignored these moves toward peace and continued the sieges at Yannina and at Scutari (Shkoder) in northern Albania. The Bulgarians and Serbs maintained their investment at Adrianople.

By 13 January 1913, the diplomatic efforts at London had turned into a shambles as the Great Powers attempted to insure their own influence in the Balkans and to further insure their share of the now almost prostrate Ottoman Empire. Completely dismayed by the events, the Young Turks overthrew the Porte on 23 January and abrogated the armistice on 3 February. One month later Yannina fell to the Greeks and on 26 March Adrianople fell to an assault that cost the Serbo-Bulgarian force almost 10,000 lives. When the citadel fell the Turks still had over 60,000 troops in the garrison. On 22 April, Scutari fell to Montenegran irregulars. A final peace was imposed on 30 May in which Turkey lost almost everything that still remained of its European possessions. Albania, which had declared its independence and its neutrality when the war had started was given Scutari at Montenegran expense and the division of Macedonia created a major squabble between Bulgaria and Serbia. Crete was given to Greece. Serbia was once again blocked in its attempt to reach the Adriatic by Austro-Hungarian and Italian support for the Albanian cause.

## THE SECOND BALKAN WAR

As the ink was drying on the London peace accords a new war began when Bulgarian forces attacked Serbian positions along the Vardar river on the night of 29-30 June 1913. The Serbians and their Greek allies were able to withstand the brunt of the attack which soon faltered and slowed. By July, both Romania and Turkey had entered the war against the Bulgarians who were now on the defensive in all sectors. On 31 July, as Romanian forces moved almost unopposed on Sofia, and Turkish forces were reoccupying Adrianople, Bulgaria asked for terms. The ensuing Treaty of Bucharest, signed on 10 August, took away all of Bulgaria's gains and set the boundaries in the Balkans that were to remain with some few adjustments to the present. The signing of the treaty at the Romanian capital took place one week less than a year before the beginning of the Great War.

There are numerous sources on the Balkan Wars that present the various important aspects of the two conflicts in different ways. Stavrianos [486] and Jelavich [276] both have good general accounts of the wars. Petrovich [389] gives a good view of the Serbian role. Dupuy's [150] chronological record is very useful although some of the dates appear to be in error. Ernst Helmreich's THE DIPLOMACY OF THE BALKAN WARS, 1912-1913 [595] is extremely useful in understanding the critical nature of the situation in relation to the tenuous balance of power in Europe. Sir George Young's NATIONALISM AND WAR IN THE NEAR EAST [576] is an excellent firsthand account of this same problem. This work has a very good bibliography. James Miller's dissertation presented at Clark University in 1969 was entitled "The Concert of Europe in the First Balkan War, 1912-1913" [356]. Dimitrije Djordjevic's REVOLUTIONS NATIONALES DES PEUPLES BALKANIQUES, 1804-1914 [139] is also quite interesting in its approach to the problem of synchronous desire for freedom held by all of the Balkan nationalities, even though the general atmosphere of enmity and suspicion made any long range association highly unlikely. Christopher Thomson's OLD EUROPE'S SUICIDE; OR, THE BUILDING OF A PYRAMID OF ERRORS [515] describes in a series of essays the Balkan situation before and during the wars and its portent of the Great War. Thomson was a general officer who wrote from personal experience and who adds great flavor to the story of the war. William Sloane's THE BALKANS: A LABORATORY OF HISTORY [481] is a excellent study of the conditions that allowed brilliant military achievement and barbarian atrocities to occur together.

Histories devoted specifically to the war include Major Clyde S. Ford's THE BALKAN WARS [179] which are a compilation of a lectures presented by this army doctor at Fort Leavenworth in 1915. Jacob Schurman's THE BALKAN WARS, 1912-1913 [448] is also a compilation of papers that were a part of the 1914 Stafford Little Lectures series. It is excellent reading. Colonel Sir Reginald Rankin's INNER HISTORY OF THE BALKAN WAR [406] uses the veteran London _Times_ Balkan correspondent, James D. Bourchier as the central figure in the book ascribing to him all sorts of heroics in uniting the Christians against the Muslim hordes of the Ottoman Empire. The book is actually quite good and very enjoyable reading. Cyril Campbell's journalistic THE BALKAN WAR DRAMA [82] is also

worthwhile. Another book by an individual who covered the war is
Henry Farnsworth's LOG OF A WOULD-BE WAR CORRESPONDENT [168] which
is a narrative account of a young American journalist who managed to
cover the war even without official Turkish sanction to do so.

Foreign language works on the war include Nicolae Iorga's
ISTORIA RAZBOIULUI BALBANIC [260] that is another compilation of
lectures published in 1915 by the University of Bucharest.
BALKANSKATA VOINA, 1912-1913 [172], by I.V. Fishev, is a 1940
publication produced in Bulgaria. Another one published in Sofia a
decade later is Militsa Ognianova's BALKANSKATA VOINA [373]. Josef
Kolejka deals with the Balkan reaction to the Young Turk uprising in
his BALKANSKA OTAZKA 1908-1914: MEZINARODI SOCIALISTICKE HNUTI O
MLADOTURECKE REVOLUCI A O BALKANSKYCH VALKACH [306]. PRVI BALKANSKI
RAT, 1912-1913 [577] was published in Belgrad, contains a number of
the war plans involved, and has an excellent bibliography. Petar
Stojanov focusses on the Macedonian problem in his MAKEDONIJA VO
POLITIKATA NA GOLEMITE SILI VO VREMETO NA BALKANSKITE VOINI
1912-1913 [493]. Another work that deals primarily with the
Macedonian issue is Savo Skoko's doctoral dissertation that was
published by the Yugoslav Institute of Military History in 1975.
This work is entitled DRUGI BALKANSKI RAT 1913. It centers upon the
Second Balkan War period. Yet another work on Macedonia is Georgi
Abadziev's BALKANSKITE VOJNI I MAKEDONIJA [1] that was published in
Skoplje in 1958. Milan Zivanovic's [582] study of the Serbo-Croatian
situation in Dubrovnik is also quite useful at this point.

The First Balkan War campaign in the eastern Balkans is the
subject of a Bulgarian state-produced work entitled VOINATA MEZHDU
B'ULGARIA I TURTSIYA 1912-1913 GOD [63]. There are two works in
French by Bernard Boncabeille that are very useful: LA GUERRE
INTERBALKANIQUE [54] and his LA GUERRE TURCO-BALKANIQUE, 1912-1913
[53]. Richard Giesche's DER SERBISCHE ZUGANG ZUM MEER UND DIE
EUROPAISCHE KRISE 1912 [202] studies the Serbian desire for access
onto the Adriatic and the stiff resistance to that idea by Italy and
Austria-Hungary. Robert Seton-Watson also deals with this topic in
his THE BALKANS, ITALY AND THE ADRIATIC [458]. An Italian document,
MOMENTI DI STORIA BALCANICA (1878-1914). ASPETTI MILITARI [50], by
Antonello Biagini, brings together reports of military observers and
diplomats who served in various locations and assignments in the
Balkans during those critical years. Ilhan Bardakci outlines the
reign of Mohammed V (1909-1918) in BIR IMPARATORLUGUN YAGMASI:
BALKAN BOZGUNU VE I, DUNYA HARBI [586]. Turkish Army of the East
operations in the Vardar and Ustruma areas are discussed by Resay
Halli in the official BALKAN HARBI, 1912-13. GARP ORDUSU. VARDAR
ORDUSU ILE USTRUMA KOLORDUSUNUN HAREKAT VE MUHAREBELERI [221].
Hikmet Suer looks at the battles of Bolayir and Katalka, the landing
at Sarkoy and the recapture of Kirklareli and Adrianople during the
First Balkan War in his TURK SILAHLI KUVVETLERI TARIHI, OSMANLI
DEVREI, BALKAN HARBI [497] in a four-volume section of the official
history of the Turkish Army. In ASKERI TARIH BELGERI DERGISI:
DOCUMENTS D'HISTOIRE MLITAIRE [529] the Turkish Department of
Military History Strategic Studies periodically publishes documents
relevant to particular periods. Number 78 of this series deals with
the Balkan Wars. Serbo-Macedonian affairs are discussed in SRBSKI
IZVORI ZA ISTORIJATA NA MAKEDONSKIOT NAROD 1912-1914 [479]. This
study has an extensive bibliography.

DOCUMENTS AND MATERIALS ON THE HISTORY OF THE BULGARIAN
PEOPLE [65] contains a number of references on the Balkan War
period. Demetrius Cassarvetti discusses the Greek role in the
struggle in his HELLAS AND THE BALKAN WARS [93]. There is coverage
of Albania and the role of the Greek Premier, Eleutherios Venizelos.
Venizelos is also discussed in Eleutherios Prevelakis' "Eleutherios
Venizelos and the Balkan Wars" [398], VENIZELOS [199] , by H.A.
Gibbons, LIFE OF VENIZELOS [103], and "Venizelos and the Struggle
Around the Balkan Pact" [403], by Bogdan Raditsa. Greco-Albanian
relations are discussed in Basil Kondis' GREECE AND ALBANIA,
1908-1914 [308]. Halpern's THE MEDITERRANEAN NAVAL SITUATION,
1908-1914 [222] is also useful in this regard. Greece's relations
with the Ottoman Empire is discussed in "The Greeks and the Turks on
the Eve of the Balkan Wars" [573], by D. Xanalatos. In 1937,
Demetrios Caslamanos' "Reminiscences of the Balkan Wars" [92] was
printed. This is one of the best accounts of what transpired within
the Greek government at the outbreak of the war. A KING'S PRIVATE
LETTERS [111] is the correspondence from King Constantine I of
Greece to Princess Paola of Saxe-Weimar during the war years.

Peter Reuter looks at French politics in DIE BALKANPOLITIK
DES FRANZOSISCHEN IMPERIALISMUS 1911-1914 [411]. In volume IX of
BRITISH DOCUMENTS ON THE ORIGINS OF THE WAR 1898-1914 [210], the
editors deal with the Balkan Wars and on the Balkan League and
Turkey. This volume is over 1,100 pages and contains British
diplomatic and other archival material on the period as it relates
to the events in the Balkans. Ivan Geshov produced L'ALLIANCE
BALKANIQUE [194] that was published the same year (1915) in London
as THE BALKAN LEAGUE [195]. Demetrios Drosos wrote LA FONDATION DE
L'ALLIANCE BALKANIQUE [145] which was published in Athens in 1929
when he was Greek Minister of Foreign Affairs. RUSSIA AND THE BALKAN
ALLIANCE OF 1912 [513] was written by Edward Thaden. It is quite
useful. John Hoffman's THE AUSTRO-RUSSIAN RIVALRY IN THE BALKANS,
1909-1912 [236] is also important reading in setting the background
to the war. Joseph Heller's BRITISH POLICY TOWARDS THE OTTOMAN
EMPIRE [227] deals with the the period from the Young Turk revolt to
the breakup of the empire. Allan Cunningham's THE WRONG HORSE? - A
STUDY OF ANGLO-TURKISH RELATIONS BEFORE THE FIRST WORLD WAR [122]
takes a different approach in studying the same problem.

In addition to the memoires already mentioned, there are a
number of others that are important. Probably the most interesting
is the account of Joyce Cary, the brilliant English novelist who
served in the British Red Cross with the Montenegran army. His
MEMOIR OF BOBOTES [91] is not well written but tells of the war as
he saw it. The University of Texas published this work after Cary's
death in 1957. In Mary Edith Durham's STRUGGLE FOR SCUTARI [151] one
finds a narrative of the personal reflections of an eyewitness to
the fighting in Albania. Doctor Hans Vogel's account in his VALJEWO,
ERINNERUNGEN EINES SCHWEIZER ARTZES AN DEN SERBISCH-TURKISCHEN KRIEG
[546] also deals with the medical and sanitation problems
encountered in this 20th-century yet primitive war. A WAR
PHOTOGRAPHER IN THRACE: AN ACCOUNT OF PERSONAL EXPERIENCES DURING
THE TURKO-BALKAN WAR, 1912 [30] is Herbert Baldwin's story. Maurice
Baring's LETTER'S FROM THE NEAR EAST, 1909-1912 [35] tells of
conditions in Constantinople, cholera at San Stefano, and the
Bulgarian and Serbian campaigns during the First Balkan War. Sir
Robert Graves' STORM CENTERS OF THE NEAR EAST: PERSONAL MEMORIES,

1879-1929 [213] is more encompassing but still interesting. The accounts of the British ambassador to Vienna from 1908 to 1913 is found in R. Vogel's "Sir Fairfax Cartwright and the Balkans" [547]. The fighting in Epirus is discussed in the firsthand account of Thomas S. Hutchinson in AN AMERICAN SOLDIER UNDER THE GREEK FLAG AT BEZANIE [253]. An Russian's account of the war is found in Evgenie N. Cherekov's POEZDKA NA BALKANII; ZAMETKI VOENNOGO KORRESPONDENTA [102]. Frederic G. Herr relates his observations of the First Balkan War in his SUR LE THEATRE DE LA GUERRE DES BALKANS: MON JOURNAL DE ROUTE (17 NOVEMBRE-15 DECEMBRE 1912) [230]. Gustava Cirilli recounts the action at Edirne in JOURNAL DU SEIGE D'ADRIANOPLE (IMPRESSIONS D'UN ASSEIGE) [105]. Georges Antoinat's LA GUERRE DES BALKANS EN 1912: CAMPAGNE DE THRACE [20], Philip Howell's THE CAMPAIGN IN THRACE [247], and Vincent Seligman's THE SALONICA SIDE-SHOW [451] complement each other.

LA GUERRE DES BALKANS [PAR] HENRY BURLEY. LES VICTOIRES SERBES [72] is an account of the Serbian army in action, while Reginald Kann looks at the army in different perspective in his LA MANOEVRE SERBE [283]. George R. Nayes and Leonard Bacon have translated a number of folksongs in HEROIC BALLADS OF SERVIA [370]. Walter Morison has added to this collection in his "Ballards of Serbian Liberation" [366]. Will Seymour Monroe's BULGARIA AND HER PEOPLE; WITH AN ACCOUNT OF THE BALKAN WARS, MACEDONIA, AND THE MACEDONIAN BULGARS [361] devotes his account to the Second Balkan War in what is admittedly a travel book. Baron Noel-Edward Buxton's WITH THE BULGARIAN STAFF [76] is the account of a member of the British parliament at the front during the war. His account lends an entirely different perspective to the struggle. Hermenegild Wagner's WITH THE VICTORIOUS BULGARIANS [553] is interesting and well illustrated but it is also mostly hearsay.

Captain Willard Vickers' "The Ottoman Army in the Balkan Wars" [544] is an unpublished thesis presented at Princeton in 1958. It is very good and worth the effort to find. Ellis Ashmead-Bartlett has, in collaboration with his brother Seabury, produced his eyewitness account of the battle at Lule Gurgaz where he was an accredited correspondent with the staff of the Grand Vizier Abdullah Pasha. His is the best record of the totally unprepared condition of the the Ottoman army at the outbreak of the fighting. Lionel James, the correspondent of the London Times takes a somewhat different view giving credit to the Turks as soldiers but not to their leaders. Another eyewitness account is G. von Hochwachter's MIT DEN TURKEN IN DER FRONT IM STABE MAHMUD MUCHTAR PASCHAS [234]. This work is in French and is a narrative of First Balkan War from 12 October to 14 November 1912. Sir Philip Gibbs and Bernard Grant have contributed BALKAN WAR: ADVENTURES OF THE WAR WITH CROSS AND CRESCENT [201]. This is most interesting as it is in fact two narratives, one from the Bulgarian side (Gibbs) and the other from the Turkish (Grant). It must be used with caution, however, as it is not always a firsthand account but has, rather, been enlarged with hearsay.

Assen Tzankov discusses the settlement of the Second Balkan War in his "The 1913 Balkan Peace of Bucharest" [532], while David Jordan eugenically compares the Balkan Wars with the American Civil War in his WARS AFTERMATH [280]. The REPORT OF THE INTERNATIONAL COMMISSION TO INQUIRE INTO THE CAUSES AND CONDUCT OF THE BALKAN WARS

[87] was sponsored by the Carnegie Endowment for International Peace and published in 1914. Another organization the "Peace Group for Conciliation" published Alfred Fried's A FEW LESSONS TAUGHT BY THE BALKAN WAR [183] also in 1914. Friedrich von Bernhardi's ON WAR OF TO-DAY [48] is an important two-volume German military treatise published in 1912 that brings together German thinking on the application of technology to warfare among its many other topics.

## THE FIRST WORLD WAR

The Great War of 1914-1918 is rightly recorded as one of the most traumatic experiences of history. The fighting caused enormous destruction, and forced tragic sacrifices upon its participants. Before its finish almost every nation on earth became involved in it. The ensuing disintegration of the old European order changed the course of future history and became the cornerstone upon which Bolshevism and National Socialism would be built. The war solved few problems and in its aftermath political turbulence and economic confusion continued to plague Europe. The incident that precipitated the long-expected conflict happened in the Balkans.

After the end of the Second Balkan War, the Ottomans withdrew completely from European Turkey. Bulgaria, defeated as it had been by Serbia, drew closer to Austria-Hungary. Seeing the growing Austro-Hungarian hostility, Serbia, already furious over the Austrian annexation of Bosnia-Herzogovina in 1908, and Montenegro grew closer to Russia while Romania began a vigorous campaign to get Transylvania away from the Austro-Hungarians. Russia was now in tenuous control of the northern Balkans, but the situation was very tricky and the slightest miscalculation could prove extremely dangerous. Russia also faced the problem of growing German interest in the Ottoman Empire. The Sultan had accepted the German offer of monetary support in building the Bagdad Railway. Russia finally agreed to German interest in the Ottoman Empire for German acknowledgment of a Russian sphere of influence in northern Persia. But Russia became alarmed in 1913 when it became apparent that Germany was moving to modernize the Turkish army and was placing Germans in command of most of the larger formations. When the Triple Entente complained, the Porte backed off; but Russia still viewed the possibility of a German-Ottoman alliance with grave concern. Thus, by the beginning of 1914, the basic elements necessary for war were all in place. The alliances had been made, small nations clustered around larger ones for protection—some by choice but most by necessity. In the Austro-Hungarian Empire, for instance, about half of the 50 million inhabitants were Slavic but had little to say about their lot in life in the German-Magyar-controlled government. Among those thought to favor governmental reforms to allow greater Slavic participation was the Archduke Franz Ferdinand, the 50-year old nephew of the aging Emperor Franz Joseph I. Franz Ferdinand had married a commoner and had apparently lost his chance for the throne. He was, however, a General of Cavalry in the Austro-Hungarian army and the Inspector General of the Armed Forces. In late June 1914, he was given the task of inspecting the maneuvers of the 15th and 16th army corps near Tarcin in Bosnia.

On 28 June 1914, on the anniversary of Serbia's defeat and subjugation by the Turks at Kosovo, at Bosnia's capital city of Sarajevo, Franz Ferdinand was assassinated by a young Bosnian member of the Black Hand Society, Gavrilo Princip, who was one of three youths, apparently equipped and supported by members of the Serbian government led by Colonel Dragutin Dimitrijevic, who was now known by the codename "Apis." Austria-Hungary seized upon this opportunity to settle the Balkan question and issued an ultimatum to the Serbians which would have, if accepted, put Serbia in the Austro-Hungarian thrall. Austria knew that, if Serbia refused, the same end could be achieved by force of arms. On 23 July the ultimatum was delivered. Russia advised Serbia to agree where it could but not to relinquish its sovereignty. On 25 July Serbia answered that it would agree to some but not all of the demands. On 27 July Russia informed Serbia that it would fight, if necessary, to preserve Serbian integrity. On 28 July the Austrians, finding the Serbian reply unacceptable, declared war whereupon Russia ordered a partial mobilization along the Austro-Hungarian frontier. France then informed Russia it would abide by its alliance obligations. Germany then ordered a partial mobilization to counter the Russian moves, even while it attempted to get Vienna to back away from the dangerous situation. On 31 July Tsar Nicholas II ordered a general mobilization and Germany, in response, declared a state of emergency issuing an ultimatum to the Russians. When this demand was refused, Germany declared war on Russia (1 August). In rapid succession, then, Germany declared war on France, Austria-Hungary on Russia, and Montenegro and England on Germany. By 4 August 1914, World War I had begun. On 12 August France and England completed the process by declaring war on Austria-Hungary.

Vladimir Dedijer's THE ROAD TO SARAJEVO [129] is an excellent account of the events that led to the war. FROM SADOWA TO SARAJEVO. THE FOREIGN POLICY OF AUSTRIA-HUNGARY, 1866-1914 [56] traces the history of the foreign policy of the empire from Konigratz to the assassination. Hans Bauer's SARAJEWO. DIE FRAGE DER VERANTWORTLICHKEIT DER SERBISCHEN REGIERUNG AN DEM ATTENTAT VON 1914 [42] deals with the question of Serbian complicity in the events at Sarajevo. Amos Simpson and Vaughan Baker produced a small, 68-page study called DEATH OF AN OLD WORLD, 1914-1945 [472] that summarizes the events and would be of help to someone needing a quick refresher. Margareta Faissler deals with Great Powers foreign policy in EUROPEAN DIPLOMACY IN THE BALKANS, AUG. 19, 1913-JUNE 28, 1914 [165]. Robert Seton-Watson also looks at these events in his SARAJEVO: A STUDY IN THE ORIGINS OF THE GREAT WAR [461] and in his THE WAR AND DEMOCRACY [454] that was published on the eve of the war. Seton-Watson's GERMAN, SLAV AND MAGYAR: A STUDY OF THE ORIGINS OF THE GREAT WAR [457] should also be looked at as it outlines the Pan-German movement in Austria-Hungary and among the Southern Slavs. Another of his books that should be read is EUROPE IN THE MELTING POT [459]. Luigi Albertini's THE ORIGINS OF THE WAR OF 1914 [9] is a three-volume translation from the Italian. Sidney Fay's THE ORIGINS OF THE WORLD WAR [170] is in two volumes. Alan Taylor's WAR BY TIMETABLE: HOW THE FIRST WORLD WAR BEGAN [508] is a chronological record of the events. Ivan August Zeibert's DER MORD VON SARAJEVO UND TISZAS SCHULD AN DEM WELTKRIEG [580] is also quite interesting. Alfred von Wegener's BIBLIOGRAPHIE ZUR VORGESCHICHTE DES WELTKRIEGES [558], which was published in 1934, is most useful. Two other good works on the war from the German view are Micheal Balfour's THE KAISER AND HIS TIMES [31] and Fritz Fisher's GERMANY'S AIMS IN THE FIRST WORLD WAR [173]. BRITISH DOCUMENTS ON THE ORIGINS OF THE WAR, 1898-1914 [210], by G.P. Gooch and Sir Harold Temperley, present archival material on the war from the English point of view.

THE ORIGINS OF A TRAGEDY: JULY 1914 [564], edited by Sam Williamson, is an attempt to reevaluate the socio-historiographical causes of the conflict. Bernadotte Schmitt looks at the military requirements of the participants in THE COMING OF THE WAR, 1914 [442] that was produced in two volumes in 1930. Paul Kennedy's THE WAR PLANS AND THE GREAT POWERS, 1880-1914 [294] is a collection of articles that explores many aspects of the origins of the conflict. LA GENESE DE LA GUERRE MONDIALE; LA DEBACLE DE L'ALLIANCE BALKANIQUE [196], by Ivan Geshov, studies the breakup of the Balkan Alliance and its effects on the gathering conflict. Count Ottokar Czernin, the Austro-Hungarian ambassador to Romania at the beginning of the war, and his country's representative at Brest-Litovsk wrote IN THE WORLD WAR [124] which was published in 1920. Arthur Frothingham's HANDBOOK OF WAR FACTS AND PEACE PROBLEMS [185] is a very useful reference arranged in 11 chapters, each on a different aspect of the war. Leon Savadjian's LES ORIGINES ET LES RESPONSIBILITES DE LA GUERRE MONDIALE [433] covers the same ground and is quite good. Lastly, General J.E. Valley and Pierre Dufourcq's LA PREMIERE GUERRE MONDIALE [540] is in two volumes the first of which covers the first two years of the war and is aptly called 1914-1916/DE SARAJEVO A VERDUN. MIROVAYA IMPERIALISTICHESKAYA VOINA 1914-1918 [297], by G. Khmelevskii, was published in Moscow in 1936 by the Frunze Academy. It contains 1,650 entries in an annotated bibliography.

The recorded history of the overall events of World War I is voluminous and defies incorporation here. There are a few works that need to be mentioned, however, including Dupuy [150], James Stokesbury's A SHORT HISTORY OF WORLD WAR I [494], C.R.M.F. Cruttwell's A HISTORY OF THE GREAT WAR, 1914-1918 [118], Francis W. Halsey's THE LITERARY DIGEST HISTORY OF THE WORLD WAR [597], and Brian Bond's excellent article in NCMH 12 entitled "The First World War" [55]. Thomas Frothingham's A GUIDE TO THE MILITARY HISTORY OF THE WORLD WAR, 1914-1918 [187] was published in 1920 and is an early synopsis of the war. Charles Horne and Walter Austin prepared the seven-volume SOURCE RECORDS OF THE GREAT WAR [241] in 1923. It is an indispensable aid to the serious researcher. John Ray's THE FIRST WORLD WAR [407] is relatively new (1975) and quite good. Martin Gilbert's A MILITARY ATLAS OF THE FIRST WORLD WAR [204] is very helpful. The cartography was done by Arthur Banks and the atlas is often listed under his name. Mircea Popa produced a Romanian-language history in PRIMUL RAZBOI MONDIAL. 1914-1918 [394] that is most interesting for its bibliography. Sir Winston Churchill's THE UNKNOWN WAR: THE EASTERN FRONT [104] is excellent.

THE FIRST WORLD WAR IN THE BALKANS

The Great War came to the Balkans when Austria-Hungary executed its Plan "R" on 29 July 1914 with the bombardment of Belgrad. The confused Austrian general staff, led by General Franz Hotzendorf, had initially issued orders to execute Plan "B", their plan to fight Serbia alone and had to rescind those orders to meet the additional threat of Russian interference in the Serbian offensive. Because of this, and the overall ineffectiveness of the Austro-Hungarian army, the relocation of units caused by the change in plans caused great confusion that affected both the Serbian and the subsequent Galician campaigns. The effects of the shelling of

Belgrad were minimal except in the hearts of the Serbians. The Romanian Crown Council met on 3 August and decided against allowing King Carol I to fulfill the Triple Alliance obligation. Instead Romania declared armed neutrality.

The real offensive began on 12 August when three of the six Austro-Hungarian armies entered Serbia by crossing the Sava and Danube rivers. The total strength of the force has been numbered at about one-quarter million men. This army was commanded by General Potiorek. They were opposed by numerically inferior numbers of Serbians under the command of Marshal Radomir Putnik, the Serbian hero of the Balkan Wars. The two forces met near Cer Mountain in northern Serbia 15-16 August, where the Serbians eventually prevailed after four days of fighting forcing the Austrians out of Serbian territory. At the behest of the Allies, Serbia then mounted an offensive to clear Austrian-controlled Bosnia. In the Galician campaign the Austrians performed better and dislodged the Russian Southwestern Army Group northeast of Lvov (Lemberg) (23 August-2 September 1914).

Fighting renewed in the Balkans on 7 September when the Austrians counterattacked into Serbia forcing a withdrawl of Serbian forces from Bosnia primarily because of ammunition and other critical supply shortages. The Austrian bridgehead thus secured (17 September), the Serbians were forced to withdraw south of Belgrad which was finally abandoned on 2 December. The mass exodus of the civilian population further hindered Serbian defensive activities. An Allied ammunition resupply through Thessalonike allowed for a significant Serbian victory on the Kolubara (Kolubra) river. Once again, Serbian territory was rid of the Austrians who were forced to use their river flotillas on the Sava and Danube to screen the Austrian withdrawal. In 1914 the Austrians had over 225,000 casualties, 50,000 of them on the Kolubara, from a total force of about 450,000, while the Serbians lost nearly one-half of their effective strength. On 1 October King Carol I of Romanian had died and was replaced by his nephew, Ferdinand I (1914-1927).

The war in 1915 greatly expanded the scope and participation in the fighting. In October 1914 Turkey had joined the Germans which prompted a declaration of war on 2 November by Russia and Serbia. Then bickering began when the Entente, in attempting to entice Bulgaria and Romania into the war, allowed Russia to offer all of Macedonia to the Bulgarians at Serbian expense. In the meantime, Germany labored to supply Turkey by sending them across neutral Romania, who apparently allowed it in recompense for not joining the German alliance as promised. By June 1915 this communications and supply route between the Germans and the Turks was closed. Bulgaria, on the other hand, held aloof until after the disaster at Gallipoli. This campaign had been designed to open an Allied supply route to Russia. At that point, Bulgaria joined the Triple Alliance (14 October 1915). This added Bulgarian forces to the already started Austro-German offensive (6 October) which had crossed the Sava-Danube line into Serbia. In early October, the Venizelos government of Greece requested Entente support for Serbia and an Anglo-French force was put ashore at Thessalonike (Salonika). The Greek king, Constantine, faced with unrest at home, dismissed Venizelos and declared his country neutral. Both French and English forces were turned back in attempts to link up with the Serbians

(October-November) and by late November the Serbians were forced
into a horrible retreat into Albania and Montenegro. The remnants of
the Serbian army were evacuated by the French to the island of Corfu
where many more died of disease. Some were eventually relocated to
Bizerte in North Africa. Montenegro was occupied by the Austrians.
By the end of 1915, it is estimated that Serbia lost an additional
150,000 troops with an additional 160,000 taken prisoner.

The Balkan situation in 1916 remained relatively static
until mid-summer. During those early months the Allied positions
around Thessalonike (Salonika) were reinforced and the Serbian army
reconstituted. In all, about 250,000 French, British, and Serbian
troops were within the Salonika perimeter by August and were
preparing an offensive up the Vardar. Also during the spring and
early summer, Romania was suffering unrest primarily regarding
anti-war sentiments; but, on 17 August, Romania, having abrogated
its treaty with Germany and Austria, declared for the Entente. Ten
days later, Romania declared war on Austria-Hungary and moved a
large force into Transylvania where they were thrown back (Battle of
Sibiu, 26-28 September) by German forces commanded by General Erich
von Falkenhayn. The Battles of Praid-Sovata (29 September-3 October)
and Petrosani (1-3 October) both ended in defeat and the Romanians
were forced to back to the Romano-Transylvanian frontier. On 8
October Brasov was retaken by the Germans.

At Salonika, as the Allies were about to open their
offensive, a Bulgarian-German army attacked driving back the
defenders. (Battle of Florina, 17-27 August 1916.) On 31 August
Bulgarian troops attacked into Dobrudja one day before Sofia
declared war on Romania. Also, on 1 September Turkey declared war on
Romania. In a six-day battle at Turtucaia (Tutrakhan) (1-6
September) the Romanian army was badly defeated and forced to
retire. A subsequent counter-offensive (1-5 October) slowed in the
face of stiff resistance and the threat along the Transylvanian
border required that the campaign be abandoned and the bulk of the
troops shifted to that sector. Before they could arrive, however,
the Battle of Brasov took place (8 October) that forced a further
retreat of the Romanians. In a number of battles that lasted into
November the Romanians were able stop the German-Austrian advance,
only to have their lines penetrated at Tirgu-Jiu (Targu Jiu) on 17
November allowing the enemy penetration into the Oltenian plain of
Wallachia. On 24 November a Germany-Bulgarian army crossed the
Danube at Zimnicea threatening Bucharest. The next day the Romanians
moved their capital out of Bucharest to Jassy (Iasi). Bucharest was
subsequently captured on 6 December after a week-long battle. The
remnants of the Romanian army were then pushed into Russia. One
estimate claims the Romanians lost between 300,000 and 400,000 men
in the campaign. German allied losses are placed at about 60,000.

Following the Battle of Florina in the Salonika sector, an
Allied counteroffensive (10 September-19 November) successfully
moved into the Vardar capturing Monastir (Bitola) on 19 November. At
the same time another Austrian army moved into Albania where it was
met by an Italian force that was finally able to repel them and link
up with the Salonika force in the Vardar. The entire Balkan front
then stalemated until June of 1917 because of widespread disease.
There were some actions fought in the Vardar that were inconclusive.
Then, in June 1917, King Constantine of Greece was forced to

abdicate because of his pro-German leanings. The new king, Alexander
(1917-1920), immediately appointed Venizelos as premier. On 27 June
Greece entered the war on the side of the Allies. Before the end of
the year, the Allied command at Salonika underwent a major
reorganization. The French general, M.L.A. Guillaumat, was put in
charge.

In Romania the reconstituted army was further reinforced
with 30,000 prisoners of Romanian descent who had been in the hands
of the Russians. This force was later joined by a Transylvanian
corps of volunteers. At approximately the same time, Germany and
Austria concluded an agreement placing occupied Romania under
Austro-Hungarian control after a victorious conclusion to the war
(Vienna Document, 26 March 1917). By July-August the Romanian army
was on the move and fought a successful battle at Marasti (24 July-1
August). A strong German counterattack at Marasesti (6-19 August)
was finally repelled by a Russo-Romanian force. This action was
followed by others that destroyed the German timetable in the
region. The year ended in a major Russo-Romanian defeat, however, at
Ciresoaia (12 September). On 7 November 1917 the Bolsheviks took
power in Russia.

The breakdown of the Eastern Front after the Bolshevik
takeover in Petrograd created a respite of sorts from major military
operations in the Balkans although the region was far from calm. In
January 1918, a major strike developed in Austria-Hungary that
spread to the armed forces by February. Romanian sailors joined in
the mutiny on 9 February. The next day Romania sued for peace which
was concluded on 7 May (Treaty of Bucharest). In the meantime, of
course, the Treaty of Brest-Litovsk (3 March 1918) had taken Russia
out of the war. Beginning in September the Allied armies in the
Balkans succeeded in penetrating the enemy lines in the Vardar with
about 200,000 troops. The only opposition by this time was from the
Bulgarians as the Germans had almost all been withdrawn to the
Western Front. After Skolpje fell on 29 September the Bulgarians
sued for peace. The Allies concluded an armistice with the
Bulgarians but continued clearing the Balkans of German resistance
and were preparing to attack Budapest when Germany capitulated on 11
November 1918 ending the Great War (Hungary surrendered on 13
November).

There are a number of sources of general information on the
war in the Balkans. A good place to start is Harold Lake's memoire
CAMPAIGNING IN THE BALKANS [316] that was published in 1918. In the
anonymously produced THE NEAR EAST FROM WITHIN [598] is the
political memoire of an allegedly high-ranking person that relates
the intrigues of the 1915-1916 period. Vladislav R. Savic's
SOUTH-EASTERN EUROPE: THE MAIN PROBLEM OF THE PRESENT WORLD STRUGGLE
[435] is another account of those same early days of the war period.
Another view is presented in the U.S. Army's THE BALKANS, 1915 [536]
that was produced in 1915. William Bailey's SLAVS IN THE WAR ZONE
[27] covers all of Slavic Eastern Europe but describes in detail
some of the important events in the Balkans especially the the early
Serbian debacle and the terrorism conducted by the Austro-Hungarians
in Bosnia. Margareta Faissler's EUROPEAN DIPLOMACY IN THE BALKANS,
AUG. 19, 1913-JUNE 28, 1914 [165] should be looked at here to
understand the political ramifications of the events. In the second
edition of William Sloan's THE BALKANS: A LABORATORY OF HISTORY

[481], seven chapters are devoted to the war and immediate postwar periods. Marion Newbigin's GEOGRAPHICAL ASPECTS OF THE BALKAN PROBLEMS IN THEIR RELATION TO THE GREAT EUROPEAN WAR [371] describes the geographic factors that made the Balkans the strategically important area that it was.

LA NOSTRA SPEDIZIONE IN ALBANIA (1915-1916) [49], by E. Bertotti, deals with the Italian operations against the Austro-Hungarians. Paolo Giordani looks at another aspect of Italian involvement in his LA MARINE ITALIENNE DANS LA GUERRE EUROPEENE POUR L'ARMEE SERBE [206]. Alan Moorehead's GALLIPOLI: ACCOUNT OF THE 1915 CAMPAIGN [364] is all anyone needs to understand the ramifications of that ill-fated Allied operation. Leon Savadjian tells Bulgaria's story of the early events in the war in LA BULGARIE EN GUERRE [429]. Another interesting work on Bulgarian involvement in the war is the MEMOIRES OF THE BULGARIAN LEGIONARIES FROM MACEDONIA AND THRACE PRESENTED BY THE CENTRAL COMMITTEE OF LEGIONARIES TO REPRESENTATIVES OF THE GREAT POWERS OF THE ENTENTE AND THE UNITED STATES OF AMERICA [68] in 1919.

Cazan and Radelescu-Zoner's ROMANIA SI TRIPLA ALANTA [95] deals with Romanian disengagement at the beginning of the war. Glenn Torrey describes "The Rumanian-Italian Agreement of 23 Sept. 1914" [520], "Rumania and the Belligerents, 1914-1916" [518] and "The Rumanian Campaign of 1916: Its Impact on the Belligerents" [519] in three related articles. The Romano-Italian Agreement mentioned by Torrey dealt with an obligation to notify the other signatory eight days in advance of any change from the neutral status each had declared. Robert Seton-Watson's ROUMANIA AND THE GREAT WAR [455] relates the struggles of Romanians in Transylvania and the role played by Romanians in Russia, both residents and POWs. Dimitrii Draghicescu's LES ROUMAINES DE SERBIE [141] looks at another group of Romanians living away from their native land. Nicholas Lupu's RUMANIA AND THE WAR [334], Ernst Kabisch's DER RUMANIENKRIEG 1916 [282], and ROMANIA IN PRIMUL RAZBOI MONDIAL [418] are all different and each is of some interest. Vasile Maciu's "The Romanian Army in the First World War (1916-1918) [342] blames World War I on "monopoly capitalism" but interestingly points out that the Romanian Social Democratic Party advocated war if Romanian territorial integrity was threatened. There are two works that deal with the Battle of Marasti which took place in August 1917: "The 'Marasti' Society and Its Main Achievements" [527], by Florian Tuca, and MARASTI, MARASESTI, OITUZ. DOCUMENTE MILITARE [96], which was prepared by Constantin Cazanisteanu. Colonel Cazanisteanu's work deals with other battles as well and contains 215 pertinent documents including some foreign, primarily French, ones. Zoltan Szaz discusses "The Transylvanian Question: Romania and the Belligerents, July-October 1914" [502] in his article in the January 1954 JCEA. The first volume of Ion Suta's INFANTERIA ROMANA [499] deals with the early stages of the war.

The events that affected Serbia are found in a number of good selections. Petrovich [389] has a fairly detailed account of the fighting. Dupuy's [150] chronology is very good. Jelavich [276] and Stavrianos [486] both have good coverage of the war in Serbia. John C. Adams' "Serbia in the First World War" [4] was written as a part of the United Nations Series. Lazar Markovich edited a collection of articles entitled SERBIA AND EUROPE, 1914-1920 [346] that was originally published in French in Geneva. Doctor Markovich was a Serbian representative at the Paris Peace Conference. It is quite valuable in the facts it portrays in its condemnation of British and French policies that seemingly ignored the growing German menace to the Balkans, particularly to Serbia, before the war. Also of great interest is Victor Komski's account of his service in the Serbian army before immigrating to the United States. His BLACKBIRD'S FIELD [307] was published in 1934 and may have suffered from the passage of time, but it is still excellent. Helen Losanitch Frothingham's MISSION FOR SERBIA [186] is also quite interesting. Lieutenant Milutin Krunich's SERBIA CRUCIFIED; THE BEGINNING [311] relates four sketches of the war written by a serving officer in the Serbian army. It is one of the most moving and vivid accounts of war that can be found. Robert Seton-Watson's SERBIA'S WAR OF LIBERATION [456] deals with the early part of the struggle. Spiro Kitintcheff deals with the Macedonian problem in his QUELQUES MOTS DE RESPONSE AUX CALOMNIATEURS DES MACEDONIENS [300]. LA DEBACLE SERBE [44], by G. Bechirowsky, deals with the initial Serbian defeats. This same topic is covered by Gerald Silberstein in "The Serbian Campaign of 1915: Its Military Implications" [470]. Rodolphe Reiss' THE KINGDOM OF SERBIA: REPORT UPON THE ATROCITIES COMMITTED BY THE AUSTRO-HUNGARIAN ARMY DURING THE FIRST INVASION OF SERVIA: SUBMITTED TO THE SERBIAN GOVERNMENT [409] and his HOW AUSTRIA HUNGARY WAGED WAR IN SERBIA: PERSONAL INVESTIGATIONS OF A NEUTRAL [408] show a different side of the war that is a very serious indictment of the conduct of the Austro-Hungarian army. Lojze Ude's SLOVENCI IN JUGOSLOVANSKA SKUPNOST [533] is a collection of the author's writings that include his opinions on a number of topics related to the war as viewed from the Slovenian perspective. Milan Zivanovic's DUBROVNIK U BORBI ZA UJEDIN'EN'IE 1908-1918 [582] tells the story of the war in that region. Lastly, Professor Wayne Vucinich's SERBIA BETWEEN EAST AND WEST [549] is especially good and has an outstanding bibliography.

The Austro-Hungarian role in the war in the Balkans is covered in most of the standard references and also in a few specialized studies. The Dual Monarchy and the Southern Slav are the general subjects of Robert Seton-Watson's THE WAR AND DEMOCRACY [454]. "Austria-Hungary and the War - The October 1913 Crisis, Prelude to July 1914" [190] is found in EHH [251]. Rudolf Kiszling edited OSTERREICH-UNGARNS LETZTER KRIEG, 1914-1918 [299]. Leo Valiani's THE END OF AUSTRIA-HUNGARY [539] deals largely with the Italian aspects of a number of the key Balkan issues involved in the Empire's demise. In Arthur May's two-volume THE PASSING OF THE HABSBURG MONARCHY [351] deals at length with both the political and military developments on the Balkan and Russian fronts. Gunther Rothenberg's THE ARMY OF FRANCIS JOSEPH [420] is also important reading at this point. Reiss's [408, 409] indictments of Austro-Hungary conduct in the field are similarly important. Helmut Rumpler discusses Austro-Hungarian war aims in the Balkans at the beginning of the war, Richard Plaschka studies the Czech rebellion in Russia, and Reinhold Lorenz surveys the diary of General von Marterer in OSTERREICH UND EUROPA: FESTGABE FUR HUGO HANTSCH ZUM 70. GEBURTSTAG [378]. Wladimir Aichelberg deals with the unlikely phenomenon of Austro-Hungarian submarines in World War I in DIE UNTERSEEBOOTE OSTERREICH-UNGARNS [6]. This study is in two volumes.

Aichelberg and a group of colleagues discuss Austro-Hungarian warships in DIE "TEGETTHOFF" KLASSE. OSTERREICH-UNGARNS GROSSTE SCHLACHTSCHIFFE [7].

Norman Stone looks at "Hungary and the Crisis of July 1914" [496], while THE HUNGARIAN PROBLEM [250] is discussed in a report the centers upon Hungarian responsibilities for the war and the treatment of enemy aliens in Hungary during the war. The siege at Przemsyl by the Russians is the topic of Laszlo Szabo's A NAGY TEMETO/PRZEMYSL OSTROMA 1914-1915 [501]. Tibor Hajdu studies the political history of Hungary from the beginning of the Great War to 1919 in AZ OSZIROZSAS FORRADOLOM [220]. Bertita Harding relates the war years in respect to the activities of King Charles IV and Queen Zita of Hungary in IMPERIAL TWILIGHT: THE STORY OF KARL AND ZITA OF HUNGARY [225]. Sandor Petho deals with the period 1848 to the 1920 Treaty of Trianon in VILAGOSTOL TRIANONIG; A MAI MAGYARORSZAG KIALAKULASANAK TORTENETE [601]. A few of the studies on the participation of the later Czechoslovakian states include Edward Benes' MY WAR MEMOIRES [45] and Vera Olivova's THE DOOMED DEMOCRACY: CZECHOSLOVAKIA IN A DISRUPTED EUROPE, 1914-38 [375]. In TAJNY VYBOR (MAFFIE) A SPOLUPRACE S JIHOSLOVANY V LETECH 1916-1918 [385], by Milada Paulova, deals with Czech-Yugoslav cooperation and with a Czech underground that functioned during the period.

Particular attention is paid to the Salonika front in Petar Opacic's SOLUNSKI FRONT-ZEJTINLIK [377] and in his SOLUNSKA OFANZIVA 1918. GODINE [376]. Charles Packer's RETURN TO SALONIKA [379] is also interesting reading. GREECE AND THE ALLIES [2] is the subject of G.F. Abbott's study that covers the period 1914-1922. Christos Theodoulou looks at Greco-Allied relations in the period before Greece entered the war in GREECE AND THE ENTENTE, AUGUST 1, 1914-SEPTEMBER 25, 1916 [514], while George Leon discusses GREECE AND THE GREAT POWERS, 1914-1917 [326]. Harry Psomiades looks at Greco-Ottoman relations up to the 1923 Treaty of Lausanne in THE EASTERN QUESTION: THE LAST PHASE. A STUDY IN GREEK-TURKISH DIPLOMACY [401]. Elie Kedourie's ENGLAND AND THE MIDDLE EAST: THE DESTRUCTION OF THE OTTOMAN EMPIRE, 1914-1921 [291] is a comprehensive look at British policy toward the Ottomans during and immediately after the war. Although it deals with subjects outside of the Balkans they are closely connected with British policy that did impact upon the them. Another example of this may be found in Morris Jastrow's THE WAR AND THE BAGDAD RAILWAY [270]. Halsey deals more directly with the subject in TURKEY AND THE BALKANS, AUGUST 1914-OCTOBER 1918 [223] which is volume 8 in the 10-volume LITERARY DIGEST HISTORY OF THE GREAT WAR [597]. This volume is divided into two sections one of which deals with Turkey while the other concentrates upon the Balkans and Greece. "Turkey in the First World War" [100], by F. Celiker, is found in RIHM 46. "Die Turkei seit dem Weltkrieg." [262] and "Der Turanismus der Jungturken. Zur osmanischen Aussenpolitik im Weltkrieg" [264] are both by G. Jaschke. Ahmed Emin's TURKEY IN THE WORLD WAR [159] was published in America in 1930 and is quite informative. The impressively titled BIRINCI DUNYA HARBINDE TURK HARBI. SINA-FILISTIN CEPHESI, HARBIN BASLANGICINDAN IKINCI GAZZE MUHAREBELERI SONUNA KADAR [374], by Yaha Okcu and Hilmi Ustunsoy, is another view of the Turkish involvement in World War I in the Sinai. Its value here is in the details it presents about the structure of the Turkish army at war. TURK SILHALI KUVVETLERI TARIHI. OSMANLI DEVRI. BIRINCI DUNYA HARBI [509], by Irfan Teksut and Necati Okse,

deals with the Dardanelles campaign. This study is complemented by
BIRINCI DUNYA HARBINDE TURK HARBI. CANAKKALE CEPHESI [575], by Remzi
Yigitguden and others. Pertev Demirhan's GOLTZ PASANIN HATIRASI VE
HAL TERCUMESI [132] is the memoires and biography of the German
general Kolmar von der Goltz whose influence was felt in every part
of Turkish military life since 1882. Goltz commanded Turkish forces
in Mesopotamia during the war. A broader view of Turco-German
relations may be found in Ulrich Trumpener's GERMANY AND THE OTTOMAN
EMPIRE, 1914-1918 [525] and in Professor Silberstein's "The Central
Powers and the Second Turkish Alliance" [471].

## THE INTERWAR YEARS

As always, peace was a frail commodity in the Balkans; and
1918 witnessed a rebirth of the same fundamental problems that had
existed before the war only this time they centered around the
victor Succession States of Czechoslovakia, Romania, and Yugoslavia,
on the one hand, and the vanquished nations of Austria, Hungary,
Turkey, and Bulgaria on the other. The manifestation of these
problems gave some pause to reflect that the seeds of another
conflict were already flourishing.

Not the least of these problems, albeit externally created,
was the repercussions of the Bolshevik Revolution that had shaken
Europe to the core. The enmity that existed between Greece and
Turkey was to continue until 1922 and, indeed, be brought back to
life on occasion even into the post-World War II period.
Cross-border incidents were common: Romania attacked Hungary in 1919
and the Yugoslav army seemed to spend as much time in Austrian
territory as it did at home until after 1921. There was a major
revolt in Turkey and widespread disorder in Albania until a stable
government could be established there. And there was, of course,
considerable feuding over the prospects of the formation of the
Southern Slav coalition of states that would become Yugoslavia. What
happened in many of these situations was directly related to what
was going on in Russia and Western desires to build a buffer of
stable, friendly states between itself and the Red Menace. This
notion, in turn, ran afoul of differing Franco-British views on the
balance of power and how it should be attained. For the Balkans all
this really meant was that, once again, they lay between East and
West and that their futures would be dealt away by others. Greece,
for example, was expelled from Asia Minor and Albania allowed to
return to its prewar status.

One of the best sources of information on this period is
INDEPENDENT EASTERN EUROPE: A HISTORY [339], by C.A. Macartney and
A.W. Palmer. This work points out the fundamental errors that were
made at Paris and how they affected the Danubian states' later
ability to withstand outside pressure. REVOLUTION IN CENTRAL EUROPE,
1918-1919 [89] deals with the postwar problems of Germany and
Austria. In Austria the army of the ancien regime disbanded almost
immediately to be replaced by a people's militia. In Germany, of
course, the army never disbanded and the General Staff continued
almost as if nothing had occurred. Karl Nowak takes a somewhat
different look at conditions in THE COLLAPSE OF CENTRAL EUROPE
[372]. Joseph Rothschild's EAST CENTRAL EUROPE BETWEEN THE TWO WORLD
WARS [421] is in the HECE series and is most useful. Joseph Roucek
looks at BALKAN POLITICS; INTERNATIONAL RELATIONS IN NO MAN'S LAND

[422]. There are a number of errors of fact in this book, but it is still of some benefit to the cautious reader. David Mitrany's THE EFFECT OF THE WAR IN SOUTHEASTERN EUROPE [359] is also quite helpful. Volume 4 of A DOCUMENTARY HISTORY OF MODERN EUROPE is BREAKDOWN AND REBIRTH: 1914 TO THE PRESENT [38]. This is the last of a four-volume series and is a quite useful reference source. Robert Wolff's THE BALKANS IN OUR TIME [567] deals with the spread of communism in the Balkans and has a good bibliography. Alan J.P. Taylor's FROM SARAJEVO TO POTSDAM [507] is fair. James Shotwell's BALKAN MISSION [468] is a narration of a 1925 journey through the Balkans on behalf of the Carnegie Endowment for International Peace. Hamilton Fish Armstrong's NEW BALKANS [22] also studies the problems that beset the Balkan states, especially the border disputes, which hindered any real hope of peace in the region. This book was published in 1926. Anderson's THE GREAT POWERS AND THE NEAR EAST (1774-1923) [18] and his EASTERN QUESTION, 1774-1923 [17] are two versions of the same theme; but either one is worth the reading. Fernand Grinard's GRANDEUR ET DECADENCE DE L'ASIE [216] and Jacques Ancel's MANUEL HISTORIQUE DE LA QUESTION D'ORIENT: 1792-1923 [15] are also both very good.

Frank Marston's THE PEACE CONFERENCE OF 1919: ORGANIZATION AND PROCEDURE [349] points out the utter lack of preparation that went into the Paris meeting. THE HISTORY OF PEACE CONFERENCE OF PARIS [511] which was edited by Sir Harold Temperley is a six-volume collection that contains all the data one should need on the various treaties that settled the affair. In a two-volume set, the Carnegie Endowment puts forth THE TREATIES OF PEACE, 1919-1923 [88]. Colonel Iskender Akbaba deals with the July 1923 agreement that restored Turkish Thrace to the Maritza river in his "The Peace Treaty of Lausanne" [8]. Leon Savadjian's BIBLIOGRAPHIE BALKANIQUE [432] is a two-volume set, volume 1 of which covers the 1920-1930 period. This reference contains short accounts and statistics in English, French, Italian, and German. There are also a few short biographical sketches that will be of some use.

That there was little respite from violence in the Balkans is amply illustrated in the battles that went on in the Apuseni Mountains in northern Transylvania between Royal Romanian army units and Hungarian soviet military units in April 1919. The issue of Transylvania was settled in June when that province was given to Romania by the Allied Supreme Council in Paris. In turn, Bukovina was given to the Romanians as a result of the Austro-Allied Peace Treaty of Saint-Germain that was signed on 10 September 1919. On 27 November the Bulgarian-Allied Peace Treaty was signed at Neuilly-sur-Seine. A peace agreement was not concluded with Hungary until 4 June 1920 (Treaty of Trianon) after Hungary had invaded Czechoslovakia in March 1919 and had been invaded by Romania in April of that same year.

This initial postwar period in Romania is discussed in Keith Hitchins' "The Russian Revolution and the Romanian Socialist Movement" [233]. The article in SLAVIC REVIEW is excellent and important reading at this point. David Mitrany's THE LAND AND THE PEASANT IN RUMANIA: THE WAR AND AGRARIAN REFORM, 1917-21 [360] is also quite good. Andrei Popovici's THE POLITICAL STATUS OF BESSARABIA [395] was published in 1931 and deals with the always touchy situation of the location of the Russo-Romanian border. Boris

Ranghet studies Romano-American relations in his RELATIILE ROMANO-AMERICANE IN PERIOADA PRIMULUI RAZBOI MONDIAL, 1916-1920 [405]. Ranghet states that United States entry into the First World War helped pave the way for the Romanian decision to join the Entente. Gheorghe Unc and Augustin Deac's 1918. GARZILE NATIONALE ROMANE DIN TRANSILVANIA [534] deals with the role of the national guard in Transylvania in the unification. Professor Olivova [375] addresses the problems faced by the Czechs in this same period.

LA BULGARIE A LA CONFERENCE DE LA PAIX [430] is Leon Savadjian's contribution to the understanding of the impact of the Paris Peace Conference on the future of the Balkans especially in regard to the territorial question. Nikola Dimitrov's L'ORGANISATION MILITAIRE ILLEGALE DU PARTI COMMUNISTE BULGARE, 1919-1923 [137] is an interesting, if somewhat inflated, account of the communist organization in Bulgaria. CONTEMPORARY HISTORY OF THE GREEKS AND OF THE OTHER PEOPLES OF THE EAST FROM 1821 TO 1921 [290], by Professor P. Karolides, closes with the immediate post-World War I period and, in doing so, lays the groundwork for future Greco-Turkish problems. Harry Psomiades' THE EASTERN QUESTION: THE LAST PHASE. A STUDY OF GREEK-TURKISH DIPLOMACY [401] looks at the minorities problem and the genocide practiced by the Turks against Christian Greeks and Armenians in Anatolia. The Lausanne Agreement is given very detailed coverage. Charles Eddy also looks at some of these issues in his GREECE AND THE GREEK REFUGEES [156]. James Barros examines the events surrounding a Greco-Bulgarian border incident that occurred on October 19, 1925, that rapidly involved the Great Powers and, subsequently, the League of Nations. It demonstrates one of the few times when the League was able to act with some resolve.

Yugoslavia's story during this period is discussed in Ivo Lederer's YUGOSLAVIA AT THE PEACE CONFERENCE: A STUDY IN FRONTIERMAKING [322] and in Robert Kerner's YUGOSLAVIA AND THE PEACE CONFERENCE [599]. Dimitrije Djordjevic has edited 11 essays on the establishment of a new state in THE CREATION OF YUGOSLAVIA, 1914-1918 [140]. Each essay has an excellent bibliography. Henry Baerlien's two-volume THE BIRTH OF YUGOSLAVIA [25] does much the same thing but in greater detail and in a single vernacular. Desanka Todorovic has given us an excellent narrative of postwar relations between the various Balkan states in JUGOSLAVIJA I BALKANSKE DRZAVE 1918-1923 [517]. Charles Beard and George Radin look at the government and administration of the new Yugoslav state in BALKAN PIVOT: YUGOSLAVIA [43]. Another interesting work is Jovan Cvijic's BALKANSKO POLNOSTROVO I JUGOSLOVENSKE ZEMLJE [123] which is also in two volumes. One of Yugoslavia's numerous crises is discussed in LES CAUSES DE LA CRISE YOUGOSLAVE [289]. Leon Savadjian's BIBLIOGRAPHIE YOUGOSLAVE 1933 [434] will be helpful at this point. Charles Jelavich looks at "Nikola Pasic: Greater Serbia or Jugoslavia" [275] in a July 1951 article in JCEA. He refers, of course, to Nikola Pashich, the Serbian premier, who finally decided to cooperate with the Yugoslav Committee in the signing of the Corfu Declaration of 1917 which was the keystone for the unification of the Southern Slavs. Lazare Marcovich looks at the problems of the Balkans issue from a different perspective in his "Lord Curzon and Pashitch: Light on Yugoslavia, Turkey and Greece in 1922" [345]. Hermann Wendel studies the Macedonian problem in MAKEDONIEN UND DER FRIEDE [559], while Josef Bajza's DIE KROATISCHE FRAGE [28] and Vladko Macek's THE STRUGGLE FOR FREEDOM [340] look at Croatia.

Tibor Hajdu's AZ OSZIROZSAS FORRADALOM [220] relates to the period in Hungary from the outbreak of the war until March 1919 with emphasis on the October Revolution of 1918. Alfred D. Low's THE SOVIET HUNGARIAN REPUBLIC AND THE PARIS PEACE CONFERENCE [331] describes how Bela Kun's Soviet regime, which was established on 21 March 1919, was allowed to survive even as long as it did because the Peace Conference failed to stop it. This is an important study and should not be overlooked. HISTORY OF HUNGARY, 1920-1944 [336], by C.A. Macartney, is also extremely valuable as is A MAGYAR VOROS HADSEREG 1919; VALOGATOTT DOKUMENTUMOK [231] which is a history of the Hungarian Red Army told through a collection of documents edited by Tibor Hetes. Other good studies include Leon Savadjian's THE CAMPAIGN AGAINST THE TREATY OF TRIANON [431]; David Cattell's "The Hungarian Revolution of 1919 and the Reorganization of the COMINTERN in 1920" [94]; and HUNGARY IN REVOLUTION, 1918-1919: NINE ESSAYS [548], which was edited by Ivan Volgyes. Oscar Jaszi's REVOLUTION AND COUNTER-REVOLUTION IN HUNGARY [271] deals with the collapse of Austria-Hungary, the October 1918 revolution, the Karolyi government, the Soviet republic in 1919, and the counterrevolutionary reign of terror that followed. Hungary's invasion of Slovakia on 28 March 1919 is mentioned in Dupuy [150]. Petho [601] and Butler [74] have accounts of the Trianon agreement. Erno Garami looks at the Hungarian Soviet period through the eyes of an exiled Socialist leader in his FORRONGO MAGYARORSZAG EMLEKEZESEK ES TANULSAGOK [191]. Gustav Gratz equates the October revolt with the Soviet republic in A FORRADALMAK KORA: MAGYARORSZAG TORTENETE 1918-1920 [212]. Of special interest is Harry Bandholtz' AN UNDIPLOMATIC DIARY, BY THE AMERICAN MEMBER OF THE INTER-ALLIED MILITARY MISSION TO HUNGARY, 1919-1920 [33]. Lastly, Norbert Csanadi and others have prepared a history of Hungarian aviation called A MAGYAR REPULES TORTENETE [119].

Along with the standard references on Austria that have already been cited, there are a few other works that deserve mention: Z.A.B. Zeman's THE BREAK-UP OF THE HABSBURG EMPIRE, 1914-1918; A STUDY IN NATIONAL AND SOCIAL REVOLUTION [580], Arthur May's THE PASSING OF THE HAPSBURG MONARCHY [351], and Oscar Jaszi's THE DISSOLUTION OF THE HABSBURG MONARCHY [272]. Leo Valiani's THE END OF AUSTRIA-HUNGARY [539] is also very useful.

The history of the other chief contender in the Balkans, Russia, is covered extensively, especially the period of the Bolshevik Revolution. There are, however, several works that should be mentioned. Peter Lee and Graham Bearman's RUSSIA IN REVOLUTION [323] is nicely organized and is only 80 pages. THE RUSSIAN REVOLUTION: DISORDER OR NEW ORDER? [58], that was edited by Daniel Brower, covers a wide range of opinion on this crucial question. There is a good bibliographical essay and a useful chronology. Richard Charques' TWILIGHT OF IMPERIAL RUSSIA [101] is also quite interesting. Lastly, there is a collection of SECRET DIPLOMATIC DOCUMENTS AND TREATIES FROM THE ARCHIVES OF THE MINISTRY OF FOREIGN AFFAIRS OF THE FORMER RUSSIAN GOVERNMENT [449] which was published in Petrograd in 1918. This work has an introduction written by Leon Trotsky whose sole purpose in publishing these important state secrets was to incite revolution. Trotsky's harangue aside, it is a valuable source of information.

There is also a wealth of information available on Turkey's plight during this postwar period. Shaw [466] should be looked at as he devotes a full chapter to those times. Harry N. Howard's THE PARTITION OF TURKEY, 1913-1923; A DIPLOMATIC ACCOUNT [246] is good and is heavily documented. Wilbur White's THE PROCESS OF CHANGE IN THE OTTOMAN EMPIRE [562] looks at the dissolution of the empire after World War I. It has a very good bibliography. THE GREAT POWERS AND THE END OF THE OTTOMAN EMPIRE [295] was edited by Professor Marion Kent and looks at a broad range of questions that deal with how far the Great Powers were willing to go to extend their influence in the empire or over its corpse. Lieutenant General Cemal Enginsoy, a retired Turkish officer, discusses the Turkish revolution in a paper presented at the CIHM colloquy at Montpellier in 1981. His paper, "The Place of the Turkish War of Independence (1919-1922) in the World Military History," [160] outlines the phases of the struggle that lasted from 1919 until 1922. Two other articles by General Enginsoy that deal with this period are " The Main Factors Affecting on the Gradual Inefficiency of the Kuvayi Milliye for Decisive Operations Against Strong Enemy Regular Forces During the Turkish National Struggle (1919-23)" [161] and "Operations on the Western Front During the Turkish War of Independence" [162]. The Kuvayi Milliye is the Turkish phrase for the nationalist militia and this paper would be of extreme interest to anyone studying this period in any detail. In his article on the western front operations, General Enginsoy outlines the entire struggle and then concentrates on the Turkish Greek War which is the generally accepted western title for this phase of the conflict. Dupuy's [150] account of this war is very good. Dakin [126] and Stavrianos [486] both have good coverage of the struggle from different perspectives. Psomiades [401] should be read for details on the Treaty of Lausanne (24 July 1923) that gave back to Turkey much that had been taken from it at Sevres. Iskender Akbaba gives a Turkish view of the agreement in "The Peace Treaty of Lausanne" [8] that is in RIHM 46.

The role played in the revolution by Mustafa Kemal Pasha, who took the name Ataturk, is studied in S.R. Sonyel's excellent TURKISH DIPLOMACY 1918-1923: MUSTAFA KEMAL AND THE TURKISH NATIONAL MOVEMENT [483]. The article by G. Jaschke entitled "Das Ende des osmanischen Sultanats" [267] is also interesting reading. Paul C. Helmreich's FROM PARIS TO SEVRES: THE PARTITION OF THE OTTOMAN EMPIRE AT THE PEACE CONFERENCE OF 1919-1920 [228] deals with the outcome of the treaty negotiations that saw Greek expansion into Thrace and the development of Italian spheres of influence among the outcomes. Cevdet Timur's contribution to the Turkish official military history series, TURK ISTIKLAL HARBI, volume 7: IDARI LIYETLER (15 MAYIS 1919-2 KASIM 1923) [516], is excellent but it is in Turkish. This is an administrative history of the period between May 1919 and November 1923. Volumes 79 and 80 of the official ASKERI TARIH DERGISI: DOCUMENTS D'HISTOIRE MILITAIRE [529] deal with military documents of the 1919-1922 period. The Soviet BIBLIOGRAFIYA TURTSII (1917-1958) [537] is also useful. Two other works of peripheral interest to this main theme are Wilbur White's THE STATUS IN INTERNATIONAL LAW OF FRAGMENTS OF THE OTTOMAN EMPIRE [563] and THE UNITED STATES RESPONSE TO TURKISH NATIONALISM AND RFORM, 1914-1939 [522], by Richard Trask. Lastly, the Allied force that

that landed in Constantinople in March 1920 to ensure a supply line to the White Russian forces in southern Russia is mentioned briefly in Dupuy [150] and in Enginsoy [162].

## THE LITTLE ENTENTE AND THE BALKAN LEAGUE

For the nations of the Balkans one of the primary concerns was a revival of the old systems that had oppressed them. For Czechoslovakia the principle threat to survival was a renewal of the Austrian-Hungary Empire in the general sense and the threat posed by Hungary in the particular. Following the Hungarian declaration of war on Czechoslovakia on 28 March 1919 and the subsequent events that witnessed the eventual flight of the Bela Kun Soviet government from Budapest, the Czechs moved to secure support through the establishment of the Little Entente. Yugoslavia joined first on 14 August 1920, followed by Romania on 23 April 1921. A Romano-Yugoslav treaty was then concluded on 7 June 1921. This alliance was extended by the Prague Protocol of 7 May 1923 and a series of other protocols through 1929. France, now without the support of Russia, sought other East European alliances, first with Poland in 1921, then with the Little Entente by linking itself in a treaty of friendship and alliance with Czechoslovakia in 1924, with Romania in 1926, and with Yugoslavia in 1927. Italy's rivalry with France dictated its support of Hungary and the equally ostracized Bulgaria and Albania through this period. Already, in October 1922, Benito Mussolini had marched on Rome. The 1929 meeting of the Little Entente took place in Belgrade and extended the various bilateral conventions for an additional five-year period. Even so, the international tensions that were building in Europe and the growing worldwide economic depression were being felt in the Balkans in a number of ways, even though relations were better than they had been in years.

As a result, a Balkan organization strong enough to withstand these pressures was felt to be needed, and a move in that direction was begun in Athens in October 1930 with the convening of the first Balkan Conference. One offshoot of these meetings was the Treaty of Ankara (30 October 1930) that advocated Greco-Turkish naval parity in the eastern Mediterranean and the freezing of present territorial frontiers. Before the conference ended the drafting of a Balkan Pact had been decided upon. There were a total of four conferences held, the last one at Salonika in 1933. In sum, the Balkan Conferences proved no more successful than the League of Nations in preventing the polarization of Europe and the threat of another conflict. In 1933, however, the Little Entente did make some positive moves toward a lasting peace through the establishment of a standing council and the indefinite extension of the alliance. In March of that year, the new council took, as one of its first actions, a stand against the Four Power Pact that Mussolini had proposed for Great Britain, France, Germany, and Italy as a substitute for the League. The Pact was approved in a greatly watered-down form in June 1933 and was put to the test when Germany began threatening its neighbors. In the case of Austria, France and England vacillated and Italy offered support (7 August 1933). In that same year, Hitler's propaganda campaign against the Sudetenland began and, before year's end, Romania concluded a non-aggression pact (17 October 1933) with its old master, Turkey.

On 9 February 1934, the Entente signed a pact at Athens that bound Yugoslavia, Turkey, Greece, and Romania to the guaranteed security of frontiers and mutual consultation on Balkan policy and issued an invitation to other Balkan countries to join this new endeavor. This was followed by a military convention between Romania, Turkey, and Yugoslavia initialed at Belgrad on 28 November but not put into force until February 1937. A military coup d'etat put a military dictatorship in place in Bulgaria after the former government had rejected the Balkan Pact. King Boris was soon able to reestablish the throne, however, establishing a royal dictatorship in the process. In Yugoslavia, the assassination of King Alexander (9 October 1934) by a revolutionary thought to be in the pay of Hungary almost triggered a war.

In 1935 Czechoslovakia signed a mutual assistance agreement with the Soviet Union that stipulated support if the USSR received French support first. In Romania, in March 1935, the once illegal "Iron Guard" began operating in the open under the title of the "Everything for the Country" party. In October of that year, the long simmering dispute between Italy and Ethiopia broke into open warfare that lasted until 1936 when Haile Selassie was captured and his nation annexed by Mussolini. The Rhineland was reoccupied by Germany on 7 March 1936 and the Berlin-Rome Axis was established on 27 October. The world once again moved toward war.

These events are discussed in a number of documents including Shaw [466], Stavrianos [486], Macartney [336], Jelavich [276], and Dupuy [150]. Robert Kerner studies some of these issues in his YUGOSLAVIA AND THE PEACE CONFERENCE [599] and, with Harry Howard, looks into THE BALKAN CONFERENCES AND THE BALKAN ENTENTE, 1930-1935; A STUDY IN THE RECENT HISTORY OF THE BALKAN AND NEAR EAST PEOPLES [296]. Eliza Campus' THE LITTLE ENTENTE AND THE BALKAN ALLIANCE [84] presents the Romanian view, while the League of Nation's view is discussed in John Crane's THE LITTLE ENTENTE [116]. Robert Machray's THE LITTLE ENTENTE [341] is also good. Theodore Geshkoff's BALKAN UNION; A ROAD TO PEACE IN SOUTHEASTERN EUROPE [193] outlines the development of a Balkan federation from the earliest times concentrating on the events of the 1930s. It has an excellent bibliography. Doctor Campus has also produced INTEREGEREA BALCANICA [83]. Another Romanian study is "Das balkanische Militarbundnis (1934-1940)" [257], by Micheal Ionescu. Marin Pundeff presents a different aspect of this period in his AJIL article entitled " The Balkan Entente Treaties" [402]. The Bulgarians have published (1977) LA PREPARATION DIPLOMATIQUE DU PACTE BALKANIQUE 1934: RECHERCHES SUR L'HISTOIRE DES RELATIONS INTERNATIONALES DANS LES BALKANS DANS LA PREMIERE MOITIE DES ANNEES 30 [67]. Another publication from this same source is LA POLITIQUE FRANCAISE ET LES BALKANS, 1933-1936 [66] which is the ACTA of a Franco-Bulgarian conference held in Paris in 1972. Henryk Batowski investigates "The Failure of the Balkan Alliance" [41] in his fine article in BALKAN STUDIES.

Some of the other references important to this period include Brian Bond's BRITISH MILITARY POLICY BETWEEN THE TWO WORLD WARS [593] and Philip Reynolds' BRITISH FOREIGN POLICY IN THE INTER-WAR YEARS [412]. John Lukacs' THE GREAT POWERS AND EASTERN

EUROPE [333] begins its coverage with 1934, when the Soviet Union entered the League of Nations. It is quite interesting and useful as background for what is to come. Another interesting work is GENERAL STAFFS AND DIPLOMACY BEFORE THE SECOND WORLD WAR [396], that was edited by the Canadian scholar Professor Adrian Preston. It covers the developments between 1931 and 1941 in essays by six recognized experts and is very good reading. YUGOSLAVIA IN CRISIS: 1934-1941 [239], by J.B. Hoptner, shows Yugoslavia's problems in the context of the larger European struggle that was developing. Professor Olivova's THE DOOMED DEMOCRACY: CZECHOSLOVAKIA IN A DISRUPTED EUROPE, 1914-38 [375] shows the Czech determination to be free at a time when the freedom of all hung in the balance. Nina Smirnova gives the Soviet view of Italy's role in the Balkans as of 1979 in POLITIKA ITALII NA BALKANAKH: OCHERK DIPLOMATICHESKOI ISTORII: 1922-1935 GG. [482]. Francis Carsten's FASCIST MOVEMENTS IN AUSTRIA [90] deals in depth with the events leading up to the assassination of Austrian Premier Englebert Dollfuss after the Vienna <u>Putsch</u> in July 1935 and the subsequent attempts to strengthen Austria in the face of growing Nazi interference. Admiral Miklos Horthy's MEMOIRES [242] concentrate on the 1930s although the overall coverage extends into the Second World War period. Horthy was Regent of Hungary from 1920 until 1944 when he was removed by the Germans.

REGIMURILE FASCISTE SI TOTALITARE DIN EUROPE [417] is a Romanian collection of studies on Fascist regimes including those that developed in Hungary, Italy, Bulgaria, and elsewhere in Europe between 1920 and 1945. Conspicuous by its absence is the one that developed in Romania. Colonel A.G. Savu has an article in ARS entitled "The Type of Defensive War Envisaged by the Romanian Inter-War Military Policy" [438]. In that same volume, Captain Ioan Talpes has "The Dynamics of the Organizational Structure of the Romanian Army (1919-1939)" [503]. Yet another article in ARS is Colonel Paul Baltagi's "Beginning of Aviation Integration into Romania's Military System" [32]. BEHIND CLOSED DOORS: SECRET PAPERS ON THE FAILURE OF ROMANIAN-SOVIET NEGOTIATIONS, 1931-1932 [24], which was translated by Walter Bacon, is a most interesting account of this little-studied aspect of the times. "Die Turkei in den Jahren 1933 und 1934. Geschichtskalender [268] and DIE TURKEI IN DEN JAHREN 1935-1941 [266] were both written by G. Jaschke.

## BIBLIOGRAPHICAL LISTING

1. Abadziev, G. BALKANSKITE VOJNI I MAKEDONIJA. Skopje: 1958.

2. Abbott, G.F. GREECE AND THE ALLIES. London: 1922.

3. Adams, A.E., et al. AN ATLAS OF RUSSIAN AND EAST EUROPEAN HISTORY. New York: 1967 [1966].

4. Adams, J.C. "Serbia in the First World War." UNS. Berkeley & Los Angeles: 1949.

5. Ahmad, F. "Great Britain's Relations with the Young Turks, 1908-1914." MES II/4 (1966), 302-309.

6. Aichelburg, W. DIE UNTERSEEBOOTE OSTERREICH-UNGARNS. 2 vols. Graz: 1981.

7. _____., et al. DIE "TEGETTHOFF" KLASSE. OSTERREICH-UNGARNS GROSSTE SCHLACHTSCHIFFE. Mistelbach: 1979.

8. Akbaba, I. "The Peace Treaty of Lausanne." RIHM 46 (1980), 234-238.

9. Albertini, L. THE ORIGINS OF THE WAR OF 1914. 3 vols. Edit. & trans. by Isabella M. Massey. London & New York: 1952-1957.

10. Albrecht-Carrie, R. THE MEANING OF THE FIRST WORLD WAR. Englewood Cliffs: 1965.

11. Alger, J.I. THE QUEST FOR VICTORY: THE HISTORY OF THE PRINCIPLES OF WAR. CMH 30. Westport: 1981.

12. Anastasoff, C. A CENTURY OF BALKAN TURMOIL. 2 vols. Indianapolis: 1942.

13. _____. THE TRAGIC PENINSULA: A HISTORY OF THE MACEDONIAN MOVEMENT FOR INDEPENDENCE SINCE 1878. St. Louis: [c.1938].

14. _____. THE BULGARIANS: FROM THEIR ARRIVAL IN THE BALKANS TO MODERN TIMES, THIRTEEN CENTURIES OF HISTORY. Hicksville: c.1977.

15. Ancel, J. MANUEL HISTORIQUE DE LA QUESTION D'ORIENT: 1792-1923. Paris: 1923.

16. Anderson, F.M., & Hershey, A.S. HANDBOOK FOR THE DIPLOMATIC HISTORY OF EUROPE, ASIA AND AFRICA, 1870-1914. New York: 1969 [1918].

17. Anderson, M.S. THE EASTERN QUESTION, 1774-1923. London & New York: 1966.

18. _____. THE GREAT POWERS AND THE NEAR EAST (1774-1923). London: 1970.

19. Andreski, S. MILITARY ORGANIZATION AND SOCIETY. Berkeley: 1968.

20. Antoinat, G.M. LA GUERRE DES BALKANS EN 1912: CAMPAGNE DE THRACE. Paris: 1913.

21. Archer, L. BALKAN JOURNAL. New York: 1944.

22. Armstrong, H.F. NEW BALKANS. New York 1926.

23. Ashmead-Bartlett, E., & Ashmead-Bartlett, S. WITH THE TURKS IN THRACE. London: 1913.

24. Bacon, W.M., Jr., trans. BEHIND CLOSED DOORS: SECRET PAPERS ON THE FAILURE OF ROMANIAN-SOVIET NEGOTIATIONS, 1931-1932. Stanford: 1979.

25. Baerlein, H.P.B. THE BIRTH OF YUGOSLAVIA. 2 vols. London: 1922.

26. Omitted

27. Bailey, W.F. SLAVS IN THE WAR ZONE. London: 1917 [1916].

28. Bajza, J. DIE KROATISCHE FRAGE. Budapest: 1941.

29. Balck, W. TACTICS. 2 vols. Trans. by Walter Krueger. Ft. Leavenworth: 1911-1914.

30. Baldwin, H. A WAR PHOTOGRAPHER IN THRACE: AN ACCOUNT OF PERSONAL EXPERIENCES DURING THE TURCO-BALKAN WAR, 1912. London: [1913].

31. Balfour, M.L.G. THE KAISER AND HIS TIMES. London: [1964].

32. Baltagi, P. "Beginning of Aviation Integration into Romania's Military System." ARS. Bucharest: 1980.

33. Bandholtz, H. AN UNDIPLOMATIC DIARY, BY THE AMERICAN MEMBER OF THE INTER-ALLIED MILITARY MISSION TO HUNGARY, 1919-1920. New York: 1933.

34. Banks, A. A WORLD ATLAS OF MILITARY HISTORY, 1860-1945. New York: 1978.

35. Baring, M. LETTERS FROM THE NEAR EAST, 1909 AND 1912. London: 1913.

36. Barker, E. MACEDONIA: ITS PLACE IN BALKAN POWER POLITICS. RIIA. Westport: 1980 [1950].

37. Barnes, T.G., & Feldman, G.D., eds. A DOCUMENTARY HISTORY OF MODERN EUROPE. Vol. 3: NATIONALISM, INDUSTRIALIZATION, AND DEMOCRACY, 1815-1914. Washington: 1980 [1972].

38. _____. A DOCUMENTARY HISTORY OF MODERN EUROPE. Vol. 4:
    BREAKDOWN AND REBIRTH, 1914 TO THE PRESENT. Washington:
    1982 [1972].

39. Omitted

40. Barros, J. THE LEAGUE OF NATIONS AND THE GREAT POWERS: THE
    GREEK-BULGARIAN INCIDENT, 1925. Oxford: 1970.

41. Batowski, H. "The Failure of the Balkan Alliance." BS VII/1
    (1966), 111-122.

42. Bauer, H. DIE FRAGE DER VERANTWORTLICHKEIT DER SERBISCHEN
    REGIERUNG AN DEM ATTENTAT VON 1914. Stuttgart: 1930

43. Beard, C.A., & Radin, G. BALKAN PIVOT: YUGOSLAVIA. New York:
    1929.

44. Bechirowsky, G. LA DEBACLE SERBE. Berne: 1917.

45. Benes, E. MY WAR MEMOIRES. Trans. by P. Selver. London: 1928.

46. Berard, V. LA REVOLUTION TURQUE. Paris: 1909.

47. Berghahn, V.R. THE HISTORY OF AN INTERNATIONAL DEBATE. New
    York: 1982.

48. Bernhardi, F. von. ON WAR OF TO-DAY. 2 vols. London: 1912.

49. Bertotti, E. LA NOSTRA SPEDIZIONE IN ALBANIA (1915-1916).
    Milan: 1926.

50. Biagini, A. MOMENTI DI STORIA BALCANICA ASPETTI MILITARI
    (1878-1914). Rome: 1981.

51. Birdeanu, N., & Nicholescu, D. CONTRIBUTII LA ISTORIA MARINEI
    ROMANE. DIN CELE MAI VECHE TIMPURI PINA IN 1918.
    Bucharest: 1979.

52. Bombaci, A. "Le fronti turcho della battaglia delle Gerbe. RSO
    19 (1941), 193-248.

53. Boncabeille, B.P.L. LA GUERRE TURCO-BALKANIQUE, 1912-1913.
    Paris: 1913.

54. _____. LA GUERRE INTERBALKANIQUE. Paris, Nancy & Chapelot:
    1914.

55. Bond, B. "The First World War." NCMH 12. Cambridge: 1968.

56. Bridge, F.R. FROM SADOWA TO SARAJEVO. THE FOREIGN POLICY OF
    AUSTRIA-HUNGARY, 1866-1914. London & Boston: 1972.

57. Brierly, J.L. "The League of Nations." NCMH 12. Cambridge:
    1968.

58. Brower, D.R., ed. THE RUSSIAN REVOLUTION: DISORDER OR NEW ORDER? St. Louis: c.1919.

59. Omitted.

60. Brusilov, A.A. A SOLDIER'S NOTE-BOOK, 1914-1918. London: 1930.

61. Bujac, J.L.E. PRECIS DE QUELQUES CAMPAGNES CONTEMPORAINES. Vol. 1: DANS LES BALKANS. 6 vols. Paris: 1893-1908.

62. Bulatovic, M. THE WAR WAS BETTER. Trans. by B. Brusar. New York: (c.1972).

63. Bulgaria. VOINATA MEZHDU B'ULGARIA I TURTSIYA, 1912-1913 GOD. Sofia: 19??.

64. _____. LES GRANDES PUISSANCES ET LES BALKANS A LA VEILLE ET AU DEBUT DE LA DEUXIEME GUERRE MONDIALE, 1937-1941. Sofia: 1973.

65. _____. Academy of Sciences. DOCUMENTS AND MATERIALS ON THE HISTORY OF THE BULGARIAN PEOPLE. Edited by M. Voynov & L. Panayotov. Sofia: 1969.

66. _____. LA POLITIQUE FRANCAISE ET LES BALKANS, 1933-1936. COLLOQUE HISTORIQUE FRANCO-BULGARE, PARIS: 18-19 NOVEMBER 1972. Sofia: 1975.

67. _____. LA PREPARATION DIPLOMATIQUE DU PACTE BALKANIQUE 1934: RECHERCHES SUR L'HISTOIRE DES RELATIONS INTERNATIONALES DANS LES BALKANS DANS LA PREMIERE MOITIE DES ANNEES 30. Edit. by Nikolay Todorov & Christina Daneva-Mihova. Sofia: 1977.

68. Bulgarian Legionaries. MEMOIRES OF THE BULGARIAN LEGIONARIES FROM MACEDONIA AND THRACE PRESENTED BY THE CENTRAL COMMITTEE OF LEGIONARIES TO REPRESENTATIVES OF THE GREAT POWERS OF THE ENTENTE AND THE UNITED STATES OF AMERICA. Sofia: 1919.

69. Bullen, R., & Bridge, R. THE GREAT POWERS AND THE EUROPEAN STATES SYSTEM, 1815-1914. New York: 1980.

70. Bulow, Prince B. von. MEMOIRES OF PRINCE VON BULOW. 4 vols. Boston: 1931.

71. Burbulea, E. APARAREA NATIONALA SI CALITATILE LUPTATORILOR. Bucharest: 1981.

72. Burley, H. LA GUERRE DES BALKANS [PAR] HENRY BURLEY. LES VICTOIRES SERBS. Paris: 1913.

73. Bury, J.P.T. "Diplomatic History, 1900-1912." NCMH 12. Cambridge: 1968.

74. Butler, R. "The Peace Settlement of Versailles, 1918-1933." NCMH 12. Cambridge: 1968.

75. Buxton, C.R. TURKEY IN REVOLUTION. London: 1909.

76. Buxton, N.E., Baron. WITH THE BULGARIAN STAFF. New York: 1913.

77. _____. EUROPE AND THE TURKS. London: 1907.

78. Omitted

79. Buxton, N.E., Baron & Buxton, C.R. WAR AND THE BALKANS. London: 1915.

80. Buxton, N.E., Baron & Lease, C.S. BALKAN PROBLEMS AND EUROPEAN PEACE. New York: 1919.

81. Cammarata, F. ALBANICA. Palermo: 1968.

82. Campbell, C. THE BALKAN WAR DRAMA. New York: 1913.

83. Campus, E. INTEREGEREA BALCANICA. Trans. by Delia Razdolescu. BHR 36. Bucharest: 1972.

84. _____. THE LITTLE ENTENTE AND THE BALKAN ALLIANCE. BHR Studies 59. Bucharest: 1978.

85. Cantor, N.F., & Berner, S., eds. THE MODERN ERA, 1815 TO THE PRESENT. PEH III. Arlington Heights: 1967.

86. Cantor, N.F., & Werthman, M.S., eds. THE MAKING OF THE MODERN WORLD, 1815-1914. Arlington Heights: 1967.

87. Carnegie Endowment for International Peace. REPORT OF THE INTERNATIONAL COMMISSION TO INQUIRE INTO THE CAUSES AND CONDUCT OF THE BALKAN WARS. Washington: 1914.

88. _____. THE TREATIES OF PEACE, 1919-1923. 2 vols. Washington:1924

89. Carsten, F.L. REVOLUTION IN CENTRAL EUROPE, 1918-1919. Berkeley & Los Angeles: 1972.

90. _____. FASCIST MOVEMENTS IN AUSTRIA. London: 1977.

91. Cary, (A.)J. MEMOIR OF BOBOTES. Austin: [1960].

92. Caslamanos, D. "Reminiscences of the Balkan Wars." SEER XVI (1937), 113-128.

93. Cassavetti, D.J. HELLAS AND THE BALKAN WARS. London: 1914.

94. Cattell, D. "The Hungarian Revolution of 1919 and the Reorganization of the COMINTERN in 1920." JCEA XI:1 (January-April 1951), 27-38.

95. Cazan, G.N., & Radelescu-Zoner, S. ROMANIA SI TRIPLA ALIANTA 1878-1914. Bucharest: 1979.

96. Cazanisteanu, C., ed. MARASTI, MARASESTI, OITUZ. DOCUMENTE MILITARE. Bucharest: 1977.

97. Ceaucescu, I. ed. PAGES FROM THE MILITARY HISTORY OF THE
    ROMANIAN PEOPLE. Bucharest: 1980.

98. _____. THE ENTIRE PEOPLE'S WAR FOR THE HOMELAND'S DEFENCE
    WITH THE ROMANIANS. Bucharest: 1980.

99. _____., ed. THE ROAD TO INDEPENDENCE. EEM CXXXV. New York:
    1983.

100. Celiker, F. "Turkey in the First World War." RIHM 46 (1980),
     163-205.

101. Charques, R. THE TWILIGHT OF IMPERIAL RUSSIA. Oxford: 1974.

102. Cherekov, E.N. POEZDKA NA BALKANII; ZAMETKI VOENNOGO
     KORRESPONDENTA. Moscow: 1913.

103. Chester, S.B. LIFE OF VENIZELOS. London: 1921.

104. Churchill, W.S., Sir. THE UNKNOWN WAR: THE EASTERN FRONT. New
     York: 1932.

105. Cirilli, G. JOURNAL DU SIEGE D'ADRIANOPLE (IMPRESSIONS D'UN
     ASSIEGE). Paris: 1913.

106. Clarke, J.J. "World Military History." GSUMH. Washington: 1979.

107. Clarkson, J.D. A HISTORY OF RUSSIA. New York: 1961.

108. Cleator, P.E. WEAPONS OF WAR. New York: 1968.

109. Clogg, R. A SHORT HISTORY OF MODERN GREECE. Berkeley: 1979.

110. Colby, E. MASTERS OF MODERN WARFARE. Princeton: 1943.

111. Constantine I, King of Greece. A KING'S PRIVATE LETTERS.
     London: [1925].

112. Cooper, M.B. "British Policy in the Balkans, 1908-1909." HIST J
     VII/2 (1964), 258-279

113. Cordier, L. CAMPAIGNS - WORLD WAR, 1914-1918. Aurillac: 1970
     [1969].

114. Omitted

115. Cowles, V. THE RUSSIAN DAGGER: COLD WAR IN THE DAYS OF THE
     CZARS. New York & Evanston: 1969.

116. Crane, J.O. THE LITTLE ENTENTE. New York: 1931 [1928].

117. Crankshaw, E. THE FALL OF THE HOUSE OF HABSBURG. New York:
     1983.

118. Cruttwell, C.R.M.F. A HISTORY OF THE GREAT WAR, 1914-1918. 2nd
     ed. Oxford: 1961 [1934].

119. Csanadi, N., et al. A MAGYAR REPULES TORTENETE. 2nd ed.
     Budapest: 1977.

120. Csendes, L. A HABSBURG BIRDODALOM ES AZ OSZTRAK-MAGYAR
     MONARCHIA TERKEPEINEK KATAOLGUSA 1700-1919. Budapest:
     1981.

121. Cucu, M. FACTORUL GEOGRAFIC IN ACTINUNILE MILITARE. SECVENTE
     DIN ISTORIA MILITARA ROMANEASCA. Bucharest: 1981.

122. Cunningham, A. THE WRONG HORSE? - A STUDY OF ANGLO-TURKISH
     RELATIONS BEFORE THE FIRST WORLD WAR. St. Anthony's Papers
     No. 17, MEA IV. Oxford: 1965.

123. Cvijic, J. BALKANSKO POLNOSTROVO I JUGOSLOVENSKE ZEMLYE. 2
     vols. Belgrad: 1922.

124. Czernin, O. IN THE WORLD WAR. New York: 1920.

125. Dakin, D. THE GREEK STRUGGLE IN MACEDONIA, 1897-1913. Salonica:
     1966.

126. _____. THE UNIFICATION OF GREECE, 1770-1923. London: 1972.

127. Dawn, C.E. FROM OTTOMANISM TO ARABISM. Urbana: 1973.

128. Dedijer, V. THE BELOVED LAND. New York: 1961.

129. _____. THE ROAD TO SARAJEVO. New York: 1966.

130. Delmas, J. "L'Alliance militaire Fanco-Russe et la Revolution
     Bolchevique." Paper presented at CIHM, Montpellier, 1981.

131. del Vayo, J. "Balkan Triangle." NATION CLXXV (September 20,
     1952), 224.

132. Demirhan, P. GOLTZ PASANIN HATIRASI VE HAL TERCUMESI. Istanbul:
     1949.

133. Denison, G.T. HISTORY OF CAVALRY. 2nd ed. London: 1913.

134. Denton, W. MONTENEGRO: ITS PEOPLE AND THEIR HISTORY. New York:
     1982 [1877].

135. Deutscher, I. "The Russian Revolution." NCMH 12. Cambridge:
     1968.

136. Dimakis, J. LA PRESSE FRANCAISE FACE A LA CHUTE DE MISSOLONGHI
     ET A LA BATAILLE NAVALE DE NAVARIN: RECHERCHES SUR LES
     SOURCES DU PHILHELLENES FRANCAIS. Thessaloniki: 1976.

137. Dimitrov, N. L'ORGANISATION MILITAIRE ILLEGALE DE PARTI
     COMMUNISTE BULGARE, 1919-1923. Sofia: 1977.

138. Djordjevic, D. CARINSKI RAT AUSTRO-UGARSKE I SRBIJE, 1906-1911.
     Belgrad: 1962.

139. _____. REVOLUTIONS NATIONALES DES PEUPLES BALKANIQUES, 1804-1914. Edit. by Jorjo Tadic & Margita Ristic. Belgrad: 1965.

140. _____. THE CREATION OF YUGOSLAVIA, 1914-1918. Santa Barbara: 1980.

141. Draghicescu, D. LES ROMAINES DE SERBIE. Paris: 1919.

142. _____. LA TRANSYLVANIE. EDQR III. Paris: 1918.

143. Dragnic, A.N. SERBIA, NIKOLA PASIC, AND YUGOSLAVIA. New Brunswick: 1974.

144. Driault, E. LA QUESTION D'ORIENT. 5th ed. Paris: 1912.

145. Drosos, D.I. LA FONDATION DE L'ALLIANCE BALKANIQUE. Athens: 1929.

146. Duff, J.D., ed. RUSSIAN REALITIES AND PROBLEMS. Cambridge: 1917.

147. Duffy, T.G. RUSSIA'S BALKAN POLICY, 1894-1905. New York: c.1975.

148. Duggan, S.P.H. THE EASTERN QUESTION. New York: 1970.

149. Dujcev, I. MAZEDONIEN IN DER BULGARISCHEN GESCHICHTE. Sofia: 1941.

150. Dupuy, R.E., & Dupuy, T.N. THE ENCYCLOPEDIA OF MILITARY HISTORY. Rev. ed. New York: 1977 [1970].

151. Durham, M.E. THE STRUGGLE FOR SCUTARI. London: 1914.

152. _____. TWENTY YEARS OF BALKAN TANGLE. London: 1920.

153. _____. HIGH ALBANIA. New York: 1971.

154. Earle, E.M. TURKEY, THE GREAT POWERS, AND THE BAGDAD RAILWAY. New York: 1966.

155. _____, ed. THE MAKERS OF MODERN STRATEGY: MILITARY THOUGHT FROM MACHIAVELLI TO HITLER. Princeton: 1943.

156. Eddy, C.B. GREECE AND GREEK REFUGEES. London: 1931.

157. Eidelberg, P.G. THE GREAT RUMANIAN PEASANT REVOLT OF 1907: ORIGINS OF A MODERN JACQUERIE. SIECE. Leiden: 1974.

158. Elliot, H., Sir. SOME REVOLUTIONS AND OTHER DIPLOMATIC EXPERIENCES. London: 1922.

159. Emin, A. TURKEY IN THE WORLD WAR. New Haven: 1930.

160. Enginsoy, C. "The Place of the Turkish War of Independence (1919-1922) in the World Military History." CIHM Acta Tehran, 1978.

161. _____. "The Main Factors Affecting on the Gradual Inefficiency of the Kuvayi Milliye for Decisive Operations Against Strong Enemy Regular Forces During the Turkish Nation Struggle." CIHM Montpellier, 1981.

162. _____. "Operations on the Western Front During the Turkish War of Independence." RIHM 46 (1980), 205-231.

163. Essame, H. THE BATTLE OF EUROPE 1918. London: 1972.

164. Evrygenis, D. ION DRAGHOUMIS AND THE MACEDONIAN STRUGGLE. Thessalonike: 1961.

165. Faissler, M. EUROPEAN DIPLOMACY IN THE BALKANS, AUG. 19, 1913-JUNE 28, 1914. Chicago: 1936.

166. Falls, C. THE ART OF WAR. New York: 1961.

167. Farkas, M. A CSASZARI SAS LEHULL. Budapest: 1982.

168. Farnsworth, H.W. LOG OF A WOULD-BE CORRESPONDENT. New York: 1913.

169. Omitted.

170. Fay, S. THE ORIGINS OF THE WORLD WAR. New York: 1930.

171. Fehmi, Y. LA REVOLUTION OTTOMANE (1908-1910). Paris: 1911.

172. Fichev, I.V. BALKANSKATA VOINA, 1912-1913. Sofia: 1940.

173. Fisher, F. GERMANY'S AIMS IN THE FIRST WORLD WAR. New York: 1967.

174. Fisher, S. "Ottoman Feudalism and Its Influence Upon the Balkans." HISTORIAN XV (Autumn 1952), 3-22.

175. Fisher-Galati, S. TWENTIETH CENTURY RUMANIA. New York: 1970.

176. _____. "The Habsburg Monarchy and Balkan Revolution." AHY II (1966), 1-10.

177. Florinsky, M.T. RUSSIA: A HISTORY AND AN INTERPRETATION. New York: 1953.

178. Forbes, N. et al. The BALKANS; A HISTORY OF BULGARIA, SERBIA, GREECE, RUMANIA, TURKEY. New York: [1970].

179. Ford, C.S. THE BALKANS WARS: BEING A SERIES OF LECTURES DELIVERED AT THE ARMY SERVICE SCHOOLS FORTLEAVENWORTH, KANSAS. Ft. Leavenworth: 1915.

180. Forster, E.S. A SHORT HISTORY OF MODERN GREECE, 1821-1956. 3rd ed., rev. London: 1958.

181. Forster, G., et al. UNIFORMEN EUROPAISCHER ARMEEN. Berlin, DDR: 1978.

182. France. Commission de Publication des Documents Relatifs aux Origines de la Guerre de 1914, eds. Third Series. 7 vols. Paris: 1933-1934.

183. Fried, A.H. A FEW LESSONS TAUGHT BY THE BALKAN WAR. New York: 1914.

184. Frischauer, P. THE IMPERIAL CROWN: THE STORY OF THE RISE AND FALL OF THE HOLY ROMAN AND AUSTRIAN EMPIRES. London: 1939.

185. Frothington, A.L. HANDBOOK OF WAR FACTS AND PEACE PROBLEMS. 4th ed. New York: 1919.

186. Frothington, H.L. MISSION IN SERBIA. New York: 1970.

187. Frothington, T.G. A GUIDE TO THE MILITARY HISTORY OF THE WORLD WAR, 1914-1918. Boston: 1920.

188. Fuller, J.F.C. A MILITARY HISTORY OF THE WESTERN WORLD. 3 vols. New York: 1954-1955.

189. Fussel, P. THE GREAT WAR AND MODERN MEMORY. Oxford: 1975.

190. Galantai, J. "Austria-Hungary and the War - the October 1913 Crisis, Prelude to July 1914. EHH. 1980.

191. Garami, E. FORRONGO MAGYARORSZAG EMLEKEZESEK ES TANULSAGOK. Leipzig & Vienna: 1922.

192. Gaumant, E. LA FORMATION DE LA YOUGOSLAVIE, XV$^e$-XX$^e$ SIECLES. Paris: 1931.

193. Geshkoff, T.I. BALKAN UNION: A ROAD TO PEACE IN SOUTHEASTERN EUROPE. New York: 1940.

194. Geshov, I.E. L'ALLIANCE BALKANIQUE. Paris: 1915.

195. _____. THE BALKAN LEAGUE. London: 1915.

196. _____. LA GENESE DE LA GUERRE MONDIALE; LA DEBACLE DE L'ALLIANCE BALKANIQUE. Berne: 1919.

197. Gewehr, W.M. THE RISE OF NATIONALISM IN THE BALKANS, 1800-1930. Hamden: 1967 c.1931.

198. Gibb, H.A.R., Sir, et al., eds. ENCYCLOPEDIA OF ISLAM. New ed. Leiden: 1954-.

199. Gibbons, H.A. VENIZELOS. New York: 1920.

200. _____. THE NEW MAP OF EUROPE (1911-1914). 10th ed. New York: 1923 [1914].

201. Gibbs, P.H., Sir, & Grant, B. BALKAN WAR: ADVENTURES OF WAR WITH THE CROSS AND CRESCENT. Boston: 1913.

202. Giesche, R. DER SERBISCHE ZUGANG ZUM MEER UND DIE EUROPAISCHE KRISE, 1912. Stuttgart: 1932.

203. Gilbert, F. THE END OF THE EUROPEAN ERA, 1890 TO THE PRESENT. 2nd ed. New York: 1970.

204. Gilbert, M. A MILITARY ATLAS OF THE FIRST WORLD WAR. Arthur Banks, Cartographer. New York: [c.1970].

205. _____. RUSSIAN HISTORY ATLAS. New York: 1972.

206. Giordani, P. LA MARINE ITALIENNE DANS LA GUERRE EUROPEEN POUR L'ARMEE SERBE. Milan: c.1917.

207. Giurescu, C.C., et al. CHRONOLOGICAL HISTORY OF ROMANIA. Bucharest: 1972.

208. Gollwitzer, H. EUROPE AND THE AGE OF IMPERIALISM, 1880-1914. LWC. New York & London: 1969.

209. Omitted.

210. Gooch, G.P., & Temperley, H., Sir. BRITISH DOCUMENTS ON THE ORIGINS OF THE WAR, 1898-1914. London: 1928-1933.

211. Grassi, M.A. CHARTE TURQUE ON ORGANIZATION RELIGIEUSE, CIVILE ET MILITAIRE DE L'EMPIRE OTTOMAN. Paris: 1925.

212. Gratz, G. A FORRADALMAK KORA; MAGYARORSZAG TORTENETE 1918-1920. Budapest: 1935.

213. Graves, R.W., Sir. STORM CENTRES OF THE NEAR EAST: PERSONAL MEMORIES, 1879-1929. New York: [1975].

214. Great Britain. Foreign Office Historical Section. THE BALKAN STATES. 2 vols. Wilmington: 1973 [1920].

215. Grimsted, P.K. ARCHIVES AND MANUSCRIPT COLLECTIONS IN THE USSR: MOSCOW AND LENINGRAD. Zug: nd.

216. Grinard, F. GRANDEUR ET DECADENCE DE L'ASIE. Paris: 1947.

217. Grothe, H. DAS ALBANISCHE PROBLEM. Halle:

218. Gulick, E.V. EUROPE'S CLASSICAL BALANCE OF POWER: A CASE HISTORY OF THE THEORY AND PRACTICE OF ONE OF THE GREAT CONCEPTS OF EUROPEAN STATECRAFT. Ithaca: 1956.

219. Gyoerkei, J. MAGYAR ONKENTESEKA SPANYOL POLGARHABORUBAN. Budapest: 1977.

220. Hajdu, T. AZ OSZIROZSAS FORRADALOM. Budapest: 1963.

221. Halli, R. BALKAN HARBI, 1912-1913. GARP ORDUSU. VARDAR ORDUSU ILE USTRUMA KOLORDUSUNUN HAREKAT VE MUHAREBELERI. Ankara: 1979.

222. Halpern, P.G. THE MEDITERRANEAN NAVAL SITUATION, 1908-1914. Boston: 1971.

223. Halsey, F.W. TURKEY AND THE BALKANS, AUGUST 1914-OCTOBER 1918. Vol. 8 in THE LITERARY DIGEST HISTORY OF THE WORLD WAR. New York & London: 1919.

224. Hantsch, H. DAS GESCHICHTE OSTERREICHS. Vol. II. Vienna: 1950.

225. Harding, B. IMPERIAL TWILIGHT: THE STORY OF KARL AND ZITA OF HUNGARY. Indianapolis: 1939.

226. Heller, J. BRITISH POLICY TOWARDS THE OTTOMAN EMPIRE 1908-1914. Totowa: 1983.

227. Helmreich, P.C. THE DIPLOMACY OF THE BALKAN WARS, 1912-1913. New York: [1969, c.1938].

228. _____. FROM PARIS TO SEVRES: THE PARTITION OF THE OTTOMAN EMPIRE AT THE PEACE CONFERENCE OF 1919-1920. Columbus: 1974.

229. Heppell, M., & Singleton, F.B. YUGOSLAVIA. New York: 1961.

230. Herr, F.G. SUR LE THEATRE DE LA GUERRE DES BALKANS; MON JOURNAL DE ROUTE (17 NOVEMBRE-15 DECEMBRE). Paris: 1913.

231. Hetes, T., ed. A MAGYAR VOROS HADSEREG 1919; VALOGATOTT DOKUMENTUMOK. Budapest: 1959.

232. Heymann, E. BALKAN: KRIEGE, BUNDNISSE, REVOLUTIONEN; 150 JAHRE POLITIK UND SCHICKSAL. Berlin: 1938.

233. Hitchins, K. "The Russian Revolution and the Romanian Socialist Movement." SR XXVII No. 2 (June 1968), 268-289.

234. Hochwachter, G. von. MIT DEN TURKEN IN DER FRONT IM STABE MAHMUD MUCHTAR PASCHAS. In French: AU FEU AVEC LES TURCS; JOURNAL D'OPERATIONS (CAMPAGNE DE THRACE: 12 OCTOBRE-14 NOVENBRE 1912). Trans. to German by Commandant Minart. Paris: 1913.

235. Hoensch, J.K. DER UNGARISCHE REVISIONISMUS UND DIE ZERSCHLAGUNG DER TSCHECHSLOWAKEI. Tubingen: 1967.

236. Hoffman, J.W. THE AUSTRO-RUSSIAN RIVALRY IN THE BALKANS, 1909-1912. Chicago: 1937.

237. Hogg, I. A HISTORY OF ARTILLERY. London: 1974.

238. Holt, P.M., et al., eds. CAMBRIDGE HISTORY OF ISLAM. 2 vols. Cambridge: 1977-1978.

239. Hoptner, J.B. YUGOSLAVIA IN CRISIS, 1934-1941. New York: 1962.

240. Horecky, P.L. SOUTHEASTERN EUROPE; A GUIDE TO BASIC PUBLICATIONS. Chicago: 1969.

241. Horne, C.F., & Austin, W.F. SOURCE RECORDS OF THE GREAT WAR. 7 vols. USA: 1923.

242. Horthy, M. MEMOIRES. New York: 1957.

243. Hosch, E. THE BALKANS: A SHORT HISTORY. Trans. by Tania Alexander. New York: 1972.

244. Hourani, A.H. THE OTTOMAN BACKGROUND OF THE MODERN MIDDLE EAST. Harlow: 1970.

245. Houtsma, T. ed. ENCYCLOPEDIA OF ISLAM. 1st ed. 4 vols. w/suppl. Leiden: 1913-1938.

246. Howard, H.N. THE PARTITION OF TURKEY; A DIPLOMATIC ACCOUNT, 1913-1923. New York: 1966 [c.1931].

247. Howell, P. THE CAMPAIGN IN THRACE. London: 1913.

248. Hristov, H., et al. THE ILINDEN-PREOBRAZHENIE UPRISING OF 1903. Sofia: 1983.

249. Hunczak, T. RUSSIAN IMPERIALISM FROM IVAN THE TERRIBLE TO THE REVOLUTION. New Brunswick: 1974.

250. Hungarian Frontier Readjustment League. THE HUNGARIAN PROBLEM. Budapest: 1928.

251. Hungary. Akademiai Kiado. ETUDES HISTORIQUES HONGROIS. 2 vols. Budapest: 1980.

252. Hurd, A.S. THE BRITISH FLEET IN THE GREAT WAR. London: [1918].

253. Hutchinson, T.S. AN AMERICAN SOLDIER UNDER THE GREEK FLAG AT BEZANIE. Nashville: 1913.

254. Ignotus, P. "Czechs, Magyars, Slovaks." THE POLITICAL QUARTERLY 40 No. 2 (June 1969), 187-204.

255. Inal, I.M.K. OSMANLI DEVRINDE SON SADRIAZAMLAR. 6 vols. Istanbul: 1940-1953.

256. Omitted

257. Ionescu, M. E. Das balkanische Militarbundnis (1934-1940). RIHM 36 (1977), 228-236.

258. Iorga, N. HISTOIRE DES ROUMAINES DE LA PENINSULE DES BALKANS. Bucharest: 1919.

259. _____. GESCHICHTE DES OSMANISCHEN REICHES. 5 vols. Gotha: 1908-1913.

260. _____. ISTORIA RAZBOIULUI BALCANIC. BUCHAREST: 1915.

261. James, L. WITH THE CONQUERED TURK. Boston: 1913.

262. Jaschke. G. "Die Turkei seit dem Weltkrieg. Turkische
     Geschichtskalender fur 1929 mit neuen Nachtrag zu
     1918-1928." WI XII (1930-1931), ii 1-50; iii 137-166; XV
     (1933), iv 1-33.

263. _____. " Die grosseren Verwalttungsbezirke der turkei seit
     1918." MSOS XXXVIII (1935), 81-104.

264. _____. "Der Turanismus der Jungturken. Zur osmanischen
     Aussenpolitik im Weltkrieg." WI XXIII (1941), 1-54.

265. _____. "Der Freiheitskampf des turkischen Volkes." WI XIV
     (1932), 6-21.

266. _____. DIE TURKEI IN DEN JAHREN 1935-1941. Leipzig: 1943.

267. _____. "Das Ende des osmanischen Sultanats. SAV I/i (1944)
     113-136.

268. _____. "Die Turkei in den Jahren 1933 und 1924.
     Geschichtskalender. MSOS XXXVIII (1935), 105-142.

269. Jaschke, G., & Pritsch, E. "Die Turkei seit dem Weltkrieg.
     Turkische Geschichtskalender 1918-1928." WI X (1927-1929),
     1-154.

270. Jastrow, M. THE WAR AND THE BAGDAD RAILWAY. Philadelphia &
     London: 1917.

271. Jaszi,O. REVOLUTION AND COUNTER-REVOLUTION IN HUNGARY. New
     York: 1939.

272. _____. THE DISSOLUTION OF THE HABSBURG MONARCHY. Chicago:
     1961 [1929].

273. Jelavich, B. A CENTURY OF RUSSIAN FOREIGN POLICY, 1814-1914.
     New York: 1964.

274. Jelavich, C., ed. THE HABSBURG MONARCHY; TOWARD A MULTINATIONAL
     EMPIRE OR NATIONAL STATES? New York: 1959.

275. _____. "Nicola Pasic: Greater Serbia or Jugoslavia." JCEA
     XI:2 (July 1951), 133-152.

276. Jelavich, C., & Jelavich, B. THE ESTABLISHMENT OF THE BALKAN
     NATIONAL STATES, 1804-1920. HECE 8. Seattle, Washington &
     London: 1977.

277. _____., eds. THE BALKANS IN TRANSITION. REES. Berkeley &
     Los Angeles: 1963.

278. Jessup, J.E., & Coakley, R.W., eds. A GUIDE TO THE STUDY AND
     USE OF MILITARY HISTORY. Washington: 1979.

279. Johnston, R.W. TRADITION VERSUS REVOLUTION: RUSSIA AND THE
     BALKANS IN 1917. EEM 28. New York: 1977.

280. Jordan, D.S. WAR'S AFTERMATH. Boston & New York: 1914.

281. Jordan, G., ed. NAVAL WARFARE IN THE TWENTIETH CENTURY,
     1900-1945. London & New York: c.1977.

282. Kabisch, E. DER RUMANIENKRIEG 1916. Berlin: c.1938.

283. Kann, R. LA MANOEVRE SERBE. Paris: 1913.

284. Kann, R.A. THE MULTINATIONAL EMPIRE; NATIONALISM AND NATIONAL
     REFORM IN THE HABSBURG MONARCHY, 1848-1918. 2 vols. New
     York: 1950.

285. _____. THE HABSBURG EMPIRE: A STUDY IN INTEGRATION AND
     DISINTEGRATION. New York: 1979.

286. _____. A HISTORY OF THE HABSBURG EMPIRE, 1526-1918.
     Berkeley: 1974.

287. Omitted

288. Kann, R.A., & David, Z. THE PEOPLES OF THE EASTERN HABSBURG
     LANDS, 1526-1918. HECE 6. Seattle & London: 1983.

289. Karayovoff, T. LES CAUSES DE LA CRISE YOUGOSLAVE. Budapest:
     1929.

290. Karolides, P. CONTEMPORARY HISTORY OF THE GREEKS AND OF THE
     OTHER PEOPLES OF THE EAST FROM 1821 TO 1921. Athens: 1929.

291. Kedourie, E. ENGLAND AND THE MIDDLE EAST: THE DESTRUCTION OF
     THE OTTOMAN EMPIRE, 1914-1921. Totowa: 1977 [1956].

292. _____. "The Middle East, 1900-1945." NCMH 12. Cambridge:
     1968.

293. Kennan, G. "The Soviet Union, 1917-1939." NCMH 12. Cambridge:
     1968.

294. Kennedy, P.M., ed. THE WAR PLANS OF THE GREAT POWERS 1880-1914.
     London: 1979.

295. Kent, M., ed. THE GREAT POWERS AND THE END OF THE OTTOMAN
     EMPIRE. Totowa: 1984.

296. Kerner, R.J., & Howard, H.N. THE BALKAN CONFERENCES AND THE
     BALKAN ENTENTE, 1930-1935; A STUDY IN THE RECENT HISTORY
     OF THE BALKAN AND NEAR EAST PEOPLES. Westport: [1970].

297. Khmelevskii, G. MIROVAYA IMPERIALISTICHESKAYA VOINA 1914-1918.
     Moscow: 1936.

298. Kinross, Lord. (J.P.D. Balfour) THE OTTOMAN CENTURIES: THE RISE
     AND FALL OF THE TURKISH EMPIRE. London: 1977.

299. Kiszling, R. OSTERREICH-UNGARNS LETZTER KRIEG 1914-1918.
     Vienna: 1930-1938.

300. Kitintcheff, S. QUELQUES MOTS DE RESPONSE AUX CALOMNIATEURS DES MACEDONIENS. Lausanne: 1919.

301. Klyuchevski, V.O. KURS RUSSKOI ISTORII. 5 vols. Moscow: 1937 [1921-1923].

302. _____. A HISTORY OF RUSSIA. 2 vols. Trans. by C.J. Hogarth. New York: 1911-1912.

303. Knight, E.F. THE AWAKENING OF TURKEY: A HISTORY OF THE TURKISH REVOLUTION. London: 1909.

304. Knotel, R., et al. UNIFORMS OF THE WORLD. Trans. by Ronald G. Ball. New York: 1980 [1937].

305. Kohn, H. THE HABSBURG EMPIRE, 1804-1918. Princeton: 1961.

306. Kolejka, J. BALKANSKA OTAZKA 1908-1914: MEZINARODNI SOCIALISTICKE HNUTI O MLADOTURECKE REVOLUCI A O BALKANSKYCH VALKACH. Brno: 1979.

307. Komski, V. BLACKBIRD'S FIELD. New York: c.1934.

308. Kondis, B. GREECE AND ALBANIA, 1908-1914. Thessaloniki: 1976.

309. Kosary, D.G. BEVEZETES A MAGYAR TORTENELEM FORRASAIBA ES IRADALMABA. Vol. 1. Budapest: 1970.

310. Kratchunov, K. LA POLITIQUE EXTERIEURE DE LA BULGARIE, 1880-1920. Vol. 1. Sofia: 1928-.

311. Krunich, M. SERBIA CRUCIFIED: THE BEGINNING. Boston & New York: 1918.

312. Kuepfer, E. LA MACEDOINE ET LES BULGARES. Lausanne: 1918.

313. Omitted.

314. Kushner, D. THE RISE OF TURKISH NATIONALISM, 1876-1908. Totowa: 1977.

315. Kyrou, A. OUR BALKAN NEIGHBORS. Athens: 1962.

316. Lake, H. CAMPAIGNING IN THE BALKANS. New York: 1918.

317. Lampe, J.R., & Jackson, M.R. BALKAN ECONOMIC HISTORY, 1550-1950: FROM IMPERIAL BORDERLANDS TO DEVELOPING NATIONS. Bloomington: 1982.

318. Langer, W.L., ed. THE RISE OF MODERN EUROPE. 20+ vols. New York: 1936-.

319. Lausanne, Conference on Near Eastern Affairs, 1922-1923. RECUEIL DES ACTES DE LA CONFERENCE. Turkish ed. by Ahmet Yavuz. Ankara: 1968-.

320. Lazarovich-Hrebelianovich, Prince. SERVIAN PEOPLE. 2 vols. New York: 1910.

321. Lederer, I.J., ed. RUSSIA AND THE BALKANS IN RUSSIAN FOREIGN
     POLICY: ESSAYS IN HISTORICAL PERSPECTIVE. New Haven: 1962.

322. _____. YUGOSLAVIA AT THE PEACE CONFERENCE: A STUDY IN
     FRONTIERMAKING. New Haven & London: 1963.

323. Lee, P., & Bearman, G. RUSSIA IN REVOLUTION. Exeter: 1974.

324. Legrand, E.L.J. BIBLIOGRAPHIE ALBANAISE. Leipzig: 1973.

325. Lengyel, E. 1000 YEARS OF HUNGARY. New York: 1958.

326. Leon, G. GREECE AND THE GREAT POWERS, 1914-1917. Thessaloniki:
     1974.

327. Lessner, E.C., & Lessner, A.M.L. THE DANUBE: THE DRAMATIC
     HISTORY OF THE GREAT RIVER AND THE PEOPLE TOUCHED BY ITS
     FLOW. Garden City: 1961.

328. Lewinsohn, R. THE PROFITS OF WAR THROUGH THE AGES. New York:
     1979.

329. Lewis, B. THE EMERGENCE OF MODERN TURKEY. London: 1961.

330. Logoreci, A. THE ALBANIANS. London: 1977.

331. Low, A.D. THE SOVIET HUNGARIAN REPUBLIC AND THE PARIS PEACE
     CONFERENCE. TAPS 53:10. New Series. Philadelphia: 1963.

332. Lowe, J.T. GEOPOLITICS AND WAR: MACKINDER'S PHILOSOPHY OF
     POWER. Washington: c.1981.

333. Lukacs, J.A. THE GREAT POWERS AND EASTERN EUROPE. New York:
     [1953].

334. Lupu, N. RUMANIA AND THE WAR. Boston: 1919.

335. Luvaas, J. "The Great Military Historians and Philosophers."
     GSUMH. Washington: 1979.

336. Macartney, C.A. HISTORY OF HUNGARY, 1920-1944. New York: 1956.

337. _____. THE HABSBURG EMPIRE, 1790-1918. New York: 1969.

338. _____. HUNGARY, A SHORT HISTORY. Chicago: 1962.

339. Macartney, C.A., & Palmer, A.W. INDEPENDENT EASTERN EUROPE: A
     HISTORY. New York: 1966 [1962].

340. Macek, V. THE STRUGGLE FOR FREEDOM. University Park & London:
     1968.

341. Machray, R. THE LITTLE ENTENTE. London & New York: 1929.

342. Maciu, V. "The Romanian Army in the First World War
     (1916-1918)." PHRA. Bucharest: 1975.

343. Magocsi, P.R. THE SHAPING OF NATIONAL IDENTITY: SUBCARPATHIAN
RUS', 1848-1948. HUS. Cambridge: 1978.

344. Makkai, L. HISTOIRE DE TRANSYLVANIE. Paris: 1946.

345. Marcovich, L. "Lord Curzon and Pashitch - Light on Yugoslaviia,
Turkey and Greece in 1922." JCEA XIII (January 1954),
329-337.

346. _____., ed. SERBIA AND EUROPE, 1914-1920. London: [1920].

347. Margutti, A.A.V. Freiherr von. THE EMPEROR FRANCIS JOSEPH AND
HIS TIMES. London: [1921].

348. Marriott, J.A.R., Sir. THE EASTERN QUESTION. 3rd ed. Oxford:
1930.

349. Marston, F.S. THE PEACE CONFERENCE OF 1919: ORGANIZATION AND
PROCEDURE. RIIA. London: 1944.

350. Mavrocordato, J. MODERN GREECE, 1800-1931. London: 1931.

351. May, A.J. THE PASSING OF THE HABSBURG MONARCHY, 1914-1918. 2
vols. Philadelphia: 1966.

352. Mayer, A.J. DYNAMICS OF COUNTER-REVOLUTION IN EUROPE,
1870-1956: AN ANALYTIC FRAMEWORK. New York: 1971.

353. McEvedy, C. THE PENQUIN ATLAS OF RECENT HISTORY. New York:
1982.

354. McNeill, W.H. A WORLD HISTORY. 3rd ed. Oxford: 1979.

355. Meyer, K. BIBLIOGRAPHIE DER ARBEITEN ZUR OSTEUROPAISCHEN
GESCHICHTE AUS DEN DEUTSCHSPRACHIGEN FACHZEITSCHRIFTEN,
1858-1964. BMO 9. Berlin: 1966.

356. Miller, J.M. "The Concert of Europe in the First Balkan War,
1912-1913." Unpublished dissertation, Clark University,
1969.

357. Miller, W. THE OTTOMAN EMPIRE AND ITS SUCCESSORS, 1801-1927.
Cambridge: 1936.

358. Mitchell, R. THE SERBS CHOOSE WAR. Garden City: 1943.

359. Mitrany, D. THE EFFECT OF THE WAR IN SOUTHEASTERN EUROPE. New
York: 1973 [c.1936].

360. _____. THE LAND AND THE PEASANT IN RUMANIA: THE WAR AND
AGRARIAN REFORM, 1917-21. London: 1930.

361. Monroe, W.S. BULGARIA AND HER PEOPLE; WITH AN ACCOUNT OF THE
BALKAN WARS, MACEDONIA, AND THE MACEDONIAN BULGARS.
Boston: 1914.

362. Montross, L. WAR THROUGH THE AGES. New York: 1944.

363. Moore, F. THE BALKAN TRIAL. New York: 1971.

364. Moorehead, A. GALLIPOLI: ACCOUNT OF THE 1915 CAMPAIGN. New York: 1956.

365. Mordal, J. TWENTY-FIVE CENTURIES OF SEA WARFARE. New York: 1965.

366. Morison, W., ed."Ballards of Serbian Liberation". SEER XVIII No. 52 (July 1939), 1-17.

367. Morris, J., & Roberts, J.M. EUROPE 1880-1945. New York: 1967.

368. Murray, W.S. THE MAKING OF THE BALKAN STATES. New York: 1967 [1910].

369. Musat, M. "Military Factors and National Development: The Impact of Foreign Pressures." TRTI. New York: 1983.

370. Nayes, G.R., & Bacon, L., Trans. HEROIC BALLADS OF SERVIA. Boston: 1913.

371. Newbigin, M.I. GEOGRAPHICAL ASPECTS OF BALKAN PROBLEMS IN THEIR RELATION TO THE GREAT EUROPEAN WAR. New York: 1915.

372. Nowak, K.F. THE COLLAPSE OF CENTRAL EUROPE. London: 1924.

373. Ognianova, M. BALKANSKATA VOINA. Sofia: 1949.

374. Okcu, Y., & Ustunsoy, H. BIRINCI DUNYA HARBINDE TURK HARBI. SINA-FILISTIN CEPHESI, HARBIN BASLANGICINDAN IKINCI GAZZE MUHAREBELERI SONUNA KADAR. 9 vols. Ankara: 1975.

375. Olivova, V. THE DOOMED DEMOCRACY: CZECHOSLOVAKIA IN A DISRUPTED EUROPE, 1914-38. Trans. by George Theiner. London & Montreal: 1972.

376. Opacic, P. SOLUNSKA OFANZIVA 1918. GODINE. Belgrad: 1980.

377. _____. SOLUNSKI FRONT-ZEJTINLIK. Belgrad: 1978.

378. OSTERREICH UND EUROPE: FESTGABE FUR HUGO HANTSCH ZUM 70. GEBURTSTAG. Graz, Vienna & Cologne: 1965.

379. Packer, C. RETURN TO SALONIKA. London: [1964].

380. Pakalm, M.Z. SON SADRAZAMLAR VE BASVEKILLER. 5 vols. Istanbul: 1940-1948.

381. Pallis, A.A. GREECE'S ANATOLIAN VENTURE AND AFTER. London: 1937.

382. Palmer, A.W. THE PENGUIN DICTIONARY OF TWENTIETH CENTURY HISTORY, 1900-1978. New York: 1979.

383. Pandevski, M. ILINDENSKOTO VOSTANIE VO MAKEDONIJA 1903. Skopje: 1978.

384. Pauley, B. HABSBURG LEGACY, 1867-1939. New York: 1972.

385. Paulova, M. TAJNY VYBOR (MAFFIE) A SPOLUPRACE S JIHOSLOVANY V
LETECH 1916-1918. Prague: 1968,

386. Pavlowitch, K. St. "Yugoslavia and Romania." JCEA XXIII No. 4
(January 1964), 451-485.

387. Pentzopoulos, D. THE BALKAN EXCHANGE OF MINORITIES AND ITS
IMPACT UPON GREECE. Paris: 1962.

388. Petrovic, V.M. SERBIA; HER PEOPLE , HISTORY, ASPIRATIONS. New
York: 1915.

389. Petrovich, M.B. A HISTORY OF SERBIA, 1804-1918. 2 vols. New
York & London: 1976.

390. Omitted.

391. Pinkney, D.H. THE NINETEENTH CENTURY, 1815-1914. WE. Ed. by
Neil J. Hackett. St. Louis: c.1979.

392. _____., ed. PROBLEMS OF CIVILIZATION. 10+ vols. Lexington:
1977-.

393. Poletica, N.P. SARAEVSKOE UBIISTVO: ISSLEDOVANIE PO ISTORII A
AVSTRO-CERBSKIKH OTNOSHENII I BALKAMSKOI POLITIKI POSSII V
PERIOD 1903-1914 G.G. Leningrad: 1930.

394. Popa, M.N. PRIMUL RAZBOI MONDIAL. 1914-1918. Bucharest: 1979.

395. Popovici, A. THE POLITICAL STATUS OF BESSARABIA. Washington:
1931.

396. Preston, A., ed. GENERAL STAFFS AND DIPLOMACY BEFORE THE SECOND
WORLD WAR. Totowa: 1978.

397. Preston, R.A., et al. MEN IN ARMS. New York: 1956.

398. Prevelakis, E. "Eleutherios Venizelos and the Balkan Wars." BS
VII/2 (1966), 363-378.

399. Pribram, A.F. AUSTRIA-HUNGARY AND GREAT BRITAIN, 1908-1914. New
York: 1951.

400. Price, C. THE REBIRTH OF TURKEY. New York: 1923.

401. Psomiades, H.J. THE EASTERN QUESTION: THE LAST PHASE. A STUDY
IN GREEK-TURKISH DIPLOMACY. Thessaloniki: 1968.

402. Pundeff, M.V. "The Balkan Entente Treaties." AJIL XLVIII
(1954), 630-635.

403. Raditsa, B. "Venizelos and the Struggle Around the Balkan
Pact." BS VI/1 (1965), 119-130.

404. Ramsaur, E.E. THE YOUNG TURKS; PRELUDE TO THE REVOLUTION OF
1908. Princeton: 1958.

405. Ranghet, B. RELATIILE ROMANO-AMERICANE IN PERIODA PRIMULUI
     RAZBOI MONDIAL, 1916-1920. Cluj-Napoca: 1975.

406. Rankin, R., Lt. Col. Sir. INNER HISTORY OF THE BALKAN WAR.
     London: 1914.

407. Ray, J. THE FIRST WORLD WAR. Exeter: 1975.

408. Reiss, R.A. HOW AUSTRIA HUNGARY WAGED WAR IN SERBIA: PERSONAL
     INVESTIGATIONS OF A NEUTRAL. SDW. Paris: 1916.

409. _____. THE KINGDOM OF SERBIA: REPORT UPON THE ATROCITIES
     COMMITTED BY THE AUSTRO-HUNGARIAN ARMY DURING THE FIRST
     INVASION OF SERVIA: SUBMITTED TO THE SERBIAN GOVERNMENT.
     Trans. by F. Copeland. London: nd.

410. Renn, L. WARFARE: THE RELATION OF WAR TO SOCIETY. New York:
     1939.

411. Reuter, P. DIE BALKANPOLITIK DES FRANZOSISCHEN IMPERIALISMUS
     1911-1914. Frankfurt am Main & New York: 1979.

412. Reynolds, P.A. BRITISH FOREIGN POLICY IN THE INTER-WAR YEARS.
     London: [1954].

413. Riasonovsky, N. A HISTORY OF RUSSIA. 4th ed. New York & Oxford:
     1984.

414. Roider, K.A., & Youngs, F.A., eds. THE WORLD OF EUROPE. 9 vols.
     St. Louis: c.1979-.

415. Romania. STUDII DE ISTORIE SI TEORIE MILITARA. RETROSPECTIVE
     ISTORICE ANALIZE CONTEMPORANE. Bucharest: 1980.

416. _____. ENCICLOPEDIA ISTORIOGRAFIEI ROMANESTI. Bucharest:
     1978.

417. _____. REGIMURILE FASCISTE SI TOTALITARE DIN EUROPA. Vol.
     1. Bucharest: 1979.

418. _____. ROMANIA IN PRIMUL RAZBOI MONDIAL. Bucharest: 1979.

419. Ropp, T. WAR IN THE MODERN WORLD. Durham: 1959.

420. Rothenberg, G.E. THE ARMY OF FRANCIS JOSEPH. West Lafayette:
     1976.

421. Rothschild, J. EAST CENTRAL EUROPE BETWEEN THE TWO WORLD WARS.
     HECE 9. Seattle & London: [1974].

422. Roucek, J.S. BALKAN POLITICS; INTERNATIONAL RELATIONS IN NO
     MAN'S LAND. Westport: 1971 [c.1948].

423. _____. "Rumania, Albania, and Bulgaria, At the End of the
     Beginning." WAI XV (Spring 1944), 88-101.

424. Ruchti, J. DIE REFORMAKTION OSTERREICH-UNGARNS UND RUSSLANDS IN MAZEDONIEN 1903-1908. Gotha: 1918.

425. Rundle, R.N. INTERNATIONAL AFFAIRS, 1890-1939. New York: 1979.

426. RUSSIA, U.S.S.R., EASTERN EUROPE: ALPHABETICAL CUMULATIVE CATALOGUE. Cumulative IDC Catalogue. Zug: nd.

427. Russian Institute (Columbia University) Occasional Papers. RUSSIAN DIPLOMACY IN EASTERN EUROPE, 1914-1917. New York: 1963.

428. Sanness, J. EUROPE AND THE BALKANS. PAST TERRITORIAL DISPUTES AND SOCIOPOLITICAL VARIETY. Oslo: 1972.

429. Savadjian, L. LA BULGARIE EN GUERRE. Geneva: 1917.

430. _____. LA BULGARIE A LA CONFERENCE DE LA PAIX. Paris: 1918.

431. _____. THE CAMPAIGN AGAINST THE TREATY OF TRIANON. Paris: 1929.

432. _____. BIBLIOGRAPHIE BALKANIQUE. 2 vols. Paris: 1931-.

433. _____. LES ORIGINES ET LES RESPONSIBILITES DE LA GUERRE MONDIALE. Paris: 1933.

434. _____. BIBLIOGRAPHIE YOUGOSLAVE, 1933. Paris: 1934.

435. Savic, V.R. SOUTH-EASTERN EUROPE: THE MAIN PROBLEM OF THE PRESENT WORLD STRUGGLE. New York: c.1918.

436. Savu, A.G. PAGES FROM THE HISTORY OF THE ROMANIAN ARMY. BHR Monograph XV. Bucharest: 1975.

437. _____. THE ARMY AND ROMANIAN SOCIETY. Bucharest: 1980.

438. _____. "The Type of Defensive War Envisaged by the Romanian Inter-War Policy." ARS. Bucharest: 1980.

439. Scherer, A. SUDOSTEUROPA-DISSERTATIONEN, 1918-1960. EINE BIBLIOGRAPHIE DEUTSCHER, OSTERREICHISCHER UND SCHWEIZERISCHER HOCHSCHULSCHRIFTEN. Graz, Vienna, Cologne & Bohlau: 1968.

440. Schevill, F. HISTORY OF THE BALKAN PENINSULA. New York: 1971 [c.1922].

441. Schlozer, L. von. DAS TURKISCHE HEER. Leipzig: 1901.

442. Schmitt, B.E. THE COMING OF WAR, 1914. 2 vols. New York: 1930.

443. _____. SERBIA, YUGOSLAVIA, AND THE HABSBURG EMPIRE. UNS. Berkeley & Los Angeles: 1949.

444. _____. THE ANNEXATION OF BOSNIA, 1908-1909. New York: 1970 [1937].

445. Schmitthenner, P. KRIEG UND KRIEGFUHRUNG IM WANDEL DER WELTGESCHICHTE. Potsdam: 1930.

446. Schnitzer, E. (Emin Pasha). EMIN PASHA, HIS LIFE AND WORK. 2 vols. Westminister: 1898.

447. Schreiber, G. BALKAN AUS ESTER HAND. GESCHICHTE UND GEGENWART IN BERICHTEN VON AUSGENZUEGEN UND ZEITGENOSSEN. Wurzburg: 1971.

448. Schurman, J.G. BALKAN WARS, 1912-1913. Stafford Little Lectures for 1914. Princeton: 1914.

449. SECRET DIPLOMATIC DOCUMENTS AND TREATIES FROM THE ARCHIVES OF THE MINISTRY OF FOREIGN AFFAIRS OF THE FORMER RUSSIAN GOVERNMENT. Intro. by Leon Trotsky. Petrograd: 1918.

450. Seemann, K.-D., & Siegman, F. BIBLIOGRAPHIE DER SLAVISTISCHEN ARBEITEN AUS DEN DEUTSCHSPRACHIGEN FACHZEITSCHRIFTEN 1876-1963. Vol. 8 of BIBLIOGRAPHISCHE MITTEILUNGEN DES OSTEUROPA-INSTITUTS AN DER FREIEN UNIVERSITAT BERLIN. Wurzburg: 1965.

451. Seligman, V.J. THE SALONICA SIDE-SHOW. London: 1919.

452. Senkowitsch, I. DIE KULTURBEDEUTUNG SERBIENS. Zurich: 1917.

453. Serbia, Ministry of Foreign Affairs. DAS SERBISCHE BLAUBUCH, DAS RUSSISCHE ORANGEBUCH. Vienna: 1915.

454. Seton-Watson, R.W. THE WAR AND DEMOCRACY. London: 1914.

455. _____. ROUMANIA AND THE GREAT WAR. London: 1915.

456. _____. SERBIA'S WAR OF LIBERATION. London: 1916.

457. _____. GERMAN, SLAV AND MAGYAR: A STUDY OF THE ORIGINS OF THE GREAT WAR. London: 1916.

458. _____. THE BALKANS, ITALY AND THE ADRIATIC. 2nd ed. London: 1916 [1915].

459. _____. EUROPE IN THE MELTING POT. London: 1919.

460. _____. THE EMANCIPATION OF SOUTH-EASTERN EUROPE. London: 1923.

461. _____. SARAJEVO: A STUDY IN THE ORIGINS OF THE GREAT WAR. London: 1926.

462. _____. THE RISE OF NATIONALITY IN THE BALKANS. New York: 1966.

463. _____. THE SOUTHERN SLAV QUESTION AND THE HABSBURG MONARCHY. New York: 1969.

464. Sforza, C., Count. FIFTY YEARS OF WAR AND DIPLOMACY IN THE BALKANS. New York: 1940.

340

465. Shaw, S.J. "The Ottoman View of the Balkans." In THE BALKANS IN TRANSITION. Ed. by Charles & Barbara Jelavich. Berkeley: 1963.

466. Shaw, S.J., & Shaw, E.K. HISTORY OF THE OTTOMAN EMPIRE AND MODERN TURKEY. Vol. 2: REFORM, REVOLUTION AND REPUBLIC: THE RISE OF MODERN TURKEY, 1808-1975. Cambridge, London & New York: 1977.

467. Shepherd, W.R. HISTORICAL ATLAS. 8th ed. London: 1956.

468. Shotwell, J.T. BALKAN MISSION. New York: 1949.

469. Sidak, J., et al. PROIJEST HRVATSKOG NARODA G. 1860-1914. Zagreb: 1968.

470. Silberstein, G.E. "The Serbian Campaign of 1915: Its Military Implications." IRHPS III:2 (December 1966), 115-132.

471. _____. "The Central Powers and the Second Turkish Alliance." SR XXIV/1 (March 1965), 77-89.

472. Simpson, A.E., & Baker, V.B. DEATH OF AN OLD WORLD, 1914-1945. Arlington Heights: 1979.

473. Singer, J.D., et al. eds. EXPLAINING WAR: SELECTED PAPERS FROM THE CORRELATES OF WAR PROJECT. Beverly Hills: c.1979.

474. Singer, J.D., & Small, M. THE WAGES OF WAR: A STATISTICAL HANDBOOK. New York: 1972.

475. Sinor, D. HISTORY OF HUNGARY. New York: 1961.

476. Skendi, S. ALBANIAN POLITICAL THOUGHT AND REVOLUTIONARY ACTIVITY, 1881-1912. Munich: 1954.

477. _____. THE ALBANIAN NATIONAL AWAKENING, 1878-1912. Princeton: 1967.

478. Skoko, S. DRUGI BALKANSKI RAT 1913. Belgrad: 1975.

479. Skopje. Institute of National History. SRBSKI IZVORI ZA ISTORIJATA NA MAKEDONSKIOT NAROD 1912-1914. Ed. by Gligor Todorovski. Skopje: 1979.

480. Slijepcevic, D. THE MACEDONIAN QUESTION; THE STRUGGLE FOR SOUTHERN SERBIA. Chicago: 1958.

481. Sloane, W.M. THE BALKANS: A LABORATORY OF HISTORY. 2nd ed. New York: [c.1920].

482. Smirnova, N.D. POLITIKA ITALII NA BALKANAKH: OCHERK DIPLOMATICHESKOI ISTORII: 1922-1935 GG. Moscow: 1979.

483. Sonyel, S.R. TURKISH DIPLOMACY 1918-1923: MUSTAFA KEMAL AND THE TURKISH NATIONAL MOVEMENT. London & Beverly Hills: c.1975.

484. Spaulding, O.L., et al. A STUDY OF MILITARY METHODS FROM THE EARLIEST TIMES. New York: 1925.

485. Stavrianos, L.S. THE BALKAN FEDERATION; A HISTORY OF THE MOVEMENT TOWARD BALKAN UNITY IN MODERN TIMES. Northhampton: [1944].

486. _____. THE BALKANS SINCE 1453. New York: 1958.

487. _____. THE BALKANS, 1815-1914. Huntington: 1974 [c.1963].

488. Steed, H.W. THROUGH THIRTY YEARS, 1892-1922: A PERSONAL NARRATIVE. London: 1924.

489. Stephenson, G. RUSSIA FROM 1812 TO 1945: A HISTORY. New York & Washington: 1970.

490. Stevenson, F.S. A HISTORY OF MONTENEGRO. New York: 1971.

491. Stieve, F. ISVOLSKY AND THE WORLD WAR. London: 1926.

492. Stoianovich, T. "Factors in the Decline of Ottoman Society in the Balkans." SR XXI No. 4 (December 1962), 623-632.

493. Stojanov, P. MAKEDONIJA VO POLITIKATA NA GOLEMITE SILLI VO VREMETO NA BALKANSKITE VOINI 1912-1913. Skopje: 1979.

494. Stokesbury, J.L. A SHORT HISTORY OF WORLD WAR I. New York: 1981.

495. Stone, N. THE EASTERN FRONT, 1914-1917. New York & London: 1975.

496. _____. "Hungary and the Crisis of July 1914." JCH I,3 (1966), 147-164.

497. Suer, H. TURK SILAHLI KUVVETLERI TARIHI, OSMANLI DEVRI, BALKAN HARBI. 4 vols. Ankara, 1981.

498. Sugar, P.F., & Treadgold, D.W., eds. HISTORY OF EAST CENTRAL EUROPE. 11 vols. Seattle & London: 1974-.

499. Suta, I. INFANTERIA ROMANA. Vol. I: DE LA INCEPUTURI PINA LA PRIMUL RAZBOI MONDIAL. Bucharest: 1977.

500. Swire, J. ALBANIA, THE RISE OF A KINGDOM. London: 1929.

501. Szabo, L. A NAGY TEMETO/PRZEMYSL OSTROMA 1914-1915. Budapest: 1982.

502. Szaz, Z. "The Transylvanian Question: Romania and the Belligerents, July-October 1914." JCEA XII:4 (January 1954), 338-351.

503. Talpes, I. "The Dynamics of the Organizational Structures of the Romanian Army (1919-1939)." ARS. Bucharest: 1980.

504. Tanty, M. KONFLIKTY BALKANSKIE W LATACH 1878-1918. Warsaw: 1968.

505. Taylor, A.J.P. THE STRUGGLE FOR MASTERY IN EUROPE, 1848-1914. Oxford: 1952 [1931].

506. _____. THE HABSBURG MONARCHY, 1809-1918. 2nd ed. London: 1964 [1948].

507. _____. FROM SARAJEVO TO POTSDAM. New York: 1967.

508. _____. WAR BY TIMETABLE: HOW THE FIRST WORLD WAR BEGAN. Vol. 5 in LIBRARY OF THE 20th CENTURY. J.M. Roberts, Gen Ed. London: 1969.

509. Teksut, I., & Okse, N. TURK SILHALI KUVVETLERI TARIHI. OSMANLI DEVRI. BIRINCI DUNYA HARBI. Ankara: 1980.

510. Temperley, H.W.V., Sir. HISTORY OF SERBIA. London: 1917.

511. _____. HISTORY OF THE PEACE CONFERENCE OF PARIS. 6 vols. Oxford & London: 1920-1924.

512. _____. FOUNDATIONS OF BRITISH FOREIGN POLICY FROM PITT TO SALISBURY. London: 1966.

513. Thaden, E.C. RUSSIA AND THE BALKAN ALLIANCE OF 1912. University Park: [1965].

514. Theodoulou, C. GREECE AND THE ENTENTE, AUGUST 1, 1914-September 25, 1916. Thessaloniki: 1971.

515. Thomson, C.B. OLD EUROPE'S SUICIDE; OR, THE BUILDING OF A PYRAMID OF ERRORS. London: [1920].

516. Timur, C. TURK ISTIKLAL HARBI. Vol. 7: IDARI FAALIYETLER (15 MAYIS 1919-2 KASIM 1923). Ankara: 1975.

517. Todorovic, D. JUGOSLAVIJA I BALKANSKE DRZAVE 1918-1923. Belgrad: 1979.

518. Torrey, G.E. "Rumania and the Belligerents, 1914-1916." JCH I,3 (1966), 165-184.

519. _____. "The Rumanian Campaign of 1916: Its Impact on the Belligerents." SR XXXIX/1 (March 1980), 27-43.

520. _____. "The Rumanian-Italian Agreement of 23 Sept. 1914." SEER XLIV, 103 (July 1966), 403-420.

521. Toynbee, A.J. THE WESTERN QUESTION IN GREECE AND TURKEY. New York: 1970.

522. Trask, R.R. THE UNITED STATES RESPONSE TO TURKISH NATIONALISM AND REFORM, 1914-1939. Minneapolis: [1971].

523. Trebilcock, C. THE INDUSTRIALIZATION OF THE CONTINENTAL POWERS, 1780-1914. New York & London: 1981.

524. Trouton, R. PEASANT RESISTENCE IN YUGOSLAVIA, 1900-1950. London: 1952.

525. Trumpener, U. GERMANY AND THE OTTOMAN EMPIRE, 1914-1918. Princeton: 1968.

526. Tsvetkova, B.A. LES INSTITUTIONS OTTOMANES EN EUROPE. Wiesbaden: 1978.

527. Tuca, F. "The 'Marasti' Society and Its Main Achievements." ARS. Bucharest: 1980.

528. Tucker, J. "The Rumanian Peasant Revolt of 1907." Unpublished dissertation. University of Chicago, 1972.

529. Turkey. ASKERI TARIH BELGERI DERGISI: DOCUMENTS D'HISTOIRE MILITAIRE. Nos. 78-80. Ankara: 1980-1981.

530. _____. TURK SILAHLI KUVVETLERI TARIHI. 1978.

531. Turkiye Cumhuriyeti, Maarif Vekaleti. ISLAM ANSIKLOPEDISI. Istanbul & Ankara: 1940-.

532. Tzankov, A. "The 1913 Balkan Peace of Bucharest." BR IV (December 1965), 2-11.

533. Ude, L. SLOVENCI IN JUGOSLOVANSKA SKUPNOST. Maribor: 1972.

534. Unc, G., & Deac, A. 1918. GARZILE NATIONALE ROMANE DIN TRANSILVANIA. Bucharest: 1979.

535. Upward, A. THE EAST END OF EUROPE: THE REPORT OF AN UNOFFICIAL MISSION TO THE EUROPEAN PROVINCES OF TURKEY ON THE EVE OF THE REVOLUTION. London: 1908.

536. U.S. Army. THE BALKANS, 1915. Fort Leavenworth: 1915.

537. USSR, Academy of Sciences. BIBLIOGRAFIYA TURTSII (1917-1958). Moscow: 1959.

538. Vagts, A. A HISTORY OF MILITARISM. New ed. New York: 1959.

539. Valiani, L. THE END OF AUSTRIA-HUNGARY. New York: 1973.

540. Valley, J.E., & Dufourcq, P. LA PREMIERE GUERRE MONDIALE. 2 vols. Vol. 1: 1914/1916 DE SARAJEVO A VERDUN. Paris: 1968.

541. Van Creveld, M.L. SUPPLYING WAR: LOGISTICS FROM WALLENSTEIN TO PATTON. New York: 1977.

542. Van Vollenhaven, C. THE LAW OF PEACE. London: 1936.

543. Vesa, V. ROMANIA SI FRANTA LA INCEPUTUL SECOLULUI AL XX-LEA, 1900-1916. Cluj-Napoca: 1975.

544. Vickers, W. "The Ottoman Army in the Balkans". Unpublished
     Dissertation, Princeton: 1958.

545. Vital, D. THE SURVIVAL OF SMALL STATES: STUDIES IN SMALL
     POWER/GREAT POWER CONFLICT. Toronto: 1971.

546. Vogel, H., MD. VALJEWO, ERINNERUNGEN EINES SCHWEIZER ARZTES AN
     DEN SERBISCH-TURKISCHEN KRIEG. Rorschach: [194?].

547. Vogel, R. "Sir Fairfax Cartwright and the Balkans." NR V 2/3
     (January-September), 9-16.

548. Volgyes, I., ed. HUNGARY IN REVOLUTION, 1918-1919: NINE ESSAYS.
     Lincoln: 1971.

549. Vucinich, W.S. SERBIA BETWEEN EAST AND WEST. New York: 1968.

550. _____. "Jelacic and the Frontier of Modern History." AHY I
     (1965), 68-71.

551. Vukcevic, R. RAZVOJ PRIVREDE CRNE GORE. Titograd: 1974.

552. Vyvyan, J.M.K. "The Approach of the War of 1914." NCMH 12.
     Cambridge: 1968.

553. Wagner, H. WITH THE VICTORIOUS BULGARIANS. Boston: 1913.

554. Walichnowski, T. BALCANICA: GUIDE TO THE POLISH ARCHIVES
     RELATIVE TO THE HISTORY OF THE BALKAN COUNTRIES. Warsaw:
     1979.

555. Wandruszka, A. THE HOUSE OF HABSBURG: SIX HUNDRED YEARS OF A
     EUROPEAN DYNASTY. Garden City: 1964.

556. Watt, D.C. "Diplomatic History, 1930-1939." NCMH 12. Cambridge:
     1968.

557. Weber, E.J. EUROPE SINCE 1715: A MODERN HISTORY. New York:
     1972.

558. Wegener, A. von. BIBLIOGRAPHIE ZUR VORGESCHICHTE DES
     WELTKRIEGES. Berlin: 1934.

559. Wendel, H. MAKEDONIEN UND DER FRIEDE. Munich: 1919.

560. West, R. (pseud.). BLACK LAMB AND GREY FALCON. London: 1967
     [1941].

561. Westwood, J.N. ENDURANCE AND ENDEAVOUR: RUSSIAN HISTORY,
     1812-1980. 2nd ed. SOHMW. OOxford: 1981.

562. White, W.W. THE PROCESS OF CHANGE IN THE OTTOMAN EMPIRE.
     Chicago: [1937].

563. _____. THE STATUS IN INTERNATIONAL LAW OF THE FRAGMENTS OF
     THE OTTOMAN EMPIRE. [Chicago]: 1935.

564. Williamson, S.R., ed. THE ORIGINS OF A TRAGEDY: JULY 1914. St. Louis: c.1981.

565. Wiskeman, E. "Germany, Italy and Eastern Europe." NCMH 12. Cambridge: 1968.

566. Wolfe, E.R. PEASANT WARS OF THE TWENTIETH CENTURY. New York: [1969].

567. Wolff, R.L. THE BALKANS IN OUR TIME. New York & Cambridge: 1956.

568. Woodruff, W. THE STRUGGLE FOR WORLD POWER, 1500-1980. New York: 1981.

569. Woodward, E.L., Sir. PRELUDE TO MODERN EUROPE, 1815-1914. London: [1972].

570. Wright, Q. THE STUDY OF WAR. London & Chicago: 1965 [1942].

571. Wright, W.L. OTTOMAN STATECRAFT. Princeton: 1925.

572. Wyon, R. THE BALKANS FROM WITHIN. London: 1904.

573. Xanalatos, D. "The Greeks and the Turks on the Eve of the Balkan Wars." BS III 91963), 277-296.

574. Yasar, R., & Kabasakal, H. TURK SILHALI KUVVETLERI TARIHI. OSMANLI DEVRI. BALKAN HARBI. 4 vols. Ankara: c.1981.

575. Yigitguden, R., et al. BIRINCI DUNYA HARBINDE TURK HARBI. CANAKKALE CEPHESI. Ankara: 1978.

576. Young, G., Sir. NATIONALISM AND WAR IN THE NEAR EAST. Ed. by Leonard H. Courtney, 1st Baron of Penwith. New York: 1971.

577. Yugoslavia. PRVI BALKANSKI RAT, 1912-1913. Belgrad: 1959.

578. Zakythinos, D.A. THE MAKING OF MODERN GREECE. Trans. by K.R. Johnston. Totowa: 1976.

579. Zannas, A. THE MACEDONIAN STRUGGLE, RECOLLECTIONS. Thessaloniki: 1961.

580. Zeibert, I.A. DER MORD VON SARAJEVO UND TISZAS SCHULD AN DEM WELTKRIEG. Vienna: 1918.

581. Zeman, Z.A.B. THE BREAK-UP OF THE HABSBURG EMPIRE, 1914-1918; A STUDY IN NATIONAL AND SOCIAL REVOLUTION. London & New York: 1961.

582. Zivanovic, M. DUBROVNIK U BORBA ZA UJEDIN'EN'EI 1908-1918. Belgrad: 1962.

583. Zook, D.H., & Higham, R. A SHORT HISTORY OF WARFARE. New York: 1966.

584. Zwitter, F. LES PROBLEMES NATIONAUX DANS LA MONARCHIE DES
HABSBOURG. Belgrad: 1960.

ADDITIONS

585. Braun, M. "Turkenherrschaft und Turkenkampf bei den
Balkenslawen." WaG VI (1940), 124-139.

586. Barber, N. THE SULTANS. New York: 1973.

587. Seton-Watson, H. THE DECLINE OF IMPERIAL RUSSIA, 1855-1914. New
York: 1964.

588. Babin, A.I., et al. ISTORIYA OTECHESTVENNOI VOENNO-
ENTSIKLOPEDICHESKOI LITERATURI. Moscow: 1980.

589. Kochan, L., & Abraham, R. THE MAKING OF MODERN RUSSIA. New ed.
Harmondsworth & New York: 1983.

590. Clayton, G.D. BRITAIN AND THE EASTERN QUESTION: MISSALONGHI TO
GALLIPOLI. New York: 1974.

591. Bradley, J.F.N. CZECHO-SLOVAKIA: A SHORT HISTORY. Edinburgh:
1971.

592. Sugar, P.F. ETHNIC DIVERSITY AND CONFLICT IN EASTERN EUROPE.
Santa Barbara: 1980.

593. Bond, B. BRITISH MILITARY POLICY BETWEEN THE TWO WORLD WARS.
Oxford: 1980.

594. Bulgaria. LA POLITIQUE FRANCAISE ET LES BALKANS, 1933-1936.
Sofia: 1975.

595. Helmreich, E.C. THE DIPLOMACY OF THE BALKAN WARS, 1912-1913.
Boston: 1939.

596. Bardakci, I. BIR IMPORATORLUNGUN YAGMASI: BALKAN BOZGUNU VE I,
DUNYA HARBI. Ankara(?): 197-.

597. Halsey, F.W. THE LITERARY HISTORY OF THE WORLD WAR. 10 vols.
New York & London: 1919.

598. Anonymous. THE NEAR EAST FROM WITHIN. New York: 1915.

599. Kerner, R.J. YUGOSLAVIA AND THE PEACE CONFERENCE. UNS. Berkeley
& Los Angelos: 1949.

600. Bond, B. BRITISH MILITARY POLICY BETWEEN THE TWO WORLD WARS.
Oxford: 1980.

601. Baker, B. THE PASSING OF THE TURKISH EMPIRE IN EUROPE. London:
1913.

602. Petho, S. VILAGOSTOL TRIANONIG; A MAI MAGYARORSZAG
KIALAKULASANAK TORTENETE. 5th ed. Budapest: 1926.

# CHAPTER NINE

## 1936-1984

### BACKGROUND TO ARMAGEDDON

This short period of less than 50 years marks the last chapter in the history of the Balkans to the present decade. As time passes more events will occur that will impact either directly or indirectly upon the nations of the Balkans and will, in turn, become history. The process never ends and will continue as long as time itself continues. During this particular period, two mighty empires, Nazi Germany and the Soviet Union, both sought to dominate the Balkans and both, in different ways, were successful.

Germany's role began as a result of the death of Frederick Ebert, the Weimar Republic's first president, in 1925 and the subsequent installation of Field Marshal Paul von Beneckendorf und Hindenberg, who was both a national hero and symbol of the _ancien regime._ In his second term, the worldwide depression was felt in Germany and was perceived by many Germans as another example of the West's determination to keep the nation down in punishment for World War I. Hindenberg, feeble and in fear of death, was induced by Germany's upper-class "Junkers" to install Adolf Hitler as Chancellor. This began one of the blackest chapters in history and changed the course of human development forever.

The first German move toward the Balkans came about when Hitler tested his strength on the Austria republic that had been founded when the Dual Monarchy was dismembered. Hitler carefully planned this takeover, including a purge of his own military forces, before he provoked an incident that would allow his invasion and annexation of the now landlocked vestige of the former Austro-Hungarian Empire. Accusing the Austrian Chancellor, Kurt von Schusschnigg, of treaty violations, Hitler attempted to force the pro-German Artur von Seyss-Inquart on the Austrian leader as Minister of Interior. When Schusschnigg fought back, Hitler provoked rioting in Vienna and, when Schusschnigg resigned in despair, put Seyss-Inquart in power. Then, without waiting for a proper "request" for aid, Hitler sent in the Wehrmacht (12 March 1938). Germany then had strategic control of the middle Danube and was on the frontiers of Yugoslavia, Czechoslovakia, Hungary, and Italy. The Great Powers failed to act and Hitler had a _fait accompli_ . Europe moved closer to World War II and the Balkans were now directly threatened by a new invader.

The Soviet Union had just passed a major turning point when this period opened. This was brought about by the Seventh Comintern Congress' adoption of the Popular Front policy and by Soviet entry into the League of Nations. The long period of isolation that had followed the Soviet refusal to abide by international law and diplomacy after it seized power in 1917 was over. Beginning in 1936, the Soviet Union was providing active support to the Loyalist side in the Spanish Civil War. The Germans and Italians had begun full-scale support to Franco during the summer. This led to a straining of relations between Berlin and Moscow.

Two other events occurred during this period that also were important to the future of the Balkans and to the world in general. The first was the establishment of the Berlin-Rome axis in October 1936 and the subsequent German-Japanese Anti-Comintern Pact of 25 November 1936. The second came two years later immediately following the _Anschluss_ in Austria. At that point, Hitler demanded autonomy for the predominantly German-speaking Sudetenland region of Czechoslovakia. Moscow immediately suggested a joint declaration by the USSR, France, and Great Britain to the effect that they were prepared, if necessary, to fight. Stalin then notified Prague that the Soviet Union was ready to honor its 1935 assistance agreement, if the Czech government could solicit a similar statement from Paris. Even the United States became involved when it offered to mediate the ever-deepening Czech Crisis. When the West vacillated in its response (Munich Pact of 29 September 1938), Hitler used the occasion to act and invaded Czechoslovakia. Neither the Soviet Union nor Czechoslovakia had been invited to Munich. Czechoslovakia was forced to accede to the terms and was further humiliated by having to agree to additional terms put forth by Poland and Hungary. Hungary, for example, annexed the Carpato-Ukraine (Ruthenia) on 15 March 1939.

Another matter of importance was Stalin's purges of 1937 and 1938 that crippled the Red Army and left its remnants in the hands of an inferior officer corps. There can be little question that this fact was known in Berlin and because of it, Hitler, in his paranoia, felt a little more secure in his ultimate plan of complete destruction of the Soviet Union. The Balkans suffered indirectly from this as the purges caused such weakness in the Red Army that there was a lessening of the traditional Russian watchfulness over that region and a subsequent greater latitude of action for the Nazis. (Soviet weakness would be subsequently borne out in the Russo-Finnish War (1939).)

In 1939 events moved rapidly toward war. English and French diplomatic advances aimed at an alliance with the USSR were rebuked when Vyacheslav Molotov replaced Maxim Litvinov as Soviet foreign minister (3 May 1939). At the same time Germany was annexing Memel (Klaipeda, today in the USSR)(23 March 1939) and was demanding the port of Danzig and a corridor through northern Poland. In April, both England and France guaranteed Polish security. Three weeks later, on 28 April, Hitler abrogated the German-Polish Non-Aggression Treaty of 1934 and the Anglo-German Naval Agreement of 1935. Within a month, Hitler was planning the invasion of Poland. A part of this planning was secret negotiations with Stalin that culminated in the Nazi-Soviet Nonaggression Pact of 23 August 1939 that, among other things, gave the Soviet Union the right to annex eastern Poland and Bessarabia. On 1 September 1939, Nazi forces crossed into Polish territory marking the traditional beginning of Second World War.

GENERAL HISTORICAL LITERATURE OF THE PERIOD

The history of this period is the history of the Second
World War and its aftermath. There were, of course, other events
which transpired during these years, but none of them affected the
Balkans as did the impact of the war and its subsequent absorption
into the Soviet sphere of influence. The general literature on this
period is so extensive, in fact, that any attempt at exhaustive
compilation is impractical. There are a few studies that can be
mentioned, however, that will serve as a starting point for the
reader. William McNeill's A WORLD HISTORY [341] is still the best
general history in one volume. John M. Roberts' EUROPE, 1880-1945
[438] is excellent for the period up to and through the Second World
War. A.W. Palmer's THE PENGUIN DICTIONARY OF TWENTIETH CENTURY
HISTORY, 1900-1978 [387] is a comprehensive reference that can be
quite valuable to the practiced reader. Norman Cantor and Samuel
Berner's THE MODERN ERA, 1815 TO THE PRESENT [87] is also very good.
Cantor and Berner edited this work in 1967, and present a number of
excellent articles on the period. Another worthwhile study is Felix
Gilbert's THE END OF A EUROPEAN ERA, 1890 TO THE PRESENT [189]. This
book was published as a second edition in 1970. Volume 12, THE
SHIFTING BALANCE OF WORLD FORCES 1898-1945 [359] is in NCMH and was
edited by Professor C.L. Mowat. Richard Vaughan traces the
development of hopes for European unity after World War I and how
those hopes survived in this period of turmoil in TWENTIETH CENTURY
EUROPE: PATHS TO UNITY [547]. The fourth and last volume in A
DOCUMENTARY HISTORY OF MODERN EUROPE [44], that was edited by Thomas
Barnes and Gerald Feldman, deals with BREAKDOWN AND REBIRTH: 1914 TO
THE PRESENT. This volume was published in 1982.

The two volumes of R.N. Rundle's INTERNATIONAL AFFAIRS are
most valuable. Volume one [609] ends with 1939 and the emergence of
the final provocations by the totalitarian states that led to World
War II. Volume two [610] is an excellent guide to the Second World
War and the subsequent reorganization of Europe up to 1979. Jacob
Talmon deals with the question of THE ORIGINS OF TOTALITARIAN
DEMOCRACY [501] while Edward Gulick's EUROPE'S CLASSICAL BALANCE OF
POWER: A CASE HISTORY OF THE THEORY AND PRACTICE OF ONE OF THE GREAT
CONCEPTS OF EUROPEAN STATECRAFT [208] studies the effects of this
concept on the course of European history. Alan Hodgart's THE
ECONOMICS OF EUROPEAN IMPERIALISM [220] looks at the base cause of
many of Europe's problems leading up to this period. THE POLITICS OF
WAR AND PEACE: A SURVEY OF THOUGHT [67] surveys the lives of a
number of the great military leaders, statesmen, and scholars of
this period. This study is extremely helpful in understanding the
socio-political relationships involved in a man's allegiance to his
country.

GENERAL MILITARY STUDIES

An excellent place to begin is with Geoffrey Blainey's THE
CAUSES OF WAR [56]. Professor Blainey deals extensively with the
period under discussion in this fine book. Another excellent
selection is V.R. Berghahn's MILITARISM: THE HISTORY OF AN
INTERNATIONAL DEBATE, 1860-1979 [51]. This study traces the history
of the use of the term "militarism" from its inception in 1860 and
explains its several applications in contemporary times. A HISTORY

OF MILITARISM [541], by Alfred A. Vagts, is better. KRIEG UND KRIEGFUHRUNG IM WANDEL DER WELTGESCHICHTE [450], by P. Schmitthenner, is also usable, but is not as good as Vagts. Ludwig Renn's WARFARE: THE RELATION OF WAR TO SOCIETY [429] was published in 1939 but still contains many truths applicable to later times. It is especially useful to the reader in gaining an understanding of the origins of the Second World War. Theodore Ropp's WAR IN THE MODERN WORLD [606] is also very valuable as it traces the relationship of warfare to the political, socio-economic, and technological changes that have occurred especially in the decades preceding World War II. EXPLAINING WAR: SELECTED PAPERS FROM THE CORRELATES OF WAR PROJECT [467] was edited by Joel David Singer and a group of associates. It has numerous valuable parts and some brilliant articles. Stanislav Andreski's MILITARY ORGANIZATION AND SOCIETY [20] is also useful and should be studied along with Hew Strachen's EUROPEAN ARMIES AND THE CONDUCT OF WAR [490]. This study devotes three chapters to this period.

James Lowe's GEOPOLITICS AND WAR: MACKINDER'S PHILOSOPHY OF POWER [320] is particularly applicable at this time as the point of Lowe's discussion is application of Mackinder's formula to World War II and the emergence of Stalin as the arbiter of policy. WAR, DIPLOMACY, AND HISTORY [375] by Raymond O'Connor is a collection of commentaries on the use of armed forces and foreign policy as instruments of national political policy and strategy in war and peace. John Alger's THE QUEST FOR VICTORY: THE HISTORY OF THE PRINCIPLES OF WAR [12] stresses the relationship between power and intellect in the military and between the military and civilian leadership. David Vital's THE SURVIVAL OF SMALL STATES: STUDIES IN SMALL POWER/GREAT POWER CONFLICT [549] presents evidence that might be applied to any of the Balkan countries in this period.

Other useful works include MEN IN ARMS [409], by R.A. Preston, S.F. Wise, and H.O. Werner and THE MAKERS OF MODERN STRATEGY: MILITARY THOUGHT FROM MACHIAVELLI TO HITLER [148], which was edited by Edward M. Earle and published in 1943. These and other works of this genre are discussed in several chapters in A GUIDE TO THE STUDY AND USE OF MILITARY HISTORY [248], edited by John E. Jessup and Robert W. Coakley. Roger Parkinson's THE ENCYCLOPEDIA OF MODERN WAR [393] is also quite useful for this period although it does not have the overall scope of R. Ernest and Trevor Dupuy's THE ENCYCLOPEDIA OF MILITARY HISTORY [607]. The Dupuy book devotes over 300 pages to the present period. A SHORT HISTORY OF WARFARE [607], by David H. Zook and Robin Higham, devotes one-third of its total coverage to these years. THE NEW MILITARY AND NAVAL DICTIONARY [182], edited by Frank Gaynor, was published in 1951 is somewhat out of date although still useful. Elbridge Colby's MASTERS OF MOBILE WARFARE [114] and P.E. Cleator's WEAPONS OF WAR [102] are both worthwhile reading at this point. Martin Van Creveld's SUPPLYING WAR: LOGISTICS FROM WALLENSTEIN TO PATTON [543]; Richard Lewinsohn's THE PROFITS OF WAR THROUGH THE AGES [308]; and THE WAGES OF WAR: A STATISTICAL HANDBOOK [466], by Joel David Singer and Melvin Small, give different perspectives to the problems of reporting wars.

## HITLER AND NAZI GERMANY

Adolf Hitler was one of the most evil men who ever lived. His leadership of the German National Socialist Party and its assumption of power at a critical time in Europe's historical development condemned millions to untold suffering and death. Much that would happen in the Balkans can be laid at Hitler's feet. Thus, although Hitler and his Nazi Germany fall outside the most ambitious definition of the Balkans, it is important, much as it was in tracing Imperial Russian and Austrian development, to understand how Germany came to affect the entire course of human history.

While there are probably more scholarly works on the subject, there are few works that are as readable as William L. Shirer's THE RISE AND FALL OF THE THIRD REICH: A HISTORY OF NAZI GERMANY [462]. It is all the average reader will need to gain a comprehensive understanding of the state and its leaders. Alan Cassels' FASCISM [90] is a brilliant study of one of the major forces of the 20th century. Both Hitler's German variety of fascism and that practiced by Mussolini in Italy are described along with the spread of the two into central and eastern Europe. Hitler's first attempted putsch is described in great detail in MUNICH 1923 [611], by John Dornberg. Keith Eubank's MUNICH [159] is also useful. Bela Vago's THE SHADOW OF THE SWASTIKA: THE RISE OF FASCISM AND ANTISEMITISM IN THE DANUBE BASIN, 1936-1939 [539] is extremely important to an understanding of this period in the Balkans. This work by an Israeli historian focuses on the problems faced by Jews in Romania, Czechoslovakia, and Hungary. In describing their plight he exposes the insidious nature of Nazism even as it was practiced through those early years in the Balkans. Walter Ansel describes German aims in the Mediterranean in his HITLER AND THE MIDDLE SEA [21]. THE WAR PATH: HITLER'S GERMANY 1933-1939 [240], by D. Irving, is engrossing reading. A recent Soviet study on the subject is M.I. Semiryaga's NEMETSKO-FASHISTSKAYA POLITIKA NATSIONAL'NOGO PORABOSHCHENIYA V OKKUPIROVANNIKH STRANAKH ZAPADNOI I SEVERNOI EVROPII [456]. This book was published in 1980.

The story of the German takeover of Austria is told in ANSCHLUSS 1938. PROTOKOLL DES SYMPOSIUM IN WIEN AM 14. UND 15. MARZ 1978 [366]. This is a compilation of material from 14 lectures that were edited by Rudolf Neck, Adam Wandruszka, and Isabella Ackerl. Two of the lectures deal with the role played by the Austrian army and with Austrian operational plans in case of an attack from Germany, Czechoslovakia, or Yugoslavia. HITLER'S ROUTE TO BAGDAD [162] was prepared by London's Fabian Society in 1971. It is a series of five essays dealing with German plans and aspirations in Yugoslavia, Romania, Bulgaria, Greece, and Turkey. Martin Van Creveld wrote HITLER'S STRATEGY, 1940-1941: THE BALKAN CLUE [544] in which the author takes a controversial look at German planning during the period June 1940-June 1941. Van Creveld sheds new light on Hitler's view of the Balkans, and why he chose to allow Mussolini to invade Greece only to have to send in German troops when the Italians failed. Another interesting book is Norman Rich's HITLER's WAR AIMS [433].

Marcel Fodor treats the subject of German moves into Southeastern Europe in his SOUTH OF HITLER [170] which is a new and enlarged version of his earlier PLOT AND COUNTERPLOT IN CENTRAL EUROPE. The new version deals with the invasion of Czechoslovakia and German entry into the Balkans. This subject is also dealt with in Dietrich Orlov's THE NAZIS IN THE BALKANS: A CASE STUDY IN TOTALITARIAN POLITICS [380]. This is the story of the Nazi wartime policy-making body for the Balkans, the Sudosteuropa-Gesellschaft (SOEG). The book is excellent and contains a very helpful bibliography. Another interesting look at this area is found in Stojan Pribecevic's "The Nazi Drive to the East: Yugoslavia, Rumania, Hungary" [415]. Andreas Hillgruber's HITLER'S STRATEGIE: POLITIK UND KRIEGFUHRUNG 1940-1941 [217] deals with the German leader's decision during the crucial 12 months following the fall of France. Another valuable, albeit more focused, work by Professor Hillgruber is his HITLER, KONIG CAROL UND MARSCHALL ANTONESCU: DIE DEUTSCH-RUMANISCHEN BEZIEHUNGEN, 1938-1944 [612].

Two works of considerable interest at this point are Nicholas Nagy-Talavera's THE GREEN SHIRTS AND THE OTHERS: A HISTORY OF FASCISM IN HUNGARY AND RUMANIA [365] and THE DANUBE SWABIANS: GERMAN POPULATIONS IN HUNGARY, RUMANIA AND YUGOSLAVIA AND HITLER'S IMPACT ON THEIR PATTERNS [385], by G.C. Paikert. The former work is a comprehensive, if not unbiased, account of the chronological development of Fascism in Romania and Hungary with particular emphasis on the people involved. The latter book deals with the ethnic German populations in the three countries from an eye-witness vantage point. (The only real detail concerns the Hungarian Germans.) Both are well worth reading. Another work of similar nature is Dusan Biber's NACIZEM I NEMCI V JUGOSLAVIJI, 1933-1941 [613]

THE HISTORY OF THE SECOND WORLD WAR

The very magnitude of the events that transpired between 1939 and 1945 indicate the amount of literature that has been published about World War II. Official histories abound, with nearly every nation that participated having some form of written record of the events as they affected the particular nation. BIBLIOGRAPHIE ZUR INTERNATIONALEN MILITAR-AMTICHEN KRIEGSGESCHICHTSSCHREIBUNG UBER DEN ZWEITEN WELTKRIEG [425] is based on the official histories of 34 nations. The data that has accrued from the war has been examined and reexamined using every form of interpretation and analysis known to man and new studies on some phase of the war are constantly being published. The international body of knowledge about the war probably transcends any other period in history and it is obviously beyond the scope of this undertaking to enumerate more than just a very few of the more pertinent works. No better place could be found to begin than with Sir Winston Churchill's six-volume THE SECOND WORLD WAR [97]. It is a truly outstanding example of historical literature in particular and is of such stylistic excellence as to make a contribution to English literature in general. The treatment is, of course, general with a majestic sweep that often overlooks important details. As a starting point, however, there is nothing better.

Among the other works that might be considered are Keith Eubank's THE ORIGINS OF WORLD WAR II [157], which was published in 1969. His WORLD WAR II, ROOTS AND CAUSES [158], published about 1975, is also worthwhile reading and is in reality a update of the earlier work. Eubank also edited THE ROAD TO WORLD WAR II: A DOCUMENTARY HISTORY [156] which is a representative collection of documents relating to the background of the war. This 304-page compilation is an excellent supplement to either of the two aforementioned studies. TOTAL WAR: CAUSES AND COURSES OF THE SECOND

WORLD WAR [84], by Peter Calvocoressi and Guy Wint, is a comprehensive (992 page) account of the war. THE MAKING OF THE SECOND WORLD WAR [5], edited by Anthony Adamthwaite, has an exceptional collection of documents dealing with the policies and actions that led to the war.

James Stokesbury's A SHORT HISTORY OF WORLD WAR II is a good one-volume survey of the war. John Ray's THE SECOND WORLD WAR [426] is also useful. Gordon Wright's THE ORDEAL OF TOTAL WAR, 1939-1945 [584] is probably the best single-volume history available in English. Professor Wright concentrates more on the western arena, however, and details on the war in eastern Europe become somewhat diluted. LOUIS SNYDER'S HISTORICAL GUIDE TO WORLD WAR II [473] emphasizes the non-military aspects of the war, although there are sections on the "Weapons of War," "Code Names," and "Spies, Counterspies, and Hoaxes." WORLD WAR II POLICY AND STRATEGY: SELECTED DOCUMENTS WITH COMMENTARY [244], by Hans-Adolf Jacobsen and Arthur Smith, presents an array of documents in chronological order. DICTIONNAIRE DE LA SECONDE GUERRE MONDIALE [333], that was edited by Philippe Masson, is an excellent reference work with a variety of articles on people, places, events, and weapons. A SUBJECT BIBLIOGRAPHY OF THE SECOND WORLD WAR; BOOKS IN ENGLISH, 1939-1974 [151] was compiled by A.G.S. Enser. Its 592 pages contain thousands of citations. Rene Kraus' EUROPE IN REVOLT [291] deals with underground movements during the war. WHO WERE THE ARMIES? AXIS ORDER OF BATTLE, 1939-1945 [569] is actually seven volumes of order of battle data on the Wehrmacht and its allies on all fronts. Two volumes are devoted to southeastern Europe.

The best source of information in the United States is the publications of the American Committee on the History of the Second World War. One of these, published in 1972, was compiled by Professor Arthur Funk and is called THE SECOND WORLD WAR: A BIBLIOGRAPHY [13]. A second, larger publication which contains hundreds of citations is the Spring 1981 edition (No. 25) of the Committee's NEWSLETTER [14] which is entitled "Cumulative Listing of Bibliographical and Archival Resources." This compilation was prepared by William J. Dougherty and contains a listing of publications of the International Committee on the History of the Second World War since 1975. There is a large amount of material on the Balkans in this listing.

As is the case in any war, the use of good maps is crucial to understanding the effects of the terrain on the outcome of battle. Arthur Banks' A WORLD ATLAS OF MILITARY HISTORY, 1860-1945 [37], W.R. Shepherd's HISTORICAL ATLAS [461], Colin McEvedy's THE PENGUIN ATLAS OF RECENT HISTORY (EUROPE SINCE 1815) [339], and the BIBLIOGRAPHIC GUIDE TO MAPS AND ATLASES: 1981 [52] should provide all that might be required.

Among other important sources on German participation in the war, General Burkhart Muller-Hillebrand's GERMANY AND ITS ALLIES IN WORLD WAR II: A RECORD OF AXIS COLLABORATION PROBLEMS [362] is particularly useful. Written in 1954 as a part of the US Army's historical program, it is an authoritative account of a German General Staff officer who served in a position where he was able to judge the results of collaboration. Part two of this study is particularly valuable as it describes the collaboration by country.

Another useful tool is U.S. MILITARY INTELLIGENCE REPORTS: GERMANY, 1919-1941 [528], which has been reproduced on microfilm by University Publications of America in 28 reels. This collection includes data on the German Balkan Campaign, the Eastern Front, and occupation problems. Coverage from 1942 into the Cold War period is provided in a similar collection, OSS/STATE DEPARTMENT INTELLIGENCE AND RESEARCH REPORTS [523] which includes coverage on the Yugoslav partisan movement among its nearly 1,350 subject titles. The World War II part of this collection is made up of 22 reels. GERMAN MILITARY INTELLIGENCE,1939-1945 [529] is the result of allied exploitation of captured Nazi records and interrogations. A significant portion of the work is devoted to the Russian campaign. WORLD WAR II GERMAN MILITARY STUDIES [136] is a 24-volume series edited by Donald Detwiler. Among its numerous parts are sections on the Balkans, including the invasions of Yugoslavia and Greece by General Hans von Greiffenberg. Nikolaus von Prerardovich's DIE MILITARISCHE UND SOZIALE HERKUNFT DER GENERALITAT D. DEUTSCHEN HEERES 1. MAI 1944. [408] addresses the social origins and military backgrounds of 1,446 officers of the Wehrmacht. THE RUSSIAN FRONT: GERMANY'S WAR IN THE EAST, 1941-1945 [146], which was edited by James Dunnigan, deals particularly with the struggle from the operations research point of view. John Erickson's THE ROAD TO STALINGRAD [152] is an excellent account of the war on the Eastern Front up to the great turning-point on the Volga. Professor Erickson is one of the very few western historians to have been given extensive access to Soviet military records. His works are, therefore, quite valuable.

## GENERAL HISTORIES ON THE BALKANS

Leften Stavrianos' THE BALKANS SINCE 1453 [482] is still among the best general accounts of the course of events in the Balkans during this critical period. His BALKAN FEDERATION; A HISTORY OF THE MOVEMENT TOWARD BALKAN UNITY IN MODERN TIMES [483] is also quite valuable. Edgar Hosch's THE BALKANS: A SHORT HISTORY [228] provides very little coverage of the period preceding the outbreak of the Second World War. THE BALKANS IN TRANSITION [246], edited by Charles and Barbara Jelavich, has an excellent essay called "Historical Studies in the Balkans in Modern Times" by George C. Soulis which contains an excellent bibliography. Edmund Stillman's THE BALKANS [488] centers on Albania, Romania, Yugoslavia, and Bulgaria and is a Time-Life publication. Peter Sugar's ETHNIC DIVERSITY AND CONFLICT IN EASTERN EUROPE [492] is an excellent assemblage of essays. BALKAN AUS ESTER HAND [452], by George Schreiber, is a collection of eyewitness accounts and reports on developments in the Balkans. John Sanness' EUROPE AND THE BALKANS. PAST TERRITORIAL DISPUTES AND SOCIOPOLITICAL VARIETY [443] is exceptionally good as background reading on foreign economic relations. Paul Ignotus' article entitled "Czechs, Magyars, Slovaks" [236] is especially valuable in its study of Czecho-Hungarian relations. Dragos Kostich's THE LAND AND PEOPLE OF THE BALKANS: ALBANIA, BULGARIA, YUGOSLAVIA [284] is good reading but not very detailed. It is listed in the Library of Congress as a juvenile-level work but has some merit as background reading. Bernard Newman's BALKAN BACKGROUND [371] treats each country individually and, although it is not thorough in its treatment, it is interesting reading. John Lukacs' THE GREAT POWERS AND EASTERN EUROPE [321] deals with the events between 1934, when the Soviet

Union joined the League of Nations, and 1945. Its importance lies in its almost chronological description of the fates of each of the 13 eastern European nations at the hands of the Germans and Russians. BALKAN ECONOMIC HISTORY, 1550-1950 [295], by John Lampe and Marvin Jackson, describes the economic situation in the Balkans through the war period and into the immediate post-war era.

The BIBLIOGRAPHIC GUIDE TO SOVIET AND EAST EUROPEAN STUDIES: 1981 [53] is a listing of publications catalogued during that year that includes entries on all of the Balkan nations except Greece and Turkey. There are over 40,000 items listed. The 1981 edition is in three volumes. The same type of material is found in Klaus Meyer's BIBLIOGRAPHIE DER ARBIETEN ZUR OSTEUROPAISCHEN GESCHICHTE AUS DEN DEUTSCHSPRACHIGEN FACHZEITSCHRIFTEN, 1858-1964 [343] which covers German-language publications. SUDOSTEUROPA-DISSERTATIONEN, 1918-1960. EINE BIBLIOGRAPHIE DEUTSCHER, OSTERREICHISCHER UND SCHWEIZERISCHER HOCHSCHULSCHRIFTEN [449], by Anton Scherer, deals with German-language dissertations. The CHECKLIST OF PAPERBOUND BOOKS ON RUSSIA AND EAST EUROPE [476], edited by Sherman Spector and Lyman Legters, was last revised in 1966. The IDC microfiche RUSSIA, U.S.S.R., EASTERN EUROPE, ALPHABETICAL CUMULATIVE CATALOGUE [620] contains more than 6,500 titles. OSTERREICH UND EUROPA: FESTGABE FUR HUGO HANTSCH ZUM 70. GEBURTSTAG [381] contains three articles that deal with Austria's fate under Hitler. AN ATLAS OF RUSSIAN AND EAST EUROPEAN HISTORY [4], compiled by Arthur Adams and others, is also useful.

## THE BALKANS IN WORLD WAR II

OSTMITTELEUROPA IM ZWEITEN WELTKRIEG (HISTORIOGRAPHISCHE FRAGEN) [192] was edited by Ferenc Glatz and published in Budapest in 1978. It is a collection of international papers dealing with research on the Second World War conducted during the 1960s. UNDECLARED WAR [575], by Elizabeth Wiskemann, was a 1940 attempt to set forth the methods by which the Nazis forced their neighbors to accept overlordship without recourse to arms. This book deals primarily with the Danubian situation up to that time. Robert Lee Wolfe's THE BALKANS IN OUR TIME [577] has a good bibliography and covers events in Yugoslavia, Romania, and Bulgaria from 1939 to 1955. Wolfe served in the Balkan section of OSS, and his well-written book reflects a considerable knowledge of the region. John Erickson's THE SOVIET HIGH COMMAND [619] deals with events in Yugoslavia, Romania, Czechoslovakia, Bulgaria, and Hungary in the period between the wars. Of importance also is Erickson's description of Romanian order of battle for the German invasion of Russia in 1941. LES GRANDES PUISSANCES ET LES BALKANS A LA VEILLE ET AU DEBUT DE LA DEUXIEME GUERRE MONDIALE 1937-1941 [72] was published in Bulgaria in 1973 and is the ACTA of an international conference held in Sofia in 1971. Stephan Borsody's THE TRAGEDY OF CENTRAL EUROPE [59] was originally published as THE TRIUMPH OF TYRANNY and deals with the Nazi and Soviet conquests of Central Europe. Stojan Pribicevic's SPOTLIGHT ON THE BALKANS [413] deals with the period of the buildup before the war. Franz C. Weiskorf, writing under the pseudonym of Frederick W.L. Kovacs, has written THE UNTAMED BALKANS [288] the first part of which deals with the German conquest of Yugoslavia. Published in 1941, it presents a leftist and quite accurate view of what was to be the future of the Balkans. Svetozar Vukmanovic-Tempo's BORBA ZA BALKAN [553] is a 1981 Yugoslav publication that presents a latter-day view of the struggle in the Balkans. Leigh White's THE LONG BALKAN NIGHT [568] is a personal narrative on the situation in 1940-1941. White's insight into the Balkan future is remarkable. George Eric Gedye's BETRAYAL IN CENTRAL EUROPE (FALLEN BASTIONS) [641] is a resume of the events in the conquest of Austria and Czechoslovakia as perceived by an English journalist. He is especially critical of the parts played by England and France in the affair. It is excellent. Peter Lane's dissertation that was presented at the University of Washington deals with "The United States and the Balkan Crisis of 1940-1941" [296]. THE GERMAN CAMPAIGN IN THE BALKANS (SPRING 1941) [518] is one of a number of fine pamphlets turned out by the US Army in the 1950s. Another of these is GERMAN ANTIGUERRILLA OPERATIONS IN THE BALKANS (1941-1945) [519] which deals with the methods used in attempts to quell the resistance that sprang up all over the Balkans. Martin Van Creveld's HITLER'S STRATEGY, 1940-1941: THE BALKAN CLUE [544] is also quite useful. There is coverage of the Italian attack on Greece, the invasion of Yugoslavia, and the problem of bringing Bulgaria into the Nazi camp. Van Creveld also demonstrates the relationship between Hitler's plans for Southeastern Europe and his plan for the Soviet Union.

## THE OCCUPATION OF CZECHOSLOVAKIA

Following years of subversion in the Sudetenland and Great Power appeasement of Hitler, the German annexation of Czechoslovakia (10-16 March 1939) signalled the beginning of the military campaign into Central Europe. Although not technically a part of the Balkans, the fall of the Czechs is a good place to start in developing an understanding of the events that would transpire later. One of the better books on the general area is with J.F.N. Bradley's CZECHO-SLOVAKIA: A SHORT HISTORY [63]. Vera Olivova's THE DOOMED DEMOCRACY: CZECHOSLOVAKIA IN A DISRUPTED EUROPE, 1914-38 [376] was published in Prague in 1972. It is relatively free of ideological jargon and is extremely perceptive and well written. MEMOIRS: FROM MUNICH TO NEW WAR AND NEW VICTORY [49], by the Czech hero Edvard Benes, is absolutely indispensable to the serious student. Vojtech Mastny's THE CZECHS UNDER NAZI RULE: THE FAILURE OF NATIONAL RESISTANCE, 1939-1942 [334] describes the fall of Czechoslovakia, the occupation, and the rise of resistance. Mastny closes with an account of the terrible retribution brought upon the Czechs by the assassination of SS Obergruppenfuhrer Reinhard Heydrich. This last subject is also covered in Jan Wiener's THE ASSASSINATION OF HEYDRICH [573] in which he describes the London-directed operation that was carried out by Czech parachutists in May 1942. This book needs to used carefully as it contains a number of errors and omissions. CZECHOSLOVAKIA'S FIGHT: DOCUMENTS ON THE RESISTANCE MOVEMENT OF THE CZECHOSLOVAK PEOPLE, 1938-1945 [139], by Jiri Dolezol and Jan Kren, and "The Communist Party of Czechoslovakia and the Czech Resistance, 1939-1945" [323] both tell the same story from different perspectives.

## THE ITALIAN INVASION OF ALBANIA

There was a period of relative calm in this tiny Adriatic country following the rebellion (May 1937) against the infamous rule of Ahmed Bey Zog I (Zogu), who was both President (1925-1928) and King (1929-1945). On Good Friday, 7 April 1939, Mussolini invaded

Albania because of Zog's reluctance to accept Italian overlordship and because of his refusal to repay just loans. Zog fled first to France and then to England (1940), where he was instrumental in organizing the Albanian underground. The Italian invasion alerted Yugoslavia and Greece to the danger, but the warning came too late.

Very few definitive works are available in English that deal with this period. Anton Logoreci's THE ALBANIANS: EUROPE'S FORGOTTEN SURVIVORS [317] deals with the war period. BIBLIOGRAPHIE ALBANAISE [303], by E.L.J. Legrand, is a good source of additional material. Julian Amery's SONS OF THE EAGLE, A STUDY IN GUERRILLA WARFARE [15] is an excellent account of the resistance. PRECIS D'HISTOIRE DE LA LUTTE ANTIFASCISTE DE LIBERATION NATIONALE DU PEUPLE ALBANAISE [116] is a France version of LUFTA NACIONAL CLIRIMTARE KUNDER PUSHTUESVE ITALIANE E GJERMANE GJATE LUFTES SE DYTE BOTERORE. It was produced by the Committee on Cultural Relations in Tirana in 1975 and deals with the underground movement in Albania during the war years. FRONTE GRECO-ALBANESE, C'ERO ANCH'IO [48] was edited by Giulio Bedeschi. It is a series of personal narratives from participants in the Italian, Albanian and Greek campaigns. Enzo Misefari's LA RESISTENZA DEGLI ALBANESI CONTRO L'IMPERIALISMO FASCISTA [349] was produced in 1976 and deals with the Albanian resistance. Lefter Kasneci's TREMPEE DANS LE FEU DE LA LUTTE, BREF APERCU DE L'HISTOIRE DE L'ARMEE DE LIBERATION NATIONALE DU PEUPLE ALBANAISE (1941-1944) [266] was published in French but is the work of an Albanian. This work deals with the role of the People's National Liberation Army led by Enver Hoxha as the only savior of the nation. Ndreci Plasari's HISTORIA E LUFTES ANTIFASHISTE NACIONALCLIRIMTARE TE POPULLIT HQIPTAR [402] does the same thing in Albanian. Two other works of that same type are GRUAJA SHQIPTARE NA LUFTEN ANTIFASHISTE. NACIONALCLIRIMTARE [7], published in Tirana in 1975, and the ACTA [8] of the 1975 National Conference on the Antifascist War of National Liberation of the Albanian People held in Tirana. Riccardo Crespi's SQUADRISTI IN ALBANIA [119] is an Italian propaganda piece published in 1941.

## THE ITALIAN ATTACK ON GREECE

After Albania the Italians turned southward and attacked Greece (28 October 1940) with eight divisions. Italian ineptitude and a determined Greek defense stopped the Italians and resulted in a Greek counteroffensive which was supported by RAF elements sent from Egypt and by British surface units which bombarded Italian positions near the coast. By the end of 1940, the Italian position was at best precarious. British ground forces comprising four divisions began landing in mid-March. The Italian invasion had not been coordinated with Berlin and Hitler was furious.

In consort with planning to invade Yugoslavia (see below) the German leader was determined to seize Greece. German troop dispositions in Hungary and Romania enabled the German offensive to begin ten days after Hitler issued his directive. The Germans quickly broke through the Metaxas Line and soon held Salonika. This forced the surrender of the Greek Second Army. In a subsequent campaign in central Greece, the Greeks were forced to abandon positions near the Albanian border while the British were forced back to Thermopylae. The Greek commander, General Alexander Papagos, gallantly offered to cover a British withdrawal (begun 24 April

1941) through the Peloponnesus, even though Greece was about to surrender (23 April 1941). Although nearly cut off by a German airborne landing near Corinth on 26 April, the British were able to withdraw some 45,000 troops but were forced to abandon huge stores of materiel.

On 20 May, the Germans opened their attack on Crete with the first major airborne assault in history. Elements of the 7th Parachute Division were dropped in several locations and were promptly cut to pieces by British and Greek forces on the island. A second wave of the German 7th landed on 21 May. With a fragile airhead established, the Germans attempted to airland a mountain division. Air defense destroyed most of the planes but enough got through to begin tipping the balance in favor of the Germans. Although attempts to reinforce by sea were beaten back by the British Royal Navy with heavy casualties, continued airlift enabled the Germans to overcome the resistance. By 31 May the fighting was over. Some 12,000 British troops were taken prisoner although the Royal Navy had performed heroically in evacuating as many defenders as they did.

There is a rich collection of literature on the history of Greece in this period and on the Greek campaigns. THE MAKING OF MODERN GREECE [597], by D.A. Zakythinos, is a good place to start. Richard Clogg's A SHORT HISTORY OF MODERN GREECE [111] concentrates on the 19th and 20th centuries although it begins with Byzantine times. A SHORT HISTORY OF MODERN GREECE, 1821-1952 [173], by E.S. Forster, is also worthwhile reading.

Laird Archer's BALKAN JOURNAL [25] is a collection of excerpts from the diary he maintained from mid-1934 to August 1941 when he was Director of the Near East Foundation. It deals chiefly with the political and international affairs of that period and is very entertaining reading. APPLE OF DISCORD [582], by C.M. Woodhouse, covers much of the same material in a somewhat more scholarly fashion. WAR IN THE AEGEAN [472], by Peter Smith and Edwin Walker, is useful. THE BATTLE OF GREECE, 1940-1941 [391], by General Alexander Papagos, is excellent. LA CAMPAGNA DI GRECIA [242] is three-volume official Italian history of the war. It contains a thorough account of the action plus numerous documents, maps, and photos. The Greek version is told in a seven-volume collection that is found under French title: L'ARMEE HELLENIQUE PENDANT LA SECONDE GUERRE MONDIALE [200]. Unfortunately, this excellent edition has not been translated from the original Greek. It is extremely detailed, the last volume dealing with the battle for Crete. There is a similar two-volume set [201] that deals with the Greek Navy in World War II. Robin Higham's "British Intervention in Greece 1940-1941: The Anatomy of a Grand Deception" [215] is an excellent account of British problems in Greece. Higham has also produced "A Limited War in a Total War: the Coming of the Graeco-German War, 1940-1941" [216] which is a case study in military-diplomatic command and deals with British aid to Greece. Another of this series is "'General' and Guarantees -- Some Aspects of Aid to Greece in 1940-1941" [214]. FRONTE GRECO-ALBANESE, C'ERO ANCH'IO [48], edited by Giulio Bedeschi, discusses the activity connected with the Italian invasion of Greece from Albania. NAZI VICTORY: CRETE 1941 [507], by D. Thomas, deals with that phase of the German push into the Aegean. Dominick Eudes' THE KAPENTANIOS: PARTISANS AND CIVIL WAR IN GREECE,

1943-1949 [160] deals in part with the resistance and with the intertwined affair of ELAS and the communist attempt to seize power even before the Germans were defeated. Henry Maule's SCOBIE: HERO OF GREECE. THE BRITISH CAMPAIGN 1944-45 [336] deals with the campaign of Lieutenant General Sir Ronald Scobie to bring order to the chaos in Greece.

## YUGOSLAVIA

Following the Italian invasion of Albania in April 1939, England and France assured Yugoslavia, Romania, and Greece of support against further Nazi aggression. The Yugoslav regency council, which had ruled since the death of King Alexander (1918-1934), was to continue its ineffective leadership. Yugoslavia declared its neutrality, but the council appeared to favor the Germans. This position was generally opposed by the people, however, who rose against the government on 26-27 March 1941. Prince Regent Paul, chief among the three-man regency, was ousted and a new anti-German government, headed by Prince Peter, installed. German pressure had already been felt in Yugoslavia as Hitler, intent upon his plan to invade the Soviet Union, sought a secure southern flank. With the Yugoslav governmental shift and with the debacle going on in Greece, Hitler moved to immediately attack both Yugoslavia and Greece.

The Yugoslav coup d'etat took place within days of the signing of the Tripartite Agreement in Vienna. Thus, Hitler decided that, in view of his plans to attack the Soviet Union, he could not afford a hostile country on his southern flank. The attack opened on 6 April 1941, just hours after the announcement of the Soviet-Yugoslav Treaty of Friendship and Non-aggression (5 April). German forces entered Yugoslavia from Austria, Hungary, and Romania in a classic blitzkrieg maneuver. The pre-invasion terrorist bombings of key Yugoslav command and control facilities, especially in Belgrad, helped prevent the mobilization of the armed forces. After the capture of most of the major cities, Yugoslavia was forced to surrender on 17 April. Yugoslavia lost about 400,000 troops killed, captured or wounded compared to the German loss of less than 600 men. King Peter and his cabinet were forced to flee into exile, first to Jerusalem, then to London, then to Cairo (1943).

In Yugoslavia, a major resistance campaign was mounted by General Draza Mihailovic (named Minister of War - 13 January 1942) and the reports received in London convinced the Allies that the Chetniks alone were fighting the Germans. Thereafter, a Lend-Lease agreement was signed (18 March 1942) by the government-in-exile to supply the Chetnik forces, but nothing was allocated for the communist-inspired Partisans led by Josip Broz who was known as Tito. By the autumn of 1942, western capitols were aware that a deep rift had developed between Mihailovic and Tito. Soon open civil war existed (Uzice - 1 November 1942) between the two resistance groups. Tito's major problem was supplying his forces. He drove his men intent upon proving to the Allies, especially the Soviet Union, that support of the Partisans was the key to success. He was in daily communication with Moscow pleading for supplies but to no avail. Thereafter, he turned to the west where he received promises but very little substantive assistance. Eventually, British agents reported that the Chetniks were dealing more in collaboration than in resistance. The truth of this assertion notwithstanding, Tito began to emerge as the central figure in the struggle against the Germans and Italians. Although both groups continued to receive aid throughout the war, recognition of Mihailovic was withdrawn in 1943. The United State's position was one of reluctant support for Tito but it did accede to British requests to do so. In September 1944 Tito met with Stalin to avert a Soviet takeover of Yugoslav operations. Stalin allowed Tito to retain command; and when Soviet forces entered Yugoslavia, Partisan forces joined them in liberating Belgrad (20 October 1944). Tito then set up a provisional government (March 1945).

No review of the literature that deals with this period in Yugoslav history would be complete without mention of Dame Rebecca West's BLACK LAMB AND GREY FALCON [563] which is a record of a journey through Yugoslavia in 1937. It is considered a brilliant example of journalistic exposition that reveals the ways that country embodied all the central conflicts that troubled Europe at the time. YUGOSLAVIA [212], by Muriel Heppell and Frank B. Singleton, outlines this period in an often ambivalent manner. The second half of the book was written by Singleton and at times seems to be an apologia for Tito's rise to power. This may be the result of a lack of clarity in the events of the more modern era. YUGOSLAVIA [268], edited by Robert Kerner, is somewhat better. THE BELOVED LAND [131], by Vladimir Dedijer, is an excellent account told by a man who was, until 1954, one of Tito's lieutenants. It is autobiographical and contains many worthwhile excerpts from his wartime diary. A SHORT HISTORY OF YUGOSLAVIA: FROM EARLY TIMES TO 1966 [108], by S. Clissold, is very useful and can be combined with Clissold's YUGOSLAVIA AND THE SOVIET UNION, 1939-1973 [107]. Dragisa N. Ristic's YUGOSLAVIA'S REVOLUTION OF 1941 [435] discusses the overthrow of the regency government. It is interesting in its detail of the military coup that placed King Peter II on the throne.

Histories devoted to the war years include YUGOSLAVIA IN THE SECOND WORLD WAR [29] which was authored by Borisan Atanackovic and others. This work is in English and was published in Belgrad in 1965. It is heavily weighted towards Tito's role in the war to the exclusion of other forces involved. Dusan Biber deals with the German threat in NACIZEN I NEMCI V JUGOSLAVIJI, 1933-1941 [613]. Pero Moraca looks at the war and the aftermath in THE WAR AND REVOLUTION OF THE PEOPLES OF YUGOSLAVIA, 1941-1945 [356]. THE SERBS CHOOSE WAR [350], by Ruth Mitchell, is the story of General Billy Mitchell's sister and her travels through Albania and Yugoslavia. It is self-serving, full of errors, and not worthy of the serious reader. Mitchell did manage to get herself arrested by the Gestapo and spent 13 months in a German prison, and in this sense the book might make interesting reading as an autobiographical novel. Vladko Macek's THE STRUGGLE FOR FREEDOM [325] touches upon the war in Croatia. Milovan Djilas' THE EVE OF WAR [137] is another history written by one of Tito's former lieutenants who broke with him over his policies. Djilas' MONTENEGRO [138] is also worthwhile. Alfredo Breccia's JUGOSLAVIA 1939-1941: DIPLOMAZIA DELLA NEUTRALITA [68] focuses on the years immediately preceding the outbreak of hostilities. Ljubomir Bosnjak's ZBORNIK DOKUMENTA O NARODNOOSLOBODILACKOM RATU NARODA JUGOSLAVIJE [61] contains documents and data on the war. Antun Miletic's ZBORNIK DOKUMENTA I PODATAKA O NARODNOOSLOBODILACKOM RATU NARODA JUGOSLAVIJE [346] is a three-volume collection of German documents outlining the 1943 campaign.

The sensitive issues involved in the Yugoslav resistance and the Mihailovic-Tito controversy are discussed in various aspects in a number of worthwhile studies. THE EMBATTLED MOUNTAIN [640], by F.W.D. Deakin, is the story of Deakin's mission to Yugoslavia in which he became convinced Mihailovic was a collaborator. Matteo Milazzo's THE CHETNIK MOVEMENT AND THE YUGOSLAV RESISTANCE [345], Jozo Tomasevich's THE CHETNIKS: WAR AND REVOLUTION IN YUGOSLAVIA, 1941-1945 [510]; Branko Latas and Milovan Dzelebdzic's CETNICKI POKRET DRAZ MIHAILOVICA 1941-1945 [301], and Walter Roberts' TITO, MIHAILOVIC AND THE ALLIES, 1941-1945 [439] are all good with the last being the best. The Mihailovic issue is summed up in PATRIOT OR TRAITOR: THE CASE OF GENERAL MIHAILOVICH. PROCEEDING AND REPORT OF THE COMMISSION OF INQUIRY OF THE COMMITTEE FOR A FAIR TRAIL OF DRAJA MIHAILOVICH [621]. In the introduction to this report, which was published by the Hoover Institute, David Martin substantially refutes most of the allegations placed against Mihailovich as nothing more than Tito's ensuring himself, in the best tradition of rising dictators everywhere, unopposed and unbridled leadership. Bogdan Krizman's ANTE PAVELIC I USTASE [292] deals with the resistance group called "Ustasi" headed by the Croatian nationalist leader Ante Pavelic (1889-1959). The book deals with the Ustasi military organization and its terrorist activities. Apparently more interested in Croatian independence than in an overall Yugoslav victory over the Nazis, Pavelic countenanced widespread collaboration with the Germans and Italians during the war. Fikreta Jelic-Butic's USTASE I NEZAVISNA DRZAVA HRVATSKA [247] is an analysis of the terrorist activities of the Ustase in support of the Axis cause.

Radoje Pajovic's KONTRA REVOLUCIJA U CRNOJ GORI. CETNICKI I FEDERALISTICKI POKRET 1941-1945 [386] describes the Chetnik movement as "reactionary" in this outline of its operations in Montenegro and states its members were drawn from adherents of the Triple Regency. SRBIJA U RATU I REVOLUCIJA, 1941-1945 [590] is a 1976 publication of the Yugoslav Institute of Military History and describes "the war of national liberation" and the ensuing revolution in terms of activities in the Serbian region. Petar Kacavenda's SKOJ I OMLADINA U NARODNOOSLOBODILACKOJ VOJSCI I PARTIZANSKIM ODREDIMA JUGOSLAVIJE 1941-1945 [259] is a historiographical description of the League of Communist Youth in the army and Partisan detachments. 1941-1942. U SVEDOCANSTVIMA UCESNIKA NARODOOSSLOBODILACKE BORBE [591] is a 25-volume collection of eyewitness accounts of the war. Djordje Dragic's SANITETSKA SLUZBA U PARTIZANSKIM USLOVIMA RATOVANJA [142] is an account of terrible health conditions that pervaded the course of the war for the Partisans. Tone Ferenc's NASCISTICKA POLITIKA DENACIONALIZACIJE U SLOVENIJI U GODINAMA OD 1941. DO 1945 [166] is a new interpretation of the Nazi occupation. Branko Petranovic's AVNOJ [398] is the story of the Antifascist Council for National Liberation which functioned throughout the war. Svetozar Vukmanovic-Tempo's REVOLUCIJA KOJA TECE: MEMOARI [554] is a two-volume memoire by a high-ranking Yugoslav official that begins in 1912 but deals chiefly with Tito's rise to power and the war. NARODNOOSLOBODILACKI POKRET NOP BEOGRADA 1941-1945 [594] is a 1974 official publication dealing with Partisan activities in and around Belgrad. Milan Basta's RAT JE ZAVRSEN 7 DANA KASNIJE [45] is an account of the cessation of hostilities in Yugoslavia seven days after the Nazi capitulation.

Friedrich Wiener's PARTISANENKAMPF AM BALKAM: DIE ROLLE DES PARTISANENKAMPFS IN D. JUGOSLAWISCHEN LANDESVERTEIDIGUNG [571] is a history of the Axis occupation and underground movement that fought against it. Another German work is Dirk-Gerd Erpenbeck's SERBIEN 1941. D. MILITARVERWALTUNG UND SERBISCHER WIDERSTAND [155] which discusses German difficulties in consolidating their power after the takeover of Serbia. Karl Hnilicka's DAS ENDE AUF DEM BALKAN 1944/45; DIE MILITARISCHE RAUMUNG JUGOSLAVIENS DURCH DIE DEUTSCHE WEHRMACHT [219] is an uneven, anti-Yugoslav, anti-communist account of the war. It cannot be safely used by any except the most skilled historian who may find some stray bits of useful information. It does contain a 20-page bibliography that is quite useful and interesting. Milivoj Sudjic's YUGOSLAVIA IN ARMS [491] was published in 1942 and discusses the rise of Yugoslav resistance in patriotic terms. Svetislav-Sveta Petrovic's FREE YUGOSLAVIA CALLING [399] is a collection of articles by a Yugoslav radio journalist that concern the German conquest up to 1941. Ruth Trouton's PEASANT RESISTANCE IN YUGOSLAVIA, 1900-1950 [515] takes a much broader view of the resistance movement. This book grossly exaggerates Tito's accomplishments. Another panegyric to Tito is found in TITOVE ISTORIJSKE ODLUKE [592] which was published in Belgrad in 1978 and purports to demonstrate Tito's overall influence on Yugoslav history. THE LIBERATION STRUGGLE OF THE YUGOSLAV PEOPLES [593] does much the same thing. Slobodan Nesovic's JUGOSLAVIJA-BULGARSKA, RATNO VREME, 1941-1945 [370] is a Yugoslav account of the Bulgaria occupation of Macedonia and the subsequent renewal of accords when Bulgaria switched sides in 1944.

THE YUGOSLAV STRUGGLE THROUGH AMERICAN EYES [332] was written by Ralph Martin in collaboration with Stojan Pribicevic. It is a first-person account of the war. Three books by Charles W. Thayer: GUERRILLA [503], BEARS IN THE CAVIAR [504], and HANDS ACROSS THE CAVIAR [505], were written by a former OSS officer serving with Tito's Partisans. All three are excellent, even if they cannot be properly categorized as history. James Inks' EIGHT BAILED OUT [237] is the story of an American bomber crew forced to bail out over Yugoslavia which managed to survive by living as Chetniks among the German occupation forces. DAS BULGARISCHE HEER IN JUGOSLAWIEN 1941-1945 [351], by Boro Mitrovski, Venceslav Glisic, and Tomo Ristovski, deals with the Bulgarian military occupation of Yugoslavia. One section of the book purports the inevitable spirit of brotherhood and cooperation that existed between the Yugoslav Partisans and the rank and file of the Bulgarian forces. Another combat history that is very interesting is Erich von Stering's JEDER WAS EIN STUCH VON UNS; LEBEN UND KAMPF EINER KOMPANIE AUF IHREM WEG VON ATTIKA NACH SARAJEWO, HERBST 1944 [485].

## BULGARIA'S ROLE IN THE WAR

Bulgaria signed a non-aggression pact with the Balkan Entente on 31 July 1938 and began to rearm in 1939 with money lent by England and France. There was an immediate demand for restitution of the old borders by certain factions within the government, but these were overtaken by the outbreak of World War II. The Filov government, which was installed in Feb 1940, along with King Boris, were pro-German. When Germany forced Romania to cede southern Dobrudja back to Bulgaria (7 September 1940), Bulgaria was obliged to reciprocate by joining the Anti-Comintern Pact (1 March 1941) and by permitting the stationing of German troops on Bulgarian soil. These troops were used in the invasions of Greece and Yugoslavia as discussed above. Bulgarian troops were eventually used to occupy the northeastern part of Greece (Thrace), Macedonia, and part of Serbia. When Germany attacked the Soviet Union, however, Bulgaria refused to join in, but did declare war on Great Britain and, later, the United States. When King Boris died under mysterious circumstances in 1943, a regency council was formed to rule until the six-year-old Simeon came of age.

From 1943 the Bozhilov government was a puppet of the Germans. Resistance, formed around a coalition of several groups including the Communists (Fatherland Front), was growing and eventually forced the Bozhilov government to resign (May 1944). By late August Bulgaria had cut its ties with the Germans. On 5 September 1944 a policy of strict neutrality was proclaimed. That same day the Soviet Union declared war on Bulgaria. By midnight Bulgaria had declared war on Germany and asked for a Soviet armistice; Soviet troops thereafter entered Bulgaria unopposed. A long-planned uprising began on 2 September, and a provisional government was soon formed from among the leadership of the Fatherland Front. On 28 October an armistice was signed with the Allies; the Bulgarian army was placed under Soviet control, and Bulgarian troops were used to help defeat the Wehrmacht in Yugoslavia, Austria, and Hungary.

As in all cases, historical literature on Bulgarian is scarce. Christ Anastasoff's THE BULGARIANS: FROM THEIR ARRIVAL IN THE BALKANS TO MODERN TIMES [18] is a good place to start. Jerzy Jackowicz's BULGARIA AND THE WESTERN POWERS, 1941-1944 [243] is a recent Sofia publication in English. Marshall Lee Miller's BULGARIA DURING THE SECOND WORLD WAR [347] is a little more substantial although it is primarily a politico-diplomatic history. Two German works published at the beginning of the war are G.P. Genoff's DAS SCHICKSAL BULGARIENS [184] and Rudolf Haider's DIE BULGARISCHE WIEDERGEBURT [210]. Both are propaganda. Bulgarian foreign policy is discussed in Dimiter Sirkov's LA POLITIQUE ETRANGERE BULGARE, 1938-1941. MONOGRAPHIE [470] which was published in Sofia in 1979. LES GRANDES PUISSANCES ET LES BALKANS A LA VEILLE ET AU DEBUT DE LA DEUXIEME GUERRE MONDIALE 1937-1941 [72] is an account of Great Power activities in the Balkans, but it focuses on Bulgaria.

One aspect of the resistance is discussed in LA BRIGADE DE PARTISANS "TSCHAVDAR". RESUME HISTORIQUE [76] which is, in effect, a unit history. Georgi Georgiev's PRINOSUT NA BULGARSKIIA NAROD V ANTIFASHISTKATA NARODOOSVOBODITELNA BORBA NA BALKANSKITE NARODI: 1941-1945 G. [186] deals with Bulgarian relations in the Balkans during the war. Mihajlo Apostolski's POGLEDI NA JUGOSLOVENSKO-BULGARSKE ODNOSE [24] is a study of Bulgaria's part in the liberation of Yugoslavia with all of the credit going to the Worker's Party. Another view of this is presented in the more encompassing MAZEDONIEN IN DER BULGARISCHEN GESCHICHTE [145], by Iwan Dujcev. This is also a Bulgarian publication. HISTOIRE MILITAIRE DE LA BULGARIE, 681-1945. BIBLIOGRAPHIE [75] is a two-volume collection of titles published to the end of 1972. LA GUERRE PATRIOTIQUE EN BULGARIE, 1944-1945. DOCUMENTS [77] is an impressive four-volume selection of carefully chosen documents. Volume I, for example, covers the period from 9 September to 7 October 1944, which includes the crucial days of the uprising. DOCUMENTS AND MATERIALS ON THE HISTORY OF THE BULGARIAN PEOPLE [73] contains numerous English translations of documents dealing with this period. LA LUTTE DU PEUPLE BULGARE POUR LA PROTECTION ET LA DELIVRANCE DES JUIFS EN BULGARIE PENDANT LA SECONDE GUERRE MONDIALE. DOCUMENTS [78] is an interesting collection of documentation on the attempts of Bulgarians to protect Jews from the terror of the Holocaust. Frederick B. Chary studied the same question in his dissertation, "Bulgaria and the Jews; 'The Final Solution' 1940 to 1944" [96] which was presented at the University of Pittsburgh in 1968. Micheal Padev's ESCAPE FROM THE BALKANS [384] is a personal narrative. Nicholas Balabanov's "A Year in Ankara: December 1st 1943 to January 9th 1945" [36] outlines the attempts made to conclude an armistice between Bulgaria and the Western Powers.

## ROMANIA AND THE SECOND WORLD WAR

Romania's fate was similar to that suffered by Bulgaria. Following the annexation of Austria and the Czech invasion, Romania rapidly began to understand its danger. The agreements it had with Italy quickly disappeared (1936) after Bucharest imposed sanctions on Rome for the Abyssinian affair. Yet, Romania was prepared to honor its commitments and had been prepared to intervene in Czechoslovakia. Activity went so far as a secret accord with the Soviet Union to allow passage of Red Army units through Romanian territory. When Poland offered Romania the Ruthenian section of Czechoslovakia, Bucharest refused. As events progressed, however, Germany began to move into the Danube; first, by admission to the European Danube Commission (1 March 1939) and second, under pressure from Berlin, Bucharest signed an economic agreement with the Third Reich which gave the Germans almost complete control over Romania's economic life.

On 14 March 1939, King Carol II (1930-1940) mobilized to prevent an attack from either Germany or Hungary. Germany invaded Czechoslovakia the next day. Along with other Balkan nations, Great Britain and France guaranteed Romania's independence on 13 April 1939. Then, on 6 September 1939, six days after Germany invaded Poland, Romania declared its neutrality. From September through November of that year, Romania attempted to form a neutral coalition around the Balkan Entente to no avail. On 26 June 1940, the Soviet Union, using the chaos in Europe and the protection of the Nazi-Soviet Pact, issued an ultimatum to Bucharest demanding and getting northern Bukovina and Bessarabia. Hitler then addressed a letter to King Carol (15 July 1940) demanding a settlement of Hungarian territorial claims and a cessation of what were termed "Hostile policies" toward Berlin. When arbitration failed, Hitler ordered Romanian and Hungarian representatives to Vienna out of which the "Vienna Diktat" was issued by which northern Transylvania was ceded to Hungary. Angry protests ensued in Romania that led to the collapse of the government (4 September) and the installation (5 September) of Ion Antonescu as virtual dictator. The next day the discredited Carol abdicated in favor of his 19-year-old son, Mihai. The following day, 7 September, Romania was forced to give up southern Dobrudja (the Quadrilateral) to Bulgaria. A "National Iron-Guardist State" was declared on 14 September signifying the place of the Iron Guard which had sprung up in the early-1930s as a quasi-Fascist organization in support of the crown against left-wing activities. Antonescu suspended the constitution and assumed full power. Romania was now a German vassal.

German troops began pouring into Romania on 10 October, ostensibly in response to a request from Antonescu. By the end of the year, more than 20,000 German troops were stationed there with their major headquarters in Bucharest. On 23 November 1940, Romania adhered to the Tripartite Pact and was then an Axis partner. On 28 November, a German-instigated Iron Guard massacre took place in which 64 prominent anti-Fascists were killed. The purpose of this incident was a Nazi attempt to play Antonescu off against the Iron Guard so as to break down the last mechanism of power in the country. A second Iron Guard uprising in January 1941 was put down with much bloodshed and the Iron Guard was removed from power. By February, 500,000 German troops were in Romania. That same month Great Britain broke diplomatic relations with Bucharest. When Hitler demanded Romanian troops to support his invasion of Yugoslavia, Antonescu refused. Yet, Antonescu found popular support when asked to join the invasion of the Soviet Union. This point is loudly disputed by present-day Romanian historians, but it is clearly true. Romanian willingness to fight the Russians was in part due to long-standing animosity and the fact the Germans promised restoration of the recently seized Bessarabia. Great Britain declared war on Romania on 7 December 1941; and six days later, Romania declared war on the United States. By 1942, large Romanian military formations were on the Eastern Front at Stalingrad as a part of the Wehrmacht.

Resistance to the Antonescu regime surfaced after the Romanian army crossed the Dniester into the USSR in 1942, but its strength did not develop until after the German disaster at Stalingrad. By the spring of 1944, a coalition of leftist organizations determined to get Romania out of the war. The coup d'etat that overthrew Antonescu (23 August 1944) was engineered by King Michael (1940-1947) himself, however, with a wide spectrum of support from both right and left. The ouster was accompanied by widespread fighting against the German forces in Romania. By the end of August, Soviet troops had occupied much of the country and remained there until after the war. An armistice with the Soviet Union was signed in Moscow on 12 September 1944. Romania had exchanged one master for another.

Romanian military units were absorbed in Soviet formations with most of them going to the Second Ukrainian Front in early September. A general offensive was then undertaken to clear Transylvania (9 September). The operation was completed on 25 October 1944. On 29 October the Romanians took part in Operation Budapest in which two Soviet fronts invaded Hungary. By December Romanian units were fighting in Czechoslovakia.

The presentation of Romania's part in the war is uneven. A considerable amount of material is available on the Soviet period, but not very much is available that deals with the Antonescu-German period. This is unfortunate, but it is a fact of life within the Soviet bloc that the history of non-communist times is often neglected. It is also the case that little data is available, even if the desire to utilize it were present. Stephen Fisher-Galati's TWENTIETH CENTURY RUMANIA [168] is a sound political history of the period. Andreas Hillgruber's HITLER, KONIG CAROL UND MARSCHALL ANTONESCU: DIE DEUTSCH-RUMANISCHEN BEZIEHUNGEN, 1938-1941 [612] deals with the early, critical period in relations between Berlin and Bucharest. Philippe Marguerat's LE IIIe REICH ET LE PETROLE ROUMAINE, 1938-1940: CONTRIBUTION A L'ETUDE DE LA PENETRATION ECONOMIQUE ALLEMANDE DANS LES BALKANS A LA VEILLE ET AU DEBUT DE LA SECONDE GUERRE MONDIALE [328] deals with the Nazi economic campaign which preceded the military one. ROMANIAN NATIONALISM: THE LEGIONARY MOVEMENT [11] was written by E. Alexander and M.D. Ronnett and was published by the Loyola University Press in 1974. It is blatantly anti-semitic and an attempt to purify the Iron Guard. It must, therefore, be used with the greatest caution. The only real value to be seen in this study is that it serves as an example of the American concept of freedom of the press.

Jurgen Forster has written "Rumaniens weg in die deutsche abhangigkeit" [174] which deals with the role of the German mission in Romania in 1940-1941. VERRATINE SCHLACHTEN; DIE TRAGODIE DER DEUTSCHEN WEHRMACHT IN RUMANIEN UND UNGARN [176] is a series of personal narratives prepared by Generaloberst a. D. Hans Friessner. RUMANIENS HEILIGER KRIEG, RUNDFUNKREDE, GEHALTEN AM TAGE VON RUMANIENS KRIEGSEINTRITT, 22 JUNE 1941 [22], by Mihail Antonescu, is an interest vignette of the war. It was published in Bucharest in 1941 and deals with radio broadcasts made on the day of Romania's entrance in the "Holy War" against the Soviet Union. Alexandre Cretzianu's "The Soviet Ultimatum to Romania (26 June 1944)" [121] deals with a little-known aspect of the Soviet takeover in the Balkans. His "Romanian Armistice Negotiations, Cairo 1944" [120] deals with an even less-understood aspect of Romania's attempt to leave the war. Cretzianu's THE LOST OPPORTUNITY [122] is an interesting and well-written personal narrative of the 1939-1945 period in Romania. Barry Brannen's "The Soviet Conquest of Rumania" [64] is the first-hand account of a member of the Allied Control Commission who arrived in Bucharest in October 1944. Silviu Cruciunas' THE LAST FOOTSTEPS [124] is a story of the Romanian underground.

The Romanians have turned out a considerable volume of material on the World War II period, but very little of it accurately covers the period when the nation was in the German thrall. The CHRONOLOGICAL HISTORY OF ROMANIA [622], which was a collaborative effort under the direction of Constantin Giurescu, has considerable information on the period but much of it has suffered from ideological editing. THE ARMY AND THE ROMANIAN SOCIETY [448], edited by Colonel Alexandre Savu, contains a number of articles on the period, none of which deal with the Romanian military during the German period. Eugen Bantea and Michael Ionescu's "Neutrality Policy in the First Stage of World War II: The Romanian Case" [41] is worth reading. PAGES FROM THE HISTORY OF THE ROMANIAN ARMY [447] contain 19 articles, four of which deal with the war period; none deal with the period between 1940 and the insurrection of August 1944.

THE ANTI-FASCIST RESISTANCE IN THE NORTH-EAST OF TRANSYLVANIA [595], was written by G. Zaharia and others. Another work on the subject is Nicolae Stan's REFLECTARI ISTORICO-LITERARE ALE REZISTENTEI ROMANESTI [479]. A significant part of the book deals with anti-German resistance. A third work is Antone Marinescu and Gheorghe Romanescu's ARMATA ROMANA IN RAZBOIUL ANTIHITLERIST [329] which contains 60 maps and sketches of the main operations of the Romanian forces involved in the drive into Czechoslovakia. PARTICIPAREA ROMANIEI LA RAZBOIUL ANTIHITLERIST OGLINDITA IN LITERATURA ISTORICA SI MEMORIALISTICA, IN LITERATURA BELETRISTICA, DRAMATURGIA SI CINEMATIGRAFIA ROMANEASCA. BIBLIOGRAFIE SELECTIVA [440] is a bibliography based on Romania's role against Germany as seen in several different media.

DOCUMENTE PRIVIND ISTORIA MILITARA A POPORULUI ROMAN [624] is a multivolumed collection of Romanian and foreign documents dealing with the insurrection and its aftermath. Volumes 1-4 contain more than 1,100 documents. There are presently six volumes in the set. LES COMBATS EN VUE DE LA LIBERATION DE LA ROUMANIE [23] is a Moscow-produced study that deals with the Soviet forces involved in "liberation" of Romania. Ion Babici's SOLIDARITATES ROMANEASCA CU LUPTA ANTIFASCISTA DIN BALCANI [32] takes a broader view of the same events. Constantin Nicolae and P. Ilie deal with the uprising in Bucharest in BUCURESTIUL IN INSURECTIE [372]. Gheorghe Zaharia's INSURECTIA POPORULUI ROMAN DIN AUGUST 1944 [596] deals with the coordination, secrecy, and precision required in preparing for the uprising. Ion Cuspa's CONTRIBUTA ROMANIEL LA RAZBOIUL ANTI-HITLERIST (23 AUGUST 1944-9 MAY 1945) [126] is a general review of Romania military developments during the period. This study was also produced in the Russian language. INSURECTIA DIN AUGUST 1944 SI SEMNIFICATIA SI ISTORICA [625] was produced in 1974 and is a series of 31 articles in Romanian with French and Russia summaries. Major General Eugen Bantea has also produced three studies of the uprising and Romania participation in the war against Germany; "National Antifascist and Anti-Imperialist Insurrection of August 1944 - Expression of the Romanian People's Will of Independence" [39], (with others) ROMANIA IN THE WAR AGAINST HITLER'S GERMANY [42], INSURECTIA ROMANA IN JURNALUL DE RAZBOI AL GRUPULUI DE ARMATA GERMAN "UCRAINA DE SUD" [40]. In the last study, Bantea analyzes the uprising based on German records.

Eugen Preda wrote a diplomatic history of Romania in the Second World War; called "SARITURA DE PISICA": [INSEMNARI DESPRE AL II-LEA RAZBOI MONDIAL], it was published in Bucharest in 1976. ENCICLOPEDIA ISTORIOGRAFIEI ROMANESTI [623] is a reference work containing biographical notes, works, and bibliographies covers Romanian history from early times to the present. It also contains documentary sources and lists of training and research facilities.

## HUNGARY'S ROLE IN THE WAR

The annexation of Austria put the Third Reich on the Hungarian frontier and added to the problems of the already shaky Hungarian government under the regime of Admiral Miklos(Nicholos) Horthy. The grumblings of the German population in Hungary helped point the nation into the Nazi camp, and Hungary gave open support when the Wehrmacht moved into Czechoslovakia. On 2 November 1938, Hitler gave a large chunk of southern Slovakia to Hungary and then, on 15 March 1939, Hungary annexed the Carpatho-Ukrainian region of Ruthenia which gave it a common border with Poland. Less than a month later (11 April 1939), Hungary withdrew from the League of Nations. Among the requirements imposed upon Hungary in return for

Hitler's favors was one allowing German troops passage through the nation for the attack on Yugoslavia. The continuing cooperation between the Hungarian General Staff and the German High Command eventually led to the suicide of the Hungarian Premier, Count Pal Teleki.

His replacement, Laszlo Bardossy, developed even stronger ties with the Reich which led to Hungarian participation in the invasion of the USSR in June 1941. By the end of the year, Hungary was at war with the United States and Great Britain. Bardossy apparently acted in each case without consultation. Horthy then relieved Bardossy and replaced him with Miklos Kallay who was anti-Nazi and, at the same time, anti-communist. Kallay's attempts to achieve a separate peace with the Allies probably helped save Hungary from the bombing that was ravaging the rest of Hitler's empire. Hitler, incensed with what appeared to be less than wholehearted Hungarian cooperation, called Horthy to Berlin where he ordered him to dismiss Kallay and put in his place the Nazi sympathizer Dome Sztojay. If Horthy refused, Hitler noted, Hungary would be occupied. Sztojay immediately imposed the "Final Solution," and over 600,000 Hungarian Jews were slaughtered. German troops occupied Hungary in early 1944. In October 1944 Horthy broke away from the Axis and arranged an armistice for which he was promptly arrested and put into a German prison. The advancing Soviet armies turned Hungary into a battleground as Nazi sympathizers, especially Ferenc Szalasi and his Arrow-Cross Party, in charge of the Hungarian government refused to surrender. On 24 December 1944 Soviet troops were in Budapest which had ben destroyed by departing Wehrmacht forces. Fighting did not stop in Hungary until April 1945, at which point Hungary was already a Soviet satellite.

There are three good general histories of Hungary: HUNGARY, A SHORT HISTORY [324], by C.A. Macartney; HISTORY OF HUNGARY [468], by Denis Sinor; and 1000 YEARS OF HUNGARY [307], by Emil Lengyel. Jeno Gyoerkei's MAGYAR ONKENTESEKA SPANYOL POLGARHABORUBAN [209] deals with Hungarian volunteers in the Spanish Civil War. Nicholas M. Nagy-Talavera's THE GREEN SHIRTS AND THE OTHERS: A HISTORY OF FASCISM IN HUNGARY AND RUMANIA [365] is a chronology of events. Jorg K. Hoensch's DER UNGARISCHE REVISIONISMUS UND DIE ZERSCHLAGUNG DER TSCHECHOSLOWAKEI [221] focuses on the part played by Hungary in the breakup of Czechoslovakia. John Pelenyi's "The Soviet Plan for a Hungarian Government in the West at the Outbreak of World War II" [394] deals with a little-known aspect of the war. DIPLOMACY IN A WHIRLWIND: HUNGARY BETWEEN NAZI GERMANY AND THE SOVIET UNION [269], by S.D. Kertesz, was published in 1956 and deals with the diplomatic pressures felt in Budapest during the war.

John F. Montgomery's HUNGARY: THE UNWILLING SATELLITE [353] is the eyewitness report of the United States Minister to Hungary between 1933 and 1941. Montgomery covers the period to the end of the war. Vasyl Markus' "The Carpato-Ukraine Under Hungarian Occupation, (1939-1944) [330] deals with the German-inspired move to place the Hungarians on the Polish border. Gyula Kallai's A MAGYAR FUGGETLENSEGI MOZGALOM, 1936-1945 [263] deals chiefly with the World War II period including the country's occupation by the Wehrmacht. It stresses the role of the Hungarian Communist Party in the resistance movement. Andras Kiz' AZ ANTIFASISZTA MAGYAR KATONSI HAGYOMAMANYOKROL 1945 [278] is a study of the anti-German military movement that is heavily laced with propaganda. Istvan Nemeskurty's REQUIEM EGY HADSEREGERT [368] is a memorial to the 2nd Hungarian Army that perished on the Don. It too is propaganda but worth reading. Jozsef Gazsi's FENYEK A BORSONYBEN. EGY ANTIFASISZTA ZASZLOALJ TORTENETE [183] deals with the history of the Gorgey Battalion that was formed as a part of a detachment to be used against the Soviets. Instead, the battalion operated as a sabotage unit against the Germans.

Mario D. Fenyo's HITLER, HORTHY AND HUNGARY: GERMAN-HUNGARIAN RELATIONS, 1941-1944 [165] deals with foreign relations more than with individuals. THE CONFIDENTIAL PAPERS OF ADMIRAL HORTHY [499], edited by Miklos Szinai and Laszlo Szucs, are a good reinforcement for MEMOIRS [227] by Horthy himself. Admiral Horthy's memoires have been published in several languages. The wartime career of Nicholas Kallay is discussed in his HUNGARIAN PREMIER: A PERSONAL ACCOUNT OF A NATION'S STRUGGLE IN THE SECOND WORLD WAR [264]. Peter Bokor's VEGJATEK A DUNA MENTEN. INTERJUK EGY FILMSOROZATHOZ [57] is a selection from interviews made for a series of Hungarian television presentations on the war. Laszlo Suranyi's A MAGYARORSZAGI TANACSKOZTARSASAG BELYEGKIADAAINAK ES A VOROS HADSEREG TABORI POSTAJANSK TORTENETE [496] deals with the issuance of Hungarian stamps and the Red Army postal service. Mihaly Korom's MAGYARORSZAG IDEIGLENES NEMZETI KORMANYA ES A FEGYVERSZUNET/1944-1945 [283] is a study of the Hungarian caretaker government and the armistice. HOSOK. A SZOVJETNIO HOSEI A MAGYARORSZAGI FELSZABADITO HARCOKBAN 1944-1945 [312], by Ervin Liptai and others, is a biographical study of the Soviet heroes of the Hungarian campaign. This work was published in Budapest in 1981.

## TURKEY IN THE SECOND WORLD WAR

The Kemal government was able to refortify the Straits after the Montreux Agreement was signed (20 July 1936) and joined the Saadabad Pact, an agreement similar to the Balkan Pact (1934). The new arrangement with Iran, Iraq, and Afghanistan was signed 9 July 1937. That same year Turkey nearly went to war with Syria and France over its claims to the port of Alexandretta (Iskenderun), but the issue was finally settled when France ceded the city to Turkey (23 June 1939). On 10 November 1938, Kemal died and the nation went into mourning. The new Turkish president, Ismet Inonu, was almost immediately beset by the problems of the Second World War in Europe. Great Britain did sign a mutual assistance pact with Turkey on 12 May 1939, but the signing of the Soviet-German Treaty in August shocked Turkey and required it to strengthen its own position. Subsequently, on 19 October 1939, an Anglo-French-Turkish mutual assistance pact was signed. Supplies began to flow into Turkey, but the treaty was never honored, and Turkey remained neutral throughout the war. This served Allied strategy and probably saved Turkey from disaster. When Germany attacked the Soviet Union in June 1941, Turkey was isolated from the West but this too worked in its favor because it prevented the execution of a German plan to drive into Palestine from the north and from out of Africa. Turkey had signed a non-aggression pact with Germany in 1941 but was able to maintain good relations with the Allies. In fact, Turkey supplied aid to both sides during the war, until March 1944, when strained relations with Great Britain created problems. Only after it became clear the United Nations would invite only belligerents to San Francisco did

Turkey declare war on Germany (1 March 1945).

Although no longer a part of the Balkans, it is worthwhile to include Turkey in an overall reading plan. A few of the better general histories on Turkey during this period include THE NEAR EAST IN MODERN TIMES: FORTY CRUCIAL YEARS, 1900-1940 [28], by George Arnakis and Wayne Vucinich; REFORM, REVOLUTION AND REPUBLIC: THE RISE OF MODERN TURKEY, 1808-1975 [460], by Stanford and E.K. Shaw; THE OTTOMAN BACKGROUND TO THE MODERN MIDDLE EAST [229], by Albert Hourani; THE EMERGENCE OF MODERN TURKEY [309], by Sir Bernard Lewis; and TURKEY, IRAN, AND THE MIDDLE EAST, 1919-1939 [54], by Robin Bidwell. The CAMBRIDGE HISTORY OF ISLAM [225], edited by P.M. Holt and others; the ENCYCLOPEDIA OF ISLAM [188], edited by Sir H.A.R. Gibb and others; and ISLAM ANSIKLOPEDISI [516] are the best general references available. Leon Dennen adds an interesting sidebar to the history of these times in his TROUBLE ZONE; BREWING POINT OF WORLD WAR III? [134] which is in part an eyewitness account of the author's sojourn in Turkey in 1944 where he worked with anti-Nazi refugees.

## THE SOVIET UNION AND THE END OF WORLD WAR II IN THE BALKANS

The part played by the Soviet Union in the winning of the war is a subject of considerable literary effort and a number of works dealing with it are mentioned elsewhere in this chapter. Among the extensive array of other studies that are important here are RUSSIA AND THE BALKANS IN RUSSIAN FOREIGN POLICY: ESSAYS IN HISTORICAL PERSPECTIVE [302], edited by Ivo Lederer. The SOVETSKAYA VOENNAYA ENTSIKLOPEDIYA [537] is an eight-volume source reference that is a requirement for the truly serious student. ISTORIYA VTOROI MIROVOI VOINII 1939-1945 GG. [534] is presently a nine-volume history of the Second World War which is told with some interesting interpretations of the facts. ISTORIYA OTECHESTVENNOI VOENNO-ENTSIKLOPEDICHESKOI LITERATURII [33], by A.I. Babin and others, is a resume of historical literature. Manfred Kehrig's STALINGRAD - ANALYSE UND DOKUMENTATION EINER SCHLACHT [267] has a considerable amount of material taken from both German and Soviet sources on the Germano-Romanian crisis that arose after the defeat at Stalingrad. THE SOVIET UNION, 1941-1949 is part of the OSS/STATE DEPARTMENT INTELLIGENCE AND RESEARCH REPORTS [523]. This segment constitutes eight reels of microfilm contains 170 separate reports that include: "Soviet Guerrilla Warfare," "Soviet Relations With Czechoslovakia," and "Capabilities and Intentions of the U.S.S.R. in the Postwar Period."

The RECORDS OF THE JOINT CHIEFS OF STAFF [525] is in two parts one of which deals with the Soviet Union. This collection is on two reels and deals with the period 1942-1945. CHETYRE GODA VOINY [599], by A.S. Zhadov, is the personal story of an army commander who participated in the drive on Prague. SOVETSKII SOYUZ I BOR'BA NARODOV TSENTRAL'NOI I YUGOVOSTOCHNOI EVROPY ZA CVOBODY I NEZAVISIMOST' 1941-1945 [535] describes the Soviet view of the commonalty of effort of the nations of Central and Southeastern Europe in the defeat of Nazi Germany. Yugoslavia, Romania, Greece, Albania, Hungary, and Bulgaria are all discussed. VELIKAYA POBEDA 1941-1945. RECOMENDATEL'NYI BIBLIOGRAFICHESKII UKAZATEL' [536] is a handy bibliography on Soviet sources about the war. RUSSIAN HISTORY ATLAS [190], by Martin Gilbert, is quite useful. Lew Shankowsky's

"Soviet and Satellite Sources on the Ukrainian Insurgent Army" [459] is a useful reference for sources on the Ukrainian guerrilla army that fought alongside the Germans until Hitler told them they would not be granted independence. At that point they turned on the Germans creating a multi-sided struggle for control of Volhynia (1942). Two very interesting stories are told by Harold Lehrman in RUSSIA'S EUROPE [304] and Il'ia Ehrenburg in EUROPEAN CROSSROAD; A SOVIET JOURNALIST IN THE BALKANS [150]. Both men were journalists, the first a pro-Soviet liberal and the second a well-known Soviet correspondent. The first account is one of disillusionment with the Soviet domination in the Balkans, the second is a paean to the great Soviet accomplishments in the region. The latter book needs to be read carefully, however, as the observant reader may note more than a little irony in the writing.

## THE ROLE OF THE BRITISH IN THE BALKANS

As the British played an important role in the development of events in the Balkans, a number of sources of information exist that may be of some value. THE RUSSIA CORRESPONDENCE OF THE BRITISH FOREIGN OFFICE, 1906-1948 [199] is one part of a larger collection under the same title that contains files on microfilm back to 1883. It is a very complete and well-organized collection. BRITISH FOREIGN POLICY IN THE INTER-WAR YEARS [431], by Philip Alan Reynolds, is only 182 pages and is an excellent refresher. BRITISH FOREIGN POLICY [298], by R. Victor Langford, is much more complete, but ends its coverage in 1939. BRITISH POLICY IN SOUTH-EAST EUROPE IN THE SECOND WORLD WAR [43], by Elizabeth Barker, is excellent but somewhat difficult to wade through if prior knowledge is lacking. BRITISH POLICY TOWARD WARTIME RESISTANCE IN YUGOSLAVIA AND GREECE [31], by Phyllis Auty and Richard Clogg, is an absolute requirement for the serious student. BRITAIN AND EUROPEAN RESISTANCE 1940-1945 [478], by David Stafford, is a survey of the Special Operations Executive (SOE) in its fostering of non-communist controlled resistance on the continent. It deals more directly with western Europe, but the lessons are fundamentally the same. The ultra-secret "Enigma" operations conducted by the British are discussed in "The British Knowledge of German Movements into the Balkans before the Operations 'Marita' and 'Barbarossa,' through the ULTRA Intelligence" [445] was the title of a paper presented by Alberto Santoni. Stephen Xydis' "The Secret Anglo-Soviet Agreement on the Balkans of October 8, 1944" [586] tells of another little-known facet of the war. Henry Martin's EAGLES VICTORIOUS: THE OPERATIONS OF THE SOUTH AFRICAN FORCES OVER THE MEDITERRANEAN AND EUROPE, IN EUROPE, IN ITALY, THE BALKANS AND THE AEGEAN, AND FROM GIBRALTAR AND WEST AFRICA [331] is the history of South African aerial operations some of which dealt with the Balkans.

There are in addition, a number of Italian works of interest here. Angelo Lodi's L'AERONAUTICA ITALIANA NELLA GUERRA DI LIBERAZIONE 1943-1945 [315] deals with operations in the Balkans, especially in Yugoslavia. Nino Arena's LA REGIA AERONAUTICA 1943-1946. -DALL'ARMISTIZIO ALLA COBELLIGERANZA [26] is the first of a two-volume set that deals in part with operations in the Balkans. L'ESERCITO ITALIANO NELLA 2. GUERRA MONDIALE. IMMAGINI [241] is an official pictorial that includes some otherwise unavailable photography on Italian operations in the Balkans

## RESISTANCE IN GENERAL

PARTISAN WARFARE IN THE BALKANS [626] was originally prepared by the Historical Division of European Command under the title "Partisan Warfare in the Mountains of Greece and Southern Albania 1943/44." It was subsequently published by GPO in 1950. Ronald Bailey's PARTISANS AND GUERRILLAS [35] was produced jointly with the editors of Time-Life Books and deals with underground movements in the Balkans. Stowers Johnson's AGENTS EXTRAORDINARY [254] does about the same thing but deals more directly with British operations in the region. Costa de Loverdo's LES MAQUIS ROUGE DES BALKAN, 1941-1945 [319] studies communist-inspired resistance movements in Greece, Yugoslavia, and Albania. Ernstgert Kalbe's ANTIFASCHISTISCHER WIDERSTAND UND VOLKSDEMOKRATISCHE REVOLUTION IN SUDOSTEUROPA: DAS HINUBERWACHSEN D. WIDERSTANDKAMPFS GEGEN D. FASCHISMUS IN D. VOLKSREVOLUTION (1941-1944/45) [261] deals with anti-Fascist resistance in the Balkans, how it developed, and how it theoretically became the basis for popular revolution. Ferdinand Miksche's SECRET FORCES: THE TECHNIQUE OF UNDERGROUND MOVEMENTS [344] is another account of the development of resistance movements. REZISTENTA EUROPEANA, 1938-1945 [118] was produced by N. Copoiu and a group of colleagues from the Romanian Institute of Historical and Socio-Political Studies. A periodical on the subject is RESISTANCE EUROPIENE [430] which is published periodically in Turin. Reuben Ainsztein produced a voluminous volume entitled JEWISH RESISTANCE IN NAZI-OCCUPIED EASTERN EUROPE [6]. In this study the author presents evidence that the Jews did fight and were not all led passively to their deaths. Vera Laska has edited WOMEN IN THE RESISTANCE AND IN THE HOLOCAUST: THE VOICES OF EYEWITNESSES [300] in which resistance in the Balkans, especially Yugoslavia is covered in some detail. Another, similar study, FEMALE SOLDIERS - COMBATANTS OR NON-COMBATANTS? HISTORICAL AND CONTEMPORARY PERSPECTIVES [193], edited by Nancy Goldman, contains information on women in Yugoslavian, Greek and Soviet wartime operations.

## THE COLD WAR BEGINS

The end of the war was, in some respects, as traumatic for the people of the Balkans as was the war itself. For some, the end of the war did not mean an end to the fighting; for others it meant exchanging a Nazi master for a Soviet one. The result was the same in either case, a continuation of the centuries-old struggle for independence and freedom of choice and expression.

The Paris Peace Treaty (10 February 1947) that the Allies concluded with Romania, Bulgaria, and Italy did three things. It declared Trieste a Free Territory, a status that would remain until 1954, when the territory was divided between Italy and Yugoslavia. Second, it ceded the major part of the region known as Venezia Giulia (in the northeast corner of old Italy), plus the Adriatic islands, including Zadar, to Yugoslavia. Lastly, it confirmed the 1940 transfer of southern Dobrudja from Romania to Bulgaria. For Bulgaria, Romania, Albania, Yugoslavia, Hungary, and Czechoslovakia the future was dictated by the Soviet Union. Austria was initially divided into four zones for occupation purposes; not until 1955 were the Allies, including the Soviet Union, able to reach agreement and restore Austria to its pre-war boundaries under the proviso that it thereafter remain completely neutral. Greece was not as fortunate and the end of the war found the nation caught up in a civil war.

Probably the best place to start any survey of this period in the Balkans is with the series of books published by the US Government under the general title of AREA HANDBOOKS [627]. There is one for each of the principal countries normally accepted as being in the Balkans, plus one for Czechoslovakia (DA Pamphlet 550-158), that became swept up in the same kinds of problems as those seen in the Balkans. Each of these handbooks contains a good historical summary of the events as they transpired in the postwar years and much other useful information as well. Klaus Knorr's THE WAR POTENTIAL OF NATIONS [279] is also valuable as a general primer on military power. Lynn Davis' THE COLD WAR BEGINS: SOVIET-AMERICAN CONFLICT OVER EASTERN EUROPE [128] is a 1978 Princeton publication that ties the present situation in Eastern Europe to events that preceded World War II. John A Lukacs' THE GREAT POWERS AND EASTERN EUROPE [321] contains much information on this period especially in the part entitled "The Russian Era Begins." Zbigniew Brzezinski's THE SOVIET BLOC: UNITY AND CONFLICT [628] is good for the period up to 1959. THE NEW EASTERN EUROPE: THE KHRUSHCHEV ERA AND AFTER [629] deals with the time from the death of Stalin in 1953 until 1966. The 1973 Supplement to the STRATEGIC STUDIES READING GUIDE [358], edited by Lt. Col. Motiuk, contains dozens of titles of both individual national and regional interest at this point. This bibliography is an official publication of the Canadian armed forces. There are also many titles useful here in the American Committee of the History of the Second World War's NEWSLETTER No. 25 [14]. The second part of the RECORDS OF THE JOINT CHIEFS OF STAFF [525] is a nine-reel microfilm collection dealing with "Europe and NATO." Although these records are more western Europe-oriented, there are some valuable insights into Allied policy toward the central and southeastern regions. The GUIDE TO FOREIGN MILITARY STUDIES, 1945-54: CATALOG AND INDEX [533] is also quite useful at this point.

Bogdan Szajkowski's THE ESTABLISHMENT OF MARXIST REGIMES [498] is an interesting study presenting one approach to communist takeovers. This work is valuable in that it contains a rather thorough summation of the other writing on the subject. THE TRAGEDY OF CENTRAL EUROPE [59], by Stephan Borsody, deals in part with the Soviet takeover in the Balkans. The same is true of Arnold and Veronica Toynbee's THE REALIGNMENT OF EUROPE [513]. Another interesting account may be found in THE OTHER EUROPEANS [604] which was written by A. Zischka and published in 1962. An operations research approach to this problem is stated in Richard Beal's SYSTEMS ANALYSIS OF INTERNATIONAL CRISES, 1948-1962 [46]. Redvers Opie and his colleagues at the Brookings Institute have produced THE SEARCH FOR PEACE SETTLEMENTS [378] as a reference survey of treaties with several of the Balkan states and the negotiations leading up to their signing. William King and Frank O'Brien's THE BALKANS, FRONTIER OF TWO WORLDS [273] reports on postwar developments in the Balkans as viewed by two American journalists. The title of Joseph Roucek's BALKAN POLITICS: INTERNATIONAL RELATIONS IN NO MAN'S LAND [441] tells the story and needs no further elaboration. This book was originally published in 1948. COMMUNIST POWER IN EUROPE, 1944-1949 [338], edited by Martin McCauley, is a collection of lectures presented at the University of London.

Henry Roberts' THE SATELLITES IN EASTERN EUROPE [436] is a publication of the American Academy of Political and Social Science. Paul Lendvai's EAGLES IN THE COBWEBS; NATIONALISM AND COMMUNISM IN THE BALKANS [306] deals with developments in several of the Balkan states. It covers Yugoslavia, Romania, Bulgaria, and Albania. Robert King's MINORITIES UNDER COMMUNISM: NATIONALITIES AS A SOURCE OF TENSION AMONG BALKAN COMMUNIST STATES [272] is another interesting study that also has an extensive bibliography. Bela Vago's "Popular Fronts: Popular Fronts in the Balkans" [540] deals with the techniques of conquest used by the Soviets to seize power in the Balkans after World War II. Louis Adamic's LIBERATION [2] was published in 1945 by the United Committee of South Slavic Americans. Robert Drechsler's KREUZWEG DER DEUTSCHEN IM SUDOSTEN 1944-1950: "DEN DEUTSCHEN DER TOD": DAS "ANDERE" HOLOCAUST: DOKUMENTATION [144] is about German influence in the Balkans during this period.

## THE GREEK CIVIL WAR

Even before the general armistice ending the Second World War, Greek communist forces attempted the overthrow of the just reestablished government. The uprising took place between 3 December 1944 and 11 January 1945 and was suppressed by British occupation forces. On 1 September 1945, the monarchy was restored and King George II (1945-1947) put on the throne. Then, in May 1946, a major outbreak of fighting began that would last until October 1949 in which communist guerrilla forces supported from Yugoslavia, Albania, and Bulgaria attempted to seize power. The British, who supported the Royal government, soon found themselves in dire economic straits and were forced to suspend further aid. At that point, the United States moved to fill the void with President Truman announcing his determination to support both Turkey and Greece in their struggle against the communists (Truman Doctrine - 12 March 1947). In the meantime, in December 1946, the United Nations Security Council had established a special commission to investigate the alleged border violations. The commission reported their findings on 23 May 1947, presenting proof that the Yugoslavs, Albanians, and Bulgarians had violated the UN Charter.

With American materiel and advisors, the Greek army was rebuilt and was able to restore order in all of Greece except along the northern borders. In 1948 a series of Greek offensives were begun that eventually drove most of the communist forces out of the country. Incidents continued, however, with artillery fire being directed against Greek army positions out of Bulgaria. After a series of condemnations by the United Nations and a climactic battle at Mount Grammos (28 August 1949), the Greek Civil War ended (16 October 1949). Two years later, on 20 September 1951, Greece joined NATO and, on 9 August 1954, signed a long-term military treaty with Yugoslavia and Turkey. Relations with Turkey rapidly deteriorated, however, over the Cyprus situation.

## THE TURKISH INVASION OF CYPRUS

There had been a long dispute between the Greek majority and the Turkish minority of this British colony over the island's future. This dispute erupted into guerrilla warfare in 1952 when Greek Cypriot sentiments toward union with Greece turned to acts of

terrorism against the Turkish Cypriot population. The union movement
was lead by Mihail Khristodolous Mouskos, the island's Greek
Orthodox Archbishop who was Makarios III. The Greek guerrilla forces
were commanded by Colonel Georgios Grivas, a legendary wartime hero.
The fighting lasted for seven years until a cease-fire was arranged
(13 March 1959) among the British and the Greek and Turkish
Cypriots. Both Greece and Turkey accepted the terms of this accord.

Thereafter, an independent Cypriot state was established
with Makarios as its president (14 December 1959). The situation did
not improve, however, as those favoring union with Greece continued
their agitation. By 1963 fighting had again broken out as the
Makarios government appeared bent on depriving the Turkish Cypriots
of their equal rights. The following year, a United Nations
peacekeeping force was introduced (27 March 1964) following a UN
Security Council resolution. By August Turkish warplanes were
attacking Greek Cypriot positions in retaliation for attacks on
Turkish Cypriot villages. As war loomed, the UN was able to obtain a
new ceasefire.

When the Makarios government failed to lift the restrictions
placed on the Turkish Cypriots, tensions once again mounted (1966).
The UN Secretary General, U Thant, was able to head off a Turkish
threat of intervention by forcing Makarios to lift the restrictions.
More trouble erupted in 1967 and war was averted only by US
mediation. Then, on 15 July 1974, a Greek-instigated coup d'etat
took place. Makarios was forced to flee the country. Five days
later, Turkish forces occupied the northern coast of the island. War
was again averted only by the Greek military leadership's
acknowledgement of its own weakness against the Turks and because of
a lack of popular support in Athens.

## THE GREEK MILITARY DICTATORSHIP

The tensions that developed between Greece and Turkey led to
other serious complications at home; and in 1967, a right-wing
military junta carried out a coup d'etat (21 April) to prevent the
election of the leftist candidate, George Popandreou. A second coup
attempt by King Constantine failed (13 December 1967), and the junta
made their leader, Colonel Georgios Papadopolous, prime minister.
Two resistance organizations began to attack the government. In 1969
Greece withdrew from the Council of Europe. Following the coup, the
US had stopped military aid to Greece, but this was restored in
1970. On 1 June 1973, Papadopolous declared himself president of the
new Republic of Greece only to be deposed by the junta on 23
November. A military officer, General Phaidon Gizikis became
president and remained in office until 23 July 1974 when the junta
relinquished control to the government of Konstantinos Karamanlis.
The constitution was restored and martial law lifted (9 October),
but the restoration of the monarchy was rejected (8 December 1974).
Greece partially withdrew from NATO after the Turkish invasion of
Cyprus. In 1975 another right-wing coup was attempted but failed
with the resultant repression of opposition.

Greece then began fortifying and reinforcing its islands
along the Turkish Anatolian coast. In addition, a new army corps was
organized in Thrace. Greece then went about attempting to form a new
Balkan coalition with some political and economic success. Tensions

remained high (1976) at home during this period with a number of dead due to the rioting. A lessening of international tensions came about when Greek and Turk representatives began a series of discussions to find amicable ways of settling their disputes (1977). Then, in 1978, the Soviets made arrangements to have their naval vessels repaired in Greek shipyards. The resulting uproar led to a worsening of relations with the United States and NATO. In the latter case, Turkey also pledged to block any attempts to reintegrate Greece to full NATO status. When these obstacles were overcome (20 October 1980) and Greece was readmitted to NATO, major demonstrations broke out but order was soon restored.

The military history of Greece during this period is found in a number of useful sources. THE STRUGGLE FOR GREECE, 1941-1949 [580], by C.M. Woodhouse, breaks the period into three phases; guerrilla movements against the Germans, 1941-1943; British intervention, 1944-1945; and the US-backed government victory in the Greek Civil War, 1946-1949. Another, more detailed source on US involvement may be found in John Iatrides' "From Liberation to Civil War. The United States and Greece, 1944-46" [234]. Iatrides also wrote REVOLT IN ATHENS: THE GREEK COMMUNIST "SECOND ROUND," 1944-1945 [235] which deals with the attempt of the Greek Communist Party to seize power in December 1944. Floyd Spencer's WAR AND POST-WAR GREECE [477] and George Grivas-Dighenis' GUERRILLA WARFARE AND EOKA'S STRUGGLE: A POLITICO-MILITARY HISTORY [204] are both interesting. Stephen Xydis' GREECE AND THE GREAT POWERS, 1944-1947: PRELUDE TO THE "TRUMAN DOCTRINE" [587] is probably the best single volume on the Greek crisis. Edgar O'Ballance's THE GREEK CIVIL WAR, 1944-1949 [374], C.M. Woodhouse's APPLE OF DISCORD [582] and D.G. Kousoulas' REVOLUTION AND DEFEAT: THE STORY OF THE GREEK COMMUNIST PARTY [287], when taken together, form a thorough exposition of the political and military factors involved in this extremely complicated period in Greek history. Harry Howard's "Greece and Its Balkan Neighbors: 1948-1949, The United Nations' Attempts at Reconciliation" [231] which was published in BALKAN STUDIES is also quite useful. OSDIRR [523] has an interesting study on "The Role of the Army in Greek Politics (1946)."

THE GREEK UPHEAVAL: KINGS, DEMOGOGUES, BAYONETS [506], by Taki Theodoracopolous, deals with the period after 1967. GREECE UNDER MILITARY RULE [112], edited by Richard Clogg and George Yannopoulos, has a number of excellent articles on this period. "The Military Coup d'Etat in Twentieth Century Greece" [390] was the title of a paper given by S. Victor Papacosma at the AHA conference in New Orleans in 1972. George Yannopoulos' "The Tradition of Dictatorship" [589] was published in 1975. Andreas Papandreou's DEMOCRACY AT GUNPOINT: THE GREEK FRONT [392] is worthwhile reading, as is "The Role of the Military in Greek Politics" [286], by G.A. Kourvetaris, and "Greece and the Crisis in the Mediterranean" [546], by P.J. Vatikiotis. Stephen Xydis' "Coups and Countercoups in Greece, 1967-1973" [588] is excellent. KARAMANLIS: THE RESTORER OF GREEK DEMOCRACY [581], by C.M. Woodhouse, is one of the few in-depth studies of this Greek leader to be found in English. Francis Lincoln's UNITED STATES AID TO GREECE: 1947-1962 [311] and BRITISH POLICY TOWARDS THE CHANGE OF DYNASTY IN GREECE [411], by E. Prevelakis, are each interesting in their individual coverages of events.

CYPRUS: CONFLICT AND RECONCILIATION, 1954-1958 [636], by Stephen Xydis, deals with the early phases of the Cyprus problem. THE STRUGGLE FOR CYPRUS [171] by C. Foley and W.J. Scobie; CYPRUS AND MAKARIOS [634], by Stanley Mayes; CYPRUS: A PLACE OF ARMS [635], by Robert Stephens; and Lawrence Stern's article, "Bitter Lessons: How We Failed in Cyprus" [487] are probably sufficient direct sources for the latter phases of the crisis.

## TURKEY

The end of the Second World War witnessed a renewal of the "Eastern Question" as the Soviet Union used both military and political pressure to gain concessions in the Turkish Caucasus and the Straits. In August 1946, for instance, Moscow demanded joint basing rights in the Dardanelles. These demands were rejected by Turkey on 18 October 1946. The following year, massive US aid (Truman Doctrine) began to flow into Turkey as a means of reinforcing its resolve against the Soviet Union. During the Korean War (1950-1953), The Turks sent a brigade-size unit to fight as a part of the United Nations Command. Turkey joined NATO in 1951. In the period of the Cyprus problem, serious anti-Greek rioting broke out in several large cities in Turkey, especially in September 1955 when major problems developed in Istanbul and Izmir.

Turkey also felt pressure from the south during this period and several major border clashes with Syria occurred in late-1957. In 1960 widespread rioting began again in a number of major cities when students opposed the dictatorial methods used by the Menderes government. Rioting increased and, in Ankara, the cadets at the military academy mutinied and joined the protest (21 May 1960). The army was then brought in to put down the trouble but, instead, took over the government (26-27 May 1960) arresting the president and most of the other Democratic Party functionaries in the process. In the political struggle that followed, a Republican People's Party slate and a new constitution won by only slim majorities (October 1961). Attempted coups occurred in 1962 and 1963, but both were put down with a minimum of violence. In 1963 Turkey signed a nuclear weapons agreement with the United States in which the last of a group of obsolescent Jupiter missiles on Turkish soil were removed.

Internal tensions began to develop and martial law was imposed in some areas in June 1970, but trouble continued. On 12 March 1971, the army demanded and got sweeping changes in the government. Even so, the rioting continued and martial law was extended to most of Turkey in April 1971. The strife continued and political assassination became a way of life in Turkey. In 1978, Turkey took part in NATO exercises which also included Greek forces for the first time since the Cyprus Crisis.

Much of Turkey's military role in Balkan developments has been discussed above in connection with affairs on the island of Cyprus. Some additional information dealing with earlier times in Turkey can be found in DIE TURKEI IN DEN JAHREN 1942-1951 [631] which was done by G. Jaschke. Shaw [460] is also useful. Walter Weiker's THE TURKISH REVOLUTION, 1960-61: ASPECTS OF MILITARY POLITICS [562] deals with the military coup.

ALBANIA

The tiny nation of Albania found itself embroiled in a confrontation with the British and Greeks over passage rights in the Corfu Channel in 1946. The affair continued until 1949, but was resolved only in the courts. Following the death of Stalin (1953) and his subsequent denunciation by Khrushchev (1956), Albania broke diplomatic relations with the Soviet Union and allied itself with the People's Republic of China.

Albanian military history during this period may be found in "Focus on Albania" [290] by Rexhep Krasniqi and in a 1969 State Department publication entitled "People's Republic of Albania." One of the better accounts of this period may be found in Anton Logoreci's THE ALBANIANS: EUROPE'S FORGOTTEN SURVIVORS [317]. Nicholas Pano's THE PEOPLE'S REPUBLIC OF ALBANIA [389]; THE ALBANIAN STRUGGLE IN THE OLD WORLD AND THE NEW [163], which was a part of the 1975 Federal Writer's Project; Abdal Sula's ALBANIA'S STRUGGLE FOR INDEPENDENCE [494]; and the British Naval Intelligence Division's ALBANIA [198] are all useful. Lastly, Joseph S. Roucek's "Rumania, Albania, and Bulgaria. At the End of the Beginning" [442] is a 1944 article of some interest as background reading. The OSDIRR [523] has, in its "Postwar Europe (1945-1949)" section, a number of useful references, at least one of which deals with Albania.

Anton Logoreci discusses "Albania and China: The Incongruous Alliance" [318] in a 1967 article in CURRENT HISTORY. Jan Myrdal and Gun Kessle's ALBANIA DEFIANT [363] was originally published in Swedish. David Egli's "Albania: Mediterranean Maoists" [149] is a 1967 firsthand report of conditions in Albania by a NEWSWEEK reporter who was one of the very few westerners allowed into the country. In 1968 Lieutenant Commander Leslie Gardiner described the military structure of the country in "Albania: The People's Army" [181]. Gardiner also wrote "Albania: The Last Lonely Stronghold" [180]. Horst Topp's DIE ALBANISCHE MILITARFUHRUNG UND DIE BEZIEHUNGEN ZWISCHEN DER VR ALBANIEN, DER VR CHINA UND DEN USA [511] is a 44-page pamphlet that is well worth the reading.

YUGOSLAVIA AND TITO

Robert Kerner's YUGOSLAVIA [268] is a good place to begin reading on that nation during this period. YUGOSLAVIA, ROMANIA, BULGARIA; NEW ERA IN THE BALKANS [396], by Lila Perl, was written as a primer for younger audiences but has some value as a quick review. THE COMMUNIST REGIMES OF EASTERN EUROPE [481], by R.F. Starr, is useful. TITO AND GOLIATH [27], by H. Armstrong, BALKAN CAESAR; TITO VERSUS STALIN [567], and Phyllis Auty's TITO [30] provide more than sufficient coverage of the Yugoslav leader. George Radin's ECONOMIC RECONSTRUCTION IN YUGOSLAVIA; A PRACTICAL PLAN FOR THE BALKANS [419] is a Carnegie Endowment for International Peace publication. It is not indexed. Louis Adamic's THE EAGLE AND THE ROOTS [3] is the record of the author's 1949 visit to Yugoslavia. The author died before the manuscript was completed, so it is difficult to tell whether the excessive errors in fact and orientation are his or belong to those who finished the book for him. A part of the book is a panegyric to Tito. Another attempt at secular beatification may be found in TITO-STRATEGIST OF THE REVOLUTION AND FOUNDER OF THE PEOPLE'S ARMY [196]. Milla Z. Logan's COUSINS AND COMMISSARS (AN

INTIMATE VISIT TO TITO'S YUGOSLAVIA) [316] is an entirely different type of report on travel in Yugoslavia in the late 1940's. It is a humorous account that gives a good understanding of life in the Yugoslav countryside. Stephen Clissold's WHIRLWIND: AN ACCOUNT OF MARSHAL TITO'S RISE TO POWER [105] ends its account with the beginning of this era.

Vladimir Dedijer's "Sarajevo Fifty Years After" [129] is a FOREIGN AFFAIRS article that must be read. OPERATION SLAUGHTERHOUSE: EYEWITNESS ACCOUNTS OF POSTWAR MASSACRES IN YUGOSLAVIA [406] was edited by John Prcela and Stanko Guldescu. It is a emotion-filled account of massacres, real and imagined, carried out against those Tito saw as his enemies (principally in this case, Croatians who fought with the Ustasi and Domobran forces). Vladko Macek's THE STRUGGLE FOR FREEDOM [325] is also useful at this point as it deals with the Croatian situation after the war in its last chapters. Djoko Slijepcevic's THE MACEDONIAN QUESTION: THE STRUGGLE FOR SOUTHERN SERBIA [471] is a study of the events that evolved from this problem in the 1920-1957 period. Slobodan Nesovic's DIPLOMATSKA IGRA OKO JUGOSLAVIJE 1944-1945 [369] is an analysis of the positions taken by the Great Powers on the fate of postwar Yugoslavia. THE CRIME OF GENOCIDE (A PLEA FOR THE RATIFICATION OF THE GENOCIDE PACT) [457] is self-serving but well-worth reading in the context of the almost constant struggle that has gone on over the fate of southern Serbia. Vladimir Dedijer's DOKUMENTI 1948 [130] contains historical documents on the Yugoslav Revolution that followed the end of World War II.

YUGOSLAVIA AND STALIN'S SUCCESSORS, 1968-69 [637], by Dennison I. Rusinow, deals with Yugoslav reaction to the Czech invasion. THE ROLE OF THE MILITARY IN COMMUNIST YUGOSLAVIA: AN HISTORICAL SKETCH [250] was written by A. Ross Johnson for the Rand Corporation. He also did TOTAL NATIONAL DEFENSE IN YUGOSLAVIA [251], YUGOSLAVIA IN THE TWILIGHT OF TITO [253], and THE FUTURE OF YUGOSLAVIA [249]. Sir Duncan Wilson's TITO'S YUGOSLAVIA [574] is an account of Yugoslav development since 1948. Alex N. Dragnich's TITO'S PROMISED LAND: YUGOSLAVIA [143] is one of the best works on the subject in English. Constantin Fotitch's THE WAR WE LOST: YUGOSLAVIA'S TRAGEDY AND THE FAILING OF THE WEST [175] is an account written by the exiled ex-ambassador to the United States. It deals primarily with the wartime period but has some excellent insights into the future as it was viewed from the perspective of how the Allies let transpire those events that placed Yugoslavia in the communist thrall.

Stephen Clissold has also written CROAT SEPARATISM [106] which deals with the vexing problem of nationalism within a multi-nation state. THE SOVIET-YUGOSLAV DISPUTE: TEXT OF THE PUBLISHED CORRESPONDENCE [475] deals with the on-going struggle between national communist movements and the Soviet brand of microcosmic communism. Evangelos Kofos' work is aptly titled NATIONALISM AND COMMUNISM IN MACEDONIA [280]. Risto Vukcevic studies economic conditions in Montenegro in his RAZVOI PRIVREDE CNRE GORE [552]. John Iatrides' BALKAN TRIANGLE: BIRTH AND DECLINE OF AN ALLIANCE ACROSS IDEOLOGICAL BOUNDARIES [233] is a description of relations among Yugoslavia, Greece, Turkey, and Albania which led to the Treaties of Ankara (1953) and Bled (1954) which allied these nations and which failed after about one year. This excellent study outlines the effects of a "marriage of convenience" that became inoperative because of the differing national political objectives of each of the signators.

## ROMANIA

COMMUNISM IN RUMANIA, 1944-1962 [239], by Ghita Ionescu, is a thoroughly researched history of the establishment and operation of a communist-inspired government in a Balkan country. CAPTIVE RUMANIA [123], which was the work of Alexandre Cretzianu and others, is a more passionate account of how Romania succumbed to communism. Mercia Carp's "The Armed Forces of Captive Romania" [88] is one of the contributions in the Cretzianu study. Another view of this same subject is presented in Colonel Constantin Toderascu's "The Romanian Army's Participation in the Reconstruction of the National Economy in the 1944-1947 Period" [508]. Constantin Oprita's "Development of the Education System of the Romanian Army Over the Post-War Years" [379] is also interesting. George Cioranescu's "Rumania After Czechoslovakia: Ceaucescu Walks the Tightrope" [98] demonstrates how small states can defy large ones but only at great risk. Aurel Braun's ROMANIAN FOREIGN POLICY SINCE 1965: THE POLITICAL AND MILITARY LIMITS OF AUTONOMY [65] is an excellent discussion of the glass house in which Romania dwells and the types of problems that could shatter its fragile relationship with the Soviet Union.

STUDII DE ISTORIE SI TEORIE MILITARA. RETROSPECTIVE ISTORICE ANALIZE CONTEMPORANE [638] is a collection of studies on military thought and practice with particular attention paid to the political and ideological indoctrination of the soldier. LA DEFENSE NATIONALE DANS LA CONCEPTION ROUMAINE [639] deals with the Romanian concept of universal military training. It emphasizes the external nature of the threat posed to the nation. NATIONAL DEFENSE, THE ROMANIAN VIEW [94] was edited by I. Cernat and E. Stanislav and outlines the main characteristics of Romanian military doctrine. Colonel Traian Grozea wrote "The National Defence of Socialist Romania" [205] and edited ARMATA REPUBLICII SOCIALISTE ROMANIA. SINTEZA SOCIAL-POLITICA SI MILITARA [206]. The latter work is a collection of articles that deal with the organization and training of the army to defend the homeland. Grozea is one of Romania's leading theoreticians.

Constantin Olteanu's THE ROMANIAN ARMED POWER CONCEPT [377] is another example of this same genre. Information on the military and higher academic accomplishment may be found in Demitru Matei's "Officers and Generals in the Membership of the Romanian Academy" [335]. Colonel General Ion Coman, the former Minister of Defense and present Party Secretary, wrote "Landmarks of the Evolution of the Army of the Socialist Republic of Romania" [115]. Coman's deputy at the time, Lieutenant General Gheorghe Gomiou, presented a paper at the CIHM Bucharest Conference, 1980 entitled DES MILITAIRES PARTICIPANTS A LA VIE CULTURELLE ET SCIENTIFIQUE DE LA ROUMAINE [194]. Emil Burbulea's APARAREA NATIONALA SI CALITATILE LUPTATORILOR [80] deals with the complex problems of national defense and soldierly qualities and human qualities and leadership. LA DEFENSE NATIONALE DANS LA PENSEE ROUMAINE [185], edited by Maria Georgescu and others, is full of additional references. The present Romanian Minister of Defense, Ilie Ceaucescu, has written a study on guerrilla warfare entitled HARTUIREA IN ACTIUNILE DE LUPTA DUSE IN

RAZBOIUL INTREGULUI POPOR PENTRU APARAREA PATRIEI [92]. Mihai Cucu's FACTORUL GEOGRAFIC IN ACTINUNILE MILITARE. SECVENTE DIN ISTORIA MILITARA ROMANEASCA [125] is a study of Romanian victories as a function of terrain analysis.

## BULGARIA

BULGARIA [132] was edited by L.A.D. Dellin and is one of a series of handbooks published by the Mid-European Studies Center of the Free Europe Committee. Minko Minkov's BULGARIA AND THE ECONOMIC DEVELOPMENT OF THE BALKANS [348] was published in Sofia in 1962. The Soviet Union published SOVETSKO-BOLGARSKIE OTNOSHENIYA I SVYAZI: DOKUMENTY I MATERIALY [538] deals with Soviet assistance in building the Bulgarian army between September 1944 and December 1958. A brief history of "The Bulgarian Army" [79] is found in a 1965 article dealing with both army and navy activities.

## THE HUNGARIAN UPRISING, 1956

One of the most dramatic events of the postwar era came when the overwhelming anti-communist sentiment in Hungary erupted into open rebellion in 1956. In 1947 a communist coup unseated the government of Ferenc Nagy. From that point until 1956, communist control in Hungary went largely unchallenged. There were, however, signs in early 1956 that the regime was in the throes of a severe internal battle. This resulted in a major shake-up of the government in late July 1956. There is some evidence to suggest that what happened next may have been inspired by the new communist leaders who hoped to flush out dissident elements by authorizing a massive demonstration in Budapest on 23 October 1956. A major revolt followed in which the Hungarian "Freedom Fighters" all over the country moved quickly to oust the communists (25 October) by both paramilitary and parliamentary means. In the process, many communist officials, including members of the secret police, fled into Austria. A new government was installed under the leadership of the moderate communist, Imre Nagy.

In the meantime, the ousted communist party secretary, Erno Gero, asked the Soviet Union for support. Fighting had now erupted across the country in which the Hungarian Freedom Fighters battled both communist Hungarian and Soviet forces. On 28 October the Soviets, in a move designed to mask their real intentions, offered to negotiate a withdrawal. Three days later, on 1 November, about 200,000 Soviet troops, some from as far away as Uzbekistan, invaded Hungary. Budapest was surrounded and Nagy and his cabinet arrested. Fighting continued, however, with a resulting loss of more than 30,000 Hungarians and about 7,000 Soviets. Before the end of November, more than 175,000 Hungarians fled their homeland as a result of the Soviet suppression. Nagy and a number of other Hungarians were executed by the Soviets and a puppet government was installed.

The history of this series of events depends upon who is telling the story. One study of interest on Hungary is THE STRUGGLE BEHIND THE IRON CURTAIN [364] which is the personal reminiscences of Ferenc Nagy, the Prime Minister of Hungary in 1946-1947. His work is, however, undocumented. A study entitled "New Light on the Hungarian Political Crisis (1947)" may be found in the OSDIRR [523].

MAGYAR HARCOSOK BAJTARSI KOGOSSEGE [417] is a white paper on Hungarian prisoners of war illegally detained by the Soviets. It was prepared by the PW Service of Hungarian Veterans in Munich.

For the anti-communist view of the tragic events surrounding the Hungarian Uprising, one should read Paul E. Zinner's REVOLUTION IN HUNGARY [602], Miklos Molnar's BUDAPEST 1956: A HISTORY OF THE HUNGARIAN REVOLUTION [352], or Ferenc Vali's RIFT AND REVOLT IN HUNGARY; NATIONALISM VERSUS COMMUNISM [542]. Vali's is an eyewitness account and is excellent. TEN YEARS AFTER: THE HUNGARIAN REVOLUTION IN THE PERSPECTIVE OF HISTORY [1], edited by Tamas Aczel, contains 12 essays including a chronology of the period 1953-1965. It is probably the most profound view of the uprising available. Another good collection of essays is presented in THE HUNGARIAN REVOLUTION IN PERSPECTIVE [556] which was edited by Francis S. Wagner. George Heltai's article, "November 1956: The End in Budapest" [211], is also quite good.

Janos Radvanyi's HUNGARY AND THE SUPERPOWERS: THE 1956 REVOLUTION AND REALPOLITIK [421] exposes the diplomatic aspects of this affair. Bela Kiraly's "The Organization of National Defense During the Hungarian Revolution" [276] is especially useful. BOOKS ON THE HUNGARIAN REVOLUTION: A BIBLIOGRAPHY [500] was compiled by Zoltan Sztaray and is very thorough. Peter I. Gosztony has produced "General Maleter: A Memoir" [197]. General Pal Maleter was a hero of the uprising who was arrested while negotiating with the Soviets and executed. A British dissertation entitled "The United States and the Hungarian Revolution of 1956: A Case Study of American Policies Towards East Central Europe from 1945 to 1957" [289] was presented at the University of London by B. Kovig. David Pryce-Jones prepared a pictorial chronology of the uprising entitled THE HUNGARIAN REVOLUTION [416] which is very useful.

Two works of some interest that cover certain aspects of this period were produced in Budapest. A MAGYAR NEPHADSEREG TORTENETE 1945-1959 [361], by Sandor Mucs and Erno Zagoni, is a history of the Hungarian army. A MAGYAR FORRADALMI HONVED KARTHATALOM 1956, NOVEMBRE-1957, JUNIUS [497], by Arpad Szabo, deals with the Hungarian armed forces during the months following the uprising. An entirely different view of the uprising may be found in Manfred Rauchensteiner's SPATHERBST 1956. DIE NEUTRALITAT AUF DEM PRUFSTAND [424] which is a reflection upon the role played by the year-old Austrian army in controlling the Austro-Hungarian border during the crisis and the politico-military realities of neutrality in the face of armed threat.

THE CZECHOSLOVAKIA SPRING

Within three years of the end of the war another tragedy unfolded in Czechoslovakia. In February 1948 the communist premier, Klement Gottwald, demanded and got total control of the placement of his National Front personnel in all key positions in the government, except the post of foreign minister which was held by Jan Masaryk. Even so, all of Masaryk's aides were Gottwald's men. On 10 March 1948, Masaryk was murdered by the communists either with or without Soviet approval. Then, in May, in a rigged election Gottwald replaced Benes as president with Antonin Zapotocky as prime minister. A series of purges followed (1951-1953) that led to extremely rigid rule. Gottwald died in 1953 and was replaced by Zapotocky. He died in 1957 and Antonin Novotny became the Czech leader. Novotny lasted until 1968 when economic problems led to his ouster as party leader; Alexander Dubcek then took over the leadership.

Beginning in 1962 the Czech communist party began a series of inquiries into the injustices committed by preceding regimes. This led to a certain "democratization" of a number of aspects of Czech social and political life and, in July 1968, to a demand to the Soviet Union to revise the Warsaw Pact Treaty to clearly establish its purely defensive nature. In answer, the Soviets invaded Czechoslovakia on 20 August 1968 with a combined force of about one-half million troops representing the Soviet Union, East Germany, Poland, Hungary, and Bulgaria. The liberal Dubcek government was deposed and Gustav Husak was installed as party leader. Although the other members of the Warsaw Pact withdrew their troops, nearly 70,000 Soviet troops remained to ensure against further demonstrations.

There are good books that deal with Czechoslovakia during this time. Among these are THE MASARYK CASE [486], by Claire Sterling; JAN MASARYK: A PERSONAL MEMOIRE [314], by Sir R.H.B. Lockhart; and Z. Zeman's THE MASARYKS: THE MAKING OF CZECHOSLOVAKIA [598]. Paul Zinner's COMMUNIST STRATEGY AND TACTICS IN CZECHOSLOVAKIA, 1918-48 [602] deals with the communist seizure of the country as one of the most fateful events of the Cold War. The OSDIRR [523] has a study on "Soviet Relations with Czechoslovakia (1946)," and another on "Purges in the Communist Party of Czechoslovakia (1953)." THE SOVIET INVASION OF CZECHOSLOVAKIA: ITS EFFECTS ON EASTERN EUROPE [127] was edited by E.J. Czerwinski and J. Pilkolkiewicz. John Kalvoda's CZECHOSLOVAKIA'S ROLE IN SOVIET STRATEGY [265] deals with both Edvard Benes and Thomas Masaryk and has excellent documentation. Walter Kotsch's "The Tanks of August 1968" [285] examines how the Soviet attack did what history had not done -- unify the Czechs and Slovaks. Jeffrey Simon uses the Czech invasion as one of his case studies in COHESION AND DISSENSION IN EASTERN EUROPE: SIX CRISES [465].

## THE WARSAW PACT AND THE SOVIETIZED BALKANS

Under the grandiloquent title of "The East European Treaty of Friendship, Cooperation, and Mutual Assistance," the Warsaw Pact was established on 14 May 1955 as a counter to NATO. The 10-article treaty claims its authority from the United Nations Organization and has, as a supplemental instrument, the "Establishment of a Joint Command of the Armed Forces of the Signatories to the Treaty ..." From that moment, the majority of the military history of the Balkans has been associated with that Soviet-sponsored and Soviet-led organization. The Warsaw Pact includes the Balkan states of Bulgaria, Romania, Hungary, their neighbors, Czechoslovakia and Poland, and East Germany. A wealth of published material is available on the organization, leadership, capabilities, deployments, technologies, and training of the member forces of the Warsaw Pact. Additional studies are available on all other phases of its existence, not the least of which are assessments of the reliability the Soviet Union can place in each of its allies. A large part of this information is found in unclassified writings that are available to the average reader. There is, of course, an equally large amount of data that is considered sensitive and which is therefore kept under lock and key. This information is protected for a number of reasons, one of the principal being the protection of the means by which the information was collected. The average reader will have to be satisfied with what is available and should find ample material for any purpose. The following selections are representative of the material as it may be applied against the Balkans.

A good place to begin is by reading William Woodruff's THE STRUGGLE FOR WORLD POWER, 1500-1980 [583]; Eugen Weber's EUROPE SINCE 1715: A MODERN HISTORY [561], and his TWENTIETH CENTURY EUROPE [560]; Harriet Ward's WORLD POWERS IN THE TWENTIETH CENTURY [558]; and Christopher D. Jones' SOVIET INFLUENCE IN EASTERN EUROPE: POLITICAL AUTONOMY AND THE WARSAW PACT [256]. This study deals with the politico-military structure of the Warsaw Pact and points out areas where the Pact works and where it does not. The author makes an interesting argument for the thesis that Moscow's control over the satellite states is based upon their capacity and will for military self-defense. EASTERN EUROPE SINCE 1945 [357] is a history of the development of communism up to 1983. William Kintner and Wolfgang Klaiber's EASTERN EUROPE AND EUROPEAN SECURITY [275] appears to be more a collection of studies rather than an integrated volume. It is still quite good. BALKAN SECURITY [299] by F. Stephen Larrabee, deals with both military and political factors in the Balkans. Peter Mooney examines the Soviet Union and Eastern Europe in one chapter in THE SOVIET SUPERPOWER: THE SOVIET UNION, 1945-1980 [354]. Richard Starr's "The East European Alliance System" [480] and his THE COMMUNIST REGIMES IN EASTERN EUROPE [481] are both excellent. COMMUNISM IN EASTERN EUROPE [422], edited by Teresa Rakowska-Harmstone and Andrew Gyorgy, is a valuable source of data on socio-political and economic conditions. Gordon Brook-Shepherd's RUSSIA'S DANUBIAN EMPIRE [69] is an interesting assessment of Soviet successes in the Balkans to about 1953. Henry Roberts' EASTERN EUROPE: POLITICS, REVOLUTION, AND DIPLOMACY [437] is also quite useful. Peter Summerscale's THE EAST EUROPEAN PREDICAMENT [495] is an assessment of the alignment changes that have occurred over the last two decades.

Another excellent study is Wayne Vucinich's "Sovietization in the Balkans" [551] which was published in CURRENT HISTORY in 1954. It lays the background for the institutionalization of the Warsaw Pact. Thomas Wolfe looks at the same problem from a different angle in his SOVIET POWER AND EUROPE, 1945-1970 [578]. Dimitri Analis' LES BALKANS 1945-1960: LA PRISE DU POUVOIR [17] is excellent. Hugh Seton-Watson produced THE EAST EUROPEAN REVOLUTION [458]. In Stephen Anderson's "Soviet Relations with East Europe" [19], which was written in 1966, the author points out the three main lines the Soviets followed in developing organizational cohesiveness in the Balkans. THE NEW EASTERN EUROPE: THE KHRUSHCHEV ERA AND AFTER [66] is good in its coverage of the period from Khrushchev's assumption of power to 1965, after his ouster. Robert King's MINORITIES UNDER COMMUNISM; NATIONALITIES AS A SOURCE OF TENSION AMONG BALKAN COMMUNIST STATES [272] is an interesting assessment of the problems faced in tying to integrate the Balkan nations into the communist sphere. Roy Mellor's EASTERN EUROPE: A GEOGRAPHY OF THE COMECON COUNTRIES [342] explores a different aspect of Soviet relations with the Balkans. EASTERN EUROPE AND THE THIRD WORLD: EAST VS. SOUTH [420], edited by Michael Radu, is extremely important in its evaluation of non-Soviet gains in the developing nations.

Francois Fejto's A HISTORY OF THE PEOPLE'S DEMOCRACIES: EASTERN EUROPE SINCE STALIN [164] is useful for its period of coverage, but the translation into English makes it hard to follow. CIVIL-MILITARY RELATIONS IN COMMUNIST SYSTEMS [213], edited by Dale Herspring and Ivan Volgyes, has 12 essays that attempt to explain this relationship. It is not very helpful although the articles taken separately are quite good. THE DYNAMICS OF COMMUNISM IN EASTERN EUROPE [81], by R.V. Burks, is also useful at this point. Lilita Dzirkals and A. Ross Anderson edited SOVIET AND EAST EUROPEAN FORECASTS OF EUROPEAN SECURITY for the Rand Corporation. The collected material is the ACTA of the 1972 Varna Conference. George Hoffman's THE BALKANS IN TRANSITION [223] is also quite useful. The two works edited by Stephen Kertesz: THE FATE OF EAST CENTRAL EUROPE [271] and EAST CENTRAL EUROPE AND THE WORLD; DEVELOPMENTS IN THE POST-STALINIS ERA [270] are both excellent. The former contains 16 articles dealing with the creation of the Soviet empire in Eastern Europe while the latter surveys the history of the region after Stalin. Both are very useful. Although Rudolf Bahro uses East Germany as his case study in THE ALTERNATIVE IN EASTERN EUROPE [34], he does address the 1968 Czech situation. Bahro is an East German dissident who is an avowed communist and Marxist even though he has rejected Leninism.

Another useful study is Phillip Petersen's SOVIET POLICY IN THE POST-TITO BALKANS [397]. Lawrence Whetten's THE SOVIET PRESENCE IN THE EASTERN MEDITERRANEAN [565], his "The Military Consequences of Mediterranean Super Power Parity" [566], Howard Chambers' DETENTE AND THE EASTERN MEDITERRANEAN [95], and Jesse Lewis' THE STRATEGIC BALANCE IN THE MEDITERRANEAN [310] are all quite interesting. Robert L. Wolfe's THE BALKANS IN OUR TIME [577] and Charles and Barbara Jelavich's THE BALKANS IN TRANSITION [246] are both quite good. The OSS/STATE DEPARTMENT INTELLIGENCE AND RESEARCH REPORTS [523] and the SPECIAL STUDIES SERIES [526] contain hundreds of titles for the period after 1945 a number of which deal with the Balkans in this period. George Schopflin edited THE SOVIET UNION AND EASTERN EUROPE: A HANDBOOK [451] in 1970. Another handy reference is AN HISTORICAL GEOGRAPHY OF THE BALKANS [89] edited by Francis W. Carter. SOUTH-EASTERN EUROPE: A POLITICAL AND ECONOMIC SURVEY [434] was prepared by RIIA in 1972. In 1971 the United States Army produced COMMUNIST EASTERN EUROPE: ANALYTIC SURVEY OF LITERATURE [522]. It contains a wealth of data, maps, and other information plus hundreds of additional titles. Ivan Berend and Gyorgy Ranki's ECONOMIC DEVELOPMENT IN EAST CENTRAL EUROPE IN THE 19TH AND 20TH CENTURIES [50] also has some utility at this point.

One means of gaining an understanding of the Warsaw Pact is by using DIE ORGANISATION DES WARSCHAUER VERTRAGES. DOKUMENTE UND MATERIALIEN, 1955-1980 [187]. This is a compendium of reports and meetings of a number of the more important committees of the organization. This collection of documents was produced in East Germany. Ithiel de Sola Pool's SATELLITE GENERALS: A STUDY OF MILITARY ELITES IN THE SOVIET SPHERE [403] looks at the problems involved in choosing between capable commanders and loyal ones. In

1965 MILITARY AFFAIRS published "The Satellite Armies - A Soviet Asset?" [427] by James T. Reitz. In this article Colonel Reitz assesses the results of the years of effort the Soviet Union had put into attempting to turn a liability into an asset. The HANDBOOK ON THE WARSAW PACT ARMIES OF EASTERN EUROPE [531] is a 1966 publication of the Defense Intelligence Agency. Thomas W. Wolfe's "The Warsaw Pact in Evolution" [579] deals with the direction of Soviet policy toward the Warsaw Pact. A digested version of a 1966 NATO publication on the subject may be found in "The Warsaw Pact" [559] published in 1967 in MILITARY REVIEW. This article has a good explanation of the top-level organization of the Pact.

After the Soviet invasion of Czechoslovakia, John W. DePauw's "Soldiers of the Warsaw Pact" [135] looks at the characteristics of the satellite soldiers of the Pact in an article prepared as a part of the US Army's troop indoctrination program. Walter Clemens' "The Changing Warsaw Pact" [104] and his "The Future of the Warsaw Pact" [103] are much alike but are both worth reading. Malcolm Mackintosh's THE EVOLUTION OF THE WARSAW PACT [326] is an excellent review published in the ADELPHI PAPERS by an authority on how the Soviet military system works. Another excellent article, this time in MILITARY AFFAIRS, is R. Rockingham Gill's "Europe's Military Balance After Czechoslovakia" [191]. Gill postulates that the Czech invasion caused the balance to tilt in the Soviet's favor. Henrik Birnbaum and Speros Yryonis edited ASPECTS OF THE BALKANS; CONTINUITY AND CHANGE [55] which is the ACTA of the 1969 International Conference on the Balkans held at UCLA. A DOCUMENTARY STUDY OF THE WARSAW PACT [245], by J.R. Jain, is also interesting in its portrayal of the development of the organization up to 1967 through the use of its own official records. Micheal Boll's "The Dilemma of the Warsaw Pact" [58] deals with the apparent loss of domination of the Pact by the Soviets following Czechoslovakia. Paul Shirk's "Warsaw Treaty Organization" [463] is a study that deals with emphasis placed on military integration by the USSR. Otto von Pivka's THE ARMIES OF EUROPE TODAY [401] deals with the early 1970s. Bela Kiraly's "Why the Soviets Need the Warsaw Pact" [277] explains how the Soviets use the Pact to sustain their political posture in relation to the other political forces in Europe. Andrzej Korbonski's THE WARSAW PACT [282] is an example of the fine work done by the Carnegie Endowment for International Peace. In THE WARSAW PACT: CASE STUDIES IN COMMUNIST CONFLICT RESOLUTION [428], by Robin Remington, three examples are given, one of which deals with Czechoslovakia and another with Romania. THE WARSAW PACT'S CAMPAIGN FOR "EUROPEAN SECURITY" [252] is another Rand publication by A. Ross Johnson.

Ian McGeoch's "The Defence of NATO's Southern Flank" [340] is a 1972 RUSI study that deals in some aspects with the possible employment of Balkan Warsaw Pact forces. Two years later, in 1976, Mean Johnston looked at the same problem in "The Southern Flank of NATO: Problems of the Southern Region in the Post-1973 October War Period" [255]. Friedrich Wiener's THE ARMIES OF THE WARSAW PACT NATIONS [570] is a quite useful pamphlet but is out-of-date. A more recent study is THE WARSAW PACT: POLITIC PURPOSE AND MILITARY MEANS [101], edited by Robert Clawson and Lawrence Kaplan, is a collection of 14 articles on political and military aspects of the organization. John K. Campbell's "Soviet Strategy in the Balkans" [86] was published in PROBLEMS OF COMMUNISM in 1974. Another up-to-date work is NATO AND THE WARSAW PACT: A COMBAT ASSESSMENT which is Volume 1 in FIGHTING ARMIES [178], edited by Richard Gabriel. Gabriel has also produced THE NEW RED LEGIONS [179], Volume 2 of which is a survey data book on the Soviet army. SOVIET ALLIES: THE WARSAW PACT AND THE ISSUE OF RELIABILITY [367], which was edited by Daniel Nelson, contains a number of articles arranged in two sections: one dealing with concepts and systems and another with country studies. This work was published in 1984. As a last entry for this period, one should not overlook Friedrich Wiener's DIE ARMEEN DER NEUTRALEN UND BLOCKFREIEN STAATEN EUROPAS. ORGANISATION-KRIEGBILD- WAFFEN UND GERAT [572]. This is an overview of the military organizations and doctrines of Austria, Yugoslavia, Albania, and other non-Warsaw Pact or neutral nations. Wiener's work is always excellent.

**BIBLIOGRAPHIC LISTING**

1. Aczel, T., ed. TEN YEARS AFTER: THE HUNGARIAN REVOLUTION IN THE PERSPECTIVE OF HISTORY. New York: 1966.

2. Adamic, L. LIBERATION. New York: 1945.

3. _____. THE EAGLE AND THE ROOTS. Garden City: 1952.

4. Adams, A.E., et al. AN ATLAS OF RUSSIAN AND EAST EUROPEAN HISTORY. New York: 1967 [1966].

5. Adamthwaite, A.P., ed. THE MAKING OF THE SECOND WORLD WAR. London: 1977.

6. Ainsztein, R. JEWISH RESISTANCE IN NAZI-OCCUPIED EASTERN EUROPE. New York: 1974.

7. Albania. GRUAJA SHQIPTARE NA LUFTEN ANTIFASHITE. NACIONALCLIRIMTARE. Tirana: 1975.

8. _____. CONFERENCE NATIONALE DES ETUDES SUR LA LUTTE ANTIFASCISTE DE LIBERATION NATIONALE DU PEUPLE ALBANAIS. Tirana: 1975.

9. _____. KONFERENZA E STUDIMEVE ALBANOLOGJIKE 2D. Tirana: 1969-.

10. Albrecht, U., ed. A RESEARCH GUIDE TO ARMS AND ARMED FORCES. Totowa: 1979.

11. Alexander, E., & Ronnet, M.D. ROMANIAN NATIONALISM: THE LEGIONARY MOVEMENT. Chicago: 1974.

12. Alger, J.I. THE QUEST FOR VICTORY: THE HISTORY OF THE PRINCIPLES OF WAR. CMH 30. Westport: 1981.

13. American Committee on the History of the Second World War. THE SECOND WORLD WAR: A BIBLIOGRAPHY. Compiled by Arthur L. Funk. Gainesville: 1972.

14. _____. "Cumulative Listing of Bibliographic and Archival Resources." NEWSLETTER No. 25 (Spring 1981).

15. Amery, J. SONS OF THE EAGLE, A STUDY IN GUERRILLA WARFARE. London: 1948.

16. _____. APPROACH MARCH; A VENTURE INTO AUTOBIOGRAPHY. London: 1973.

17. Analis, D. LA BALKANS 1945-1960: LA PRISE DU POUVOIR. [Paris]:
    c.1978.

18. Anastasoff, C. THE BULGARIANS: FROM THEIR ARRIVAL IN THE
    BALKANS TO MODERN TIMES. THIRTEEN CENTURIES OF HISTORY.

19. Anderson, S.S. "Soviet Relations with East Europe." CURRENT
    HISTORY (October 1966), 200-205.

20. Andreski, S. MILITARY ORGANIZATION AND SOCIETY. 2nd ed.
    Berkeley: 1968.

21. Ansel, W. HITLER AND THE MIDDLE SEA. Durham: 1972.

22. Antonescu, M.A. RUMANIENS HEILIGER KRIEG, RUNDFUNKREDE,
    GEHALTEN AM TAGE VON RUMANIENS KRIEGSEINTRITT, 22 JUNI
    1941. Bucharest: 1941.

23. Antosiak, A.V. LES COMBATS EN VUE LA LIBERATION DE LA ROUMANIE.
    Moscow: 1974.

24. Apostolski, M. POGLEDI NA JUGOSLOVENSKO-BULGARSKE ODNOSE.
    Belgrad: 1980.

25. Archer, L. BALKAN JOURNAL. New York: 1944.

26. Arena, N. LA REGIA AERONAUTICA 1943-1946. -DALL'ARMISTIZIO ALLA
    COBELLIGERANZA. Vol. 1: DALLA GUERRA DE LIBERAZIONE ALLA
    REPUBLICA. Rome: 1977.

27. Armstrong, H. TITO AND GOLIATH. New York: 1951.

28. Arnakis, G.G., & Vucinich, W.S. THE NEAR EAST IN MODERN TIMES.
    Vol. 2: FORTY CRUCIAL YEARS, 1900-1940. Austin & New York:
    1972.

29. Atanackovic, B., et al. YUGOSLAVIA IN THE SECOND WORLD WAR.
    Trans. by Lovett F. Edwards. Belgrad: 1965.

30. Auty, P. TITO. New York: 1972.

31. Auty, P., & Clogg, R. BRITISH POLICY TOWARD WARTIME RESISTANCE
    IN YUGOSLAVIA AND GREECE. ULSEE. London: 1974.

32. Babici, I. SOLIDARITATES ROMANEASCA CU LUPTA ANTIFASCISTA DIN
    BALCANI. Bucharest: 1979.

33. Babin, A.I., et al. ISTORIYA OTECHESTVENNOI
    VOENNO-ENTSIKLOPEDICHESKOI LITERATURII. Moscow: 1980.

34. Bahro, R. THE ALTERNATIVE IN EASTERN EUROPE. New York: 1978.

35. Bailey R., et al. PARTISANS AND GUERRILLAS. Alexandria: c.1978.

36. Balabanov, N. "A Year in Ankara: December 1st 1943 to January
    9th 1945." BR V (December 1945), 49-55.

37. Banks, A. A WORLD ATLAS OF MILITARY HISTORY, 1860-1945. New York: 1978.

38. Bantea, E., Maj. Gen. "Political and Military Considerations on the Insurrection of August 1944." PHRA BHR Mongraph 15. Bucharest: 1975.

39. _____. "National Antifascist and Anti-Imperialist Insurrection of August 1944 - Expression of the Romanian People's Will of Independence." RIHM 36 (1977), 178-189.

40. _____. INSURECTIA ROMANA IN JURNALUL DE RAZBOI AL GRUPULUI DE ARMATA GERMAN "UCRAINA DE SUD." Bucharest: 1974.

41. Bantea, E., Maj. Gen., & Ionescu, M. "Neutrality Policy in the First Stage of World War II: The Romanian Case." CIHM ACTA, 1978.

42. Bantea, E., et al. ROMANIA IN THE WAR AGAINST HITLER'S GERMANY. Bucharest: 1970.

43. Barker, E. BRITISH POLICY IN SOUTH-EAST EUROPE IN THE SECOND WORLD WAR. New York: 1976.

44. Barnes, T.G., & Feldman, G.D. A DOCUMENTARY HISTORY OF MODERN EUROPE. 4 vols. Washington: 1979-1982.

45. Basta, M. RAT JE ZAVRSEN 7 DANA KASNIJE. Zagreb: 1978.

46. Beal, R.S. SYSTEMS ANALYSIS OF INTERNATIONAL CRISIS, 1948-1962. Washington: 1979.

47. Becker, A.S., & Horelick, A.L. SOVIET POLICY IN THE MIDDLE EAST. Santa Monica: 1970.

48. Bedeschi. G., ed. FRONTE GRECO-ALBANESE, C'ERO ANCH'IO. Milan: 1977.

49. Benes, E. MEMOIRS: FROM MUNICH TO NEW WAR AND NEW VICTORY. Trans. by Godfrey Lias. London: 1954.

50. Berend, I.T., & Ranki, G. ECONOMIC DEVELOPMENT IN EAST CENTRAL EUROPE IN THE 19TH AND 20TH CENTURIES. New York: 1974.

51. Berghahn, V.R. MILITARISM: THE HISTORY OF AN INTERNATIONAL DEBATE, 1860-1979. New York: 1982.

52. BIBLIOGRAPHIC GUIDE TO MAPS AND ATLASES: 1981. Boston: 1982.

53. BIBLIOGRAPHIC GUIDE TO SOVIET AND EAST EUROPEAN STUDIES: 1981. 3 vols. Boston: 1981.

54. Bidwell, R., ed. TURKEY, IRAN, AND THE MIDDLE EAST, 1919-1939. 35 vols. Frederick: 1984.

55. Birnbaum, H., & Vryonis, S., eds. ASPECTS OF THE BALKANS; CONTINUITY AND CHANGE. Contributions of the International Balkan Conference, UCLA, 1969. The Hague: 1972.

56. Blainey, G. THE CAUSES OF WAR. New York: 1973.

57. Bokor, P. VEGJATEK A DUNA MENTEN. INTERJUK EGY FILMSOROZATHOZ. Budapest: 1982.

58. Boll, M.M. "The Dilemma of the Warsaw Pact." MR 49/7 (July 1969), 89-95.

59. Borsody, S. THE TRAGEDY OF CENTRAL EUROPE. London: [1960].

60. _____. "Modern Hungarian Historiography." JMH XXIV No. 4 (December 1952), 398-405.

61. Bosnjak, L. ZBORNIK DOKUMENATA O NARADNOOSLOBODILACKOM RATU NARODA JUGOSLAVIJE. Vol. 9. Belgrad: 1975.

62. Bourne, K., & Watt, D.C., gen. eds. BRITISH DOCUMENTS ON FOREIGN AFFAIRS: REPORTS AND PAPERS FROM FOREIGN OFFICE CONFIDENTIAL PRINT: THE SOVIET UNION, 1917-1939. 15 vols. Frederick: 1984.

63. Bradley, J.F.N. CZECHO-SLOVAKIA: A SHORT HISTORY. Edinburgh: 1971.

64. Brannen, B. "The Soviet Conquest of Rumania." FA 30:3 (April 1952), 466-488.

65. Braun, A. ROMANIAN FOREIGN POLICY SINCE 1965: THE POLITICAL AND MILITARY LIMITS TO AUTONOMY. New York & London: 1978.

66. Braun, J.F. THE NEW EASTERN EUROPE: THE KHRUSHCHEV ERA AND AFTER. New York, Washington & London: 1966.

67. Brayton, A.A., & Landwehr, S.J. THE POLITICS OF WAR AND PEACE: A SURVEY OF THOUGHT. Washington: [1981].

68. Breccia, A. JUGOSLAVIA 1939-1941: DIPLOMAZIA DELLA NEUTRALITA. FDSP 25. Rome: 1978.

69. Brook-Shepherd, G. RUSSIA'S DANUBIAN EMPIRE. New York & London: c.1954.

70. Bulatovic, M. THE WAR WAS BETTER. Trans. by G. Brusar. New York: (c.1970).

71. Omitted.

72. Bulgaria., Academy of Sciences. LES GRANDES PUISSANCES ET LES BALKANS A LA VEILLE ET AU DEBUT DE LA DEUXIEME GUERRE MONDIALE 1937-1941. Sofia: 1973.

73. _____. DOCUMENTS AND MATERIALS ON THE HISTORY OF THE BULGARIAN PEOPLE. Sofia: 1969.

74. Omitted.

75. _____. HISTOIRE MILITAIRE DE LA BULGARIE, 681-1945. BIBLIOGRAPHIE. 2 vols. Sofia: 1973.

76. _____. LA BRIGADE DE PARTISANS "TSCHAVDAR". RESUME
HISTORIQUE. 2d ed. Sofia: 1979.

77. _____. LA GUERRE PATRIOTIQUE EN BULGARIE, 1944-1945.
DOCUMENTS. 4 vols. Sofia: 1978.

78. _____. Institute of History. LA LUTTE DU PEUPLE BULGARE
POUR LA PROTECTION ET LA DELIVRANCE DES JUIFS EN BULGARIE
PENDANT LA SECONDE GUERRE MONDIALE. DOCUMENTS. Sofia:
1979.

79. "The Bulgarian Army." AU COSANTOIR 25/9 (September 1965),
467-468.

80. Burbulea, E. APARAREA NATIONALA SI CALITATILE LUPTATORILOR.
Bucharest: 1981.

81. Burks, R.V. THE DYNAMICS OF COMMUNISM IN EASTERN EUROPE.
Princeton: 1961.

82. Byrnes, R.F. BIBLIOGRAPHY OF AMERICAN PUBLICATIONS ON EAST
CENTRAL EUROPE, 1945-1957. Bloomington: 1961.

83. Calafeteanu, I. DIPLOMATIA ROMANEASCA IN SUD-ESTUL EUROPEI
(MARTIE 1938-MARTIE 1940). Bucharest: 1980.

84. Calvocoressi, P., & Wint, G. TOTAL WAR: CAUSES AND COURSES OF
THE SECOND WORLD WAR. New York & London: [1972].

85. Cammarata, F. ALBANICA. Palermo: 1968.

86. Campbell, J.K. "Soviet Strategy in the Balkans." PC 23
(July-August 1974), 1-16.

87. Cantor, N.F., & Berner, S., eds. THE MODERN ERA, 1815 TO THE
PRESENT. PEH III. Arlington Heights: 1967.

88. Carp, M. "The Armed Forces in Captive Romania." In A.
Cretzianu. CAPTIVE ROMANIA. New York: 1956.

89. Carter, F.W., ed. AN HISTORICAL GEOGRAPHY OF THE BALKANS.
London & New York: 1977.

90. Cassels, Alan  FASCISM. New York: [1975].

91. Ceaucescu, I. "Partial Mobilization in the Spring of 1939."
PHRA. BHR 15. Bucharest 1975.

92. _____. HARTUIREA IN ACTIUNILE DE LUPTA DUSE IN RAZBOIUL
INTREGULUI POPOR PENTRU APARAREA PATRIEI. Bucharest: 1981.

93. _____. RAZBOIUL INTREGULUI POPOR PENTRU APARAREA PATRIEI LA
ROMANI. Bucharest: 1981.

94. Cernat, I., & Stanislav, E., eds. NATIONAL DEFENSE, THE
ROMANIAN VIEW. Bucharest: 1976.

95. Chambers, H.L. DETENTE AND THE EASTERN MEDITERRANEAN. SSI. Carlisle Barracks: 1957.

96. Chary, F.B. "Bulgaria and the Jews: 'The Final Solution' 1940 to 1944." Unpublished Doctoral Dissertation. University of Pittsburgh, 1968.

97. Churchill, Winston., Sir. THE SECOND WORLD WAR. 6 vols. Cambridge: 1948-1953.

98. Cioranescu, G. "Rumania After Czechoslovakia: Ceaucescu Walks the Tightrope." EE 18:6 (June 1969), 2-7.

99. Clarke, J.J. "World Military History." GSUMH. Washington: 1979.

100. Clarkson, J.D. A HISTORY OF RUSSIA. New York: 1961.

101. Clawson, R. W., & Kaplan, L.S. THE WARSAW PACT: POLITICAL PURPOSE AND MILITARY MEANS. Wilmington: 1982.

102. Cleator, P.E. WEAPONS OF WAR. New York: 1968.

103. Clemens, W.C. "The Future of the Warsaw Pact." ORBIS 11:4 (Winter 1968), 996-1033.

104. _____. "The Changing Warsaw Pact." EE 17:6 (June 1968), 7-12.

105. Clissold, S. WHIRLWIND: AN ACCOUNT OF MARSHAL TITO'S RISE TO POWER. London: 1949.

106. _____. CROAT SEPARATISM. ISC. London: 1979.

107. _____. YUGOSLAVIA AND THE SOVIET UNION, 1939-1973. RIIA. Oxford: 1975.

108. _____. A SHORT HISTORY OF YUGOSLAVIA: FROM EARLY TIMES TO 1966. Cambridge: 1966.

109. Clogg, R. "The Ideology of the Revolution of 21 April 1967." In Richard Clogg & George Yannopoulos. GREECE UNDER MILITARY RULE. New York: 1972.

110. _____. "A Hand in the Resistance." TIMES (London) LITERARY SUPPLEMENT. 14 November 1975, 1362-1363.

111. _____. A SHORT HISTORY OF MODERN GREECE. Berkeley: 1979.

112. Clogg, R., & Yannopoulos, G. GREECE UNDER MILITARY RULE. New York: 1972.

113. Cockburn, A. THE THREAT: INSIDE THE SOVIET MILITARY MACHINE. New York: 1983.

114. Colby, E. MASTERS OF MODERN WARFARE. Princeton: 1943.

115. Coman, I. "Landmarks of the Evolution of the Army of the Socialist Republic of Romania." PHRA. BHR 15. Bucharest: 1975.

116. Comite des Relations Culturelles de Tirana. PRECIS D'HISTOIRE DE LA LUTTE ANTIFASCISTE DE LIBERATION NATIONALE DU PEUPLE ALBANAISE: 1939-1944. Paris: 1975.

117. Copley, G.R., ed. DEFENSE AND FOREIGN POLICY HANDBOOK. Bi-annual. New York: 1976-.

118. Copoiu, N., et al. REZISTENTA EUROPEANA, 1938-1945. 2 vols. Bucharest: 1973-1976.

119. Crespi, R. SQUADRISTI IN ALBANIA. Milan: 1941.

120. Cretzianu, A. "Romanian Armistice Negotiations, Cairo 1944." JCEA XI:3 (October 1951), 243-258.

121. _____. "The Soviet Ultimatum to Romania (26 June 1944)." JCEA IX (January 1950), 396-403.

122. _____. THE LOST OPPORTUNITY. London: [1957].

123. Cretzianu, A., et al. CAPTIVE RUMANIA. New York: 1956.

124. Cruciunas, S. THE LAST FOOTSTEPS. London: 1961.

125. Cucu, M. FACTORUL GEOGRAFIC IN ACTINUNILE MILITARE. SECVENTE DIN ISTORIA MILITARA ROMANEASCA. Bucharest: 1981.

126. Cuspa, I., et al. CONTRIBUTA ROMANIEL LA RAZBOIUL ANTI-HITLERIST (23 AUGUST 1944-9 MAY 1945). Bucharest: 1958.

127. Czerwinski, E.J., & Pilkolkiewicz, J., eds. THE SOVIET INVASION OF CZECHOSLOVAKIA: ITS EFFECTS ON EASTERN EUROPE. New York, Washington & London: 1972.

128. Davis, L.E. THE COLD WAR BEGINS: SOVIET-AMERICAN CONFLICT OVER EASTERN EUROPE. Princeton: 1974.

129. Dedijer, V. "Sarajevo Fifty Years After." FA XLII No. 4 (July 1964), 569-584.

130. _____. DOKUMENTI 1948. Belgrad: 1979.

131. _____. THE BELOVED LAND. New York: 1961.

132. Dellin, L.A.D., ed. BULGARIA. New York: [1957].

133. del Vayo, A.V. "Balkan Triangle." NATION CLXXV (September 20, 1952), 224.

134. Dennen, L. TROUBLE ZONE; BREWING POINTS OF WORLD WAR III?. New York: [1945].

135. DePauw, J.W. "Soldiers of the Warsaw Pact." AD 24:5 (May 1969), 20-27.

136. Detwiler, D.S., ed. WORLD WAR II GERMAN STUDIES. 24 vols. New York: 1971 [1980].

137. Djilas, M. THE EVE OF BATTLE. New York: 1962.

138. _____. MONTENEGRO. New York: 1963.

139. Dolezol, J., & Kren, J. CZECHOSLOVAKIA'S FIGHT: DOCUMENTS ON THE RESISTANCE MOVEMENT OF THE CZECHOSLOVAK PEOPLE, 1938-1945. Prague: 1964.

140. Dombrady, L. A MAGYAR GAZDASAG ES A HADFELSZERELES 1938-1944. Budapest: 1981.

141. Dornberg, J. EASTERN EUROPE: A COMMUNIST KALEIDOSCOPE. New York: c.1980.

142. Dragic, D. SANITETSKA SLUZBA U PARTIZANSKIM USLOVIMA RATOVANJA. Belgrad: 1977.

143. Dragnich, A.N. TITO'S PROMISED LAND: YUGOSLAVIA. New Brunswick: 1954.

144. Drechsler, R.H. KREUZWEG DER DEUTSCHEN IM SUDOSTEN 1944-1950: "DEN DEUTSCHEN DER TOD": DAS "ANDERE" HOLOCAUST: DOKUMENTATION. Vienna: 1979

145. Dujcev, I. MACEDONIEN IN DER BULGARISCHEN GESCHICHTE. Sofia: 1941.

146. Dunnigan, J.F., ed. THE RUSSIAN FRONT: GERMANY'S WAR IN THE EAST, 1941-1945. London & Melbourne: 1978.

147. Dzirkals, L., & Johnson, A.R., eds. SOVIET AND EAST EUROPEAN FORECASTS OF EUROPEAN SECURITY: PAPERS FROM THE 1972 VARNA CONFERENCE. A REPORT PREPARED BY USAF PROJECT REACH. Santa Monica: 1973.

148. Earle, E.M., ed. THE MAKERS OF MODERN STRATEGY: MILITARY THOUGHT FROM MACHIAVELLI TO HITLER. Princeton: 1943.

149. Egli, D. "Albania: Mediterranean Maoists." NEWSWEEK 70 No. 7 (14 August 1967), 49.

150. Ehrenburg, I.G. EUROPEAN CROSSROAD: A SOVIET JOURNALIST IN THE BALKANS. New York: 1947.

151. Enser, A.G.S., comp. A SUBJECT BIBLIOGRAPHY OF THE SECOND WORLD WAR; BOOKS IN ENGLISH, 1939-1974. Boulder & London: 1977.

152. Erickson, J. THE ROAD TO STALINGRAD. New York; 1975.

153. _____. THE ROAD TO BERLIN. Boulder: 1983.

154. _____. SOVIET MILITARY POWER. RUSI. London: 1971.

155. Erpenbeck, D.-G. SERBIEN 1941. D. MILITARVERWALTUNG UND
     SERBISCHER WIDERSTAND. Osnabruch: 1976.

156. Eubank, K., ed. THE ROAD TO WORLD WAR II: A DOCUMENTARY
     HISTORY. New York: 1973.

157. _____. THE ORIGINS OF WORLD WAR II. New York: 1969.

158. _____. WORLD WAR II, ROOTS AND CAUSES. Lexington: c.1975.

159. _____. MUNICH. Westport: 1984.

160. Eudes, D. THE KAPENTANIOS: PARTISANS AND CIVIL WAR IN GREECE,
     1943-1949. New York: 1973.

161. Evangelos, K. NATIONALISM AND COMMUNISM IN MACEDONIA.
     Thessaloniki: 1964.

162. Fabian Society, London. HITLER'S ROUTE TO BAGDAD. Freeport:
     1971.

163. Federal Writer's Project. THE ALBANIAN STRUGGLE IN THE OLD
     WORLD AND THE NEW. New York: 1975.

164. Fejto, F. A HISTORY OF THE PEOPLE'S DEMOCRACIES: EASTERN EUROPE
     SINCE STALIN. Trans. by Daniel Weissbort. New York,
     Washington & London: 1971.

165. Fenyo, M.D. HITLER, HORTHY AND HUNGARY: GERMAN-HUNGARIAN
     RELATIONS, 1941-1944. YREES 11. New Haven & London: 1972.

166. Ferenc, T. NASCISTICKA POLITIKA DENACIONALIZACIJE U SLOVENIJI U
     GODINAMA OD 1941. DO 1945. Belgrad: 1979.

167. Finer, S.E. "The Man on Horseback." AFS I/1 (November 1974),
     5-27.

168. Fisher-Galati, S. TWENTIETH CENTURY RUMANIA. New York: 1970.

169. Florinsky, M.T. RUSSIA: A HISTORY AND AN INTERPRETATION. 2
     vols. New York: 1953.

170. Fodor, M.W. SOUTH OF HITLER. A NEW AND ENLARGED EDITION OF PLOT
     AND COUNTERPLOT IN CENTRAL EUROPE. New ed. Boston: 1939.

171. Foley, C., & Scobie, W.J. THE STRUGGLE FOR CYPRUS. Stanford:
     1976.

172. Fontaine, A. HISTORY OF THE COLD WAR: FROM THE KOREAN WAR TO
     THE PRESENT. New York: 1969.

173. Forster, E.S. A SHORT HISTORY OF MODERN GREECE, 1821-1956. 3rd
     ed. rev. Ed. & enlarged by Douglas Dakin. London: 1958.

174. Forster, J. "Rumaniens weg in die deutsche abhangigkeit." MGM
     XXV No. 1 (1979), 47-77.

175. Fotitch, C. THE WAR WE LOST: YUGOSLAVIA'S TRAGEDY AND THE
FAILING OF THE WEST. New York: 1948.

176. Friessner, H. VERRATINE SCHLACHTEN; DIE TRAGODIE DER DEUTSCHEN
WEHRMACHT IN RUMANIEN UND UNGARN. Hamburg: 1956.

177. Fuller, J.F.C. THE CONDUCT OF WAR, 1789-1961. New Brunswick:
1961.

178. Gabriel, R.A., ed. FIGHTING ARMIES. 3 vols. Westport: 1983.

179. _____. THE NEW RED LEGIONS. 2 vols. Westport: 1980.

180. Gardiner, L. "Albania: 'Last Lonely Stronghold'." USNIP 93:10
(October 1967), 54-59.

181. _____. "Albania: The People's Army." MR 48:5 (May 1968),
32-40.

182. Gaynor, F., ed. THE NEW MILITARY AND NAVAL DICTIONARY. New
York: 1951.

183. Gazsi, J. FENYEK A BORSONYBEN. EGY ANTIFASISZTA ZASZLOALJ
TORTENETE. Budapest: 1976.

184. Genoff, G.P. DAS SCHICKSAL BULGARIENS. Berlin: 1940.

185. Georgescu, M., et al. LA DEFENSE NATIONALE DANS LA PENSEE
ROUMAINE. Budapest: 1980.

186. Georgiev, G.I. PRINOSUT NA BULGARSKIIA NAROD V ANTIFASHISTKATA
NARODOOSVOBODITELNA BORBA NA BALKANSKITE NARODI: 1941-1945
G. Sofia: 1979.

187. German Democratic Republic. DIE ORGANISATION DES WARSCHAUER
VERTRAGES. DOKUMENTE UND MATERIALIEN, 1955-1980. Berlin:
1980.

188. Gibb, H.A.R., Sir., et al. ENCYCLOPEDIA OF ISLAM. New ed.
Leiden: 1954-.

189. Gilbert, F. THE END OF A EUROPEAN ERA, 1890 TO THE PRESENT. 2d
ed. New York: 1970.

190. Gilbert, M. RUSSIAN HISTORY ATLAS. New York: 1972.

191. Gill, R.R. "Europe's Military Balance after Czechoslovakia." MR
49:1 (January 1969), 47-55.

192. Glatz, F., ed. OSTMITTELEUROPA IM ZWEITEN WELTKRIEG
(HISTORIOGRAPHISCHE FRAGEN). Budapest: 1978.

193. Goldman, N.L., ed. FEMALE SOLDIERS - COMBATANTS OR
NON-COMBATANTS?: HISTORICAL AND CONTEMPORARY PERSPECTIVES.
Westport: 1982.

194. Gomoiu, Gh. DES MILITAIRES PARTICIPANTS A LA VIE CULTURELLE ET
     SCIENTIFIQUE DE LA ROUMANIE. CIHM. Bucharest: 1980.

195. Gorlitz, W. PAULUS AND STALINGRAD. Trans. by R.H. Stevens. New
     York: 1963.

196. Gosnyak, I. TITO - STRATEGIST OF THE REVOLUTION AND FOUNDER OF
     THE PEOPLE'S ARMY. Belgrad: 1963.

197. Gosztony, P.I. "General Maleter: A Memoir." PC XV 3-4
     (March-April 1966), 54-61.

198. Great Britain. Naval Intelligence Division. ALBANIA. London:
     1945.

199. _____. Foreign Office. THE RUSSIA CORRESPONDENCE OF THE
     BRITISH FOREIGN OFFICE, 1906-1948. Foreign Office File
     371. On microfilm. Wilmington: n.d.

200. Greece, General Staff of the Army. Department of History of the
     Army. L'ARMEE HELLENIQUE PENDANT LA SECONDE GUERRE
     MONDIALE. 7 vols. Athens: 1959-1967.

201. _____. General Staff of the Navy. RAPPORT SUR L'ACTION DE
     LA MARINE ROYALE PENDANT LA SECONDE GUERRE MONDIALE. 2
     vols. Athens: 1952-1954.

202. "Greece and Turkey." KCA 27987, Looseleaf Series (8 October
     1976).

203. Grimsted, P.K., ed, ARCHIVES AND MANUSCRIPT COLLECTIONS IN THE
     USSR. Zug: n.d.

204. Grivas-Dighenis, G. GUERRILLA WARFARE AND EOKA'S STRUGGLE: A
     POLITICO-MILITARY STUDY. London: 1964.

205. Grozea, T. "The National Defence of Socialist Romania." PHRA.
     Bucharest: 1975.

206. _____., ed. ARMATA REPUBLICII SOCIALISTE ROMANIA. SINTEZA
     SOCIAL-POLITICA SI MILITARA. Bucharest: 1978.

207. Omitted.

208. Gulick, E.V. EUROPE'S CLASSICAL BALANCE OF POWER: A CASE
     HISTORY OF THE THEORY AND PRACTICE OF ONE OF THE GREAT
     CONCEPTS OF EUROPEAN STATECRAFT. Ithaca: 1955.

209. Gyoerkei, J. MAGYAR ONKENTESEKA SPANYOL POLGARHABORUBAN.
     Budapest: 1977.

210. Haider, R. DIE BULGARISCHE WIEDERGEBURT. Berlin: 1941.

211. Heltai, G. "November 1956: The End in Budapest." EE 15:10
     (October 1966), 10-15.

212. Heppell, M., & Singleton, F.B., YUGOSLAVIA. New York: 1961.

213. Herspring, D.R., & Volgyes, I., eds. CIVIL-MILITARY RELATIONS IN COMMUNIST SYSTEMS. Boulder & Folkstone: 1978.

214. Higham, R. "'General' and Guarantees -- Some Aspects of Aid to Greece in 1940-1941." Unpublished Paper. KSU. Manhattan: n.d.

215. _____. "British Intervention in Greece 1940-1941: The Anatomy of a Grand Deception." BS 23. (1982), 101-126.

216. _____. "A Limited War in a Total War: The Coming Graeco-German War, 1940-1941." KSU. Manhattan: 1983.

217. Hillgruber, A. HITLER'S STRATEGIE: POLITIK UND KRIEGFUHRUNG 1940-1941. Frankfurt/Main: 1965.

218. _____. " Hitler's Strategy and Politics in the Second World War." Unpublished Paper. n.d.

219. Hnilicka, K. DAS ENDE AUF DEM BALKAN 1944/45; DIE MILITARISCHE RAUMUNG JUGOSLAVIENS DURCH DIE DEUTSCHE WEHRMACHT. Gottingen: 1970.

220. Hodgart, A. THE ECONOMICS OF EUROPEAN IMPERIALISM. New York: 1978.

221. Hoensch, J.K. DER UNGARISCHE REVISIONISMUS UND DIE ZERSCHLAGUNG DER TSCHECHOSLOWAKEI. Turbingen: 1967.

222. Hoffman, G.W. REGIONAL DEVELOPMENT STRATEGY IN SOUTHEAST EUROPE; A COMPARATIVE ANALYSIS OF ALBANIA, BULGARIA, GREECE, ROMANIA AND YUGOSLAVIA. New York: 1972.

223. _____. THE BALKANS IN TRANSITION. Princeton: 1963.

224. Hogg, I. A HISTORY OF ARTILLERY. London: 1974.

225. Holt, P.M., et al. CAMBRIDGE HISTORY OF ISLAM. 2 vols. Cambridge: 1977-1978.

226. Horecky, P.L. SOUTHEASTERN EUROPE: A GUIDE TO BASIC PUBLICATIONS. Chicago: 1969.

227. Horthy, M. MEMOIRS. New York: 1957.

228. Hosch, E. THE BALKANS: A SHORT HISTORY. Trans. by Tania Alexander.New York: 1972.

229. Hourani, A.H. THE OTTOMAN BACKGROUND OF THE MODERN MIDDLE EAST. Harlow: 1970.

230. Houtsma, T. ed. ENCYCLOPEDIA OF ISLAM. 4 vols. w/suppl. Leiden: 1913-1938.

231. Howard, H.N. "Greece and Its Balkan Neighbors: 1948-1949, The United Nations Attempts at Reconciliation." BS 7:1 (1966), 1-23.

232. Hungary. FEGYVERREL A HAZAERT. MAGYAR ELLENALLASI ES PARTIZANHARCOK MASODIK VILAGHABORU IDEJEN. Budapest: 1980.

233. Iatrides, J.O. BALKAN TRIANGLE: BIRTH AND DECLINE OF AN ALLIANCE ACROSS IDEOLOGICAL BOUNDARIES. SEH 12. The Hague & Paris: 1968.

234. _____. "From Liberation to Civil War. The United States and Greece, 1944-46." US Department of State. OERP. No. FAR 23890.

235. _____. REVOLT IN ATHENS: THE GREEK COMMUNIST "SECOND ROUND," 1944-1945. Princeton: 1972.

236. Ignotus, P. "Czechs, Magyars, Slovaks." PQ 40:2 (June 1969), 187-204.

237. Inks, J.M. EIGHT BAILED OUT. Ed. by Lawrence Klingman. London: [1955].

238. International Institute for Strategic Studies, London. THE MILITARY BALANCE. Annual.

239. Ionescu, G. COMMUNISM IN ROMANIA, 1944-1962. London & New York: 1964.

240. Irving, D. THE WAR PATH: HITLER'S GERMANY 1933-1939. New York: 1978.

241. Italy. Army General Staff, Official History. L'ESERCITO ITALIANO NELLA 2. GUERRA MONDIALE. IMMAGINI. Rome: 1976.

242. _____. LA CAMPAGNA DI GRECIA. 3 vols. Rome: 1980.

243. Jackowicz, J. BULGARIA AND THE WESTERN POWERS, 1941-1944. Sofia: 1981.

244. Jacobsen, H.-A., & Smith, A.L. WORLD WAR II POLICY AND STRATEGY: SELECTED DOCUMENTS WITH COMMENTARY. Santa Barbara: 1979.

245. Jain, J.R. A DOCUMENTARY STUDY OF THE WARSAW PACT. The Hague: 1968.

246. Jelavich, C., & Jelavich, B., eds. THE BALKANS IN TRANSITION. REES. Berkeley & Los Angeles: 1963.

247. Jelic-Butic, F. USTASE I NEZAVISNA DRZAVA HRVATSKA. Zagreb: 1977.

248. Jessup, J.E., Coakley, R.W. A GUIDE TO THE STUDY AND USE OF MILITARY HISTORY. Washington: 1979.

249. Johnson, A.R. THE FUTURE OF YUGOSLAVIA. Santa Monica: 1974.

250. _____. THE ROLE OF THE MILITARY IN COMMUNIST YUGOSLAVIA: AN HISTORICAL SKETCH. Santa Monica: 1978.

251. _____. TOTAL NATIONAL DEFENSE IN YUGOSLAVIA. Rand RCP
     P-4746. Santa Monica: 1971.

252. _____. THE WARSAW PACT'S CAMPAIGN FOR "EUROPEAN SECURITY."
     Rand RCR 565-PR. Santa Monica: 1970.

253. _____. YUGOSLAVIA IN THE TWILIGHT OF TITO. Beverley Hills:
     [1974].

254. Johnson, S. AGENTS EXTRAORDINARY. London: 1975.

255. Johnston, M. "The Southern Flank of NATO: Problems of the
     Southern Region in the Post-1973 October War Period." MR
     56/4 (April 1976), 22-29.

256. Jones, C.D. SOVIET INFLUENCE IN EASTERN EUROPE: POLITICAL
     AUTONOMY AND THE WARSAW PACT. New York: 1981.

257. Jones, D., ed. THE MILITARY-NAVAL ENCYCLOPEDIA OF RUSSIA AND
     THE SOVIET UNION. Vols. 1 & 2. Gulf Breeze: 1978-1980.

258. _____. SOVIET ARMED FORCES REVIEW ANNUAL. 1977-.

259. Kacavenda, P. SKOJ I OMLADINA U NARODNOOSLOBODILACKOJ VOJSCI I
     PARTIZANSKIM ODREDIMA JUGOSLAVIJE 1941-1945. Belgrad: n.d.

260. Kahn, D. HITLER'S SPIES: GERMAN MILITARY INTELLIGENCE IN WWII.
     New York: 1978.

261. Kalbe, E. ANTIFASCHISTISCHER WIDERSTAND UND VOLKSDEMOKRATISCHE
     REVOLUTION IN SUDOSTEUROPPA: DAS HINUBERWACHSEN D.
     WIDERSTANDKAMPFS GEGEN D. FASCHISMUS IN D. VOLKSREVOLUTION
     (1941-1944/45). Berlin: 1974.

262. Kalezic, Z. STRUKTURNE PROMJEME NA CRNOGORSKOM SELU U XX
     UIJEKU. Titograd: 1976.

263. Kallai, G. A MAGYAR FUGGETLENSEGI MOZGALOM, 1936-1945. 5th ed.,
     rev. Budapest: 1965.

264. Kallay, N. HUNGARIAN PREMIER: A PERSONAL ACCOUNT OF A NATION'S
     STRUGGLE IN THE SECOND WARLD WAR. New York: 1954.

265. Kalvoda, J. CZECHOSLOVAKIA'S ROLE IN SOVIET STRATEGY.
     Washington: 1978.

266. Kasneci, L. TREMPEE DANS LE FEU DE LA LUTTE, BREF APERCU DE
     L'HISTOIRE DE L'ARMEE DE LIBERATION NATIONALE DU PEUPLE
     ALBANAIS (1941-1944). Paris: 1969.

267. Kehrig, M. STALINGRAD - ANALYSE UND DOKUMENTATION. EINER
     SCHLACHT. Stuttgart: 1974.

268. Kerner, R., ed. YUGOSLAVIA. Berkeley: 1949.

269. Kertesz, S.D. DIPLOMACY IN A WHIRLWIND: HUNGARY BETWEEN NAZI
     GERMANY AND THE SOVIET UNION. South Bend: 1956 [1953].

270. _____., ed. EAST CENTRAL EUROPE AND THE WORLD; DEVELOPMENTS
     IN THE POST-STALIN ERA. South Bend: 1962.

271. _____., ed. THE FATE OF EAST CENTRAL EUROPE. South Bend:
     1956.

272. King, R.R. MINORITIES UNDER COMMUNISM; NATIONALITIES AS A
     SOURCE OF TENSION AMONG BALKAN COMMUNIST STATES.
     Cambridge: 1973.

273. King, W.B., & O'Brien, F. THE BALKANS, FRONTIER OF TWO WORLDS.
     New York: 1947.

274. Kinross, Lord (J.P.D. Balfour). THE OTTOMAN CENTURIES: THE RISE
     AND FALL OF THE TURKISH EMPIRE. London: 1977.

275. Kintner, W.R, & Klaiber, W. EASTERN EUROPE AND EUROPEAN
     SECURITY. New York: 1971.

276. Kiraly, B. "The Organization of National Defense During the
     Hungarian Revolution." CEF 14:1 (July 1966), 12-22.

277. _____. "Why the Soviets Need the Warsaw Pact." EE 12:4
     (April 1969), 8-17.

278. Kiz, A. AZ ANTIFASISZTA MAGYAR KATONSI HAGYOMAMANYOKROL 1945.
     Budapest: 1978.

279. Knorr, K.E. THE WAR POTENTIAL OF NATIONS. Princeton: 1956.

280. Kofos, E. NATIONALISM AND COMMUNISM IN MACEDONIA. Salonika:
     1964.

281. Kolarz, W. MYTHS AND REALITIES IN EASTERN EUROPE. London:
     [1946].

282. Korbonski, A. THE WARSAW PACT. New York: 1969.

283. Korom, M. MAGYARORSZAG IDEIGLENES NEMZETI KORMANYA ES A
     FEGYVERSZUNET/1944-1945. Budapest: 1981.

284. Kostich, D.D. THE LAND AND PEOPLE OF THE BALKANS: ALBANIA,
     BULGARIA, YUGOSLAVIA. Rev. ed. Philadelphia: 1973.

285. Kotsch, W. "The Tanks of August 1968." USNIP 95:5 (May 1969,
     86-93.

286. Kourvetaris, G.A. "The Role of the Military in Greek Politics."
     IRHPS 8/3 (August 1971), 91-111.

287. Kousoulos, D.G. REVOLUTION AND DEFEAT: THE STORY OF THE GREEK
     COMMUNIST PARTY. Oxford: 1965.

288. Kovacs, F.W.L. (pseud.) THE UNTAMED BALKANS. New York: 1941.

289. Kovig, B. "The United States and the Hungarian Revolution of 1956: A Case Study of American Policies Towards East Central Europe from 1945 to 1957." Unpublished dissertation at University of London, 1967.

290. Krasniqi, R. "Focus on Albania." ACEN NEWS No. 141 (July-August 1968), 3-13.

291. Kraus, R. EUROPE IN REVOLT. London & New York: [1943].

292. Krizman, B. ANTE PAVELIC I USTASE. Budapest: 1978.

293. Kulic, D. MAKEDONIA I SOCIJALISTICKA REVOLUCIJA U JUGOSLAVIJI. Belgrad: 1979.

294. Kveder, D. "Territorial War: A New Concept of Resistence." FA 32 (1953/54), 91-108.

295. Lampe, J.R., & Jackson, M.R. BALKAN ECONOMIC HISTORY, 1550-1950. Bloomington: 1982.

296. Lane, P.B. "The United States and the Balkan Crisis of 1940-1941." Unpublished doctoral dissertation. University of Washington at Seattle, 1972.

297. Langer, W.L., ed. THE RISE OF EUROPE. 20+ vols. New York: 1936-.

298. Langford, R.V. BRITISH FOREIGN POLICY. Washington: [1942].

299. Larrabee, F.S. BALKAN SECURITY. IISS. London: 1977.

300. Laska, V., ed. WOMEN IN THE RESISTANCE AND IN THE HOLOCAUST: THE VOICES OF EYEWITNESSES. CWS 37. Westport: 1983.

301. Latas, B., Dzelebdzic, M. CETNICKI POKRET DRAZE MIHAILOVICA 1941-1945. Belgrad: 1979.

302. Lederer, I.J., ed. RUSSIA AND THE BALKANS IN RUSSIAN FOREIGN POLICY: ESSAYS IN HISTORICAL PERSPECTIVE. New Haven: 1962.

303. Legrand, E.L.J. BIBLIOGRAPHIE ALBANAISE. Leipzig: 1973.

304. Lehrman, H.A. RUSSIA'S EUROPE. New York: [1947].

305. Leites, N. SOVIET STYLE IN WAR. RCRS. Santa Monica: 1982.

306. Lendvai, P. EAGLES IN THE COBWEBS; NATIONALISM AND COMMUNISM IN THE BALKANS. Garden City: 1969.

307. Lengyel, E. 1000 YEARS OF HUNGARY. New York: 1958.

308. Lewinsohn, R. THE PROFITS OF WAR THROUGH THE AGES. New York: 1979.

309. Lewis, B., Sir. THE EMERGENCE OF MODERN TURKEY. London: 1961.

310. Lewis, J.W. THE STRATEGIC BALANCE IN THE MEDITERRANEAN. FAS 29.
     AEIPPR. 1976.

311. Lincoln, F.F. UNITED STATES AID TO GREECE, 1947-1962.
     Germantown: 1975.

312. Liptai, E., et al. HOSOK. A SZOVJETNIO HOSEI A MAGYARORSZAGI
     FELSZABADITO HARCOKBAN 1944-1945. Budapest: 1981.

313. Omitted.

314. Lockhart, R.H.B., Sir. JAN MASARYK: A PERSONAL MEMOIRE. London:
     [1951].

315. Lodi, A. L'AERONAUTICA ITALIANA NELLA GUERRA DI LIBERAZIONE
     1943-1945. Rome: 1975.

316. Logan, M.Z. COUSINS AND COMMISSARS (AN INTIMATE VISIT TO TITO'S
     YUGOSLAVIA). New York: 1949.

317. Logoreci, A. THE ALBANIANS: EUROPE'S FORGOTTEN SURVIVORS.
     Boulder: 1977.

318. _____. "Albania and China: The Incongruous Alliance." CR
     52:308 (April 1967), 227-231.

319. Loverdo, C. de. LES MAQUIS ROUGE DES BALKAN, 1941-1945. Paris:
     1967.

320. Lowe, J.T. GEOPOLITICS AND WAR: MACKINDER'S PHILOSOPHY OF
     POWER. Washington: c.1981.

321. Lukacs, J.A. THE GREAT POWERS AND EASTERN EUROPE. New York:
     [1953].

322. Luvaas, J. "The Great Military Historians and Philosophers."
     GSUMH. Washington: 1979.

323. Luza, R. "The Communist Party in Czechoslovakia and the Czech
     Resistance, 1939-1945." SR XXVIII No. 4 (December 1969),
     561-576.

324. Macartney, C.A. HUNGARY, A SHORT HISTORY. Chicago: 1962.

325. Macek, V. THE STRUGGLE FOR FREEDOM. University Park & London:
     1968.

326. Mackintosh, M. THE EVOLUTION OF THE WARSAW PACT. ISS. London:
     1969.

327. Magocsi, P.R. THE SHAPING OF A NATIONAL IDENTITY: SUBCARPATHIAN
     RUS', 1848-1948. Cambridge: 1978.

328. Marguerat, P. LE III$^e$ REICH ET LE PETROLE ROUMAIN,
     1938-1940: CONTRIBUTION A L'ETUDE DE LA PENETRATION
     ECONOMIQUE ALLEMANDE DANS LES BALKANS A LA VEILLE ET AU
     DEBUT DE LA SECONDE GUERRE MONDIALE. Leiden: 1977.

329. Marinescu, A., & Romanescu, G. ARMATA ROMANA IN RAZBOIUL
     ANTIHITLERIST. (ALBUM DE SCHEME). Bucharest: 1980.

330. Markus, V. "The Carpato-Ukraine Under Hungarian Occupation,
     (1939-1944)." UQ X (1954), 252-256.

331. Martin, H.J. EAGLES VICTORIOUS: THE OPERATIONS OF THE SOUTH
     AFRICAN FORCES OVER THE MEDITERRANEAN AND EUROPE: IN
     ITALY, THE BALKANS AND THE AEGEAN, AND FROM GIBRALTAR AND
     WEST AFRICA. Cape Town: c.1977.

332. Martin, R.G. THE YUGOSLAV STRUGGLE THROUGH AMERICAN EYES. New
     York: 1944.

333. Masson, P., ed. DICTIONNAIRE DE LA SECONDE GUERRE MONDIALE. 2
     vols. Paris: n.d.

334. Mastny, V. THE CZECHS UNDER NAZI RULE: THE FAILURE OF NATIONAL
     RESISTANCE, 1939-1942. New York & London: 1971.

335. Matei, D. "Officers and Generals in the Membership of the
     Romanian Academy." ARS. Bucharest: 1980.

336. Maule, H. SCOBIE: HERO OF GREECE. THE BRITISH CAMPAIGN 1944-45.
     London: 1975.

337. Mayer, A.J. DYNAMICS OF COUNTER-REVOLUTION IN EUROPE,
     1870-1956: AN ANALYTICAL FRAMEWORK. New York: 1971.

338. McCauley, M., ed. COMMUNIST POWER IN EUROPE, 1944-1949. London:
     1977.

339. McEvedy, C. THE PENQUIN ATLAS OF RECENT HISTORY (EUROPE SINCE
     1815). New York: 1982.

340. McGeoch, I. "The Defence of NATO's Southern Flank." JRUSI
     117:166 (June 1972), 3-10.

341. McNeill, W.H. A WORLD HISTORY. 3rd ed. Oxford: 1979.

342. Mellor, R.E.H. EASTERN EUROPE: A GEOGRAPHY OF THE COMECON
     COUNTRIES. New YOrk: 1975.

343. Meyer, K. BIBLIOGRAPHIE DER ARBEITEN ZUR OSTEUROPAISCHEN
     GESCHICHTE AUS DEN DEUTSCHSPRACHIGEN FACHZEITSCHRIFTEN,
     1858-1964.

344. Miksche, F.O. SECRET FORCES: THE TECHNIQUE OF UNDERGROUND
     MOVEMENTS. London: 1950.

345. Milazzo, M.J. THE CHETNIK MOVEMENT AND THE YUGOSLAV RESISTANCE.
     Baltimore: 1975.

346. Miletic, Antun. ZBORNIK DOKUMENATA I PODATAKA O
     NARODNOOSLOBODILACKOM RATU NARODA JUGOSLAVIJE. 3 vols.
     Belgrad: n.d.

347. Miller, M.L. BULGARIA DURING THE SECOND WORLD WAR. Stanford: 1975.

348. Minkov, M. BULGARIA AND THE ECONOMIC DEVELOPMENT OF THE BALKANS. Sofia: 1962.

349. Misefari, E. LA RESISTENZA DEGLI ALBANESI CONTRO L'IMPERIALISMO FASCISTA. Milan: 1976.

350. Mitchell, R. THE SERBS CHOOSE WAR. Garden City: 1943.

351. Mitrovski, B., ed. THE BULGARIAN ARMY IN YUGOSLAVIA, 1941-1945. Trans. by Kordija Kveder. Belgrad: 1971.

352. Molnar, M. BUDAPEST 1956: A HISTORY OF THE HUNGARIAN REVOLUTION. Trans. by Jennetta Ford. London: 1968.

353. Montgomery, J.F. HUNGARY: THE UNWILLING SATELLITE. New York: 1947.

354. Mooney, P.J. THE SOVIET SUPERPOWER: THE SOVIET UNION, 1945-80. Exeter: 1982.

355. Moore, J.E., ed. JANE'S FIGHTING SHIPS. New York: annual.

356. Moraca, P. THE WAR AND REVOLUTION OF THE PEOPLES OF YUGOSLAVIA, 1941-1945. New York: 1965.

357. Morris, L.P. EASTERN EUROPE SINCE 1945. Exeter: 1984.

358. Motiuk, L., ed. STRATEGIC STUDIES READING GUIDE. w/suppl. Canadian Forces Publications. Ottawa: 1972-.

359. Mowat, C.L., ed. THE SHIFTING BALANCE OF WORLD FORCES 1898-1945. 2d ed. NCMH 12. Cambridge: 1968.

360. Mrazkova, D., & Remes, V. THE RUSSIAN WAR, 1941-1945. New York: 1977 [c.1975].

361. Mucs, S., & Zagoni, E. A MAGYAR NEPHADSEREG TORTENETE 1945-1959. Budapest: 1979.

362. Muller-Hillebrand, B. GERMANY AND ITS ALLIES IN WORLD WAR II: A RECORD OF AXIS COLLABORATION PROBLEMS. Frederick: 1979.

363. Myrdal, J., & Kessle, G. ALBANIA DEFIANT. Trans. by Paul B. Austin. New York: c.1976.

364. Nagy, F. THE STRUGGLE BEHIND THE IRON CORTAIN. Trans. by Stephan K. Swift. New York: 1948.

365. Nagy-Talavera, N.M. THE GREEN SHIRTS AND THE OTHERS: A HISTORY OF FASCISM IN HUNGARY AND RUMANIA. Stanford: 1970.

366. Neck, R., et al. ANSCHLUSS 1938. PROTOKOLL DES SYMPOSIUM IN WIEN AM 14. UND 15. MARZ 1978. Vienna: 1981.

367. Nelson, D.N., ed. SOVIET ALLIES: THE WARSAW PACT AND THE ISSUE OF RELIABILITY. Boulder: 1984.

368. Nemeskurty, I. REQUIEM EGY HADSEREGERT. Budapest: 1982.

369. Nesovic, S. DIPLOMATSKA IGRA OKO JUGOSLAVIJE 1944-1945. Zagreb, Pvro & Stvarnost: 1977.

370. _____. JUGOSLAVIJA-BULGARSKA, RATNO-VREME, 1941-1945. Belgrad & Sarajevo: 1979.

371. Newman, B. BALKAN BACKGROUND. New York: 1945.

372. Nicolae, C., & Ilie, P. BUCURESTIUL IN INSURECTIE. Bucharest: 1975.

373. _____. "The Participation of the Romanian Army in the Anti-Hitler War." PHRA, BHR Monograph 15. Bucharest: 1975.

374. O'Ballance, E. THE GREEK CIVIL WAR, 1944-1949. New York & Washington: [1966].

375. O'Connor, R.G. WAR, DIPLOMACY, AND HISTORY. Washington: 1979.

376. Olivova, V. THE DOOMED DEMOCRACY: CZECHOSLOVAKIA IN A DISRUPTED EUROPE, 1914-38. Trans. by George Theiner. London: 1972.

377. Olteanu, C. THE ROMANIAN ARMED POWER CONCEPT. Bucharest: 1982.

378. Opie, R., et al. THE SEARCH FOR PEACE SETTLEMENTS. Washington: 1951.

379. Oprita, C. "The Development of the Educational System of the Romanian Army Over the Post-War Years." RIHM 46 (1980), 157-166.

380. Orlov, D. THE NAZIS IN THE BALKANS: A CASE STUDY IN TOTALITARIAN POLITICS. Pittsburgh: [1968].

381. OSTERREICH UND EUROPE: FESTGABE FUR HUGO HANTSCH ZUM 70. GEBURTSTAG. Graz, Vienna, & Cologne: 1965.

382. Overy, R.J. THE AIR WAR 1939-1945. London: 1980.

383. Pacor, M. ITALIA E BALCANI DAL RISORGIMENTO ALLA RESISTENZA. Milan: 1968.

384. Padev, M. ESCAPE FROM THE BALKANS. Indianapolis: 1943.

385. Paikert, G.C. THE DANUBE SWABIANS: GERMAN POPULATIONS IN HUNGARY, RUMANIA AND YUGOSLAVIA AND HITLER'S IMPACT ON THEIR PATTERNS. SSL 10. The Hague: 1967.

386. Pajovic, R. KONTRA REVOLUCIJA U CRNOJ GORI. CETNIKI I FEDERALISTICKI POKRET 1941-1945. Titigrad: 1977.

387. Palmer, A.W. THE PENGUIN DICTIONARY OF TWENTIETH-CENTURY HISTORY, 1900-1978. New York: 1979.

389. Pano, N.C. THE PEOPLE'S REPUBLIC OF ALBANIA. Baltimore: 1968.

390. Papacosma, S.V. "The Military Coup d'Etat in Twentieth Century Greece." Paper presented at AHA Conference, New Orleans, 1972.

391. Papagos, A. THE BATTLE OF GREECE, 1940-1941. Athens: 1949.

392. Papandreou, A. DEMOCRACY AT GUNPOINT: THE GREEK FRONT. Garden City: 1970.

393. Parkinson, R. THE ENCYCLOPEDIA OF MODERN WAR. New York: 1977.

394. Pelenyi, J. "The Secret Plan for a Hungarian Government in the West at the Outbreak of World War II." JMH XXXVI No. 2 (June 1964), 170-177.

395. Pentzopoulos, D. THE BALKAN EVCHANGE OF MINORITIES AND ITS IMPACT UPON GREECE. Paris: 1962.

396. Perl, L. YUGOSLAVIA, ROMANIA, BULGARIA; NEW ERA IN THE BALKANS. Camden: [1970].

397. Petersen, P.A., ed. SOVIET POLICY IN THE POST-TITO BALKANS. Washington: [1979?].

398. Petranovic, B. AVNOJ. Belgrad: 1976.

399. Petrovic, S. FREE YUGOSLAVIA CALLING. Ed. & trans. by Joseph C. Peters. New York: 1941.

400. Pines, R., ed. SOVIET STRATEGY IN EUROPE. New York: 1976.

401. Pivka, O. von. THE ARMIES OF EUROPE TODAY. Reading, Berks: 1972.

402. Plasari, N. HISTORIA E LUFTES ANTIFASCHISTE NACIONALCLIRIMTARE TE POPULLIT HQIPTAR. Tirana: 1975-.

403. Pool, I. de S. SATELLITE GENERALS: A STUDY OF MILITARY ELITES IN THE SOVIET SPHERE. Stanford: 1955.

404. Potholm, C.P. STRATEGY AND CONFLICT: THE SEARCH FOR HISTORICAL MALLEABILITY. Frederick: 1979.

405. Omitted.

406. Prcela, J., & Guldescu, S. eds. OPERATION SLAUGHTERHOUSE: EYEWITNESS ACCOUNTS OF POSTWAR MASSACRES IN YUGOSLAVIA. Philadelphia: 1970.

407. Preda, E. "SARITURA DE PISICA": [INSEMNARI DESPRE AL II-LEA RAZBOI MONDIAL]. Bucharest: 1976.

408. Prerardovich, N. von. DIE MILITARISCHE UND SOZIALE HERKUNFT DER GENERALITAT D. DEUTSCHEN HEERES 1. MAI 1944. SMMK 14. Osnabruck: 1978.

409. Preston, R.A., et al. MEN AT ARMS. New York: 1956.

410. Pretty, R.T., ed. JANE'S WEAPONS SYSTEMS. New York: biannual.

411. Prevelakis, E. BRITISH POLICY TOWARDS THE CHANGE OF DYNASTY IN GREECE. Athens: 1953.

412. Pribicevic, S. THE BALKANS AND CENTRAL EUROPE. Three lectures at the Foreign Policy Council meeting, Cleveland, Ohio. December 1938.

413. _____. SPOTLIGHT ON THE BALKANS. New York: 1940.

414. _____. WORLD WITHOUT END; THE SAGA OF SOUTHEASTERN EUROPE. New York: [1939].

415. _____. "The Nazi Drive to the East: Yugoslavia, Rumania, Hungary." FPR XIV No. 15 (October 15, 1938).

416. Pryce-Jones, D. THE HUNGARIAN REVOLUTION. New York: 1970.

417. PW Service of Hungarian Veterans. MAGYAR HARCOSOK BAJTARSI KOGOSSEGE. Munich: 1951.

418. Ra'anan, U. "The USSR and the Middle East: Some Reflections on the Soviet Decision-making Process." ORBIS (Fall 1973), 946-977.

419. Radin, G. ECONOMIC RECONSTRUCTION IN YUGOSLAVIA; A PRACTICAL PLAN FOR THE BALKANS. New York: 1946.

420. Radu, M., ed. EASTERN EUROPE AND THE THIRD WORLD: EAST VS. SOUTH. New York: 1981.

421. Radvanyi, J. HUNGARY AND THE SUPERPOWERS: THE 1956 REVOLUTION AND REALPOLITIK. Stanford: 1972.

422. Rakowska-Harmstone, T., & Gyorgy, A., eds. COMMUNISM IN EASTERN EUROPE. Bloomington: 1979.

423. Rand Corporation. A BIBLIOGRAPHY OF SELECTED RAND PUBLICATIONS. Santa Monica: 1983.

424. Rauchensteiner, M. SPATHERBST 1956. DIE NEUTRALITAT AUF DEM PRUFSTAND. Vienna: 1981.

425. Rausch, J. BIBLIOGRAPHIE ZUR INTERNATIONALEN MILITARISCH-AMTLICHEN KRIEGSGESCHICHTSSCHREIBUNG UBER DEN ZWEITEN WELTKRIEG. Vienna: 1978.

426. Ray, J. THE SECOND WORLD WAR. Exeter: 1977.

427. Reitz, J.T. "The Satellite Armies - A Soviet Asset?" MR (October 1965), 28-35.

428. Remington, R.A. THE WARSAW PACT: CASE STUDIES IN COMMUNIST CONFLICT RESOLUTION. SCRR 17. Cambridge & London: 1971.

411

429. Renn, L. WARFARE: THE RELATION OF WAR TO SOCIETY. New York: 1939.

430. RESISTANCE EUROPIENE. Turin: periodically from 1976.

431. Reynolds, P.A. BRITISH FOREIGN POLICY IN THE INTER-WAR YEARS. London: [1954].

432. Riasanovsky, N. A HISTORY OF RUSSIA. 2nd ed. New York: 1969.

433. Rich, N. HITLER'S WAR AIMS. New York: 1973.

434. RIIA. Information Department. SOUTH-EASTERN EUROPE: A POLITICAL AND ECONOMIC SURVEY. New York: [1972].

435. Ristic, D.N. YUGOSLAVIA'S REVOLUTION OF 1941. HIP. University Park: 1966.

436. Roberts, H.L., ed. THE SATELLITES IN EASTERN EUROPE. Philadelphia: 1958.

437. _____. EASTERN EUROPE: POLITICS, REVOLUTION, AND DIPLOMACY. New York: 1970.

438. Roberts, J.M. EUROPE, 1880-1945. New York: 1967.

439. Roberts, W.R. TITO, MIHAILOVIC AND THE ALLIES, 1941-1945. New Brunswick: 1973.

440. Romania. PARTICIPAREA ROMANIEI LA RAZBOIUL ANTIHITLERIST OGLINDITA IN LITERATURA ISTORICA SI MEMORIALISTICA, IN LITERATURA BELETRISTICA, DRAMATURGIA SI CINEMATIGRAFIA ROMANEASCA. BIBLIOGRAFIE SELECTIVA. Bucharest: 1980.

441. Roucek, J.S. BALKAN POLITICS: INTERNATIONAL RELATIONS IN NO MAN'S LAND. Westport: 1971 [1948].

442. _____. "Rumania, Albania, and Bulgaria. At the End of the Beginning." WAI XV (Spring 1944), 88-101.

443. Sanness, J. EUROPE AND THE BALKANS. PAST TERRITORIAL DISPUTES AND SOCIOPOLITICAL VARIETY. Oslo: 1972.

444. Santoni, A. "Le Functionnement de l'alliance germano-itallienne dans la guerre de Mediterranee." Paper presented at CIMH, Montpellier, September 1981.

445. _____. "The British Knowledge of the German Movements into the Balkans Before the Operations 'Marita' and 'Barbarossa' through the ULTRA Intelligence." Paper presented at CIHM, Bucharest, 1980.

446. Savu, A.G. "Romania's Neutrality at the Start of World War II." PHRA, BHR 15. Bucharest: 1975.

447. _____. PAGES FROM THE HISTORY OF THE ROMANIAN ARMY. BHR 15. Bucharest: 1975.

448. _____. THE ARMY AND THE ROMANIAN SOCIETY. Bucharest: 1980.

449. Scherer, A. SUDOSTEUROPA-DISSERTATIONEN, 1918-1964. EINE BIBLIOGRAPHIE DEUTSCHER, OSTERREICHISCHER UND SCHWEIZERISCHER HOCHSCHULSCHRIFTEN. Graz, Vienna, Cologne & Bohlau: 1968.

450. Schmitthenner, P. KREIG UND KREIGFUHRUNG IM WANDEL DER WELTGESCHICHTE. Potsdam: 1930.

451. Schopflin, G., ed. THE SOVIET UNION AND EASTERN EUROPE; A HANDBOOK. New York & Washington: 1970.

452. Schreiber, G. BALKAN AUS ESTER HAND. GESCHICHTE UND GEGENWART IN BERICHTEN VON AUGENZEUGEN U. ZEITGENOSSEN. Wurzburg: 1971.

453. Scott. W.F. SOVIET SOURCES ON DOCTRINE AND STRATEGY. New York: c.1975.

454. Scott, W.F., & Scott, H.F. THE ARMED FORCES OF THE USSR. 2nd ed. Boulder: 1981.

455. Seaton, A. THE RUSSO-GERMAN WAR. New York & Washington: 1972.

456. Semiryaga, M.I. NEMETSKO-FASHISTSKAYA POLITIKA NATSIONAL'NOGO PORABOSHCHENIYA V OKKUPIROVANNIKH STRANAKH ZAPADNOI I SEVERNOI EVROPII. Moscow: 1980.

457. Serbian National Defense Council of American. THE CRIME OF GENOCIDE (A PLEA FOR THE RATIFICATION OF THE GENOCIDE PACT). Chicago: 1951.

458. Seton-Watson, H. THE EAST EUROPEAN REVOLUTION. 3rd ed. New York: 1961.

459. Shankowsky, L. "Soviet and Satellite Sources on the Ukrainian Insurgent Army." AUAAS IX, Nos. 1-2 (1961), 234-261.

460. Shaw, S.J., & Shaw, E.K. HISTORY OF THE OTTOMAN EMPIRE AND MODERN TURKEY. Vol. 2: REFORM, REVOLUTION AND REPUBLIC: THE RISE OF MODERN TURKEY, 1808-1975. Cambridge, London and New York: 1977.

461. Shepherd, W.R. HISTORICAL ATLAS. 8th ed. London: 1956.

462. Shirer, W.L. THE RISE AND FALL OF THE THIRD REICH: A HISTORY OF NAZI GERMANY. New York: 1960.

463. Shirk, P.R. "Warsaw Treaty Organization." MR 19:5 (May 1969), 28-37.

464. Sick, G.G. "Russia and the West in the Mediterranean: Perspectives for the 1970's." NWCR (June 1970), 49-67.

465. Simon, J. COHESION AND DISSENSION IN EASTERN EUROPE: SIX CRISES. FPI. New York: 1983.

413

466. Singer, J.D., & Small, M. THE WAGES OF WAR: A STATISTICAL HANDBOOK. New York. 1972.

467. Singer, J.D., et al, eds. EXPLAINING WAR: SELECTED PAPERS FROM THE CORRELATES OF WAR PROJECT. Beverly Hills: c.1979.

468. Sinor, D. HISTORY OF HUNGARY. New York: 1961.

469. SIPRI. ARMS TRADE REGISTERS: THE ARMS TRADE WITH THE THIRD WORLD. Cambridge: 1975.

470. Sirkov, D. LA POLITIQUE ETRANGERE BULGARE, 1938-1941. MONOGRAPHIE. Sofia: 1979.

471. Slijepcevic, D. THE MACEDONIAN QUESTION: THE STRUGGLE FOR SOUTHERN SERBIA. Chicago: 1958.

472. Smith, P.C., & Walker, E. WAR IN THE AEGEAN. London: 1974.

473. Snyder, L.L. LOUIS SNYDER'S HISTORICAL GUIDE TO WORLD WAR II. Westport: 1981.

474. Sokolovsky, V.D. SOVIET MILITARY STRATEGY. Ed. by Harriet Fast Scott. 3rd ed. New York: 1975 [1968].

475. THE SOVIET-YUGOSLAV DISPUTE: TEXT OF THE PUBLISHED CORRESPONDENCE. London & New York: 1948.

476. Spector, S., & Legters, L., eds. CHECKLIST OF PAPERBOUND BOOKS ON RUSSIA AND EAST EUROPE. 2nd ed., rev. Albany: 1966.

477. Spencer, F.A. WAR AND POST-WAR GREECE. Washington: 1952.

478. Stafford, D. BRITAIN AND EUROPEAN RESISTANCE 1940-1945. A SURVEY OF THE SPECIAL OPERATIONS EXECUTIVE. London: 1980.

479. Stan, N. REFLECTARI ISTORICO-LITERARE ALE REZISTENTEI ROMANESTI. Bucharest: 1979.

480. Starr, R.F. "The East European Alliance System." NIP (September 1964).

481. _____. THE COMMUNIST REGIMES IN EASTERN EUROPE. HIP. Stanford: 1971.

482. Stavrianos, L.S. THE BALKANS SINCE 1453. New York: 1958.

483. _____. BALKAN FEDERATION; A HISTORY OF THE MOVEMENT TOWARD BALKAN UNITY IN MODERN TIMES. Northhampton: [1944].

484. Stephensen, G. RUSSIA FROM 1812 TO 1945: A HISTORY. New York & Washington: 1970.

485. Stering, E. von. JEDER WAS EIN STUCK VON UNS; LEBEN UND KAMPF EINER KOMPANIE AUF IHREM WEG VON ATTIKA NACH SARAJEWO, HERBST 1944. Neckarmund, 1959.

486. Sterling, C. THE MASARYK CASE. New York, Evanston & London: 1979.

487. Stern, L. "Bitter Lessons: How We Failed in Cyprus." FP (Summer 1975), 34-78.

488. Stillman, E.O. THE BALKANS. New York: 1964.

489. Stokesbury, J.L. A SHORT HISTORY OF WORLD WAR II. New York: 1980.

490. Strachen, H. EUROPEAN ARMIES AND THE CONDUCT OF WAR. Winchester: 1983.

491. Sudjic, M. YUGOSLAVIA IN ARMS. London: 1942.

492. Sugar, P.F. ETHNIC DIVERSITY AND CONFLICT IN EASTERN EUROPE. Santa Barbara: 1980.

493. Sugar, P.F., & Treadgold, D.W. HISTORY OF EAST CENTRAL EUROPE. 11 vols. Seattle & London: 1974-.

494. Sula, A.B. ALBANIA'S STRUGGLE FOR INDEPENDENCE. New York: 1967.

495. Summerscale, P.W. THE EAST EUROPEAN PREDICAMENT. New York: 1982.

496. Suryani, L. A MAGYORORSZAGI TANACSKOZTARSASAG BELYEGKIADAAINAK ES A VOROS HADSEREG TABORI POSTAJANSK TORTENETE. Budapest: 1978.

497. Szabo, A. A MAGYAR FORRADALMI HONVED KARTHATALOM 1956, NOVEMBRE-1957, JUNIUS.

498. Szajkowski, B. THE ESTABLISHMENT OF MARXIST REGIMES. London: 1982.

499. Szinai, M., & Szucs., eds. THE CONFIDENTIAL PAPERS OF ADMIRAL HORTHY. Budapest: 1965.

500. Sztaray, Z., comp. BOOKS ON THE HUNGARIAN REVOLUTION: A BIBLIOGRAPHY. Brussels: 1960.

501. Talmon, J.L. THE ORIGINS OF TOTALITARIAN DEMOCRACY. London: 1952.

502. Taylor, J.W.R., et al, eds. JANE'S ALL WORLD AIRCRAFT. New York: 1972-.

503. Thayer, C.W. GUERRILLA. London: c.1963.

504. _____. BEARS IN THE CAVIAR. Philadelphia: [1951].

505. _____. HANDS ACROSS THE CAVIAR. Philadelphia: [1952].

506. Theodoracopolous, T. THE GREEK UPHEAVAL: KINGS, DEMOGOGUES, BAYONETS. London: 1976.

507. Thomas., D. NAZI VICTORY: CRETE 1941. New York: 1972.

508. Toderascu, C. "The Romanian Army's Participation in the
     Reconstruction of the National Economy in the 1944-1947
     Period." ARS. Bucharest: 1980.

509. Todorov, K. BALKAN FIREBRAND, THE AUTOBIOGRAPHY OF A REBEL¼
     SOLDIER AND STATESMAN. Chicago: 1943.

510. Tomasevich, J. THE CHETNIKS: WAR AND REVOLUTION IN YUGOSLAVIA,
     1941-1945. Stanford: 1975.

511. Topp, H.D. DIE ALBANISCHE MILITARFUHRUNG UND DIE BEZIEHUNGEN
     ZWISCHEN DER VR ALBANIEN, DER VR CHINA UND DEN USA.
     Cologne-Ehrenfeld: 1975?

512. Toynbee, A.J. THE WESTERN QUESTION IN GREECE AND TURKEY. New
     York: 1970.

513. Toynbee, A.J., & Toynbee, V.M. THE REALIGNMENT OF EUROPE. RIIA.
     New York: 1955.

514. Treholt, A. "Europe and the Greek Dictatorship." In GREECE
     UNDER MILITARY RULE, R. Clogg & G. Yannopolous, eds. New
     York: 1972.

515. Trouton, R. PEASANT RESISTANCE IN YUGOSLAVIA, 1900-1950.
     London: 1952.

516. Turkiye Cumhuriyeti, Maarif Vekaleti. ISLAM ANSIKLOPEDISI.
     Istanbul & Ankara: 1940-.

517. United States. THE GERMAN CAMPAIGN IN RUSSIA - PLANNING AND
     OPERATIONS (1940-1942). DA Pamphlet No. 2-261a. March
     1955.

518. _____. THE GERMAN CAMPAIGN IN THE BALKANS (SPRING 1941). DA
     Pamphlet No. 20-260. November 1953.

519. _____. GERMAN ANTIGUERRILLA OPERATIONS IN THE BALKANS
     (1941-1944). DA Pamphlet No. 20-243. August 1954.

520. _____. OPERATIONS OF ENCIRCLED FORCES: GERMAN EXPERIENCES
     IN RUSSIA. DA Pamphlet 20-234. January 1952.

521. _____. CASE STUDY IN GUERRILLA WARFARE: GREECE DURING WORLD
     WAR II. SORO. 1961.

522. _____. COMMUNIST EASTERN EUROPE: ANALYTIC SURVEY OF
     LITERATURE. 1971.

523. _____. OSS/STATE DEPARTMENT INTELLIGENCE AND RESEARCH
     REPORTS. 14 parts on microfilm. Frederick: n.d.

524. _____. CONFIDENTIAL U.S. DIPLOMATIC POST RECORDS: RUSSIA
     AND THE SOVIET UNION. 3 parts on microfilm. Frederick:
     n.d.

525. _____. RECORDS OF THE JOINT CHIEFS OF STAFF. 2 parts on microfilm. Frederick: n.d.

526. _____. SPECIAL STUDIES SERIES. 3 parts, with 2 supplements, on microfilm. Frederick: n.d.

527. _____. CENTRAL INTELLIGENCE AGENCY RESEARCH REPORTS. 3 parts on microfilm. Frederick: n.d.

528. _____. U.S. MILITARY INTELLIGENCE REPORTS: GERMANY, 1919-1941. On microfilm. Frederick: n.d.

529. _____. Military Intelligence Division, U.S. War Department. GERMAN MILITARY INTELLIGENCE, 1939-1945. Frederick: 1984 [1983].

530. _____. U.S. MILITARY INTELLIGENCE REPORTS: THE SOVIET UNION, 1919-1941. Frederick: n.d.

531. _____. HANDBOOK ON THE WARSAW PACT ARMIES OF EASTERN EUROPE. DIA AP-1-220-3-7-66-INT. Washington: 1966.

532. _____. Central Intelligence Agency. EASTERN EUROPE. Washington: 1972.

533. _____. US Army Europe Historical Division. GUIDE TO FOREIGN MILITARY STUDIES, 1945-54: CATALOG AND INDEX. c.1955.

534. USSR. ISTORIYA VTOROI MIROVOI VOINII 1939-1945 GG. 9 vols. Moscow: 1973-.

535. _____. SOVETSKII SOYUZ I BOR'BA NARODOV TSENTRAL'NOI I YUGOVOSTOCHNOI EVROPY ZA CVOBODY I NEZAVISIMOST' 1941-1945 GG. Moscow: 1978.

536. _____. VELIKAYA POBEDA 1941-1945. RECOMENDATEL'NYI BIBLIOGRAFICHESKII UKAZATEL'. Moscow: 1979.

537. _____. SOVETSKAYA VOENNAYA ENTSIKLOPEDIYA. 8 vols. Moscow: 1976.

538. _____. SOVETSKO-BOLGARSKIE OTNOSHENIYA I SVYAZI. DOKUMENTY I MATERIALY. Vol. 2: SENTYABR' 1944-Dekabr' 1958. Moscow: 1981.

539. Vago, B. THE SHADOW OF THE SWASTIKA: THE RISE OF FASCISM AND ANTISEMITISM IN THE DANUBE BASIN, 1936-1939. London: 1975.

540. _____. "Popular Fronts: Popular Fronts in the Balkans." JCH 5:3 (July 1970), 2-157.

541. Vagts, A. A HISTORY OF MILITARISM. New ed. New York: 1959.

542. Vali, F.A. RIFT AND REVOLT IN HUNGARY; NATIONALISM VERSUS COMMUNISM. Cambridge: 1961.

543. Van Creveld, M.L. SUPPLYING WAR: LOGISTICS FROM WALLENSTEIN TO PATTON. New York: 1977.

544. _____. HITLER'S STRATEGY, 1940-1941: THE BALKAN CLUE. London: 1973.

545. Vandevoorde, P. PARAS DU MONDE ENTIER. Brussels: 1981.

546. Vatikiotis, P.J. "Greece and the Crisis in the Mediterranean." MILLENIUM IV:4 (Spring 1975), 75-81.

547. Vaughan, R. TWENTIETH CENTURY EUROPE: PATHS TO UNITY. New York: 1979.

548. Vigor, P.H. SOVIET BLITZKRIEG THEORY. New York: 1983.

549. Vital, D. THE SURVIVAL OF SMALL STATES: STUDIES IN SMALL POWER/GREAT POWER CONFLICT. Toronto: 1971.

550. Von der Porten, E. THE GERMAN NAVY IN WORLD WAR II. New York: 1969.

551. Vucinich, W.S. "Sovietization in the Balkans." CH XXVI (June 1954), 339-346.

552. Vukcevic, R. RAZVOJ PRIVREDE CRNE GORE. Titograd: 1974.

553. Vukmanovic-Tempo, S. BORBA ZA BALKAN. Zagreb: 1981.

554. _____. REVOLUCIJA KOJA TECE: MEMOARI. 2 vols. Belgrad: 1971.

555. Omitted.

556. Wagner, F.S., ed. THE HUNGARIAN REVOLUTION IN PERSPECTIVE. Washington: 1967.

557. Walichnowski, T. BALCANICA: GUIDE TO THE POLISH ARCHIVES RELATIVE TO THE HISTORY OF THE BALKAN COUNTRIES. Warsaw: 1979.

558. Ward, H. WORLD POWERS IN THE TWENTIETH CENTURY. Exeter: 1978.

559. "The Warsaw Pact." MR 47:10 (October 1967), 18-21.

560. Weber, E.J., ed. TWENTIETH CENTURY EUROPE. St. Louis: 1980.

561. _____. EUROPE SINCE 1715: A MODERN HISTORY. New York: 1972.

562. Weiker, W.F. THE TURKISH REVOLUTION, 1960-61: ASPECTS OF MILITARY POLITICS. Washington: 1963.

563. West, R.(Pseud.) BLACK LAMB AND GREY FALCON. New York: 1937.

564. Westwood, J.N. ENDURANCE AND ENDEAVOUR: RUSSIAN HISTORY, 1812-1980. 2nd ed. New York: 1982.

565. Whetten, L.L. THE SOVIET PRESENCE IN THE EASTERN MEDITERRANEAN. New York: 1971.

566. _____. "The Military Consequences of Mediterranean Super Power Parity." NME (November 1971), 14-25.

567. White, L. BALKAN CAESAR; TITO VERSUS STALIN. New York: 1951.

568. _____. THE LONG BALKAN NIGHT. New York: 1944.

569. WHO WERE THE ARMIES? AXIS ORDERS OF BATTLE, 1939-1945: GERMAN
     ARMY. 4 vols.; SOUTHEASTERN EUROPE AXIS. 2 vols.; SOVIET
     UNION. 1 vol. Allentown: n.d.

570. Wiener, F. THE ARMIES OF THE WARSAW PACT NATIONS. 3rd ed., rev.
     Vienna: 1981.

571. _____. PARTISANENKAMPF AM BALKAN: DIE ROLLE DES
     PARTISANENKAMPFS IN D. JUGOSLAWISCHEN LANDESVERTEIDIGUNG.
     Vienna: [1976].

572. _____. DIE ARMEEN DER NEUTRALEN UND BLOCKFREIEN STAATEN
     EUROPAS. ORGANISATION- KRIEGSBILD- WAFFEN UND GERAT.
     Vienna: 1978.

573. Wiener, J.G. THE ASSASSINATION OF HEYDRICH. New York: 1969.

574. Wilson, D., Sir. TITO'S YUGOSLAVIA. Cambridge: 1980.

575. Wiskemann, E. UNDECLARED WAR. London: 1940.

576. Wolfe, E.R. PEASANT WARS OF THE TWENTIETH CENTURY. London: 1971
     [1969].

577. Wolfe, R.L. THE BALKANS IN OUR TIME. Rev ed. Cambridge: 1974.

578. Wolfe, T.W. SOVIET POWER AND EUROPE, 1945-1970. Baltimore &
     London: 1970.

579. _____. "The Warsaw Pact in Evolution." TWT 22:5 (May 1966),
     191-198.

580. Woodhouse, C.M. THE STRUGGLE FOR GREECE, 1941-1949. London:
     1976.

581. _____. KARAMANLIS: THE RESTORER OF GREEK DEMOCRACY. New
     York: 1983.

582. _____. APPLE OF DISCORD. London & New York: 1948.

583. Woodruff, W. THE STRUGGLE FOR WORLD POWER, 1500-1980. New York:
     1981.

584. Wright, G. THE ORDEAL OF TOTAL WAR, 1939-1945. New York: 1968.

585. Wright, Q. THE STUDY OF WAR. London & Chicago: 1965 [1942].

586. Xydis, S.G. "The Secret Anglo-Soviet Agreement on the Balkans
     of October 8, 1944." JCEA XV (October 1955), 248-271.

587. _____. GREECE AND THE GREAT POWERS, 1944-1947: PRELUDE TO
     THE "TRUMAN DOCTRINE." Salonika: 1963.

588. _____. "Coups and Countercoups in Greece, 1967-1973." PSQ 89:3 (Fall 1974), 507-538.

589. Yannopoulos, G.N. "The Tradition of Dictatorship." TLS 3844 (14 November 1975), 1367.

590. Yugoslavia. SRBIJA U RATU I REVOLUCIJE, 1941-1945. Belgrad: 1976.

591. _____., Institute of Military History. 1941-1942. U SVEDOCANSTVIMA UCESNIKA NARODNOOSLOBODILACKE BORBE. Belgrad: 1975.

592. _____. TITOVE ISTORIJSKE ODLUKE. Belgrad: 1978.

593. _____. THE LIBERATION STRUGGLE OF THE YUGOSLAV PEOPLES. Trans. by Z. Spaleta. Belgrad: 1961.

594. _____. NARODNOOSLOBODILACKI POKRET NOP BEOGRADA 1941-1944. Belgrad: 1974.

595. Zaharia, G., et al. THE ANTI-FASCIST RESISTANCE IN THE NORTH-EAST OF TRANSYLVANIA. BHR Studies No. 61. Bucharest: 1979.

596. _____. INSURECTIA POPORULUI ROMAN DIN AUGUST 1944. Bucharest: 1979.

597. Zakythinos, D.A. THE MAKING OF MODERN GREECE. Trans. by K.R. Johnson. Totowa: 1976.

598. Zeman, Z. THE MASARYKS: THE MAKING OF CZECHOSLOVAKIA. New York: 1976.

599. Zhadov, A.S. CHETYRE GODA VOINY. Moscow: 1978.

600. Zhilin, P.A. THE SECOND WORLD WAR AND OUR TIME. PCW 69. Moscow: 1978.

601. _____. "Some Problems of Counteroffensive in Wars of the 19th-20th Centuries." CIHM, Sandhurst, 1974.

602. Zinner, P.E. REVOLUTION IN HUNGARY. New York: 1962.

603. _____. COMMUNIST STRATEGY AND TACTICS IN CZECHOSLOVAKIA, 1918-48. New York & London: 1963.

604. Zischka, A. THE OTHER EUROPEANS. London: 1962.

605. Zoppo, C. "Soviet Ships in the Mediterranean and the U.S.-Soviet Confrontation in the Middle East." ORBIS (Spring 1970), 109-128.

## ADDITIONS

606. Ropp, T. WAR IN THE MODERN WORLD. Durham: 1959.

607. Dupuy, R.E., Dupuy, T.N. THE ENCYCLOPEDIA OF MILITARY HISTORY. Rev. ed. New York: 1977 [1970].

608. Zook, D.H., & Higham, R. A SHORT HISTORY OF WARFARE. New York: 1966.

609. Rundle, R.N. INTERNATIONAL AFFAIRS 1890-1939. New York: 1979.

610. _____. INTERNATIONAL AFFAIRS 1939-1975. New York: 1981.

611. Dornberg, J. MUNICH 1923: THE STORY OF HITLER'S FIRST GRAB FOR POWER. New York: c.1982.

612. Hillgruber, A. HITLER, KONIG CAROL UND MARSCHALL ANTONESCU: DIE DEUTSCH-RUMANISCHEN BEZIEHUNGEN, 1939-1944. Wiesbaden: 1954.

613. Biber, D. NACIZEM I NEMCI V JUGOSLAVIJI, 1933-1941. Lyubyana: 1966.

614. Armajani, Y. MIDDLE EAST PAST AND PRESENT. Englewood Cliffs: 1970.

615. Peretz, D. THE MIDDLE EAST TODAY. 2nd ed. New York: 1971 [1963].

616. Seton-Watson, H. EASTERN EUROPE BETWEEN THE WARS, 1918-1941. 3rd ed. rev. New York, Evanston & London: 1967 [1945].

617. Korbel, J. THE COMMUNIST SUBVERSION OF CZECHOSLOVAKIA, 1938-1948; THE FAILURE OF COEXISTENCE. Princeton: 1959.

618. Kennan, G.F. FROM PRAGUE AFTER MUNICH: DIPLOMATIC PAPERS, 1938-1940. Princeton: 1968.

619. Erickson, J. THE SOVIET HIGH COMMAND. New York: 1962.

620. RUSSIA, U.S.S.R., EASTERN EUROPE: ALPHABETICAL CUMULATIVE CATALOGUE. Cumulative IDC Catalogue. Zug: nd.

621. Hoover Institute. PATRIOT OR TRAITOR: THE CASE OF GENERAL MIHAILOVICH. PROCEEDINGS AND REPORT OF THE COMMISSION OF INQUIRY OF THE COMMITTEE FOR A FAIR TRIAL FOR DRAJA MIHAILOVICH. HIP 191. Intro. by David Martin. Stanford: 1978.

622. Giurescu, C.C., et al. CHRONOLOGICAL HISTORY OF ROMANIA. Bucharest: 1972.

623. Stefanescu, S., ed. ENCICLOPEDIA ISTORIOGRAFIEI ROMANESTI. Bucharest: 1978.

624. Romania. DOCUMENTE PRIVIND ISTORIA MILITARA A POPORULUI ROMAN. Vols. 1-6. Bucharest: 1977-1980.

625. _____. INSURECTIA DIN AUGUST 1944 SI SEMNIFICATIA EI ISTORICA. Bucharest: 1974.

626. United States. Department of Army. PARTISAN WARFARE IN THE
     BALKANS. Orig. publ. as "Partisan Warfare in the Mountains
     Based On Experiences in Greece and Southern Albania."
     Historical Division, European Command. 1950.

627. _____. Foreign Area Studies, The American University. AREA
     HANDBOOKS: ALBANIA. DA Pamph. 550-98, 1971; BULGARIA. DA
     Pamph. 550-168, 1974; CZECHOSLOVAKIA. DA Pamph. 550-158,
     1972; GREECE. DA Pamph. 550-87, 1977; HUNGARY. DA Pamph.
     550-165, 1973; ROMANIA. DA Pamph. 550-160, 1972; TURKEY.
     DA Pamph. 550-80, 1970; YUGOSLAVIA. DA Pamph. 550-99,
     1973.

628. Brzezinski, Z.K. THE SOVIET BLOC: UNITY AND CONFLICT. Rev. ed.
     New York: 1960.

629. Brown, J.F. THE NEW EASTERN EUROPE: THE KHRUSHCHEV ERA AND
     AFTER. New York, Washington, & London: 1966.

630. United States. Department of State. PEOPLE'S REPUBLIC OF
     ALBANIA. Background Notes No. 8217. February 1969.

631. Jaschke, G. DIE TURKEI IN DEN JAHREN 1942-1951. Wiesbaden:
     1955.

632. Goerlitz, W. PAULUS AND STALINGRAD. New York: 1963.

633. Ziemke, E.F. STALINGRAD TO BERLIN: THE GERMAN DEFEAT IN THE
     EAST. Washington: 1968.

634. Mayes, S. CYPRUS AND MAKARIOS. London: 1960.

635. Stephens, R. CYPRUS: A PLACE OF ARMS. London & New York: 1966.

636. Xydis, S.G. CYPRUS: CONFLICT AND RECONCILIATION, 1954-1958.
     Columbus: 1967.

637. Rusinow, D.I. YUGOSLAVIA AND STALIN'S SUCCESSORS, 1968-69.
     Hanover, 1969.

638. Romania. STUDII DE ISTORIE SI TEORIE MILITARA. RETROSPECTIVE
     ISTORICE ANALIZE CONTEMPORANE. Bucharest: 1980.

639. _____. LA DEFENSE NATIONALE DANS LA CONCEPTION ROUMAINE.
     Bucharest: 1976.

640. Deakin, F.W.D. THE EMBATTLED MOUNTAIN. New York & London: 1971.

641. Gedye, G.E. BETRAYAL IN CENTRAL EUROPE (FALLEN BASTIONS). New
     York: 1938.

# ABBREVIATIONS

The following list of abbreviations and acronyms are used as a practical means of conserving space. Standard or common abbreviations are used whenever possible. Except at the beginnings of sentences or notes these abbreviations are used throughout the text and bibliographical sections of this book.

| ABBREVIATION | PUBLICATION OR ORGANIZATION |
|---|---|
| AAAPSS | Annals of the American Academy of Political and Social Sciences |
| AAASS | American Association for the Advancement of Slavic Studies |
| ABREES | American Bibliography of Russian and East European Studies |
| ACFA | American Council on Foreign Affair |
| AD | Army Digest |
| AEIPPR | American Enterprise Institute for Public Policy Research |
| AFS | Armed Forces and Society |
| AHA | American Historical Association |
| AHR | American Historical Review |
| AJIL | American Journal of International Law |
| AMSL | Aldershot Military Society Lectures |
| ARS | The Army and the Romanian Society |
| AUAAS | Annals of the Ukrainian Academy of Arts and Sciences |
| BCSSC | Brooklyn College Studies on Society in Change |
| BHR | Bibliotheca Historica Romaniae |
| BJRL | Bulletin of the John Ryland Library |
| BMO | Bibliographische Mitteilungen des Osteuropa |
| BR | Bulgarian Review |
| BS | Balkan Studies |
| BSOAS | Bulletin of the School of Oriental and African Studies |
| BTTD | Begelere Turk Tarih Dergisi |
| BWS | Bartholomew's World Series |
| CaMH | Cambridge Medieval History |
| CEEASL | Communist East Europe Analytic Survey of Literature |
| CEF | Central European Federalist |

| | |
|---|---|
| CEIP | Carnegie Endowment for International Peace |
| CH | Current History |
| CHI | Cambridge History of Islam |
| CHJ | Cambridge Historical Journal |
| CHR | Catholic Historical Review |
| CIA | Central Intelligence Agency |
| CIHM | Commission International d'Histoire Militaire |
| CIHS | Congress of Historical Sciences |
| CL | Convorbiri Literare |
| CMH | Contributions in Military History |
| CPHEI | Conference Permanente des Hautes Etude Internationale |
| CR | Croatian Review |
| CUSL | Columbia University Studies in Libraries |
| CUSM | Colburn's United Services Magazine |
| CWS | Contributions to Women's Studies |
| DA | Dissertation Abstracts |
| DHME | Documentary History of Modern Europe |
| DHWC | Documentary History of Western Civilization |
| DIA | Defense Intelligence Agency |
| EABS | Edition de l'Academie Bulgare des Sciences |
| EARSR | Editura Academici Republicii Socialiste Romania |
| EB | Etudes Balkaniques |
| EE | East Europe |
| EEM | East European Monographs |
| EDQR | Etudes Documentaires sur la Question Roumaines |
| EEQ | East European Quarterly |
| EH | Etudes Historiques |
| EHH | Etudes Historiques Hongroises |
| EHR | English Historical Review |
| EI | Encyclopedia of Islam |
| FAS | Foreign Affairs Studies |
| FDSP | Facolta di Scienze Politiche, Rome |
| FH | Feuilles d'Histoire |
| FILE | File din Istoria Militara a Poporului Roman |
| FMES | Foundations of Modern Europe Series |
| FP | Foreign Policy |
| FPI | Foreign Policy Issues |
| FRP | Foreign Policy Report |
| FSEH | Forum Series in European History |
| GPO | Government Printing Office |
| GSUMH | Guide to the Study and Use of Military History |
| GSW | Geschichte der Stadt Wien |
| HECE | History of East Central Europe Series |

| | |
|---|---|
| HES | History of Europe Series |
| HHM | Harvard Historical Monographs |
| Hist J | History Journal |
| HIP | Hoover Institute Publications |
| HMCH | Hidryma Meleton Chersonou tou Haimou |
| HTD | Harp Tarihi Dairesi |
| HUS | Harvard Ukrainian Series |
| HZ | Historische Zeitschrift |
| | |
| IA | Islam Antsiklopedisi |
| IAM | Istanbul Archaeological Museum |
| IBS | Institute of Balkan Studies |
| IISS | International Institute For Strategic Studies |
| IRHPS | International Review of History and Political Science |
| ISC | Institute for the Study of Conflict |
| ISS | Institute of Strategic Studies, London |
| ISSS | Illinois Studies in Social Studies |
| | |
| JAOS | Journal of the American Oriental Society |
| JCEA | Journal of Central European Affairs |
| JCH | Journal of Contemporary History |
| JES | Journal of European Studies |
| JMH | Journal of Modern History |
| JMSI | Journal of the Military Services Institute |
| JRCAS | Journal of the Royal Central Asian Society |
| JRUSI | Journal of the Royal United Services Institute |
| JWH | Journal of World History |
| | |
| KCA | Keesing's Contemporary Archives |
| KSU | Kansas State University |
| | |
| LECS | Library of European Civilization Series |
| LMM | Lippincott's Monthly Magazine |
| LSSEES | London School of Slavonic and East European Studies |
| LWC | Library of World Civilization |
| | |
| MA | Military Affairs |
| MEA | Middle East Affairs (St. Anthony's Papers) |
| MEJ | Middle East Journal |
| MES | Middle East Studies |
| MGM | Militar-geschichteliche Mitteilungen |
| MIOG | Mitteilungen des Instituts fur Osterreichische Geschichts-Forschung |
| MR | Military Review |
| MS | Militarhistorische Schriftenreihe |
| MSOS | Mitteilungen des Seminars fur Orientalische Sprachen |
| | |
| NAR | North American Review |

| NCMH | New Cambridge Modern History |
| NHME | Norton History of Modern Europe Series |
| NME | New Middle East |
| NR | New Review |
| NWCR | Naval War College Review |
| | |
| OCMH | Office of the Chief of Military History, Department of Army |
| OERP | Office of External Research Papers, Department of State |
| OGL | Osterreich in Geschichte und Literatur |
| OSDIRR | OSS/State Department Intelligence and Research Reports |
| | |
| PBA | Proceedings of the British Academy |
| PC | Problems of Communism |
| PCRI | Papers on the Centennial of Romanian Independence |
| PCW | Problems of the Contemporary World |
| PEC | Problems in European Civilization Series |
| PEEI | Publications of the East European Institute (Munich) |
| PEH | Problems in European History Series |
| PHRA | Pages From the History of the Romanian Army |
| PIC | Problems in Civilization |
| PMHRP | Pages From the Military History of the Romanian People |
| PNYSHS | Proceedings of the New York State Historical Society |
| PRASGI | Proceeding of the Royal Asiatic Society of Great Britain and Ireland |
| | |
| RCRS | Rand Corporation Research Study |
| REES | Russian and East European Studies |
| REHPB | Recherches et Etudes sur l'Histoire ou Peuple Bulgare |
| REIOP | Royal Engineer Institute, Occasional Papers |
| RESEE | Revue des Etudes Sud-Est Europeens |
| RHMC | Revue d'Histoire Moderne et Contemporaire |
| RIEB | Revue Internationale des Etudes Balkaniques |
| RIFA | Royal Institute of Foreign Affairs |
| RIHM | Revue Internationale d'Histoire Militaire |
| RIIA | Royal Institute of International Affairs |
| RME | Rise of Modern Europe Series |
| RMW | Revolutions in the Modern World Series |
| RO | Rivista Orientalni |
| RR | Russian Review |
| RRH | Revue Roumaine d'Histoire |
| RSO | Revista Studi Orientali |

426

| | |
|---|---|
| RUSI | Royal United Services Institute |
| | |
| SA | Sudosteuropaische Arbeiten |
| SAV | Studien zur Auslandeskunde, Vorderarien |
| S&CED | South and Central European Division, Library of Congress |
| SCRR | Studies in Communism, Revisionism, and Revolution |
| SDW | Studies and Documents on the War |
| SEER | Slavonic and East European Review |
| SEES | Etudes Slaves et Est-Europeens |
| SEH | Structure of European History Series |
| SES | Southeast Europe Series |
| SHBF | Southern Hungary and Balkan Studies |
| SI | Studia Islamica |
| SIECE | Studies of the Institute of East Central Europe, Columbia University |
| SIHC | Studies in Islamic History and Civilization. Scripta Hierosolymitana |
| SIPRI | Stolkholm International Peace Research Institute |
| SMMK | Studien z. Militargeschichte, Militarwiss, und Konflictforschung |
| SOB | Sudosteuropa Bibliographie |
| SOF | Sudost Forschungen |
| SOHMW | Short Oxford History of the Modern World |
| SoR | Social Research |
| SORO | Special Operations Research Office |
| SR | Slavic Review |
| SREEH | Studies in Russian and East European History |
| SSL | Studies in Social Life |
| StEH | Studies in European History Series |
| SY | Slavic Yearbook |
| | |
| TAD | Tarih Arastirmalari Dergisi |
| TAPS | Transactions of the American Philosophical Society |
| TCAAS | Transactions of the Connecticut Academy of Arts and Sciences |
| TD | Tarihi Dergisi |
| THSA | Turkish Historical Society of Ankara |
| TK | Turk Kulturu |
| TM | Tarihi Mecmuasi |
| TPQ | The Political Quarterly |
| TRET | Turcica: Revue d'Etudes Turques |
| TRTI | The Road To Independence |
| TWT | The World Today |
| | |
| UAS | Uralic & Altaic Series |
| ULSEE | University of London Slavonic and East European Series |

| | |
|---|---|
| UNR | United Nations Review |
| UNS | United Nations Series |
| UQ | Ukrainian Quarterly |
| USDS | United States Department of State |
| USM | United Services Magazine |
| USMHI | United States Army Military History Institute |
| USNIP | United States Naval Institute Proceedings |
| VI | Voprosy Istorii |
| WaG | Die Welt al Geschichte |
| WAI | World Affairs Interpreter |
| WE | The World of Europe |
| WI | Welt des Islam |
| WP | World Politics |
| WSECE | War and Society in East Central Europe |
| YREES | Yale Russian and East European Studies |
| ZHVS | Zeitschrift des historischen Vereins fur Steiermark |

# INDEX OF SUBJECTS

This index is established using the most frequently encountered forms of the subject titles or words. Where alternate usages are common, the other forms are also indicated.

Abbas, Shah of Persia, 96
Abdalla Pasha, 276
Abdulaziz, 233
Abdul Hamid I (Abdulhamit I), 142, 144, 147
Abdul Hamid II (Abdulhamit II), 233, 242, 294
Abyssinian Affair, 366
Acre, occupied, 188
Adolphus, Gustavus, 92
Adrianople, seizure of, 38; capital of Musa, 44; Truce of, 75, Treaty
   of, 184, "... Affair," 130; fall of, 296; recapture of, 298
Afghanistan, 371
Afumati, Radu de la, 67
Ahmed I, 95, 96, 97
Ahmed III, 130, 131, 133, 135, 136
Ahmed Sidi Pasha, 99
Aix-la-Chapelle, Treaty of, 127
Albania, 5,18, 108, 125, 173, 176, 177, 185, 214, 220, 280, 356, 372,
   374, 376, 381, 389; benefits of Second Balkan War, 296; ceases to
   exist, 48; general information, 1, 6, 71, 380; insurrection in,
   295; Italian invasion of, 358-359; siege of, 48; Turkish captive,
   64; Turkish troops sent to, 184; under Soviet Union, 374
Albert of Habsburg, 46
Alb Iulia, Treaty of 76; refuted, 77
Albrecht, Archduke, 233
Alexander, King of Greece, 306
Alexander, King of Yugoslavia, assassinated (1934), 316
Alexander I of Battenberg, 239, 247, 293
Alexander I, Emperor of Russia, 170, 172, 173, 180, 181
Alexander II, Emperor of Russia, 211, 226, 247
Alexander III, Emperor of Russia, 247, 248
Alexander the Great, 10
Alexandretta (Iskenderun), 371
Alexandria, surrender at, 188; Convention of, 188
Alexandru the Kind, Prince of Moldavia, 43
Alexinatz, Battle of, 234
Algiers, seized by French, 187
Ali Pasha, Grand Vizier, 39
Ali Pasha, (Old Lion of Janinas), 183
Ali the Moldavian, 140
Allied Christian Fleet, 75
Allied Control Commission, 368
Allied Supreme Council in Paris, 311
America - See United States
Amiens, Treaty of, 179
Anatolia, 69, 96; religious revolts, 78
Andrassy, Count Julius, 233

Anglo-French-Turkish Mutual Assistance Pact, 371
Anglo-German Naval Agreement, 350
Anglo-Soviet Agreement, 373
Angora, Battle of, 43
Ankara, Treaty of (1930), 315; (1953), 381
Anna, Empress of Russia, 136
Anti-Comintern Pact, 365
Antifascist Council for National Liberation (Yugoslavia), 363
Antonescu, Ion, 366, 367
Apuseni Mountains, Battles in, 311
Aron the Tyrant, Prince of Moldavia, 76
Arrow-Cross Party, 370
Arslan Pasha of Buda, 74
Asaf Pasha, 246
Asia Minor, Turkish campaign into, 43; Turkish ouster from, 44
Asir Pasha, 228
Astrakhan, Russo-Turkish conflict over, 75
Ataturk (Mustafa Kemal Pasha), 314
Augustus III of Saxony, 128
Austria (See also Austro-Hungarian Empire), 126-127, 171, 216, 293,
    310, 313, 357, 358, 389; Anschluss, 350; Defeats Turks, 76;
    divided; 375; First Balkan War, 295; German takeover, 349-353;
    holds Hungary, 7; involved in Hungarian Civil War, 69; Long War,
    76-79; Rakoczi defeated by, 130; revolts in, 211; Russo-Turkish
    War, 144-145; sides with Hungarian rebels, 93; takes Hungary and
    Transylvania, 105; taken by Charles V, 63; Thirty Years' War, 98;
    treaty with England and France, 228; Turko-Venetian-Austrian War,
    133-135; Turks campaign against, 70-71, 74, 101-105; war among
    Turkey, Russia and Austria, 136-138; War of the Austrian
    Succession, 128, 137; war with Prussia, 229
Austrian Succession, War of the (1740-1748), 128, 137
Austro-Allied Peace Treaty of Saint-Germain (1919), 311
Austro-French-Piedmontese War (1859), 228
Austro-German Treaty of 1879, 246
Austro-Hungarian Empire (See also Austria, Habsburg Empire), 3, 13,
    168, 186, 230, 248, 287, 288, 307, 308; alliance with Romania, 247;
    Austro-German Treaty, 246; collapse of, 313; demands on Serbia,
    302; general information, 221-222, Hugarian revolts, 190;
    involvement in World War I, 303-306; Romania's struggle with, 175;
    Russo-Turkish War, 235; Slavic problem, 301
Austro-Prussian War of 1866 (Seven Weeks' War), 229, 233
Austro-Russian Defense Alliance (1781), 143, 191
Austro-Russian-Turkish War (1736-1739), 128
Austro-Turkish conflicts, 79, 96
Aynali Kavak, Agreement of (1784), 144
Azov, Fortress of, 132, 137, 142

Baghdad Railroad, 292, 309
Baia, Battle of, 52-53
Bairactar Pasha, Mustafa, 182, 185
Bakhchisaray, Treaty of, 109
Bakunin, Michael, 233
Balkan Conferences, 315
Balkan Entente, 364, 366
Balkan League, 295, 299, 315-317
Balkan Pact, 315

Balkans, name source, 1, location, 1, strategic importance, 1,
    histories, 3-6, 174, 214-216
Balkan Wars, First, 9, 295-297; Second, 11, 297-301; settlement and
    aftermath, 301
Barbarossa, Hayreddin, 71
Barcsai, Akos (Acatiu), 99-100
Bardossy, Laszlo, 370
Basta, General George, 93-94
Bathory, Gabriel, 96-97
Batory, Sigismund, Prince of Transylvania, 76, 77, 94
Batory, Stefan I, Prince of Transylvania, 53
Batory, Stefan II, Prince of Transylvania, 68
Bavaria, 229; troops of, 98, 104
Bayazid I, Sultan, 14, 40, 41, 43, 44
Bayazid II, Sultan, 53, 66
Bedreddin, Seyr, 76
Beg Mezit, 47
Beirut occupied, 188
Bela Kun, Soviet government of (in Hungary), 313, withdraws from
    Budapest, 315
Belgrad (Belgrade, Beograd), abandoned, 304; bombed, 303, 361;
    captured, 145; general information, 74, 103-105; partisans in,
    363-364; Pashalik uprising, 180; siege of, 128; liberated by
    Soviets, 362; struggle for independence, 228; Treaty of, 137, Turks
    attack, 50-51; Turks defeated at, 134; under a Pasha, 183
Belogradchik, Battle of, 190
Benes, Edvard, 358, 384, 385
Bercenyi, Laszlo, 100
Berczenyi, Nicholas, 130
Berlin, Congress of, 171, 246, 288; conference in, 235
Berlin-Rome Axis, 316, 350
Bessarabia, 144, 145, 350, 366, 367
Bethlen, Gabriel (Bethlen Gabor), 97, 98
Beust, Count Friedrich von, 233
Bihach, Fortress of, 134
Bismarck, Otto von, 211, 229, 230, 232, 233, 246, 292
Black Hand Society, 302
Black Sea, Conference on the, 232
Blaj, Treaty of, 105
Bled, Treaty of, 381
Bobilna (Bobolna) Mountain, Battle of, 46
Bocskai, Stefan, 94-95
Bohemia, 37; mercenaries of, 68, 98 100, 137, 221; Protestant uprising
    in, 95; French policy toward, 170, 224
Boiacikoy, Treaty of (1854), 225
Bolayir, Battle of, 298
Bolshevik Revolution, 306; results of, 310, 313
Bonneval, Claude Alexandre (Bombadier Ahmed Pasha, Bonneval Pasha),
    138
Boris, King of Bulgaria, 316, 365
Bosnia (See also Bosnia-Herzogovina), 10, 90, 96, 126, 176, 238, 290,
    307; Austrian troops in, 137; Battle of Sizzek, 76; fighting in
    WWI, 304; annexation of Herzogovina, 295; Ottoman conquest, 52;
    revolt in, 234; semi-autonomy, 235; Serbs fail, 134; Turks attack,
    145
Bosnia-Herzogovina (See also Bosnia), 188, 238; annexed by Bosnia,
    295, 301
Bozhilov government in Bulgaria, 365
Brasov, Battles of, 97, 305

Brest-Litovsk, Treaty of, 306
Brigandage, 101
Brincoveanu, Constantine, 131, 133, 134
Broz, Josef - See Tito
Bucharest, captured/occupied, 53, 77, 145, 305; uprising (1956) in,
    383; Russian forces, 140-141; Treaties of, (1812), 181; (1886),
    247; (1913), 11, 297; (1918), 306; Turkish siege, 181
Bucov, Battle of, 94
Buda (Budapest), 68-69; fall of, 70, 73, 104
Bukovina, 366
Bulgaria, 5, 16, 18, 19, 42, 90, 108, 126, 133, 148, 173, 185, 192,
    214, 218, 224, 288, 307, 312, 356, 358, 364, 372, 374, 376, 383;
    alliance with Serbia, 295; against Turks, 47-48; Balkan Wars,
    295-297; brigandage, 101; British influence, 177; capital sacked,
    40; Crimean War, 225; Dark Era, 64; disaster at the Pruth, 133;
    divided, 235, 247; general information, 1, 6-7, 176, 310; German
    plans for, 353; given Macedonia, 11; military coup, 316; Ottomans
    in, 38; Russo-Turkish War, 186, 238, 239; struggle for
    independence, 228; under Soviet domination, 374; uprisings in, 72,
    190, 228; Warsaw Pact, 385; involvement in WWI, 301, 304-306;
    involvement in WWII, 364-366
Bulgarian-Allied Peace Treaty, 311
Burebista (Dacian King), 7
Byzantine Empire, 4, 12, 17; Empire's end, 37, 50; general
    information, 3, 6, 11; New Empire, 144; Second Rome, 48-49

Calugareni, Battle of, 77-79
Candia, defeat of French and Venetians at, 103
Cannon, early use of, 92
Cantacuzino, Stephan, 133
Capodistrias, John (Ioannius Kapodistrias), 184, 186
Carol I of Hohenzollern-Sigmaringer, Prince and King of Romania, 230,
    231, 234, 247, 249, 354, 366
Carpato-Ukraine (Ruthenia), annexed by Hungary, 350, 369
Catherine II the Great, Empress of Russia, 127, 140-144, 146
Catholic League, 90
Catlabuga, Battle of, 53
Celali (Jelali) uprising, 96
Cem Sultan, 66
Central Powers, 218
Cer Mountain, Battle of, 304
Cetatea-Alba (Belgorog-Denestrovski, USSR), 45, 53
Charles IV, King of Hungary, 309
Charles V, Holy Roman Emperor, 63, 66, 69-71
Charles V of Lorraine, 103, 104
Charles VI, Emperor of Austria, 128, 137
Charles X, King of Sweden, 99
Charles XII, King of Sweden, 131, 132
Charles Albert, Elector of Barvaria, 104, 128
Cherniaev, Gen. Mikhail G., 240
Chesme, naval battle at, 140, 141
Chetniks, 361, 363
Chilia, attack on fortress at, 53
Chocim, castle, 100; city, 144
Chorlulu Ali, 133
Ciamurli, Battle of, 44
Cimpia Turzii, murder of Michael the Brave, 94
Ciresoaia, Battle of, 306

Cirmen (Cernomen), Battle of (1371), 38
Cluj, Diet of, 97
Cold War, 374-376, 385
Comona Monastery, Battle of, 140
Compromise of 1867, 233
Concert of Europe, 226, 227
Confederation of Bar, 139
Constantine, Crown Prince and King of Greece, 295, 296, 299, 305, 306, 377
Constantine XI Paleologus, Byzantine Emperor, 49
Constantinople, 3, 15, 49, 67, 69, 74, 130, 235; Allied forces land, 315; capture of, 11; Conference of, 234; fall of, 48; retreat of Mohammed II to, 51; siege of, 14;, Sublime Porte in, 50; Treaty of, 184
Corfu, 134, 305; channel dispute, 380; Declaration of 1917, 312
Corinth, 134
Cosmin Forest (Codrul Cosminului), Battle of, 54
Council of Europe, Greek withdrawal from, 377
Cretan campaign, 100
Crete, revolution, 230; uprising, 249; given to Greece, 296; German attack on, 360; Battle of 360
Crimean War, 172, 214, 217, 225, 226; aftermath of, 227, 239
Croatia, 96, 134, 138, 218, 230, 290, 293; revolution, 190; Habsburg defensive line, 10; national feeling in, 222
Csaki, Prince Nicolae, 46
Curtea de Arges, Battle of, 94
Cuza, Prince Alexandru Ioan, 228, 230, 231
Cyprus, Turkish invasion of, 376, 379
Czechoslovakia, 309, 310, 317, 357, 375, 388; agreement with Russia, 316; Czech Legion rebellion in Russia, 308; general information, 315, 367, 374, 384, 385; German occupation of, 350, 353, 358-359; invasion by Hungary, 311; Jewish problem, 353; Soviet relations with, 316, 372, 374; Warsaw Pact, 385
Czerny Ostrov, Battle of, 99

Dan II, Prince of Wallachia, 45
Danilevsky, Nicholas, 240
Danubian Principalities, 40, 64, 75, 76, 136, 144; Russia enters, 225; Turkish and Austrian occupation, 227-228
Dardenelles, closed, 188, 379
Delcasse, Theophile, 292
Deli Hassan (Hassan the Mad), 96
Devsirme, 66, 72
Dilessi Affair, 232
Dimitriev, Gen. Radko, 296
Dimitrijevic, Col. Dragutin, 293, known as "Apis," 302
Djunas, Battle of, 234
Dobrotich of Dobrudja, 38-39
Dobrudja, area, 12, 41; province, 43, 44; Serban's Turkish campaign, 94; returned to Bulgaria, 365, southern region (The Quadrilateral) to Romania, 366; returned to Bulgaria, 374
Doja, Gheorghe, 65
Dolfuss, Englebert, Premier of Austria, 317
Domobran forces, 381
Doria, Adm. Andrea, 71
Dracsani, Moldo-Polish defeat at, 97
Dracul, Vlad (Dracula), Prince of Wallachia, 47

Dragasani, Ypsilanti's defeat at, 183
Dual Alliance, 292
Dual Monarchy, 308; establishment, 231; dismemberment, 349
Dubcek, Alexander, 385
Dusan, Stephen (Nemanja), 6, 9

Eastern Question, 20, 143, 146-147, 170-172, 174, 175, 189, 191, 214,
     216, 225, 227, 236-238, 244, 246, 283, 287; renewal of, 379
East Germany (German Democratic Republic), in the Warsaw Pact, 385
Ebert, Frederick, President of the Weimar Republic, 349
Economics, impact of war on, 38; condition of Europe in 18th century,
     122, Balkan factors, 123, 128
Edriou, Nicolai, 143
Elphinstone, Admiral, 140
England (Great Britain), 3, 171, 172, 237, 309; agreement with Turkey,
     371; alliance against Russia, 228, declares war (1914), 302;
     diplomatic break with Romania, 367; general information, 37, 121,
     128, 135, 139, 144, 167, 244; guarantees Polish security, 350;
     guarantees Romanian independence, 366; role in Balkans, 373-374;
     refuses support for Greek claims, 246; Soviet rebuke, 350;
     support in WWII, 361; units in Greece, 359, 360; Triple Entente,
     292; at war with Hungary, 370
Epirus, fighting in, 300
Ethiopia, 316
Eugene, Prince of Savoy, 105, 130, 131, 133, 134, 137, 138
European Danube Commission, 366
Evrenos-Bey, 43

Fakhir-ad-Din, 97
Falkenhayn, Gen. Erich von, 305
Farmagusta, siege of, 75
Fatherland Front, 365
Feldioara, Battle of, 70
Fenes (Floresti), defeat of George II, 99
Feodar I, Moscovite Tsar, 63
Feodar III, Muscovite Tsar, 109
Ferdinand, Archduke, 65, 69-73
Ferdinand, Archduke Franz, 301; assassination, 302
Ferdinand, Archduke of Stria, 95
Ferdinand I of Romania, 304
Ferdinand II, Holy Roman Emperor, 98
Ferdinand of Saxe-Coburg, 247
Filov government in Bulgaria, 364-365
"Final Solution," 370
Fintinele, defeat at, 190
Firearms, introduced, 91
Florina, Battle of, 305
Focsani, Battle of, 145
Four Power Pact, 315
France, 3, 106, 146, 232, 237; absolutism in, 89; aids in Hungarian
     revolt, 103; allied with the Ottomans, 71; Anglo-French-Turkey
     Mutual Non-Aggression Pact, 371; Austrian involvement, 143; cedes
     Alexandretta, 371; Crimean War, 225-226; colonial rivalry, 121;
     fall of, 354; First Balkan War, 295; general information, 37, 167,
     179, 224, 292; guarantees Polish security, 350; guarantees Romanian
     independence, 360; republic proclaimed, 189; revolution in, 122,
     128, 168, 189; Second Republic, 211; East European allies, 315;

France (Cont'd), Seven Weeks' War, 229; squadrons in Black Sea, 225;
    support in WWII, 361; Treaty of Paris (1856), 228
Franco-Prussian War, 229, 232-234, 249
Frangepani, Count, 103
Frankfurt Assembly, 211
Frankish Empire, 10
Franz Joseph, Emperor of Austria-Hungary, 190, 191, 228, 230, 231,
    233, 288, 301
Fratia (Fraternity), 189
Frederick, Elector of the Palatine, 98
Frederick II the Great, 128, 138, 139, 147
Friederich, Prince of Saxe-Coburg, 145
Friedrich Wilhelm, Crown Prince, commands the Second Army, 229

Galician campaign, 304
Gallipoli (WWI), 304, 307, captured (1354), 38
Garibaldi, Guiseppe, 211
General Staff, concept, 232
Genoa, 38, 39; fleet, 47
George I, King of Greece, 230, 246
George II, King of Greece, 376
German Balkan campaign, 356
German High Command, in Hungary, 370
German-Japanese Anti-Comintern Pact, 350
German National Socialist (Nazi) Party, 352
Germano-Romanian crisis, 372
German Polish Non-Aggression Treaty, 350
Germany (See also Prussia), alliance with Austria-Hungary, Romania,
    247; confederation, 229; general information, 292; relations with
    Russia, 246; rise of militarism, 285; unification, 211, 222; view
    of war, 93; World War I, investment in Ottoman Empire, 301;
    involvement in war, 304-306; partial mobilization, 302; post-WWI
    period, 310-311; World War II, annexation of Czechoslovakia,
    358-359; annexation of Memel, 350; events of 1936-1939, 349-350;
    Hitler and Nazi Germany, 352-354; Hitler's demand on Romania, 366;
    Hitler's favors to Hungary, 369-370; in Bulgaria, 364-366; in
    Hungary, 369-371; in Romania, 366-369; in Yugoslavia, 361-364;
    Turkey's non-aggression pact with, 371
Gero, Erno, 383
Ghaza (Mohammedan concept), 14
Ghica III, Prince Grigore, 142
Giurgiu, Battle of, 77, 140
Gizikis, Gen. Phaidon, 377
Golbac, Battle of, 45
Golitsen, Prince Basil, 109
Golitsyn, Prince Alexandre, 139, 140
Goltz, Gen. Kolmar von der (Goltz Pasha), 310
Goraslau, Battle of, 94
Gorgey Battalion, 371
Gottwald, Klement, 384
Gran, 77; Battle of, 77
Gratiani, Gaspar, 98
Great Britain - See England
Great Northern War, 128, 130
Great Powers, 3, 170, 183, 184, 186, 188, 224, 246, 283, 284, 296,
    302, 312, 314, 317, 349, 356, 358, 365, 381
Great Revolution of 1848, 189-191

Greco-Byzantine Phase, 3

Greece, 5, 16, 17, 21, 91, 125, 214, 221, 228, 309, 312, 372, 374, 381; civil war in, 375-376; Dilessi Affair, 232; First Balkan War, 295-297; general information, 1, 11-12, 64, 124, 310; German plan for, 353; independent kingdon of, 184; problems, 377-378; Italian attack on, 359-361; invasion of, 356, 358; Ottoman invasion of, 42; ports blockaded, 225; rebellion in, 140, 145, 170; reestablishment of Turkish rule, 135; revolution (1821), 182-187, (1843), 189; Second Balkan War, 297; Second War for Independence, 230; Turkish campaign in, 133; unrest in, 91; uprising on Crete, 249; World War I, declares neutrality, 305; enters war, 306

Greek Cypriots, 377

"Greek Plan," 144

Greiffenberg, Gen Hans von, 356

Grivas, Col. Georgios, 377

Guillaumat, Gen. M.L.A., 306

Guns (Koszeg), defense of, 71

Gustavus Adolphus, 92

Gyor, Turkish garrison at, 103

Gyula, attack on, 74


Habsburg Empire (See also Vienna), anti-Habsburg uprising in Croatia, 130; clashes with Turks, 73; dynastic rivals in France, 89; fosters revolt, 75; general information, 12-14, 143; Hungarian fear of, 67; importance of Croatia to, 10; moves in Balkans, 69; Transylvanian involvement, 76, 99; war with Ottomans, 107

Haile Selassie, Emperor of Ethiopia, 316

Halil, Patrona, 136

Hamadan, Battle of, 135

Hamid, Abdul, 182

Hamid Pasha, Halil, Grand Vizier, 144, 147

Harkany (Nagyharsany), Battle of, 104

Heretiai (Philhellene), 183, 185

Hermannstadt, Battle of, 47

Herzogovina, 10; Ottoman conquest of, 52; Christian massacre, 234; uprising in, 234; semi-autonomous, 235, 238; annexed, 295

Heydrich, Reinhard, assassination of, 358

Hindenberg, Fld. Marsh. Paul von Beneckendorf und, 349

Hindov, Battle of, 41

Hitler, Adolf, 283, 349, 352, 358, 371

Holland, 135

Holstein (Holsten), Christian von, 101

Holy League, 75, 76, 104

Holy Roman Empire, 13, 37; Sigismund of Luxembourg, Emperor of, 41; confronts Balkan conflict, 54; decline and rebirth, 63, 65, 73, 102, 104; Ottoman Empire against, 71

Holy See, 97

Horea, Vasili Ursu Nicola, 143

Horthy, Adm. Miklos (Nicholas), 7, 317, 369, 371

Hotzendorf, Gen. Franz, 303-304

Hoxha, Enver, 359

Hunedoara, county of, 43; (See also Iancu of)

Hungarian Freedom Fighters, 383

Hungarian General Staff, 370

Hungarians, imprisonment of Vlad Tepes, 52; overlordship of Transylvania, 46; territorial claims, 366

Hungary (See also Austria-Hungary), 15, 18, 19, 37, 90, 147, 170, 222, 288, 309, 313, 354, 357, 372; against Moldavia, 41; annexes Ruthenia, 350; anti-Habsburg revolt, 130; civil war, 69, 73; discontent in, 102-105; divided, 70; Dual Monarchy, 231; French policiy toward, 224, general information, 1, 7, 63, 65, 126, 174-175, 231, 310; revolution, 189; Habsburg Hungary, 95, 103; invaded by Austria, 77; Jewish problem, 353; liberation from Turkish rule, 135; Ottoman cultural impact, 108; Protestant rights in, 99; revolts in, 136, 145; threats from, 39, 40; Turkish campaigns in, 66-70, 76; under Soviet domination, 374; 1956 Uprising, 383-384; Warsaw Pact, 385; in World War II, 369-371
Hunyadi, Janos (John) - See Iancu of Hunedoara
Husak, Gustav, 385
Hussite movement in Bohemia, 46

Iancu, Avram, 190
Iancu of Hunedoara, 43, 46-51
Ibraham, Grand Vizier, 68, 74, 77
Ibrahim Pasha (of Egypt), 187-188
Iezerul Cahulului (Kagul), Battle of, 75
Ignatiev, Count Nicholas, 240
Industrial Revolution, 167, 168, 212
Inonu, Ismet, 371
Iran, 371
Iraq, 371
"Iron Gate," 45
Iron Guard, 367-368
Isabella, Regent of John II, 73
Ishak Bey, 46
Iskenderun - See Alexandretta
Ismail, fort at, 145
Italo-Turkish War (Tripoli War), 295
Italy, 305, 307, 317, 374; attack on Greece, 356-359; forces in Albania, 306; invasion of Albania, 358 operations against Austria-Hungary, 307; war with Turks, 295; agree with Romania, 307, 366; post-WWI alinement, 315; conflict with Ethiopia, 316;
Ivan III, Moscovite Tsar, 63
Ivan IV, Moscovite Tsar, 63
Ivanco, 39

Jacobin Movement, 147
Jadwiga, Queen of Poland, 41
Janissaries, 43, 72, 76, 78, 93, 97, 103, 135, 180, 181, 182
Janos, Kardas, 46
Jassy (Iasi), 139, 144; capture of 140; Treaty of, 145; Romanian capital moved to, 305
Jews, of Romania, Czechoslovakia, and Hungary, 353, 370; in Bulgaria, 366; resistance, 374
Jihad (Holy War), 14, 50, 72
John I Albert, King of Poland, 54
John I Tzimisces, Byzantine Emperor, 12
John III Sobieski, King of Poland, 104
John V Paleologus, Byzantine Emperor, 49
Jones, Adm. John Paul, 144
Joseph I, King of Hungary
Joseph II, Emperor of Austria-Hungary, 143, 144, 147
Kagageorgevic, Peter, 293

Kalender Revolt, 69
Kallay, Miklos, 370-371
Kalolyi, Count Michael, 288, government of, 313
Kanlice Conference, 229
Kapikulu, military corps, 66
Kapodistrias, Ioannis - See Capodistrias
Karageorge (George Petrovic), 180-182
Karamanlis, Konstantinos, 377
Kara-Yaziji, 96
Karlowitz, Peace at, 105, 107, 124, 133
Katalka, Battle of, 298
Kemel government, 371
Kemel Pasha, Mustafa - See Ataturk
Kemeny, Ioan (Janos), 101
Kereste, Battle of, 77
Khalil Pasha, 134
Khmelnitsky, Bogdan, 109
Khotin, fortress of, 139-140
Khrushchev, Nikita, 375, 380, 386
Kipchak tribe, 14
Kirklareli, recapture of, 298
Kizluca (Korludzha), Battle of 140
Koca Yusuf Pasha, 144
Komarno, surrender of, 190
Koniggratz (Sadowa), Battle of, 229, 233, 248
Konigsegg-Rothenfels, Col. Lothar J.G., 137
Konya (Koniah), Battle of, 187
Koprulu, Fazil Ahmed, 102
Koprulu, Mohammed, 99
Koprulu, Mustafa, Grand Vizier, 105
Kossovo (Kosovo), 10 14; First Battle of, 39-40; Second Battle of, 48
Kossuth, Louis, 190-192
Koubara (Kolubra) River, Battle of, 304
Koumoundouros, Alexandros, 246
Kroszka, Battle of, 137
Kruje, Neopolitan garrison at, 48
Krummau, capture of, 95-96, 98
Kuchuk-Kainardji (Kucuk Kaynarca), peace accord, 140; Treaty of, 144, 146
Kurdzhali movement, 148, 182
Kuvayi Milliye (nationalist militia), 314

Lackfy, Nicolae, Szekler Viovode of Transylvania, 39
Ladislas II, King of Bohemia, and as Ladislas VI, King of Hungary, 65
Lasislas III, King of Poland, and as Ladislas V, King of Hungary, 47, 49
Larga and Cahul (Kartal), Tiurkish defeat near, 140
Lattas, Michael (Omar Pasha), 225
Laudon, Gen. Gideon von, 145
Lausanne, Peace Treaty of, 309, 311-312, 314
Lavrov, Peter, 233
Lazar I of Serbia, 38
Lazarevich, Stefan, 42, 43
League of Communist Youth, 363
League of Nations, 312, 316, 356, 369
Leopold I, Holy Roman Emperor, 103
Lepanto, First Battle, 52, 65; Second Battle, 65; naval 75

Linz, Treaty of, 99
Little Entente, 315-317
Livinov, Maxim, 350
London, 225, Treaty of 184; Conference of 1871, 227; Conference of
    1883 247; Peace Conference of 1912, 296
Long (Bulgarian) Campaign, 47-48
Long War, 76-78
Louis I the Great of Anjou, 39
Louis (Ludwig or Lajos) II, 66, 68
Louis XIV, King of France, 103, 131
Louis of Baden, 105
Louis Philip of France, 189
Lublin, Treaty of, 40
Luck-Volhynia, Russo-Moldavian Alliance of, 131
Luders, Gen. A.N., 190
Lule Gurgaz, Battle of, 300
Lvov (Lemberg), Battle near, 304

Macedon, Philip of, 10
Macedonia, 19, 298, 299, 308, 312, 364, 381, general information,
    9-11, 176-177, 218, 290; Ottoman vassal, 38; Romanians in, 125;
    partition of 295; insurrection in, 295;
Magyar Arpad, dynasty of, 7
Mahmud I, 135, 136
Mahmud (Mahmoud) II, 147, 182, 187, 188
Makarios III, 377
Maleter, Gen. Pal, 384
Marasesti, Battle of, 306
Marasti, Battle of, 306, 307
Maria Theresa, 128, 137, 138, 143
Maritsa River, Battle of Cirmen, 38
Marxist regimes, establishment of, 375
Masaryk, Jan, 384, 385
Masaryk, Thomas, 385
Mathias Corvinus, King of Hungary, 54; attack of Austria, 54
Matthias, Count of Thurn, 95; leader of Protestant revolt, 98
Matthias, Holy Roman Emperor, 95, King of Austria, Bohemia, Habsburg
    Hungary, 98
Mavrocordata, Nicolae, 133
Maximilian II, 73
Maximilian, Archduke, 54, 63, 77
Medjid, Abdul, Sultan, 188, 225
Mehmed Pasha, Baltaji, Grand Vizier, 132, 133
Mehmet III, Sultan, 77
Mehmet IV, Sultan, 99, 100, 103, 107
Mehmet Ali-Bey of Egypt, 184, 187-188
Mehmet Raghib Pasha, Grand Vizier, 124
Memel, annexed by Germany, 350
Menderes government in Turkey, 379
Metaxas Line, 359
Metternich, Klemens Fust von, 169, 190
Michael, King of Romania, 367
Michael the Brave (Mihai Viteazul), Prince of Wallachia, 76, 77, 93,
    94
Midhat Pasha, 234
Mihai I Apafi, 101-104
Mihail I, son of Mircea, 45

Mihailovic, Gen. Draza, 361, 363
Mihal Ogullari clan, 72
Mihnea, Radin, 97
Miklov (Nicholsburg), Treaty of, 98
Milescu, Nicolae, 101
Military Science and History, 22, 64, 91-93, 128-131, 178-179,
    216-217, 284-285; changes in warfare, 121; 18th century literature,
    123, Militarism, 351
Miraslau, Battle of, 94
Mircea the Old, Viovode of Wallachia, 39-41, 43-45
Mohacs, Battle of, 68-69
Mohammed Emin (Mehmet Emin Pasha), 139, 140
Mohammed Pasha, Grand Vizier, 51
Mohammed the Restorer, Sultan, 44
Mohammed II the Conquerer, 3, 48-53
Mohammed V, 298
Moldavia,9, 20, 41; alliance with Poland, 44; army defeated, 75;
    attacked by Poland, 70; Austro-Russian attack into, 145; Bukovina
    ceded, 142; general information, 52-53, 67, 69, 72-73, 96, 97, 99,
    104-105; revolution, 109, part of the "Greek Plan," 144; Russian
    intervention into, 126, 132, 140, 226; sacked, 99; Turkish attack,
    43, 45; Turks settle in, 76; unification with Wallachia, 219;
    Ypsilanti's independent state, 181; Zapolya's treaty with, 70
Moldowandji, Ali (Ali the Moldavian), 140
Molotov, Vyacheslav, 350
Moltke, Capt, Helmuth von,188, 211, 229, 230, 232
Monastir (Bitola), Battle of, 296; captured, 306
Mongol forces, 14
Montecuccoli, Raimondo, 101, 102, 107
Montenegro, 5, 9, 90, 126, 218, 290, 381; Austrian occupation, 305;
    Chetnik operations, 363; First Balkan War, 295-296; general
    information, 176, 301; independent, 235; Ottoman conquest, 52;
    rebels  in, 134, 139; Russian intervention, 133
Montreux Agreement, 371
Moravia, 100
Morea, (The Peloponnesus), 48, 133; given to Venice, 105; Turkish
    victories, 134-135
Moscow, as the Third Rome, 49, 63
Mount Grammos, Battle of, 376
Mouskos, Mihail Khristodolous - See Makarios III
Movila, Ieremia, 94
Movila, Simeon, 94
Munich Pact, 350
Murad I, 14, 38
Murad II, 45, 47, 48
Murad III, 75,
Murad IV, 97, 100
Murad V, 233, 242
Musa, son of Bayazid, 44
Mussolini, Benito, 315, 353
Mustafa I, 97
Mustafa II, 105, 130
Mustafa  III, 139, 141, 142
Mustafa IV, 182, 185
Mustafa Kara, 103, 104, 106
Mustafa Kemal Pasha (Ataturk), 314
Mustafa the Pretender, 44

Nadasdi, Count Ferenc, 102
Nadir Shah, 135-136
Nagy, Ferenc, 383
Nagy, Imre, 383
Nagyvarad, Treaty of, 73; besieged, 99
Napoleon Bonaparte, 13, 167, 168, 170, 172, 181
Napoleon III, 211, 212, 225, 228, 232, 233
National Front (Czechoslovakia), 384
"National Iron—Guardist State," 366-367
National Socialism, 301
Naval warfare, 179
Navarino, 140; bay, 184; Battle of Navarino, 186
Nazi-Soviet Non-Agression Pact, 350, 366
Nemanja (Dusan), Stephen, 6, 9
Nenodovic, Matija, 180, 186
"New World," 37, 121, 128
Nezib, Battle of, 188
Nicephorus II Phocas of Byzantium, 12
Nicholas I, Emperor of Russia, 172, 173, 191, 226, 227
Nicholas II, Emperor of Russia, 291
Nicholas, Grand Duke, 234
Nicopolis (Nigbolu), Battle of, 14, 41-42
Nissa, Treaty of, 137
North Atlantic Treaty Organization (NATO), partial Greek withdrawal,
    377; Greece readmitted, 378; Turkey joins, 379; Warsaw Pact
    counter, 385
Nove Zamky (Neuhaus), defense of the fortress, 102
Novi, defense of the fortress, 134
Novotny, Antonin, 385

Obrenovic, King Milan, 247, 293
Obrenovich, Prince Milos of Serbia, 183
October Diploma, 228
October Revolution of 1918, 313
Oglu, Bali-Beg Malcoci (Pasha of Silistra), 53
Ogullari clan, 72
Old Lion of Janina, 183
Omar Pasha, (Michael Lattas), 188, 225
Opanez, Battle of, 235
"Operation Budapest," 367
Oradea, Peace of, 72; Treaty of 73
Orlov, Russian Admiral, 140
Osman Pasha, 235
Osman I, Prince, 14
Osman II, 97
Otho of Bavaria, King of Greece, 184, 188, 189, 230
Ottoman Empire, (See also Turks, Turkey and the Sublime Porte), 2, 3,
    91, 108, 123-125, 127, 222-223, 290-291, 309; Adrianople Affair,
    130; anti-Ottoman coalition, 76, 77, 94; anti-Ottoman Crusade, 65;
    apex of power, 64; Austria's peace, 145; bandits in, 101, Bagdad
    Railway, 292, 301; Black Sea forces, 121; Bulgarian campaign, 40,
    47; civil war, 44, claim on Romanian principalities, 228;
    Constantinople falls to, 11; Crimean War, 225-226, 227; decline of,
    75, 211, 295; dissolution of, 314; early conquests, 6, 7, 11;
    European help, 188; expansion of, 40-45, 52; French alliance, 71;
    general information, 89, 177-178, 190; relations with Greece, 299;
    Holy League against, 75, 76, 78, 94, 104; internal problems, 66;
    invasion of Greece, 42; name origin; 14;

Ottoman Empire (Cont'd), new sultans, 53-54; political and diplomatic
retreats, 107; Osman, 14, Osmanli, 14, Othman, 14; recovery from
Karlowitz, 124; rule in Europe, 96; Russo-Turkish Wars, 1710-1711,
131-133; 1768-1774, 139-142; 1787-1792, 144-145; 1806-1812,
180-182; 1877-1878, 233-243; structure of the state, 72, 124; Tatar
vassals of, 98-99; 14th century threat from, 38-39; war with
Austria, 133-137; war with Venice, 65, 93, 133-136; withdrawal from
Europe, 301
Ouchy, Treaty of, 295

Pahlen, Count Peter, 184
Paisie, Radu, Viovode of Wallachia, 72
Pan-Slavic Committee, 240; movement, 240
Papagos, Gen. Alexander, 359
Paris Peace Conference, 312, 313
Paris Peace Treaty, WWII, 374
Paris, Treaty of, 226-228; accords of 1856, 233
Pashich, Nicola, 218, 289, 312
Paskevich, Gen. Fld. Marshal Prince Ivan, 225
Passarowitz (Pazarevac), Treaty of, 54; aftermath, 135-136
Paul I, Emperor of Russia, 179
Paul, Prince Regent of Yugoslavia, 361
Pavelic, Ante, 363
Peace of Szatmar (Satu Mare), 130
Pechenegs, 12
People's National Liberation Army, 359
People's Republic of China, 380
Persia, four year war with Turks, 137; Mudad III at war with, 76,
Selim I at war with, 66; Turkish conflicts with, 71, 95, 97;
victory over Turks, 135
Pest (Budapest), revolt in, 189
Peter I the Great, Emperor of Russia, 89, 101, 108, 121, 127, 131, 133
Peter, Prince and King of Yugoslavia, 361, 362
Peter, Prince of Montenegro, 145
Peterwardein (Petervarad) Fortress, defense of, 68; Battle of, 134
Petrosani, Battle of, 305
Petrovich, George (Karageorge), 180-182
Peur, Jean Sans, Duke of Burgundy, 41
Philip V of Spain, 128
Pilsen, taken, 98
Pius V, establishes Holy League, 75
Plevna, Battle of, 234-236
Pobedonostsev, Constantin, 248
Poland, 170; allied with Moldavia, 43-44; attempted coup, 49; attacks
Moldavia, 70, 94; civil war, 139; designs on Hungary; 63; first
partition, 139; in new Holy League, 104; invades Wallachia, 94;
Germans enter, 350; Podolian region returned, 105; second
revolution, 233; Soviet annexation, 350; against Khmelnitsky, 109;
war with Turks, 47-48, 50, 52, 97, 103-104; uprising in, 75; war
with Moldavia, 70, 94; war with Transylvania, 99-101; Warsaw Pact,
385
Polish-Moldavian Alliance, 44
Polish Succession, War of, 128, 136
Poltava, aftermath of battle, 126
Popandreou, George, 377
Potemkin, Grigori Aleksandrovich, 145
Potiorek, Gen. Oskar, 304
Pozsony, election at, 69
Pragmatic Sanction, 128

Prague, peace at, 73, 98; Treaty of 229; Protocol, 315, 372
Praid-Sovata, Battle of, 305
Princip, Gavrilo, 302
Proclamation of Pades, 183
Prussia (See also Germany), 143, 144, 167, 225, 232
Pruth, Treaty of the, 132, 133; surrender on the, 132
Przemsyl, siege of, 309
Putineiu, Battle of, 76
Putnik, Gen. Radomir, 296, 304
Putsch, Vienna, 317; Munich, 353

Quadruple Alliance, War of the, 128

Radeysky, Marshal Josef, 221
Radu the Handsome, 52
Rahova (Orekhovo), Battle of, 235
Rakoczi, Francis, 130
Rakoczi, George II, 99
Rakoczi movement, 131
Reinsurance Treaty, 292
Resistance during WWII, 374
Rhineland, reoccupied, 316
Rhodes, Turkish siege, 52, objective of Suleimann, 67
Ribbentrop, Joachim von, 283
Rimnik, Battle of, 145
Romania, 6, 16, 18, 19, 20, 95, 101, 125, 126, 170, 185, 186, 192,
    214, 226, 237, 289, 307, 312, 354, 356, 361, 372, 374, 376, 388;
    agreement with Italy, 307; allegiance to Catherine, 140; campaign
    for Transylvania, 301; French policy, 224; general information, 1,
    7-9, 175-175, 219-220, 230-231, 310, 382-383; German plans, 353;
    given Transylvania, 311; revolution, 189, 190; independence, 235;
    "Iron Guard," 316; Jewish problem, 353; joins Little Entente, 315;
    lose of Bessarabia, 181; non-aggression pact with Turkey, 316;
    relations with Russia, 108, Second Balkan War, 297; secret
    agreement with Russia, 234; siege of Vienna, 104; situation in
    provinces, 67, 72; Treaty of Lublin, 40; Triple Alliance, 292;
    Turkish attacks, 40; under Soviet domination, 374; unification of
    principalities, 93, 228; uprisings, 75, 94, 294; war of
    independence, 243-245; Warsaw Pact, 385; WWI involvement, 304-306;
    WWII involvement, 366-369; Ypsilanti enters, 184
Roscani (Ryskany), Battle of, 75
Rovine, Battle of, 40
Royal Air Force (RAF), in Greece, 359
Rudolph, Emperor of Austria, 76, 94, 95
Rumelia, 44, 108
Rumiantsev, Count Peter, 140, 145
Russia (See also Soviet Union), 3, 90, 109, 127-128, 171, 172-173,
    186, 191, 216, 248, 291; alliance against, 228; Bolshevik
    Revolution, 306, 310, 313; Catherine's Second War with Turkey,
    142-143; conflict with Turks, 75; Crimean War, 225-227; defeated by
    Turks, 103; defense alliance with Turks, 187-188; general
    information, 12-13, 63, 108-109, 167, 223-224, 283; WWI
    involvement, 302, 304, 306; joins Holy League, 104; moves toward
    Black Sea, 229; navy, 121; preoccupation with Balkans and Ottoman
    Empire, 12; protector of Balkans, 49; relations with Romania, 108;
    rise of militarism, 285; rivalry with Austria, 239; influence in
    northern Persia, 301; war with Turkey and Austria, 136-137;
    withdraws from Wallachia, 183; with Serbs against Turks, 228
Russo-Finnish War, 350

Russo-Greek relations, 127
Russo-Moldavian alliance (of Luck-Volynia), 131
Russo-Turkish Wars, 1710-1711, 131-133, 135; 1768-1774, 127, 139-142;
    1787-1792, 144-146; 1806-1812, 180-182, 186; 1877-1878, 10, 11,
    176, 233-243

Saadabad Pact, 371
Saguna, Bishop Andreiu, 192
Saint Germain, Austro-Allied Peace Treaty of, 311
Saint Gotthard Abbey, Battle of, 102
Salonika, during WWI, 309; Allied reinforcements, 305; Allied
    reorganization, 306; invasion of, 313; WWII, 359
Sanjaks, 72
San Stefano, Treaty of, 235, 246
Sarajevo, 9, 248; assassination of Franz Ferdinand, 302
Sarkoy, landing at, 298
Scheia, Battle of, 53
Schiopul, Petru, 75
Schulenberg, Marshal Johann Mathis von der, 134
Schusschnigg, Kurt von, Chancellor of Austria, 349
Scobie, Lt. Gen. Sir Robert, 361
Scolari, Filippo de, 45
Sebastiani, Gen. 180, 181
Second Coalition, War of the, 179
Second Hungarian Army, 371
Second Ukrainian Front, 367
Secuiul, Moise, 94
Seghedinat, Pero, 136
Seleusul Mare (Oradea), Battle of, 101
Selim I, Sultan, 66
Selim II the Sot, 75
Selim III, 145, 147, 179, 181, 179
Seljuks, 14
Semendria (Smederevo) Fortress, 46
Senova, Battle of, 235
Senyavin, Adm., 181
Serbia (See also Serbians), 5, 9, 16, 96, 126, 173, 192, 214, 217,
    218, 293, 381; alliance with Bulgaria, 295; Austrian attacks on,
    134,
Serbia (Cont'd), 137, 145; blocked from Adriatic, 297; British
    influence in, 177; cleared of Turks, 104; declares war on Turkey,
    235; declares war, WWI, 304; free state ends, 51; general
    information, 176, 183, 228, 239, 289, 301, 308; German takeover,
    364; revolution, 190; independence confirmed, 235; Second Balkan
    War, 297; Macedonia given to, 11; Montenegro absrbed by, 10; prior
    to WWI, 302; Turks return, 105; turns to Russia, 109, 133; under
    Austria-Hungary, 247; war of national liberation, 363
Serbian campaign, WWI, 304
Serbians (See also Serbia), 185, 222; against Wallachia, 40; defeated
    by Ottomans, 38; detachment used by Bayazid, 43; at Kossovo, 39; as
    a part of Yugoslavia,9; occupy Albania, 6; part of Ypsilanti's
    independent state, 181; revolt, 180
Serbin, Radu, 94, 96, 97
Serbo-Balkan War, 218
Seventh Comintern Congress, 349
Seven Weeks War (Austro-Prussian War), 229, 233
Seven Years' War (Great War for Empire), 128, 139
Severin Fortress, 45

Seyss-Inquart, Artur von, 349
Shabotz, Battle of, 66-67
Shishman, Ivan, Tsar of Turnovo, 40
Sibiu, Battle of, 305
Sigismund, John II of Hungary, 73
Sigismund of Luxembourg, King of Hungary & Bohemia, 41, 43, 45
Silahdar Ali Pasha, 133
Sinan Pasha, Grand Vizier of Wallachia, 76-77
Siniser, Bilal, 229
Sinope, destruction of Turkish fleet, 225
Sintimbru, Battle of, 46
Sissek, Battle of, 76
Sistiva, Treaty of, 145
Skanderbeg (Gjergi Kastrioti), 48
Skolpje, fall of, 306
Slavs, 5, 6, 9, 68, 127; Southern, 21, 147; Eastern, 41; Southern
    problem, 287, 308
Slobozia, armistice, 181, 182; defeat at, 183
Slovakia, ceded to Hungary, 369
Smirdan, Battle of, 235
Sofia, Battle of, 235; declares war on Romania, 305
Sophia, Regent of Russia, 109
Soviet-German Treaty, 371
Soviet Union (See also Russia), 12-13, 108, 375, 385-388; accord with
    Romania, 366, 367, 382; agreement with Czechoslovakia, 316; allies
    of China, 380; Bolshevik Revolution, 306, 313; declares war on
    Bulgaria, 365, enters League of Nations, 317, 349, 356; Hungarian
    uprising, 383; interaction with Yugoslavia, 361; techniques to
    seize power in the Balkans, 376; Warsaw Pact, 385; WWII, 356, 370
Soviet-Yugoslav Traty of Friendship and Non-Aggression, 361
Spanish Civil War, 350, 370
Spanish Succession, War of the, 127, 128, 131, 132
Special Operations Executive (SOE), 373
Srazhimir, Tsar Ivan, of the Tsarate of Vidin, 40, 42
Stalin, Josef, 350, 352, 375, 380, 387; purges, 350; meets Tito, 362
Starhemberg, Count Rudiger von, 103
Stefan I, of Hungary, 7
Stefan I, Viovode of Moldavia, 41
Stefan the Great 51-52, 53, 64
Straits, closed 188, 397
Straits Convention, 188, 189, 225
Sturdza, Prince, 190
Styria, Turks invade, 52, 134
Sublime Porte (See also Ottoman Empire, Turkey), 75, 89, 94, 97, 101,
    108, 142; "Adrianople Affair," 130; French alliance with, 71;
    Mehmet Ali's revolt, 187; tribute increased by, 131; overthrow by
    Young Turks, 296
Suceava, fortress at, 53
Sudetenland, campaign against, 315; Hitler requests autonomy for, 350,
    358
Sudosteuropa-Gesellschaft (SOEG) (Nazi Balkan policy office), 353
Suleiman II, 105
Suleiman, son of Bayazid, 44
Suleiman the Magnificent, 66, 69-75; death of, 74
Sutu, Prince Alexandru, 183
Suvorov, Alexandre, 140, 142, 144, 145
Sviatoslav I, Grand Duke of Kiev, 12, 108, 131-132

Sweden, 128
Syria, 97, 98, 187, 371, 379
Szalasi, Ferenc, 370
Szatmar (Satu Mare), Treaty of, 130-131
Szatojay, Dome, 370
Szechenyi, Count Stephen, 192
Szigeth (Szigetvar), attack on, 74; Turks attack, 76

Tanzimat epoch, 223, 233
Targul-Mures (Maros-Vasarkely), 130
Tatars, 75, 76, 105, 127, 136, 139; support Turks, 52; with Bayazid,
    53; defeated, 76; Crimean Tatars, 96, 98, 99; Bugeac, 98; in
    Bulgaria, 228
Tepes, Vlad (Vlad the Impaler), 50, 51-53
Thant, U, 377
Thessalonike - See Salonika
Third Coalition, 180, 181
Third Estate, 179
Thirty Years' War, 89-92; Bohemian phase, 95, 98, 100
Thokoly, Count Imre, 103, 105
Three Emperors League, 246, 247
Thrace, 11
Timisoara, Battle of, 65; fortress at 134, 135
Timur (Tamerlane), 43
Tirgoviste, Battle of, 77
Tirgu-Jiu (Tagu-Jiu), Battle of, 305
Tito, (Josef Broz), 361, 362, 363, 364, 380-382; after his death, 387
Tokay (Tokaj), Zapolya defeated at, 69
Tott, Baron Francois de, 142
Transylvania, 20, 40, 175, 289; acknowledged, 105; Austrian garrison,
    105; Catholics persecuted, 94; ceded to Hungary, 366; declared
    autonomous, 228; defends Belgrad, 50; divided, 143; given to
    Romania, 311; revolution, 189, 190; independence acknowledged, 95;
    Iron Gate defeat, 45; part of Austro-Hungarian Empire, 9; removed
    from anti-Ottoman coalition, 94; revolts, 44, 46, 52, 93, 103, 136,
    247; struggle for control, 39; troops used, 48, 67, 98, 99, 103;
    Turkish penetration, 43; Turhish puppet, 101
Trentschin (Trencin), Battle of 130
Trianon, Treaty of, 309, 311, 313
Trieste, Free, 374
Tripartite Agreement of Vienna, 361, 366
Triple Alliance, 145, 292, 294, 304
Triple Entente, 292; Serbis requests support of, 305
Triple Regency of Yugoslavia (Yugoslav Regency Council), 361, 363
Tripoli (Italo-Turkish) War, 295
Tripolitsa, massacre of garrison at, 184
Truman Doctrine, 376, 378, 379
Truman, Harry S., 376
Turkey (See also Ottoman Empire, Turks, Sublime Porte), 129, 214, 239,
    309, 357, 379, 381; conflict with Greece, 376-377; declares war on
    Romania, 305; Democratic Party, 379; general information, 1, 14-15,
    20-21, 44, 106, 177-178, 310; German plan for, 353; invasion of
    Cyprus, 376-377; Koprulu period, 100, non-aggression pact with
    Romania, 316; Ottoman withdrawal from, 310; reform movement, 172;
    Republican Peoples' Party, 379; revolt in Cyprus, 249; rioting in,
    379, Serbia declares war on, 235; U.S. support, 376;

Turkey (Cont'd), war with Egypt, 188; war with Greece, 245-246; war of
    independence, 314; war with Italy, 294; war with Persia, 137-138;
    war with Poland, 97; wars with Russia, 1710-1711, 131-133, 135;
    1768-1774, 127, 139-142; 1787-1792, 144-146; 1806-1812, 180-182,
    186; 1877-1878, 10, 11, 176,  233-243; WWI, 304; WWII, 371-372
Turkish-Austrian Convention, 228
Turkish Caucasus, 379
Turkish Cypriots, 377
Turkish-Greek War, 314
Turkish non-aggression pact with Germany, 371
Turko-Austrian War, 134
Turko-Egyptian Wars, 188
Turko-French relations, 100
Turko-Hungarian armistice, 45
Turko-Persian War of Nadir Shah, 136
Turko-Russian War, 226
Turko-Venetian-Austrian War, 133-135
Turko-Venetian War, 93
Turks (See also Turkey, Ottoman Empire, Sublime Porte), against
    Austria, 70-71, 76-78, 102-103; against France, 179; against the
    Holy Roman Empire, 71; against Hungary, 66-70, 73-74, 102-103;
    against Poland, 103; attack the Banat, 53; capture Constantinople,
    37; capture Gallipoli, 38; conflict with Russia, 109; cross the
    Danube, 183, defeat at Valea-Alba, 53; defeat in Austria, 54; Iancu
    against the, 46-51; in the Danube valley, 2; revolution, 189-191;
    in Transylvania, 101, 105; Long War, 76-79, 94; rig Romanian
    election, 228; Serbian campaign against, 94; Vlad Tepes against,
    51-52; westernization attempts, 90
Turnovo, sacked, 40
Turtucaia (Tutrakhan), Battle of, 305
Tutora, Battle of, 98

Ukrainian Guerrilla Army, 373
Ukrainian uprising, 109
Ulema (council), 144
United Nations, 372, 376, 377, 378, 379, 385
United States, 192, 312, 315, 384; Czech Crisis, 349; general
    information, 167, 283; Hungary at war with, 370; nuclear weapons
    agreement with Turkey, 379; revolution, 122, 128, 139; Romania
    declares war on, 367; supports Tito, 362
Unkiar-Skelessi, Treaty of, 187, 188
USSR - See Soviet Union
Ustasi, 363, 381

Valea-Alba (Razboieni), Turks defeated at, 53
Valide, Sultana, 97
Varna, Battle of 14, failure at, 47, importance, 48
Varpolota Fortress, 74
Vasili Basil, Tsar of Russia, 63
Vaslui, Battle of, 49, 52
Vasvar, Treaty of, 102
Vauban, Marquis Sabastien le Prestre de, 130
Venetians, 134-135; naval units, 47; war with Turks, 75; Cretan
    campaign, 100; defeat at Candia, 103, given Morea, 105
Venice, 10, 38, 133; naval war with, 45; Turk's wars with, 52, 64, 71;
    new Holy League, 104
Venizelos, Eleutherios, Premier of Greece, 299, 305, 306
Vesprism (Beszprem) captured, 76

Victor II Emmanuel, 211
Vidin, captured, 42; retaken, 45; Mezit Beg of, 47; Battle of 243
Vienna (See also Austria), 106, 107, 231; Bukovina district ceded to,
    142; Catholic resurgence in, 95; Great Siege of, 103; revolt in
    189-190; sieges of, 70, 98, 102-103
"Vienna Diktat," 366
Vlad the Usurper (Iron Vlad), 40, 42
Vladimerescu, Tudor, 183, 186
Vladislav III, 67
Voicu, Romanian Knaz, 43

Wallachia, 9, 20, 101, 125; Austrian occupation, 134, 137; Fratia,
    189; general information, 44, 64, 67, 70, 72, 93, 96, 97; Germans
    enter, 305; revolution, 189; Hungarian campaign, 39; part of "Greek
    Plan," 144; Polish invasion, 94; revolts in, 73, 139, 186; Russian
    operations in, 226; Russo-Turkish War involvement, 131; sacked by
    Turks, 99; troops used, 40, 47, 48, 53, 75; Turkish retribution,
    133; Turkish raids, 38, 39, 43, 45 98, 190; unification with,
    Moldavia, 219
Wallis, Count Georg O. von, 137
Warsaw occupied, 99
Warsaw Pact Treaty, 387, 388, 389
Wehrmacht, 349, 355, 356, 365, 367, 369, 370
Westphalia, Peace of, 90
White Hill (Weisser Berg), Battle of, 98
White Russian forces, 315
Wilhelm II, 292
Worker's Party, 365
World War I, 212, 213, 215, 232, 233, 235, 242, 283, 284, 285, 293,
    301-306; Romanian role, 289; role of Nicholas II, 291, peace
    conference, 311, 351
World War II, 283, 284, 316, 349, 350, 351, 357; Balkan involvement,
    356-372

Young Turk Association, 294-295; overthrow of Sublime Porte, 296, 298,
    299
Ypsilanti, Constantin, Prince of Wallachia, 181
Ypsilanti, Alexandros, 183
Yugoslavia, 5, 18, 20, 90, 126, 214, 293, 312, 317, 354, 356, 366,
    372, 373, 376, 389; general information, 1, 9-11, 310, 374,
    380-382; German plan for, 353; German invasion, 356, 358, 367; WWII
    involvement, 361-364; joins Little Entente, 315; partisan movement,
    356, 361, 362, 363; resistance in, 374; Tito, 380-382; under Soviet
    domination, 374
Yugoslav Regency Council (Triple Regency), 361, 363

Zamoyski, John, 94
Zapolya, John, Viovide of Transylvania, 65, 67-73
Zapotocky, Antonin, 384, 385
Zarnesti, Austrian defeat at, 105
Zenta on the Tisza, Battle of, 105
Zeta District, rebel haven in, 10
Zog I, Ahmed Bey (Zogu), 358
Zrinyi, Count Miklos, 103
Zsibo, Rakoczi's defeat at, 130
Zsitvatorok, Treaty of, 95
Zurich, Treaty of, 228
Zvornik, fortress at, 134

# INDEX OF AUTHORS

This index contains an alphabetized listing of all of the authors, editors, compilers, and translators whose names are generally associated with the particular works mentioned in this volume. In some cases, the page designator refers only to an entry in the bibliographic section rather than in text and indicates a study that was, for a number of reasons, not placed in the textual material, but is worthy of mention here. In all other cases, the page number refers to the text. This index does not reflect volumes published by institutes or other collective or anonymous works. Names are spelled as they are presented either in the front matter of the study or as listed in the Library of Congress catalog. In one or two instances, more than one entry may appear for an individual based upon a different presentation of the name.

Abadziev, Georgi, 298
Abbott, G.F., 309
Abbott, J.S.C., 232
Abdi, (fnu), 136
Abou El-Haj, Refik A., 107
Abraham, Richard (w/Lionel Kochan), 291
Achtermeier, William O., 242
Aczel, Tamas, 384
Adamic, Louis, 376, 380
Adams, A.E., et al, 129, 170, 224, 291, 357
Adams, John C., 308
Adamthwaite, Anthony P., 355
Adaniloaie, Nichita, 244, 245; (w/Dan Berindei), 192
Adil, Ordaz bin, 41
Adnan, Abdulhak, 227
Ahmad, F., 295
Ahmed, Ali Mustafa ben, 72
Aichelberg, Wladimir, 309
Ainsztein, Reuben, 374
Akbaba, Col. Iskender, 311, 314
Akdag, Mustafa, 78, 91, 96
Aktepe, Munir, 97, 136, 230
Alasya, Col. Kadri, 226
Albertini, Luigi, 302
Albion, R.G., 122
Albrecht, U. 390
Aleksandrescu, Col. Vasile, 243, 245
Aleksic-Pejkovic, L., et al, 237
Alexander, E. (w/M.D. Ronnett), 368
Alexandrescu, V. 250
Alexandrescu-Dersca (Bulgaru), M., 43
Alger, John I., 178, 217, 285, 352
Allen, W.E.D., 15, 66
Allmayer-Beck, J.C. (w/E. Lessing), 54, 80, 110, 250
Almas, D. 77, 95

Almedingen, E.M., 173
Alston, R.C., 123
Altundag, Sinasi, 97
Amery, Julian, 359
Analis, D. 390
Anastasoff, Christ, 7, 215, 248, 286, 288, 290, 365
Ancel, Jacques, 146, 171, 214, 311
Anderson, A. Ross, (w/Lilita Dzirkals), 387
Anderson, D.P. 251
Anderson, Frank Meloy, (w/Amos Hershey), 236, 284
Anderson, J.H. 251
Anderson, M.S. 122, 141, 146, 170, 213, 214, 311
Anderson, R.C. 78, 93, 127, 129, 135, 179, 217
Anderson, Stephen S., 386
Andics, Mrs. E., 191
Andreski, Stanislav, 178, 216, 285, 352
Andrews, Byron, 238
Angeli, Moritz von, 137
Angelov, D.S., 100
Ansel, Walter, 353
Anthing, Johann F., 142
Antip, Maj. Gen. Constantine, 244; (w/Maj. Gen. Eugen Bantea), 244
Antoinat, Georges M., 300
Antonescu, Mihail A., 368
Apostolski, Mihajlo, 365
Archer, Laird, 360
Arena, Nino, 373
Arkayin, Asir, 107
Armayani, Y., 421
Armstrong, Hamilton Fish, 311, 380
Arnakis, George G., 15, 45, 89, 124, 177, 222, 247; (w/Wayne S.
    Vuchinich), 372
Arneth, A. von, 131
Ash, William, 248
Ashmead-Bartlett, Ellis & Seabury, 300
Asim Efendi, A. 147, 178, 182
Aston, Trevor H., 90
Atanackovic, Borisan, et al, 362
Atiya, A.S. 42
Austin, Walter, (w/Charles Horne), 303
Auty, Phyllis, 373; (w/Richard Clogg), 380
Ayers, P. 102
Ayverdis, A., 223

Babici, Ion, 369
Babin, A.I., et al, 173,224, 372
Babinger, Franz C.H., 5, 20, 39, 47, 74, 173, 215, 240
Bacon, Leonard (w/George R. Nayes), 300
Bacon, Walter M., Jr., 317
Baerlien, Henry P.B., 312
Bahro, Rudolf, 387
Bailey, F.E., 172, 224
Bailey, Ronald, et al, 374
Bailey, William F., 306
Baines, N.H. (w/H.St.L.B. Moss), 12
Bajza, Josef, 313
Baker, B. 347

Baker-Pasha, Lt. Gen. Valentine, 242
Baker, Vaughan (w/Amos Simpson), 302
Balabanov, Nicholas, 366
Balcescu, Nicolae, 8
Balck, William, 178, 217, 285
Baldwin, Herbert, 299
Balfour, Michael L.G., 303
Baltagi, Col. Paul, 317
Bandholtz, Harry, 313
Banks, Arthur, 230, 303, 355
Bannon, Alfred J. (w/Achilles Edelenyi), 16
Bantea, Maj. Gen Eugen, 369; (w/Constantine Antip), 244; (w/ Michael
    Ionescu), 368
Banyai, Ladislau, 51
Barber, Noel, 192, 223, 291
Bardakci, Ilhan, 298
Baring, Maurice, 300
Barker, Col. A.J., 226
Barker, Elizabeth, 11, 125, 177, 218, 290, 373
Barker, Thomas M., 102, 103, 106, 107, 138
Barnes, Thomas G. (w/Gerald D. Feldman), 168, 169, 213, 284, 311, 351
Barnwell, Grant R., 237
Barros, James, 312
Bartholomew, John., 1
Basila, I., 252
Basri Beg, 176, 220
Basta, Milan, 364
Bastav, S., 80
Bastelberger, J., 188
Batowski, Henryk, 316
Bauer, Hans, 302
Bayerle, Gustav, 79
Baykal, B.S., 141, 226
Baysum, Mohammed Cavid, 96, 100, 105, 142
Beal, Richard S., 375
Beard, Charles (w/George Radin), 312
Bearman, Graham (w/Peter Lee), 313
Bechirowsky, G., 308
Becker, A.S. (w/Arnold L. Horelick), 392
Beckinsale, Monica & Robert, 2
Beckman, G. 42
Bedeschi, Giulio, 359, 360
Beer, A., 147
Belder, E.A., 100
Beldiceanu, Nicoara, 44, 50, 53, 72
Belin, F.A., 72
Benaglia, Giovanni, 107
Benda, K, 131, 147
Benedict, Heinrich, 138
Benes, Edvard, 309
Benzoin, A., 150
Berard, V. 320
Bercovici, Konrad, 5
Berend, Ivan T. (w/ Gyorgy Ranki) 174, 215, 387
Berghahn, V.R., 216, 285, 351
Berindei, Dan, 231, 244; (w/Nichita Adaniloaie), 192
Berner, Samuel (w/Norman Cantor), 168, 169, 212, 283, 351

Bernhardi, Frederich von, 301
Bertotti, E. 307
Besbelli, Saim, 45, 71
Beskrovnyi, Luibomir G., 128
Best, Geoffrey, 179, 213
Betts, R.R., 111
Bezoin, Antonio, 137
Biaggi, A., 247
Biagini, Antonello, 298
Biber, Dusan, 354, 362
Bidwell, Robin, 372
Bigg, W., 103
Bindreiter, U., 253
Birdeanu, N. (w/D. Nicholescu), 176, 220, 289
Birke, Ernest, 170, 224
Birkos, Alexander, 17
Birnbaum, Henryk (w/Speros Yryonis), 388
Bishop, Robert (w/E.S. Crayfield), 13
Bitoleanu, Ion (w/ Adrian Radulescu), 39, 41
Black, Cyril, 5
Blainey, Geoffrey, 129, 142, 216, 351
Blind, K., 192
Bliss, Porter C. (w/Linus P. Brockett), 238
Bliss, Lt. Tasker H., 242
Blum, Jerome, et al, 168
Bode, Andreas, 141, 146
Bodea, Cornelia, 192, 219, 243
Body, P. 147
Bogaiavlenskii, S., 133
Boia, Lucian, 175, 219, 248
Bokor, Peter, 371
Boll, Michael M., 388
Bolsover, G.H., 226
Bombaci, A., 320
Boncabeille, Bernard, 298
Bond, Brian, 303, 316
Bonneval, Comte de Claude Alexandre, 138
Boniface, Antun, 10
Boppe, Auguste, 137, 185
Borsody, Stephan, 357, 375
Bosnjak, Ljubomir, 362
Bourne, K. (w/D.C. Watt), 393
Bousquit, George, 7
Bowen, H. 74, 89, 136
Bowen, R. 124
Boyle, Frederich, 240
Bozkurt, Riza, 49, 50
Braddock, Joseph, 12, 185
Bradford, E., 80
Bradley, J.F.N., 175, 218, 291, 358
Brailsford, Henry N., 11
Brainard, A.P., 253
Brannen, Barry, 368
Braubach, M., 131, 133
Braun, Aurel, 382
Braun, E. von, 8
Braun, J.F. 386

Braun, Maximilian, 5, 40, 108, 124, 177, 223, 290
Brayton, Abbott A. (w/Stephana J. Landwehr), 178, 216
Breccia, Alfredo, 362
Breunig, Charles, 146, 169
Brewster, J.W. (w/ J.A. McLeod), 24
Bridge, F.R. 229, 248, 288, 292, 302
Bridge, Roy (w/Roger Bullen), 169, 186, 284
Brierly, J.L., 321
Brinton, Crane C., 122
Brockett, Linus P. (w/Porter C. Bliss), 238
Bromley, J.S., 111, 121; (w/A.A. Goodwin), 123, 168; (w/A.N. Kurat),
    124, 132, 135; (w/A.N. Ryan), 151
Brooke, Z.N. (w/C.W. Previte-Orton), 59
Brook-Shepherd, Gordon, 386
Brower, Daniel R., 313
Brown, A.D. (w/ H.D. Jones), 17
Brown, J.F., 422
Brown, J.H. (w/S.A. Grant), 27
Brunker, Lt. Col. Howard M.E., 237
Brusatti, Alois, 222
Brusilov, A.A., 321
Bruun, Geoffrey, 122, 170
Bryce, James, 13
Brzezinski, Zbigniew K., 375
Bujac, Jean L.E., 191, 217, 285
Bulatovic, M., 393
Bullen, Roger (w/Roy Bridge), 169, 186, 284
Bulow, Prince B. von, 321
Burbulea, Emil, 382
Burks, Richard V., 243, 387
Burley, Henry, 300
Burski, A.A. von, 65
Bury, John B., 11
Bury, J.P.T., 195, 212, 213, 254, 321
Butler, R., 313
Buxton, Baron Noel-Edward, 300; (w/C.S. Lease) 322
Buxton, Charles R., 294
Byrnes, R.F., 24, 394

Calvocoressi, Peter (w/Guy Wynt), 354
Camesina, Albert, 106
Cammarata, Felice, 176, 220, 288
Campbell, Cyril, 298
Campbell, George Douglas, 8th Duke of Argyll, 227
Campbell, John, 192
Campbell, John K., 388
Campus, Eliza, 316
Candea, Sandra, 20
Cantimir, Prince Dimitri, 14
Cantor, Norman F. (w/Samuel Berner), 168, 169, 212, 283 351;
    (w/Michael S. Werthman), 169, 212, 284
Carp, Mercia, 382
Carsten, Francis L., 100, 317; et al, 171, 221
Carter, Francis, W., 2
Cary, (A.) Joyce, 299
Caslamanos, Demetrios, 299
Cassarvetti, Demetrius J., 299

Cassels, Alan, 353
Cassels, Lavender, 124
Cattell, David, 313
Cazan, Gheorghe N., (w/Serban Radelescu-Zoner), 248, 294, 307
Cazanisteanu, Col. Constantin, 8, 192, 220, 245, 307; (w/Michael
    Ionescu), 245; et al, 248
Ceaucescu, General Ilie, 45, 175, 219, 220, 289, 382; (w/Maj. Gen.
    Constantin Olteanu), 245; (w/V. Mocanu), 245; et al, 244
Celebi, Evliya, 96
Celiker, F. 309
Cernat, I. (w/ E. Stanislav), 382
Cernovodeanu, Paul, 101,125
Cesar, J., 81
Cevad Eren, Ahmed, 147, 182, 188, 242
Cevat Pasha Efendi, Ahmed, 187
Chambers, Howard, 387
Chandler, David G., 2, 38, 93, 121, 128, 132, 170, 179, 217
Charnaris, P. 42
Charques, Richard, 313
Chary, Frederick, 366
Chekrezi, Constantin A., 6
Cherekov, Evgenie N., 300
Chesney, Col. F.R., 185
Chester, S.B., 323
Churchill, Sir Winston S., 303, 354
Ciachir, Nicholae, 219, 220, 244
Cioranescu, George, 382
Cipolla, Carlo, 90
Cirilli, Gustava, 300
Clark, Sir G.N., et al, 90
Clarke, Jeffery, 22, 217, 285
Clarkson, Jesse D., 90, 127, 132, 172, 223, 236, 291
Clausewitz, Carl von, 178
Clauson, Sir Gerald L.M., 20
Clawson, Robert (w/Lawrence Kaplan), 388
Clayton, Gerald D., 171, 224, 291
Cleator, P.E., 92, 129, 179, 217, 285, 352
Clissold, Stephen, 9, 362, 381
Clogg, Richard, 148, 177, 185, 221, 360; (w/Phyllis Auty), 373;
    (w/George Yannopoulos), 378
Coakley, Robert W. (w/John E. Jessup), 22, 93, 178, 217, 285, 352
Cobden, Richard, 223
Cohen, William B., 213
Colby, Elbridge, 92, 129, 179, 217, 285, 352
Coles, Paul, 15, 42, 89, 124
Coman, Col. Gen Ion, 244, 382
Constantine I, King of Greece, 299
Constantini, Colonel Aime, 106
Cook, M.A., 124, 132
Cooke, William S., 45
Cooper, J.P., 92
Cooper, M.B., 294
Copoiu, N., et al, 374
Coquelle, P. 10, 52, 90, 126, 176, 218
Cordier, L. 323
Corivan, Nicholae, 244
Corvisier, Andre, 93, 129

Courteille, Michel Pavet de, 68
Cowles, Virginia, 191, 223, 226, 238, 248, 291
Coxe, William, 13
Craig, Gordon A., 169, 213, 229, 230
Crainiceanu, Gen. G., 257
Crane, John O., 316
Crankshaw, Edward, 138, 287
Crawley, C.W., 179, 182, 185
Crayfield, E.S., 13
Creasy, Sir Edward S., 14, 141, 142, 146, 177, 180, 181, 187, 188,
    222, 226, 230, 236
Crespi, Riccardo, 359
Cretzianu, Alexandre, 368, 382
Crouzenac, S. de (Saunier de Beaumont), 152
Crowe, Maj. John H.V., 241
Cruciunas, Silviu, 368
Cruttwell, C.R.M.F., 303
Csanadi, Norbert, et al, 313
Csendes, L., 324
Cucu, Mihai, 289, 382
Cunningham, Allen, 299
Curtiss, John Shelton, 226
Cuspa, Ion, 52, 53, 54, 369
Cvijic, Jovan, 312
Czernin, Count Ottokar, 303
Czerwinski, E.J. (w/J. Pilkolkiewicz), 385

Dakin, Douglas, 141, 184, 185, 186, 188, 189, 221, 230, 232, 246,
    288, 293, 314
Dalton, Maj. Gen. J.C., 241
Dan, Mihail, 47, 48, 51
Darby, H.C., 63
David, Zdanek (w/Robert Kann), 14, 71, 90, 126, 173, 214, 287
Davis, Lynn, 375
Davison, R.H., 21, 227, 242
Dawn, C.E., 257, 324
Deac, Augustine (Georghe Unc), 312
Deakin, F.W.D., 363
De Bazancourt, L., 257
de Bonnac, Marquis, 237
Dedijer, Vladimir, 290, 302, 362, 381
Delafield, Richard, 226
Delbruck, Hans, 93, 129
Dellin, L.A.D., 383
Delmas, J., 130
del Vayo, J.A., 257
De Maderiaga, I., 146
Demirhan, Pertev, 249, 310
Denison, George, 179, 217
Dennen, Leon, 372
Denton, Rev. William, 10
Deny, J., 106
De Pauw, John W., 388
Detwiler, Donald, 356
Deutscher, I., 324
Diehl, Charles, 50
Dimakis, J., 324

Dimitrov, Nikola, 312
Dinic, M., 39
Dioszegi, I., 237
Dirimtekin, Feridun, 50
Djevad Bey, Ahmed, 72, 93
Djilas, Milovan, 10, 363
Djordjevic, Dimitriji, 6, 180, 182, 185, 191, 215, 293, 297, 312
d'Ohsson, I.M., 124
Dojnov, Dojno, 238
Dolezol, Jiri (w/Jan Kren), 358
Dontas, Doman, 185, 230, 232, 246
Dorn, Walter, 122
Dornberg, John, 353
Dougherty, William J., 355
Doyle, William, 90, 122, 131
Dragan, Joseph, 6
Draghicescu, Dimitrii, 289, 307
Dragic, Djordje, 363
Dragnic, Alex N., 290, 381
Drechsler, Robert, 376
Driault, Edouard, 146, 171, 214
Drosos, Demetrios I., 299
Ducas, I., 45
Duff, James D., 291
Duffy, Christopher, 138
Duffy, Thomas G., 249, 293
Dufourcq, Pierre (w/Gen. J.E. Valley), 303
Duggan, Stephen P.H., 171, 214
Dujcev, Iwan, 290, 365
Dunn, Richard S., 63, 122
Dunnigan, James, 356
Dunn-Pattison, R.P., 170
Dupuy, R. Ernest & Trevor N., 37, 47, 49, 52, 64, 68, 70, 70, 78, 92,
    130, 131, 135, 137, 141, 146, 179, 182, 187, 188, 191, 216, 230,
    236, 246, 247, 249, 284, 295, 297, 303, 308, 313, 314, 315, 316,
    352
Dupuy, Trevor N., 93
Durham, Mary Edith, 293, 299
Dvoichenko-Markov, Demetreous, 146
Dwight, Henry O., 242,
Dwyer, F.J., 236
Dzelebdzic, Milovan (w/Branko Latas), 363
Dzirkals, Lilita (w/A. Ross Anderson), 387

Earle, Edward M., 130, 178, 216, 285, 351
Eddy, Charles B., 312
Edelenyi, Achilles, 16
Edroiu, N., 153
Edwards, Lovett, 180, 186
Egerton, Hugh E., 172, 224
Egli, David, 380
Ehreburg, Il'ia, 373
Eidelberg, Philip G., 294
Einhorn, V., 112
Eisenmann, Louis, 231
Ekren, (fnu), 102
Elagin, S.I., 119
Eliot, Sir Charles, 15, 89

Ellesmere, Earl of, 70, 106
Elliot, Sir H., 325
Elton, G.R., 63
Emin, Ahmed, 309
Enginsoy, Lt. Gen. Cemal, 314, 315
Enser, A.G.S., 355
Epanchin, Col. Nicholai, 240
Epstein, F.T., 26
Erendil, Muzaffer, 14, 39, 42, 44, 47, 48
Erickson, John, 356, 357
Erpenbeck, Dirk-Gerd, 364
Eskenasi, Viktor, 45
Essame, H., 325
Eton, William, 14, 124
Eubank, Keith, 353, 354
Eudes, Dominick, 360
Evans, Arthur J., 238
Evans, Stanley G., 6
Eversley, Lord G.J. Shaw-Levre, 14
Evrygenis, Dimitrios, 293
Eyck, Erich, 230

Faissler, Margareta, 302, 308
Falls, Cyril B., 129, 178, 216, 284
Farkas, C., 326
Farnsworth, Henry W., 298
Farquhar-Bernard, Alfred, 240
Fay, Sidney, 302
Fehleisen, Egmont, 232
Fehmi, Youssouf, 294
Fejto, Francois, 387
Feldman, Gerald (w/Thomas Barnes), 168, 169, 213, 284, 311, 351
Fenenc, Tone, 363
Fenyo, Mario D., 371
Fichev, I.V., 326
Fichtner, Paula S., 68
Fife-Cooksen, Lt. Col. John C., 241
Finer, S.E., 398
Finlay, George, 11, 39, 90, 125, 176, 184, 221
Fisher, Allen, 141
Fisher, Fritz, 303
Fisher, Sidney N., 65, 66, 74, 108, 124, 222, 290
Fisher-Galati, Stephen, 6, 7, 19, 221, 289, 368
Fishev, I.V., 298
Florinsky, Michael T., 127, 172, 223, 291
Floyd, Dale E., 178, 217
Fodor, Marcel S., 353
Foley, C. (w/W.J. Scobie), 379
Fontaine, A., 398
Foot, M., 259
Forbes, Archibald, 240
Forbes, Neville, et al, 5, 174, 214, 286
Ford, Maj. Clyde S., 297
Formby, John, 242
Forst de Battaglia, Otto, 106
Forster, E.S., 12, 185, 221, 288, 360
Forster, Gerhard, 285

Forster, Jurgen, 368
Fortunatow, P., 239
Fotitch, Constantin, 381
Fraser, Charles, 91
Fraser, Maj. Gen. Sir Thomas, 241
Fried, Alfred, 301
Friessner, Generaloberst a.D. Hans, 368
Frischauer, P. 126, 171 221, 287
Frothingham, Arthur L., 303
Frothingham, Helen Losanovitch, 308
Frothingham, Thomas L., 303
Fuller, J.F.C., 37, 92, 129, 178, 216, 284
Funk, Arthur, 355
Furneaux, Rupert, 242
Fussel, P., 327
Fuyet, Herve, 180

Gabriel, Richard A., 389
Galantai, J., 288
Garami, Erno, 313
Gardiner, Lt. Cmdr. Leslie, 380
Gardiner, Samuel R., 100
Gaumant, E., 217, 290
Gaynor, Frank, 352
Gazsi, Jozsef, 371
Gedye, George Eric, 358
Gegaj, Athanase, 48
Genoff, G.P., 219, 365
Genova, Liudmila, 219
Georgescu, Maria, et al, 192, 382
Georgiev, Georgi I., 365
Gershoy, Leo, 146
Geshkoff, Theodore I., 316
Geshov, Ivan E., 299, 303
Gewehr, Wesley Marsh, 3, 174, 215, 286
Gibb, Sir Harold A.R. (w/H. Bowen), 74, 89, 124; et al, 372
Gibbon, E. 27
Gibbons, H.A., 41, 299
Gibbs, W.H., 122, 182
Gibbs, Sir Philip H. (w/Bernard Grant), 300
Giesche, Richard, 298
Gilbert, Felix, 169, 212, 284, 351
Gilbert, Martin, 13, 170, 224, 291, 303, 373
Gill, R.R., 399
Gines, D.S. (w/ B.G. Mexas), 7
Giordani, Paolo, 307
Girvidan, H.H., 78
Giurescu, Constantin C., et al, 8, 39, 40, 44, 51, 54, 67, 97, 125, 135, 219, 231, 289, 294, 368
Giurescu, Dinu, 8
Gladt, Karl, 180, 182, 185
Glatz, Ferenc, 357
Goerlitz, W., 422
Gokbilgin, M. Tayyip, 78, 108
Goldman, Nancy L., 374
Gollner, Carl, 74
Gollwitzer, Heinz, 248, 283

Golovachev, Viktor F., 141
Goltz, Gen. Baron Kolmar von der, 249
Gomiou, Lt. Gen. Gheorghe, 382
Gooch, Brison, 226
Gooch, George P., 138; (w/Sir Harold Temperley), 303
Goodwin, A., 122, 123, 168
Gorceix, Septima, 138
Gordon, Thomas, 185
Gorlitz, W., 399
Gosnyak, I., 381
Gossip, Robert, 172, 222
Gosztony, Peter I., 384
Grachev, V.P., 41
Gragger, Robert, 107
Grant, A.J., 90
Grant, Bernard (w/Sir Philip Gibbs), 300
Grant, S.A. (w/J.H. Brown), 27
Grassi, M.A., 178, 223, 291
Gratz, Gustav, 313
Graves, Sir Robert W., 248, 300
Graviere, Jurien de la, 71, 78
Greckov, I.B., 79
Greene, F.V., 241, 248
Grenadier, Robin L., 82
Grey of Fallodon, Viscount, 261
Grimstead, Patricia K., 21, 291
Grinard, Fernand, 178, 214, 223, 311
Grivas-Dighenis, George, 378
Grothe, H., 328
Grozea, Col. Traian, 382
Guldescu, Stanko, 74; (w/John Prcela), 381
Gulick, Edward V., 122, 168, 178, 213, 284, 351
Gyoerkei, Jeno, 370
Gyorgy, Andrew (w/Teresa Rakowska-Harmstone), 386

Hadrovics, L., 113
Haider, Rudolf, 365
Hajdu, Tibor, 309, 313
Hajek, Alois, 78, 239
Hale, J.R., 63, 68, 79
Halecki, Oskar, 4, 47
Halli, Resay, 298
Halpern, Paul G., 295, 299
Halsey, Francis W. 303, 309
Hamley, Sir Edward B., 226
Hammer-Purgstall, Joseph von, 15, 124, 177
Hammond, Nicholas G.L., 11, 42
Hammond, R.A., 237
Hampson, Norman, 146, 169
Hantsch, H. 126, 171, 221, 287
Harding, Bertita, 309
Hardoin, N. (Dick le Lonlay, pseud.), 261
Harris, David, 237
Haskell, Arnold L., 239
Headley, Phineas C., 191
Heer, Friedrich, 13, 71, 78, 90
Held, Joseph, 46

Heller, Joseph, 294, 299
Helmreich, Ernst C., 297
Helmreich, Paul C., 314
Heltai, George, 384
Henderson, Nicholas, 133
Hengelmuller von Hengervar, Ladislas Freiherr, 130
Heppel, Muriel (w/Frank B. Singleton), 9, 90, 126, 176, 217, 290, 362
Herbert, Frederick W. von, 243
Herr, Frederic G., 300
Hershey, Amos (w/Frank M. Anderson), 236, 284
Herspring, Dale R. (w/Ivan Volgyes), 387
Hess, A., 65
Hetes, Tibor, 313
Heurtley, W.A., et al, 27
Heyd, Uriel, 147
Heymann, Egon, 174, 215, 286
Heymann, F.G., 57
Higham, Robin, 360; (w/David H. Zook), 37, 64, 78, 92, 121, 130, 179,
     216, 236, 284, 352
Hillgruber, Andreas, 354, 368
Himes, Capt. (fnu), 240
Hink, Helma, 248
Hinsley, Francis H., 212, 236
Hitchins, Keith T., 175, 192, 311
Hnilicka, Karl, 364
Hobsbawm, E.J., 146, 169
Hochwachter, G. von, 300
Hodgart, Alan, 122, 168, 351
Hodgetts, E.A.B., 154
Hoensch, J.K., 329
Hoffman, George W., 387
Hoffman, John Wesley, 295, 299
Hogg, Ian, 179, 217
Holborn, Hajo, 249
Holt, P.M., et al, 372
Hoptner, J.B., 317
Horak, Stephen, 16
Horecky, Paul L., 15, 16, 169, 215, 286
Horelick, Arnold L. (w/A.S. Becker), 365
Horetsky, Adolf von, 241
Horne, Alistair, 170
Horne, Charles F. (w/Walter F. Austin), 303
Horthy, Adm. Miklos(Nicholas), 317, 371
Hosch, Edgar, 5, 123, 173, 214, 286, 356
Hourani, Albert Habib, 14, 124, 177, 222, 290, 372,
Houtsma, T., 28
Howard, Harry N., 314, 378; (w/ Robert Kerner), 316
Howard, Michael E., 217, 232
Howell, Philip, 300
Hozier, Col. Sir H.M., 229, 237
Hristov, H., et al, 293
Huart, C.L., 72
Hummelberger, Walter, 102
Hunczak, Taras, 127, 173, 223, 291
Hurd, A.S., 252
Hurowitz, J.C., 146, 171
Hussey, John, 12

Hutchinson, Thomas, S., 300
Hutton, R,M. 132
Huyshe, Wentworth, 238

Iatrides, John, 378, 381
Ignat'ev, Pavel, 240
Ignotus, Paul, 126, 175, 218, 291, 356
Ilie, P. (w/Col. Constantin Nicholae), 369
Il'in, Lt. D.S., 141
Immich, Max, 102
Inal, Ibnulemin Mahmud Kemel, 249
Inalcik, Halil, 15, 39, 44, 45, 47, 51, 52, 67, 68, 71, 78, 93, 242
Inks, James, 364
Ionescu, Ghita, 382
Ionescu, Michael, 316; (w/ Maj. Gen. Eugen Bantea), 368; (w/Col.
    Constantin Cazanisteanu), 245
Iorga, Nicolae, 8, 39, 47, 52, 76, 95, 125, 146, 175, 177, 219, 223,
    289, 290, 298
Iosipescu, Sergie, 45
Irving, D., 353
Iseminger, George L., 227
Itzkowitz, Norman, 124
Izzi, Suleyman, 138

Jackowicz, Jerzy, 365
Jackson, Marvin R. (w/ John Lampe), 123, 174, 215, 287, 357
Jacobs, I., 135
Jacobson, Hans-Adolp (w/Arthur L. Smith), 355
Jahn, Max, 123
Jain, J.R., 388
James, Lionel, 300
Janetta, M.J., 123
Jaschke, G., 294, 309, 314, 317, 379
Jastrow, Morris, 309
Jaszi, Oscar, 287, 288, 313
Jelavich, Barbara & Charles, (Barbara), 222, 223, 227, 248 291;
    (Charles), 221, 248, 287, 312; (together), 3, 173, 188, 191, 214,
    231, 236, 247, 286, 288, 297, 308, 316, 256, 387
Jelic-Butic, Fikreta, 363
Jenkins, H.D., 74
Jenkins, Romilly, 232
Jessup, John E., 241, 243; (w/Robert W. Coakley), 22, 93, 178, 217,
    285, 352
Jirecik, Konstantin, 41
Johnson, A. Ross, 381
Johnson, Mean, 388
Johnson, Stowers, 374
Johnston, M., 403
Johnston, R.W., 331
Jomini, Alexander G., 241
Jomini, Baron H., 178
Jones, Christopher, D., 386
Jones, David, 403
Jones, H.D., 17
Jones, Tom, 168
Jonquiere, A.de la, 41
Jordan, David S., 301

Jordan, G., 332
Jovanovic, V.M., 28
Juchereau de Saint-Denys, A. de, 58

Kabasakai, H. (w/R. Yosar), 346
Kabisch, Ernst, 307
Kacavenda, Petar, 363
Kahn, D., 403
Kalbe, Ernstgert, 374
Kaldis, William P., 186
Kalezic, Z., 403
Kallai, Gyula, 370
Kallay, N., 403
Kalvoda, John, 385
Kaminsky, Howard, 46
Kanet, Roger E., 18
Kann, Reginald, 300
Kann, Robert A., 13, 171, 191, 221, 287; (w/Zdanec David), 14, 71,
    90, 126, 173, 214, 287
Kaplan, H.H., 155
Kaplan, Lawrence (w/Robert Clawson), 388
Karal, Enver Z., 71, 133, 223
Karasz, A., 264
Karayovoff, T., 332
Karolides, P., 185, 191, 221, 246, 249, 312
Karol of Romania, 264
Karpat, Kemal, 16
Kasneci, Lefter, 359
Kaynar, R., 264
Kedourie, Elie, 295, 309
Keep, J.L.H., 223, 236, 248
Kehrig, Manfred, 372
Kellenbenz, Herbert, 122
Kellogg, Frederick, 243
Kemeny, Gabor G., 19
Kennan, G. F., 332
Kennedy, Paul M., 122, 303
Kent, Marion, 314
Kerner, Robert J., 9, 126, 312, 316, 362, 380; (w/Harry Howard), 316
Kertesz, Stephen D., 387
Kessle, Gun (w/Jan Myrdal), 380
Khalifeh, Hajji, 65, 93, 135
Khitrova, Ina, 224
Khmelevskii, G., 303
Khristov, Khristo, 239
Kindinger, Rudolph, 102
King, Edward, 240, 243
King, Robert R., 376, 386
King, William B. (w/ Frank O'Brien), 375
Kinross, Lord J.P.D. Balfour, 14, 52, 67, 68, 71, 77, 78, 89, 96, 97,
    100, 106, 124, 177, 22, 290
Kintner, William R. (w/Wolfgang Klaiber), 386
Kiraly, Bela K., 123, 384, 388
Kissling, Hans J., 96
Kissling, Rudolph, 191
Kiszling, Rudolf, 308
Kitintcheff, Spiro, 308

Kiz, Andras, 370
Klaiber, Wolfgang (w/William Kintner), 386
Klaic, Vjekoslav, 10
Klokman, I.R., 141
Klyuchevski, Vasili O., 127, 133, 172, 223, 291
Knapp, V.J., 264
Knight, E.F., 294
Knorr, Klaus E., 375
Knotel, R., et al, 333
Knox, Gen. Sir W.G., 242
Kochan, Lionel (w/Richard Abraham), 291
Koehler, Kurt, 106
Kofos, Evangelos, 246, 381
Kohn, Hans, 171, 187, 191, 221, 287
Kolarz, Walter, 6
Kolejka, Josef, 298
Komski, Victor, 308
Kondis, Basil, 299
Kontogiannes, P.M., 127
Koprulu, Mehmet Fuat, 15
Korbel, J., 421
Korbonski, Andrzej, 388
Korom, Mihaly, 371
Kortepeter, Carl M., 78
Kosary, D.G., 7, 46, 47, 174, 186, 222
Kosev, Konstantine, 238
Kostelski, Z., 9
Kostich, Dragos D., 356
Kotsch, Walter, 385
Koumoulides, John T.A., 221
Kourvetaris, G.A., 378
Kousoulas, D.G., 378
Kovacs, Frederick W.L. (pseud.), 357
Kovig, B., 384
Kowalski, T., 74, 108
Krallert-Sattler, G., 29
Kramers, J.H., 70
Krasniqi, Rexhep, 380
Kratchunov, K., 333
Kraus, Rene, 355
Kren, Jan (w/Jiri Dolezol), 358
Kreutel, R., 114
Krieger, Leonard, 156
Krinitsyn, F.S., 141
Krizman, Bogdan, 363
Krunich, Lt. Milutin, 308
Kuepfer, Emile, 177, 290
Kukiel, Marian, 106
Kulic, D., 405
Kunitz, George C., 106
Kurat, A.N., 100, 107, 124, 132, 135; (w/J.S. Bromley), 156
Kushner, D., 291
Kutukoglu, Bekir, 78, 105, 142
Kverer, D., 405
Kyrou, Alexis, 293

Lachouque, Henri, 170

Laffan, R.G.D., 54
Lahrkamp, Helmut, 101
Lake, Harold, 306
Lamb, Harold, 83
Lamouche, L. 223
Lampe, John R. (w/Marvin R. Jackson), 123, 174, 215, 287, 357
Landwehr, Stephana J. (w/Abbott A. Brayton), 178, 216
Lane, Peter B., 358
Langer, William L. 122, 169, 212, 233, 237, 248
Langford, R. Victor, 373
Langlois, Gen. Hippolyte, 241
Larrabee, F. Stephen, 386
Larrabee, S.A., 186, 221
Laska, Vera, 374
Latas, Branko (w/Milovan Dzelebdzic), 363
Lazarovich-Hrebelianovich, Prince, 176, 218, 289
Lazelle, Henry, 248
Lease, C.S. (w/N.E. Buxton), 323
Leathers, Noel L., 237
Lecomte, Ferdinand, 238
Lederer, Ivo J., 13, 127, 172, 223, 291, 312, 372
Lee, Peter (w/Graham Bearman), 313
Le Faure, Amedee J., 238
Lefebvre, G., 156
Legrand, E.L.J., 6. 7. 18, 125, 220, 288, 359
Legters, L., 16, 357
Lehrman, Harold A., 373
Leites, N., 405
Lendvai, Paul, 376
Lengyel, Emil, 7, 46, 47, 65, 68, 69, 90, 96, 103, 126, 174, 191,
    222, 288, 370
Lentin, A., 127
Leo, Michel, 78, 91, 126, 176, 219
Leon, George, 309
Lessing, E. (w/J.C. Allmayer-Beck), 54
Lessner, Ann M.L. & Erwin C., 4, 67-71, 76,78, 90, 96, 103, 106, 123,
    173, 214, 230, 236, 286, 293
Levend, Agah Sirri, 72
Levy, Armand, 191
Levy, Avigdor, 188
Lewinsohn, Richard, 38, 217, 285, 352
Lewis, Sir Bernard, 15, 50, 147, 222, 290, 372
Lewis, Jesse W., 387
Lewis, Michael, 217, 230
Liddell-Hart, Basil H., 217, 230
Liess, Otto R.I., 6
Lincoln, Francis F., 378
Lincoln, W. Bruce, 173, 227
Lindsay, Jack O., 12
Liptai, Ervin, et al, 371
Livescu, Jean (w/Stefan Pascu), 245
Lloyd, C.C. 122, 182
Lobanov-Rostovsky, A., 146, 172, 186
Lockhart, Sir R.H.B., 385
Lodi, Angelo, 373
Loebl, Alfred, 96
Logan, Milla Z., 381

Logoreci, Anton, 6, 288, 359, 380
Lorenz, Reinhold, 309
Loverdo, Costa de, 374
Low, Alfred D., 313
Lowe, James T., 216, 285, 352
Lufti Pasha, 74
Lukacs, John A., 317, 356, 375
Lukinich, Imre, 74, 95, 131
Lupu, Nicholas, 307
Luther, Martin, 70
Luvaas, Jay, 130, 216, 285
Luza, R., 358
Lybyer, Albert H., 72
Lyons, M., 128, 240

Macartney, C.A., 7, 14, 54, 63, 96, 97, 99, 100, 125, 127, 137, 146,
    171, 174, 191, 221, 222, 230, 231, 287, 288; (w/A.W. Palmer), 313,
    316, 370
MacDermott, Mercia, 7, 42, 72, 78, 90, 96, 97, 126, 133, 148, 176,
    182, 186, 192, 218, 22, 236, 239, 248
Macek, Vladko, 293, 313, 362, 381
MacGahan, Januarius, 242
Machray, Robert, 316
Maciu, Vasile, 307
Mackenzie, David, 236, 239
Mackintosh, Malcolm, 388
Madden, H.M., 267
Maderiaga, Isalda de, 142, 146
Magocsi, P.R., 335, 406
Maior, Liviu, 244
Makkai, Ladislav, 8, 53, 102, 125, 175, 219, 289
Makriyannis, 186
Mamatey, Victor S., 71, 90, 126, 171
Mange, Alyce E., 224
Marcovich, Lazare, 312
Marczali, H. 126
Marguerat, Philippe, 368
Margutti, Albert A.V. Freiherr von, 191, 230, 288
Marinescu, Antone (w/Gheorghe Romanescu), 369
Markopoulos, G., 246
Markovich, Lazar, 308
Markus, Vasyl, 370
Marlow, John, 172, 224
Marmullaku, Ramadan, 6
Marriott, Sir John A.R., 146, 170, 214
Marston, Frank S., 311
Martin, Henry J., 373
Martin, Ralph G., (w/Stojan Pribicevic), 364
Martinov, (fnu), 267
Marx, Karl, 146, 171
Massie, Robert K., 133
Masson, Philippe, 355
Mastecky, Vaslac, 7
Mastny, Vojtech, 358
Matei, Demitru, 382
Matley, Ian, 8
Matuschka, L., 135

Maule, Henry, 361
Maurice, Maj. Gen. Sir Frederich B., 237
Mavrocordato, J., 176, 184, 221, 288
May, Arthur J., 248, 308, 313
Mayer, A.J., 335
Mayes, S., 422
McCauley, Martin, 376
McClellan, George B., 241
McConnell, Allen, 173
McCullagh, F., 242
McEvedy, Colin, 2, 38, 216, 284
McGeoch, Ian, 388
McLaughlin, Louisa A. (w/Emma M. Pearson), 239
McMunn, Sir George F., 93
McNeill, William H., 37, 168, 212, 351
Mediger, W., 127
Medlicott, W.N., 221, 236, 248
Mehmet, Mustafa M., 125
Mellor, Roy E.H., 386
Menage, Victor L., 66
Menning, Bruce W., 127, 173
Merei, G., 147
Merriman, Roger, 74
Mexas, B.G., 17
Meyer, Klaus, 229, 357
Michiewicz, A., 202
Mijatovich, Chedomille, 9
Miksche, Ferdinand O., 374
Milazzo, M.J., 407
Miletic, Antun, 362
Milic, Danica, 185
Miller, A.F., 185
Miller, James M., 297
Miller, Marshall Lee, 365
Miller, William, 5, 17, 135, 141, 222, 290
Millman, Richard, 233
Milutinovic, K.N., 268
Milyoukan, Paul N., 291
Minkov, Minko, 383
Misefari, Enzo, 359
Mishev, Dimitrie, 7
Mitchell, Ruth, 362
Mitrany, David, 311, 312
Mitrovski, Boro, 364
Mocanu, V. (w/Gen. Ilie Ceaucescu), 245
Molnar, Miklos, 384
Moltke, H.K.B. Graf von, 185, 217
Monroe, Will Seymour, 300
Montagu, Irving, 241
Montagu, Lady M.M., 158
Montgomery, John F., 370
Montross, Lynn, 216, 284
Mooney, Peter J., 386
Moore, Frederick, 249, 294
Moorehead, Alan, 307
Moraca, Pero, 362
Mordal, Jacques, 179, 217, 285

Mordtmann, A., 50
Mordtmann, Johannes H., 66, 68
Morison, Walter, 300
Morris, Lady Constance, 138
Morris, John, 248; (w/J.M. Roberts), 283
Morris, L.P., 386
Morris, W.O'C., 268
Morton, Frederic, 249
Mosely, Philip E., 191
Moss, H.St.L.B. (w/N.H. Baines), 12
Mosse, W.E., 227
Motiuk, Lt. Col. L. 375
Mouzaffer-Talaat Pasha Bey, 238, 243
Mowat, C.L., 351
Mrazkova, D. (w/V. Remes), 408
Mucs, Sandor (w/Erno Zagoni), 384
Muhtar Pasha, Ahmed, 185
Muhtar Pasha, Ferik Ahmed, 102
Muller-Hillebrand, Gen. Burkhart, 355
Munson, William B., 103, 106, 107
Murad, Anatol, 191, 230
Muresan, Camil, 46
Murray, William S., 215, 286
Musat, Mircea, 43, 244
Mutafeieva, Vera P., 78
Mylonas, George, 5
Myrdal, Jan (w/ Gun Kessle), 380
Myshlaevskii, Col. Aleksandr Z., 127

Naff, Thomas, 123, 124, 147; (w/R. Owen), 158
Nagy, Ferenc, 383
Nagy-Talavera, Nicholas M., 354, 370
Nami, Mustafa, 91
Namier, Lewis B., 191
Narochnitskaya, Lydia I., 240
Nayes, George R. (w/Leonard Bacon), 300
Naylor, Kenneth E., et al, 16
Neagoe, Manole, 64, 77
Neck, Rudolf, et al, 353
Needham, John L., 241
Nelson, Daniel N., 389
Nembigin, Marion I., 307
Nemes, D., 203
Nemeskurty, Istvan, 371
Nenadovic, M., 203
Nesovic, Slobodan, 364, 381
Newman, Bernard, 356
Newman, James R., 37
Nicholae, Col. Constantin, 244; (w/P. Ilie), 369
Nicholescu, D. (w/ N. Birdeanu), 176, 220, 289
Nikitin, S.A. 224, 227, 239
Niven, Alexander, 170
Noli, Fan S., 48
Nouzille, Jean, 137
Novikova, Olga, 241
Nowak, Karl F., 311
Nowak, Tadeusz, 100, 107

O'Ballance, Edgar, 378
Obolensky, Dimitri, 12
O'Brien, C.B., 109
O'Brien, Frank (w/William King), 375
O'Connor, J.D., 237
O'Connor, Raymond G., 178, 352
Odlozilnik, O., 59
Ogg, David, 90, 122
Ognianova, Militsa, 298
Okcu, Yaha (w/Hilmi Ustunsoy), 310
Okse, Necati (w/Irfan Teksut), 310
Oliva, L. Jay, 109, 133
Olivier, Lewis P.F., 218
Olivova, Vera, 309, 312, 358
Ollier, Edmund, 238
Olteanu, Maj. Gen. Constantin, 8, 42, 186, 243, 244; (w/Gen. Ilie
    Ceaucescu), 245, 382
Oman, Sir Charles, 37, 64
Ondes, O., 242
Opacic, Petar, 309; (w/Savo Skoko), 239
Opie, Redvers, 375
Oprita, Constantin, 382
Orhunlu, Cenzig, 100, 105, 107, 108, 229
Orlov, Dietrich, 353
Ostrogorski, George, 11, 50
Overy, R.J., 409
Owen, Roger, 123, 124
Ozkaya, Yucel, 141
Oztuna, T.Y., 242

Packer, Charles, 309
Pacor, M., 409
Padev, Michael, 366
Padover, Saul K., 146
Paget, John, 175
Paikert, G.C., 354
Pajol, C.V.P., 158
Pajovic, Radoje, 363
Pakalm, Mehmed Ziki, 249, 291
Palanceanu, Elena, et al, 245
Pall, Frederick, 48
Pallis, A.A., 336
Palmer, A.W., 284, 351; (w/C.A. Macartney), 310
Palmer, J.A.B., 43
Panaretoff, Stephen, 5
Pandevski, Manol, 293
Panitescu, P.P., 77, 95
Pano, Nicholas C., 380
Papacosma, S. Victor, 378
Papacostea, Serban, 51, 52
Papadopoulos, G.S., 249
Papadopoullos, T.H., 30
Papagos, Gen. Alexander, 360
Papandreou, Andreas, 378
Papavici, A., 270
Pargellis, Stanley M., 123
Parkinson, Roger, 352

Parnell, Arthur, 131
Parry, J.H., 38
Parry, V.J., 52, 65, 67, 78, 96
Parvan, V., 59
Pascu, Stefan, 40, 244; (w/Jean Livescu), 245, 289, 294
Pataki, I., 79
Pauley, B., 221, 287
Paulova, Milada, 309
Pavlovska, Zvetana, 239
Pavlowitch, K.St., 218
Pears, Sir Bernard, 242
Pears, Sir Erwin, 50
Pearson, Emma M. (w/ Louisa A. McLaughlin), 239
Peball, Kurt, 102
Pelagic, Vasa, 218
Pelenyi, John, 370
Penkov, Stojan, 238
Penson, Lillian, 172
Pentzopoulos, D., 337
Perceval, Caussin de, 187
Peretz, D., 421
Perl, Lila, 380
Pestich, S.L., 127
Petersen, Phillip A., 387
Petho, Sandor, 222, 288, 309, 313
Petranovic, Branko, 363
Petrosian, Y.A., 271
Petrovic, Svetislav-Sveta, 364
Petrovic, Vojislav M., 9, 126, 218, 229, 239, 289
Petrovich, Michael Boro, 176, 185, 192, 218, 230, 247, 289, 297, 308
Pheil-Burghaus, R.F.A. Graf von, 271
Phousaras, G.I., 17
Pick, Robert, 138
Pieri, Piero, 93
Pilkolkiewicz, J. (w/E.J. Czerwinski), 385
Pines, R., 410
Pinkney, David H., 169, 170, 212, 284
Pinson, M., 227
Pittara, E., 108
Pivka, Otto von, 388
Plasari, Ndreci, 359
Plaschka, Richard, 308
Plomer, W., 185
Poletica, N.P., 293
Polianski, H.A., 177
Polisensky, J.V., 90, 100
Pollo, Stefanaq, 6
Poloskei, F., 192, 222
Pool, Ithiel de Sola, 387
Popa, Mircea N., 303
Pope, Dudley, 38
Popescu-Puturi, I., 271
Popovic, M.R., 107
Popovici, Andrei, 312
Portal, R., 127
Potholm, C.P., 410
Potter, G.R., 59

Pounds, Norman J.G., 4, 170
Prance, Gerald (w/Reginald Wyon), 10
Pravan, Vasile, 53
Prcela, John (w/Stanko Guldescu), 381
Preclin, E. (w/V.L. Tapie), 122
Preda, Dumitru, 231
Preda, Eugen, 369
Prerardovich, Nikolaus von, 356
Preston, Adrian, 317
Preston, R.A., et al, 129, 178, 216, 285, 351
Pretty, R.T., 410
Prevelakis, Eleutherios, 299, 379
Previte-Orton, C.W. (w/Z.N. Brooke), 59
Pribecevic, Stojan, 3, 354, 357; (w/Ralph G. Martin), 364
Pribram, A.F., 288, 295
Price, Clair, 294
Prpic, G.J., 85
Pryce-Jones, David, 384
Psomiades, Harry J., 309, 312, 314
Pundeff, Marin V., 19, 316
Puryear, V.J., 224

Quimby, Robert S., 129, 179

Ra'anan, U., 411
Rabb, T.K., 91, 100, 122
Radelescu-Zoner, Serban (w/Gheorghe Cazan), 248, 294, 307
Radin, George, 380; (w/Charles A. Beard), 312
Raditsa, Bogdan, 299
Radu, Michael, 387
Radulescu, Adrian (w/I. Bitoleanu), 39, 41
Radvanyi, Janos, 384
Ragib Pasha, 141
Raif, (fnu) (w/(fnu) Ekrem), 102
Rakowska-Harmstone, Teresa (w/Andrew Gyorgy), 386
Rambaud, Alfred N., 127, 172, 223
Ramm, A., 271
Ramsaur, E.E., 338
Ramsay, G.D., 79
Ranghet, Boris, 312
Ranke, Leopold von, 72, 89, 135
Ranki, Gyorgy (w/Ivan Berend), 174, 215, 387
Rankin, Col. Sir Reginald, 297
Ransel, David L., 142, 146
Rapoport, A., 178
Rasid, Mehmet, 125
Rath, Rueben John, 191
Rauchensteiner, Manfred, 384
Rausch, J., 411
Ray, John, 303, 354
Reddaway, W.F., 90, 122, 169
Reed, H.A., 187
Refik, Ahmed, 78, 91, 108, 126, 178
Regnault, Elias, 176, 215
Reinach, Joseph, 176, 239
Reiss, Rodolphe A., 308
Reitz, Col. James T., 388

Remington, Robin A., 388
Renn, Ludwig, 178, 216, 285, 352
Resid Efendi, Cesmi Zade Mustafa, 141
Reuter, Peter, 299
Reynolds, Philip A., 316, 373
Rheindorf, Kurt, 227
Riasonovsky, Nicholas V., 90, 127, 132, 172, 223, 236, 291
Rich, Norman, 213, 236, 353
Ristelhueber, Rene, 4
Ristic, Dragisa N., 362
Ritter, Monika, 227
Roberts, Henry L., 8, 51, 376, 386
Roberts, John M., 351; (w/John Morris), 283
Roberts, Penfield, 122
Roberts, Walter R., 363
Robson, Eric, 121
Rock, Kenneth W., 19, 191
Roider, Karl A., 159; (w/F.A. Youngs), 137, 169, 212
Romanescu, Gheorghe, 45, 51-53, 77, 245; (w/Antone Marinescu), 369
Ronnett, M.D. (w/E. Alexander), 368
Ropp, Theodore, 64, 93, 178, 216, 285, 352
Rose, John H., 129, 179
Rosetti, R., 273
Rostovzeff, Mihail, 10, 11
Rothenberg, Gunther E., 74, 78, 106, 123, 138, 182, 191, 218, 230, 231, 288, 308
Rothrock, George, 168
Rothschild, Joseph, 311
Roucek, Joseph S., 311, 375, 380
Roy, I., 116
Rubin, Alexandre, 244
Ruchti, Jacob, 293
Rude, George F., 146, 169
Ruggles, Melville (w/Vaslac Mastecky), 17
Rumenin, Rumen, 273
Rumpler, Helmut, 222, 308
Runciman, Sir Stephen, 42, 50
Rundle, R.N., 249, 284, 351
Rupp, George, H., 236
Rusinow, Dennison I., 381
Rusu, Dorina N., 186
Ryan, A.N., 121
Ryan, Sir Charles S. (w/John Sandes), 242
Rycault, Sir Paul, 91, 106

St. Clair, W., 186
Saint-Denys, A. de Juchereau de, 41, 185, 188
Saints-Priest, M. LeComte, 237
Sakellariou, M.B. 135
Sale, Col. M.T., 241
Salusbury, Philip H.B., 240, 243
Samoilov, S.I., 186
Sanda, G., 274
Sandes, John (w/Sir Charles Ryan), 242
Sani-zade, Mehmed Ataullah, 182
Sanness, John, 215, 286, 356
Santoni, Alberto, 373

Sargent, Lyman T., 185, 221
Saul, Norman E., 146, 172
Savadjian, Leon, 17, 303, 307, 311-313
Savant, J., 186
Savic, Vladislav R., 306
Savu, Col. Alexandru G., 175, 176, 219, 220, 245, 289, 317, 368
Scammell, G.V., 90
Schechta-Wesseherd, Ottokar von, 185
Schem, Alexander J., 237
Scherer, Anton, 21, 123, 174, 216, 287, 357
Schevill, Bernard, 173
Schevill, Ferdinand, 3, 38, 123, 135, 137, 141, 146, 214, 286
Schlozer, L. von, 242, 291
Schlumberger, G., 50
Schmitt, Bernadotte E., 172, 224, 290, 295, 303
Schmitthenner, P., 129, 179, 285, 352
Schnitzer, E. (Emin Pasha), 340
Schopflin, George, 387
Schreiber, George, 215, 286, 356
Schroeder, Maj. Gen. G. von, 242
Schroeder, Paul W., 227
Schultz, Eberhard, 186
Schurman, Jacob G., 297
Schuyler, Eugene, 133
Schwarz, Berhard, 176, 218
Schwoebel, Robert, 50, 66
Scobie, W.J. (w/C. Foley), 379
Scott, Henry Lee, 38
Scott, William L. & Harriet F., 413
Seaton, A., 413
Seemann, Klaus-Dieter (w/Frank Siegmann), 236
Segvic, Cherubin, 10
Sehsuvaroglu, Haluk Y., 242
Seligman, Vincent J., 300
Semiryaga, M.I., 353
Senior, N.W., 275
Senkowitsch, Ivo, 218
Seton-Watson, Hugh, 172, 291, 386
Seton-Watson, Robert W., 4, 8, 10, 51, 90, 125, 147, 171, 174, 175,
    215, 219, 222, 236, 237, 247, 286-289, 298, 302, 307, 308
Seyfi, Ali Riza, 71
Sforza, Count Carlo, 218, 289
Shandanova, Liliana, 123, 215
Shankowsky, Lew, 373
Shannon, R.T., 23
Shaw, E.K. (Stanford Shaw), 290, 372
Shaw, Stanford J., 15, 21, 41, 47, 51, 52, 66-68, 70, 71, 78, 89, 96,
    100, 124, 141, 146, 147, 177, 181, 188, 192, 222, 226, 290, 314,
    316; (w/E.K. Shaw), 290, 372
Shay, Mary Lucille, 136
Shepherd, W.R., 128, 170, 216, 284, 355
Shirer, William L., 353
Shirk, Paul R., 388
Shotwell, James T., 311
Shukla, Ram Lakham, 227
Shupp, Paul, 171, 180
Sick, G.G., 413

Sidak, Jaroslav, et al, 218, 290
Siegman, Frank (w/Klaus-Deiter Seemann), 236
Silberstein, Gerald E., 308, 310
Simon, Jeffery, 385
Simpson, Amos E. (w/Vaughan B. Baker), 302
Singer, J. David (w/M. Small), 217; et al, 285, 352
Singleton, Frank B. (w/Muriel Heppell), 9, 90, 126, 176, 217, 290, 362
Siniser, Bilal, 239
Sinor, Denis, 7, 102, 103, 126, 174, 191, 222, 370
Sirkov, Dimiter, 365
Sisac, Ferdnand, 10
Skafesh, Cornel (w/Col. Florian Tuca), 244
Sked, Alan, 171, 221
Skendi, Stavro, 6, 248, 288
Skiotes, Dennis N., 185
Skoko, Savo, 298; (w/Petar Opacic), 239
Slijepcevic, Djoko, 290, 381
Sloane, William M., 293, 297, 307
Small, Melvin (w/J. David Singer), 217, 285, 352
Smirnova, Nina D., 317
Smith, Arthur (w/Hans-Adolf Jacobson), 355
Smith, Colin L., 249
Smith, F.B., 227
Smith, Peter C. (w/Edwin Walker), 360
Snyder, Louis, 355
Sokolovsky, V.D., 414
Sonyel, S.R., 314
Sorel, Albert, 146
Soulis, George C., 215, 287, 356
Soures, G.M., 514
Spaulding, O.L., et al, 93, 121, 129, 178, 217, 284
Spector, Sherman D. (w/L. Legters), 4, 16, 357
Speire, H., 129
Spencer, Floyd A., 378
Spinka, Matthew, 4
Spira, Gyorgy, 192
Spiridonakis, Basile, 125, 170, 221
Stadtmuller, George, 5
Stafford, David, 373
Stan, A., 161
Stan, Nicholae, 186, 220, 368
Stanescu, Eugen, 77, 79
Stanislav, E. (w/I. Cernat), 382
Starr, Richard F., 380, 386
Stavrianos, Leften S., 4, 38, 74, 78, 90, 101, 107, 123, 135, 137, 141, 147, 173, 180, 181, 186, 187, 191, 214, 230, 231, 236, 247, 286, 288, 297, 308, 314, 316, 356
Stearn, Peter N., 191
Steblau, Erich Lassota von, 79
Steed, H.W., 342
Stefanescu, Stefan, 39, 40, 220
Stephens, Robert, 379
Stephenson, Graham, 172, 223, 291
Stering, Erich von, 364
Sterling, Claire, 385
Stern, Lawrence, 379

473

Sterns, P.N., 207
Stevenson, Francis S., 10, 176, 218, 290
Stieve, F., 342
Stiles, William H., 191
Stillman, Edmund O., 356
Stillman, William, 177, 223, 238
Stoianovich, Trian, 4, 38, 107, 124, 177, 223, 290
Stoicescu, Nicholae, 39, 40, 51, 52, 72, 77, 79, 101
Stoikov, A., et al, 239
Stojanov, Petar, 298
Stojanovic, Mihailo D., 237
Stokesbury, James L., 303, 355
Stone, Norman, 309
Stoye, John, 102, 103, 121, 127, 131
Strachen, Hew, 352
Sturminger, Walter, 70, 107
Subhi, M., et al, 136
Sudi, Suleyman, 182, 223
Sudjic, Milivoj, 364
Suer, Hikmet, 298
Sugan, Istvan, 69
Sugar, Peter F., 39, 90, 96, 100, 147, 173, 174, 356; (w/Ivo
    Lederer), 33; (w/Donald W. Treadgold), 4, 123, 215, 286
Sula, Abdal B., 380
Summerscale, Peter W., 386
Sumner, Benedict H., 109, 127, 132, 133, 237
Suranyi, Laszlo, 371
Suta, Ion, 307
Swire, Joseph, 6, 125, 176, 220, 288
Sydenham, First Baron Col. G.S., 242
Szabo, Arpad, 384
Szabo, Laszlo, 309
Szajkowski, Bogdan, 375
Szakaly, Ferenc, 68
Szaz, Zoltan, 307
Szilassy, S., 192
Szinai, Miklos (w/Laszlo Szucs), 371
Sztaray, Z., 415
Szucs, Laszlo (w/Miklos Szinai), 371

Tacan, Necati Salim, 107
Taillemite, Etienne, 91
Takats, Sandor, et al, 79
Talmon, Jacob L., 169, 351
Talpes, Capt. Ioan, 317
Tambs, Lewis A. (w/A.S. Birkos), 17
Tanner, J.R., 61
Tansel, Salahaddin, 53, 65, 138
Tanty, Mieczysaw, 248, 286
Tapie, Victor L., 14, 96, 106, 135; (w/E. Preclin), 122
Tarle, Evgenie V., 141, 146
Tauer, F., 86
Taylor, A.J.P., 213, 214, 221, 284, 302, 311
Taylor, J.W.R., et al, 415
Tefft, Benjamin F., 192
Teksut, Irfan (w/Necati Okse), 310
Teleki, Ladislas, 191

Teleki, P. 7
Temperley, Sir Harold W. V., 9, 147, 171, 172, 218, 224, 239, 289, 311; (w/George P. Gooch), 303
Tevik, Suleyman (w/A. Zuhdi), 249
Thadin, Edward C., 299
Thayer, Charles, 364
Theodoracopolous, Taki, 378
Theodoulou, Christos, 309
Thierfelder, Franz, 4
Thim, Josef, 192
Thomas, D., 360
Thomson, Christopher B., 297
Thomson, Gladys Scott, 141
Thornton, A.P., 213, 236
Tileston, M.W. (Foote), 278
Timur, Cevdet, 314
Tingas, Gerald, 100
Toderascu, Col. Constantin, 382
Todleben, Gen. Count F.E., 242
Todorov, K., 415
Todorov, Nicholai, 6, 7, 185, 191
Todorovic, Desanka, 312
Tomasevich, Jozo, 363
Tomassino, Luciano, 102
Tomson, G.S., 146
Topp, Horst, 380
Topping, P.W., 7
Torrey, Glenn E., 307
Tott, Baron de., 162
Toumanoff, Cyril M., 48
Toynbee, Arnold J., 14, 186, 215, 286; (w/Veronica Toynbee), 375
Trask, Richard R., 315
Treadgold, Donald (w/Peter Sugar), 4, 123, 215, 286
Trebilcock, Clive, 168, 214, 284
Treholt, A., 416
Treue, Wilhelm, 226
Trotha, Lt. Col. Thilo von, 242
Trouton, Ruth, 290, 364
Trowbridge, W.R.H., 162
Trumpener, Ulrich, 310
Trypucko, J., 34
Tsvetkova, Bistra A., 50, 100, 101, 108, 124, 126, 178, 223, 239, 290
Tuca, Col. Florian, 244; (w/Cornel Skafesh), 244
Tucker, Jack, 294
Tukin, C., 249
Tupetz, Theodor, 137
Turan, Serafeddin, 78
Turat, A., 249
Tushin, Y.P., 119
Tutoveanu, Gen. Ion, 245
Tveritinova, A., 96
Tzankov, Assen, 301

Ude, Lojze, 308
Uhlirz, Matilde & Karl, 171
Ulucay, Mohammed Cagatay, 101
Unc, George (w/Augustin Deac), 312

Upton, Maj. Gen. Emory, 216
Upward, Allen, 293
Urban, Aladar, 192
Urbansky, Andrew B., 39
Ursu, I., 64
Ustunsoy, Hilmi, (w/Yaha Oksu), 310
Uzuncarsili, Ismail Hakki, 66, 72, 89, 100, 125, 141, 147, 242

Vacalopoulos, Apostollos, 42, 91
Vago, Bela, 353, 376
Vagts, Alfred A., 129, 178, 216, 285, 351
Vali, Ferenc A., 384
Valiani, Leo, 287, 308, 313
Valley, Gen. J.E. (w/Pierre Dufourcq), 303
Van Creveld, Martin L., 93, 129, 179, 217, 285, 352, 353, 358
Vandal, Albert, 138
Vandervoorde, P., 417
Vansca, Max, 106
Van Vollenhaven, C., 129, 178, 216, 285
Varkonyi, A.R., 131
Vasif Efendi, Ahmed, 141, 142, 182
Vasiliev, A.A., 12
Vatikiotis, P.J., 378
Vaughn, D.M., 34
Vaughn, Richard, 351
Veenendal, A.J., 131
Velicki, Constantin N., 239
Ventre-Nouvel, J., 163
Veristchagin, A.V., 279
Vernadsky, George, 109, 127, 172, 223
Vesa, Vasile, 289, 294
Vickers, Capt. Willard
Vigor, P.H., 418
Viskovatov, A.V., 119
Vital, David, 168, 214, 284, 352
Vladescu, Christian M., 220
Vladimirescu, Tudor, 220
Vogel, Hans, 299
Vogel, R., 300
Volgyes, Ivan, 313; (w/Dale Herspring), 387
Volkl, Ekkehard, 95
Voltz, G.B., 138
Von der Porten, E., 418
Voynov, M., et al, 176, 219
Vryonis, S., 34
Vucinich, Wayne S., 14, 293, 386; (w/George Arnakis), 15, 372
Vukcevic, Risto, 381
Vukmanovic-Tempo, Svetozar, 357, 263
Vyvyan, J.M.K., 223, 230

Wagner, Arthur L., 229
Wagner, Maj. Eduard, 92
Wagner, Francis S., 384
Wagner, Georg, 102
Wagner, Hermenegild, 300
Walichnowski, Tadeus, 216
Waliszewski, K., 133

Walker, Edwin (w/Peter Smith), 360
Wandruszka, Adam, 13, 71, 90, 126, 171, 221
Wangerman, E., 127
Wanklyn, H.G., 35
Ward, Harriet, 386
Warner, Philip, 226
Watt, D.C., 345
Weber, Eugen J., 122, 168, 213, 283, 386
Weber, S.H., 17
Weddern, Cardinal von, 241
Wedgewood, C.V., 100
Wegener, Alfred von, 303
Weiker, Walter F., 380
Weiner, M. 169, 231
Weissmann, N., 72, 93
Weld, Stuart F., 237
Wellesley, Col. The Hon. Frederich A., 241
Wendel, Hermann, 313
Wernham, R.B., 87, 118
Werthman, Michael, 169, 212, 284
West, Dame Rebecca (pseud.), 290, 362
Western, J.R., 164
Westwood, J.N., 173, 223, 291
Whetten, Lawrence L., 387
White, Leigh, 358
White, R.J., 122
White, Wilber W., 290, 314, 315
Wiener, Fredrich, 364, 388, 389
Wiener, Jan G., 358
Wijn, J.W., 92
Willey, Basil, 90
Williams, E.N., 90, 122
Williams, Roger L., 233
Williamson, Sam R., 303
Wilson, C., 91
Wilson, Sir Duncan, 381
Wint, Guy (w/Peter Calvocoressi), 354
Winter, J.M., 38
Wirthwein, Walter G., 237
Wiskemann, Elizabeth, 357
Wittek, P., 61
Wittram, Reinhard, 109, 133
Wolf, John B., 122
Wolfe, E.R., 346
Wolfe, Robert Lee, 357, 387
Wolfe, Thomas W., 386, 388
Wolff, Robert L., 42, 107, 311
Woloch, Isser, 122
Woodhouse, C.M., 185-187, 360, 378
Woodruff, William, 168, 213, 284, 386
Woodward, Sir Ernest Llewellyn, 284
Wren, Melvin C., 248
Wright, Alfred, 240
Wright, Gordon, 355
Wright, John W., 121
Wright, Quincy, 64, 92, 121, 129, 178, 216, 284
Wright, Walter L., 124, 177, 222, 290

Wyon, Reginald, 293; (w/Gerald Prance), 10

Xanalatos, D., 299
Xydis, Stephen G., 373, 378, 379

Yannopolous, George N., 378; (w/Richard Clogg), 378
Yasar, R. (w/H. Kabasakai), 346
Yigitguden, Remzi, et al, 310
Young, Sir George, 297
Youngs, Frederic A., Jr. (w/K.A. Roider), 137, 169 212
Yriarte, Charles, 238
Yryonis, Speros (w/Henrik Birnbaum), 388
Yurtseven, R., 185

Zacek, Vaclav, et al, 9
Zacher, Josef, 100
Zade Efendi, C.M.R., 164
Zagoni, Erno (w/Sandor Mucs), 384
Zaharia, Gheorghe, 369; et al, 368
Zakythinos, Dionysios A., 12, 185, 221, 288, 360
Zannas, Alexandros, 290
Zeibert, Ivan August, 302
Zeman, Z.A.B., 313, 385
Zhadov, A.S., 372
Zhilin, P.A., 281
Ziemke, E.F., 422
Zinkeisen, J.W., 124, 136, 177
Zinner, Paul F., 384, 385
Zischka, A., 375
Zivanovic, Milan, 293, 295, 298, 308
Zlatarski, V.N., 6
Zmajevic, Vicko, 108, 125
Zmie, Gorjanin, 239
Zook, David H. (w/Robin Higham), 37, 64, 78, 92, 121, 130, 179, 216, 236, 284, 352
Zoppo, C., 420
Zuhdi, A. (w/Suleyman Tevik), 249
Zujovic, Mladen J., 248
Zwiedinich-Sudenhorst, Hans von, 106
Zwitter, Fran, 222, 287